Organizational Behavior
Seventh Edition
Update

ASSESSMENT UPDATE

John R. Schermerhorn, Jr.
Ohio University

James G. Hunt
Texas Tech University

Richard N. Osborn
Wayne State University

 John Wiley & Sons, Inc.

New York   Chichester   Weinheim   Brisbane   Singapore   Toronto

Acquisitions Editor	Jeff Marshall
Marketing Manager	Charity Robey
Senior Production Editor	Patricia McFadden
Cover Designer	Madelyn Lesure
Text Designer	Laura C. Ierardi
OB Skills Workbook Designer	Kenny Beck
Illustration Editor	Anna Melhorn
Photo Manager	Hilary Newman
Photo Researcher	Jennifer Atkins
Front Cover Photo	William R. Salaz/Duomo Photography, Inc.
Back Cover Photo	@ Duomo Photography, Inc.

This book was set in ITC Garamond Light by LCI Design and printed and bound by Von-Hoffmann Press. The cover was printed by Lehigh Press.

This book is printed on acid-free paper. ∞

ISBN: 0-471-43571-6

Printed in the United States of America.

10 9 8 7 6 5 4 3 2 1

Contributors

■ CASES FOR CRITICAL THINKING

Barry R. Armandi, *State University of New York*, Forrest F. Aven, *University of Houston, Downtown*, Kim Cameron, *Brigham Young University*, David S. Chappell, *Ohio University*, Anne C. Cowden, *California State University, Sacramento*, Bernardo M. Ferdman, *California School of Professional Psychology*, Placido L. Gallegos, *Southwest Communications Resources, Inc. and the Kaleel Jamison Consulting Group. Inc.*, Ellen Ernst Kossek, *Michigan State University*, Barbara McCain, *Oklahoma City University*, Mary McGarry, *Empire State College*, Aneil Mishra, *Pennsylvania State University*, Karen Mishra, *Pennsylvania State University*, Marc Osborn, *Arizona Chamber of Commerce*, V. Jean Ramsey, *Texas Southern University*, Franklin Ramsoomair, *Wilfrid Laurier University*.

■ EXPERIENTIAL EXERCISES AND SELF-ASSESSMENT INVENTORIES

Barry R. Armandi, *State University of New York, Old Westbury*, Ariel Fishman, *The Wharton School, University of Pennsylvania*, Barbara K. Goza, *University of California, Santa Cruz*, D.T. Hall, *Boston University*, F.S. Hall, *University of New Hampshire*, Lady Hanson, *California State Polytechnic University, Pomona*, Conrad N. Jackson, *MPC, Inc.*, Mary Khalili, *Oklahoma City University*, Robert Ledman, *Morehouse College*, Paul Lyons, *Frostburg State University*, J. Marcus Maier, *Chapman University*, Michael R. Manning, *New Mexico State University*, Barbara McCain, *Oklahoma City University*, Annie McKee, *The Wharton School, University of Pennsylvania*, Bonnie McNeely, *Murray State University*, W. Alan Randolph, *University of Baltimore*, Paula J. Schmidt, *New Mexico State University*, Susan Schor, *Pace University*, Timothy T. Serey, *Northern Kentucky University*, Barbara Walker, *Diversity Consultant*, Paula S. Weber, *New Mexico Highlands University*, Susan Rawson Zacur, *University of Baltimore*.

About the Authors

Dr. John R. Schermerhorn, Jr., is the Charles G. O'Bleness Professor of Management in the College of Business Administration at Ohio University. He earned a Ph.D. in organizational behavior from Northwestern University, after receiving an M.B.A. (with distinction) from New York University, and a B.S. from the State University of New York at Buffalo. He has served as Director of the Center for Southeast Asia Studies at Ohio University and also as on-site Coordinator of Ohio University E.M.B.A. and M.B.A. programs in Malaysia. He was a Visiting Professor of Management at the Chinese University of Hong Kong as well as Visiting Scholar at Liaoning University in China and the Technical University of Wroclaw in Poland. Dr. Schermerhorn has won awards for teaching excellence at Tulane University, the University of Vermont, and Ohio University, where he has been named a University Professor, the university's leading award for undergraduate teaching. He is the author and coauthor of over 50 journal articles, book chapters, and proceedings. His other Wiley books include *Management* (Wiley, Sixth Edition, 1999), *Introducing Management* (Wiley, First Edition, 2000), and *Basic Organizational Behavior* (Wiley, Second Edition, 1998).

Dr. James G. (Jerry) Hunt is the Paul Whitfield Horn Professor of Management, Professor of Health Organization Management, Director, Institute for Leadership Research, and former department chair of Management, Texas Tech University. He received his Ph.D. and Master's degrees from the University of Illinois, after completing a B.S. (with honors) at Michigan Technological University. Dr. Hunt has coauthored an Organization Theory text and *Basic Organizational Behavior* (Wiley, Second Ed., 1998) and has authored or coauthored three leadership monographs. He founded the Leadership Symposia Series and coedited the eight volumes based on the series. He has presented or published nearly 200 articles, papers, and book chapters, and among his most recent books are *Leadership: A New Synthesis*, published by Sage, and *Out-of-the-Box Leadership*, published by JAI. The former was a finalist for the Academy of Management's 1993 Terry Distinguished Book Award. Recently, Dr. Hunt received the Distinguished Service

Award from the Academy of Management and the Barnie E. Rushing. Jr. Distinguished Researcher Award from Texas Tech University for his long-term contributions to management research and scholarship. He has lived and taught in England and Finland.

Dr. Richard N. Osborn is Professor of Management and Organizational Sciences in the School of Business Administration, Wayne State University. He has received teaching awards at Southern Illinois University at Carbondale and Wayne State University, and he has also taught at Monash University (Australia), Tulane University, and the University of Washington. He received D.B.A. from Kent State University after earning an M.B.A. at Washington State University and a B.S. from Indiana University. With over 150 presentations and publications, Dr. Osborn is a leading authority on international alliances in technology-intensive industries and is co-author of an Organization Theory text and *Basic Organizational Behavior* (John Wiley & Sons, 1995, 1998). He has served as a member of the editorial boards of the *Academy of Management Journal, Technology Studies, Journal of High Technology Management, The Academy of Management Review, The Journal of Management* and Editor of International Strategy for the *Journal of World Business*. He is very active in the Academy of Management, having served as divisional program chair and president, as well as the Academy representative for the International Federation of Scholarly Associations of Management. Dr. Osborn's research has been sponsored by the Department of Defense, Ford Motor Company, National Science Foundation, Nissan, and the Nuclear Regulatory Commission, among others. In addition to teaching, Dr. Osborn spent a number of years in private industry, including a position as a senior research scientist with the Battelle Memorial Institute in Seattle, where he worked on improving the safety of commercial nuclear power.

Preface

"Fast!" That's the word one hears most frequently these days when people describe high performance organizations. "Fast," is also what you should think when you look at the cover of this book. And inside its pages, you'll find an emphasis on what might be called—"Fast OB." There is no denying the great opportunities and challenges of our ever-changing environment. Accordingly, *Organizational Behavior* Seventh Edition has been designed and updated to meet the demanding tests faced by organizations and their members in the emerging 21st century. While retaining the emphasis on the fundamentals of organizational behavior that has characterized past editions, this edition grounds the study of OB in the fast-paced action context of today's organizations and careers.

Organizational Behavior Seventh Edition has been developed on the premise that the study of organizational behavior is essential for everyone seeking career success in the modern workplace. It doesn't matter whether that career unfolds in the arena of business, government, education, or public service. It does matter that the individual is prepared to perform in organizations challenged by uncertainty, bound for continuous change, and affected by the forces of high technology.

The goal of this book is to help today's students become leaders of tomorrow's organizations. The twenty-first century is here, and its character belongs to everyone who studies with us today. What they do as managers and leaders will not only shape the contributions of the institutions of society, but also fundamentally alter lives around the globe.

Organizations aren't just fast today, they also increasingly differ from past traditions in their essential forms and characters. We are in an era that values entrepreneurship, horizontal structures, knowledge management, virtual organizations, work-life balance, and more. At the same time that borderlines are disappearing in the global economy, functional lines are disappearing within organizations. One has only to read the pages of *The Wall Street Journal*, FAST COMPANY *Magazine, Fortune, Business Week, The Economist,* and other periodicals and local newspapers to realize how dominant and persistant are the forces of continuous change. These changes affect work and education alike and they call ceaselessly for a commitment to integrated learning and teamwork.

As management educators, we bear an important responsibility—one that cannot deny that the old ways and standards just aren't good enough anymore. We live, work and learn in a society that expects high performance and high quality-of-work-life to go hand in hand; that considers ethics and social responsibility paramount measures of individual and organizational performance; that respects the talents of workforces increasingly rich in demographic and cultural diversity; and that knows the imprint of globalization.

The seventh edition of *Organizational Behavior* was revised with these realities in mind. The book has been redesigned and substantially redeveloped from the foundations set by its predecessors. Our recommitment to organizational behavior and its central role in the learning environment is well illustrated by the "OB Skills Workbook" that is included as an essential component in the textbook. This unique feature has been expanded and enriched based upon the enthusiastic feedback of those using the last edition. We are especially pleased to include in this OB Skills Workbook the FASTCOMPANY *Collection*, a carefully selected group of full-text articles from the innovative FASTCOMPANY magazine.

Consistent also with feedback on the last edition, we have retained the trim and professional format of the book. We are convinced that by content and design *Organizational Behavior* Seventh Edition can well serve the needs of your OB course and help to inform and enthuse students who must face the challenges of tomorrow's workplace, not yesterday's. We have written this book for students who want to understand the discipline of OB in full awareness of its practical value and importance to their future careers. And we have written this book to meet the needs of instructors who want to give their students a solid introduction to the discipline, a rich array of alternative learning activities, and a strong emphasis and commitment to skill development. *Organizational Behavior,* Seventh Edition is our contribution to the study of a dynamic discipline that becomes increasingly relevant as our society and its institutions rush forward into an uncertain future.

John R. Schermerhorn, Jr.
Ohio University

James G. (Jerry) Hunt
Texas Tech University

Richard N. Osborn
Wayne State University

About This Book

Organizational Behavior, Seventh Edition brings to its readers the solid and complete content core of prior editions, the exciting "OB Skills Workbook," and many revisions, updates, and enhancements that reflect today's dynamic times. The book covers the discipline in an orderly progression, but allows for parts and/or chapters to be used out of sequence at the instructor's prerogative. We do strongly suggest, however, that the first two opening chapters in Part 1: The Environment—Chapter 1, "Organizational Behavior Today," and Chapter 2, "The High Performance Organization"—be used in sequence to set the context for the course.

Parts 2, 3, 4, and 5 offer the basic building blocks for understanding OB—the study of individuals, groups, organizations, and processes, respectively. In each of these parts, readers will find chapters offering solid coverage of the basic theories and concepts of organizational behavior, along with many examples and guidelines emphasizing their practical application to the 21st century workplace.

■ CHANGES AND UPDATES

In addition to the foundations provided in preceding editions, *Organizational Behavior, Seventh Edition* offers new and expanded coverage of the following topics.

- *Chapter 1: Organizational Behavior Today*—Intellectual Capital, e-commerce, virtual organizations, life-long learning, ethical behavior, social responsibility
- *Chapter 2: High Performance Organizations*—Change and high performance organizations, characteristics and challenges of high performance organizations, organizational learning, building a high performance organization
- *Chapter 3: Global Dimensions of Organizational Behavior*—Regional economic alliances, values and national cultures, cultural relativism, ethical imperialism, expatriate work, global organizational learning
- *Chapter 4: Diversity and Individual Differences*—Workforce diversity, demographic differences, personality differences, valuing and managing diversity

- *Chapter 5: Perception and Attribution*—Perception as an influence in organizational behavior, attribution theory and implications
- *Chapter 6: Motivation and Reinforcement*—Motivation across cultures, motivation and job satisfaction, social learning, behavioral self management, classical & operant conditioning
- *Chapter 7: Human Resource Management Systems*—Human resource management, career planning and development, performance evaluation, reward systems
- *Chapter 8: High Performance Job Designs*—Technology and job design, process reengineering, goal setting and MBO, flexible working hours
- *Chapter 9: The Nature of Groups*—Group contributions to organizations, foundations of group effectiveness, group dynamics and decision making
- *Chapter 10: Teamwork and High Performance Teams*—High-performance teams, team building, employee involvement teams, self-managing teams, virtual teams
- *Chapter 11: Basic Attributes of Organizations*—Organizational goals, formal structures and the division of labor, horizontal specialization, coordination, bureaucracy, alternative structures
- *Chapter 12: Information Technology and Organizational Design*—Contingency influences of size, information technology, operations technology, environment, and strategy
- *Chapter 13: High Performance Organizational Cultures*—The functions of culture, common assumptions and culture, values and organizational culture, subcultures, culture building through organizational development
- *Chapter 14: Leadership*—Behavioral and contingency theory updates, attribution theory and the new leadership, leadership and high performance organizations
- *Chapter 15: Power and Politics*—Gaining and using power, empowerment, understanding and dealing with organizational politics, organizational politics and self protection
- *Chapter 16: Informational Communication*—Effective communication, technology and communication, the electronic office, virtual meetings, cultural differences in communication
- *Chapter 17: Decision Making*—Decision-making approaches, garbage can view, judgmental heuristics, creativity, participation, cultural differences
- *Chapter 18: Conflict and Negotiation*—Constructive conflict, conflict management, win-win conflict, distributive negotiation, integrative negotiation
- *Chapter 19: Change, Innovation, and Stress*—Continuous change, strategies of change, resistance to change, innovation processes, stress management
- *Module: Research Foundations of OB*—Research designs, working with data, ethical considerations

■ PEDAGOGICAL FEATURES

As always, a primary goal in writing this book is to create a textbook that appeals to the student reader, while still offering solid content. Through market research surveys and focus groups with students and professors, we learned what features worked best from previous editions, what could be improved, and what could be added to accomplish this goal both effectively and efficiently. The participants in the focus groups in particular were quite forthcoming about their likes and dislikes. They told us what worked for them and what didn't. The outcome is the following list of pedagogical elements that appear in every chapter of *Organizational Behavior, Seventh Edition*.

- *Chapter-Opening Photo Essays* Each chapter opens with a "real world" vignette that is linked to the chapter content. These real-world examples show how people can make a difference in the way organizations operate and offer a visionary stimulus to start students on a voyage of discovery as they examine the content that follows. Internet Web Site addresses for many of the organizations are included in these essays.
- *Study Questions* Following the opening vignette, the chapter focuses the reader's attention through a set of boxed study questions that are tied to both the major headings of the chapter and the concluding summary.
- *Embedded Boxes* Throughout the chapter, embedded boxes are used to further illustrate best practices applications. These short and photo enhanced boxes provide concise and relevant examples without disrupting the flow of the text. *Entrepreneurship, Ethics and Social Responsibility, Globalization, High Performance Organizations, Technology,* and *Workforce Diversity* issues are the themes of these visual examples.
- *OB Across Functions* Unique and new to this edition is a timely feature that provides in each chapter clear and real examples of how OB plays a role in all aspects of an organization, and in all the various roles and functions that make them work.
- *Annotated margin photos* add variety to the content without breaking up the flow of text. These annotated margin photos provide additional current real-world examples of OB in practice. Many include the organization's Web Site address so that the student can peruse additional information about the company on the Internet.
- *Effective Manager boxes* are integrated into the text as practical tips and applications. They offer useful action guidelines on topics relevant to skills development and career readiness.
- *Running glossary* The most important and relevant concepts are boldfaced and defined in the margin as key terms. All of the boldfaced key terms and additional italicized important terms are included in a comprehensive *glossary* at the end of the book, providing one-stop definitions of all the terms introduced in the book.
- *Margin list identifiers* call out important lists for the reader's attention. As with the last edition, the use of lists has been minimized.
- *Chapter Study Guide* At the end of each chapter is a total learning feature that includes three components to help students consolidate their learning and prepare for quizzes and examinations. A *bullet-list summary* is tied back to the chapter-opening study questions. A *list of key terms*, with page references, links them back to the boldfaced terms in the text and their margin definitions. A chapter *self-test* serves as a built-in study guide, offering multiple-choice, true–false, short response, and applications essay questions. Specifically added at the request of students, the format of the self-tests reflects the types of questions students will be expected to answer on in-class

exams. Students can access an interactive version of the self-tests on the Schermerhorn Web Site at www.wiley.com/college/schermerhorn.

■ THE OB SKILLS WORKBOOK

A collection of FASTCOMPANY magazine articles, along with numerous *case studies for critical thinking, experiential exercises*, and *self-assessment inventories* have been contributed by a number of professors of Organizational Behavior throughout the United States and Canada, and assembled in this update of our regular *OB Skills Workbook*. This selection represents a collection of both tried-and-true and unique cases, exercises, and assessments. We have brought them to you in one self-contained section of this book to help you enrich your class sessions. Rather than tie this vast portfolio of choices to specific chapters, we have offered a matrix of choices for you to select from. Most importantly, we have gathered these from colleagues who are known for their innovative teaching.

■ SUPPORT PACKAGE

Organizational Behavior, Seventh Edition is supported by a comprehensive learning package that assists the instructor in creating a motivating and enthusiastic environment.

A new exciting, interactive web site supports the Seventh Edition of *Organizational Behavior*. This incredibly rich source of materials contains a wide variety of student and instructor resources including Interactive Self-Testing; Internet Exercises for each chapter; On-Line Cases; a Cross-Functional On-Line Case; Interactive Self-Assessments; The FASTCOMPANY Collection; a link to BusinessExtra; The Career Advancement Portfolio; and Instructor's Resources.

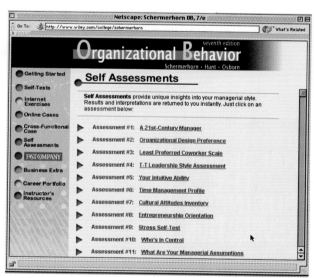

The *Cross-Functional Integrating Case* is on Trilogy Software, Inc. This case is timely, hot linked and rich in integrative learning opportunities.

Bruse Barringer of the University of Central Florida has extensively revised the *Instructor's Resource Guide*. The Instructor's Resource Guide contains numerous resources for each chapter, including Course Development, Sample Assignments and Innovative Instructional Designs; Teaching Suggestions for how to use and integrate the media components; Lecture Outline and Lecture Notes, and much more.

Bruce Barringer also has extensively revised the *Test Bank*. The expanded Test Bank now includes approximately 125 questions per chapter, which include 75-100 multiple choice questions, 25 True/False questions, and 4 essay questions with suggested responses.

The *Computerized Test Bank* is available for IBM and compatible computers, and contains an electronic version of the test bank with full custom test design features.

John Schermerhorn's personal and class-tested *PowerPoint® Slides* are available on the Web Site for downloading and on the Instructor's CD-ROM.

The *Instructor's CD-ROM* features the electronic files for the Instructor's Manual, Test Bank, Computerized Test Bank, and PowerPoint Presentations.

A comprehensive *Video Package* ties directly to the core topics of the text and brings to life real-world examples of organizational behavior in practice. *The Wiley Nightly Business Report-Organizational Behavior Video Series* contains segments from the highly respected Nightly Business Report, which have been selected for their applicability to organizational behavior principles and for their reinforcement of key concepts in the text. Each of the segments is approximately three to seven minutes long and can be used to introduce topics to the students, enhance lecture material, and provide real-world context for related concepts. Bruce Barringer of the University of Central Florida culled Nightly Business Report segments to create an expanded video package for the Seventh Edition.

A *WebCT* course is available with *Organizational Behavior*, Seventh Edition. WebCT is a course management tool that facilitates the organization and delivery of course materials on the Web.

Packaging Options for Customer Value

The new FAST COMPANY *Handbook of the Business Revolution*, sponsored by John Wiley & Sons, Inc., provides six insightful articles reprised from past issues of the magazine about the changing landscape of leadership, work and careers. These thought-provoking articles are sure to challenge, stimulate, and inspire your students. To help you use this Handbook in your course, we created a teaching guide on the Schermerhorn Web Site that provides:

- A correlation guide to using the handbook articles with *Organizational Behavior*, Seventh Edition
- A brief summary of each article
- Discussion questions for each article

The Handbook of the Business Revolution can be packaged with *Organizational Behavior*, Seventh Edition for a nominal fee by using this special set ISBN: 0-471-36106-2. Ask your local Wiley representative about receiving a free six month gift subscription to FAST COMPANY magazine (instructors only).

The new *Student Video CD-ROM* is available to package with *Organizational Behavior* for a nominal fee by using this special set ISBN: 0-471-38057-1. This CD-ROM includes key NBR videos and accompanying video viewing questions.

Acknowledgments

Organizational Behavior, Seventh Edition benefits from insights provided by a dedicated group of management educators from around the globe who carefully read and critiqued draft chapters of this edition. We are pleased to express our appreciation to the following colleagues for their contributions to this new edition.

Forrest Aven
University of Houston

Michal Cakrt
Czech management Center

Nina Cole
York University

Janice M. Feldbauer
Austin Community College

Lady Alice Hanson
Claifornia State Polytechnic University Pomona

Andrew Klein
Keller Graduate School of Management

Kristi M. Lewis
Oregon State University

Judy C. Nixon
University of Tennessee at Chattanooga

L. David Schuelke
Bethel College

Ronni Stephens
Central Missouri State University

Romuald Stone
Keller Graduate School of Management

Donald White
University of Arkansas

We also thank those reviewers who contributed to the success of previous editions, setting the groundwork for this sixth edition:

Merle Ace
Chi Anyansi-Archibong
Terry Armstrong
Leanne Atwater
Steve Axley
Abdul Aziz
Richard Babcock
Robert Barbato
Richard Barrett
Nancy Bartell

Anna Bavetta
Robb Bay
Hrach Bedrosian
Bonnie Betters-Reed
Gerald Biberman
Mauritz Blonder
Dale Blount
G. B. Bohn
Joseph F. Byrnes
Gene E. Burton

Daniel R. Cillis
Paul Collins
Ann Cowden
Deborah Crown
Roger A. Dean
Delf Dodge
Dennis Duchon
Michael Dumler
Ken Eastman
Theresa Feener

Dalmar Fisher
J. Benjamin Forbes
Cynthia V. Fukami
Normandie Gaitley
Daniel Ganster
Joe Garcia
Robert Giambatista
Manton Gibbs
Eugene Gomolka
Barbara Goodman
Stephen Gourlay
Frederick Greene
Richard Grover
Bengt Gustafsson
Peter Gustavson
Don Hantula
Kristi Harrison
William Hart
Nell Hartley
Neil J. Humphreys
David Hunt
Eugene Hunt
Howard Kahn
Harriet Kandelman
Paul N. Keaton
Peter Kreiner

Donald Lantham
Beverly Linnell
Kathy Lippert
Michael London
Carol Lucchesi
David Luther
Lorna Martin
Douglas McCabe
James McFillen
Charles Milton
Herff L. Moore
David Morean
Sandra Morgan
Paula Morrow
Richard Mowday
Linda Neider
Dennis Pappas
Edward B. Parks
Robert F. Pearse
Lawrence Peters
Joseph Porac
Samuel Rabinowitz
Franklin Ramsoomair
Charles L. Roegiers
Steven Ross
Michael Rush

Richard J. Sebastian
Anson Seers
R. Murray Sharp
Allen N. Shub
Dayle Smith
Walter W. Smock
Pat Sniderman
Ritch L. Sorenson
Shanthi Srinivas
Paul L. Starkey
Sharon Tucker
Ted Valvoda
Joyce Vincelette
David Vollrath
W. Fran Waller
Charles Wankel
Fred A. Ware, Jr.
Andrea F. Warfield
Harry Waters, Jr.
Joseph W. Weiss
Deborah Wells
Bobbie Williams
Barry L. Wisdom
Wayne Wormley
Barry Wright
Raymond Zammuto

Efforts to extend *Organizational Behavior,* Seventh Edition in new directions have benefited greatly from those educators whose works are represented in *The OB Skills Workbook.* These colleagues are identified in the workbook with their contributions, and we greatly appreciate the range of innovative pedagogical options they help provide users of this book.

We are grateful for all the hard work of the supplements authors and our supplements editor, Cynthia Rhoads, who worked to develop the comprehensive ancillary package described above. We thank Bruce Barringer of the University of Central Florida for authoring the Instructor's Resource Guide and the Test Bank, and assisting in the development of the *Nightly Business Report AT&T* video series. We also thank Diane Hunt-Wagner of the University of Phoenix for creating Internet Exercises available on the Web Site, and David Chappell of Ohio University for contributing several cases to the book and Web Site.

As always, the support staff at John Wiley & Sons was most helpful in the various stages of developing and producing this edition. Our editor, Brent Gordon, applied the very best of OB to build a committed high performance team to work with us on the book. We thank him for maintaining the quest for quality and timeliness—in all aspects of the book's content and design. Maddy Lesure was the creative force behind the new design, while Hilary Newman's special talent as photo researcher resulted in the beautiful use of photography that enhances this edition. We also thank Kelly Tavares of Wiley for her excellent production assistance, Betty Pessagno for copyediting, Anna Melhorn for overseeing the illustration program, and Carlise Paulson for leading the marketing campaign. The extraordinary efforts of David Kear (media editor) in providing the best in Web support were indispensable for a true 21st century product. Thank you everyone!!

Brief Contents

Contents

■ Chapter 8
High Performance Job Designs 153

PART 4   MANAGING ORGANIZATIONS

■ Chapter 11
Basic Attributes of Organizations   213

■ Chapter 12
Information Technology and Organizational Design   239

■ Chapter 13
High Performance Organizational Cultures   263

PART 5   MANAGING PROCESSES

■ Chapter 14
High Performance Leadership   285

■ Chapter 15
Power and Politics   309

■ Chapter 16
Information and Communication   333

THE OB SKILLS WORKBOOK   419

Organizational Behavior Today

GOOD IDEAS + ENTREPRENEURSHIP = SUCCESS

The beaches of Ibiza, Spain, were delightful. But when Dalia Almanza-Smith picked up a free postcard from a local restaurant, her honeymoon took an unusual twist. Dalia and her husband spent the next two months not just traveling in Europe, but also planning a new business venture based on postcard advertising. The idea was unique— give away postcards instead of charging for them. Instead of charging the customer, charge an advertiser whose message was carried on the back of the card.

Next came the entrepreneurship. Dalia had experience in advertising, while her husband was a management consultant. They used savings and credit to come up with $40,000 to invest in a new business called Frankie Freecards. Dalia quit her job to work full time on the business plan. After identifying two other competitors, she

contacted them, and together they formed a new company called Go Card. With a lot of hard work, the company grew to $5 million in revenues. Dalia took back her part of the business and renamed it HotStamps, and joined a partnership with another entrepreneurial firm, Network Event Theater. It offers a Web site dedicated to the information needs of the 15 million students enrolled in colleges and universities.

Success is motivating according to Dalia, who hopes to have racks with her cards displayed all over the country. "It motivated me to do more," she says: "There is no way to stop me now." Born in Mercedes, Texas, Dalia says she learned to trust in her talents as a Hispanic woman. In her words: "I learned early to persevere…. I was not going to inherit any money…I had to invent myself."

Dalia Almanza-Smith is not alone in her quest for success. The U.S. Small Business Administration reports a 114 percent growth rate for businesses started by Hispanic women. This compares with a 26 percent growth rate for businesses overall.[1]

*O*rganizational Behavior 7/E is about people, everyday people like you and us, who work and pursue careers today in new and highly demanding settings. It is about people who seek fulfillment in their lives and jobs in a variety of ways and in uncertain times. It is about common themes that now characterize the modern workplace, including high performance, productivity improvement, technology utilization, product and service quality, workforce diversity, work-life balance, and competitive advantage in a global economy. This book is also about how a complex environment challenges people and organizations to change, learn, and continuously develop themselves in the quest for promising futures.

Dalia Almanza-Smith, featured in the opening example, has gotten the message. Striking out on the entrepreneurial path, she recognizes the need to take personal charge of her career destiny. And she demonstrates the capacity to take risk in pursuit of unprecedented opportunities. But whether your career unfolds in entrepreneurship, corporate enterprise, public service, or any other occupational setting, one thing remains sure: Success for people and organizations requires flexibility, creativity, learning, and a willingness to change. That is the message of today, and it will be the message for tomorrow.

Study Questions

Chapter 1 introduces the field of organizational behavior as a useful knowledge base for achieving career success in today's dynamic environment. As you read the chapter, keep in mind these key questions.

- What is organizational behavior and why is it important?
- How do we learn about organizational behavior?
- What are organizations like as work settings?
- What is the nature of managerial work?
- How do ethics influence human behavior in organizations?

Organizational Behavior Today

People at work in organizations today are part of a new era. The institutions of society and the people who make them work are challenged in many and very special ways. Society at large increasingly expects high performance and high quality of life to go hand-in-hand, considers ethics and social responsibility core values, respects the vast potential of demographic and cultural diversity among people, and accepts the imprint of a globalization on everyday living and organizational competitiveness. In this new era of work and organizations, the body of knowledge we call "organizational behavior" offers many insights of great value.

■ WHAT IS ORGANIZATIONAL BEHAVIOR?

Formally defined, **organizational behavior**—OB for short—is the study of individuals and groups in organizations. Learning about OB will help you develop a better work-related understanding about yourself and other people. It can also expand your potential for career success in the dynamic, shifting, complex, and challenging *new* workplaces of today…and tomorrow.

■ **Organizational behavior** is the study of individuals and groups in organizations.

Figure 1.1 shows how *Organizational Behavior 7/E* progresses logically from the current environment—including an emphasis on high performance organizations and implications of globalization, to dimensions of individual and group behavior in organizations, to the nature of organizations themselves, and

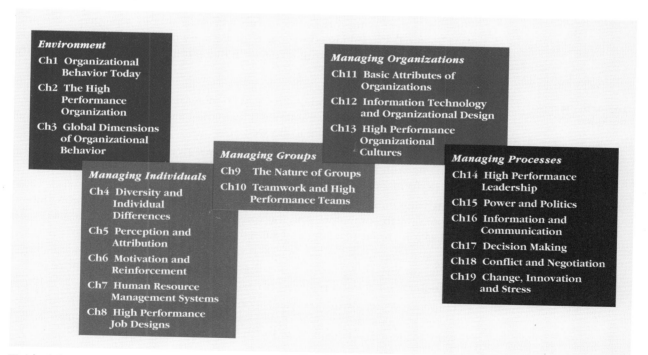

Environment
Ch1 Organizational Behavior Today
Ch2 The High Performance Organization
Ch3 Global Dimensions of Organizational Behavior

Managing Individuals
Ch4 Diversity and Individual Differences
Ch5 Perception and Attribution
Ch6 Motivation and Reinforcement
Ch7 Human Resource Management Systems
Ch8 High Performance Job Designs

Managing Groups
Ch9 The Nature of Groups
Ch10 Teamwork and High Performance Teams

Managing Organizations
Ch11 Basic Attributes of Organizations
Ch12 Information Technology and Organizational Design
Ch13 High Performance Organizational Cultures

Managing Processes
Ch14 High Performance Leadership
Ch15 Power and Politics
Ch16 Information and Communication
Ch17 Decision Making
Ch18 Conflict and Negotiation
Ch19 Change, Innovation and Stress

Figure 1.1
Major topics in the study of OB: *Organizational Behavior 7/E.*

MIT's Center for Coordination Science

www.mit.edu

Researchers at MIT's Center for Coordination Science study the "wired economy," where the Internet and computer networks are changing commerce and organizations. A current initiative focuses on "inventing the organizations of the twenty-first century."

to core processes of OB—including leadership, power and politics, information and communication, decision making, conflict and negotiation, and change, innovation, and stress.

■ SHIFTING PARADIGMS OF ORGANIZATIONAL BEHAVIOR

Progressive workplaces today look and act very differently from those of the past. They have new features, they approach work processes in new ways, and they serve different customer and client markets. The last decade of the twentieth century was especially dramatic in both the nature and pace of change. One observer called it a "revolution that feels something like this: scary, guilty, painful, liberating, disorienting, exhilarating, empowering, frustrating, fulfilling, confusing, challenging. In other words, it feels very much like chaos."[2] But what began as a revolution has become everyday reality as we start a new century. Intense global competition, highly interdependent national economies, constantly emerging computer and information technologies, new forms of organizations, and shifting population demographics are now part of the norm. Today we are surrounded by both change and its implications for organizations—just look at the new world of electronic commerce,[3] and for individuals—look also at the demand for competencies with new technologies and commitment to continuous personal improvement.[4] What remains is the struggle to deal best with these changes, individually and institutionally, and to keep up the pace as further changes emerge.[5]

In an article entitled "The Company of the Future," Harvard Professor and former Secretary of Labor Robert Reich says: "Everybody works for somebody or something—be it a board of directors, a pension fund, a venture capitalist, or a traditional boss. Sooner or later you're going to have to decide who you want to work for."[6] In making this decision, you will want to join a progressive workplace that reflects values consistent with your own. This book can help you prepare for such choices in full recognition that our transition to the new century includes these trends:[7]

Trends in the new workplace

- Demise of "command-and-control"—with increasing competitiveness in organizational environments, traditional hierarchical structures are proving too unwieldy, slow, and costly to do well.

- Emergence of new workforce expectations—a new generation of workers is bringing with it less tolerance for hierarchy, more informality, and concerns for performance merit rather than status.

- Increasing impact of information technologies—organizations are now burgeoning with computers, and the consequent implications for information utilization are far reaching and substantial.

- Belief in empowerment—a dynamic and complex environment places a premium on knowledge, experience, and commitment, all of which thrive in high-involvement and participatory work settings.

- Emphasis on teamwork—organizations today are less vertical and more horizontal in focus; driven by complex environments and customer demands, work is increasingly team based with a focus on peer contributions.

- Concern for work-life balance—as society increases in complexity, organizations are paying more attention to how members balance the sometimes-conflicting demands and priorities of work and personal affairs.

■ ORGANIZATIONAL BEHAVIOR AND DIVERSITY

An important watchword in the twenty-first century is **workforce diversity**— the presence of differences based on gender, race and ethnicity, age, and able-bodiedness.[8] Success in the new workplace requires a set of skills for working successfully with a broad mix of people from different racial and ethnic backgrounds, of different ages and genders, and of different domestic and national cultures. *Valuing diversity* is an OB theme. It refers to managing and working with others in full respect for their individual differences. Interpersonal sensitivity and cultural respect are indispensable to valuing diversity.

> ■ **Workforce diversity** involves differences based on gender, race and ethnicity, age, and able-bodiedness.

Even though valuing diversity is emphasized in our books and classrooms, much remains to be accomplished. A **glass ceiling effect** acts as a hidden barrier limiting the career advancement of minorities and women in some situations. A *Harvard Business Review* forum on "Race in the U.S. Workplace," for example, included these opening statements: "Many people of color themselves still struggle with the closed doors of institutional racism…ignorance and prejudice have by no means disappeared from the U.S. workforce." The article went on to conclude: "Yet there are signs of headway."[9] A recent study of 860 U.S. companies indicates that the number of African-Americans serving as board directors increased 18 percent in a two-year period; the number of women directors increased 4 percent.[10] Yet, as one indicator of lingering disparities in diversity representation in the executive ranks, women are reported as holding only about 11 percent of corporate officerships in Fortune 500 companies (see The Effective Manager 1.1). They also earn as senior executives only 68 cents to the dollar earned by the highest-paid men.[11]

> ■ The **glass ceiling effect** is a hidden barrier limiting advancement of women and minorities in organizations.

THE EFFECTIVE MANAGER 1.1

HOW TO MAKE DIVERSITY STICK

- Focus on getting the best talent.
- Develop career plans for *all* employees.
- Provide career mentoring by diversity cohorts.
- Promote minorities to responsible positions.
- Maintain accountability for diversity goals.
- Make diversity part of organizational strategy.
- Build diversity into senior management.

Learning About Organizational Behavior

We live and work in a knowledge-based economy that is continually laced with the winds of change. This places a great premium on "learning" by organizations as well as individuals. Only the learners, so to speak, will be able to maintain the pace and succeed in a constantly changing environment.[12]

■ ORGANIZATIONAL BEHAVIOR AND THE LEARNING IMPERATIVE

Consultants and scholars emphasize **organizational learning** as the process of acquiring knowledge and utilizing information to adapt successfully to changing circumstances.[13] Organizations must be able to change continuously and positively while searching continuously for new ideas and opportunities. The same is true for each of us. We must strive for continuous improvement to keep pace with a dynamic and complex environment.

> ■ **Organizational learning** is the process of acquiring knowledge and using information to adapt successfully to changing circumstances.

Life-long learning is a popular concept these days, and the message is relevant. You can and must learn from day-to-day work experiences, conversations with colleagues and friends, counseling and advice from mentors, success models, training seminars and workshops, and the information available in the popular press and mass media. This book contains a special section, *The Organizational Behavior Workbook*, designed specifically to help you begin this process. Included in the workbook are many opportunities for you, individually and in student study groups, to analyze readings and cases, participate in experimental exercises, and complete skills-assessment inventories to advance your learning.

www.eyi.com

HIGH PERFORMANCE ORGANIZATION

Organizations that offer learning cultures are highly sought after by today's college graduates. Ernst & Young LLP, an accounting and consulting firm with over 80,000 employees and $9 billion in annual revenues, is one of them. Visit the firm's Center for Business Innovation, and you'll find a professional staff and facility dedicated to learning. John Jordan, the center's director for electronic commerce, says: "Working here has given me a rich Rolodex.... It's a group I could never assemble on my own.... I'm learning too much here to make going out on my own an attractive option."[14]

■ SCIENTIFIC FOUNDATIONS OF ORGANIZATIONAL BEHAVIOR

As far back as a century ago, consultants and scholars were giving increased attention to the systematic study of management. Although most attention was initially on physical working conditions, principles of administration, and industrial engineering principles, by the 1940s the focus had broadened to include the essential human factor. This gave impetus to research dealing with individual attitudes, group dynamics, and the relationships between managers and workers. Eventually, the discipline of organizational behavior emerged as a broader and encompassing approach. Today, it continues to evolve as a discipline devoted to scientific understanding of individuals and groups in organizations, and of the performance implications of organizational structures, systems, and processes.[15]

Interdisciplinary Body of Knowledge   OB is an interdisciplinary body of knowledge with strong ties to the behavioral sciences—psychology, sociology, and anthropology, as well as to allied social sciences—such as economics and political science. Organizational behavior is unique, however, in its devotion to applying and integrating these diverse insights to achieve a better understanding of human behavior in organizations.

Use of Scientific Methods   OB uses scientific methods to develop and empirically test generalizations about behavior in organizations. Figure 1.2 describes research methodologies commonly used. Scientific thinking is important to OB researchers and scholars for these reasons: (1) the process of data collection is controlled and systematic; (2) proposed explanations are carefully tested; and (3) only explanations that can be scientifically verified are accepted. Research concepts and designs in OB are explained further in the module "Research Methods in Organizational Behavior."

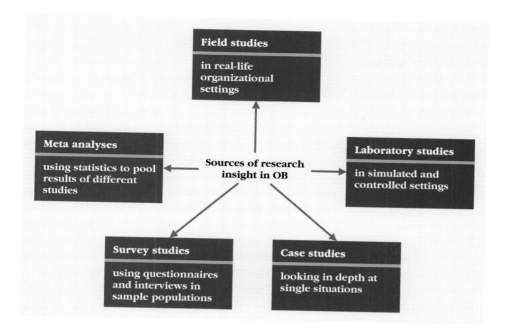

Figure 1.2
Research methods in organizational behavior.

Focus on Application   The field of organizational behavior focuses on applications that can make a real difference in how organizations and people in them perform. Outcome or dependent variables studied by researchers, for example, include task performance, job satisfaction, job involvement, absenteeism, and turnover. It is in this sense that OB is an applied social science that can ultimately help to improve the functioning of organizations and the work experiences of their members. Among the practical questions addressed by the discipline and in this book are: How should rewards such as merit pay raises be allocated? When should jobs be designed for individuals and for groups? What are the ingredients of successful teamwork? How can organizational cultures be changed? Should decisions be made by individual, consultative, or group methods? In a negotiation, what is the best way to achieve "win-win" outcomes?

Contingency Thinking   Rather than assume that there is one "best" or universal way to manage people and organizations, OB recognizes that management practices must be tailored to fit the exact nature of each situation. Using a **contingency approach**, researchers try to identify how different situations can best be understood and handled. In Chapter 3, for example, we recognize that culture can affect how OB theories and concepts apply in different countries.[16] What works well in one culture may not work as well in another. Other important contingency variables addressed in this book include environment, technology, task, structure, and people.

■ The **contingency approach** seeks ways to meet the needs of different management situations.

Organizations as Work Settings

The study of organizational behavior must be framed in an understanding of organizations as work settings. An **organization** is formally defined as a collection of people working together in a division of labor to achieve a common purpose. This definition describes a wide variety of clubs, voluntary organizations, and religious

■ **Organizations** are collections of people working together to achieve a common purpose.

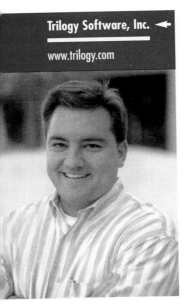

Trilogy Software, Inc. ◄

www.trilogy.com

At Trilogy Software, Inc., in Austin, Texas, CEO and founder Joe Liemandt says: "There's nothing more important than recruiting and growing people." He's abandoned the traditional employer-employee relationship in favor of workers becoming shareholders and partners in business. This gives Trilogy an important edge in the competitive market for high-tech talent.

bodies, as well as entities such as small and large businesses, labor unions, schools, hospitals, and government agencies. The insights and applications of OB can be applied to help all such organizations perform up to expectations as social institutions.

■ PURPOSE, MISSION, AND STRATEGIES

The *core purpose* of an organization may be stated as the creation of goods or services for customers. Nonprofit organizations produce services with public benefits, such as health care, education, judicial processing, and highway maintenance. Large and small for-profit businesses produce consumer goods and services such as automobiles, banking, travel, gourmet dining, and accommodations.

Missions and *mission statements* focus the attention of organizational members and external constituents on the core purpose.[17] For example, the pharmaceutical giant Merck states that its purpose is "to preserve human life." The retailer Wal-Mart states that it seeks "to give ordinary folk the chance to buy the same things as rich people."[18] Increasingly, mission statements are written to communicate a clear *vision* in respect to long-term goals and future aspirations. The corporate vision at America West Airlines expresses the desire "to be known for its focus on customer service and its high performance culture."[19] Bold and challenging visions can attract attention and help draw members together in the quest for high performance. As Robert Reich states in his description of the company of the future: "Talented people want to be part of something that they can believe in, something that confers meaning on their work, on their lives—something that involves a mission."[20]

Given a sense of purpose and a vision, organizations pursue action *strategies* to accomplish them. The variety of mergers and acquisitions common in business today, such as the Daimler-Chrysler combination, are examples of corporate strategies to achieve and sustain advantage in highly competitive environments. In this context, strategies must be both well formulated and well implemented for the organization to succeed.[21] The plan alone is insufficient to the broader strategic goal: To get and stay ahead of the competition. It is here, at the level of action, that the field of organizational behavior becomes especially important. A knowledge of OB is essential to effective strategy implementation. Things happen in organizations because of the efforts of people, and how people work together in organizations is what OB is all about.

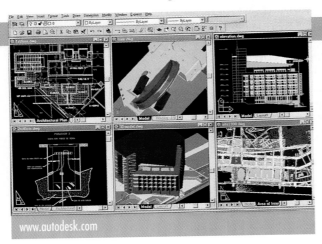

www.autodesk.com

✛ WORKPLACE DIVERSITY

Autodesk, a California-based leading developer of computer-aided design software, makes a commitment to people in its quest for success. Headed by CEO Carol Bartz, the global firm is the fourth-largest PC software firm in the world. It is also devoted to maintaining a high-performance culture that supports motivated and visionary people. At the Web site, you can read how a program called "Future Work Now" uses technology to bring flexibility to work schedules—allowing employees to work in the office, on the road, and at home. The firm also allows casual dress every day and offers paid sabbaticals after four years. And, at Autodesk, you can even bring your dog to work![22]

■ PEOPLE AND WORK SYSTEMS

When CEO Richard Kovacevic of Norwest was asked to comment on the bank's performance, he said: "Our success has to do with execution...talented, professional, motivated people who care...that's our competitive advantage."[23] Leaders of today's organizations recognize the importance of putting people first. They understand the new significance of the old concept—people are an organization's most critical assets.

One of the important directions in OB today is the emphasis on **intellectual capital** as represented by the sum total of knowledge, expertise, and dedication of an organization's workforce.[24] It recognizes that even in the age of high technology, people are the indispensable **human resources** whose knowledge and performance advance the organization's purpose, mission, and strategies. Only through human efforts can the great advantages be realized from other *material resources* of organizations such as technology, information, raw materials, and money. A recent *Fortune* survey of America's most-admired firms goes so far as to report that "the single best predictor of overall success was a company's ability to attract, motivate, and retain talented people."[25]

Today's strategic emphasis on customer-driven and market-driven organizations places great significance on understanding the relationship between an organization and its environment. As shown in Figure 1.3, organizations can be viewed as **open systems** that obtain resource inputs from the environment and transform them into outputs that are returned to the environment in the form of finished goods or services. If everything works right, the environment values these outputs and creates a continuing demand for them. This sustains operations and allows the organization to survive and prosper over the long run. But things can and sometimes do go wrong in the organization/environment relationship. If the value chain breaks down and an organization's goods or services

■ **Intellectual capital** is the sum total of knowledge, expertise, and energy available from organizational members.

■ **Human resources** are the people who do the work that helps organizations fulfill their missions.

■ **Open systems** transform human and material resource inputs into finished goods and services.

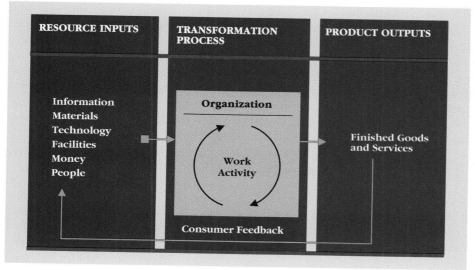

Figure 1.3
Organization and environment relationships.

become unpopular, it will sooner or later have difficulty obtaining the resources it needs to operate. In the extreme case, it will be forced out of existence.

Organizational Behavior and Management

Regardless of your career direction and entry point, the field of organizational behavior will someday become especially important as you try to master the special challenges of working as a **manager**. In all organizations, managers perform jobs that involve directly supporting the work efforts of others. Being a manager is a unique challenge that carries distinct performance responsibilities. Managers help other people get important things done in timely, high-quality, and personally satisfying ways. In the new workplace, this is accomplished more through "helping" and "supporting" than through traditional notions of "directing" and "controlling." Indeed, the word "manager" is increasingly being linked in the new workplace to roles described by such titles as "coordinator," "coach," or "team leader."[26]

■ **Managers** are formally responsible for supporting the work efforts of other people.

■ THE NATURE OF MANAGERIAL WORK

Anyone who serves as a manager or team leader assumes a unique responsibility for work that is accomplished largely through the efforts of other people. The result is a very demanding and complicated job that has been described by researchers in the following terms.[27] *Managers work long hours.* A work week of more than the standard 40 hours is typical. The length of the work week tends to increase as one advances to higher managerial levels; heads of organizations often work the longest hours. *Managers are busy people.* Their work is intense and involves doing many different things on any given workday. The busy day of a manager includes a shifting mix of incidents that require attention, with the number of incidents being greatest for lower-level managers. *Managers are often interrupted.* Their work is fragmented and variable. Interruptions are frequent, and many tasks must be completed quickly. *Managers work mostly with other people.* In fact, they spend little time working alone. Time spent with others includes working with bosses, peers, subordinates, subordinates of their subordinates, as well as outsiders, such as customers, suppliers, and the like. *Managers are communicators.* In general, managers spend a lot of time getting, giving, and processing information. Their work is often face-to-face verbal communication that takes place during formal and informal meetings. Higher level managers typically spend more time in scheduled meetings than do lower level managers.

■ THE MANAGEMENT PROCESS

An *effective manager* is one whose organizational unit, group, or team consistently achieves its goals while members remain capable, committed, and enthusiastic. This definition focuses attention on two key results. The first is *task performance*—the quality and quantity of the work produced or the services provided by the work unit as a whole. The second is *job satisfaction*—how people feel about their work and the work setting. Just as a valuable machine should not be allowed to break down for lack of proper maintenance, the valuable contribu-

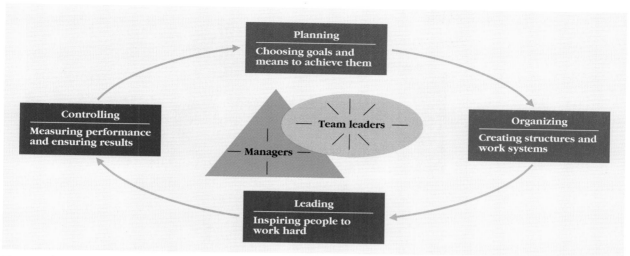

Figure 1.4
The management process of planning, organizing, leading, and controlling.

tions of the human resource should never be lost for lack of proper care. Accordingly, OB directs a manager's attention to such matters as job satisfaction, job involvement, and organizational commitment, as well as measures of actual task performance.

The job of any manager or team leader is largely one of adding value to the work setting by doing things that help others to accomplish their tasks. A traditional and still relevant way of describing this job is as a set of tasks or functions that must be performed constantly and often simultaneously. As shown in Figure 1.4, these four *functions of management* are planning, organizing, leading, and controlling. They form a framework for managerial action that can be described as follows:[28]

- **Planning**—Defining goals, setting specific performance objectives, and identify the actions needed to achieve them.
- **Organizing**—Creating work structures and systems, and arranging resources to accomplish goals and objectives.
- **Leading**—Instilling enthusiasm by communicating with others, motivating them to work hard, and maintaining good interpersonal relations.
- **Controlling**—Ensuring that things go well by monitoring performance and taking corrective action as necessary.

■ MANAGERIAL ROLES AND NETWORKS

In what has become a classic study of managerial behavior, Henry Mintzberg moved beyond this functional description and identified three sets of roles that managers must be prepared to perform on a daily basis.[29] These roles are shown in Figure 1.5. In the first category are *interpersonal roles* that involve working directly with other people. They include hosting and attending official ceremonies (figurehead), creating enthusiasm and serving people's needs (leader), and

Four functions of management

■ **Planning** sets objectives and identifies the actions needed to achieve them.

■ **Organizing** divides up tasks and arranges resources to accomplish them.

■ **Leading** creates enthusiasm to work hard to accomplish tasks successfully.

■ **Controlling** monitors performance and takes any needed corrective action.

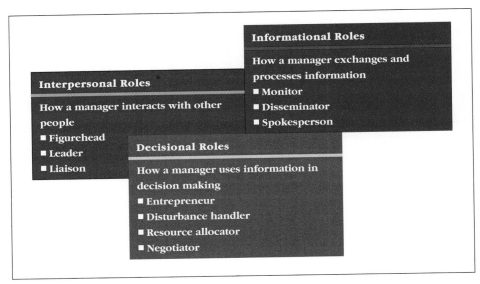

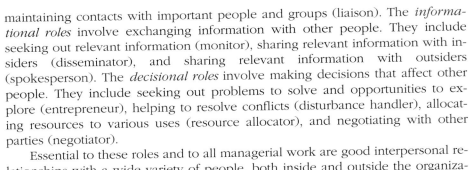

Figure 1.5
Ten roles of effective managers.

Florida A & M University ◄

www.famu.edu

Dean Sybil Mobley welcomes corporate visitors to Florida A&M's business school. And the firms are glad to come. They get the inside track on recruiting the school's graduates, known for their high caliber and immersion in corporate culture. Says Mobley: "We want them to hit the ground running."

maintaining contacts with important people and groups (liaison). The *informational roles* involve exchanging information with other people. They include seeking out relevant information (monitor), sharing relevant information with insiders (disseminator), and sharing relevant information with outsiders (spokesperson). The *decisional roles* involve making decisions that affect other people. They include seeking out problems to solve and opportunities to explore (entrepreneur), helping to resolve conflicts (disturbance handler), allocating resources to various uses (resource allocator), and negotiating with other parties (negotiator).

Essential to these roles and to all managerial work are good interpersonal relationships with a wide variety of people, both inside and outside the organization.[30] Managers and team leaders should be able to develop, maintain, and work well within *task networks*—of specific job-related contacts, *career networks*—of career guidance and opportunity resources and *social networks*—of trustworthy friends and peers.[31]

■ MANAGERIAL SKILLS AND COMPETENCIES

A *skill* is an ability to translate knowledge into action that results in a desired performance. Robert Katz divides the essential managerial skills into three categories: technical, human, and conceptual.[32] He further suggests that the relative importance of these skills varies across the different levels of management. Technical skills are considered more important at entry levels of management, where supervisors and team leaders must deal with job-specific problems. Senior executives are concerned more with issues of organizational purpose, mission, and strategy. Broader, more ambiguous, and longer term decisions dominate attention at these higher levels, and conceptual skills gain in relative importance. Human skills, which are strongly grounded in the foundations of organizational behavior, are consistent in their importance across all managerial levels.

Technical Skills A **technical skill** is an ability to perform specialized tasks. Such ability derives from knowledge or expertise gained from education or experience. This skill involves proficiency at using select methods, processes, and procedures to accomplish tasks. Perhaps the best current example is skill in using the latest communication and information technologies. In the "high-tech" workplaces of today, technical proficiency in word processing, database management, spreadsheet analysis, E-mail, and communications networks are often hiring prerequisites. Some technical skills require preparatory education, whereas others are acquired through specific training and on-the-job experience.

Human Skills Central to managerial work and team leadership are **human skills**, or the ability to work well with other people. They emerge as a spirit of trust, enthusiasm, and genuine involvement in interpersonal relationships. A person with good human skills will have a high degree of self-awareness and a capacity for understanding or empathizing with the feelings of others. People with this skill are able to interact well with others, engage in persuasive communications, deal successfully with disagreements and conflicts, and more. Human skills are indispensable in the new age of organizations where traditions of hierarchy and vertical structures are giving way to lateral relations and peer structures.[33]

Conceptual Skills All good managers are able to view the organization or situation as a whole and to solve problems to the benefit of everyone concerned. This capacity to analyze and solve complex and interrelated problems is a **conceptual skill**. It involves the ability to see and understand how the whole organizational system works, and how the parts are interrelated. Conceptual skill is used to identify problems and opportunities, gather and interpret relevant information, and make good problem-solving decisions that serve the organization's purpose.

OB Across Functions

FINANCE

New CFO Key to Turnaround

With a strong background in finance and information systems, Deborah Hopkins also drew upon her people skills and experience with diversity and mentoring programs when taking on her new job as CFO of Boeing Aircraft. One of her first public events was a company retreat attended by 280 corporate executives. She presented basic financial formulas carefully, concerned that her audience not think she was talking beneath them. The praise flowed, and many attendees thanked her for clarifying basic business concepts. Hopkins has the experience and skills to make a difference at Boeing by teaching the managers about business, increasing the sophistication of managerial decision making, and helping to increase the integration of accounting and financial systems. Harry Stonecipher, Boeing's President and CEO, says that Hopkins is "a good communicator and she knows what she is talking about." This combination of technical and human skills is beneficial for both Boeing and Hopkins's career.

■ **Technical skill** is an ability to perform specialized tasks.

■ **Human skill** is the ability to work well with other people.

■ **Conceptual skill** is the ability to analyze and solve complex problems.

Ethics and Organizational Behavior

The word "ethics" is important in OB. **Ethical behavior** is that accepted as morally "good" and "right," as opposed to "bad" or "wrong," in a particular setting.[34] Is it ethical to withhold information that might discourage a job candidate from joining your organization? Is it ethical to ask someone to take a job you know will not be good for his or her career progress? Is it ethical to ask so much of someone that they continually have to choose between "having a 'career' and having a 'life'?" The list of questions can go on and on, but an important point

■ **Ethical behavior** is morally accepted as "good" and "right."

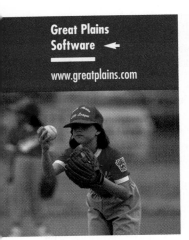

Great Plains Software ◄

www.greatplains.com

Doug Burgum, chairman and CEO of this Fargo, North Dakota, software firm believes in work-life balance. He says: "Balance is what's needed when your kids are playing in a softball tournament, and they really want you to be there. We want parents to be able to say 'yes' to their kids...to say 'yes' to things that are important to them but that may conflict with their regular working hours."

■ **Procedural justice** is the degree to which policies and procedures are properly followed.

■ **Distributive justice** is the degree to which all people are treated the same under a policy.

■ An **ethical dilemma** requires a person to choose among actions that offer possible benefits while also violating ethical standards.

remains: The public is increasingly demanding that people in organizations and the organizations themselves all act in accordance with high ethical and moral standards.

■ WAYS OF THINKING ABOUT ETHICAL BEHAVIOR

Ethical behavior conforms not only to the dictates of law but also to a broader moral code that is common to society as a whole. Just exactly what moral code governs a person's choices, however, is a subject of debate. At least four ways of thinking about ethical behavior in and by organizations can be identified.

The *utilitarian view* considers ethical behavior to be that which delivers the greatest good to the greatest number of people. Those who subscribe to the results-oriented utilitarian logic assess the moral aspects of their decisions in terms of the consequences they create. Utilitarianism believes that the needs of the many outweigh the needs of the few. From such a perspective, it may be ethical to close a factory in one town in order to keep the parent corporation profitable and operating in several other towns.

The *individualism view* considers ethical behavior to be that which is best for an individual's long-term self-interests. In principle, at least, someone who acts unethically in the short run—such as by denying a qualified minority employee a promotion, should *not* succeed in the long run because the short-run action will not be tolerated. Thus, if everyone operated with long-term self-interest in mind, their short-run actions would be ethical.

The *moral-rights view* considers ethical behavior to be that which respects fundamental rights shared by all human beings. This view is tied very closely to the principle of basic human rights, such as those of life, liberty, and fair treatment by law. In an organization, this principle is reflected in such issues as rights to privacy, due process, and freedom of speech. Ethical behavior does not violate any of these fundamental human rights.

The *justice view* considers ethical behavior to be that which is fair and impartial in its treatment of people. It is based on the concept of equitable treatment for all concerned. In OB, two issues address this view of ethical behavior.[35] **Procedural Justice** is the degree to which the rules and procedures specified by policies are properly followed in all cases under which they are applied. In a sexual harassment case, for example, this may mean that required hearings are held for every case submitted for administrative review. **Distributive justice** is the degree to which all people are treated the same under a policy, regardless of race, ethnicity, gender, age, or any other demographic characteristic. In a sexual harassment case, this might mean that a complaint filed by a man against a woman would receive the same hearing as one filed by a woman against a man.

■ ETHICAL DILEMMAS IN THE WORKPLACE

An **ethical dilemma** is a situation in which a person must decide whether or not to do something that, although benefiting them or the organization, or both, may be considered unethical. It is difficult to predict exactly what ethical dilemmas you will someday face. However, research suggests that people at work often encounter such dilemmas in their relationships with superiors, subordinates, customers, competitors, suppliers, and regulators. Common issues underlying the dilemmas involve honesty in communications and contracts, gifts and entertainment, kickbacks, pricing practices, and employee terminations.[36] More and more organizations are offering ethics training programs that offer advice (see The Effective Manager 1.2) for handling ethical dilemmas.[37] In addition, the training helps participants learn how to identify and deal with these common rationalizations that are sometimes used to help justify actual or potential misconduct.[38]

- Pretending the behavior is not really unethical or illegal.
- Excusing the behavior by saying it's really in the organization's or your best interest.
- Assuming the behavior is okay because no one else is expected to find out about it.
- Presuming your superiors will support and protect you if anything should go wrong.

THE EFFECTIVE MANAGER 1.2

HOW TO DEAL WITH ETHICAL DILEMMAS

1. Recognize and clarify the dilemma.
2. Get all the possible facts.
3. List all of your options.
4. Test each option by asking:
   Is it legal? Is it right? Is it beneficial?
5. Make your decision.
6. Double check your decision by asking:
   How will I feel if my family finds out? How will I feel if this is printed in the newspaper?
7. Then, and only then, take action.

Ways to rationalize unethical behavior

ORGANIZATIONAL SOCIAL RESPONSIBILITY

Closely related to the ethics of workplace behavior is **social responsibility**—the obligation of organizations to behave in ethical and moral ways as institutions of the broader society. This concept suggests that members must ensure that their ethical frameworks extend to the organization as a whole. Managers and leaders should commit organizations to actions that are consistent with both the quest for high productivity and the objective of corporate social responsibility. Unfortunately, it doesn't always turn out this way. Some years ago, for example, two Beech-nut senior executives were sentenced to jail for their roles in a notorious case of organizational wrongdoing. The scandal involved the sale of adulterated apple juice for infants. Although the bottles were labeled "100% fruit juice," the contents turned out to be a blend of chemical ingredients. This case, like many others that make the daily news, came to public awareness because of a *whistleblower*—someone within the organization who exposes the wrongdoings of others in order to preserve high ethical standards.[39]

■ **Social responsibility** is the obligation of organizations to behave in ethical and moral ways.

WORK AND THE QUALITY OF LIFE

In many ways, the study of organizational behavior is a search for practical ideas on how to help organizations achieve high performance outcomes while always acting in an ethical and socially responsible manner. A central concern in this quest must be the well being of an organization's entire workforce—this means everyone, not just the managers. The term **quality of work life**, or QWL, is a prominent indicator in OB of the overall quality of human experience in the workplace. It is a reminder that high performance in any work setting can and should be accomplished by high levels of job satisfaction.

■ **Quality of work life** is the overall quality of human experiences in the workplace.

www.sas.com

If you go to work in Cary, North Carolina, at SAS Institute, the world's largest closely held software company, you're unlikely to leave to take a better job with a competitor. Under the leadership of entrepreneur and founder James H. Goodnight, SAS offers impressive benefits. Goodnight says: "I like happy people." Headquarters employees have a free health clinic, a recreation facility, daily performances by a pianist during lunch, and private offices. SAS promotes families by offering flexible hours, a 35-hour-work schedule, and two on-site day-care centers. Employees get an extra week of paid vacation over the Christmas holiday, and receive a year-end bonus and profit sharing. Not surprisingly, SAS's turnover is a low 4 percent.[40]

A commitment to QWL can be considered a core value of OB. The stage was set very early in the life of the discipline by theorists with a strong human orientation, such as Douglas McGregor.[41] He contrasted what he called *Theory X assumptions*—that people basically disliked work, needed direction, and avoided responsibility, with *Theory Y assumptions*—that people liked work, were creative, and accepted responsibility. For McGregor, Theory Y assumptions were the most appropriate and tended to create positive *self-fulfilling prophecies*. That is, when people were treated well at work, the likelihood was that they would respond positively and as expected.

Today the many concepts and theories discussed in OB reflect QWL and Theory Y themes. The hallmarks of excellence in management and organizations now include *empowerment*—involving people from all levels of responsibility in decision making; *trust*—redesigning jobs, systems, and structures to give people more personal discretion in their work; *rewards*—building reward systems that are fair, relevant, and consistent, while contingent on work performance; *responsiveness*—making the work setting more pleasant and supportive of individual needs and family responsibilities; and **work-life balance**—making sure that the demands of the job are a reasonable fit with one's personal life and non-work responsibilities.[42]

A commitment to QWL is consistent with respect for what was earlier called the intellectual capital of an organization. It involves putting people first in any list of organizational priorities. The next chapter will continue to explore how people help to build high performance organizations. For now, consider the leadership challenge posed in these comments made by Jeffrey Pfeffer in his book, *The Human Equation: Building Profits by Putting People First*.[43]

■ **Work-life balance** deals with the demands from one's work and personal affairs.

The key to managing people in ways that lead to profits, productivity, innovation, and real organizational learning ultimately lie in how you think about your organization and its people.... When you look at your people, do you see costs to be reduced?... Or, when you look at your people do you see intelligent, motivated, trustworthy individuals—the most critical and valuable strategic assets your organization can have?

Chapter 1 Study Guide

Summary

What is organizational behavior and why is it important?

- Organizational behavior is the study of individuals and groups in organizations.

- Dramatic changes signal the emergence of a new workplace with high technology, global competition, demanding customers, and high performance systems.

- Valuing diversity and respecting differences is a key theme in OB; workforces are increasingly diverse in terms of gender, race and ethnicity, age, and able-bodiedness.

How do we learn about organizational behavior?

- Organizational learning is the process of acquiring knowledge and utilizing information to adapt successfully to changing circumstances.

- Learning about organizational behavior involves more than just reading a textbook; it also involves a commitment to continuous and life-long learning from experience.

- OB is an applied discipline based on scientific methods and that uses a contingency approach recognizing that management practices must fit the situation.

What are organizations like as work settings?

- An organization is a collection of people working together in a division of labor for a common purpose—to produce goods or services for society.

- As open systems, organizations interact with their environments to obtain resources that are transformed into outputs returned to the environment for consumption.

- The resources of organizations are material—such as technology, capital, and information, as well as human—the people who do the required work.

What is the nature of managerial work?

- Managers in the new workplace are expected to act more like "coaches" and "facilitators" than as "bosses" and "controllers."

- An effective manager is one whose work unit, team, or group accomplishes high levels of performance that are sustainable over the long term by enthusiastic workers.

- The four functions of management are (1) planning—to set directions, (2) organizing—to assemble resources and systems, (3) leading—to create workforce enthusiasm, and (4) controlling—to ensure desired results.

- Managers fulfill a variety of interpersonal, informational, and decisional roles while working with networks of people both inside and outside of the organization.

- Managerial performance is based on a combination of essential technical, human, and conceptual skills.

How do ethics influence human behavior in organizations?

■ Ethical behavior is that which is accepted as morally "good" and "right" instead of "bad" or "wrong."

■ Ways of thinking about an ethical behavior include the utilitarian, individualism, moral-rights, and justice views.

■ The workplace is a source of possible ethical dilemmas in which people may be asked to do or are tempted to do things that violate ethical standards.

■ Organizational social responsibility is the obligation of organizations as a whole to act in ethical ways.

■ The insights of OB can help build and maintain high performance organizations that offer their members a high quality of work life.

Key Terms

Conceptual skill (p. 13)
Contingency approach (p. 7)
Controlling (p. 11)
Distributive justice (p. 14)
Ethical behavior (p. 13)
Ethical dilemma (p. 14)
Glass ceiling effect (p. 5)
Human resources (p. 9)
Human skill (p. 13)

Intellectual capital (p. 9)
Leading (p. 11)
Managers (p. 10)
Open system (p. 9)
Organizations (p. 7)
Organizational behavior (p. 3)
Organizational learning (p. 5)
Organizing (p. 11)

Planning (p. 11)
Procedural justice (p. 14)
Quality of work life (p. 15)
Social responsibility (p. 15)
Technical skill (p. 13)
Workforce diversity (p. 5)
Work-life balance (p. 16)

Self-Test 1

■ MULTIPLE CHOICE

1. The term "workforce diversity" refers to differences in race, age, gender, ethnicity, and _____ among people at work. (a) social status (b) personal wealth (c) able-bodiedness (d) political preference

2. What is the best description of the setting facing organizational behavior today? (a) Command-and-control is in. (b) The new generation expects much the same as the old. (c) Empowerment is out. (d) Work-life balance concerns are in.

3. The interest of OB researchers in outcome variables such as _____ is an indication that the discipline is concerned with practical issues and applications. (a) absenteeism and turnover (b) job satisfaction (c) job performance (d) all of these

4. The "glass ceiling effect" in organizations is _____. (a) a hidden barrier limiting career advancement of minorities and women (b) an unpublicized limit on wages paid to top managers (c) an unpublicized limit on wages paid to operating workers (d) a restriction on the hiring of full-time permanent workers

5. Which statement about OB is most correct? (a) OB seeks "one-best-way" solutions to management problems. (b) OB is a unique science that has little relationship to other scientific disciplines. (c) OB is focused on using knowledge for practical applications. (d) OB is so modern that it has no historical roots.

6. In the open systems view of organizations, technology, information, and money are among the _____. (a) products (b) services (c) inputs (d) outputs

7. The management function of _____ is concerned with creating enthusiasm for hard work. (a) planning (b) organizing (c) controlling (d) leading

8. Justifying ethical behavior based on the greatest good for the most people is the _____ view. (a) utilitarian (b) individualism (c) moral-rights (d) justice

9. When someone excuses unethical behavior by pointing out that it is really in the organization's best interest, they are _____. (a) doing the right thing for themselves (b) doing the right thing for society (c) rationalizing the unethical conduct (d) following the rule of procedural justice

10. When facing an ethical dilemma, final action should be taken only after _____. (a) recognizing the dilemma (b) checking whether or not the action will be legal (c) making sure no one will find out if the action is wrong (d) double checking to make sure that you are personally comfortable with the decision

■ TRUE–FALSE

11. Organizational behavior is defined as the study of how organizations behave in different environments.   T   F

12. In the statement, "OB seeks to meet the needs of different management situations." the implication is one of contingency thinking.   T   F

13. Organizational learning is a process of acquiring knowledge and using information to adapt to changing circumstances.   T   F

14. The external environment is not important to organizations as open systems.   T   F

15. When a president holds frequent meetings with a task force to stay informed about its progress, she is fulfilling the planning function of management.   T   F

16. Technical skills are probably the most important skills for top-level managers.   T   F

17. Managerial work involves major use of interpersonal networks.   T   F

18. A team leader who gives a friend special preference under a vacation leave policy is violating distributive justice.   T   F

19. A whistleblower is someone who exposes unethical behavior in organizations.   T   F

20. Research suggests that organizational superiors are the causes of many ethical dilemmas faced by people at work.   T   F

■ SHORT RESPONSE

21. What does "valuing diversity" mean in the workplace?

22. What is an effective manager?

23. How would Henry Mintzberg describe a typical executive's workday?

24. Why is QWL an issue of ethics and organizational social responsibility?

■ APPLICATIONS ESSAY

25. Juanita Perez faces a dilemma in her role as the accounts manager for a local social service agency. One of the employees has reported to her that another employee is charging meals to his travel expense account even when he is attending a conference

where meals are provided. What should Juanita do in this situation that sets the stage so that (a) similar problems will not arise in the future, and that (b) the criteria of both procedural and distributive justice are satisfied?

Explore application-oriented Fast Company articles, cases, experimental exercises, and self-assessments in the OB Skills Workbook

■ **Visit the Schermerhorn Web site to find the Interactive Self-Test and Internet exercises for this chapter.**

The High Performance Organization

OWNERSHIP BEGINS AT THE GRASSROOTS

www.shell.com

To speed up its massive effort to change its complex and resistant bureaucracy, Shell Oil Company decided to bring in six- to eight-person teams from six operating companies to a "retailing boot camp." As an example, in order to help Malaysia increase service-station revenues along major highways, Shell established a set of cross-functional teams made up of four or five marketing managers, a dealer, and a union trucker. Shell prepared a

number of new marketing and leadership tools for the teams to apply in the local market. For 60 days, the first set of teams used those tools to develop plans for dealing with their problems. They then returned to "boot camp" for a peer review meeting. After the third set of teams completed boot camp, all teams met together with the high-level managing director's team to present their plans at demanding and intense sessions. They were on a "hot seat" in their presentations before their peers and the managing director's team.

The teams returned home for another 60 days during which they worked to put their plans into action. Then they reported back on their breakthroughs and their breakdowns. The managing director claims that the kind of straight talk generated by this process is new to Shell and puts pressure on him, as well as on the teams. Shell's goal of a 25:1 return on its investment in this program has been exceeded, and Shell has been encouraged to use the program in other situations and to take other related steps to increase its competitiveness in a fast-changing world.

W e live and work in an age of increasing global competition, new technologies, shifting demographics, and changing social values. A crucial reaction to these kinds of forces has been the emergence of a new breed of organization, the *high performance organization* or HPO. These are organizations intentionally designed to bring out the best in people and create an extraordinary organizational capability that delivers sustainable high performance results.[1] HPOs are fast, agile, and market driven. They emphasize respect for people, as evidenced by the involvement of workers and managers at all levels and consistent use of teams like those at Shell. Organizations with significant HPO features now make up from one-fifth to one-third of Fortune 1000 companies, and the growth trend will surely continue.[2] Increasingly, future careers will unfold in high performance work settings.

Study Questions

Chapter 2 examines trends and directions in high performance organizations, and their implications for the field of organizational behavior. As you read the chapter, keep in mind the following key questions.

- What is the high performance context of organizational behavior?
- What is a high performance organization?
- What are the management challenges of high performance organizations?
- How are high performance organizations created?

High Performance Context of Organizational Behavior

Some critical forces in the emerging high performance context involve changing customer expectations, the changing workforce, and changing organizations.

■ OB AND CHANGING CUSTOMER EXPECTATIONS

Only those organizations that deliver what customers want in terms of quality, service, and cost will prosper in today's highly competitive environments. This continues to be an age of **total quality management** (TQM)—management dedicated to ensuring that an organization and all of its members are committed to high quality, continuous improvement, and customer satisfaction. *Quality* in this sense means that customers' needs are met and that all tasks are done right the first time. An important hallmark of the total quality concept is **continuous improvement**—the belief that anything and everything done in the workplace should be continually evaluated by asking two questions: (1) Is this necessary? (2) If so, can it be done better?[3]

Consistent with this approach is the creation of customer-driven organizations that are dedicated to quality and service. Figure 2.1 expresses this notion in the form of an *upside-down pyramid* view of organizations. The figure focuses attention on total quality service to customers and clients by placing them at the top of the organization. Managing from this point of view requires that workers operate in ways that directly affect customers and clients; it requires that team

■ **Total quality management** is total commitment to high quality results, continuous improvement, and meeting customer needs.

■ **Continuous improvement** is the belief that anything and everything done in the workplace should be continually improved.

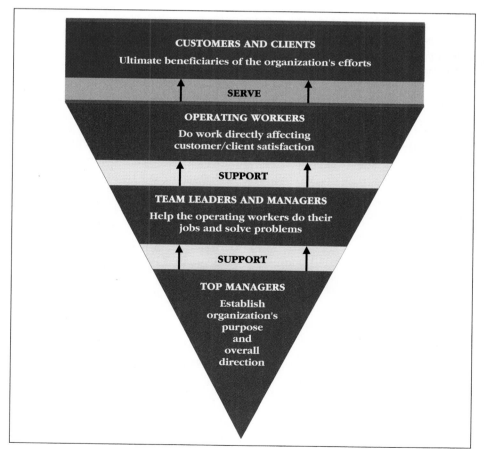

CUSTOMERS AND CLIENTS
Ultimate beneficiaries of the organization's efforts

SERVE

OPERATING WORKERS
Do work directly affecting
customer/client satisfaction

SUPPORT

TEAM LEADERS AND MANAGERS
Help the operating workers do their
jobs and solve problems

SUPPORT

TOP MANAGERS
Establish
organization's
purpose
and
overall
direction

Figure 2.1
The "upside-down pyramid" view of organizations and management.

Customers.com ◄

www.seybold.com

Organizations are supposed to serve customers. Run by Patricia Seybold, founder and CEO of the Seybold Group, Customers.com presents case studies of organizations, such as Amazon.com, that achieve success by learning about their customers, building customer loyalty, and maintaining a strong customer base.

leaders and middle managers do things that directly support the workers; and it requires that top managers clarify the organizational mission and objectives, set strategies, and make adequate resources available.[4]

■ OB AND THE CHANGING WORKFORCE

The American workforce is becoming more and more diverse with an increasing proportion of women, persons of color, and older employees. Trends in Canada and the European Union are similar.[5] Besides more diversity, two especially important and contradictory workforce characteristics are (1) the impact of **Generation X** or *"Gold-Collar" workers* (those born between 1965 and 1977), and (2) the impact of poor educational preparation of some high school graduates. In fact, U.S. test scores were the lowest in one comparison of 16 industrialized countries.[6] Both characteristics present a current OB challenge but in very different ways.

Figure 2.2 shows that Gold-Collar Generation X workers demand a lot of the company. They want challenge on the job and flexibility in work schedules; some even want to work at home. But they also want to work in teams, and they are interested in **empowerment**—being allowed as an individual or group to make decisions that affect their work. These needs, wants, and desires are likely to be strongest for **knowledge workers**—employees whose major task is to produce new knowledge, typically through computer-oriented means—and other jobs with workers in high demand and low supply. At the millennium, this condition is widespread throughout the U.S. economy, with unemployment rates the lowest in many years.[7] The level of skills and abilities among many of these workers allows them to function well in highly challenging jobs and work settings.[8]

At the opposite end of the spectrum are those high school graduates who score poorly on standardized tests and enter the workforce with skills deficiencies. In the United States, an alarming number of them require considerable basic skills training in math, writing, and reasoning to get them up to speed in

■ Generation X workers are those born between 1965 and 1977 who are knowledge workers in short supply.

■ Empowerment allows individuals or groups to make decisions that affect them or their work.

■ Knowledge workers employees whose major task is to produce new knowledge, typically through computer-oriented means.

Figure 2.2
Values and Preferences of the Generation X or "Gold-Collar" Workforce.

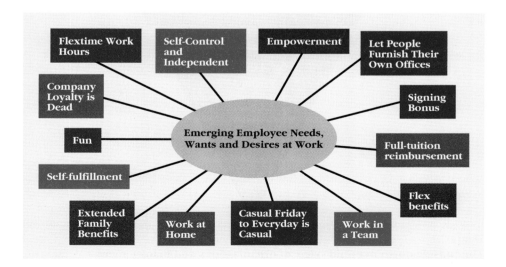

many of today's organizations.[9] In a knowledge-driven economy, high costs are associated with such remedial training and the individuals can suffer long-term career disadvantages.

■ OB AND CHANGING ORGANIZATIONS

The last decade may well be remembered as the one that fundamentally changed the way people work.[10] We experienced the stresses of downsizing and restructuring; we gained sensitivity to the peaks and valleys of changing economic times; and we witnessed the advent of the Internet with its impact on both people and organizations. Truly progressive organizations, however, are doing much more than simply cutting employees and adding technology to reduce the scale of operations in the quest for productivity. They are changing the very essence of the way things are done, and they are adding new meaning to the traditional notions of employer–employee relationships.

One characteristic of this new and fast-paced world of organizations is constant change which carries with it an emphasis on reinventing ways of doing things and continuously improving in all aspects of operations. Many organizations have pursued **process reengineering** which rethinks and radically redesigns business processes to stimulate innovation and change and improve critical performance measures such as cost, quality, service, and speed.[11] Organizations facing these new demands are being asked to "start over"—to forget how things were done in the past and to ask only how they should be done to best meet critical performance measures. Answers to these questions are used to redesign activities and workflows in order to give better value to both internal and external customers.

New information technology has seen an explosion of activity in what may become a benchmark of twenty-first-century organizations—**electronic commerce** in which business is transacted through the Internet. The popular Web-based bookseller Amazon.com is but one spectacular example of emerging **E-corporations** that utilize the Internet and information technologies to support enterprise-wide computer integration of all aspects of operations.[12] In an increasingly "Net-centric" world, technology-driven *network organizations* operate as virtual alliances of suppliers, customers, and even competitors, who link with the latest electronic information technologies and share such things as skills, costs, and access to global markets.[13] These alliances are formed, utilized, and disbanded with ease, all in quick response to business opportunities.

These and related developments are giving rise to what some call a *free-agent economy*, one in which individuals contract their services to a shifting mix of employers over time.[14] British scholar and consultant Charles Handy describes the career implications of what he calls the **shamrock organization**.[15] A shamrock, the Irish national emblem, has three leaves per stem. Each leaf represents a different group of people. The first leaf is a core group of workers made up of permanent, full-time employees with critical skills, who follow standard career paths. This is a relatively small group, perhaps made up of those who remain after major downsizing of a more traditional organization. The second leaf is a group of outside operators who are engaged contractually by the core group to perform a variety of jobs essential to the daily functioning of the organization. Many of these jobs would be performed by full-time staff, (e.g., human resource personnel) in a more traditional organization. The third leaf is a group of part-timers who can be hired

■ **Process reengineering** is the total rethinking and redesigning of organizational process to improve performance and innovation and involves analyzing, streamlining, and reconfiguring actions and tasks to achieve work goals.

■ **Electronic commerce** is where business is transacted through the Internet.

■ **E-corporations** utilize the Internet and information technologies to support enterprise-wide computer integration of operations.

■ **Shamrock organizations** are firms that operate with a core group of permanent workers supplemented by outside contractors and part-time workers.

temporarily by the core group as the needs of the business grow and who can just as easily be let go when business falls. Today's college graduates must be prepared to succeed in the second and third leaves, not just the first.

What Is a High Performance Organization?

■ The **high performance organization** is intentionally designed to bring out the best in people and produce sustainable organizational results.

The free-agent economy and shamrock organization are one aspect of the rapidly changing context of OB. Another is the **high performance organization**, introduced earlier as one intentionally designed to bring out the best in people and thereby produce organizational capability that delivers sustainable organizational results. Instead of treating people as disposable parts of constantly shifting temporary alliances, HPOs place people first.[16] They are regarded as the crucial resource in providing the capability to deliver sustainable high performance results.

■ EMPHASIS ON INTELLECTUAL CAPITAL

■ **Intellectual capital** is represented by the sum total of knowledge, expertise, and energy available from organization members.

The essential foundation for the high performance organization is **intellectual capital**, defined in Chapter 1, as represented by the sum total of knowledge, expertise, and dedication of an organization's workforce.[17] In this sense, even in the days of high technology, people are the indispensable *human resources* whose contributions advance the organization's purpose, mission, and strategies. To utilize this intellectual capital, HPOs often organize their flow of work around the key business processes and often create work teams within these processes.[18] They follow human-resource policies directed toward enhancing employee flexibility, skills, knowledge, and motivation.[19] At the same time, high performance organizations involve fewer levels of management and change the way managers operate. They become much less directive order-givers and instead emphasize coaching, integrating the work of work teams with each other, and facilitating the work of the teams so that they can best complete their jobs and meet customer expectations.[20]

www.digitalevolution.com

☐ TECHNOLOGY

A 22-member project team at Digital Evolution, a small Los Angeles software company, has just completed a successful prototype for a multimedia auto dealership management system as part of the client's larger "showroom of the future strategy." The process involved the best of both technology and teamwork. The next task is to produce a working version of the prototype to link together 12 dealerships. Digital's team members will relocate to the customer's headquarters to work with the information systems department. Once tested, each function in the multimedia system is transferred over the dealer network to the client's IS department. Digital Evolution's philosophy is to send project teams into client firms for maximum customer service and innovation.

■ KEY COMPONENTS OF HIGH PERFORMANCE ORGANIZATIONS

A high performance organization's specific form depends on its setting—for example, an HPO bank would have a form different than an auto manufacturer's.[21] But, most high performance organizations include the five components shown in Figure 2.3. The key HPO components are: employee involvement, self-directing work teams, integrated production technologies, organizational learning, and total quality management.

Employee Involvement   The amount of decision making delegated to workers at all levels reflects **employee involvement**. This can be visualized as a continuum.[22] At one end is no involvement (workers just do their jobs) or parallel involvement (there are such things as suggestion boxes, roundtable discussions concerning the jobs, and quality circles—members of a quality circle meet regularly to find ways to achieve continuous improvement of quality operations). In the middle is moderate involvement or participative management (there are increased responsibilities for making day-to-day job decisions). At the opposite end from low involvement is high involvement, or what we earlier termed empowerment—where, you will recall, there is worker responsibility for making decisions regarding themselves and their work. Typically, these decisions are of great latitude regarding virtually all aspects of the job. Increased use of employee involvement came from the realization that positive benefits could come from allowing employees' input into how their jobs were done. Research shows that employee productivity and various aspects of satisfaction tend to be higher with more involvement.[23]

Self-Directing Work Teams   Teams or workgroups that are empowered to make decisions about planning, doing, and evaluating their work are **self-directing work teams**. They sometimes have other names, such as self-managing or self-leading work teams, or autonomous work groups. We discuss them thoroughly in Chapter 10. There are at least two reasons for their role in high perfor-

■ **Employee involvement** is the amount of decision making delegated to employees.

■ **Self-directing work teams** are teams that are empowered to make decisions about planning, doing, and evaluating their work.

Hampton Inn thrives on employee involvement. When a customer complained that the complimentary continental breakfast did not make his favorite cereal available, the service representative saw an opportunity to make the guest happy. The rep gave him his money back—not for the breakfast—but for one night's stay. The rep did it on the spot without having to check with higher authority.

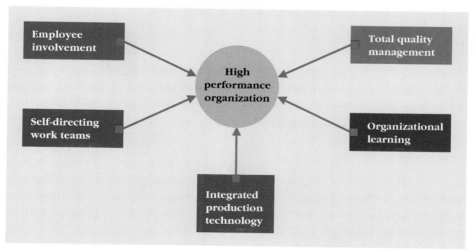

Figure 2.3
Five components of a high performance organization.

mance organizations. First, the importance of tapping employee expertise and knowledge is now well-recognized. Second, there has been an increased need for employees to manage themselves as organizations have downsized and restructured for greater competitiveness.[24] Self-directing work teams strongly affect employee satisfaction and commitment and moderately affect performance.[25]

www.nutrasweetkelco.com

✖ HIGH PERFORMANCE ORGANIZATION

When representatives of self-managing teams met at a business unit of Monsanto Company, their pride and involvement was evident—indeed, they acted like managers, even owners. They discussed strategy, organization structure, technology, implications of broadening the product line, cost controls, and many other business-related concerns handled by management in traditional types of organizations. Their work teams were newly designed and were becoming more stable as a result of changes in hiring, compensation practices, and implementation of a new integrated software system.

Integrated Production Technologies   All organizations use technology to combine the use of resources, knowledge, and techniques and create a product or service output. The concept of **integrated production technologies** focuses on providing flexibility in manufacturing and services and involves job-design and information systems. Key aspects of integrated production technologies typically involve the use of just-in-time production or service systems, and a heavy emphasis on computers to assist in designing products or services, controlling equipment in production processes, and integrating the business functions.

■ **Integrated production technologies** focus on providing flexibility in manufacturing and services and involve job design and information systems as a part of the technology.

Just-in-time systems involve working closely with suppliers to make sure just the right amount of material is available to do the job. At Honeywell, for example, this is done by having the materials suppliers work in the Honeywell plants to see that the inventory level is appropriate. McDonald's does it by keeping only a very small (just-in-time) supply of hamburgers on hand to service its customers.[26]

Computer usage includes integrating such business functions as order entry and accounting with computer-aided design of the product or service and computer-aided production to help control workflow and other product or service aspects. For example, the Technology/Clothing Technology Corporation has developed a computer design process that will allow clothing manufacturers to create "custom" clothing and then to use computers to translate the final design specifications into instructions for manufacturing the item.[27] K2 Corporation, a large U.S. manufacturer of skis, uses these approaches in producing its custom-ordered skis.[28] These design and production functions are often integrated via computer into the just-in-time systems and the integration of business functions so that placing the order, designing it, producing it, and making sure an appropriate level of parts is available are all assisted by computer.

Organizational Learning   Chapter 1 introduced *organizational learning* as a way for organizations to adapt to their settings and to gather information to anticipate future changes.[29] High performance organizations with the characteristics in this section, are designed for organizational learning. They integrate information into the organization's memory for availability and use in new situations.[30] The need for such learning resulted from the realization that traditional, hierarchically structured organizations were not very good at anticipating environmental changes or at sharing information across functions such as production, marketing, and engineering.

Total Quality Management   As introduced earlier, total quality management involves a total commitment to high-quality results, continuous improvement, and meeting customer needs. The initial push for TQM as far back as the mid-1980s tended to apply it in separate, narrowly focused groups emphasizing various aspects of quality. These groups met separately from the workers' regular jobs. Now total quality management has become a tightly integrated part of HPOs where an emphasis on employee involvement and self management encourages all workers to do their own quality planning and checking.

Self-directing production teams at Encore Computers make special-order computer systems for pilot training and other simulations. To control quality and other concerns, Encore uses a customized computerized resource planning system that generates knowledge for continuous process and output improvement to process its orders.

Management Challenges of High Performance Organizations

The journey toward becoming an HPO presents many challenges. Responding to these challenges calls for a very strong leadership commitment. For those organizations that have made the HPO commitment, it has been well worth the effort. Studies of some 1100 companies across a 30-year period show some interesting results. First, bottom-line financial performance tends to increase 30 to 50 percent over a three- to five-year time period. Second, this bottom-line financial performance has increased by a minimum of 3 to 7 percent per year faster than in traditional organizations.[31] These results, however, are dependent upon the mastery of the following challenges.

■ ENVIRONMENTAL LINKAGES

Like other organizations, high performance organizations are open systems influenced by the rapidly moving *external environment* with its global emphasis and rapidly changing customer expectations. Among the most important *inputs* are the organizational worksite's problems and opportunities and the organization's purpose, mission, and strategy, along with its vision. HPOs typically develop a mission and vision package that ties these elements together and integrates them with the organization's core values.[32] In a true HPO, this vision/direction package must involve employees and managers at all organization levels. This blending is crucial to ensuring a high level of acceptance by everybody in the organization. This high level of mutual acceptance is a key difference between HPOs and other more traditional organizations. The previously mentioned *HPO components*—employee involvement, self-directed work teams, integrated manufacturing technolo-

Saturn ◄
www.saturn.com

GM's multibillion-dollar Saturn Corporation began planning for a new kind of company with a steering committee of six high-level union and management representatives and subcommittees from 55 GM plants and 41 United Auto Worker locals. This "committee of 99," working for several years, developed what was ultimately to become Saturn's vision/direction setting package that guided the new corporation.

gies, organizational learning, and total quality management—make unique contributions to the transformation of inputs into outputs.

The *outputs* basically consist of individual, group, and organizational effectiveness and contributions to society. Organizational effectiveness looks at how well the HPO has done financially and what the quality of work life is for members of the organization. The latter includes satisfaction, commitment to the organization, and many other measures of this kind, as indicated in Chapter 1. Contributions to society are those the organization is making to society through charitable contributions, volunteer activities by managers and workers, and many other similar activities.[33]

This open systems perspective therefore means that the inputs, transformation processes, and outputs are all influenced by the external environment and all influence each other. Thus, there is feedback from the outputs to the transformation components and inputs, and there is continual adjustment to meet the environmental demands.

■ INTERNAL INTEGRATION

A difficult challenge is the integration of all five HPO components. For example, the self-directing teams must include the integrated production system in their plans and operations. Often the teams are heavily involved in the system's design. Similarly, the teams also must include total quality management considerations as part of their functioning. At the same time, they must build organizational learning and employee involvement functions and activities. In successful HPOs there is a fit among all these activities and functions, as there is with the open system inputs and outputs.

Unlike traditional organizations, in which design emanates from the top down, the design of an HPO involves a combination of top-down and bottom-up decision making. Successful design calls for a strong and sustained emphasis from the top supported by various design teams comprised of people from all levels of the organization. It also calls for staying on course in dealing with the inevitable problems introduced by change. Organizations able to do this can reap the kinds of benefits we discuss in the concluding section.

■ **HPO "islands"** are HPO units engulfed by organizations or units that do not function as HPOs and may even be opposed to them.

Sometimes **HPO "islands"** exist within a larger, more traditional organization. HPO islands are engulfed by organizations or units that do not function as HPOs and may even be opposed to them. Saturn Corporation within General Motors is one such example. Originally set up to help serve as an example for the rest of the corporation, Saturn has been in a constant struggle to maintain itself as a true HPO.[34] Some influential executives from GM and the United Auto Workers Union have not supported Saturn because they have been concerned about losing the control they maintain elsewhere in GM's more traditional organization.[35]

In spite of these internal pressures, Saturn has been quite successful as a high performance organization. At the same time, external market forces have made it very difficult for Saturn to continue its success. Well-run HPOs have generally been better able to withstand these negative pressures than have traditional ones, however.[36]

■ MIDDLE MANAGER ROLES

Middle managers must also address a number of challenges to build a true high performance organization. Many will be asked to help implement one or more of the components described earlier to help move their organization on the journey toward becoming an HPO. As an example, creating self-directing work teams can provide resistance at both manager and employee levels.[37] A key concern is that middle managers in traditional organizations may be asked to implement a change that eliminates some or all of their job.[38] Many of these functions have been shifted to the teams themselves, and the middle managers must carve out new roles and adjust their traditional role as a source of direction.

Although many Generation X employees may welcome new self-managing team environments, other workers, particularly those lacking the appropriate educational skills, may offer resistance. Some employees do not believe that working in teams is a fair way to work, and some do not like the additional challenge of teams. There is also a strong preference among many employees, especially in the United States, to do individual work. A key challenge for middle managers in implementing any of these components (see The Effective Manager 2.1) is to help deal with possible employee resistance.[39]

Another challenge for middle managers is to resolve the tensions that may exist between or among the various components. For example, in an organization on a journey toward an HPO, the total quality management component may reflect the separate, narrowly focused groups emphasizing various aspects of quality. These groups typically have lots of management control. In contrast, an employee involvement component in this same organization involves considerable worker empowerment across a great many issues, and not just quality. To reconcile the demands of these two different HPO components is very difficult for both managers and employees. The middle managers and the employees will need to be extensively trained to handle their new role in an HPO. Middle managers also will require lots of training and they must help with the design and implementation of training for other employees.[40] This much or more training is needed for employees to be able to perform their new duties and to keep up with increasing competition.

> **OB Across Functions**
>
> PRODUCT DEVELOPMENT
>
> **Customer Input Through Quality Function Deployment**
>
> Firms are increasingly using cross-functional teams to deploy the voice of the customer through all stages of the product development process. These teams have the skills to design the product, write engineering specifications, purchase materials, and prepare plans for production preparation and completion. For example, Wiremold, an electrical goods manufacturer in West Hartford, Connecticut, uses three-member design teams. These teams have a marketer, a design/product engineer, and a production engineer. The teams interview their customers—electrical contractors and architects—about their needs. These interviews lead to a broad, preliminary definition of the product. Then the teams interview other customers over and over as the product begins to develop on team members' computer screens and in their minds. When this process started, the designers did not want a production engineer involved in discussions. Ultimately, however, the process worked so well that the team could see the product through the customer's eye, and the importance of having each of the product design functions represented became obvious.
>
> The quality function deployment process cut the design process from three years to less than six months at Wiremold. Sales increased by 150 percent by creating new market niches and grabbing customers from competitors that were not using cross-functional teams and the quality function deployment process. *www.wiremold.com*

■ HIGH LEVEL LEADERSHIP

The first challenge for upper level management is to decide how far to go in becoming an HPO. Many organizations implement only one or two of the components above and are not true HPOs. They are traditional organizations with some HPO components. How far they attempt to go depends on the environment and input factors, as well as on how strongly the top level values and is committed to a true HPO. For example, HPOs are particularly useful in constantly changing environments that demand innovation. Some firms, such as Procter and Gamble, place a strong value on HPOs, and top management has a strong commitment to them.[41] Many managers simply do not want to make this kind of commitment and instead are satisfied with trying to implement one or two components or sometimes just a small portion of a single component.

Another challenge for senior managers is the internationalization of U.S. business practices. In a number of countries where status, power, and prestige are inherent in work-related values (e.g., Malaysia, Italy, Mexico) it can be very difficult to implement HPO components like self-directing teams and employee involvement. In addition, workers with the appropriate abilities and education may not be available.[42] Finally, training and development of middle managers is a challenge. As we have stated, they no longer perform many of the managerial duties in traditional organizations.

■ GREENFIELD SITES VERSUS REDESIGNS

A final challenge is the question of starting a high performance organization from scratch or redesigning a traditional organization to become one. Those started from scratch at a new site are called **greenfield sites**. Saturn Corporation is an example. It took ten years to develop Saturn from its original conception until its plant opened. During that period, everything was designed from the ground up—typical for greenfield sites.[43] In contrast, redesigns start out as more traditional organizations and try to change these designs to work toward becoming an HPO.

Organizations that have implemented new designs have experienced an average financial increase of about 10 percent a year. In contrast, organizations that have redesigned themselves have realized average increases of 6.8 percent a year. Traditional organizations that have not been redesigned have seen improvements of 3.8 percent a year.[44] So, although all three design types have experienced financial increases in response to external and internal pressures, the HPO designs have done the best.

■ **Greenfield sites** are those HPO sites started from scratch at a new site.

Illustrative Case:
Creating a High Performance Organization

One organization that is moving toward becoming a high performance organization is VF Corporation.[45] Called a "stealth giant" because it touches peoples' lives in dozens of ways without their being aware of it, VF Corporation makes Lee, Wrangler, Britannia, and Rustler jeans and sells about $2 billion of jeans a year—more than any other organization. The firm, 100 years old and headquartered in Greensboro, North Carolina is undergoing a far-reaching redesign.

■ CHANGE LEADERSHIP

In total, VF Corp. makes 17 brands of different kinds of apparel and had total sales of $5.5 billion in a recent reporting period. Until recently, each brand operated as an independent division, with its own purchasing, production, marketing and computer systems. The brands are sold in mass-market retail outlets, such as Wal-Mart and Target, as well as department stores such as Macy's.

When Mackey McDonald took over as chief executive officer, he was determined to shake up the firm. VF had long been a steady, but not spectacular performer. Its sales were almost flat and costs were increasing, its information systems costs alone rising more than 10 percent per year. Each of the brands had its own system and the systems were not able to communicate with each other. The divisions did not coordinate raw material ordering or manufacturing to maximize output. They also often competed for the same buyers. The corporation had many small-company disadvantages and few of the large-company advantages.

McDonald set a goal of $7 billion in sales within four years. He articulated a vision of "consumerization" which would tailor the firm's production and distribution systems to serve customers with maximum efficiency. VF no longer would have to depend on fuzzy national and regional forecasts, which often created shortages or gluts in inventories. McDonald said, "We had a tremendous opportunity to compete on knowledge." He envisioned using what is called a "micromarketing system" that would be able to predict that, say, a particular Wal-Mart store would sell a given number of Wranglers with a 34 inch waist size, in a given color, at the beginning of summer. VF would then make sure the jeans were in stock, so that sales would not be lost to competitors. To do this and the other things needed to carry out the vision, VF would move far toward becoming an enterprise or E-corporation. It also would be taking giant steps toward becoming a high performance organization. Let us now look at the steps taken to become a true HPO.

■ TOTAL SYSTEMS COMMITMENT

The environment facing VF Corporation was becoming increasingly complex, global, and fast moving. Low-priced foreign goods were increasing across many of VF's brands. Competitors, such as Levi Strauss, were attempting to move toward consumerization.[46] VF's sales had pretty much plateaued, and costs were increasing. These and other pressures were pushing the firm to take steps to deal with the external environmental changes.

As a response to these pressures, as well as the internal-coordination ones mentioned earlier, McDonald put forth his consumerization vision and $7 billion sales goal. McDonald's first step to establish a vision/direction setting package was to bring together 50 VF managers. They fanned out across the country looking for best practices to emulate. Firms such as Proctor & Gamble, 3M, and Caterpillar were visited.

The management group then almost literally locked itself into a conference room for about six months and developed new business processes for VF. The firm reorganized the 17 brands into five "coalitions": intimates, jeanswear (including workwear), playwear, knitwear, and international operations and marketing. It also moved the headquarters to North Carolina and set up a new unit to coordinate the coalitions. This unit was called VF Services and, in addition to coordinating the technology across the coalitions, VF Services oversaw some accounting, procurement, and human resources operations, all as part of the E-cor-

S. C. Johnson ←

www.scjohnsonwax.com

S. C. Johnson, in Racine, Wisconsin, well known for such products as Johnson's Wax, Glade, and the like, has worked hard to be a high performance organization. It has saved more than $1 billion without investing in building additional manufacturing capacity.

poration, high-tech system. To indicate the division's importance, its head was appointed as a division president and also was a long-term VF employee.

■ IMPLEMENTATION PROCESSES

The next step was to develop implementation processes for product development, production planning, and distribution. This also required development of crucial processes for routing information from unit to unit, at the employee level, departmental level, coalition level and wherever else such information was needed. At this point, VF turned to a number of outside enterprise resource planning software vendors to help tie together the above systems and vision/direction setting package, while also modifying the systems to suit its own needs. Figure 2.4 shows a simplified version of the VF enterprise-wide integrated information systems.

The figure emphasizes integrated production technology. Its core is the enterprise resource planning (ERP) function which handles order management, production planning, materials management, and finance modules, all with sophisticated software programs. All the other functions—product-development, micromarketing, warehouse control—manufacturing control, capacity and raw materials planning, and forecasting tie into ERP and to each other. Each uses its

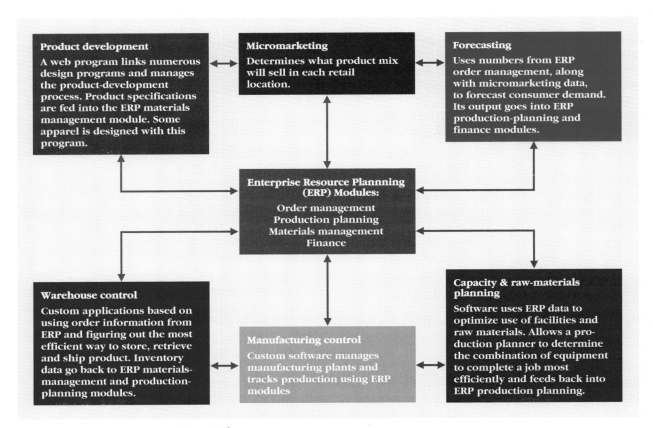

Figure 2.4
Simplified VF Corporation enterprise-wide integrated information systems.

own software. The system is designed to tie together everything from raw material ordering to supplying retailers with appropriately designed and manufactured apparel products in a timely manner.

This integrated production technology component was central to the vision/direction setting package put together by CEO McDonald and his 50 key executives, in response to the changing environment. In terms of employee involvement, we also know that 50 key executives were involved. There also is evidence that the company's computer personnel were strongly involved. We do not know how involved the production employees were and we have no information here on the extent to which self-directing work teams were used.

In terms of organizational learning, it probably will be enhanced by the enterprise-wide planning system. The system records and feeds back information across the enterprise in a very systematic way. At the same time, considerable training time is devoted to the managers and employees. For example, the VF employees responsible for getting only a single one of the software modules running have each undergone at least 14 weeks of training. They spend time at vendor organizations as well as in VF. Vendor employees also spend considerable long-term time in VF Corporation.

Figure 2.4 shows the extensive feedback among the modules in the production component. At the same time, the production component will provide financial feedback as well as whatever output information management deems to be important. Likewise, as indicated above, we are told there is feedback between the production technology component and the total quality and organizational learning components, and it is reasonable to assume with the other components as well. We also can assume that, for total quality management, computerized systems should provide a great deal of assistance.

In summary, this once-traditional organization that has used an E-corporation approach as a starting point on a journey that could lead to becoming a high performance organization. VF Corporation has demonstrated some of the characteristics of such an organization, but only time will tell whether or not it achieves its goals.

Chapter 2 Study Guide

What is the high performance context of organizational behavior?

Summary

- Total quality management deals with meeting the customer's needs, making sure all tasks are done right the first time, and with continuous improvement.

- Customer-driven organizations can be seen as upside-down pyramids where workers operate in ways directly affecting customers, and managers directly support the workers.

- The diverse and changing workforce includes new pressures from "Generation X workers" who want such things as job challenge, job flexibility, and empowerment.

- Organizations are embracing process reengineering, electronic commerce, and free-agent employees with a mix of permanent, part-time, and transitory workers.

What is a high performance organization?

■ A high performance organization is designed to bring out the best in people and achieve sustained high performance.

■ HPOs tend to organize workflow around key business processes and follow human-resource policies designed to enhance employee flexibility, skills, knowledge, and motivation.

■ The key components of HPOs include employee involvement, self-directing work teams, integrated production technologies, organizational learning, and total quality management.

What are the management challenges of high performance organizations?

■ Environmental linkages challenge HPOs to be effective open systems whose inputs, transformation processes, and outputs support a clear and relevant vision.

■ Internal integration challenges all HPO components to work successfully together in a dynamic and ever-improving fashion.

■ Middle manager challenges involve implementing the HPO components, adapting to different managerial roles, and helping with design and implementation of employee training.

■ High-level leadership challenges include determining how far to go toward becoming an HPO, training and development of middle managers, and maintaining overall positive momentum during times of great change.

How are high performance organizations created?

■ VF Corporation is an example of an organization striving to become a true HPO; it is introducing high-tech, enterprise corporation technology to deal with all facets of its apparel business.

■ Various aspects of VF's HPO initiative include an enterprise resource planning function with sophisticated software involving order management, production planning, materials management, and finance modules.

■ The integrated production HPO component at VF supports a "consumerism" vision/direction setting package to tailor the firm's production and distribution systems to serve customers with maximum efficiency.

Key Terms

Continuous improvement (p. 23)
Electronic commerce (p. 25)
Employee involvement (p. 27)
Empowerment (p. 24)
E-corporation (p. 25)
Generation X workers (p. 24)

Greenfield sites (p. 33)
High performance organization (p. 26)
HPO islands (p. 31)
Integrated production technologies (p. 28)
Intellectual capital (p. 26)
Knowledge workers (p. 24)

Process reengineering (p. 25)
Self-directing work teams (p. 28)
Shamrock organizations (p. 25)
Total quality management (p. 23)

■ MULTIPLE CHOICE

1. A high performance organization _____. (a) is similar to a traditional organization (b) automatically occurs whenever self-managing work teams are involved (c) produces organizational capability that delivers sustainable high performance results (d) must have a very specific kind of organization structure

2. One of the following is *not* listed as a characteristic of the changing workforce: _____. (a) increased ranking in high school education scores (b) decreased ranking in high school education scores (c) more diversity (d) arrival of Generation Xers

3. One of the following is *not* listed as an input of an HPO open systems model: _____. (a) organizational worksite problems/opportunities (b) external/global business environment (c) strategies (d) vision/direction package

4. The five transformation components listed in the HPO open systems model _____. (a) are independent of one another (b) need to fit or match (c) assume very few employees (d) once established require little change

5. Compared to a traditional organization, a high performance organization _____. (a) has a stronger functional orientation (b) is much simpler to design (c) is more productive (d) requires more employees

6. Because HPOs invest heavily in their employees' training they illustrate the important directions of _____ organizations. (a) learning (b) shamrock (c) vertical (d) e-commerce.

7. HPOs _____. (a) are started primarily from the bottom (b) are started primarily from the middle (c) require little top-management effort (d) require much effort from the top, middle, and bottom

8. An organization, such as Saturn, termed an "island," _____. (a) floats aimlessly (b) operates as an HPO within a larger entity that is not an HPO (c) is early in its journey toward becoming an HPO (d) tends to operate better than if it is a part of a larger HPO

9. The performance record of HPOs _____. (a) tends to be about the same as for a traditional organization (b) tends to be substantially higher than traditional organizations (c) tends to be only marginally higher than traditional organizations (d) shows benefits that are less than costs

10. Once an HPO is established, it _____. (a) changes very little (b) is in a constant process of change (c) reverts back to a traditional organization (d) trims the number of employees

■ TRUE–FALSE

11. True HPOs also must be E-corporations.   T   F

12. HPOs emphasize employee involvement and self-management.   T   F

13. Results of HPOs include organizational effectiveness, individual, team, and organizational learning, and societal benefits.   T   F

14. High performance organizations tend to have fewer hierarchical levels than traditional organizations.   T   F

15. Any organization that uses employee work teams is an HPO.   T   F

16. Greenfield sites emphasize the changing of traditional organizations to HPOs. T F
17. A traditional organization becomes an HPO from the bottom up. T F
18. Once the decision is made to go ahead, HPOs are easy to establish. T F
19. Strong, sustained, top-down leadership is required for an HPO. T F
20. HPOs appear to be a management fad. T F

■ SHORT RESPONSE

21. Briefly discuss the role of the changing workforce in an HPO.
22. Briefly compare and contrast traditional organizations and HPOs along at least three components.
23. Briefly discuss the difficulties of HPO "islands" within larger corporations.
24. Briefly discuss the major middle-management challenges in establishing an HPO.

■ APPLICATIONS ESSAY

25. Your manager has recently heard about high performance organizations and has asked you to explain them to him so that he can decide whether or not his organization should become one. Answer his request.

Explore application-oriented Fast Company articles, cases, experimental exercises, and self-assessments in the OB Skills Workbook

■ **Visit the Schermerhorn Web site to find the Interactive Self-Test and Internet exercises for this chapter.**

Global Dimensions of Organizational Behavior

CULTURE AND COMPETITIVE ADVANTAGE

www.canadiantire.ca

When Wal-Mart, Home Depot, Sports Authority and other aggressive American retailers moved into Canada, the local stalwart, Canadian Tire, was sent on the run. Many observers believed the firm would not survive the intense competition. But along came a smart new CEO, Stephen Bachand. With two decades of experience in hardware retailing in the United States, interestingly enough, Bachand spearheaded major changes in the firm's logistics, product mix, store design, office management, and customer service. He made home office executives and support staff spend time working in the retail stores to get a better sense of the business. Says Bachand: "Why is that? Because we're in the retail business." Bachand personally met with dealers and encouraged upward communication. "When we tell those at the head office things, they listen and respond," a dealer said. Bachand believes in being responsive. "When you have a good idea," he points out, "customers see, but so do competitors. I'm never satisfied. You've got to be fleet of foot." You also have to understand the culture, something American retailers struggle with as they enter the Canadian markets. When Wal-Mart pushed its "everyday low prices" strategy, popular at home, Bachand and Canadian Tire didn't follow suit. "The thing that's clear," he said, "is that Canadians like to shop where they know that the price is right." Canadian Tire's mission reflects these values: "To be the first choice for Canadians in Automotive, Sports and Leisure, and Home products, providing total customer value through customer-driven service, focused assortments and competitive operations." Watch out, Wal-Mart. It may not be long before a Canadian Tire store shows up in your home town of Bensonville, Arkansas.[1]

This is the age of globalization when corporate success is increasingly linked to worldwide operations and a global staff.[2] Stephen Bachand learned first-hand one of the foremost lessons of doing business in international markets—you've got to understand the local culture. All around the globe, people like Bachand, working in large and small businesses alike, are facing the many challenges and opportunities associated with business competition in an increasingly complex and "borderless" world.[3] The ability to respect differences and value diversity is an important key to success in managing organizational behavior across cultures.

Today's organizations need managers with global awareness and cultural sensitivity. This doesn't mean that they all must work in foreign lands. But it does mean that they must be aware of how international events may affect the well-being of organizations and that they must know how to deal with people from other countries and cultures. They must also be able to learn quickly from management practices around the world. The variety of issues and topics in the present chapter will help you to understand the important global dimensions of organizational behavior.

Study Questions

This chapter will broaden your understanding of people and organizations operating across cultures and in a complex global economy. As you read Chapter 3, keep in mind these key questions:

■ Why is globalization significant to organizational behavior?
■ What is culture?
■ How does globalization affect people at work?
■ What is a global view on organizational learning?

Organizational Behavior and Globalization

Most organizations today must achieve high performance in the context of a competitive and complex global environment.[4] As we begin the twenty-first century, we find ourselves fully in the age of **globalization** with its complex economic networks of competition, resource supplies, and product markets transcending national boundaries and circling the globe.[5] None of us can have failed to notice its impact on organizations, the people who work in them, and our everyday lives. Consider the potential effects of globalization in terms of your own life and career: (1) You already purchase many products made by foreign firms; (2) you may someday work overseas in the foreign operation of a domestic firm; (3) you may someday work overseas as an expatriate employee of a foreign firm; and (4) you may someday work as a domestic employee of a foreign firm operating in your home country. The field of organizational behavior recognizes these realities and seeks to help you understand the performance implications of work in the global economy.

■ **Globalization** involves growing worldwide interdependence of resource suppliers, product markets, and business competition.

■ A GLOBAL ECONOMY

The rapid growth of information technology and electronic communications has heightened the average person's awareness of the global economy. The international news brings the entire world into our homes and our thoughts daily. An explosion of opportunities on the Internet allows us to share and gather information from global sources at low cost and from the convenience of our desktops— at home, while traveling, or at work. And, always, the transnational movement of products, trends, values, and innovations continues to change lifestyles at a rapid pace. At the same time that valuable skills and investments move from country to country, cultural diversity among the populations is increasing. Immigration is having profound implications for many nations. Tomorrow's employers will have even greater need to deal with *multicultural workforces*—those that draw workers from nontraditional labor sources and from ethnic backgrounds representing all corners of the globe.[6]

Domestic self-sufficiency is no longer a viable option for nations or businesses.[7] Commercial investments travel the trade routes of the world. Canadian businesses, for example, have their sights set on America, with some $65 billion already invested there. Germany is a large investor in the United States, with recent mergers creating the global giants Daimler Chrysler and Deutsche Bank-Bankers Trust. The Japanese are also large investors with ownership stakes in over 1500 U.S. factories, employing over 350,000 people.[8] Crossing the Atlantic to Scotland, with its low taxes, excellent infrastructure, and skilled workers, many high-technology firms like IBM have invested over $4.5 billion in what is now being called "Silicon Glen."[9] Global supplier networks play significant roles in the operations of many industries. The U.S. automobile industry, for example, imports Japanese, Mexican, and Brazilian engines; utilizes German instruments and British electronics; and employs Italian designers. Advances in technology make it possible for software developers in places like Bangalore, India, to work for global employers without ever having to leave home.

Yahoo! operates in thirteen languages in sixteen countries, and it is considered to be one of the most popular Web sites in Japan.

■ REGIONAL ECONOMIC ALLIANCES

The importance of regional economic alliances as forces in the global economy is undeniable.[10] First and foremost, the European Union (EU) is moving forward with its agendas of political, economic, and monetary union among member countries.[11] Remarkably, it has seen the advent of a new world currency, the Euro, which will replace the traditional currencies of many member nations. Within the EU, businesses from member countries have access to a market of some 400 million customers. Agreements to eliminate border controls and trade barriers, create uniform technical product standards, open government procurement contracts, and unify financial regulations are all designed to bring economic benefit and union to Europe, a region whose economy of some $6.5 trillion closely approaches the U.S.'s $8.0 trillion economy.[12]

The EU's counterpart in North America, the North American Free Trade Agreement (NAFTA), links the economies and customer markets of Canada, the United States, and Mexico in freer trade. NAFTA has been praised for uniting in trade a region with more potential customers than the European Union. It now looks forward to a future of expanded membership to other countries of the Americas. Some business and government leaders even speak of an all-encompassing Free Trade Agreement for the Americas (FTAA) by 2005. At present, the Caribbean Community (CARICOM) is seeking to negotiate free trade agreements with Latin American countries. In addition, the Andean Pact (linking Venezuela, Colombia, Ecuador, Peru, and Bolivia) and Mercosur (linking Brazil, Paraguay, Uruguay, and Argentina) are already active in South America.[13]

Similar regional economic partnerships are being forged in other parts of the globe as well. In Asia, the Asia-Pacific Economic Co-operation Forum (APEC) is a framework designed to produce joint economic development among countries of the Asia-Pacific basin. A region that has recently experienced economic turmoil with worldwide financial implications, Asia remains a world economic power and is the home of many world-class business competitors.[14] Japan's economic influence is ever-evident, as is China's whose might may well dominate the twenty-first century. Recent events have further confirmed the importance of other Asian countries, especially Taiwan, Singapore, South Korea, Malaysia, Thailand, and Indonesia. India, with its huge population, is an economy on the move and is recognized as a world-class supplier of software expertise.

Africa, led by developments in post-Apartheid South Africa, has also become an important member of the global economy. Countries like Uganda, Ivory Coast, Botswana, South Africa, and Ghana are now recognized as positive business prospects.[15] A report on sub-Saharan Africa recently concluded that the region's contextual problems are manageable and that the continent presents investment opportunities.[16] Coca-Cola, one of the American firms responding to this call, projects 15 percent growth rates as part of its business plan for Africa. Coca Cola's CEO M. Douglas Ivester says: "We see an Africa more directly accountable for its own destiny than it has for centuries."[17]

■ GLOBAL QUALITY STANDARDS

One indicator of the importance of business globalization is the quality designation "ISO," representing quality standards set by the International Standards Organization in Geneva, Switzerland. This mark of quality excellence has become a framework for quality assurance worldwide. The European Union and more than 50 countries, including the United States, Canada, and Mexico, have endorsed the ISO's quality standard. The certification is fast becoming a goal for companies around the world who want to do business in Europe and want to win reputations as total quality "world-class" manufacturers.

■ GLOBAL MANAGERS

Along with prior developments in globalization, the search is now also on for a new breed of manager—the **global manager**, someone who knows how to conduct business across borders.[18] Often multilingual, the global manager thinks with a world view; appreciates diverse beliefs, values, behaviors, and practices; and is able to map strategy accordingly. If you fit this description (see The Effective Manager 3.1), or soon will, get ready. Corporate recruiters are scrambling to find people with these skills and interests.

The global dimension in business and management, though pervasive, poses many complications to be overcome. Even high performers with proven technical skills at home may find that their styles and attitudes just don't work well overseas. Experienced international managers indicate that a "global mindset" of cultural adaptability, patience, flexibility, and tolerance are indispensable.[19] The failure rate for Americans in overseas assignments has been measured as high as 25 percent,[20] and a study criticizes British and German companies for giving inadequate preparation to staff sent abroad.[21]

THE EFFECTIVE MANAGER 3.1

ATTRIBUTES OF THE "GLOBAL MANAGER"

- Adapts well to different business environments.
- Respects different beliefs, values, and practices.
- Solves problems quickly in new circumstances.
- Communicates well with people from different cultures.
- Speaks more than one language.
- Understands different government and political systems.
- Conveys respect and enthusiasm when dealing with others.
- Possesses high technical expertise for a job.

■ A **global manager** has the international awareness and cultural sensitivity needed to work well across national borders.

GLOBALIZATION ⊕

At the University of Michigan, executives from various nations come together to study worldwide management. In a five-week course called the Global Leadership Program, participants learn from an international team of world-class educators and engage in cutting-edge cross-cultural team exercises and projects. The program is designed to develop participants' awareness of the complications and challenges associated with global management. Participants are grouped into six-person teams. Each team develops strategic plans for doing business in foreign countries. Team members even go together on special two-week regional business assessment visits to the target countries. They then share the key learning of top management from the industries studied in the program.[22]

www.bus.umich.edu

Cultures and Cultural Diversity

■ **Culture** is the learned and shared way of thinking and acting among a group of people or society.

The word "culture" is frequently used in organizational behavior in connection with the concept of corporate culture, the growing interest in workforce diversity, and the broad differences among people around the world. Specialists tend to agree that **culture** is the learned, shared way of doing things in a particular society. It is the way, for example, in which its members eat, dress, greet and treat one another, teach their children, solve everyday problems, and so on.[23] Geert Hofstede, a Dutch scholar and consultant, refers to culture as the "software of the mind," making the analogy that the mind's "hardware" is universal among human beings.[24] But the software of culture takes many different forms.[24] Indeed, we are not born with a culture; we are born into a society that teaches us its culture. And because a culture is shared by people, it helps to define the boundaries between different groups and affect how their members relate to one another.

■ POPULAR DIMENSIONS OF CULTURE

The popular dimensions of culture are those that are most apparent to the individual traveling abroad—for example, language, time orientation, use of space, and religion.[25]

Language   Perhaps the most conspicuous aspect of culture, and certainly the one the traveler notices first, is language. The languages of the world number into the thousands. Some, such as Maltese, are spoken by only a handful of people, whereas others, such as English, Spanish, and Chinese, are spoken by millions. Some countries, such as France and Malaysia, have one official language; others, such as Canada, Switzerland, and India, have more than one; and still others, like the United States, have none.

The centrality of language to culture is represented by the *Whorfian hypothesis*, which considers language as a major determinant of our thinking.[26] The vocabulary and structure of a language reflect the history of a society and can also reveal how members relate to the environment. Arabic, for example, has many different words for the camel, its parts, and related equipment. As you might expect, English is very poor in its ability to describe camels. The fact that many people apparently speak the same language, such as English, doesn't mean that they share the same culture. Some words spoken in one language fail to carry the same meaning from culture to culture or region to region. A "truck" in Chicago is a "lorry" in London; "hydro" in Calgary is "electric power" in Boston; grocery shoppers in the American Midwest put "pop" in their "sacks," East Coast shoppers put "soda" in their "bags."

■ In **low-context cultures** messages are expressed mainly by the spoken and written word.

■ In **high-context cultures** words convey only part of a message, while the rest of the message must be inferred from body language and additional contextual cues.

The anthropologist Edward T. Hall notes important differences in the ways different cultures use language.[27] Members of **low-context cultures** are very explicit in using the spoken and written word. In these cultures, such as those of Australia, Canada, and United States, the message is largely conveyed by the words someone uses, and not particularly by the "context" in which they are spoken. In contrast, members of **high-context cultures** use words to convey only a limited part of the message. The rest must be inferred or interpreted from the context, which includes body language, the physical setting, and past relationships—all of which add meaning to what is being said. Many Asian and Middle Eastern cultures are considered high context, according to Hall, whereas most Western cultures are low context.

Time Orientation   Hall also uses time orientation to classify cultures.[28] In **polychronic cultures** people hold a traditional view of time that may be described as a "circle." This suggests repetition in the sense that time is "cyclical" and goes around and around. In this view time does not create pressures for immediate action or performance. After all, one will have another chance to pass the same way again. If an opportunity is lost today—no problem, it may return again tomorrow. Members of polychronic cultures tend to emphasize the present and often do more than one thing at a time.[29] An important business or government official in a Mediterranean country, for example, may have a large reception area outside his or her office. Visitors wait in this area and may transact business with the official and others who move in and out and around the room, conferring as they go.

Members of **monochronic cultures** view time more as a "straight line." In this "linear" view of time, the past is gone; the present is here briefly; and the future is almost upon us. In monochronic cultures time is measured precisely and creates pressures for action and performance. People appreciate schedules and appointments and talk about "saving" and "wasting" time. Long-range goals become important, and planning is a way of managing the future. In contrast to the Mediterranean official in the last example, a British manager will typically allot a certain amount of time in her daily calendar to deal with a business visitor. During this time the visitor receives her complete attention. Only after one visitor leaves will another one be received, again based upon the daily schedule.

Use of Space   *Proxemics*, the study of how people use space to communicate, reveals important cultural differences.[30] Personal space can be thought of as the "bubble" that surrounds us, and its preferred size tends to vary from one culture to another. When others invade or close in on our personal space, we tend to feel uncomfortable. Then again, if people are too far away, communication becomes difficult. Arabs and South Americans seem more comfortable talking at closer distances than do North Americans; Asians seem to prefer even greater distances. When a Saudi moves close to speak with a visiting Canadian executive, the visitor may back away to keep more distance between them. But the same Canadian may approach a Malaysian too closely when doing business in Kuala Lumpur, causing her or his host to back away. Cross-cultural misunderstandings due to different approaches to personal space are quite common.

OB Across Functions

INFORMATION SYSTEMS

Going Global by Staying High Tech

There is no shortage of assistance for those small and medium-sized businesses that want to "go global." Indeed, the information needed to get started as an exporter and participant in the marketplaces of the world is available at the touch of a keyboard—on the Internet. Those looking for a starting point can go to *www.web.idirect.com/ ~tiger/supersit.htm*. To look up travel guides and location information in a minute, *www.go-global.com* is a useful site. International business is well catalogued at *www.fita.org*, and in-depth information on free trade zones where exports are free of customs duties is available at *www.imex.com/naftz.html*. The world of international business is a world of diverse peoples and cultures. The best of the best know how to work across cultures with respect and delight. Visit *www.bena.com/ewinters/xculture.html* for essays on a variety of cross-cultural business issues. And if you want to take a miniature course in exporting, check Deloitte Touche Tohmatsu's offering at *www.dtonline. com/expand/excover.htm*. This is a small sample of rich resources available to facilitate international business ventures. But you've got to be linked and willing to explore the Web to take full advantage of them. Information technology today provides the potential for competitive advantage through expanded global commerce. It's yours for the asking.

■ In a **polychronic culture** people tend to do more than one thing at a time.

■ In a **monochronic culture** people tend to do one thing at a time.

In some cultures, often polychronic ones, space is organized in such a way that many activities can be carried out simultaneously. Spanish and Italian towns are organized around central squares (plazas or piazzas), whereas American towns typically have a traditional "Main Street" laid out in linear fashion. Similar cultural influences are seen in the layout of work space. Americans, who seem to prefer individual offices, may have difficulty adjusting to Japanese employers who prefer open floor plans.

Religion   Religion is also a major element of culture and can be one of its more visible manifestations. The influence of religion often prescribes rituals, holy days, and foods that can be eaten. Codes of ethics and moral behavior often have their roots in religious beliefs. The influence of religion on economic matters can also be significant.[31] In the Middle East, one finds interest-free "Islamic" banks that operate based on principles set forth in the Koran. In Malaysia, business dinners are scheduled after 8:00 P.M. so that Muslim guests can first attend to their evening prayer.

■ VALUES AND NATIONAL CULTURES

Cultures vary in their underlying patterns of values and attitudes. The way people think about such matters as achievement, wealth and material gain, risk and change, may influence how they approach work and their relationships with organizations. A framework developed by Geert Hofstede offers one approach for understanding how value differences across national cultures can influence human behavior at work. The five dimensions of national culture in his framework can be described as follows.[32]

Hofstede's dimensions of national cultures

■ **Power distance** is the willingness of a culture to accept status and power differences among its members.
■ **Uncertainty avoidance** is the cultural tendency to be uncomfortable with uncertainty and risk in everyday life.
■ **Individualism–collectivism** is the tendency of a culture's members to emphasize individual self-interests or group relationships.
■ **Masculinity–femininity** is the degree to which a society values assertiveness or relationships.

1. **Power distance** is the willingness of a culture to accept status and power differences among its members. It reflects the degree to which people are likely to respect hierarchy and rank in organizations. Indonesia is considered a high–power distance culture, whereas Sweden is considered a relatively low–power distance culture.

2. **Uncertainty avoidance** is a cultural tendency toward discomfort with risk and ambiguity. It reflects the degree to which people are likely to prefer structured or unstructured organizational situations. France is considered a high–uncertainty avoidance culture, whereas Hong Kong is considered a low–uncertainty avoidance culture.

3. **Individualism–collectivism** is the tendency of a culture to emphasize individual versus group interests. It reflects the degree to which people are likely to prefer working as individuals or working together in groups. The United States is a highly individualistic culture, whereas Mexico is a more highly collectivist one.

4. **Masculinity–femininity** is the tendency of a culture to value stereotypical masculine or feminine traits. It reflects the degree to which organizations emphasize competition and assertiveness versus interpersonal sensitivity and concerns for relationships. Japan is considered a very masculine culture, whereas Thailand is considered a more feminine culture.

5. **Long-term/short-term orientation** is the tendency of a culture to emphasize values associated with the future, such as thrift and persistence, versus values that focus largely on the present. It reflects the degree to which people and organizations adopt long-term or short-term performance horizons. South Korea is high on long-term orientation, whereas the United States is a more short-term-oriented country.

■ **Long-term/short-term orientation** is the degree to which a culture emphasizes long-term or short-term thinking.

The first four dimensions in Hofstede's framework were identified in an extensive study of thousands of employees of a multinational corporation operating in more than 40 countries.[33] The fifth dimension of long-term/short-term orientation was added from research conducted by cross-cultural psychologist Michael Bond and his colleagues using the Chinese Values Survey they developed.[34] Their research suggested the cultural importance of Confucian dynamism, with its emphasis on persistence, the ordering of relationships, thrift, sense of shame, personal steadiness, reciprocity, protection of "face," and respect for tradition.[35]

When using the Hofstede framework, it is important to remember that the five dimensions are interrelated and not independent.[36] National cultures may best be understood in terms of cluster maps or collages that combine multiple dimensions. For example, Figure 3.1 shows a sample grouping of countries based on individualism–collectivism and power distance. Note that high power distance and collectivism are often found together, as are low power distance and individualism. Whereas high collectivism may lead us to expect a work team in Indonesia to operate by consensus, the high power distance may cause the consensus to be heavily influenced by the desires of a formal leader. A similar team operating in more individualist and low power distance Great Britain or America might make decisions with more open debate, including expressions of disagreement with a leader's stated preferences.

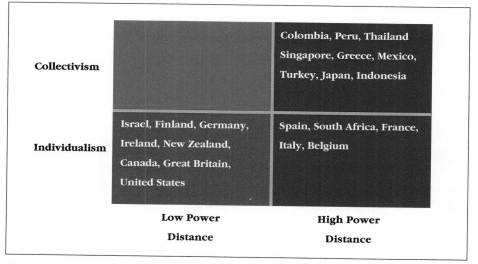

Figure 3.1
Sample country clusters on Hofstede's dimensions of individualism–collectivism and power distance.

■ UNDERSTANDING CULTURAL DIFFERENCES

To work well with people from different cultures, you must first understand your own culture. We are usually unaware of our own culture until we come into contact with a very different one. Knowing your own culture will help guard you against two problems that frequently arise in international dealings. One is the danger of *parochialism*—assuming that the ways of your culture are the only ways of doing things. The other is the danger of *ethnocentrism*—assuming that the ways of your culture are the best ways of doing things.[37] It is parochial for a traveling American businesswoman to insist that all of her business contacts speak English, whereas it is ethnocentric for her to think that anyone who dines with a spoon rather than a knife and fork lacks proper table manners.

A framework developed by Fons Trompenaars offers a useful vantage point for better understanding and, hopefully, dealing with cultural differences.[38] Working from a databank of respondents from 47 national cultures, he suggests that cultures vary in the way their members solve problems of three major types: (1) relationships with people, (2) attitudes toward time, and (3) attitudes toward the environment.

Trompenaars identifies five major cultural differences in how people handle relationships with other people. The orientations, as illustrated in Figure 3.2, are:

How cultures deal with relationships among people

1. *Universalism versus particularism*—relative emphasis on rules and consistency, or relationships and flexibility.
2. *Individualism versus collectivism*—relative emphasis on individual freedom and responsibility, or group interests and consensus.
3. *Neutral versus affective*—relative emphasis on objectivity and detachment, or emotion and expressed feelings.
4. *Specific versus diffuse*—relative emphasis on focused and narrow involvement, or involvement with the whole person.
5. *Achievement versus prescription*—relative emphasis on performance-based and earned status, or ascribed status.

With regard to problems based on attitudes toward time, Trompenaars distinguishes between cultures with sequential versus synchronic orientations. Time in

Canada, USA, Ireland	**Universalism vs. Particularism**	Indonesia, China, Venezuela
USA, Hungary, Russia	**Individualism vs. Collectivism**	Thailand, Japan, Mexico
Indonesia, Germany, Japan	**Neutral vs. Affective**	Italy, France, USA
Spain, Poland, USA	**Specific vs. Diffuse**	India, Great Britain, Egypt
Australia, Canada, Norway	**Achievement vs. Ascription**	Philippines, Pakistan, Brazil
Great Britain, Belgium, USA	**Sequential vs. Synchronic**	Malaysia, Venezuela, France

Figure 3.2
Sample country clusters on Trompenaars' framework for understanding cultural differences.

a sequential view is a passing series of events; in a synchronic view, it consists of an interrelated past, present, and future. With regard to problems based on attitudes toward the environment, he contrasts how different cultures may relate to nature in inner-directed versus outer-directed ways. Members of an inner-directed culture tend to view themselves separate from nature and believe they can control it. Those in an outer-directed culture view themselves as part of nature and believe they must go along with it.

Globalization and People at Work

OB scholars are increasingly sensitive to the need to better understand how management and organizational practices vary among the world's cultures. In this sense, we must be familiar with the importance of multinational employers, the diversity of multicultural workforces, and the special demands of international work assignments.

■ MULTINATIONAL EMPLOYERS

A true **multinational corporation**, or MNC, is a business firm that has extensive international operations in more than one foreign country. MNCs are more than just companies that "do business abroad;" they are global concerns—exemplified by Ford, Royal-Dutch Shell, Sony, and many others. The missions and strategies of MNCs are worldwide in scope. In the public sector, multinational organizations (MNOs) are those with nonprofit missions whose operations also span the globe. Examples are Amnesty International, the International Red Cross, the United Nations, and the World Wildlife Fund.

The truly global organization operates with a total world view and does not have allegiance to any one national "home." Futurist Alvin Toffler labels them *transnational organizations* that "may do research in one country, manufacture components in another, assemble them in a third, sell the manufactured goods in a fourth, deposit surplus funds in a fifth, and so on."[39] Although the pure transnational corporation may not yet exist, large firms like Nestle, Gillette, and Ford are striving hard to move in that direction. Greatly facilitating those moves are new information technologies, which allow organizations to operate through virtual linkages with components and suppliers located around the world.

The MNCs have enormous economic power and impact. Toffler, in particular, warns that "the size, importance, and political power of this new player in the global game has skyrocketed."[40] Their activities can bring both benefits and controversies to host countries. One example is in Mexico, where many *maquiladoras*, or foreign-owned plants, assemble imported parts and ship finished products to the United States. Labor is relatively inexpensive for the foreign operators, while Mexico benefits from industrial development, reduced unemployment, and increased foreign exchange earnings. But some complain about the downsides of *maquiladoras*—stress on housing and public services in Mexican border towns, inequities in the way Mexican workers are treated (wages, working conditions, production quotas) relative to their foreign counterparts, and the environmental impact of pollution from the industrial sites.[41]

Symantec ◀
www.symantec.com

If you call Symantec for assistance with the firm's popular Norton software products, your technical assistance may come from Ireland. Calls are simply rerouted by special phone lines to the Dublin office with its staff of multilingual programmers.

■ A **multinational corporation** is a business with extensive international operations in more than one country.

www.starbucks.com

Information that Guatemalan workers earn 2 cents a pound while toiling under inhumane conditions to pick coffee beans that Starbucks sold for $8 a pound brought controversy to the successful chain. CEO Howard Schultz responded by setting a new standard for socially responsible business. The new guidelines require overseas suppliers to pay wages that "address the basic needs of workers and their families," to ensure that work does not "interfere with mandated education" for children, and to help workers get "access to safe housing, clean water and health facilities and services." Global human rights activists have praised Starbucks' policy as a benchmark for importers of agricultural commodities.[42]

■ MULTICULTURAL WORKFORCES

What is the best way to deal with a multicultural workforce? There are no easy answers. Styles of leadership, motivation, decision making, planning, organizing, leading, and controlling vary from country to country.[43] Managing a construction project in Saudi Arabia with employees from Asia, the Middle East, Europe, and North America working side by side will clearly present challenges different from those involved in a domestic project. Similarly, establishing and successfully operating a joint venture in Kazakhstan, Nigeria, or Vietnam will require a great deal of learning and patience. In these and other international settings, political risks and bureaucratic difficulties further complicate the already difficult process of working across cultural boundaries.

The challenges of managing across cultures, however, are not limited to international operations. In this connection, a new term has been coined—*domestic multiculturalism*, which describes cultural diversity within a given national population: This diversity will be reflected in the workforces of local organizations.[44] Los Angeles, for example, is a popular home to many immigrant groups. Some 20 percent of the city's school children speak other languages more fluently than they speak English; in Vancouver, British Columbia, Chinese is also the mother tongue of some 20 percent of the population.

■ EXPATRIATE WORK ASSIGNMENTS

■ An **expatriate** works and lives in a foreign country for an extended time.

The human resources firm ComPsych reports there are over 350,000 Americans working abroad for U.S. employers.[45] People who work and live abroad for extended periods of time are referred to as **expatriates**. The cost of an expatriate worker can be very expensive for the employer. An executive earning $100,000 per year in the United States, for example, might cost her company more than $300,000 in the first year of an assignment in England—with the added cost tied to compensation, benefits, transfer, and other relocation expenses. Estimates are that a three-year expatriate assignment will cost the employer an average of $1 million.[46] To get the most out of the investment, progressive employers will maximize the potential of expatriate performance success by taking a variety of supportive actions.[47] They carefully recruit employees who have the right sensitivities and skills, provide them with good training and orientation to the foreign culture, actively support them while working abroad, give extra attention to the needs of the expatriate's family members, and pay careful attention to relocation when the expatriate and family return home.

Expatriates usually face their greatest problems when entering and working in a foreign culture, and when experiencing repatriation on the return home. Figure 3.3 illustrates phases in the typical expatriate work assignment, beginning with the initial assignment shock the person experiences upon being informed of a foreign posting. How recruitment, selection, and orientation are handled during this stage can have an important influence on the assignment's eventual success. Ideally, the employee, along with his or her spouse and family, is allowed to choose whether or not to accept the opportunity. Also ideally, proper pre-departure support and counseling are given to provide "realistic expectations" of what is to come.

The expatriate undergoes three phases of adjustment to the new country.[48] First is the *tourist stage*, in which the expatriate enjoys discovering the new culture. Second is the *disillusionment stage*, in which his or her mood is dampened as difficulties become more evident. Typical problems include conversing well in the local language and obtaining personal products and food supplies of preference. Third, the expatriate's mood often hits bottom in the stage of *culture shock*. Here confusion, disorientation, and frustration in the ways of the local culture and living in the foreign environment set in. If culture shock is well handled, the expatriate begins to feel better, function more effectively, and lead a reasonably normal life. If it isn't, work performance may suffer, even deteriorating to the point where a reassignment home may be necessary.

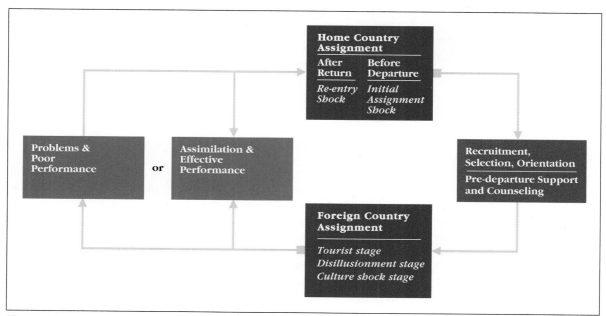

Figure 3.3
Stages in the expatriate international career cycle: potential adjustment problems in the home and foreign countries.

At the end of the expatriate assignment, perhaps after three or four years, the reentry process can also be stressful.[49] After an extended period away, the expatriate and his or her family have changed and the home country has changed as well. One does not simply "fall back in"; rather, it takes time to get used to living at home again. Furthermore, in too many instances little thought may be given to assigning the returned expatriate a job that matches his or her current skills and abilities. While abroad, the expatriate has often functioned with a great degree of independence—something that may or may not be possible at home. Problems caused by reentry shock can be minimized through careful planning. This includes maintaining adequate contact with the home office during the expatriate assignment as well as having all possible support for the move back. Employers should also identify any new skills and abilities, and assign returned expatriates to jobs commensurate with their abilities. As organizations utilize more and more expatriate assignments, their career planning and development systems must also operate on a global scale.

www.iorworld.com

⬈ ENTREPRENEURSHIP

When Noel Kreicker left the United States with her three small children for her husband's two-year business assignment in Colombia, she didn't expect to be back home within six months, but she was. Noel and her husband went to Colombia without any pre-departure cross-cultural training and no logistical support after arrival. They were on their own; they had difficulty even buying a light bulb; and after a number of mishaps, the family decided to end the assignment and return home. Now Noel has her own company, Chicago-based International Orientation Resources (IOR), which specializes in assisting others as they prepare for international assignments. IOR's Destination Assistance services help families with locating housing, schooling research, community orientation, and such day-to-day necessities as shopping, banking, and local registration requirements.

■ ETHICAL BEHAVIOR ACROSS CULTURES

The importance of ethical issues in organizational behavior and management was first introduced in Chapter 1. In the international arena, special ethical challenges arise as a result of cultural diversity and the variation in governments and legal systems that characterize our world. Prominent current issues include corruption and bribery in international business practices, poor working conditions and the employment of child and prison labor in some countries, and the role of international business in supporting repressive governments that fail to protect and respect the basic human rights of citizens.[50]

In the United States, the Foreign Corrupt Practices Act of 1977 makes it illegal for firms to engage in corrupt practices overseas, such as giving bribes to government officials in order to obtain business contracts. In 1999, member countries of the Organization for Economic Development agreed to ban payoffs to foreign officials by their countries' businesses. The United States government is pushing for more countries to join the movement against bribe giving and taking, and suggestions have been made that the World Bank consider corruption as a criterion when making loan decisions.[51]

The term *sweatshop* is increasingly in the news these days, and refers to organizations that force workers to labor under adverse conditions that may include long work days, unsafe conditions, and even the use of child labor. A variety of advocacy groups are now active in campaigning against sweatshops, and a number of well-recognized firms have been the targets of their attention—including such well-recognized multinationals as Nike, Mattel, and Disney. Watchdog groups in Asia, for example, have criticized Disney for allowing some of its contract manufacturers in China to force workers to labor seven days a week, up to 16 hours a day, and at no overtime. Mattel has been accused of engaging subcontractors who run "sweatshop Barbie" assembly lines that include extra-long work hours and heavy fines for workers' mistakes. In response to such criticisms more multinational employers are engaging outside consultants to conduct social audits of their international operations, adopting formal codes of ethical practices governing subcontractors, and backing external codes of conduct such as *Social Accountability 8000*—a certificate awarded by the Council on Economic Priorities. Nike, Disney, and Mattell have each taken steps along these lines to ensure that products made under their name are manufactured under conditions that meet acceptable standards.[52] Worth considering is the following comment by Jack Sheinkman, President Emeritus of the Amalgamated Clothing and Textile Workers Union, and member of the Council on Economic Priorities Advisory Board:

> As business becomes ever-more global in scope and its links in the chain of production extend further, the task of rating corporate social responsibility has become more complex. So, too, has the safeguarding of workers' rights…especially when responsibility is shared among manufacturers, contractors, subcontractors, buying agents,…and other parties to business agreements which transcend time-zones, language barriers, and developing and industrialized country borders alike.[53]

A continuing issue for debate in this area of international business and management practices is the influence of culture on ethical behavior. Figure 3.4 presents a continuum that contrasts "cultural relativism" with "ethical imperialism."

Council on Economic Priorities Accreditation Agency ←

www.cepaa.org

The Council on Economic Priorities Accreditation Agency accredits auditors to evaluate compliance with SA 8000. Auditors grant such certification only after consulting with human rights groups visiting and assessing businesses regarding child labor, health and safety, freedom of association and the right to collective bargaining, discrimination, disciplinary practices, working hours, compensation and management systems.

Cultural relativism	**Ethical imperialism**
←	→
No culture's ethics are superior. **The values and practices of the local setting determine what is right or wrong.**	**Certain absolute truths apply everywhere.** **Universal values transcend cultures in determining what is right or wrong.**
When in Rome, do as the Romans do.	*Don't do anything you wouldn't do at home.*

Figure 3.4
The Extremes of Cultural Relativism and Ethical Imperialism in International Business Ethics.

■ **Cultural relativism** suggests that ethical behavior is determined by its cultural context.

Business ethicist Thomas Donaldson describes **cultural relativism** as the position that there is no universal right way to behave and that ethical behavior is determined by its cultural context.[54] In other words, international business behavior is justified on the argument: "When in Rome do as the Romans do." If one accepts cultural relativism, a sweatshop operation would presumably be okay as long as it was consistent with the laws and practices of the local culture. The opposite extreme on the continuum in Figure 3.4 reflects an absolutist or universalistic assumption that there is a single moral standard that fits all situations, regardless of culture and national location. In other words, if a practice such as child labor is not acceptable in one's home environment it shouldn't be engaged in elsewhere. Critics of the absolutist approach claim that it is a form of *ethical imperialism* because it attempts to impose external ethical standards unfairly or inappropriately on local cultures and fails to respect their needs and unique situations.

Donaldson suggests that there is no simple answer to this debate and warns against the dangers of both cultural relativism and ethical imperialism. He makes the case that multinational businesses should adopt core or threshold values to guide behavior in ways that respect and protect fundamental human rights in any situation. However, he also suggests that there is room beyond the threshold to adapt and tailor one's actions in ways that respect the traditions, foundations, and needs of different cultures.[55]

A Global View of Organizational Learning

■ **Global organizational learning** is the ability to gather from the world at large the knowledge required for long-term organizational adaptation.

Organizational learning was first defined in Chapter 1 as the process of acquiring the knowledge necessary to adapt to a changing environment. In the context and themes of this chapter, the concept can be extended to **global organizational learning**—the ability to gather from the world at large the knowledge required for long-term organizational adaptation. Simply stated, people from different cultures and parts of the world have a lot to learn from one another about organizational behavior and management.

■ ARE MANAGEMENT THEORIES UNIVERSAL?

One of the most important questions to be asked and answered in this age of globalization is whether or not management theories are universal. That is, can and should a theory developed in one cultural context be transferred and used in another? The answer according to Geert Hofstede is "no," at least not without careful consideration of cultural influences. Culture can influence both the development of a theory or concept and its application. As an example, Hofstede cites the issue of motivation. He notes that Americans have historically addressed motivation from the perspective of individual performance and rewards—consistent with their highly individualistic culture. However, concepts such as merit pay and job enrichment may not fit well in other cultures where high collectivism places more emphasis on teamwork and groups. Hofstede's point, and one well worth remembering, is that although we can and should learn from what is taking place in other cultures, we should be informed consumers of that knowledge. We should always factor cultural considerations into account when transferring theories and practices from one setting to the next.[56]

A good case in point relates to the interest generated some years ago in Japanese management approaches, and based upon the success experienced at the time by Japanese industry.[57] Japanese firms have traditionally been described as favoring *lifetime employment* with strong employee-employer loyalty, seniority pay, and company unions. Their operations have emphasized a *quality commitment*, the *use of teams* and *consensus decision making*, and career development based upon *slow promotions* and *cross-functional job assignments.*[58]

Although the Japanese economy and many of its firms have had problems of their own recently, management scholars and consultants recognize that many lessons can still be learned from their practices. However, we also recognize that cultural differences must be considered in the process.[59] Specifically, what works in Japan may not work as well elsewhere, at least not without some modifications. Japan's highly collectivist society, for example, contrasts markedly with the highly individualistic cultures of the United States and other Western nations. It is only reasonable to expect differences in their management and organizational practices.

▪ BEST PRACTICES AROUND THE WORLD

An appropriate goal in global organizational learning is to identify the "best practices" found around the world. What is being done well in other settings may be of great value at home, whether that "home" is in Africa, Asia, Europe, North America, or anywhere else. Whereas the world at large once looked mainly to the North Americans and Europeans for management insights, today we recognize that potential "benchmarks" of excellence for high performance organizations can be discovered anywhere. For example, the influence of the Japanese approaches as a stimulus to global organizational learning is evident in many of the workplace themes with which you will become familiar in this book. These include growing attention to the value of teams and work groups, consensus decision making, employee involvement, flatter structures, and strong corporate cultures. These and related concepts and themes are well represented in today's high performance organizations.

As the field of organizational behavior continues to mature in its global research and understanding, we will all benefit from an expanding knowledge base that is enriched by cultural diversity. Organizational behavior is a science of contingencies, and one of them is culture. No one culture possesses all of the "right" answers to today's complex management and organizational problems. But a sincere commitment to global organizational learning can give us fresh ideas while still permitting locally appropriate solutions to be implemented with cultural sensitivity. This search for global understanding will be reflected in the following chapters as we move further into the vast domain of OB.

Chapter 3 Study Guide

Summary

Why is globalization significant to organizational behavior?

- Globalization, with its complex worldwide economic networks of business competition, resource supplies, and product markets, is having a major impact on businesses, employers, and workforces around the world.

- Nations in Europe, North America, and Asia are forming regional trade agreements, such as the EU, NAFTA, and APEC, to gain economic strength in the highly competitive global economy.

- More and more organizations, large and small, do an increasing amount of business abroad; more and more local employers are "foreign" owned, in whole or in part; the domestic workforce is becoming multicultural and more diverse.

- All organizations need global managers with the special interests and talents needed to excel in international work and cross-cultural relationships.

What is culture?

- Culture is the learned and shared way of doing things in a society; it represents deeply ingrained influences on the way people from different societies think, behave, and solve problems.

- Popular dimensions of culture include observable differences in language, time orientation, use of space, and religion.

- Hofstede's five national cultures dimensions are power distance, individualism–collectivism, uncertainty avoidance, masculinity–femininity, and long/short-term orientation.

- Trompenaars's framework for understanding cultural differences focuses on relationships among people, attitudes toward time, and attitudes toward the environment.

- Cross-cultural awareness requires a clear understanding of one's own culture and the ability to overcome the limits of parochialism and ethnocentrism.

How does globalization affect people at work?

- Multinational corporations (MNCs) are global businesses that operate with a worldwide scope; they are powerful forces in the global economy.

- Multiculturalism in the domestic workforce requires everyone to work well with people of different cultural backgrounds.

- Expatriate employees who work abroad for extended periods of time face special challenges, including possible adjustment problems abroad and reentry problems upon returning home.

- Ethical behavior across cultures is examined from the perspectives of cultural relativism and universalism.

What is a global view on organizational learning?

- A global view on learning about OB seeks to understand the best practices from around the world, with due sensitivity to cultural differences.

- Management concepts and theories must always be considered relative to the cultures in which they are developed and applied.

- Interest in Japanese management practices continues, with the traditional focus on long-term employment, emphasis on teams, quality commitment, careful career development, and consensus decision making.

- Global learning will increasingly move beyond North America, Europe, and Japan, to include best practices anywhere in the world.

Key Terms

Culture (p. 44)
Cultural relativism (p. 54)
Expatriates (p. 50)
Globalization (p. 41)
Global manager (p. 43)
Global organizational
   learning (p. 54)

High-context culture (p. 44)
Individualism–collectivism
   (p. 46)
Long-term/short-term
   orientation (p. 47)
Low-context culture (p. 44)
Masculinity–femininity (p. 46)

Monochronic culture (p. 45)
Multinational corporation
   (p. 49)
Polychronic culture (p. 45)
Power distance (p. 46)
Uncertainty avoidance
   (p. 46)

Self-Test 3

■ MULTIPLE CHOICE

1. NAFTA, APEC, and the EU are examples of _____. (a) multinational corporations (b) agencies of the United Nations (c) regional economic groupings (d) government agencies regulating international trade

2. In _____ cultures, people tend to complete one activity at a time. (a) parochial (b) monochronic (c) polychronic (d) ethnocentric

3. Cultural values emphasizing respect for tradition, ordering of relationships, and protecting one's "face" are associated with _____. (a) religious differences (b) uncertainty avoidance (c) masculinity-femininity (d) Confucian dynamism

4. One would expect to find respect for authority and acceptance of status differences in high _____ cultures. (a) power distance (b) individualism (c) uncertainty avoidance (d) aggressiveness

5. Asian countries like Japan and China are described on Hofstede's dimensions of national culture as generally high in _____. (a) uncertainty avoidance (b) short-term orientation (c) long-term orientation (d) individualism

6. _____ are foreign-owned plants that operate in Mexico, along the U.S. border, with special privileges. (a) Estrellas (b) Escuelas (c) Maquiladoras (d) Cabezas

7. In Trompenaars's framework for understanding cultural differences, _____ is used to describe different orientations toward nature. (a) inner directed versus outer directed (b) sequential versus polychronic (c) universal versus particular (d) neutral versus emotional

8. Management practices such as participative decision making and an emphasis on teamwork are often characteristic of organizations in _____ cultures. (a) monochronic (b) collectivist (c) paternalistic (d) uncertain

9. The Mercosor is an example of how different countries may cooperate in a _____ for mutual gain. (a) franchises (b) strategic alliances (c) regional economic alliances (d) chaebols

10. Which of the following is most characteristic of Japanese management practices? (a) consensus decisions (b) fast promotion (c) highly specialized career paths (d) all of these

■ TRUE–FALSE

11. Implications of globalization only apply to persons who will work in foreign countries and/or for multinational corporations.   T   F

12. The notion of "ethical imperialism" is consistant with the adage: "When in Rome, do as the Romans do."   T   F

13. Language is important as a cultural variable only when one is dealing with another person who speaks a different language.   T   F

14. A Canadian businessperson who expects foreign visitors to be able to conduct business negotiations in English is being very parochial about culture.   T   F

15. Respect earned on the basis of one's performance is associated with an achievement-oriented culture.   T   F

16. An American doing business in Hong Kong should be sensitive to the "silent language" of culture, such as that reflected in the use of space.   T   F

17. The reentry of expatriate employees returning from foreign assignments can be a source of problems for them and their employers.   T   F

18. Culture can be described as "software of the mind."   T   F

19. Promotion is typically faster in Japanese than in American businesses.   T   F

20. A global manager thinks with a world view and is tolerant of differences.   T   F

■ SHORT RESPONSE

21. Why is the individualism–collectivism dimension of national culture important in OB?

22. How do power distance values affect management practices across cultures?

23. What does the concept of ethnocentrism mean to you?

24. An organization trying to operate with Japanese management practices would do what?

■ APPLICATIONS ESSAY

25. Stephen Bachand, the CEO of Canadian Tire, featured in the chapter opener, wants to keep his company "ahead of the pack" as foreign retailers try to penetrate the Canadian market. It used to be that the American firms such as Wal-Mart and Home Depot were the major threats; now he has learned that the Asian giant Yaohan and the well-known Sainsbury's from Britain are considering operations in Canada. Bachand has heard of your special consulting expertise in "global organizational learning." He is on the telephone now and wants you to explain how the concept may help him keep his company a world-class competitor. With a large consulting contract at stake, what do you tell him about this concept?

Explore application-oriented Fast Company articles, cases, experimental exercises, and self-assessments in the OB Skills Workbook

■ **Visit the Schermerhorn Web site to find the Interactive Self-Test and Internet exercises for this chapter.**

Diversity and Individual Differences

LIFESTYLES MEET WORK STYLES

www.whirlpool.com

A few years ago you would have been hard pressed to find a corporate diversity policy with specific reference to Muslim employees. Times are changing in America's companies, as the fast-growing religion of Islam becomes a more visible presence among the nation's workers. Stop by and visit Whirlpool Corporation's Lavergne, Tennessee, plant. When other workers head off for a break, Satar Al Sorani may kneel to pray. A devout Muslim, he prays five times a day—a practice he expects his employer to allow and respect—even when prayer time falls during working hours. The Whirlpool plant has over a half dozen nationalities represented in its workforce, and at times almost 10 percent are Muslim. Management has found that changes in company policies are sometimes needed and required to accommodate this diversity.

Whirlpool isn't alone. Employees at Jeepers!, Inc.—a Waltham, Massachusetts theme park—got the firm to accept the preference of some male Muslims to wear beards. Those at Royal Caribbean Cruises of Miami, Florida, got the firm to allow the wearing of head scarves by Muslim women.

Back at Whirlpool, the extended congregational prayer service attended by Muslims at noon on Fridays created something of a problem. Now the firm allows some employees to start work at 6:00 AM, so as to be free to visit a Mosque for the prayers. As you might expect, not everyone has taken to the changes positively. One Kurd complains about being "bothered for years" by a colleague because he leaves work on Fridays to attend the Mosque. His supervisor, however, considers these absences as legitimate and excused. But the company isn't the only one to make adjustments. Ziad Barakat, who has worked at Whirlpool for ten years, has made some changes of his own. He says: "You have to compromise." That may well be a key to maintaining the balance of lifestyles and work styles.

D iversity is and should be a major concern in any organization, and valuing diversity in all aspects of operations should be a top priority. With diversity comes differences, and with differences comes the potential for problems in relationships. That cannot be denied. But importantly, too, with diversity comes the great potential for new perspective, creativity, and expanded problem solving that can be important in meeting the demands of our complex and dynamic work environments. When Whirlpool and other corporations adjust diversity policies in respect for the preferences of Muslim workers they are not only following good management practices, they are meeting part of the test continually set forth by an ever-changing society. Lifestyles should be compatible with work styles. With people indispensable to organizations and with intellectual capital the great resource of a knowledge society, those organizations that best understand and best deal with diversity and individual differences are poised to achieve competitive advantage. They will also stand forth as benchmarks among other socially responsible institutions. In this chapter, diversity and differences are examined with the framework of organizational behavior for their implications in the workplace.

Study Questions

An understanding of individual differences and similarities is crucial in today's diverse organizations. As you read Chapter 4, keep in mind these key questions.

■ What is workforce diversity, and why is it important?

■ What are demographic differences among individuals, and why are they important?

■ What are aptitude and ability differences among individuals, and why are they important?

■ What are personality determinants and differences among individuals, and why are they important?

■ What are value and attitude differences among individuals, and why are they important?

■ What does managing diversity and individual differences involve, and why is it important?

Workforce Diversity

A majority of Fortune 500 companies, including Colgate Palmolive, Corning, and Quaker Oats, are now providing incentives for executives to deal successfully with workforce diversity.[1] **Workforce diversity** refers to the presence of individual human characteristics that make people different from one another.[2] More specifically, this diversity comprises key demographic differences among members of a given workforce, including gender, race and ethnicity, age, and able-bodiedness. Sometimes they also encompass other factors, such as marital status, parental status, and religion.[3] The challenge is how to manage workforce diversity in a way that both respects the individual's unique perspectives and contributions and promotes a shared sense of organization vision and identity.

■ **Workforce diversity** is differences based on gender, race and ethnicity, age and able-bodiedness.

Workforce diversity is increasing in both the United States and Canada, as it is in much of the rest of the world. For example, in the United States, between 1990 and 2005, about 50 percent of the new entrants to the labor force will be women and racial and ethnic groups such as African Americans, Latinos, and Asians. At the same time, those 55 and older are projected to make up nearly 15 percent of the labor force. All of this is in sharp contrast to the traditional, younger, mostly white American male, labor force. Canadian and U.K. trends for women are similar.[4]

As the workforce becomes increasingly diverse, the possibility of stereotyping and discrimination increases and managing diversity becomes more important. **Stereotyping** occurs when one thinks of an individual as belonging to a group or category—for instance, elderly person—and the characteristics commonly associated with the group or category are assigned to the individual in question—for instance, older people aren't creative. Demographic characteristics may serve as the basis of stereotypes that obscure individual differences and prevent people from getting to know others as individuals and accurately assessing their performance potential. If you believe that older people are not creative, for example, you may mistakenly decide not to assign a very inventive 60-year-old person to an important task force.

Discrimination against certain people in the organization is not only a violation of U.S., Canadian, and European Union (EU) laws, but it is also counterproductive because it prevents the contributions of people who are discriminated against from being fully utilized. Many firms are increasingly recognizing that a diverse workforce that reflects societal differences helps bring them closer to their customers.

■ EQUAL EMPLOYMENT OPPORTUNITY

Equal employment opportunity involves both workplace nondiscrimination and affirmative action. Em-

OB Across Functions

HUMAN RESOURCE MANAGEMENT

Special Recruiting for Project Management

The Vera Institute of Justice was approached by the U.S. Immigration and Naturalization Service (INS) to help with a problem. On any given day INS had 80,000 people in deportation proceedings, but only 8000 beds in its detention facilities. Vera made a counterproposal to create a community supervision program along with a new screening system for detention, allowing INS to better use its space *and* improve compliance for those immigrants released. Four staff, two at Vera and two recruited for their special functional knowledge of the project area, served as a cross-functional team and devoted five months to planning for the project. The heart of the plan was a screening process to determine those immigrants whom it was safe to release and who had an incentive to appear for INS hearings. The plan was reviewed at a project meeting where all the other project directors, plus planners and key administrators met to assess it. Ultimately, INS accepted a three-year demonstration project, paying Vera $2 million per year. A national advisory board of numerous experts is involved with evaluating the project. If it appears successful, Vera will move ahead and use a similar process to develop or demonstrate eight additional programs.

Allstate Insurance ◄

www.allstate.com

Allstate Insurance has recently established a diversity training program that, among other things, trains its sales agents in diversity to capitalize on growth opportunities in diverse markets. Also, Allstate reports that those employees who have attended diversity training respond more favorably to other key indicators of management performance.

ployment decisions are nondiscriminatory when there is no intent to exclude or disadvantage legally protected groups. *Affirmative action* is a set of remedial actions designed to compensate for proven discrimination or correct for statistical imbalances in the labor force (e.g., local workers are 90 percent Hispanic, and your organization employs only 10 percent Hispanics).[5]

The most comprehensive statute prohibiting employment discrimination is Title VII of the Civil Rights Act of 1964. This act prohibits employers from discriminating against any individual with respect to compensation, terms, or conditions of employment because of race, color, religion, sex, or national origin. Affirmative action plans are required of federal government agencies and federal contractors, as well as organizations found to be in noncompliance with equal employment opportunity provisions. Many organizations also have implemented voluntary affirmative action plans.[6]

Affirmative action is legally driven by federal, state and provincial, and local laws, as well as numerous court cases. It requires written reports containing plans and statistical goals for specific groups of people in terms of such employment practices as hiring, promotions, and layoffs.[7]

■ MANAGING DIVERSITY

The concept of managing diversity in organizations emphasizes appreciation of differences in creating a setting where everyone feels valued and accepted. An organization's success or progress in managing diversity can be monitored by organizational surveys of attitudes and perceptions, among other means. Managing diversity assumes that groups will retain their own characteristics and will shape the firm as well as be shaped by it, creating a common set of values that will strengthen ties with customers, enhance recruitment, and the like. Sometimes, diversity management is resisted because of fear of change and discomfort with differences. To deal with this resistance, some countries, such as Canada, have laws designed to encourage the management of diversity at the provincial level through Employment Equity Legislation.[8]

Demographic Differences

■ **Demographic characteristics** are the background variables (e.g. age, gender) that help shape what a person becomes over time.

Demographic characteristics are the background characteristics that help shape what a person becomes. Such attributes may be thought of in both current terms—for example, an employee's current medical status—and historical terms—for instance, where and how long a person has worked at various jobs. Demographic characteristics of special interest from equal employment opportunity and workplace diversity considerations include gender, age, race, ethnicity, and able-bodiedness.

■ GENDER

The research on working women in general tells us that there are very few differences between men and women that affect job performance (see The Effective Manager 4.1). Thus, men and women show no consistent differences in their problem-solving abilities, analytical skills, competitive drive, motivation, learning ability, or sociability. However, women are reported to be more conforming and to have lower expectations of success than men do. And, women's absenteeism rates tend to be higher than those of men. This latter finding may change, however, as we see men starting to play a more active role in raising children; absenteeism is also likely to be less frequent as telecommuting, flexible working hours, and the like become more prevalent.[9] In respect to pay, women's earnings have risen slowly from 59 percent of men's in 1975 to 76 percent most recently.[10] Certainly, this rise is not consistent with the doubling of women in the labor force since 1970.[11]

■ AGE

The research findings concerning age are particularly important given the aging of the workforce. People 50 years old and older account for 85 percent of the projected labor force growth between 1990 and 2005.[12] Older workers are susceptible to being stereotyped as inflexible and undesirable in other ways. In some cases, workers as young as age forty are considered to be "old" and complain that their experience and skills are no longer valued. Age-discrimination lawsuits are increasingly common in the United States.[13] Such discrimination also operates in Britain, where 44 percent of older managers say they have experienced age discrimination.[14] On the other hand, small businesses in particular tend to value older workers for their experience, stability and low turnover. Research is consistent with these preferences and also shows lower avoidable absences.[15] Finally, to the extent age is linked to experience or job tenure, there is a positive relationship between seniority and performance. More experienced workers tend to have low absence rates and relatively low turnover.[20]

■ ABLE-BODIEDNESS

Even though recent studies report that disabled workers do their jobs as well, or better than, nondisabled workers, nearly three quarters of severely disabled persons are reported to be unemployed. Almost 80 percent of those with disabilities say they want to work.[16] Once again, the expected shortage of traditional workers is predicted to lead to a reexamination of hiring policies. More firms are expected to give serious consideration to hiring disabled workers, particularly given that the cost of accommodating these workers has been shown to be low.[17]

■ RACIAL AND ETHNIC GROUPS

Consistent with some current literature, we use the term *racial and ethnic groups* to reflect the broad spectrum of employees of differing ethnicities or races who make up an ever-increasing portion of the new workforce.[18] Of particular significance in the American workplace is diversity reflected in an increasing proportion of African Americans, Asian Americans and Hispanic Americans.

THE EFFECTIVE MANAGER 4.1

TIPS IN DEALING WITH MALE AND FEMALE MANAGERS

- Do not assume that male and female managers differ in personal qualities.
- Make sure that policies, practices, and programs minimize gender differences in managers' job experiences.
- Do not assume that management success is more likely for either females or males.
- Recognize that there will be excellent, good, and poor managers within each gender.
- Understand that success requires the best use of human talent, regardless of gender.

Mount Sinai ◄

www.msmc.com

The Mount Sinai Medical Center in New York City has pioneered several diversity strategies. The hospital's employee orientation program trains staff members to be alert to how various cultures regard pain, patients' preferences to be alone or with family members, and food preferences, among other things.

Projections by the Bureau of Labor Statistics estimate that they will constitute 27% of the workforce by the year 2005. The Hudson Institute extends this projection to 32% by the year 2020. The potential for stereotypes and discrimination to adversely affect career opportunities and progress for members of these and other minority groups must be recognized.

Even though employment decisions based on demographic differences are allowable under Title VII if they can be justified as bona fide occupational qualifications reasonable to normal business operations, race cannot be one of these. Case law has shown that these qualifications are always extremely difficult to justify.[21] In any event the flight attendant job is a case in point. When the airlines failed to show why men could not perform flight attendant duties as well as females, gender restrictions on hiring were lifted.

Aptitude and Ability

■ **Aptitude** represents a person's capability of learning something.

■ **Ability** reflects a person's existing capacity to perform the various tasks needed for a given job.

Demographic characteristics are sometimes used erroneously as stereotypes in place of assessing a person's true aptitude or ability. **Aptitude** represents a person's capability of learning something, whereas **ability** reflects a person's existing capacity to perform the various tasks needed for a given job and includes both relevant knowledge and skills.[22] In other words, aptitudes are potential abilities, whereas abilities are the knowledge and skills that an individual currently possesses.

Aptitudes and abilities are important considerations for a manager when initially hiring or selecting candidates for a job. We are all acquainted with various tests used to measure mental aptitudes and abilities. Some of these provide an overall intelligent quotient (IQ) score (e.g., the Stanford-Binet IQ Test). Others provide measures of more specific competencies that are required of people entering various educational programs or career fields. You have probably taken the ACT or SAT college entrance tests. Such tests are designed to facilitate the screening and selection of applicants for educational programs or jobs. In addition to mental aptitudes and abilities, some jobs, such as firefighters and police, require tests for physical abilities. Muscular strength and cardiovascular endurance are two of many physical ability dimensions.[23]

For legal purposes, demonstrated evidence must be presented that those scoring more favorably on the tests will tend to be more successful in their educational program, career field, or job performance than those with lower scores. In other words, there must be a fit between specific aptitudes and abilities and job requirements. If you want to be a surgeon, for instance, and cannot demonstrate good hand–eye coordination, there will not be a good ability–job fit. Such a fit is so important that it is a core concept in Chapter 7 on managing human resources.

■ **Personality** represents the overall profile or combination of characteristics that capture the unique nature of a person as that person reacts and interacts with others.

Personality

In addition to demographics and aptitude and ability, a third important individual attribute is personality. The term **personality** represents the overall profile or combination of characteristics that capture the unique nature of a person as that person reacts and interacts with others. As an example, think of a person who was the billionaire founder of a fast-growing, high-tech computer company by the time he was 30; who in his senior year in high school had turned selling newspapers into enough of a business to buy a BMW; who told his management team that his daughter's first words were "Daddy kill-IBM, Gateway, Compaq;" who learned from production mistakes and brought in senior managers to help his firm; and who is so private he seldom talks about himself: In other words, think of Michael Dell, the founder of Dell Computer, and his personality.[24]

Personality combines a set of physical and mental characteristics that reflect how a person looks, thinks, acts, and feels. Sometimes attempts are made to measure personality with questionnaires or special tests. Frequently, personality can be implied from behavior alone, such as by the actions of Michael Dell. Either way, personality is an important individual characteristic for managers to understand. An understanding of personality contributes to an understanding of organizational behavior in that we expect a predictable interplay between an individual's personality and his or her tendency to behave in certain ways.

GLOBALIZATION 🌐

Scholastic, a $630 million company, has become one of the world's leading publishers of children's books, classroom magazines, and instructional materials by emphasizing diversity strategies since the 1920s. Top management decided that one way to get input about what children from diverse backgrounds throughout the world wanted in educational materials was to hire women, minorities, and people who were bilingual and understood other cultures. This policy was unusual because, until the 1960s, the publishing industry was made up largely of white males. The firm has reinforced this diversity strategy with advice from experts concerning ways to capitalize on it. As a result, Scholastic sells 160 million books a year worldwide, and 90 percent of U.S. classrooms use its materials.

■ PERSONALITY DETERMINANTS AND DEVELOPMENT

Just what determines personality? Is personality inherited or genetically determined, or is it formed by experience? You may have heard someone say something like, "She acts like her mother." Similarly, someone may argue that "Bobby is the way he is because of the way he was raised." These two arguments illustrate the nature/nurture controversy: Is personality determined by heredity, that is, by genetic endowment, or by one's environment? As Figure 4.1 shows, these two forces actually operate in combination. Heredity consists of those factors that are determined at conception, including physical characteristics, gender, and personality factors. Environment consists of cultural, social, and situational factors.

The impact of heredity on personality continues to be the source of considerable debate. Perhaps the most general conclusion we can draw is that heredity sets the limits on just how much personality characteristics can be developed; environment determines development within these limits. For instance, a person

**Figure 4.1
Heredity and environ-
mental linkage with
personality.**

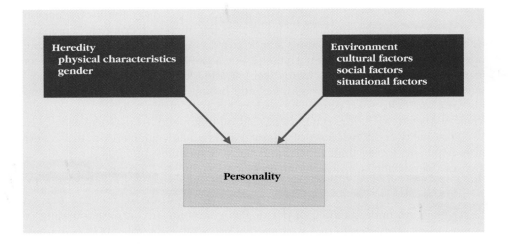

could be born with a tendency toward authoritarianism, and that tendency could be reinforced in an authoritarian work environment. These limits appear to vary from one characteristic to the next and across all characteristics there is about a 50–50 heredity–environment split.[25]

As we show throughout this book, *cultural values and norms* play a substantial role in the development of an individual's personality and behaviors. Contrast the individualism of U.S. culture with the collectivism of Mexican culture, for example.[26] Social factors reflect such things as family life, religion, and the many kinds of formal and informal groups in which people participate throughout their lives—friendship groups, athletic groups, as well as formal work groups. Finally, the demands of differing *situational factors* emphasize or constrain different aspects of an individual's personality. For example, in class you are likely to rein in your high spirits and other related behaviors encouraged by your personality. However, at a sporting event, you may be jumping up, cheering, and loudly criticizing the referees.

■ **Developmental
Approaches** are systematic
models of ways in which
personality develops across
time.

The **developmental approaches** of Chris Argyris, Daniel Levinson, and Gail Sheehy systematically examine the ways personality develops across time. Argyris notes that people develop along a continuum of dimensions from immaturity to maturity as shown in Figure 4.2. He believes that many organizations

**Figure 4.2
Argyris's Maturity–
Immaturity Continuum.**

From immaturity	To Maturity
Passivity	Activity
Dependence	Independence
Limited behavior	Diverse behavior
Shallow interests	Deep interests
Short time perspective	Long time perspective
Subordinate position	Superordinate position
Little self-awareness	Much self-awareness

treat mature adults as if they were still immature and this creates many problems in terms of bringing out the best in employees. Levinson and Sheehy maintain that an individual's personality unfolds in a series of stages across time. Sheehy's model, for example, talks about three stages—ages 18–30, 30–45, and 45–85+. Each of these has a crucial impact on the worker's employment and career, as we show in Chapter 7. The implications are that personalities develop over time and require different managerial responses. Thus, needs and other personality aspects of people initially entering an organization change sharply as they move through different stages or toward increased maturity.[27]

Personality Traits and Classifications

Numerous lists of personality traits—enduring characteristics describing an individual's behavior, have been developed, many of which have been used in OB research and can be looked at in different ways. First, recent research has examined people using extensive lists of personality dimensions and distilled them into the "Big Five:"[28]

- *Extraversion*—Outgoing, sociable, assertive
- *Agreeableness*—Good-natured, trusting, cooperative
- *Conscientiousness*—Responsible, dependable, persistent
- *Emotional stability*—Unworried, secure, relaxed
- *Openness to experience*—Imaginative, curious, broad-minded

The "Big Five" personality dimensions

Standardized personality tests determine how positively or negatively an individual scores on each of these dimensions. For instance, a person scoring high on openness to experience tends to ask lots of questions and to think in new and unusual ways. You can consider a person's individual personality profile across the five dimensions. In terms of job performance, research has shown that conscientiousness predicts job performance across five occupational groups of professions—engineers, police, managers, sales, and skilled and semiskilled employees. Predictability of the other dimensions depends on the occupational group. For instance, not surprisingly, extraversion predicts performance for sales and managerial positions.

A second approach to looking at OB personality traits is to divide them into social traits, personal conception traits, and emotional adjustment traits, and then to consider how those categories come together dynamically.[29]

■ SOCIAL TRAITS

Social traits are surface-level traits that reflect the way a person appears to others when interacting in various social settings. Problem-solving style, based on the work of Carl Jung, a noted psychologist, is one measure representing social traits.[30] It reflects the way a person goes about gathering and evaluating information in solving problems and making decisions.

Information gathering involves getting and organizing data for use. Styles of information gathering vary from sensation to intuitive. *Sensation-type individuals* pre-

■ **Social traits** are surface-level traits that reflect the way a person appears to others when interacting in various social settings.

fer routine and order and emphasize well-defined details in gathering information; they would rather work with known facts than look for possibilities. By contrast, *intuitive-type individuals* prefer the "big picture." They like solving new problems, dislike routine, and would rather look for possibilities than work with facts.

The second component of problem solving, *evaluation*, involves making judgments about how to deal with information once it has been collected. Styles of information evaluation vary from an emphasis on feeling to an emphasis on thinking. *Feeling-type individuals* are oriented toward conformity and try to accommodate themselves to other people. They try to avoid problems that may result in disagreements. *Thinking-type individuals* use reason and intellect to deal with problems and downplay emotions.

When these two dimensions (information gathering and evaluation) are combined, four basic problem-solving styles result: sensation-feeling (SF), intuitive-feeling (IF), sensation-thinking (ST), and intuitive-thinking (IT), together with summary descriptions, as shown in Figure 4.3.

Research indicates that there is a fit between the styles of individuals and the kinds of decisions they prefer. For example, STs (sensation-thinkers) prefer analytical strategies—those that emphasize detail and method. IFs (intuitive-feelers) prefer intuitive strategies—those that emphasize an overall pattern and fit. Not surprisingly, mixed styles (sensation-feelers or intuitive-thinkers) select both analytic and intuitive strategies. Other findings also indicate that thinkers tend to

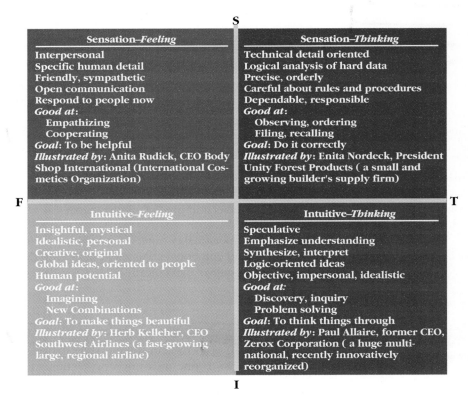

S

Sensation–*Feeling*

Interpersonal
Specific human detail
Friendly, sympathetic
Open communication
Respond to people now
Good at:
   Empathizing
   Cooperating
Goal: To be helpful
Illustrated by: Anita Rudick, CEO Body Shop International (International Cosmetics Organization)

Sensation–*Thinking*

Technical detail oriented
Logical analysis of hard data
Precise, orderly
Careful about rules and procedures
Dependable, responsible
Good at:
   Observing, ordering
   Filing, recalling
Goal: Do it correctly
Illustrated by: Enita Nordeck, President Unity Forest Products (a small and growing builder's supply firm)

Intuitive–*Feeling*

Insightful, mystical
Idealistic, personal
Creative, original
Global ideas, oriented to people
Human potential
Good at:
   Imagining
   New Combinations
Goal: To make things beautiful
Illustrated by: Herb Kelleher, CEO Southwest Airlines (a fast-growing large, regional airline)

Intuitive–*Thinking*

Speculative
Emphasize understanding
Synthesize, interpret
Logic-oriented ideas
Objective, impersonal, idealistic
Good at:
   Discovery, inquiry
   Problem solving
Goal: To think things through
Illustrated by: Paul Allaire, former CEO, Zerox Corporation (a huge multinational, recently innovatively reorganized)

F   T

I

Figure 4.3
Four problem-solving style summaries.

have higher motivation than do feelers and that individuals who emphasize sensations tend to have higher job satisfaction than do intuitives. These and other findings suggest a number of basic differences among different problem-solving styles, emphasizing the importance of fitting such styles with a task's information processing and evaluation requirements.[31]

Problem-solving styles are most frequently measured by the (typically 100-item) *Myers–Briggs Type Indicator (MBTI)*, which asks individuals how they usually act or feel in specific situations. Firms such as Apple, AT&T, and Exxon, as well as hospitals, educational institutions, and military organizations, have used the Myers–Briggs for various aspects of management development.[32]

■ PERSONAL CONCEPTION TRAITS

The *personal conception traits* represent the way individuals tend to think about their social and physical setting as well as their major beliefs and personal orientation concerning a range of issues.

Locus of Control   The extent to which a person feels able to control his or her own life is concerned with a person's internal–external orientation and is measured by Rotter's locus of control instrument.[33] People have personal conceptions about whether events are controlled primarily by themselves, which indicates an internal orientation, or by outside forces, such as their social and physical environment, which indicates an external orientation. Internals, or persons with an internal locus of control, believe that they control their own fate or destiny. In contrast, externals, or persons with an external locus of control, believe that much of what happens to them is beyond their control and is determined by environmental forces.

In general, externals are more extroverted in their interpersonal relationships and are more oriented toward the world around them. Internals tend to be more introverted and are more oriented toward their own feelings and ideas. Figure 4.4 suggests that internals tend to do better on tasks requiring complex information processing and learning, as well as initiative. Many managerial and professional jobs have these kinds of requirements.

Authoritarianism/Dogmatism   Both "authoritarianism" and "dogmatism" deal with the rigidity of a person's beliefs. A person high in **authoritarianism** tends to adhere rigidly to conventional values and to obey recognized authority. This person is concerned with toughness and power and opposes the use of subjective feelings. An individual high in **dogmatism** sees the world as a threatening place. This person regards legitimate authority as absolute and accepts or rejects others according to how much they agree with accepted authority. Superiors who possess these latter traits tend to be rigid and closed. At the same time, dogmatic subordinates tend to want certainty imposed upon them.[34]

From an ethical standpoint, we can expect highly authoritarian individuals to present a special problem because they are so susceptible to authority that in their eagerness to comply they may behave unethically.[35] For example, we might speculate that many of the Nazis who were involved in war crimes during World War II were high in authoritarianism or dogmatism; they believed so strongly in authority that they followed their unethical orders without question.

LTV ◄

www.ltvsteel.com

At the large aerospace conglomerate LTV, a manager would typically emphasize creative solutions rather than detailed facts. Ultimately, the MBTI was used to emphasize factual aspects for the sensation-thinkers, and the team moved into creative solutions. The team's effectiveness and morale improved.

■ **Authoritarianism** is a tendency to adhere rigidly to conventional values and to obey recognized authority.

■ **Dogmatism** leads a person to see the world as a threatening place and regard authority as absolute.

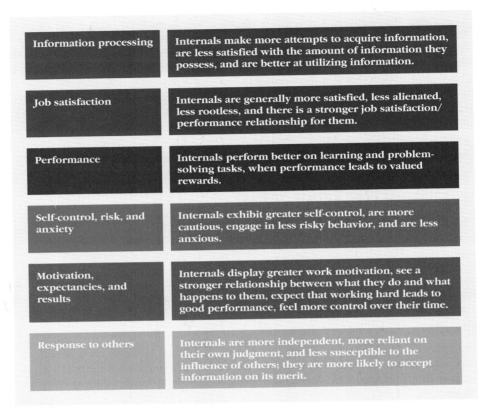

Information processing	Internals make more attempts to acquire information, are less satisfied with the amount of information they possess, and are better at utilizing information.
Job satisfaction	Internals are generally more satisfied, less alienated, less rootless, and there is a stronger job satisfaction/ performance relationship for them.
Performance	Internals perform better on learning and problem-solving tasks, when performance leads to valued rewards.
Self-control, risk, and anxiety	Internals exhibit greater self-control, are more cautious, engage in less risky behavior, and are less anxious.
Motivation, expectancies, and results	Internals display greater work motivation, see a stronger relationship between what they do and what happens to them, expect that working hard leads to good performance, feel more control over their time.
Response to others	Internals are more independent, more reliant on their own judgment, and less susceptible to the influence of others; they are more likely to accept information on its merit.

Figure 4.4
Some ways in which internals differ from externals.

Machiavellianism The third personal conceptions dimension is Machiavellian- ism, which owes its origins to Niccolo Machiavelli. The very name of this six- teenth-century author evokes visions of a master of guile, deceit, and opportunism in interpersonal relations. Machiavelli earned his place in history by writing *The Prince*, a nobleman's guide to the acquisition and use of power.[36] The subject of Machiavelli's book is manipulation as the basic means of gaining and keeping con- trol of others. From its pages emerges the personality profile of a Machiavellian— someone who views and manipulates others purely for personal gain.

Psychologists have developed a series of instruments called Mach scales to measure a person's Machiavellian orientation.[37] A high-Mach personality is someone who tends to behave in ways consistent with Machiavelli's basic princi- ples. Such individuals approach situations logically and thoughtfully and are even capable of lying to achieve personal goals. They are rarely swayed by loy- alty, friendships, past promises, or the opinions of others, and they are skilled at influencing others.

Research using the Mach scales provides insight into the way high and low Machs may be expected to behave in various situations. A person with a "cool" and "detached" high-Mach personality can be expected to take control and try to exploit loosely structured environmental situations but will perform in a perfunc- tory, even detached, manner in highly structured situations. Low Machs tend to accept direction imposed by others in loosely structured situations; they work hard to do well in highly structured ones. For example, we might expect that, where the situation permitted, a high Mach would do or say whatever it took to get his or her way. In contrast, a low Mach would tend to be much more strongly guided by ethical considerations and would be less likely to lie or cheat or to get away with lying or cheating.

Self-Monitoring   A final personal conceptions trait of special importance to managers is self-monitoring. **Self-monitoring** reflects a person's ability to adjust his or her behavior to external, situational (environmental) factors.[38]

   High self-monitoring individuals are sensitive to external cues and tend to behave differently in different situations. Like high Machs, high self-monitors can present a very different appearance from their true self. In contrast, low self-monitors, like their low-Mach counterparts, aren't able to disguise their behaviors—"what you see is what you get." There is also evidence that high self-monitors are closely attuned to the behavior of others and conform more readily than do low self-monitors.[39] Thus, they appear flexible and may be especially good at responding to the kinds of situational contingencies emphasized throughout this book. For example, high self-monitors should be especially good at changing their leadership behavior to fit subordinates with high or low experience, tasks with high or low structure, and so on.

■ **Self-monitoring** reflects a person's ability to adjust his or her behavior to external, situational (environmental) factors.

■ EMOTIONAL ADJUSTMENT TRAITS

The **emotional adjustment traits** measure how much an individual experiences emotional distress or displays unacceptable acts. Often the person's health is affected. Although numerous such traits are cited in the literature, a frequently encountered one especially important for OB is the Type A/Type B orientation.

■ **Emotional adjustment traits** measure how much an individual experiences emotional distress or displays unacceptable acts.

Type A and Type B Orientation   To get a feel for this orientation, take the following quiz and then read on.[40] Circle the number that best characterizes you on each of the following pairs of characteristics.

Casual about appointments	1 2 3 4 5 6 ⑦ 8	Never late
Not competitive	1 2 3 4 5 ⑥ 7 8	Very competitive
Never feel rushed	1 2 3 4 ⑤ 6 7 8	Always feel rushed
Take one thing at a time	1 2 3 4 5 ⑥ 7 8	Try to do many things
Do things slowly	1 2 3 4 5 ⑥ 7 8	Do things fast
Express my feelings	① 2 3 4 5 6 7 8	Hold in my feelings
Many outside interests	1 ② 3 4 5 6 7 8	Few outside interests

Total your points for the seven items in the quiz. Multiply this total by 3 to arrive at a final score. Use this total to locate your Type A/Type B orientation on the following list.

FINAL POINTS	A/B ORIENTATION
Below 90	B
90–99	B+
100–105	A-
106–119	A
120 or more	A+

■ **Type A orientations** are characterized by impatience, desire for achievement, and perfectionism.

■ **Type B orientations** are characterized by an easy going and less competitive nature than Type A.

Individuals with a **Type A orientation** are characterized by impatience, desire for achievement, and perfectionism. In contrast, those with **Type B orientations** are characterized as more easygoing and less competitive in relation to daily events.[41]

Type A people tend to work fast and to be abrupt, uncomfortable, irritable, and aggressive. Such tendencies indicate "obsessive" behavior, a fairly widespread—but not always helpful—trait among managers. Many managers are hard-driving, detail-oriented people who have high performance standards and thrive on routine. But when such work obsessions are carried to the extreme, they may lead to greater concerns for details than for results, resistance to change, overzealous control of subordinates, and various kinds of interpersonal difficulties, which may even include threats and physical violence. In contrast, Type B managers tend to be much more laid back and patient in their dealings with co-workers and subordinates.

■ PERSONALITY AND SELF-CONCEPT

■ **Personality dynamics** are the ways in which an individual integrates and organizes social traits, values and motives, personal conceptions, and emotional adjustment.

■ **Self-concept** is the view individuals have of themselves as physical, social, and spiritual or moral beings.

Collectively, the ways in which an individual integrates and organizes the previously discussed categories and the traits they contain are referred to as **personality dynamics**. It is this category that makes personality more than just the sum of the separate traits. A key personality dynamic in your study of OB is the self-concept.

We can describe the **self-concept** as the view individuals have of themselves as physical, social, and spiritual or moral beings.[42] It is a way of recognizing oneself as a distinct human being. A person's self-concept is greatly influenced by his or her culture. For example, Americans tend to disclose much more about themselves than do the English; that is, Americans' self-concept is more assertive and talkative.[43]

Two related—and crucial—aspects of the self-concept are self-esteem and self-efficacy. *Self-esteem* is a belief about one's own worth based on an overall self-evaluation.[44] People high in self-esteem see themselves as capable, worthwhile, and acceptable and tend to have few doubts about themselves. The opposite is true of a person low in self-esteem. Some OB research suggests that, whereas high self-esteem generally can boost performance and human resource maintenance, when under pressure, people with high self-esteem may become boastful and act egotistically. They also may be overconfident at times and fail to obtain important information.[45]

Self-efficacy, sometimes called the "effectance motive," is a more specific version of self-esteem; it is an individual's belief about the likelihood of successfully completing a specific task. You could be high in self-esteem, yet have a feeling of low self-efficacy about performing a certain task, such as public speaking.

Values and Attitudes

Joining demographic and personality characteristics as important individual difference characteristics are values and attitudes.

■ VALUES

■ **Values** can be defined as broad preferences concerning appropriate courses of action or outcomes.

Values can be defined as broad preferences concerning appropriate courses of action or outcomes. As such, values reflect a person's sense of right and wrong or what "ought" to be.[46] "Equal rights for all" and "People should be treated with respect and dignity" are representative of values. Values tend to influence attitudes and behavior. For example, if you value equal rights for all and you go to work for an organization that treats its managers much better than it does its workers, you may form the attitude that the company is an unfair place to work; consequently, you may not produce well or may perhaps leave the company. It's likely that if the company had had a more equalitarian policy, your attitude and behaviors would have been more positive.

Sources and Types of Values   Parents, friends, teachers, and external reference groups can all influence individual values. Indeed, peoples' values develop as a product of the learning and experience they encounter in the cultural setting in which they live. As learning and experiences differ from one person to another, value differences result. Such differences are likely to be deep seated and difficult (though not impossible) to change; many have their roots in early childhood and the way a person has been raised.[47]

The noted psychologist Milton Rokeach has developed a well-known set of values classified into two broad categories.[48] **Terminal values** reflect a person's preferences concerning the "ends" to be achieved; they are the goals individuals would like to achieve during their lifetime. Rokeach divides values into 18 terminal values and 18 instrumental values, as summarized in Figure 4.5. **Instrumental values** reflect the "means" for achieving desired ends. They represent how you might go about achieving your important end states, depending on the relative importance you attached to the instrumental values.

Illustrative research shows, not surprisingly, that both terminal and instrumental values differ by group (for example, executives, activist workers, and union members).[49] These preference differences can encourage conflict or agreement when different groups have to deal with each other.

■ **Sources and types of values** Parents, friends, teachers, and external reference groups can all influence individual values.

■ **Terminal values** reflect a person's preferences concerning the "ends" to be achieved.

■ **Instrumental values** reflect a person's beliefs about the means for achieving desired ends.

Terminal Values	Instrumental Values
A comfortable life (and prosperous)	Ambitious (hardworking)
An exciting life (stimulating)	Broad-minded (open-minded)
A sense of accomplishment (lasting contibution)	Capable (competent, effective)
A world at peace (free of war and conflict)	Cheerful (lighthearted, joyful)
A world of beauty (beauty of nature and the arts)	Clean (neat, tidy)
Equality (brotherhood, equal opportunity)	Courageous (standing up for beliefs)
Family security (taking care of loved ones)	Forgiving (willing to pardon)
Freedom (independence, free choice)	Helpful (working for others' welfare)
Happiness (contentedness)	Honest (sincere, truthful)
Inner harmony (freedom from inner conflict)	Imaginative (creative, daring)
Mature love (sexual and spiritual intimacy)	Independent (self-sufficient, self-reliant)
National security (attack protection)	Intellectual (intelligent, reflective)
Pleasure (leisurely, enjoyable life)	Logical (rational, consistent)
Salvation (saved, eternal life)	Loving (affectionate, tender)
Self-respect (self-esteem)	Obedient (dutiful, respectful)
Social recognition (admiration, respect)	Polite (courteous, well mannered)
True friendship (close companionship)	Responsible (reliable, dependable)
Wisdom (mature understanding of life)	Self-controlled (self-disciplined)

**Figure 4.5
Rokeach value survey.**

Another frequently used classification of human values has been developed by psychologist Gordon Allport and his associates. These values fall into six major types:[50]

Allport's six value categories

- *Theoretical*—Interest in the discovery of truth through reasoning and systematic thinking.
- *Economic*—Interest in usefulness and practicality, including the accumulation of wealth.
- *Aesthetic*—Interest in beauty, form, and artistic harmony.
- *Social*—Interest in people and love as a human relationship.
- *Political*—Interest in gaining power and influencing other people.
- *Religious*—Interest in unity and in understanding the cosmos as a whole.

Once again, groups differ in the way they rank order the importance of these values, as shown in the following.[51]

- *Ministers*—Religious, social, aesthetic, political, theoretical, economic.
- *Purchasing Executive*—Economic, theoretical, political, religious, aesthetic, social.
- *Industrial Scientists*—Theoretical, political, economic, aesthetic, religious, social.

The previous value classifications have had a major impact on the values literature, but they were not specifically designed for people in a work setting. A more recent values schema, developed by Maglino and associates, is aimed at people in the workplace:[52]

Maglino and associates value categories

- *Achievement*—Getting things done and working hard to accomplish difficult things in life.
- *Helping and Concern for Others*—Being concerned with other people and helping others.
- *Honesty*—Telling the truth and doing what you feel is right.
- *Fairness*—Being impartial and doing what is fair for all concerned.

These four values have been shown to be especially important in the workplace; thus, the framework should be particularly relevant for studying values in OB.

In particular, values can be influential through **value congruence**, which occurs when individuals express positive feelings upon encountering others who exhibit values similar to their own. When values differ, or are *incongruent*, conflicts over such things as goals and the means to achieve them may result. The Maglino et al. value schema was used to examine value congruence between leaders and followers. The researchers found greater follower satisfaction with the leader when there was such congruence in terms of achievement, helping, honesty, and fairness values.[53]

■ **Value congruence** occurs when individuals express positive feelings upon encountering others who exhibit values similar to their own.

Patterns and Trends in Values   We should also be aware of applied research on values trends over time. Daniel Yankelovich, for example, is known for his informative public opinion polls.[54] Among North American workers, Yankelovich notes a movement away from valuing economic incentives, organizational loyalty, and work-related identity and toward valuing meaningful work, pursuit of leisure, and personal identity and self-fulfillment. Yankelovich believes that the modern manager must be able to recognize value differences and trends among people at work. For example, he reports finding higher productivity among younger workers who are employed in jobs that match their values and/or who are supervised by managers who share their values, reinforcing the concept of value congruence.

In a nationwide sample, managers and human-resource professionals were asked to identify the work-related values they believed to be most important to individuals in the workforce, both now and in the near future.[55] The nine most popular values named were: recognition for competence and accomplishments; respect and dignity; personal choice and freedom; involvement at work; pride in one's work; lifestyle quality; financial security; self-development; and health and wellness. These values are especially important for managers because they indicate some key concerns of the new workforce. Even though each individual worker places his or her own importance on these values, and even though the United States today has by far the most diverse workforce in its history, this overall characterization is a good place for managers to start when dealing with workers in the new workplace. It is important to note, however, that, although values are individual preferences, many tend to be shared within cultures and organizations.

■ ATTITUDES

Attitudes are influenced by values and are acquired from the same sources as values: friends, teachers, parents, and role models. Attitudes focus on specific people or objects, whereas values have a more general focus and are more stable than attitudes. "Employees should be allowed to participate" is a value; your positive or negative feeling about your job because of the participation it allows is an attitude. Formally defined, an **attitude** is a predisposition to respond in a positive or negative way to someone or something in one's environment. For example, when you say that you "like" or "dislike" someone or something, you are expressing an attitude. It's important to remember that an attitude, like a value, is a hypothetical construct; that is, one never sees, touches, or actually isolates an attitude. Rather, attitudes are *inferred* from the things people say, informally or in formal opinion polls or through their behavior.

Figure 4.6 shows attitudes as accompanied by antecedents and results.[56] The beliefs and values antecedents in the figure form the **cognitive component** of an attitude: the beliefs, opinions, knowledge, or information a person possesses.

The Hanjin conglomerate's Korean Air emphasizes the individual values of service orientation, creativity, and progressiveness which are consistent with the airline's emphasis on constantly enhancing its role in the transportation business.

■ **Attitude** is a predisposition to respond in a positive or negative way to someone or something in one's environment.

■ The **cognitive component** of an attitude reflects the beliefs, opinions, knowledge, or information a person possesses.

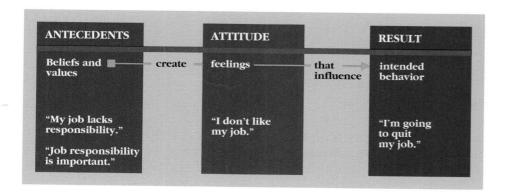

**Figure 4.6
A work-related example of the three components of attitudes.**

■ **Beliefs** represent ideas about someone or something and the conclusions people draw about them.

■ The **affective component** of an attitude is a specific feeling regarding the personal impact of the antecedents.

■ The **behavioral component** is an intention to behave in a certain way based on your specific feelings or attitudes.

Beliefs represent ideas about someone or something and the conclusions people draw about them; they convey a sense of "what is" to an individual. "My job lacks responsibility" is a belief shown in the figure. Note that the beliefs may or may not be accurate. "Responsibility is important" is a corresponding aspect of the cognitive component, which reflects an underlying value.

The **affective component** of an attitude is a specific feeling regarding the personal impact of the antecedents. This is the actual attitude itself, such as "I don't like my job." The **behavioral component** is an intention to behave in a certain way based on your specific feelings or attitudes. This intended behavior is a result of an attitude and is a predisposition to act in a specific way, such as "I'm going to quit my job."

Attitudes and Behavior   You should recognize that the link between attitudes and behavior is tentative. An attitude results in *intended* behavior; this intention may or may not be carried out in a given circumstance.

In general, the more specific attitudes and behaviors are, the stronger the relationship. For example, say you are a French-Canadian webmaster and you are asked about your satisfaction with your supervisor's treatment of French-Canadian webmasters. You also indicate the strength of your intent to look for another webmaster job in a similar kind of organization within the next six months. Here, both the attitude and the behavior are specifically stated (they refer to French-Canadian webmasters, and they identify a given kind of organization over a specific time period). Thus, we would expect to find a relatively strong relationship between these attitudes and how aggressively you actually start looking for another webmaster job.

It is also important that a good deal of freedom be available to carry out the intent. In the example just given, the freedom to follow through would be sharply restricted if the demand for webmasters dropped substantially.

Finally, the attitude and behavior linkage tends to be stronger when the person in question has had experience with the stated attitude. For example, assuming you are a business administration or management major, the relationship between your course attitude and/or your intent to drop the course and your later behavior of actually doing so would probably be stronger in your present OB course than in the first week of your enrollment in an advanced course in nuclear fission.[57]

Even though attitudes do not always predict behavior, the link between attitudes and potential or intended behavior is important for managers to understand. Think about your work experiences or conversations with other people about their work. It is not uncommon to hear concerns expressed about someone's "bad attitude." These concerns typically reflect displeasure with the behavioral consequences with which the poor attitude is associated. Unfavorable attitudes in the form of low job satisfaction can result in costly labor turnover, absenteeism, tardiness, and even impaired physical or mental health. One of the manager's responsibilities, therefore, is to recognize attitudes and to understand both their antecedents and their potential implications.

■ **Cognitive dissonance** describes a state of inconsistency between an individual's attitude and behavior.

Attitudes and Cognitive Consistency   Leon Festinger, a noted social psychologist, uses the term **cognitive dissonance** to describe a state of inconsistency between an individual's attitudes and his or her behavior.[58] Let's assume that you have the attitude that recycling is good for the economy but you don't recycle. Festinger predicts that such an inconsistency results in discomfort and a desire to reduce or eliminate it by (1) changing the underlying attitude, (2) changing future behavior, or (3) developing new ways of explaining or rationalizing the inconsistency.

Two factors that influence which of the above choices tend to be made are the degree of control a person thinks he or she has over the situation and the magnitude of the rewards involved. In terms of control, if your boss won't let you recycle office trash, you would be less likely to change your attitude than if you voluntarily chose not to recycle. You might instead choose the rationalization option. In terms of rewards, if they are high enough, rewards tend to reduce your feeling of inconsistency: If I'm rewarded even though I don't recycle, the lack of recycling must not be so bad after all.

Managing Diversity and Individual Differences

Dealing with diversity and individual differences has to be included among the most important issues challenging all managers in the quest for high performance and organizational competitiveness. This is true not only in the United States but also in Canada, European Union countries, and several countries in Asia.[59] Only the details differ.

So how do managers deal with all this? To convey the flavor of what some of the more progressive employers have done in managing diversity, let's now consider Boston-based Harvard Pilgrim Health Care (HPHC). Barbara Stern is the vice president of diversity.[60] She argues that what has traditionally been a "soft" issue is now becoming a business necessity in terms of better serving customers, understanding markets, and obtaining full benefit from staff talents. Each year, HPHC attempts to increase its diversity in terms of the proportion of women and racial minorities by 0.5 percent, which allows for continuous improvement. Such improvement raised the proportion of minority new hires from 14 to 28 percent over four years, and the total minority employees went from 16 to 21 percent over the same period.

R & D ←
ajr.newslink.org

R & D, information processing, and medical manufacturing maquiladora tours of a high-tech (twin plant) on the U.S.–Mexican border showed the importance of recognizing diversity when comparing U.S. and mexican organizations. For instance, Mexican workers emphasized family relations much more than U.S. workers.

WORKPLACE DIVERSITY ⤡

Workers at Coors attend diversity workshops and get training on sexual harassment. They can choose among eight "resource councils" or "employee networks," ranging from gays to Native Americans. Coors also has a diversity task force and a diversity management group, as well as sponsoring numerous other diversity activities, such as a black heritage festival. The firm's diversity policies are part of a larger trend toward both paternity and maternity leave, on-site day care, and "lifestyle-friendly" policies. The impetus includes a labor shortage of young "Generation X" professionals and the shifting expectations of a demographically-changing workforce.

www.coors.com

THE EFFECTIVE MANAGER 4.2

DIVERSITY CHECKUP REPORT

The Checkup Report used at Harvard Pilgrim Health Care combines interviews, internal and external data, and research results in the following areas:

- Recruitment in candidates of color
- Community demographic changes
- Women in leadership
- Attraction and retention of gays and lesbians
- Able-bodiedness among employees
- Flexible work arrangements
- Non-English-speaking customers
- White men
- Customer service

To ensure that diversity was more than just a fad, a corporate diversity council was established. This council set up specific actions to serve as the initial focus of the diversity efforts. The council determined it needed a vice presidential-level person to oversee the effort. The council's goals were: (1) to create accountability for measuring diversity (tie meeting of diversity goals into salaries of the organization's top 85 managers); (2) to provide a custom-made education program; (3) to develop an explicit code of conduct and communication with a zero-tolerance policy (for example, the code spells out inappropriate behavior such as racist jokes and creates appropriate expectations and behavior standards); (4) to commit to creating diverse candidate pools for all managerial hiring and promotion decisions (traditional closed networks that were once used are no longer appropriate); and (5) to use cultural audits, surveys, focus groups, and broad networking groups to assess diversity.

HPHC also includes seven questions in a carefully phrased opinion survey. Questions such as how employees feel they are valued; what they feel their career opportunities are; and how well the organization supports work-life balance, are asked. HPHC uses improvements in these areas as partial indicators of successful diversity.

The organization also includes the Health Triangle—networking group of more than 200 gay and lesbian employees—and the Disability Council to help the company keep on abreast of issues relevant to each group of employees. These groups also have helped to attract additional customers.

Stern, the VP, argues that simplicity and clarity are keys in diversity communication. She states that one should be able to communicate the information in 10 minutes and make it easy to understand; represent the data in a variety of ways; report on progress; and keep people at all levels informed about the progress. The Effective Manager 4.2 provides an example and illustrates insights suitable for diversity programs in general.

The following factors, encompassing and moving beyond those of HPHC, have been obtained from in-depth interviews and focus groups; they are important in tracking diversity programs: demographics, organizational culture, accountability, productivity, growth and profitability, benchmarking against the "best" programs, and measurement of the program.[61]

Some firms, such as Microsoft, have moved far toward measurement and computerization of key diversity measures. Three Microsoft employees, Stutz, Massengale, and Gordon, developed the SMG Index acronym. It provides a separate bottom-line figure, encompassing both Microsoft's women and minorities; it allows managers to analyze goals and accomplishments for both affirmative action and diversity. The lower the SMG Index (zero is best), the lower the percentage of hires, promotions, and/or retentions needed to correct group disparities. The Index is compared across groups and time.[62]

Chapter 4 Study Guide

What is workforce diversity, and why is it important?

- Workforce diversity is the mix of gender, race and ethnicity, age, and able-bodiedness in the workforce.

- Workforces in the United States, Canada, and Europe are becoming more diverse, and valuing and managing such diversity is becoming increasingly more important to enhance organizational competitiveness and provide individual development.

What are demographic differences among individuals, and why are they important?

- Demographic differences are background characteristics that help shape what a person has become.

- Gender, age, race and ethnicity, and able-bodiedness are particularly important demographic characteristics.

- The use of demographic differences in employment is covered by a series of federal, state/provincial, and local laws outlawing discrimination.

- Demographic differences can be the basis for inappropriate stereotyping that can influence workplace decisions and behaviors.

What are aptitude and ability differences among individuals, and why are they important?

- Aptitude is a person's capability of learning something.

- Ability is a person's existing capacity to perform the various tasks needed for a given job.

- Aptitudes are potential abilities.

- Both mental and physical aptitudes and abilities are used in matching individuals to organizations and jobs.

What are personality determinants and differences among individuals, and why are they important?

- Personality captures the overall profile or combination of characteristics that represent the unique nature of an individual as that individual interacts with others.

- Personality is determined by both heredity and environment; across all personality characteristics, the mix of heredity and environment is about 50–50.

- The Big Five personality framework consists of extraversion, agreeableness, conscientiousness, emotional stability, and openness to experience.

- A useful personality framework consists of social traits, personal conceptions, emotional adjustment, and personality dynamics, where each category represents one or more personality dimensions.

■ Personality characteristics are important because of their predictable interplay with an individual's behavior. Along with demographics and aptitude/ability differences, personality characteristics must be matched to organizations and jobs.

What are value and attitude differences among individuals, and why are they important?

■ Values are broad preferences concerning courses of action or outcomes.

■ Rokeach divides 18 values into terminal values (preferences concerning ends) and instrumental values (preferences concerning means).

■ Allport and his associates identify six value categories, ranging from theoretical to religious.

■ Meglino and his associates classify values into achievement, helping and concern for others, honesty, and fairness.

■ There have been societal changes in value patterns away from economic and organizational loyalty and toward meaningful work and self-fulfillment.

■ Attitudes are a predisposition to respond positively or negatively to someone or something in one's environment; they are influenced by values but are more specific.

■ Individuals desire consistency between their attitudes and their behaviors.

■ Values and attitudes are important because they indicate predispositions toward behaviors.

■ Along with demographics, aptitude/ability, and personality differences, values and attitudes need to be matched to organizations and jobs.

What does managing diversity and individual differences involve, and why is it important?

■ Managing diversity and individual differences involves striving for a match between the firm, specific jobs, and the people recruited, hired, and developed, while recognizing an increasingly diverse workforce.

■ Affirmative action; ethical considerations; local, national, and global competitive pressures; and a projected change in the nature of the workforce provide increasing workforce diversity.

■ Once a match between organizational and job requirements and individual characteristics is obtained, it is necessary to manage the increasing diversity in the workforce.

■ Firms now use a wide variety of practices in managing workforce diversity; for example: interactive networks, recruitment, education, development, promotion, pay, and assessment.

Key Terms

Ability (p. 64)	Attitude (p. 76)	Beliefs (p. 77)
Affective component (p. 77)	Authoritarianism (p. 70)	Cognitive component (p. 76)
Aptitude (p. 64)	Behavioral component (p. 77)	Cognitive dissonance (p. 78)

Demographic characteristics (p. 62)

Developmental approaches (p. 67)

Dogmatism (p. 70)

Emotional adjustment traits (p. 72)

Instrumental values (p. 74)

Personality (p. 65)

Personality dynamics (p. 73)

Self-concept (p. 73)

Self-monitoring (p. 72)

Social traits (p. 68)

Sources and types of values (p. 74)

Stereotyping (p. 71)

Terminal values (p. 74)

Type A orientations (p. 73)

Type B orientations (p. 73)

Value congruence (p. 76)

Values (p. 74)

Workforce diversity (p. 61)

■ MULTIPLE CHOICE

Self-Test 4

1. In the United States, Canada, the European Union, and much of the rest of the world, the workforce is _____. (a) becoming more homogeneous (b) more highly motivated than before (c) becoming more diverse (d) less motivated than before

2. Stereotyping occurs when one thinks of an individual _____. (a) as different from others in a given group (b) as possessing characteristics commonly associated with members of a given group (c) as like some members of a given group but different from others (d) as basically not very competent

3. Managing diversity and affirmative action are _____ (a) similar terms for the same thing (b) both mandated by law (c) different but complementary (d) becoming less and less important

4. Demographic characteristics consist of _____. (a) aptitude and ability (b) personality traits (c) background characteristics that help shape what a person has become (d) values and attitudes

5. Aptitudes and abilities are divided into _____. (a) stereotypes (b) physical and mental (c) mental and personality (d) aggressive and passive

6. Personality characteristics tend to be determined by _____. (a) environment (b) heredity (c) a mix of environment and heredity (d) a person's aptitudes and abilities

7. The Big Five Framework consists of _____. (a) five aptitudes and abilities (b) five demographic characteristics (c) extraversion, agreeableness, strength, emotional stability, and openness to experience (d) extraversion, agreeableness, conscientiousness, emotional stability, and openness to experience

8. Personality dynamics is represented by _____. (a) self-esteem, self-efficacy (b) Type A/Type B orientation (c) self-monitoring (d) Machiavellianism

9. Values and attitudes are _____. (a) similar to aptitudes and abilities (b) used interchangeably (c) related to each other (d) similar to demographic characteristics

10. Managing workforce diversity involves _____. (a) matching organizational and job requirements with increasingly diverse individuals (b) giving preference to traditional white American males (c) giving preference to nontraditional, nonwhite male workers (d) making sure quotas of workers in various categories are emphasized

■ TRUE–FALSE

11. The U.S. workforce is becoming less diverse.   T   F

12. Workforce diversity is another name for affirmative action.   T   F

13. Gender is one kind of demographic characteristic.   T   F

14. Aptitude is another name for ability.   T   F

15. Personality is determined by both environment and heredity.   T   F

16. Personality can develop across time.   T   F

17. The Big Five personality framework has been distilled from extensive lists of personality dimensions.   T   F

18. Attitudes often lead to values.   T   F

19. Both values and attitudes are predispositions to behave in certain ways.   T   F

20. An increasingly diverse workforce is exclusive to the United States.   T   F

■ SHORT RESPONSE

21. What does managing diversity and individual differences mean in the workplace?

22. Why are diversity and individual differences important in the workplace?

23. In what ways are demographic characteristics important in the workplace?

24. Why are personality characteristics important in the workplace?

■ APPLICATIONS ESSAY

25. Your boss is trying to figure out how to get the kinds of people she needs for her organization to do well, while at the same time dealing appropriately with an increasing number of nonwhite female and male workers. She has asked you to respond to this concern. Prepare a short report with specific suggestions for your boss.

Explore application-oriented Fast Company articles, cases, experimental exercises, and self-assessments in the OB Skills Workbook

■ **Visit the Schermerhorn Web site to find the Interactive Self-Test and Internet exercises for this chapter.**

Perception and Attribution

WHEN A WOMAN TAKES THE HELM

As a young girl growing up on Ghana's coast, Beatrice Vormawah wasn't allowed to go near the water. She couldn't swim, and her mother was afraid she might drown. Beatrice obeyed, but today she is the only female ship's captain in Africa and one of only about a dozen worldwide. This is particularly remarkable in West Africa, where only about half of the women are literate and less than a third go beyond primary school. On the average, Ghana's women have six children each and live only into their mid-fifties.

Two decades ago, Vormawah answered a newspaper ad for applicants to Ghana's Merchant Marine. She and two other women were accepted and graduated, and only four have done so since. A few months ago, Vormawah was promoted to captain, joining the ranks of 24 male captains. Surprisingly, Vormawah never encountered any discrimination or hostility, something she attributes to male assumptions that she would soon drop out. "They figured we'd stay on the job until we got married and had babies and then go back home."

Vormawah also differs sharply from many other African women in that her husband handles most childcare duties for their three children, ages 8 to 14. She oversees a male crew of 42, and each of her round-trip voyages usually keeps her at sea for about 24 days at a time.

Beatrice Vormawah has been successful in her career, even though she deviates substantially from the general Ghanian perceptions of woman's role in their society and their attributions about success at sea. Such gender perceptions and attributions are part of the overall perceptual and attributional processes that are critical components of OB and are the topics of this chapter.

Study Questions

Perceptions and attributions influence an individual's interpretation of his or her environment. As you read Chapter 5, keep in mind these key questions.

■ What is the perceptual process?
■ What are common perceptual distortions?
■ How can the perceptual process be managed?
■ What is attribution theory?

The Perceptual Process

A spectacular completed pass during the 1982 National Football Conference championship game helped propell Joe Montana, former San Francisco 49er quarterback, into the legendary status he enjoys today. The reverse effect apparently occurred for Danny White, Dallas Cowboys' quarterback. He fumbled in the final minute of the same game and never obtained the status of his predecessor, Roger Stauback, even though White took the Cowboys to the championship game three years in a row.[1]

■ **Perception** is the process through which people receive, organize, and interpret information from their environment.

This example illustrates the notion of **perception**, the process by which people select, organize, interpret, retrieve, and respond to information from the world around them.[2] This information is gathered from the five senses of sight, hearing, touch, taste, and smell. As Montana, White, and Stauback can attest, perception and reality are not necessarily the same thing. The perceptions or responses of any two people are also not necessarily identical, even when they are describing the same event.

Through perception, people process information inputs into responses involving feelings and action. Perception is a way of forming impressions about oneself, other people, and daily life experiences. It also serves as a screen or filter through which information passes before it has an effect on people. The

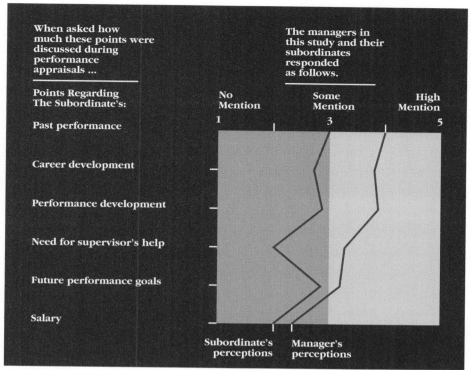

Figure 5.1
Contrasting perceptions between managers and their subordinates: The case of the performance appraisal interview.

quality or accuracy of a person's perceptions, therefore, has a major impact on his or her responses to a given situation.

Perceptual responses are also likely to vary between managers and subordinates. Consider Figure 5.1, which depicts contrasting perceptions of a performance appraisal between managers and subordinates. Rather substantial differences exist in the two sets of perceptions; the responses can be significant. In this case, managers who perceive that they already give adequate attention to past performance, career development, and supervisory help are unlikely to give greater emphasis to these points in future performance appraisal interviews. In contrast, their subordinates are likely to experience continued frustration because they perceive that these subjects are not being given sufficient attention.

■ FACTORS INFLUENCING THE PERCEPTUAL PROCESS

The factors that contribute to perceptual differences and the perceptual process among people at work are summarized in Figure 5.2 and include characteristics of the *perceiver*, the *setting*, and the *perceived*.

The Perceiver A person's past experiences, needs or motives, personality, and values and attitudes may all influence the perceptual process. A person with

Figure 5.2
Factors influencing the perceptual process.

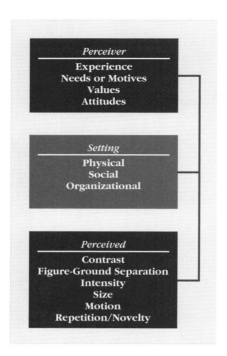

a strong achievement need tends to perceive a situation in terms of that need. If you see doing well in class as a way to help meet your achievement need, for example, you will tend to emphasize that aspect when considering various classes. By the same token, a person with a negative attitude toward unions may look for antagonisms even when local union officials make routine visits to the organization. These and other perceiver factors influence the various aspects of the perceptual process.

The Setting The physical, social, and organizational context of the perceptual setting also can influence the perceptual process. Kim Jeffrey, the recently appointed CEO of Nestle's Perrier, was perceived by his subordinates as a frightening figure when he gave vent to his temper and had occasional confrontations with them. In the previous setting, before he was promoted, Jeffrey's flare-ups had been tolerable; now they caused intimidation, so his subordinates feared to express their opinions and recommendations. Fortunately, after he received feedback about this problem, he was able to change his subordinates' perceptions in the new setting.[3]

The Perceived Characteristics of the perceived person, object, or event, such as contrast, intensity, figure–ground separation, size, motion, and repetition or novelty, are also important in the perceptual process. For example, one mainframe computer among six PCs or one man among six women will be perceived differently than one of six mainframe computers or one of six men—where there is less contrast. Intensity can vary in terms of brightness, color, depth, sound, and the like. A bright red sports car stands out from a group of gray sedans; whispering or shouting stands out from ordinary conversation. The concept is known as figure–ground separation, and it depends on which image is perceived as the background and which as the figure. For an illustration, look at Figure 5.3. What do you see? Faces or a vase?

In the matter of size, very small or very large people tend to be perceived differently and more readily than average-sized people. Similarly, in terms of motion, moving objects are perceived differently from stationary objects. And, of course, advertisers hope that ad repetition or frequency will positively influence peoples' perception of a product. Television advertising blitzes for new models of personal computers are a case in point. Finally, the novelty of a situation affects its perception. A purple-haired teenager is perceived differently from a blond or a brunette, for example.

Figure 5.3
Figure–ground
illustration.

■ STAGES OF THE PERCEPTUAL PROCESS

So far we have discussed key factors influencing the perceptual process. Now we'll look at the stages involved in processing the information that ultimately determines a person's perception and reaction, as shown in Figure 5.4. The information-processing stages are divided into information attention and selection; organization of information; information interpretation; and information retrieval.

Attention and Selection   Our senses are constantly bombarded with so much information that if we don't screen it, we quickly become incapacitated with information overload. *Selective screening* lets in only a tiny proportion of all of the information available. Some of the selectivity comes from controlled processing—consciously deciding what information to pay attention to and what to ignore. In this case, the perceivers are aware that they are processing information. Think about the last time you were at a noisy restaurant and screened out all the sounds but those of the person with whom you were talking.

In contrast to controlled processing, screening can also take place without the perceiver's conscious awareness. For example, you may drive a car without consciously thinking about the process of driving; you may be thinking about a prob-

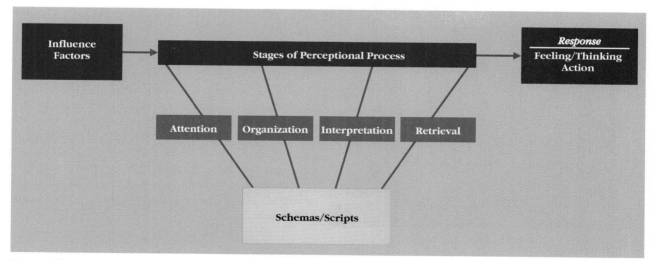

Figure 5.4
The perceptual process.

lem you are having with your course work instead. In driving the car, you are affected by information from the world around you, such as traffic lights and other cars, but you don't pay conscious attention to that information. Such selectivity of attention and automatic information processing works well most of the time when you drive, but if a nonroutine event occurs, such as an animal darting into the road, you may have an accident unless you quickly shift to controlled processing.

Organization   Even though selective screening takes place in the attention stage, it is still necessary to find ways to organize the information efficiently. **Schemas** help us do this. Schemas are cognitive frameworks that represent organized knowledge about a given concept or stimulus developed through experience.[4] A self schema contains information about a person's own appearance, behavior, and personality. For instance, a person with a decisiveness schema tends to perceive himself or herself in terms of that aspect, especially in circumstances calling for leadership.

Person schemas refer to the way individuals sort others into categories, such as types or groups, in terms of similar perceived features. The term *prototype*, or *stereotype*, is often used to represent these categories; it is an abstract set of features commonly associated with members of that category. Once the prototype is formed, it is stored in long-term memory; it is retrieved when it is needed for a comparison of how well a person matches the prototype's features. For instance, you may have a "good worker" prototype in mind, which includes hard work, intelligence, punctuality, articulateness, and decisiveness; that prototype is used as a measure against which to compare a given worker. Stereotypes, as discussed in Chapter 4, may be regarded as prototypes based on such demographic characteristics as gender, age, able-bodiedness, and racial and ethnic groups. In the case of Beatrice Vormawah, we can assume that the African Merchant Marine had established a prototype of what a good Ghanian sea captain is like, and she fit that prototype well enough to be promoted.

■ **Schemas** are cognitive frameworks that represent organized knowledge about a given concept or stimulus developed through experience.

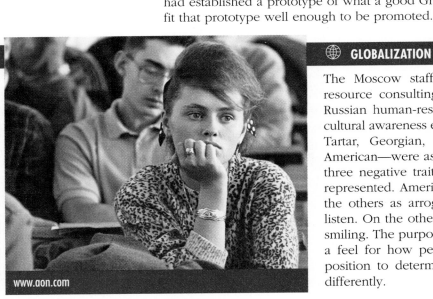

www.aon.com

🌐 GLOBALIZATION

The Moscow staff of Aon Consulting, a human-resource consulting firm, conducted a seminar for Russian human-resource managers. During a cross-cultural awareness exercise, the participants—Russian, Tartar, Georgian, British, German, Swedish, and American—were asked to identify three positive and three negative traits about each of the nationalities represented. Americans, in general, were viewed by the others as arrogant, inflexible, and unwilling to listen. On the other hand, they were seen as always smiling. The purpose of the exercise? Once you have a feel for how people perceive you, you are in a position to determine what you can or should do differently.

A *script schema* is defined as a knowledge framework that describes the appropriate sequence of events in a given situation.[5] For example, an experienced manager would use a script schema to think about the appropriate steps involved in running a meeting. Finally, *person-in-situation schemas* combine schemas built around persons (self and person schemas) and events (script schemas).[6] Thus, a manager might organize his or her perceived information in a meeting around a decisiveness schema for both himself or herself and a key participant in the meeting. Here, a script schema would provide the steps and their sequence in the meeting; the manager would push through the steps decisively and would call on the selected participants periodically throughout the meeting to respond decisively. Note that, although this approach might facilitate organization of important information, the perceptions of those attending might not be completely accurate because decisiveness of the person-in-situation schema did not allow the attendees enough time for open discussion.

As you can see in Figure 5.4, schemas are not important just in the organizing stage; they also affect other stages in the perception process. Furthermore, schemas rely heavily on automatic processing to free people up to use controlled processing as necessary. Finally, as we will show, the perceptual factors described earlier, as well as the distortions, to be discussed shortly, influence schemas in various ways.

Interpretation   Once your attention has been drawn to certain stimuli and you have grouped or organized this information, the next step is to uncover the reasons behind the actions. That is, even if your attention is called to the same information and you organize it in the same way your friend does, you may interpret it differently or make different attributions about the reasons behind what you have perceived. For example, as a manager, you might attribute compliments from a friendly subordinate to his being an eager worker, whereas your friend might interpret the behavior as insincere flattery.

Retrieval   So far, we have discussed the stages of the perceptual process as if they all occurred at the same time. However, to do so ignores the important component of memory. Each of the previous stages forms part of that memory and contributes to the stimuli or information stored there. The information stored in our memory must be retrieved if it is to be used. This leads us to the retrieval stage of the perceptual process summarized in Figure 5.4.

All of us at times can't retrieve information stored in our memory. More commonly, our memory decays, so that only some of the information is retrieved. Schemas play an important role in this area. They make it difficult for people to remember things not included in them. For example, based on your prototype about the traits comprising a "high performing employee" (hard work, punctuality, intelligence, articulateness, and decisiveness), you may overestimate these traits and underestimate others when you are evaluating the performance of a subordinate whom you generally consider good. Thus, you may overestimate the person's decisiveness since it is a key part of your high performance prototype.

Indeed, people are as likely to recall nonexistent traits as they are to recall those that are really there. Furthermore, once formed, prototypes may be difficult to change and tend to last a long time.[7] Obviously, this distortion can cause major problems in terms of performance appraisals and promotions, not to mention numerous other interactions on and off the job. By the same token, such prototypes allow you to "chunk" information and reduce overload. Thus, prototypes are a double-edged sword.

■ RESPONSE TO THE PERCEPTUAL PROCESS

Throughout this chapter, we have shown how the perceptual process influences numerous OB responses. Figure 5.4 classifies such responses into thoughts and feelings and actions. For example, in countries such as Mexico, bosses routinely greet their secretaries with a kiss, and that is expected behavior. In contrast, in this country your thoughts and feelings might be quite different about such behavior. You might very well perceive this as a form of sexual harassment. As you cover the other OB topics in the book, you also should be alert to the importance of perceptual responses covering thoughts, feelings, and actions.

Common Perceptual Distortions

Figure 5.5 shows some common kinds of distortions that can make the perceptual process inaccurate and affect the response. These are stereotypes and prototypes, halo effects, selective perception, projection, contrast effects, and self-fulfilling prophecy.

■ STEREOTYPES OR PROTOTYPES

Earlier, when discussing person schemas, we described stereotypes, or prototypes, as useful ways of combining information in order to deal with information overload. At the same time, we pointed out how stereotypes can cause inaccuracies in retrieving information, along with some further problems. In particular, stereotypes obscure individual differences; that is, they can prevent managers from getting to know people as individuals and from accurately assessing their needs, preferences, and abilities. We compared these stereotypes with research results and showed the errors that can occur when stereotypes are relied on for decision making. Nevertheless, stereotypes continue to exist at the board of directors level in organizations. A recent survey from 133 Fortune 500 firms showed that female directors were favored for membership on only the relatively peripheral public affairs committee in these organizations. Males were fa-

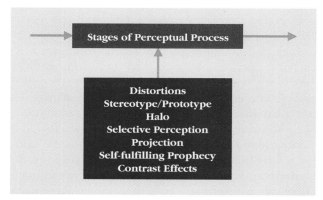

Figure 5.5
Distortions occurring in perceptual process stages.

vored for membership on the more important compensation, executive, and finance committee, even when the females were equally or more experienced than their male counterparts.[8]

Here, we reiterate our previous message: Both managers and employees need to be sensitive to stereotypes; they also must attempt to overcome them and recognize that an increasingly diverse workforce can be a truly competitive advantage.

■ HALO EFFECTS

A **halo effect** occurs when one attribute of a person or situation is used to develop an overall impression of the individual or situation. Like stereotypes, these distortions are more likely to occur in the organization stage of perception. Halo effects are common in our everyday lives. When meeting a new person, for example, a pleasant smile can lead to a positive first impression of an overall "warm" and "honest" person. The result of a halo effect is the same as that associated with a stereotype, however: Individual differences are obscured.

Halo effects are particularly important in the performance appraisal process because they can influence a manager's evaluations of subordinates' work performance. For example, people with good attendance records tend to be viewed as intelligent and responsible; those with poor attendance records are considered poor performers. Such conclusions may or may not be valid. It is the manager's job to try to get true impressions rather than allowing halo effects to result in biased and erroneous evaluations.

■ SELECTIVE PERCEPTION

Selective perception is the tendency to single out those aspects of a situation, person, or object that are consistent with one's needs, values, or attitudes. Its strongest impact occurs in the attention stage of the perceptual process. This perceptual distortion is identified in a classic research study involving executives in a manufacturing company.[9] When asked to identify the key problem in a comprehensive business policy case, each executive selected problems consistent with his or her functional area work assignments. For example, most marketing executives viewed the key problem area as sales, whereas production people tended to see the problem as one of production and organization. These differing viewpoints would affect how the executive would approach the problem; they might also create difficulties once these people tried to work together to improve things.

More recently, 121 middle- and upper-level managers attending an executive development program expressed broader views in conjunction with an emphasis on their own function. For example, a chief financial officer indicated an awareness of the importance of manufacturing, and an assistant marketing manager recognized the importance of accounting and finance along with their own functions.[10] Thus, this more current research demonstrated very little perceptual selectivity. The researchers were not, however, able to state definitively what accounted for the differing results.

These results suggest that selective perception is more important at some times than at others. Managers should be aware of this characteristic and test whether or not situations, events, or individuals are being selectively perceived.

■ **Halo effect** occurs when one attribute of a person or situation is used to develop an overall impression of the person or situation.

■ **Selective perception** is the tendency to single out for attention those aspects of a situation or person that reinforce or emerge and are consistent with existing beliefs, values, and needs.

The easiest way to do this is to gather additional opinions from other people. When these opinions contradict a manager's own, an effort should be made to check the original impression.

■ PROJECTION

■ **Projection** is the assignment of personal attributes to other individuals.

Projection is the assignment of one's personal attributes to other individuals; it is especially likely to occur in the interpretation stage of perception. A classic projection error is illustrated by managers who assume that the needs of their subordinates and their own coincide. Suppose, for example, that you enjoy responsibility and achievement in your work. Suppose, too, that you are the newly appointed manager of a group whose jobs seem dull and routine. You may move quickly to expand these jobs to help the workers achieve increased satisfaction from more challenging tasks because you want them to experience things that you, personally, value in work. But this may not be a good decision. If you project your needs onto the subordinates, individual differences are lost. Instead of designing the subordinates' jobs to fit their needs best, you have designed their jobs to fit your needs. The problem is that the subordinates may be quite satisfied and productive doing jobs that seem dull and routine to you. Projection can be controlled through a high degree of self-awareness and empathy—the ability to view a situation as others see it. In contrast with the usual negative effects of projection just described, there sometimes can be a positive ethical impact.

www.maccosmetics.com

⚖ ETHICS AND SOCIAL RESPONSIBILITY

The founders of M.A.C. Cosmetics, a Canadian firm selling a line of professional cosmetics, have successfully used perceptual projection of their ethical views onto the marketplace. Their strong views about social and charitable causes have led to shunning print and television promotion unless charitable causes are involved. Of special importance to the firm is the M.A.C. AIDS Fund to give back to the community through an AIDS-related fundraising program. That program provides contributations to HIV/AIDS organizations to be used for education, prevention, emergency services and support. Two of the firm's lipstick lines have been lauched to provide support for the AIDS Fund. Some other causes supported by M.A.C. are alternatives to animal testing for cosmetics and giving free merchandise to customers for returning containers for recycling. The support of social causes is an integral part of M.A.C.'s identity.

■ CONTRAST EFFECTS

■ **Contrast effects** occur when an individual's characteristics are contrasted with those of others recently encountered who rank higher or lower on the same characteristics.

Earlier, when discussing the perceived, we mentioned how a red sports car would stand out from others because of its contrast. Here, we show the perceptual distortion that can occur when, say, a person gives a talk following a strong speaker or is interviewed for a job following a series of mediocre applicants. We can expect a **contrast effect** to occur when an individual's characteristics are contrasted with those of others recently encountered who rank higher or lower on the same characteristics. Clearly, both managers and employees need to be aware of the possible perceptual distortion the contrast effect may create in many work settings.

■ SELF-FULFILLING PROPHECY

A final perceptual distortion that we consider is the **self-fulfilling prophecy**—the tendency to create or find in another situation or individual that which you expected to find in the first place. Self-fulfilling prophecy is sometimes referred to as the "Pygmalion effect," named for a mythical Greek sculptor who created a statue of his ideal mate and then made her come to life.[11] His prophecy came true! Through self-fulfilling prophecy, you also may create in the work situation that which you expect to find.

Self-fulfilling prophecy can have both positive and negative results for you as a manager. Suppose you assume that your subordinates prefer to satisfy most of their needs outside the work setting and want only minimal involvement with their jobs. Consequently, you are likely to provide simple, highly structured jobs designed to require little involvement. Can you predict what response the subordinates would have to this situation? Their most likely response would be to show the lack of commitment you assumed they would have in the first place. Thus, your initial expectations are confirmed as a self-fulfilling prophecy.

Self-fulfilling prophecy can have a positive side, however (see The Effective Manager 5.1). Students introduced to their teachers as "intellectual bloomers" do better on achievement tests than do their counterparts who lack such a positive introduction. A particularly interesting example of the self-fulfilling prophecy is that of Israeli tank crews. One set of tank commanders was told that according to test data some members of their assigned crews had exceptional abilities but others were only average. In reality, the crew members were assigned randomly, so that the two test groups were equal in ability. Later, the commanders reported that the so-called exceptional crew members performed better than the "average" members. As the study revealed, however, the commanders had paid more attention to and praised the crew members for whom they had the higher expectancies.[12] The self-fulfilling effects in these cases argue strongly for managers to adopt positive and optimistic approaches to people at work.

> **THE EFFECTIVE MANAGER 5.1**
>
> ### CREATING POSITIVE SELF-FULFILLING PROPHECIES FOR EMPLOYEES
>
> - Create a warmer interpersonal climate between your subordinates and you.
> - Give more performance feedback to subordinates—make it as positive as possible, given their actual performance.
> - Spend more time helping subordinates learn job skills.
> - Provide more opportunities for subordinates to ask questions.

■ **Self-fulfilling prophecy** is the tendency to create or find in another situation or individual that which one has expected to find.

Managing the Perceptual Process

To be successful, managers must understand the perceptual process, the stages involved, and the impact the perceptual process can have on their own and others' responses. They must also be aware of what roles the perceiver, the setting, and the perceived have in the perceptual process. Particularly important with regard to the perceived is the concept of impression management—for both managers and others.

Marine Midland Bank ←

www.marinemidland.com

To help its employees do their part in managing their own image as well as that of the organization, Marine Midland Bank in Buffalo, New York recently gave its 8700 employees around the country $300 gift certificates to buy professional office wear from Lands' End catalogs.

Impression
Management ◄
━━━━━━━
www.impression-
management.com

After Jack Roseman hired his two-person organization's first employee, an urgently needed computer programmer, the employee asked, "Incidentally, Jack, what's my title?" Shortly thereafter, the employee had business cards printed up and was showing them to people in an attempt at impression management.

■ IMPRESSION MANAGEMENT

Impression management is a person's systematic attempt to behave in ways that will create and maintain desired impressions in the eyes of others. First impressions are especially important and influence how people respond to one another. Impression management is influenced by such activities as associating with the "right people," doing favors to gain approval, flattering others to make oneself look better, taking credit for a favorable event, apologizing for a negative event while seeking a pardon, agreeing with the opinions of others, downplaying the severity of a negative event, and doing favors for others.[13] Successful managers learn how to use these activities to enhance their own images, and they are sensitive to their use by their subordinates and others in their organizations. In this context job titles are particularly important.

■ DISTORTION MANAGEMENT

During the attention and selection stage, managers should be alert to balancing automatic and controlled information processing. Most of their responsibilities, such as performance assessment and clear communication, will involve controlled processing, which will take away from other job responsibilities. Along with more controlled processing, managers need to be concerned about increasing the frequency of observations and about getting representative information rather than simply responding to the most recent information about a subordinate or a production order, for instance. Some organizations, including large farms, have responded to the need for representative and more accurate information by utilizing current technology. In addition, managers should not fail to seek out disconfirming information that will help provide a balance to their typical perception of information.

💻 TECHNOLOGY

Tom Melloma uses satellites 12,000 miles above the earth's surface to guide his large fertilizer rig. Inside the machine's cab, a computer screen mounted above the steering wheel displays a color-coded map of the field on his farm in the far northwest Texas panhandle. A diamond-shaped cursor on the screen follows the rig's path across the map, based on latitude and longitude. As the rig moves across the field, the computer reads color codes and tells the rig how much fertilizer to apply—more where there are low nutrients, less elsewhere. More and more farmers are turning "high tech" and replacing their subjective perceptions of where and how much fertilizer should be applied.

The various kinds of schemas and prototypes and stereotypes are particularly important at the information organizing stage. Managers should strive to broaden their schemas or should even replace them with more accurate or complete ones.

At the interpretation stage, managers need to be especially attuned to the impact of attribution on information; we discuss this concept further in the section on managing the attributional process later in the chapter. At the retrieval stage, managers should be sensitive to the fallibility of memory. They should recognize the tendency to overrely on schemas, especially prototypes or stereotypes that may bias information stored and retrieved.

Throughout the entire perception process managers should be sensitive to the information distortions caused by halo effects, selective perception, projection, contrast effects, and self-fulfilling prophecy, in addition to the distortions of stereotypes and prototypes.

Attribution Theory

Earlier in the chapter we mentioned attribution theory in the context of perceptual interpretation. **Attribution theory** aids in this interpretation by focusing on how people attempt to (1) understand the causes of a certain event, (2) assess responsibility for the outcomes of the event, and (3) evaluate the personal qualities of the people involved in the event.[14] In applying attribution theory, we are especially concerned with whether one's behavior has been internally or externally caused. Internal causes are believed to be under an individual's control—you believe Jake's performance is poor because he is lazy. External causes are seen as outside a person—you believe Kellie's performance is poor because her machine is old.

According to attribution theory, three factors influence this internal or external determination: distinctiveness, consensus, and consistency. *Distinctiveness* considers how consistent a person's behavior is across different situations. If Jake's performance is low, regardless of the machine on which he is working, we tend to give the poor performance an internal attribution; if the poor performance is unusual, we tend to assign an external cause to explain it.

Consensus takes into account how likely all those facing a similar situation are to respond in the same way. If all the people using machinery like Kellie's have poor performance, we tend to give her performance an external attribution. If other employees do not perform poorly, we attribute internal causation to her performance.

Consistency concerns whether an individual responds the same way across time. If Jake has a batch of low-performance figures, we tend to give the poor performance an internal attribution. In contrast, if Jake's low performance is an isolated incident, we attribute it to an external cause.

■ **Attribution theory** is the attempt to understand the cause of an event, assess responsibility for outcomes of the event, and assess the personal qualities of the people involved.

OB Across Functions

PUBLIC RELATIONS

Enhancing Public Image Perception Through Benchmarking

Although nationally acclaimed for its artistic quality and considered on a par with other major ballet companies, the Boston Ballet felt it lagged behind in fund-raising ability. It also worried that the perception of its image among Boston cultural institutions was too weak to support a major fund-raising expansion. The Ballet's board chair, John Humphrey, led a benchmarking effort focusing on how other organizations manage or change their public image. He established a cross-functional committee of trustees and professional staff. The committee ultimately chose three best-practice benchmark organizations in different fields: a ballet company, a museum, and a fast-growing Boston-based bakery chain—all noted for their excellent public images. Committee members developed a questionnaire and conducted followup interviews in these organizations to find out characteristics and activities that led to their superb public image perceptions. From this information, the committee made action recommendations for the Boston Ballet. Many of the recommendations were accepted, including the creation of a comprehensive image campaign for the Ballet, developed by a major Boston public relations firm, *pro bono*.

Cause of Poor Performance by Their Subordinates	Most Frequent Attribution	Cause of Poor Performance by Themselves
7	Lack of *ability*	1
12	Lack of *effort*	1
5	Lack of *support*	23

Figure 5.6
Health-care managers' attributions of causes for poor performance.

■ ATTRIBUTION ERRORS

In addition to these three influences, two errors have an impact on internal versus external determination—the *fundamental attribution error* and the *self-serving bias.*[15] Figure 5.6 provides data from a group of health-care managers.[16] When supervisors were asked to identify, or attribute, causes of poor performance among their subordinates, the supervisors more often chose the individual's internal deficiencies—lack of ability and effort—rather than external deficiencies in the situation—lack of support. This demonstrates a **fundamental attribution error**—the tendency to underestimate the influence of situational factors and to overestimate the influence of personal factors in evaluating someone else's behavior. When asked to identify causes of their own poor performance, however, the supervisors overwhelmingly cited lack of support—an external, or situational, deficiency. This indicates a **self-serving bias**—the tendency to deny personal responsibility for performance problems but to accept personal responsibility for performance success.

To summarize, we tend to overemphasize other people's internal personal factors in their behavior and to underemphasize external factors in other people's behavior. In contrast, we tend to attribute our own success to our own internal factors and to attribute our failure to external factors.

The managerial implications of attribution theory can be traced back to the fact that perceptions influence responses. For example, a manager who feels that subordinates are not performing well and perceives the reason to be an internal lack of effort is likely to respond with attempts to "motivate" the subordinates to work harder; the possibility of changing external, situational factors that may remove job constraints and provide better organizational support may be largely ignored. This oversight could sacrifice major performance gains. Interestingly, because of the self-serving bias, when they evaluated their own behavior, the supervisors in the earlier study indicated that their performance would benefit from having better support. Thus, the supervisors' own abilities or willingness to work hard were not felt to be at issue.

■ ATTRIBUTIONS ACROSS CULTURES

Research on the self-serving bias and fundamental attribution error has been done in cultures outside the United States with unexpected results.[17] In Korea, for example, the self-serving bias was found to be negative; that is, Korean managers

■ **Fundamental attribution error** is the tendency to underestimate the influence of situational factors and to overestimate the influence of personal factors in evaluating someone else's behavior.

■ **Self-serving bias** is the tendency to deny personal responsibility for performance problems but to accept personal responsibility for performance success.

attribute work group failure to themselves—"I was not a capable leader"—rather than to external causes. In India, the fundamental attribution error overemphasizes external rather than internal causes for failure. Still another interesting cultural twist on the self-serving bias and fundamental attribution error is suggested in the opening example of the Ghanian sea captain. There, Africans attributed negative consequences—driving away fish and angering mermaids into creating squalls—to women but apparently not to men. Why these various differences occurred is not clear, but differing cultural values appear to play a role. Finally, there is some evidence that U.S. females may be less likely to emphasize the self-serving bias than males.[18]

Certain cultures, such as the United States, tend to overemphasize internal causes and underemphasize external causes. Such overemphasis may result in negative attributions toward employees. These negative attributions, in turn, can lead to disciplinary actions, negative performance evaluations, transfers to other departments, and overreliance on training, rather than focusing on such external causes as lack of workplace support.[19] Employees, too, take their cues from managerial misattributions and, through negative self-fulfilling prophecies, may reinforce managers' original misattributions. Employees and managers alike (see The Effective Manager 5.2) can be taught attributional realignment to help deal with such misattributions.[20]

THE EFFECTIVE MANAGER 5.2

KEYS IN MANAGING PERCEPTIONS AND ATTRIBUTIONS

- Be self-aware.
- Seek a wide range of differing information.
- Try to see a situation as others would.
- Be aware of different kinds of schemas.
- Be aware of perceptual distortions.
- Be aware of self and other impression management.
- Be aware of attribution theory implications.

Chapter 5 Study Guide

Summary

What is the perceptual process?

- Individuals use the perceptual process to pay attention to and to select, organize, interpret, and retrieve information from the world around them.

- The perceptual process involves the perceiver, the setting, and the perceived.

- Responses to the perceptual process involve thinking and feeling and action classifications.

What are common perceptual distortions?

Common perceptual distortions include

- stereotypes or prototypes.

- halo effects.

- selective perception.

- projection.
- contrast effects.
- expectancy.

How can the perceptual process be managed?

Managing the perceptual process involves

- impression management of self and others.
- managing the information attention and selection stages.
- managing the information organizing stage.
- managing the information interpretation stage.
- managing the information storage and retrieval stage.
- being sensitive to effects of the common perceptual distortions.

What is attribution theory?

- Attribution theory involves emphasis on the interpretation stage of the perceptual process and consideration of whether individuals' behaviors result primarily from external causes or from causes internal to the individuals.
- Three factors influence an external or internal causal attribution—distinctiveness, consensus, and consistency.
- Two errors influencing an external or internal causal attribution are fundamental attribution error and self-serving bias.
- Attributions can be managed by recognizing a typical overemphasis on internal causes of behavior and an underemphasis on external causes.
- An overemphasis on internal causes tends to lead to assignment of failure to employees with accompanying disciplinary actions, negative performance evaluations, and the like.
- An underemphasis on external causes tends to lead to lack of workplace support.

Key Terms

Attribution theory (p. 95)	Halo effect (p. 91)	Selective perception (p. 91)
Contrast effects (p. 92)	Perception (p. 84)	Self-fulfilling prophecy
Fundamental attribution	Projection (p. 92)	(p. 93)
error (p. 96)	Schema (p. 88)	Self-serving bias (p. 96)

Self-Test 5   ■ MULTIPLE CHOICE

1. Perception is the process by which people _____ information. (a) generate (b) retrieve (c) transmute (d) transmogrify

2. Which of the following is not a perceptual process stage? (a) attention/selection (b) interpretation (c) follow through (d) retrieval

3. Which of the following is not a perceptual distortion? (a) stereotypes/prototypes (b) barnum effect (c) halo effect (d) contrast effect

4. Perceptual distortions _____. (a) are quite rare (b) are quite common (c) affect only the interpretation stage (d) make the perceptual process more accurate

5. Impression management _____. (a) applies only to managers (b) applies only to subordinates (c) may involve agreeing with others' opinions and doing favors for others (d) may involve disobeying a superior to show how tough one is

6. Managing the perceptual process involves being concerned with _____. (a) information organizing and interpretation (b) information processing (c) narrowing schemas (d) seeking confirming information

7. Which of the following does not influence internal or external attribution of causation? (a) distinctiveness (b) consensus (c) contrast (d) consistency

8. In the self-serving bias, the influence of _____. (a) situational factors is overestimated (b) personal factors is overestimated (c) self-factors is overestimated (d) situational factors is underestimated

9. Overemphasizing internal causes can lead to _____. (a) additional workplace support (b) training to correct deficiencies (c) promotion of managers (d) positive self-fulfilling prophecies

10. Attribution _____. (a) is a trait managers are born or not born with (b) lends itself to training (c) is almost impossible to manage (d) is strongly related to participative management

■ TRUE–FALSE

11. The perceptual process operates only in the perception of people.   T   F

12. The perceptual process involves four stages plus a response.   T   F

13. Stereotypes and prototypes are similar.   T   F

14. Expectancy is related to the self-fulfilling prophecy.   T   F

15. During the attention and selection stage, managers should concentrate primarily on automatic processing.   T   F

16. During the retrieval stage, there is a tendency to underemphasize schemas.   T   F

17. The fundamental attribution error seems to operate similarly throughout the world.   T   F

18. Distinctiveness influences internal or external causal determination.   T   F

19. There is a tendency in the United States to overemphasize internal causes of employee behavior.   T   F

20. Managerial misattributions can be influenced by training.   T   F

■ SHORT RESPONSE

21. Draw and briefly discuss the text's model of the perceptual process.

22. Select two perceptual distortions, briefly define them, and show how they influence the perceptual process.

23. What is the relation of attribution theory to the perceptual process?
24. Briefly discuss the perceptual response categories and relate them to one OB topic area.

■ APPLICATIONS ESSAY

25. Your boss has recently heard a little about attribution theory and has asked you to explain it to him in more detail, focusing on its possible usefulness in managing his department. How do you address his request?

Explore application-oriented Fast Company articles, cases, experimental exercises, and self-assessments in the OB Skills Workbook

■ **Visit the Schermerhorn Web site to find the Interactive Self-Test and Internet exercises for this chapter.**

Motivation and Reinforcement

MOTIVATION THROUGH INNOVATION

Ben Sawatzky's lumber mill in Edmonton, Canada, operates on principles that strike many as unusual, to say the least. A walk through the 160-person plant reveals a sauna and a gym with exercise machines. There are no supervisors. In teams, workers have specific production goals; once these goals are met, they get time off. The average workday is 6.75 hours. Workers are paid by the day, not the hour, and earn about double the industry average. They get a 10-day paid vacation to Hawaii or Mexico every year. Says a lumber grader: "I get paid the same as the guy next to me. I have a few more responsibilities but everything is spread out among everybody in the crew." Ben Sawatzky says, "By and large, I haven't run across any other company that has the loyalty of staff we have." All this has earned Sprucely a reputation as a high-quality maker of specialized lumber products. The firm has won a Pinnacle award for outstanding entrepreneurship. The company was started in 1983 with a personal investment of $1128, a loan of $5000, and two workers. In less than two decades, Sawatzky built Sprucely into a company whose sales now total some $60 million.

S pruceland Millworks is a refreshing story of how a firm can emphasize individuals, motivate them for excellence, and still grow profitably in a global market. Despite all the new techniques and technologies available to firms today, the long-term performance of a firm rests squarely on the behavior of individuals. Managers are not only recognizing that it is possible to build a high performance organization with loyal employees willing to stay with the firm, but that they must do so if they are to compete successfully with firms like Spruceland Millworks.

Study Questions

Motivation and reinforcement are key issues in any firm. As you read Chapter 6, keep in mind the following key questions.

- What is motivation to work?
- What are reinforcement theories, and how are they linked to motivation?
- What do the content theories suggest about individual needs and motivation?
- What do the process theories suggest about individual motivation?
- How can insights of the motivation theories be partially integrated by including job satisfaction?

What Is Motivation?

■ **Motivation** refers to forces within an individual that account for the level, direction, and persistence of effort expended at work.

If asked to identify a major concern or problem at work, a manager is very likely to cite "motivational" need to do something that will encourage people to work harder to do "what I want." Formally defined, **motivation** refers to the individual forces that account for the direction, level, and persistence of a person's effort expended at work. *Direction* refers to an individual's choice when presented with a number of possible alternatives (e.g., whether to exert effort toward product quality or toward product quantity). *Level* refers to the amount of effort a person puts forth (e.g., a lot or a little). *Persistence* refers to the length of time a person sticks with a given action (e.g., to try to achieve product quantity and give up when it is found difficult to attain).

102

■ REINFORCEMENT, CONTENT, AND PROCESS THEORIES

The theories of motivation can be divided into three broad categories.[1] **Reinforcement theories** emphasize the linkage between individual behavior and some specific outcomes to show how managers can alter the direction, level, or persistence of individual actions. They focus on the observable rather than what is inside an employee's head. Thus, reinforcement views place a premium on observing individuals to see which work-related outcomes are highly valued. By altering when, where, how, and why some types of rewards are given, the manager can change the apparent motivation of employees by providing a systematic set of consequences to shape behavior. **Content theories** focus primarily on individual needs—the physiological or psychological deficiencies that we feel a compulsion to reduce or eliminate. These theories suggest that the manager's job is to create a work environment that responds positively to individual needs. They help to explain how poor performance, undesirable behaviors, low satisfaction, and the like can be caused by "blocked" needs or needs that are not satisfied on the job. **Process theories** focus on the thought or cognitive processes that take place within the minds of people and that influence their behavior. Whereas a content approach may identify job security as an important need for an individual, a process approach probes further to identify why the person behaves in particular ways relative to available rewards and work opportunities. Ultimately, we use the insights of three sets of theories to offer an integrated view of motivational dynamics that should be useful in any work setting.[2]

> ■ **Reinforcement theories** emphasize the means through which operant conditioning takes place.

> ■ **Content theories** profile different needs that may motivate individual behavior.

> ■ **Process theories** seek to understand the thought processes that determine behavior.

■ MOTIVATION ACROSS CULTURES

Before we examine the motivation theories in detail, an important caveat is in order. Motivation is a key concern in firms across the globe. However, North American theories (and these are the only ones discussed in this chapter) are subject to cultural limitations.[3] The determinants of motivation and the best ways to deal with it are likely to vary considerably across Asia, South America, Eastern Europe, and Africa. As we pointed out in Chapter 3, individual values and attitudes—both important aspects of motivation—have strong cultural foundations. What proves "motivational" as a reward in one culture, for example, might not work in another. We should be sensitive to these issues and avoid being parochial or ethnocentric by assuming that people in all cultures are motivated by the same things in the same ways.[4]

Publix, the nation's largest employee-owned supermarket, promotes from within. Most store managers begin their careers at the bottom, working their way up from entry-level positions. Publix offers employees a generous benefits and compensation package; store managers earn bonuses based on their stores' profits.

Reinforcement

In OB, reinforcement has a very specific meaning that has its origin in some classic studies in psychology.[5] **Reinforcement** is the administration of a consequence as a result of a behavior. Managing reinforcement properly can change the direction, level, and persistence of an individual's behavior. To understand this idea, we need to review some of the concepts on conditioning and reinforcement you learned in your basic psychology course. We will then move on to applications.

> ■ **Reinforcement** is the administration of a consequence as a result of behavior.

■ CLASSICAL AND OPERANT CONDITIONING

■ **Classical conditioning** is a form of learning through association that involves the manipulation of stimuli to influence behavior.

Recall that Ivan Pavlov studied classical conditioning. **Classical conditioning** is a form of learning through association that involves the manipulation of stimuli to influence behavior. The Russian psychologist "taught" dogs to salivate at the sound of a bell by ringing the bell when feeding the dogs. The sight of the food naturally caused the dogs to salivate. Eventually, the dogs "learned" to associate the bell ringing with the presentation of meat and to salivate at the ringing of the bell alone. Such "learning" through association is so common in organizations that it is often ignored until it causes considerable confusion. Take a look at Figure 6.1. The key is to understand a stimulus and a conditioned stimulus. A **stimulus** is something that incites action and draws forth a response (the meat for the dogs). The trick is to associate one neutral potential stimulus (the bell ringing) with another initial stimulus that already affects behavior (the meat). The once-neutral stimulus is called a *conditioned stimulus* when it affects behavior in the same way as the initial stimulus. In Figure 6.1, the boss's smiling becomes a conditioned stimulus because of its linkage to his criticisms.

■ A **stimulus** is something that incites action.

Operant conditioning, popularized by B. F. Skinner, is an extension of the classical case to much more practical affairs.[6] It includes more than just a stimulus and a response behavior. **Operant conditioning** is the process of controlling behavior by manipulating its consequences. Classical and operant conditioning differ in two important ways. First, control in operant conditioning is via manipulation of consequences. Second, operant conditioning calls for examining antecedents, behavior, and consequences. The *antecedent* is the condition leading up to or "cueing" behavior. For example, in Figure 6.1, an agreement between the boss and the employee to work overtime as needed is an antecedent. If the employee works overtime, this would be the *behavior* while the *consequence* would be the boss's praise.

■ **Operant conditioning** is the process of controlling behavior by manipulating, or "operating" on, its consequences.

If a boss wants a behavior to be repeated, such as working overtime, she must manipulate the consequences. The basis for manipulating consequences is E. L. Thorndike's law of effect.[7] The **law of effect** is simple but powerful: behavior that results in a pleasant outcome is likely to be repeated while behavior that results in an unpleasant outcome is not likely to be repeated. The implica-

■ The **law of effect** is the observation that behavior that results in a pleasing outcome is likely to be repeated; behavior that results in an unpleasant outcome is not likely to be repeated.

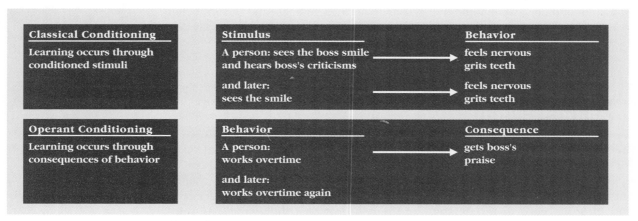

Figure 6.1
Differences between classical and operant conditioning approaches.

Contrived Rewards: Some Direct Cost		Natural Rewards: No Direct Cost	
refreshments	promotion	smiles	recognition
piped-in music	trips	greetings	feedback
nice offices	company car	compliments	asking advice
cash bonuses	paid insurance	special jobs	
merit pay increases	stock options		
profit-sharing	gifts		
office parties	sport tickets		

Figure 6.2
A sample of extrinsic rewards allocated by managers.

tions of this law are rather straightforward. If, as a supervisor, you want more of a behavior, you must make the consequences for the individual positive.

Note that the emphasis is on consequences that can be manipulated rather than on consequences inherent in the behavior itself. OB research often emphasizes specific types of rewards that are considered by the reinforcement perspective to influence individual behavior. *Extrinsic rewards* are positively valued work outcomes that are given to the individual by some other person. They are important external reinforcers or environmental consequences that can substantially influence a person's work behaviors through the law of effect. Figure 6.2 presents a sample of extrinsic rewards that managers can allocate to their subordinates.[8] Some of these rewards are contrived, or planned, rewards that have direct costs and budgetary implications. Examples are pay increases and cash bonuses. A second category includes natural rewards that have no cost other than the manager's personal time and efforts. Examples are verbal praise and recognition in the workplace.

REINFORCEMENT STRATEGIES

We now bring the notions of classical conditioning, operant conditioning, reinforcement, and extrinsic rewards together to show how the direction, level, and persistence of individual behavior can be changed. This combination is called "OB Mod" after its longer title of **organization behavior modification**. **OB Mod** is the systematic reinforcement of desirable work behavior and the nonreinforcement or punishment of unwanted work behavior. OB Mod includes four basic reinforcement strategies: positive reinforcement, negative reinforcement (or avoidance), punishment, and extinction.[9]

■ **Organization behavior modification (OB Mod)** is the systematic reinforcement of desirable work behavior and the nonreinforcement or punishment of unwanted work behavior.

Positive Reinforcement B. F. Skinner and his followers advocate **positive reinforcement**—the administration of positive consequences that tend to increase the likelihood of repeating the desirable behavior in similar settings. For example, a Texas Instruments manager nods to a subordinate to express approval after she makes a useful comment during a sales meeting. Obviously, the boss wants more useful comments. Later, the subordinate makes another useful comment, just as the boss hoped she would.

■ **Positive reinforcement** is the administration of positive consequences that tend to increase the likelihood of repeating the behavior in similar settings.

To begin using a strategy of positive reinforcement, we need to be aware that positive reinforcers and rewards are not necessarily the same. Recognition, for example, is both a reward and a potential positive reinforcer. Recognition becomes a positive reinforcer only if a person's performance later improves. Sometimes, rewards turn out not to be positive reinforcers. For example, a supervisor at Boeing might praise a subordinate in front of other group members for finding errors in a report. If the group members then give the worker the silent treatment, however, the worker may stop looking for errors in the future. In this case, the supervisor's "reward" does not serve as a positive reinforcer.

To have maximum reinforcement value, a reward must be delivered only if the desired behavior is exhibited. That is, the reward must be contingent on the desired behavior. This principle is known as the **law of contingent reinforcement**. In the previous Texas Instruments example, the supervisor's praise was contingent on the subordinate's making constructive comments. Finally, the reward must be given as soon as possible after the desired behavior. This is known as the **law of immediate reinforcement**.[10] If the TI boss waited for the annual performance review to praise the subordinate for providing constructive comments, the law of immediate reinforcement would be violated.

Now that we have presented the general concepts, it is time to address two important issues of implementation.[11] First, what do you do if the behavior approximates what you want but is not exactly on target? Second, is it necessary to provide reinforcement each and every time? These are issues of shaping and scheduling, respectively.

Shaping If the desired behavior is specific in nature and is difficult to achieve, a pattern of positive reinforcement, called shaping, can be used. **Shaping** is the creation of a new behavior by the positive reinforcement of successive approximations leading to the desired behavior. For example, new machine operators in the Ford Motor casting operation in Ohio must learn a complex series of tasks in pouring molten metal into the casting in order to avoid gaps, overfills, or cracks.[12] The molds are filled in a three-step process, with each step progressively more difficult than its predecessor. Astute master craftspersons first show neophytes how to pour the first step and give praise based on what they did right. As the apprentices gain experience, they are given praise only when all of the elements of the first step are completed successfully. Once the apprentices have mastered the first step, they progress to the second. Reinforcement is given only when the entire first step and an aspect of the second step are completed successfully. Over time, apprentices learn all three steps and are given contingent positive rewards immediately for a complete casting that has no cracks or gaps. In this way, behavior is shaped gradually rather than changed all at once.

Scheduling Positive Reinforcement Positive reinforcement can be given according to either continuous or intermittent schedules. **Continuous reinforcement** administers a reward each time a desired behavior occurs. **Intermittent reinforcement** rewards behavior only periodically. These alternatives are important

■ The **law of contingent reinforcement** is the view that, for a reward to have maximum reinforcing value, it must be delivered only if the desired behavior is exhibited.

■ The **law of immediate reinforcement** states that the more immediate the delivery of a reward after the occurrence of a desirable behavior, the greater the reinforcing effect on behavior.

■ **Shaping** is the creation of a new behavior by the positive reinforcement of successive approximations to the desired behavior.

■ **Continuous reinforcement** is a reinforcement schedule that administers a reward each time a desired behavior occurs.

because the two schedules may have very different impacts on behavior. In general, continuous reinforcement elicits a desired behavior more quickly than does intermittent reinforcement. Thus, in the initial training of the apprentice casters, continuous reinforcement would be important. At the same time, continuous reinforcement is more costly in the consumption of rewards and is more easily extinguished when reinforcement is no longer present. In contrast, behavior acquired under intermittent reinforcement lasts longer upon the discontinuance of reinforcement than does behavior acquired under continuous reinforcement. In other words, it is more resistant to extinction. Thus, as the apprentices master an aspect of the pouring, the schedule is switched from continuous to intermittent reinforcement.

As shown in Figure 6.3, intermittent reinforcement can be given according to fixed or variable schedules. *Variable schedules* typically result in more consistent patterns of desired behavior than do fixed reinforcement schedules. *Fixed interval schedules* provide rewards at the first appearance of a behavior after a given time has elapsed. *Fixed ratio schedules* result in a reward each time a certain number of the behaviors have occurred. A *variable interval schedule* rewards behavior at random times, while a *variable ratio schedule* rewards behavior after a random number of occurrences. For example, as the apprentices perfect their technique for a stage of pouring castings, the astute masters switch to a variable ratio reinforcement.

Let's look at an example from Drankenfeld Colors, Washington, Pennsylvania, with 250 employees. The absentee rate of these employees was very low, and in a recent year 44 percent of the employees had perfect attendance records. The firm wanted to use positive reinforcement to showcase perfect attendance, even though attendance was already so positive. Consequently, it gave monetary awards of $50 for perfect attendance at 6 and 12 months, with a $25 bonus for a full year of perfect attendance. In addition, the firm entered employees with perfect attendance into a sweepstakes drawing at special award banquets. The win-

■ **Intermittent reinforcement** is a reinforcement schedule that rewards behavior only periodically.

	Interval	Ratio
Fixed	**Fixed interval** Reinforcer given after a given time Weekly or monthly paychecks Regularly scheduled exams	**Fixed ratio** Reinforcer given after a given number of behavior occurrences Piece rate pay Commissioned salespeople; certain amount is given for each dollar of sales
Variable	**Variable interval** Reinforcer given at random times Occasional praise by boss on unscheduled visits Unspecified number of pop quizzes to students	**Variable ratio** Reinforcer given after a random number of behavior occurrences Random quality checks with praise for zero defects Commissioned salespeople; a varying number of calls is required to obtain a given sale
	Time based	**Behavior occurrence based**

Figure 6.3 Four types of intermittent reinforcement schedules.

Omni Royal Orleans Hotel ←

www.omnihotels.com

The Omni Royal Orleans Hotel places a heavy emphasis on its Omni Service Champion Program, recognizing desirable worker behaviors. A smiling greeting is one such desirable behavior, and the boss's praise is the consequence.

■ **Negative reinforcement** is the withdrawal of negative consequences, which tends to increase the likelihood of repeating the behavior in a similar setting; it is also known as avoidance.

■ **Punishment** is the administration of negative consequences that tend to reduce the likelihood of repeating the behavior in similar settings.

ners received an all-expense-paid trip for two to a resort. Perfect attendance increased from 44 percent to 62 percent in the program's first year.[13]

Let's consider what kind of reinforcement scheduling was used in this program. A strong argument can be made that a fixed ratio schedule was used, in conjunction with a variable ratio schedule. The first schedule rewarded attendance behaviors occurring within 6 months and 12 months, or the specific number of workday attendance occurring within these periods. Thus, for each period during which a perfect number of attendance days occurred, a person received an award—a fixed ratio schedule one.

The second schedule focuses on eligibility for the drawing. It is a variable ratio because a random number of perfect attendance days must pass before a specific employee receives a trip. Maintaining perfect attendance to qualify for the drawing is similar to playing a slot machine. In this variable ratio system, players keep putting coins in the machines because they don't have any idea when they will hit the jackpot.[14] Lotteries similar to Drankenfeld's have been used by firms as different as new car dealerships and New York Life Insurance.[15]

Negative Reinforcement (Avoidance)   A second reinforcement strategy used in OB Mod is **negative reinforcement** or avoidance—the withdrawal of negative consequences, which tends to increase the likelihood of repeating the desirable behavior in similar settings. For example, a manager at McDonald's regularly nags a worker about his poor performance and then stops nagging when the worker does not fall behind one day. We need to focus on two aspects here: the negative consequences followed by the withdrawal of these consequences when desirable behavior occurs. The term negative reinforcement comes from this withdrawal of the negative consequences. This strategy is also sometimes called avoidance because its intent is for the person to avoid the negative consequence by performing the desired behavior. For instance, we stop at a red light to avoid a traffic ticket or a worker who prefers the day shift is allowed to return to that shift if she performs well on the night shift.

Punishment   A third OB Mod strategy is punishment. Unlike positive reinforcement and negative reinforcement, punishment is not intended to encourage positive behavior but to discourage negative behavior. Formally defined, **punishment** is the administration of negative consequences or the withdrawal of positive consequences that tend to reduce the likelihood of repeating the behavior in similar settings. The first type of punishment is illustrated by a Burger King manager who assigns a tardy worker to an unpleasant job, such as cleaning the restrooms. An example of withdrawing positive consequences is a Burger King manager who docks the employee's pay when she is tardy.

Some scholarly work illustrates the importance of punishment by showing that punishment administered for poor performance leads to enhanced performance without a significant effect on satisfaction. However, punishment seen by the workers as arbitrary and capricious leads to very low satisfaction, as well as low performance.[16] Thus, punishment can be handled poorly, or it can be handled well. Of course, the manager's challenge is to know when to use this strategy and how to use it correctly.

Finally, punishment may be offset by positive reinforcement received from another source. It is possible for a worker to be reinforced by peers at the same time that the worker is receiving punishment from the manager. Sometimes the positive value of such peer support is so great that the individual chooses to put up with the punishment. Thus, the undesirable behavior continues. As many times as a experienced worker may be verbally reprimanded by a supervisor for playing jokes on new employees, for example, the "grins" offered by other workers may well justify continuation of the jokes in the future.

Does all of this mean that punishment should never be administered? Of course not. The important things to remember are to administer punishment selectively and then to do it right.

Extinction   The final OB Mod reinforcement strategy is **extinction**—the withdrawal of the reinforcing consequences for a given behavior. For example, Jack is often late for work, and his co-workers cover for him (positive reinforcement). The manager instructs Jack's co-workers to stop covering for him, withdrawing the reinforcing consequences. The manager has deliberately used extinction to get rid of an undesirable behavior. This strategy decreases the frequency of or weakens the behavior. The behavior is not "unlearned"; it simply is not exhibited. Since the behavior is no longer reinforced, it will reappear if reinforced again. Whereas positive reinforcement seeks to establish and maintain desirable work behavior, extinction is intended to weaken and eliminate undesirable behavior.

■ **Extinction** is the withdrawal of the reinforcing consequences for a given behavior.

Summary of Reinforcement Strategies   Figure 6.4 summarizes and illustrates the use of each OB Mod strategy. They are all designed to direct work behavior

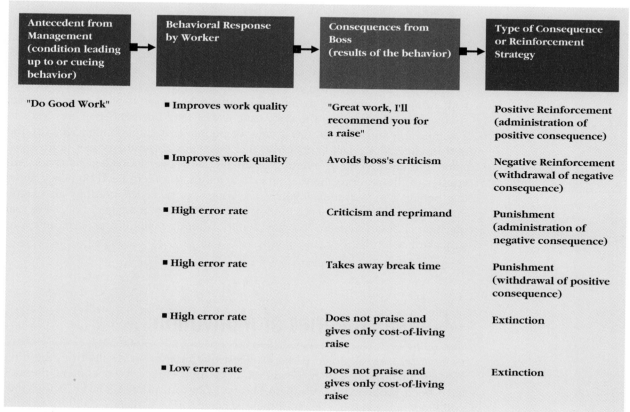

Antecedent from Management (condition leading up to or cueing behavior)	Behavioral Response by Worker	Consequences from Boss (results of the behavior)	Type of Consequence or Reinforcement Strategy
"Do Good Work"	■ Improves work quality	"Great work, I'll recommend you for a raise"	Positive Reinforcement (administration of positive consequence)
	■ Improves work quality	Avoids boss's criticism	Negative Reinforcement (withdrawal of negative consequence)
	■ High error rate	Criticism and reprimand	Punishment (administration of negative consequence)
	■ High error rate	Takes away break time	Punishment (withdrawal of positive consequence)
	■ High error rate	Does not praise and gives only cost-of-living raise	Extinction
	■ Low error rate	Does not praise and gives only cost-of-living raise	Extinction

Figure 6.4
Applying Reinforcement strategies.

toward practices desired by management. Both positive and negative reinforcement are used to strengthen the desirable behavior of improving work quality when it occurs. Punishment is used to weaken the undesirable behavior of high error rate and involves either administering negative consequences or withdrawing positive consequences. Similarly, extinction is used deliberately to weaken the undesirable high error rate behavior when it occurs. Note also, however, that extinction is used inadvertently to weaken the desirable low error rate behavior. Finally, these strategies may be used in combination as well as independently.

■ REINFORCEMENT PERSPECTIVES: USAGE AND ETHICAL ISSUES

The effective use of reinforcement strategies can help manage human behavior at work. Testimony to this effect is found in the application of these strategies in many large firms, such as General Electric and B. F. Goodrich, and even in small firms, such as Mid-America Building Maintenance. Mid-America, a janitorial services firm in Wichita, Kansas, provides an incentive program to employees who work 90 consecutive workdays without an absence.[17] Reinforcement strategies are also supported by the growing number of consulting firms that specialize in reinforcement techniques.

Managerial use of these approaches is not without criticism, however. For example, some reports on the "success" of specific programs involve isolated cases that have been analyzed without the benefit of scientific research designs. It is hard to conclude definitively whether the observed results were caused by reinforcement dynamics. In fact, one critic argues that the improved performance may well have occurred only because of the goal setting involved—that is, because specific performance goals were clarified, and workers were individually held accountable for their accomplishment.[18]

Another major criticism rests with the potential value dilemmas associated with using reinforcement to influence human behavior at work. For example, some critics maintain that the systematic use of reinforcement strategies leads to a demeaning and dehumanizing view of people that stunts human growth and development.[19] A related criticism is that managers abuse the power of their position and knowledge by exerting external control over individual behavior. Advocates of the reinforcement approach attack the problem head on: They agree that behavior modification involves the control of behavior, but they also argue that behavior control is an irrevocable part of every manager's job. The real question is how to ensure that any manipulation is done in a positive and constructive fashion.[20]

Content Theories of Motivation

Content theories, as noted earlier, suggest that motivation results from the individual's attempts to satisfy needs. Four of the better known content theories have been proposed by Abraham Maslow, Clayton Alderfer, David McClelland, and Frederick Herzberg. Each of these scholars offers a slightly different view of the needs individuals may bring with them to work.

■ HIERARCHY OF NEEDS THEORY

Abraham Maslow's **hierarchy of needs theory**, as shown in Figure 6.5, identifies five distinct levels of individual needs: from self-actualization and esteem, at the top, to social, safety, and physiological at the bottom.[21] Maslow assumes that some needs are more important than others and must be satisfied before the other needs can serve as motivators. For example, physiological needs must be satisfied before safety needs are activated, safety needs must be satisfied before social needs are activated, and so on.

Maslow's view is quite popular in U.S. firms because it appears easily implemented. Unfortunately, however, research evidence fails to support the existence of a precise five-step hierarchy of needs. The needs more likely operate in a flexible hierarchy. Some research suggests that **higher order needs** (esteem and self-actualization) tend to become more important than **lower order needs** (psychological, safety, and social) as individuals move up the corporate ladder.[22] Other studies report that needs vary according to a person's career stage, the size of the organization, and even geographical location.[23] There is also no consistent evidence that the satisfaction of a need at one level decreases its importance and increases the importance of the next higher need.[24] Finally, when the hierarchy of needs is examined across cultures, values such as those discussed in Chapter

■ Maslow's **hierarchy of needs theory** offers a pyramid of physiological, safety, social, esteem, and self-actualization needs.

■ **Higher order needs** in Maslow's hierarchy are esteem and self-actualization.

■ **Lower order needs** in Maslow's hierarchy are physiological, safety, and social.

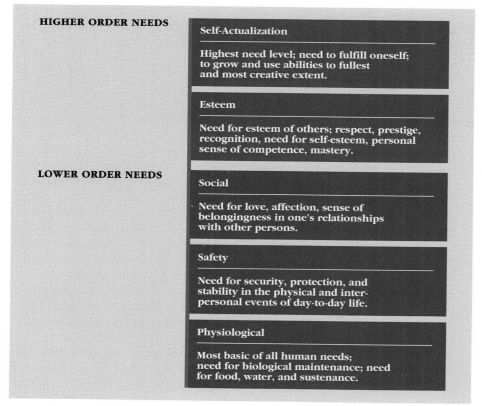

Figure 6.5
Higher order and lower order needs in Maslow's hierarchy of needs.

2 become important.[25] For instance, social needs tend to dominate in more collectivist societies, such as Mexico and Pakistan.[26]

■ ERG THEORY

■ Alderfer's **ERG theory** identifies existence, relatedness, and growth needs.

Clayton Alderfer's **ERG theory** is also based on needs but differs from Maslow's theory in three basic respects.[27] First, the theory collapses Maslow's five need categories into three: **existence needs**—desire for physiological and material well-being; **relatedness needs**—desire for satisfying interpersonal relationships; and **growth needs**—desire for continued personal growth and development. Second, whereas Maslow's theory argues that individuals progress up the "needs" hierarchy, ERG theory emphasizes a unique *frustration-regression* component. An already satisfied lower level need can become activated when a higher level need cannot be satisfied. Thus, if a person is continually frustrated in his or her attempts to satisfy growth needs, relatedness needs can again surface as key motivators. Third, unlike Maslow's theory, ERG theory contends that more than one need may be activated at the same time.

■ **Existence needs** are desires for physiological and material well-being.

■ **Relatedness needs** are desires for satisfying interpersonal relationships.

■ **Growth needs** are desires for continued personal growth and development.

Even though more research is needed to shed more light on its validity, the supporting evidence on ERG theory is encouraging.[28] In particular, the theory's allowance for regression back to lower level needs is a valuable contribution to our thinking. It may help to explain why in some settings, for example, workers' complaints focus on wages, benefits, and working conditions—things relating to existence needs. Although these needs are important, their importance may be exaggerated because the workers' jobs cannot otherwise satisfy relatedness and growth needs. ERG theory thus offers a more flexible approach to understanding human needs than does Maslow's strict hierarchy.

■ ACQUIRED NEEDS THEORY

In the late 1940s, psychologist David I. McClelland and his co-workers began experimenting with the Thematic Apperception Test (TAT) as a way of measuring human needs.[29] The TAT is a projective technique that asks people to view pictures and write stories about what they see. In one case, McClelland showed three executives a photograph of a man sitting down and looking at family photos arranged on his work desk. One executive wrote of an engineer who was daydreaming about a family outing scheduled for the next day. Another described a designer who had picked up an idea for a new gadget from remarks made by his family. The third described an engineer who was intently working on a bridge-stress problem that he seemed sure to solve because of his confident look.[30] McClelland identified three themes in these TAT stories, with each corresponding to an underlying need that he believes is important for understanding individual behavior. These needs are (1) **need for achievement (nAch)**—the desire to do something better or more efficiently, to solve problems, or to master complex tasks; (2) **need for affiliation (nAff)**—the desire to establish and maintain friendly and warm relations with others; and (3) **need for power (nPower)**—the desire to control others, to influence their behavior, or to be responsible for others.

■ **Need for achievement (nAch)** is the desire to do better, solve problems, or master complex tasks.

■ **Need for affiliation (nAff)** is the desire for friendly and warm relations with others.

■ **Need for power (nPower)** is the desire to control others and influence their behavior.

McClelland posits that these three needs are acquired over time, as a result of life experiences. He encourages managers to learn how to identify the presence of nAch, nAff, and nPower in themselves and in others and to be able to create work environments that are responsive to the respective need profiles.

The theory is particularly useful because each need can be linked with a set of work preferences. A high-need achiever will prefer individual responsibilities, challenging goals, and performance feedback. A high-need affiliator is drawn to interpersonal relationships and opportunities for communication. The high need-for-power type seeks influence over others and likes attention and recognition. If these needs are truly acquired, it may be possible to acquaint people with the need profiles required to succeed in various types of jobs. For instance, McClelland found that the combination of a moderate to high need for power and a lower need for affiliation is linked with senior executive success. High nPower creates the willingness to have influence or impact on others; lower nAff allows the manager to make difficult decisions without undue worry over being disliked.[31]

Research lends considerable insight into nAch in particular and includes some especially interesting applications in developing nations. For example, McClelland trained businesspeople in Kakinda, India, to think, talk, and act like high achievers by having them write stories about achievement and participate in a business game that encouraged achievement. The businesspeople also met with successful entrepreneurs and learned how to set challenging goals for their own businesses. Over a two-year period following these activities, the participants from the Kakinda study engaged in activities that created twice as many new jobs as those who hadn't received the training.[32]

GLOBALIZATON

In 1997 Starbucks expanded its operations to suburban Detroit following its successful openings in Tokyo and Singapore to mark its twenty-fifth anniversary. In the middle 1980s Howard Schultz took the idea of a European coffee house back to Seattle and opened IL Giornale, featuring Starbucks coffee. By the early 1990s Starbucks, as it had been renamed, had expanded to major East and West Coast cities. By the mid-1990s, Starbucks had become a hot property, opening coffee houses around the nation. Its success is attributed in part to its coffee and in part to a motivational system for all employees that reinforces respect, dignity, diversity, and excellence as well as profitability.

www.starbucks.com

■ TWO-FACTOR THEORY

Frederick Herzberg took a different approach to examining motivation. He simply asked workers to report the times they felt exceptionally good about their jobs and the times they felt exceptionally bad about them.[33] As shown in Figure 6.6, Herzberg and his associates noted that the respondents identified somewhat different things when they felt good or bad about their jobs. From this study they developed the **two-factor theory**, also known as the motivator-hygiene theory, which portrays different factors as primary causes of job satisfaction and job dissatisfaction.

According to this theory, **hygiene factors** are sources of job dissatisfaction. These factors are associated with the job context or work setting; that is, they re-

■ Herzberg's **two-factor theory** identifies job context as the source of job dissatisfaction and job content as the source of job satisfaction.

■ **Hygiene factors** in job context, the work setting, are sources of job dissatisfaction.

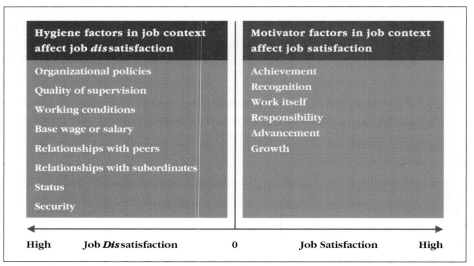

Figure 6.6
Sources of dissatisfaction and satisfaction in Herzberg's two-factor theory.

late more to the environment in which people work than to the nature of the work itself. Among the hygiene factors shown on the left in Figure 6.6 perhaps the most surprising is salary. Herzberg found that low salary makes people dissatisfied, but that paying them more does not necessarily satisfy or motivate them. In the two-factor theory, job satisfaction and job dissatisfaction are totally separate dimensions. Therefore, improving a hygiene factor, such as working conditions, will not make people satisfied with their work; it will only prevent them from being dissatisfied.

To improve job satisfaction, the theory directs attention to an entirely different set of factors—the **motivator factors** shown on the right in Figure 6.6. These factors are related to job content—what people actually do in their work. Adding these satisfiers or motivators to people's jobs is Herzberg's link to performance. These factors include sense of achievement, recognition, and responsibility.

According to Herzberg, when these opportunities are not available, low job satisfaction causes a lack of motivation and performance suffers. He suggests the technique of job enrichment as a way of building satisfiers into job content. This topic is given special attention in Chapter 8. For now, the notion is well summarized in this statement by Herzberg: "If you want people to do a good job, give them a good job to do."[34]

OB scholars continue to debate the merits of the two-factor theory and its applications.[35] Many are unable to confirm the theory. Many criticize it as being method bound. This is a serious criticism, for the scientific approach requires that theories be verifiable under different research methods. Furthermore, this theory, just like the other content theories, fails to account for individual differences, to link motivation and needs to both satisfaction and performance, or to consider cultural and professional differences.[36]

The content theories remain popular in management circles because of their simplicity and the direct apparent linkage from needs to behavior. At the same

■ **Motivator factors** in job content, the tasks people actually do, are sources of job satisfaction.

time, none of the theories links needs directly to motivated behavior desired by the manager. Rather, managers just misinterpret the theories and often inappropriately assume that they know the needs of their subordinates. Thus, we advise extreme care in simplistic application of content theories. We will return to these theories when we incorporate satisfaction into the discussion of motivation.

Process Theories

The various content theories emphasize the "what" aspects of motivation. That is, they tend to look for ways to improve motivation by dealing with activated or deprived needs. They do not delve formally into the thought processes through which people choose one action over another in the workplace. *Process theories* focus on thought processes. Although there are many process theories, we will concentrate on equity and expectancy theory.

■ Adams' **equity theory** posits that people will act to eliminate any felt inequity in the rewards received for their work in comparison with others.

■ EQUITY THEORY

Equity theory is based on the phenomenon of social comparison and is best applied to the workplace through the writing of J. Stacy Adams.[37] Adams argues that when people gauge the fairness of their work outcomes relative to others, any perceived inequity is a motivating state of mind. Perceived inequity occurs when someone believes that the rewards received for their work contributions compare unfavorably to the rewards other people appear to have received for their work. When such perceived inequity exists, the theory states that people will be motivated to act in ways that remove the discomfort and restore a sense of felt equity.

Felt negative inequity exists when an individual feels that he or she has received relatively less than others have in proportion to work inputs. *Felt positive inequity* exists when an individual feels that he or she has received relatively more than others have. When either feeling exists, the individual will likely engage in one or more of the following behaviors to restore a sense of equity.

THE EFFECTIVE MANAGER 6.1

STEPS FOR MANAGING THE EQUITY PROCESS

- Recognize that equity comparisons are inevitable in the workplace.
- Anticipate felt negative inequities when rewards are given.
- Communicate clear evaluations of any rewards given.
- Communicate an appraisal of performance on which the reward is based.
- Communicate comparison points appropriate in the situation.

How to restore perceived equity

- Change work inputs (e.g., reduce performance efforts).
- Change the outcomes (rewards) received (e.g., ask for a raise).
- Leave the situation (e.g., quit).
- Change the comparison points (e.g., compare self to a different co-worker).
- Psychologically distort the comparisons (e.g., rationalize that the inequity is only temporary and will be resolved in the future).
- Take actions to change the inputs or outputs of the comparison person (e.g., get a co-worker to accept more work).

The equity comparison intervenes between the allocation of rewards and the ultimate impact on the recipients. What may seem fair and equitable to a group leader, for example, might be perceived as unfair and inequitable by a team member after comparisons are made with other teammates. Furthermore, such feelings of inequity are determined solely by the individual's interpretation of the situation. It is not the reward-giver's intentions that count, but it is how the recipient perceives the reward that will determine actual motivational outcomes.

Research indicates that people who feel they are overpaid (perceived positive inequity) increase the quantity or quality of their work, whereas those who feel they are underpaid (perceived negative inequity) decrease the quantity or quality of their work.[38] The research is most conclusive with respect to felt negative inequity. It appears that people are less comfortable when they are underrewarded than when they are overrewarded. Such results, however, are particularly tied to individualistic cultures in which self-interests tend to govern social comparisons. In more collectivist cultures, such as those of many Asian countries, the concern often runs more for equality than equity. This allows for solidarity with the group and helps to maintain harmony in social relationships.[39]

www.oglebaynorton.com

〽 ENTREPRENEURSHIP

Although executives are quick to offer subordinates pay that is contingent on ever-upward-moving non-specific targets, when negotiating contracts with their own board of directors they want to be the ones to set the threshold for contingent bonuses and make sure it is very low. Executives also want much of the pay in salary—on a noncontingent basis. At Oglebay Norton, a provider of Great Lakes marine transportation and the mining and marketing of industrial minerals, John Lauer, the new CEO, took a stand. He does not receive his bonus until the stock price rises some 25 percent; at that point, he must present a strong case for buying the shares. Perhaps this unusual arrangement derives from Lauer's study of executive compensation in his PhD work and his finding on how debilitating huge salaries for executives can be.

■ EXPECTANCY THEORY

■ Vroom's **expectancy theory** argues that work motivation is determined by individual beliefs regarding effort/performance relationships and work outcomes.

Victor Vroom's **expectancy theory** posits that motivation is a result of a rational calculation.[40] A person is motivated to the degree that he or she believes that (1) effort will yield acceptable performance, (2) performance will be rewarded, and (3) the value of the rewards is highly positive. The interactive combination of all three influences motivation. (See Figure 6.7.) Thus, some key concepts are defined in terms of probabilities.

■ **Expectancy** is the probability that work effort will be followed by performance accomplishment.

- The probability assigned by an individual that work effort will be followed by a given level of achieved task performance is called **expectancy**. Expectancy would equal 0 if the person felt it were impossible to achieve the given performance level; it would equal 1 if a person were 100 percent certain that the performance could be achieved.

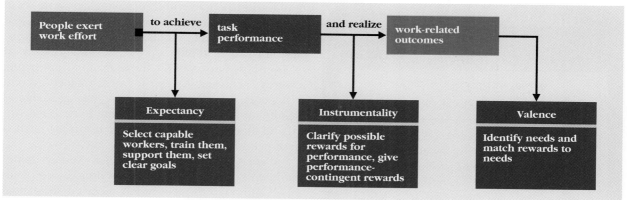

Figure 6.7
Key terms and managerial implications of Vroom's expectancy theory.

- **Instrumentality** is the probability assigned by the individual that a given level of achieved task performance will lead to various work outcomes. Instrumentality also varies from 0 to 1.*

- **Valence** is the value attached by the individual to various work outcomes. Valences form a scale from –1 (very undesirable outcome) to +1 (very desirable outcome). Vroom posits that motivation (*M*), expectancy (*E*), instrumentality (*I*), and valence (*V*) are related to one another by the equation: $M = (E) \times (I) \times (V)$. This multiplier effect means that the motivational appeal of a given work path is sharply reduced whenever any one or more of these factors approaches the value of zero. Conversely, for a given reward to have a high and positive motivational impact as a work outcome, the expectancy, instrumentality, and valence associated with the reward all must be high and positive.

Suppose that a manager is wondering whether or not the prospect of earning a merit raise will be motivational to an employee. Expectancy theory predicts that motivation to work hard to earn the merit pay will be low if *expectancy* is low—a person feels that he or she cannot achieve the necessary performance level. Motivation will also be low if *instrumentality* is low—the person is not confident a high level of task performance will result in a high merit pay raise. Motivation will also be low if *valence* is low—the person places little value on a merit pay increase. And motivation will be low if any combination of these exists. Thus, the multiplier effect requires managers to act to maximize expectancy, instrumentality, and valence when seeking to create high levels of work motivation. A zero at any location on the right side of the expectancy equation will result in zero motivation.

Expectancy logic argues that a manager must try to intervene actively in work situations to maximize work expectancies, instrumentalities, and valences that support organizational objectives.[41] To influence expectancies, managers

▪ **Instrumentality** is the probability that performance will lead to various work outcomes.

▪ **Valence** is the value to the individual of various work outcomes.

---

* Strictly speaking, Vroom's treatment of instrumentality would allow it to vary from –1 to +1. We use the probability definition here and the 0 to +1 range for pedagogical purposes; it is consistent with the instrumentality notion.

THE EFFECTIVE MANAGER 6.2

WORK GUIDELINES FOR ALLOCATING EXTRINSIC REWARDS

1. Clearly identify the desired behaviors.
2. Maintain an inventory of rewards that have the potential to serve as positive reinforcers.
3. Recognize individual differences in the rewards that will have positive value for each person.
4. Let each person know exactly what must be done to receive a desirable reward. Set clear target antecedents and give performance feedback.
5. Allocate rewards contingently and immediately upon the appearance of the desired behaviors.
6. Allocate rewards wisely in terms of scheduling the delivery of positive reinforcement.

■ **Extrinsic rewards** are given to the individual by some other person in the work setting.

■ **Intrinsic rewards** are received by the individual directly through task performance.

should select people with proper abilities, train them well, support them with needed resources, and identify clear performance goals. To influence instrumentality, managers should clarify performance–reward relationships and confirm these relationships when rewards are actually given for performance accomplishments. To influence valences, managers should identify the needs that are important to each individual and then try to adjust available rewards to match these needs.

A great deal of research on expectancy theory has been conducted, and review articles are available.[42] Although the theory has received substantial support, specific details, such as the operation of the multiplier effect, remain subject to some question. One of the more popular modifications of Vroom's original version of the theory distinguishes between work outcomes for calculating valence.[43] Researchers have separated **extrinsic rewards**—positively valued work outcomes given to the individual by some other person—from intrinsic rewards (see The Effective Manager 6.2). **Intrinsic rewards** are positively valued work outcomes that the individual receives directly as a result of task performance. A feeling of achievement after accomplishing a particularly challenging task is an example.

Expectancy theory does not specify exactly which rewards will motivate particular groups of workers. In this sense, the theory allows for the fact that the rewards and their link with performance are likely to be seen as quite different in different cultures. It helps to explain some apparently counterintuitive findings. For example, a pay raise motivated one group of Mexican workers to work fewer hours. They wanted a certain amount of money in order to enjoy things other than work rather than just more money. A Japanese sales representative's promotion to manager of a U.S. company adversely affected his performance. His superiors did not realize that the promotion embarrassed him and distanced him from his colleagues.[44]

Integrating The Motivation Theories

As you can see rewards, needs, cognitions, satisfaction, and performance are all integral to the discussion of motivation. Understanding the linkage between satisfaction and performance will help integrate all the views we have discussed.

■ JOB SATISFACTION

■ **Job satisfaction** is the degree to which individuals feel positively or negatively about their jobs.

Formally defined, **job satisfaction** is the degree to which individuals feel positively or negatively about their jobs. It is an attitude or emotional response to one's tasks as well as to the physical and social conditions of the workplace. At first glance, and from the perspective of Herzberg's two-factor theory, some aspects of job satisfaction should be motivational and lead to positive employment relationships and high levels of individual job performance. But as we will discuss, the issues are more complicated than this conclusion suggests.

HIGH PERFORMANCE ORGANIZATION

www.patagonia.com

Patagonia, a manufacturer of high-quality sports and outdoor equipment and clothing, was ranked by *Fortune Magazine* as among the 100 Best Places to work in the United States. Why? The simple—Patagonia executives see employees as the source of competitive advantage. Employees are free to schedule their own work hours, other than core time between 9 A.M. and 3 P.M.; they have the option of two- to three-month leaves of absence without pay; and they are given a lot of job involvement—with responsible tasks and decision-making input. But Patagoniacs, as they like to be called, work as hard as they play. Many of those who take off during the afternoon are back in the office in the evening working. Motivating them is a combination of a rewarding job with built-in feedback and managers who consistently reward outstanding performance.

On a daily basis, managers must be able to infer the job satisfaction of others by careful observation and interpretation of what they say and do while going about their jobs. Sometimes, it is also useful to examine more formally the levels of job satisfaction among groups of workers, especially through formal interviews or questionnaires. Increasingly, other methods are being used as well such as focus groups and computer-based attitude surveys.[45]

Among the many available job satisfaction questionnaires that have been used over the years, two popular ones are the Minnesota Satisfaction Questionnaire (MSQ) and the Job Descriptive Index (JDI).[46] Both address aspects of satisfaction with which good managers should be concerned for the people reporting to them. For example, the MSQ measures satisfaction with working conditions, chances for advancement, freedom to use one's own judgment, praise for doing a good job, and feelings of accomplishment, among others. The five facets of job satisfaction measured by the JDI are:

- *The work itself*—responsibility, interest, and growth.
- *Quality of supervision*—technical help and social support.
- *Relationships with co-workers*—social harmony and respect.
- *Promotion opportunities*—chances for further advancement.
- *Pay*—adequacy of pay and perceived equity vis-à-vis others.

Five facets of job satisfaction

■ JOB SATISFACTION, RETENTION AND PERFORMANCE

The importance of job satisfaction can be viewed in the context of two decisions people make about their work. The first is the decision to belong—that is, to join and remain a member of an organization. The second is the decision to perform—that is, to work hard in pursuit of high levels of task performance. Not everyone who belongs to an organization performs up to expectations.

The decision to belong concerns an individual's attendance and longevity at work. In this sense, job satisfaction influences *absenteeism*, or the failure of people to attend work. In general, workers who are satisfied with the job itself have more regular attendance and are less likely to be absent for unexplained reasons than are dissatisfied workers. Job satisfaction can also affect turnover, or decisions by people to terminate their employment. Simply put, dissatisfied workers are more likely than satisfied workers to quit their jobs.[47]

What is the relationship between job satisfaction and performance? There is considerable debate on this issue, with three alternative points of view evident: (1) satisfaction causes performance, (2) performance causes satisfaction, and (3) rewards cause both performance and satisfaction.[48]

Argument: Satisfaction Causes Performance   If job satisfaction causes high levels of performance, the message to managers is quite simple: To increase employees' work performance, make them happy. Research, however, indicates that no simple and direct link exists between individual job satisfaction at one point in time and work performance at a later point. This conclusion is widely recognized among OB scholars, even though some evidence suggests that the relationship holds better for professional or higher level employees than for non-professionals or those at lower job levels. Job satisfaction alone is not a consistent predictor of individual work performance.

Argument: Performance Causes Satisfaction   If high levels of performance cause job satisfaction, the message to managers is quite different. Rather than focusing first on peoples' job satisfaction, attention should be given to helping people achieve high performance; job satisfaction would be expected to follow. Research indicates an empirical relationship between individual performance measured at a certain time period and later job satisfaction. A basic model of this relationship, based on the work of Edward E. Lawler and Lyman Porter, maintains that performance accomplishment leads to rewards that, in turn, lead to satisfaction.[49] In this model rewards are intervening variables; that is, they "link" performance with later satisfaction. In addition, a moderator variable—perceived equity of rewards—further affects the relationship. The moderator indicates that performance will lead to satisfaction only if rewards are perceived as equitable. If an individual feels that his or her performance is unfairly rewarded, the performance–causes–satisfaction relationship will not hold.

Argument: Rewards Cause Both Satisfaction and Performance   This final argument in the job satisfaction–performance controversy is the most compelling. It suggests that a proper allocation of rewards can positively influence both performance and satisfaction. The key word in the previous sentence is *proper*. Research indicates that people who receive high rewards report higher job satisfaction. But research also indicates that performance-contingent rewards influence a person's work performance. In this case, the size and value of the reward vary in proportion to the level of one's performance accomplishment. Large rewards are given for high performance; small or no rewards are given for low performance. And whereas giving a low performer only small rewards initially may lead to dissatisfaction, the expectation is that the individual will make efforts to improve performance in order to obtain greater rewards in the future.

The point is that managers should consider satisfaction and performance as two separate but interrelated work results that are affected by the allocation of rewards. Whereas job satisfaction alone is not a good predictor of work performance, well-managed rewards can have a positive influence on both satisfaction and performance.

■ INTEGRATED MODEL OF MOTIVATION

Figure 6.8 outlines the integrated view. Note that the figure has much in common with Vroom's expectancy theory and the Porter–Lawler framework just discussed.[50] In the figure, job performance and satisfaction are separate, but potentially interdependent, work results. Performance is influenced most directly by individual attributes such as ability and experience, organizational support such as resources and technology, and work effort—the point at which an individual's level of motivation comes directly to bear. Individual motivation directly determines work effort, and the key to motivation is the ability to create a work setting that positively responds to individual needs and goals. Whether or not a work setting proves motivational for a given individual depends on the availability of rewards and their perceived value. Note also the importance of contingent rewards, reflecting the law of contingent reinforcement. Recall also the importance of immediacy in rewarding.

The content theories enter the model as the guide to understanding individual attributes and identifying the needs that give motivational value to the possible rewards. When the individual experiences intrinsic rewards for work performance, motivation will be directly and positively affected. Motivation can also occur when job satisfactions result from either extrinsic or intrinsic rewards that are felt to be equitably allocated. When felt negative inequity results, satisfaction will be low and motivation will be reduced.

With this discussion of reinforcement, content, and process theories, you should have a better understanding of motivation. Although it will always be difficult to motivate employees, the knowledge in this chapter should help you

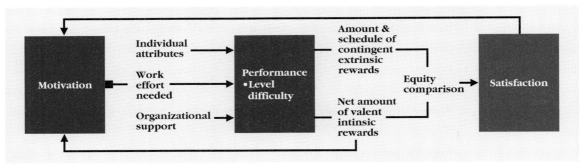

Figure 6.8
An integrated model of individual motivation to work.

reach toward higher performance and satisfaction. Finally, the integrating model rests on cultural assumptions, so that the meaning of the concepts may be culturally specific. The importance of various intrinsic and extrinsic rewards may well differ across cultures, as may the aspects of performance that are highly valued.

Chapter 6 Study Guide

Summary

What is motivation to work?

- Motivation is an internal force that accounts for the level, direction, and persistence of effort expended at work.

- Reinforcement theories emphasize the linkage between individual behavior and some specific outcomes to show how managers can alter the direction, level, or persistence of individual actions. They focus on observable aspects rather than what is inside an employee's head.

- Content theories, including the work of Maslow, Alderfer, McClelland, and Herzberg, focus on locating individual needs that influence behavior in the workplace.

- Process theories, such as equity and expectancy theory, examine the thought processes that affect decisions about alternative courses of action by people at work.

What are reinforcement theories, and how are they linked to motivation?

- Reinforcement is the means through which operant conditioning takes place and is the administration of a consequence as a result of behavior.

- The foundation of reinforcement is the law of effect, which states that behavior will be repeated or extinguished depending on whether the consequences are positive or negative.

- Positive reinforcement is the administration of positive consequences that tend to increase the likelihood of a person's repeating a behavior in similar settings.

- Positive reinforcement should be contingent and immediate, and it can be scheduled continuously or intermittently, depending on resources and desired outcomes.

- Negative reinforcement (avoidance) is used to encourage desirable behavior through the withdrawal of negative consequences for previously undesirable behavior.

- Punishment is the administration of negative consequences or the withdrawal of positive consequences, which tends to reduce the likelihood of repeating an undesirable behavior in similar settings.

■ Extinction is the withdrawal of reinforcing consequences for a given behavior.

What do the content theories suggest about individual needs and motivation?

■ Maslow's hierarchy of needs theory views human needs as activated in a five-step hierarchy ranging (lowest) physiological, safety, social, esteem, to self-actualization (highest).

■ Alderfer's ERG theory collapses the five needs into three: existence, relatedness, and growth; it maintains that more than one need can be activated at a time.

■ McClelland's acquired needs theory focuses on the needs for achievement, affiliation, and power, and it views needs as developed over time through experience and training.

■ Herzberg's two-factor theory links job satisfaction to motivator factors, such as responsibility and challenge, associated with job content.

■ Herzberg's two-factor theory links job dissatisfaction to hygiene factors, such as pay and working conditions, associated with job context.

What do the process theories suggest about individual motivation?

■ Equity theory points out that social comparisons take place when people receive rewards and that any felt inequity will motivate them to try to restore a sense of perceived equity.

■ When felt inequity is negative, that is, when the individual feels unfairly treated, he or she may decide to work less hard in the future or to quit a job.

■ Vroom's expectancy theory describes motivation as a function of an individual's beliefs concerning effort-performance relationships (expectancy), work-outcome relationships (instrumentality), and the desirability of various work outcomes (valence).

■ Expectancy theory states that Motivation = Expectancy × Instrumentality × Valence, and suggests that managers should make each factor positive in order to ensure high levels of motivation.

How can insights of the motivation theories be partially integrated by including job satisfaction?

■ Job satisfaction is a work attitude that reflects the degree to which people feel positively or negatively about a job and its various facets.

■ Common aspects of job satisfaction relate to pay, working conditions, quality of supervision, co-workers, and the task itself.

■ Job satisfaction is empirically related to employee turnover and absenteeism.

- The relationship between job satisfaction and performance is more controversial; current thinking focuses on how rewards influence both satisfaction and performance.

- Reinforcement views emphasize contingent rewards as well as the speed of the rewards.

- The content theories help identify important needs and determine what a person values by way of rewards.

- The equity theory suggests that any rewards must be perceived as equitable in the social context of the workplace.

- Although motivation predicts work efforts, individual performance also depends on job-relevant abilities and organizational support.

Key Terms

Classical conditioning (p. 104)
Content theories (p. 103)
Continuous reinforcement (p. 106)
Equity theory (p. 115)
ERG theory (p. 112)
Existence needs (p. 112)
Expectancy (p. 116)
Expectancy theory (p. 116)
Extinction (p. 109)
Extrinsic rewards (p. 118)
Growth needs (p. 112)
Hierarchy of needs theory (p. 111)
Higher order needs (p. 111)
Hygiene factors (p. 113)
Instrumentality (p. 117)

Intermittent reinforcement (p. 107)
Intrinsic rewards (p. 118)
Job satisfaction (p. 118)
Law of contingent reinforcement (p. 106)
Law of effect (p. 104)
Law of immediate reinforcement (p. 106)
Lower order needs (p. 111)
Motivation (p. 102)
Motivator factors (p. 114)
Need for achievement (p. 112)
Need for affiliation (p. 112)
Need for power (p. 112)
Negative reinforcement (p. 108)

Operant conditioning (p. 104)
Organizational behavior modification (OB Mod) (p. 105)
Positive reinforcement (p. 105)
Process theories (p. 103)
Punishment (p. 108)
Reinforcement (p. 103)
Reinforcement theories (p. 103)
Relatedness needs (p. 112)
Shaping (p. 106)
Stimulus (p. 104)
Two-factor theory (p. 113)
Valence (p. 117)

Self-Test 6 ■ MULTIPLE CHOICE

1. Reinforcement emphasizes _____. (a) intrinsic rewards (b) extrinsic rewards (c) the law of diminishing returns (d) social learning

2. OB Mod reinforcement strategies _____. (a) have much carefully controlled research support (b) have been criticized because the observed results may confuse causality (c) are not used much in large firms (d) are useful mostly in large firms

3. Negative reinforcement _____. (a) is similar to punishment (b) seeks to discourage undesirable behavior (c) seeks to encourage desirable behavior (d) is also known as escapism

4. OB Mod emphasizes _____. (a) the systematic reinforcement of desirable work behavior (b) noncontingent rewards (c) noncontingent punishment (d) extinction in preference to positive reinforcement

5. Reinforcement strategies _____. (a) violate ethical guidelines (b) involve the control of behavior (c) work best when they restrict freedom of choice (d) have largely been replaced by computer technology

6. A content theory of motivation is most likely to focus on _____. (a) contingent reinforcement (b) instrumentalities (c) equities (d) individual needs

7. A person high in need for achievement is most likely to prefer _____ in their jobs. (a) group work (b) challenging goals (c) control over other people (d) little or no feedback

8. In equity theory, the _____ is a key issue. (a) social comparison of rewards and efforts (b) equality of rewards (c) equality of efforts (d) absolute value of rewards

9. In expectancy theory, _____ is the probability that a given level of performance will lead to a particular work outcome. (a) expectancy (b) instrumentality (c) motivation (d) valence

10. Which statement about job satisfaction is most correct? (a) It causes performance. (b) It can affect turnover. (c) It cannot be measured. (d) It doesn't affect absenteeism.

■ TRUE–FALSE

11. Classical conditioning is another name for operant conditioning.   T   F

12. Because motivation is a universal concept, the theories apply equally well in all cultures.   T   F

13. The foundation for reinforcement is based on intrinsic rewards.   T   F

14. Reinforcement is the administration of a consequence as the result of behavior.   T   F

15. OB Mod especially emphasizes the concepts of punishment and extinction.   T   F

16. There is no equivalent to Maslow's social need in Alderfer's ERG theory.   T   F

17. In McClelland's acquired needs theory, a high need for socialized power involves the desire to control others for the pursuit of group or organizational goals.   T   F

18. In equity theory, felt negative inequity is a motivating state, but felt positive inequity is not.   T   F

19. An extrinsic reward is a positively valued work outcome received directly from task performance itself.   T   F

20. A reward is performance contingent when its size and value vary in proportion to the achieved performance level.   T   F

■ SHORT RESPONSE

21. Briefly compare and contrast classical conditioning and operant conditioning.

22. Briefly discuss how reinforcement is linked to extrinsic rewards.

23. What is the "frustration-regression" component in Alderfer's ERG theory?

24. What is the "multiplier effect" in expectancy theory?

■ APPLICATIONS ESSAY

25. While attending a business luncheon, you overhear the following conversation at a nearby table. Person A: "I'll tell you this, if you make your workers happy they'll be productive." Person B: "I'm not so sure, if I make them happy maybe they'll be real good about coming to work but not very good about working really hard while they are there." Which person do you agree with and why?

Explore application-oriented Fast Company articles, cases, experimental exercises, and self-assessments in the OB Skills Workbook

■ **Visit the Schermerhorn Web site to find the Interactive Self-Test and Internet exercises for this chapter.**

Human Resource Management Systems

EMPLOYEE RECRUITING GOES HIGH TECH

www.themirage.com

The newly opened Mirage Resort in Las Vegas needed to hire nearly 10,000 employees to get started. To streamline the process, it spent $1 million on a computerized process to screen 75,000 applicants in three months. Ultimately, 10 weeks were spent interviewing 26,000 finalists, and 9600 were chosen.

The high tech employee recruiting process involved these steps.

- Newspaper ad—"we are hiring." Applicants call toll free 8–8 for appointment and send an application form. Resort sends computer-generated reminder letter.

- Some 1200 applicants arrive daily. In resort parking lot, staffers confirm identity and use handsets to notify staff at the entrance. Applicants are greeted by name and refered to easy-to-use computer terminals.

- Applicants answer on-line 65 basic questions.

- Applicants go to check-out desk, where staffers check for completion, appearance, and behavior.

- Each department's staffers review database, and selected candidates are called in for interviews.

- Some 700 people are interviewed by 25 managers at a time over 12 hours. Results go into database.

- Criminal records, jobs, education, and credit histories are checked and search is narrowed.

irage shows how information technology can be used in performing the key human resource management function of employee selection in opening a gigantic new enterprise. Employee selection is part of human-resource planning for staffing needs and fulfilling those needs. The function also is part of the human resource training and career development, performance appraisal, and workforce reward functions that, along with human-resource strategic planning, are part of this chapter.

Study Questions

Management of human resources and employee rewards are increasingly important in the new workplace. As you read Chapter 7, keep in mind the following key questions.

- What are the essentials of human resource strategy and practice?
- What is training and career planning and development?
- What is performance appraisal?
- What are rewards and reward systems?

Human Resource Strategy and Practice

■ **Human resource strategic planning** hiring capable, motivated people to carry out the organization's mission and strategy.

Human-resource (HR) strategic planning is the process of providing capable and motivated people to carry out the organization's mission and strategy. A key part of this process is the *staffing function*, which involves the recruitment of employees—generating applicants; selection—making hiring decisions for each applicant; and socialization—orienting new hires to the organization.[1] This function is a critical part of an organization's job requirements—the employee characteristics match emphasized so strongly in Chapter 4. Once an HR staffing strategy is in place, managers must continue to assess current HR needs to make sure the organization continues to retain people to meet its strategic objectives.[2]

www.mattel.com

■ JOB ANALYSIS

Staffing begins with an understanding of the positions or jobs for which individuals are needed in the organization. **Job analysis** provides this information; it is the process and procedures used to collect and classify information about tasks the organization needs to complete.[3] Job analysis assists in the understanding of job activities required in a work process and helps define jobs, their interrelationships, and the demographic aptitude and ability and personality characteristics needed to do these jobs. The results can be applied to job descriptions, job evaluation and classification, training and career development, performance appraisal, and other HR aspects. Information concerned with the job itself is laid out in the job description. The job description typically contains such information as job duties and responsibilities, equipment and materials used, working conditions and hazards, supervision, work schedules, standards of performance, and relationship to other jobs.[4]

The worker characteristics of job analysis needed to meet the job requirements and specified in the job description are laid out in a job specification. For example, a safety supervisor must have a knowledge of safety regulations. The job requirements and minimum qualifications make up the job specification part of the job analysis.

In addition to other important contributions, the job content and relative importance of different job duties and responsibilities included in job analysis help organizations deal with legal requirements. Such information is useful in defending actions from legal challenges that allege discrimination or unfairness. The generic defense against a charge of discrimination is that the contested decision (hiring, providing a pay raise, termination) was made for job-related reasons, such as provided by job analy-

■ **Job analysis** is the procedure used to collect and classify information about tasks the organization needs to complete.

OB Across Functions

MEDICAL OPERATIONS

The Alphabet Soup of Medical Care

In the old days, so they say, one warm and caring physician handled many problems and even made house calls. Those days are no more, if they ever were. Now the "alphabet soup" medical jargon of today is overwhelming for many. Gayle Kataja, regional director for Connecticut Community Care, talks about APRNs, PAs, PTs, OTs, and how they and others must work together for the patient's good. An APRN is an advanced practice registered nurse, who performs many traditional physician functions. Among their tasks are taking medical histories and giving examinations. Both of these health-care providers work closely with licensed practical nurses, or LPNs, and certified nurse's aides in hospitals and in providing home health care. Those involved with rehabilitation are likely to see physical therapists, (PTs), and occupational therapists, (OTs), who help restore daily living skills. Now patients, in addition to saying *aah*, must be on top of lots of medical alphabet soup jargon to understand the team-oriented care they are getting.

sis. For example, a firefighter may be required to carry a 150-pound person from a burning building. Job analysis can help a city defend itself against sex discrimination if it can show the relevance of this requirement with a job analysis.[5]

■ RECRUITMENT

■ **Recruitment** is the process of attracting the best qualified individuals to apply for a job.

Once job analysis provides the necessary job requirements and employee characteristics, qualified people need to be drawn in to apply for various positions. **Recruitment** is the process of attracting the best qualified individuals to apply for a given job.[6]

www.digitalbase.com

📈 ENTREPRENEURSHIP

Tucked away in the medium-sized West Texas city of Lubbock is a firm called Digital Base Productions (DBP). It handles recorded phrases such as "Press one for...." or "Welcome to...." for such clients as Disney, Bell Atlantic, and Norwest Corporation. It uses high-tech state-of-the-art studios and an Avid Media Composer suite to give DBP clients access to thousands of well-known voices that can be directed to the client in real time. The three founders, David Dale, Kevin Bryan, and Berry Nelson, launched the firm 2 years ago. Bryan says the firm hires a lot of local talent and is trying to position itself as a national studio. "As Lubbock grows, we'll grow," say Bryan, as he thinks about the employee recruiting base needed.

It typically involves (1) advertisement of a position vacancy, (2) preliminary contact with potential job candidates, and (3) preliminary screening to obtain a pool of candidates. Mirage essentially followed a variation of these steps in its hiring practices. These practices are an example of external recruitment or of attracting individuals from outside the organization. External recruitment involves such sources as general advertisements, often in newspaper, trade journals, or via external Internet; word-of-mouth suggestions from current employees; use of employment agencies; and applicant walkins. By contrast, internal recruitment is a process for attracting job applicants from those currently working for the firm. Posting vacant positions on bulletin boards, in internal memos, and over intranets are frequently used ways to recruit internally.

Most firms tend to use a mix of external and internal recruitment. Some organizations, notably the United States armed forces, rely heavily on external recruitment for entry-level positions and then fill higher level positions entirely from internal promotions. Both approaches have advantages. Internal recruitment is encouraging to current employees, and external recruitment tends to bring in "new blood" and fresh ideas to the firm.

■ **Realistic job previews** provide applicants with an objective description of a job and organization.

Traditionally, firms have attempted to "sell" their organization and jobs to build up the applicant pool. More recently, an approach called a **realistic job preview**, is increasingly being used. In a realistic job preview, applicants are provided with an objective description of the prospective organization and job. Such descriptions have been found to reduce turnover and to better prepare new hires to cope with their jobs.[7]

■ SELECTION

Once an applicant pool has been recruited, the selection aspect of staffing comes into play. **Selection** involves the series of steps from initial applicant screening to final hiring of the new employee. The selection process involves completing application materials, conducting an interview, completing any necessary tests, doing a background investigation, and deciding to hire or not to hire.

■ **Selection** is the series of steps from initial applicant screening to hiring.

Application Materials   These materials may involve a traditional application form requesting various aspects of background and experience. These forms may be in traditional hard copy or on the Internet. Sometimes resume's (brief summaries of one's background and qualifications) are used in lieu of, or in addition to, other materials. Sometimes tests are included as part of the application materials.

Employment Interviews   Many of you have also probably experienced employment interviews at one time or another. Interviews are almost invariably used in the selection process (see The Effective Manager 7.1), although they are prone to the kinds of perceptual distortions discussed in Chapter 5, as well as other problems. Nevertheless, they are a mainstay of the selection process, perhaps because they can serve as public relations tools for the organization. At their best, interviews provide rough ideas concerning fit with the job and organization.[8]

Tests   Tests may be administered either before or after the interview. They include cognitive aptitude or ability and personality tests and, increasingly, tests for drug use. Intelligence tests are the most common examples of cognitive tests. Other examples are clerical and mechanical tests. Personality tests evaluate the kinds of personality characteristics discussed in Chapter 4. For example, the California Personality Inventory measures such characteristics as dominance, sociability, and flexibility. Again, whatever kind of test is used must be validated against job requirements so that the organization is not guilty of discrimination.

THE EFFECTIVE MANAGER 7.1

STEPS TO EMPHASIZE IN CONDUCTING HIRING INTERVIEWS

- Prepare yourself—check applicant's resumè and prepare agenda.
- Initially put applicant at ease—use small talk.
- Guard against stereotypes—emphasize applicant as individual.
- Emphasize results-oriented questions—not only what applicant has done but results of these actions.
- Allow for pauses to gather thoughts.
- Bring interview to a natural close.

Performance tests take many forms but often ask candidates to perform tasks that are identical to or at least closely related to what will be required on the job. As technology has become more important, performance tests involving computer skills have become more frequent. Also, a battery of tests often is used to explore a range of job behaviors.

For managerial jobs in particular, but increasingly for other jobs as well, assessment centers are often used. *Assessment centers* provide a firm with a comprehensive view of a candidate by evaluating the candidate's performance across many situations. Such assessments typically involve one to four days of various tests, simulations, role plays, and interviews, all based on dimensions the person occupying the job will need to demonstrate. AT&T has used assessment centers for many years, with considerable effectiveness, spending as much as $1500 per employee in the process.[9] IBM and the FBI are also among the more than 2000 organizations that use assessment centers for managerial selection and promotion.[10]

Background Investigation   Background investigation is yet another step that can be used either early or late in the selection process. Typically, a background investigation involves reference checks. Generally, letters of reference tend to be positively biased and so are not highly related to job performance.[11] Moreover, unless the references, either written or provided over the phone, are very carefully worded, they can lead to lawsuits. References should only disclose information about the job duties the individual in question has been performing. Any personal descriptions should involve only information that can be objectively verified.

Decision to Hire   Based on the previous steps, the organization may choose to make the hiring decision and present a formal job offer. The offer may be made by the potential employee's future boss or by a group of people. At this point, a physical examination may be required if it is shown to be relevant for job performance. For some jobs, negotiations concerning salary or other benefits may occur.

■ SOCIALIZATION

■ **Socialization** means orienting new employees to the firm and its work units.

Once hiring is completed, **socialization** is the final step in the staffing process. It involves orienting new employees to the firm and specifically to the work units in which they will be working. At this stage, the new employee is familiarized with the firm's policies and procedures and begins to get a feel for the organization's culture. Orientation can be conducted formally or informally, or it may involve a combination of the two. In complex positions, orientation may take place over an extended period of time. Socialization can help with the job requirements–employee characteristics match by helping to fill in gaps.

Training and Career Planning and Development

After an employee is selected, it is important that he or she undergo training and long-term career planning and development.

■ TRAINING

■ **Training** provides the opportunity to acquire and improve job-related skills.

Training is a set of activities that provides the opportunity to acquire and improve job-related skills.[12] In addition to initial training, training to improve skills is important and might cover such areas as: computer skills, diversity, sexual harassment, and implementation of new systems or technology.

Training can be on the job, off the job, or both. *On-the-job training* (OJT) involves job instruction while performing the job in the actual workplace. Internships, apprenticeships, and job rotation are common forms of OJT. Internships are an opportunity for students to gain real-world experience. They are often offered in the summer and may or may not be paid. *Apprenticeships* involve learning a trade from an experienced worker. They are quite common in Europe and relatively uncommon in the United States.

Related coaching or mentoring programs for managerial and professional jobs are quite common in the United States, however. *Job rotation* provides a broad range of experience in different kinds of jobs in a firm. It is often used as part of management training programs where future managers may spend from a few weeks to much longer in activities such as information processing, computer software, or computer sales. The total program could last up to one or two years, with varying amounts of mentoring.

Off-the-job training commonly involves lectures, videos, and simulations. Lectures convey specific information and work well for problem-solving and technical skills. Videos are particularly good for demonstrating various skills. Simulations, such as experiential exercises, business games, and various computer-based exercises, are particularly useful for teaching interpersonal, leadership, strategic management, and other complex skills such as those required of police officers.

A Canadian airline used a comprehensive combination of on- and off-the-job training to deal with the impact of five mergers and to cope with an extremely dynamic environment. The training was done worldwide and was conducted in combination with American Airlines. Numerous Canadian/U.S. cultural differences had to be worked through in the process.[13]

■ CAREER PLANNING AND DEVELOPMENT

In addition to employee training for short-term jobs, both the employee and the organization need to be concerned about longer term **career planning and development**, whereby individuals work with their managers and/or HR experts on career issues.[14]

Figure 7.1 offers a basic framework for formal career planning. The five steps in the framework begin with personal assessment and then progress through analysis of opportunities, selection of career objectives, and implementation of strategies, until the final step: evaluation of results. The process is recycled as necessary to allow for constructive revision of the career plan over time. Success in each of these steps entails a good deal of self-awareness and frank assessment. Thus, a successful career begins with sufficient insight to make good decisions about matching personal needs and capabilities with job opportunities over time. The manager's responsibility concerning career planning is twofold: First, planning and managing a personal career; second, assisting subordinates in assuming responsibility for their career planning and development.

Thoughts about careers take on a special relevance in the new workplace. We live and work in a time when the implications of constant change pressure us to continually review and reassess our career progress. Businesses are becoming smaller, employing fewer people, and moving beyond traditional organizational forms. Thus, there is increasing emphasis on horizontal and cross-functional relationships. Technical workers are becoming so important that they are being

■ **Career planning and development** means working with managers and/or HR experts on career issues.

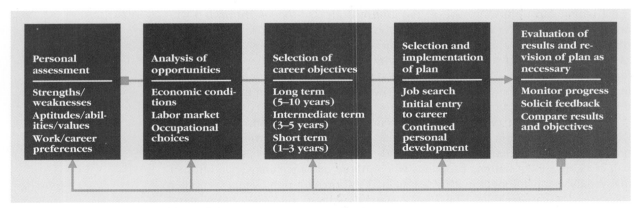

Figure 7.1
Five steps in formal career planning.

Chronic labor shortages in certain fields such as finance and computers are leading some bosses to offer CEO-style perks to recruit rank-and-file employees. Thus, employees of such firms as S.C. Johnson Wax and Ernst & Young can get free BMW leases, an errand-runner to walk their dog, and other such goodies.

treated almost like high-level managers in terms of perquisites and rewards. The nature of "work" is changing and will be less bound by "9 to 5" traditions. Continuous learning will be required, and training and electronic education marketplaces will become more and more important.

In this setting, the old notions of a career based within a single organization that takes responsibility for a person's career development are becoming increasingly obsolete. In his book, *The Age of Unreason*, British scholar and consultant Charles Handy argues forcefully that each of us must take charge of our own careers and prepare for inevitable uncertainties and changes by building a "portfolio" of skills.[15] This portfolio needs continuous development; each new job assignment must be well selected and rigorously pursued as a learning opportunity.

Initial Entry to a Career   The full implications of the new workplace become apparent at the point of initial entry to a career. Choosing a job and a work organization are difficult decisions; our jobs inevitably exert a lot of influence over our lives. Whenever a job change is considered, the best advice is to know yourself and to learn as much as possible about the new job and the organization. This helps to ensure the best person–job–organization match. By working hard to examine personal needs, goals, and capabilities and to gather relevant information, share viewpoints, and otherwise make the recruitment process as realistic as possible, you can help start a new job on the best possible note.

When considering a new job or a possible job change, a "balance sheet" analysis of possible "gains" and "losses" is important. Ask at least two questions. First, What are my potential gains and losses? Things to consider in answering this question include salary and fringe benefits, work hours and schedules, travel requirements, use and development of skills and competencies, and opportunities for challenging new job assignments. Second, What are the potential gains and losses for significant others? Here, you should consider income available to meet family responsibilities, time available to be with family and friends, implications of a geographical move on family and friends, and implications of work stress on nonwork life.

Adult Life Cycle and Career Stages   Chapter 4 showed that as people mature they pass through an adult life cycle with many different problems and prospects.

As a manager, it is especially important to recognize the effects of this cycle on the people with whom you work. Recall that the earlier-mentioned life cycle stages popularized by Gail Sheehy were: provisional adulthood (ages 18-30), first adulthood (ages 30-45) and second adulthood (ages 45-85+).[16] These are only approximate ages, and there are transitional periods in moving from one stage to the next.

Given the age of change in which we live, the stages and transitions are also much less predictable than in earlier years. Where once a person had one or two careers and a single spouse, now there also can be numerous careers and either no spouse or more than one spouse. In the provisional adult period, people may move back with their parents, stretch out their education, and try many jobs, for example. And where once people retired at age 65, now it is becoming increasingly common to start yet another career at that age.

It is useful to link the adult life cycle literature and the **career stages** literature. For those who still follow a traditional career path, we can think of it in terms of: entry and establishment—roughly comparable to the provisional adulthood stage; advancement—the first adulthood stage; and maintenance, withdrawal, and retirement—the second adulthood stage.

Entry and establishment involve on-the-job development of relevant skills and abilities. Individuals also undergo organizational and professional socialization mentioned earlier. At the same time, progressive organizations engage actively in mentoring new employees.

In the advancement stage, the individual seeks growth and increased responsibility. There may be advancement through internal career paths or external career paths, outside the organization.

During the maintenance, withdrawal and retirement stage of second adulthood individuals may experience continued growth of accomplishments or may encounter career stability. Many people encounter a **career plateau**—they find themselves in a position where they are unlikely to advance to a higher level of responsibility.

At some point during the maintenance career stage, individuals consider withdrawal and ultimate retirement. Now, some prolong this stage well into the second adulthood life cycle stage. Others, start planning for an orderly retirement at age 65 or so.

Of course, as we have said, the traditional route above is no longer typical. People may very well have many jobs and more than one career and choose not to retire until they can no longer work. All of these changes reinforce the difficulty of managers building and maintaining commitment to the job and organization and provide many OB challenges.

Performance Appraisal

Yet another key HR management function, performance appraisal, helps both the manager and subordinate maintain the organization–job–employee characteristics match. Formally defined, **performance appraisal** is a process of systematically evaluating performance and providing feedback on which performance adjustments can be made.[17] If the desired level of performance exceeds actual levels, a performance variance requiring special attention exists. For example, if you have a sales quota of 20 CD-ROM drives per month—the desired performance—and you sell only two CD-ROM drives per month—your actual

Training Resources ←

www.alx.org

America's Learning eXchange

One of the family of services in America's Career Kit.

America's Job Bank   America's Talent Bank   America's Career InfoNet

America's Learning eXchange (ALX) is a brand-new global electronic training and education marketplace on the World Wide Web. It is designed to provide one-stop electronic instructional service for employers, training providers, employees, and all those interested in life-long learning.

■ **Career stages** are different points of work responsibility and achievement through which people pass during the course of their work lives.

■ A **career plateau** is a position from which someone is unlikely to move to advance to a higher level of responsibility.

■ A **performance appraisal** is a process of systematically evaluating performance and providing feedback on which performance adjustments can be made.

performance—your performance variance of 18 CD-ROMs will require the attention of the sales manager. The performance appraisal process should be based on the job analysis mentioned earlier. The job description, describing organizational job requirements, and the job specification, describing individual worker characteristics, provide the core.

■ PURPOSES OF PERFORMANCE APPRAISAL

Any performance appraisal system is central to an organization's human-resource management activities. Performance appraisals are intended to:

Purposes of performance appraisal

- Define the specific job criteria against which performance will be measured.
- Measure past job performance accurately.
- Justify the rewards given to individuals and/or groups, thereby discriminating between high and low performance.
- Define the development experiences the ratee needs to enhance performance in the current job and to prepare for future responsibilities.

These four functions describe two general purposes served by good performance appraisal systems: evaluation, and feedback and development. From an evaluative perspective, performance appraisal lets people know where they stand relative to objectives and standards. As such, the performance appraisal is an input to decisions that allocate rewards and otherwise administer the organization's personnel functions. From a counseling perspective, performance appraisal facilitates implementing decisions relating to planning for and gaining commitment to the continued training and personal development of subordinates.

Evaluative Decisions　Evaluative decisions are concerned with such issues as promotions, transfers, terminations, and salary increases. When these decisions are made on the basis of performance criteria, as opposed to some other basis, such as seniority, a performance appraisal system is necessary.

Performance appraisal information is also useful for making selection and placement decisions. In this case, performance results are matched against individual characteristics to determine which of these characteristics are most closely related to performance. For example, management checks various individual characteristics, such as education, mathematical ability, verbal ability, mechanical ability, and achievement motivation, to see how closely they are related to performance.

Individuals who score well on those characteristics found to be closely tied to performance for a given job are considered for that position. In addition, if specific aspects of a ratee's performance are found to be inadequate, the performance appraisal process may lead to remedial training. Finally, appraisals form the basis of any performance-contingent reward system (i.e., any system that ties rewards, such as pay, to an individual's or group's performance).

Feedback and Development Decisions　Performance appraisals also can be used to let ratees know where they stand in terms of the organization's expectations and performance objectives. Performance appraisal feedback should involve a detailed discussion of the ratee's job-related strengths and weaknesses. This feedback can then be used for developmental purposes. In terms of the expectancy motivation approach discussed in Chapter 6, feedback can help clarify the ratees' sense of both instrumentality—it can help them better understand what kinds of rewards they will receive if they perform well—and expectancy—it lets them know what actions they need to take to reach that level of performance. Performance appraisal feedback also can be used as a basis for individual coaching or training by the manager to help a subordinate overcome performance deficiencies. Surveys typically indicate that around two-thirds of the sampled firms use performance appraisals for developmental purposes.

■ WHO DOES THE PERFORMANCE APPRAISAL?

Performance appraisals traditionally have been conducted by an individual's immediate superior,[18] the presumption being that since the immediate superior is responsible for the subordinate's performance, the superior should do the appraisal. In many cases, however, others may be able to better perform at least some aspects of the appraisal. For example, peers are closest to the action, and their appraisals can be especially valuable when they are obtained from several peers. Immediate subordinates also can provide insightful evaluations, as long as the ratings remain anonymous.

TECHNOLOGY 💻

www.compstar.com

CompStar Appraiser Plus is a PC program designed to provide assistance to everyone involved in the performance appraisal process: employees, administrators, department heads, and supervisors. The program uses an employee database that includes such information as salary data, EEO job category, current, last, and next appraisal dates, and the like. The evaluator selects a name from the database and then clicks on: job behaviors, goals, development plans, evaluation summary, and related areas. The program provides rating scales along with space for comments. It also includes a performance log so that the reviewer can browse through them at any time. Tight security is maintained.

To obtain as much appraisal information as possible, as many as one quarter of U.S. organizations are now using not only the evaluations of bosses, peers, and subordinates, but also self-ratings, customer ratings, and others with whom the ratee deals outside the immediate work unit. Such a comprehensive approach is called **360-degree evaluation**. The number of appraisals typically ranges from 5 to 10 per person under evaluation. Firms such as Alcoa and UPS now use 360-degree evaluations. They are made to order for the new, flatter, team-oriented organizations emphasizing total quality or high performance management, whereby input from many sources is crucial. Computer technology can now facilitate the collection and analysis of some or all of these 360-degree evaluations.[19]

One example involves the use of self- and superior ratings in an innovative way. The subordinate rates himself or herself on the importance of a given job function to the subordinate's performance and on how well the subordinate thinks he or she is performing the function. The supervisor performs a similar evaluation of the employee. A computer program then highlights those areas on

■ **360-degree evaluation** is a comprehensive approach that uses self-ratings, customer ratings, and others outside the work unit.

which there is the most disagreement. Only the associate gets the printout and may choose to discuss these areas with the supervisor. Both the timing and the specific content of such a meeting are at the discretion of the subordinate.[20]

■ DIMENSIONS AND STANDARDS OF PERFORMANCE APPRAISAL

In addition to performance outcomes, the behaviors or activities that result in these outcomes are frequently important to performance appraisal as well.

Output Measures   A number of production and sales jobs provide ready measures of *work output.* For example, a final-stage assembler may have a goal of 15 completed computer monitors per hour. The number of monitors is easily measurable, and the organization can set standards concerning how many computer monitors should be completed per hour. Here, the performance dimension of interest is a quantitative one: 15 completed computer monitors per hour. However, the organization also may introduce a *quality* dimension. The individual may be evaluated in terms not only of the number of monitors per hour but also the number of units that pass a *quality control inspection* per hour. Now, both quantity and quality are important, and the individual cannot trade one for the other. Assembling 20 monitors per hour will not do if only 10 pass inspection, nor will having a larger proportion of monitors pass inspection if only 10 monitors are assembled per hour.

In addition, management may be interested in other performance dimensions, such as downtime of the equipment used for assembling. In this case, the assembler would be evaluated in terms of quantity and quality of assembly output and equipment downtime. Management could thereby not only ensure that a desirable product is being assembled at a desirable rate but that the employee is careful with the equipment as well.

Activity Measures   In the preceding example, the output measures were straightforward, as was the measure of equipment downtime. Often, however, output measures may be a function of group efforts; or they may be extremely difficult to measure; or they may take so long to accomplish that they can't be readily determined for a given individual during a given time period. For example, it may be very difficult to determine the output of a research scientist attempting to advance new knowledge. In such a case, activity or behavioral measures may be called for, rather than output measures. The research scientist may be appraised in terms of his or her approach to problems, his or her interactions with other scientists, and the like.

Activity measures are typically obtained from the evaluator's observation and rating. In contrast, output measures are often obtained directly from written records or documents, such as production records. The difficulty of obtaining output measures may be one reason for using activity measures. Activity measures are also typically more useful for employee feedback and development than are output measures alone. For example, a salesperson may sell 20 insurance policies a month when the quota is 25. However, activities such as number of sales calls per day or number of community volunteer events attended per week (where some potential clients are likely to be found) can provide more specific information than simply the percentage of monthly quota output measures. Where jobs lend themselves to systematic analysis, important activities can be inferred from the job analysis.

■ PERFORMANCE APPRAISAL METHODS

Performance appraisal methods can be divided into two general categories: comparative methods and absolute methods.[21]

Comparative methods of performance appraisal seek to identify one's relative standing among those being rated; that is, comparative methods can establish that Bill is better than Mary, who is better than Leslie, who is better than Tom on a performance dimension. Comparative methods can indicate that one person is better than another on a given dimension, but not *how much better*. These methods also fail to indicate whether the person receiving the better rating is "good enough" in an absolute sense. It may well be that Bill is merely the best of a bad lot. Three comparative performance appraisal methods are (1) ranking, (2) paired comparison, and (3) forced distribution.

In contrast, absolute methods of performance appraisal specify precise measurement standards. For example, tardiness might be evaluated on a scale ranging from "never tardy" to "always tardy." Four of the more common absolute rating procedures are (1) graphic rating scales, (2) critical incident diary, (3) behaviorally anchored rating scales, and (4) management by objectives. The comparative methods are less likely than absolute measures to be used in more collectivist-oriented cultures because of their emphasis on the collectivity.

Ranking   **Ranking** is the simplest of all the comparative techniques. It consists of merely rank ordering each individual from best to worst on each performance dimension being considered. For example, in evaluating work quality, I compare Smith, Jones, and Brown. I then rank Brown number 1, Smith number 2, and Jones number 3. The ranking method, though relatively simple to use, can become burdensome when there are many people to consider.

■ **Ranking** is a comparative technique of performance appraisal that involves rank ordering of each individual from best to worst on each performance dimension.

Paired Comparison   In a **paired comparison** method, each person is directly compared with every other person being rated. The frequency of endorsement across all pairs determines one's final ranking. Every possible paired comparison within a group of ratees is considered, as shown below (italics indicate the person rated better in each pair):

■ **Paired comparison** is a comparative method of performance appraisal whereby each person is directly compared with every other person.

Bill vs. Mary	*Mary* vs. Leslie	*Leslie* vs. Tom
Bill vs. Leslie	*Mary* vs. Tom	
Bill vs. Tom		

Number of times Bill is better	=	3
Number of times Mary is better	=	2
Number of times Leslie is better	=	1
Number of times Tom is better	=	0

The best performer in this example is Bill, followed by Mary, then Leslie, and, last of all, Tom. When there are many people to compare, the paired comparison approach can be even more tedious than the ranking method.

■ **Forced distribution** is a method of performance appraisal that uses a small number of performance categories, such as "very good," "good," "adequate," and "very poor" and forces a certain proportion of people into each.

Forced Distribution   **Forced distribution** uses a small number of performance categories, such as "very good," "good," "adequate," "poor," and "very poor." Each rater is instructed to rate a specific proportion of employees in each of these categories. For example, 10 percent of employees must be rated very good; 20 percent must be rated good, and so on. This method *forces* the rater to use all of the categories and to avoid rating everyone as outstanding, poor, average, or the like. It can be a problem if most of the people are truly superior performers or if most of the people perform about the same.

Graphic Rating Scales   **Graphic rating scales** list a variety of dimensions that are thought to be related to high performance outcomes in a given job and that the individual is accordingly expected to exhibit, such as cooperation, initiative, and attendance. The scales allow the manager to assign the individual scores on each dimension. An example is shown in Figure 7.2. These ratings are sometimes given point values and combined into numerical ratings of performance.

The primary appeal of graphic rating scales is their ease of use. In addition, they are efficient in the use of time and other resources, and they can be applied to a wide range of jobs. Unfortunately, because of generality, they may not be linked to job analysis or to other specific aspects of a given job. This difficulty can be dealt with by ensuring that only relevant dimensions of work based on sound job analysis procedures are rated. However, there is a tradeoff: the more the scales are linked to job analyses, the less general they are when comparing people on different jobs.

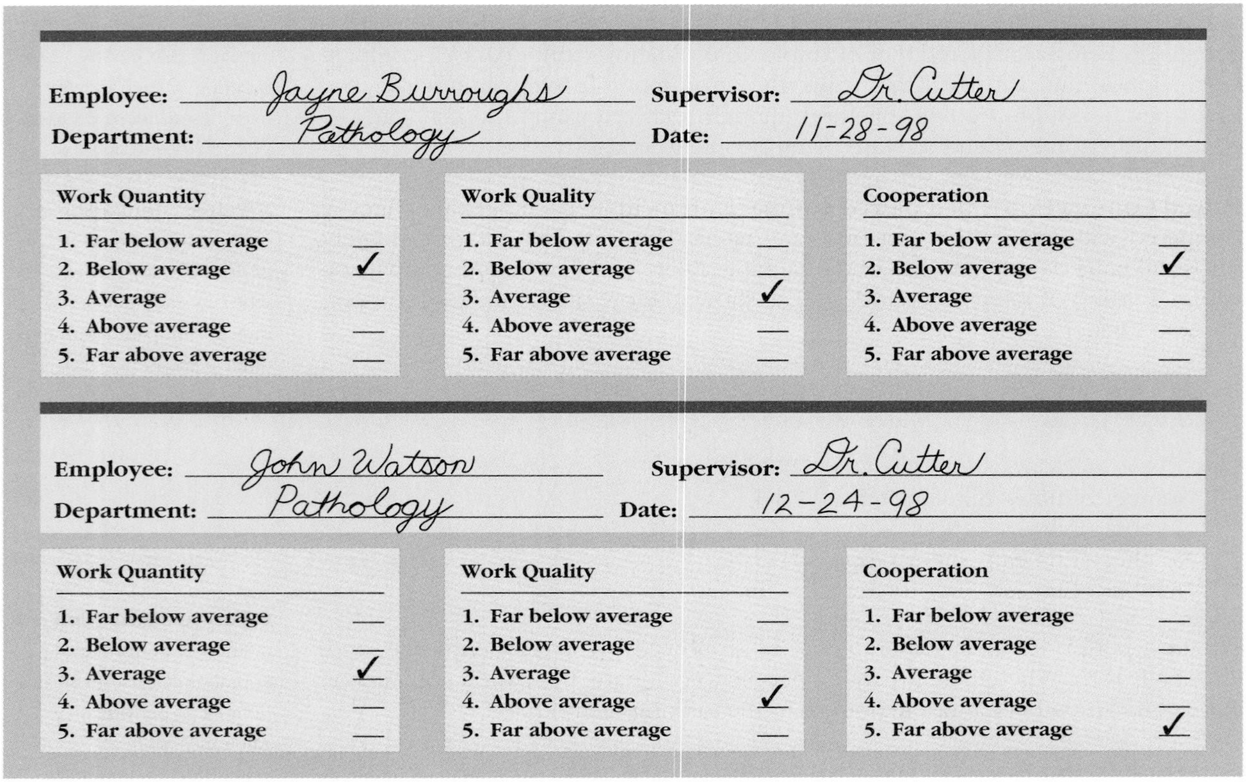

■ A **graphic rating scales** is a scale that lists a variety of dimensions thought to be related to high performance outcomes in a given job and that the individual is expected to exhibit.

| Employee: *Jayne Burroughs* | Supervisor: *Dr. Cutter* |
| Department: *Pathology* | Date: *11-28-98* |

Work Quantity		Work Quality		Cooperation	
1. Far below average	—	1. Far below average	—	1. Far below average	—
2. Below average	✓	2. Below average	—	2. Below average	✓
3. Average	—	3. Average	✓	3. Average	—
4. Above average	—	4. Above average	—	4. Above average	—
5. Far above average	—	5. Far above average	—	5. Far above average	—

| Employee: *John Watson* | Supervisor: *Dr. Cutter* |
| Department: *Pathology* | Date: *12-24-98* |

Work Quantity		Work Quality		Cooperation	
1. Far below average	—	1. Far below average	—	1. Far below average	—
2. Below average	—	2. Below average	—	2. Below average	—
3. Average	✓	3. Average	—	3. Average	—
4. Above average	—	4. Above average	✓	4. Above average	—
5. Far above average	—	5. Far above average	—	5. Far above average	✓

Figure 7.2
Sixth-month performance reviews for Burroughs and Watson.

Critical Incident Diary Supervisors may use **critical incident diaries** to record incidents of each subordinate's behavior that led to either unusual success or failure in a given performance aspect. These incidents are typically recorded in a diary-type log that is kept daily or weekly under predesignated dimensions. In a sales job, for example, following up sales calls and communicating necessary customer information might be two of the dimensions recorded in a critical incident diary. Descriptive paragraphs can then be used to summarize each salesperson's performance for each dimension as it is observed.

This approach is excellent for employee development and feedback. Since the method consists of qualitative statements rather than quantitative information, however, it is difficult to use for evaluative decisions. To provide for such information, the critical incident technique is sometimes combined with one of the other methods.

■ A **critical incident diary** is a method of performance appraisal that records incidents of unusual success or failure in a given performance aspect.

Behaviorally Anchored Rating Scales The **behaviorally anchored rating scales** (BARS) is a performance appraisal approach that has received increasing attention. The procedure for developing this type of scale starts with the careful collection of descriptions of observable job behaviors. These descriptions are typically provided by managers and personnel specialists and include both superior and inferior performance. Once a large sample of behavioral descriptions is collected, each behavior is evaluated to determine the extent to which it describes good versus bad performance. The final step is to develop a rating scale in which the anchors are specific critical behaviors, each reflecting a different degree of performance effectiveness. An example of a BARS is shown in Figure 7.3 for a retail department manager. Note the specificity of the behaviors and the scale values for each. Similar behaviorally anchored scales would be developed for other dimensions of the job.

As you can see, the BARS approach is detailed and complex. It requires lots of time and effort to develop. But the BARS also provides specific behaviors that are useful for counseling and feedback, combined with quantitative scales that are useful for evaluative comparative purposes. Initial results of the use of BARS suggested that they were less susceptible to common rating errors than were more traditional scales. More recent evidence suggests that the scales may not be as superior as originally thought, especially if an equivalent amount of developmental effort is put into other types of measures.[22] A somewhat simpler variation of behaviorally anchored scales is the *Behavioral Observation Scale* (BOS), which uses a five-point frequency scale (ranging from almost always to almost never) for each separate statement of behavior.

■ A **behaviorally anchored rating scale (BARS)** is a performance appraisal approach that describes observable job behaviors, each of which is evaluated to determine good versus bad performance.

Management by Objectives Of all the appraisal methods available, **management by objectives (MBO)** is linked most directly to means–ends chains and goal setting, as discussed in Chapter 8.[23] When an MBO system is used, subordinates work with their supervisor to establish specific task-related objectives that fall within their domains and serve as means to help accomplish the supervisor's higher level objectives. Each set of objectives is worked out between a supervisor and a subordinate for a given time period. The establishment of objectives is similar to a job analysis, except that it is directed toward a particular individual in his or her job rather than toward a particular job type alone. The increased discretion of the MBO approach means that each specific person is likely to have

■ **Management by objectives (MBO)** is a process of joint goal setting between a supervisor and a subordinate.

Figure 7.3
Example of a behaviorally anchored rating scale dimension.

Supervising Sales Personnel

Gives sales personnel a clear idea of their job duties and responsibilities; exercises tact and consideration in working with subordinates; handles work scheduling efficiently and equitably; supplements formal training with his or her own "coaching"; keeps informed of what the salespeople are doing on the job; and follows company policy in agreements with subordinates.

Effective 9 Could be expected to conduct full day's sales clinic with two new sales personnel and thereby develop them into top salespeople in the department.

8 Could be expected to give his or her sales personnel confidence and strong sense of responsibility by delegating many important tasks.

7 Could be expected never to fail to conduct weekly training meetings with his or her people at a scheduled hour and to convey to them exactly what is expected.

6 Could be expected to exhibit courtesy and respect toward his or her sales personnel.

5 Could be expected to remind sales personnel to wait on customers instead of conversing with one another.

4 Could be expected to be rather critical of store standards in front of his or her own people, thereby risking their development of poor attitudes.

3 Could be expected to tell an individual to come in anyway even though he or she called in to say he or she was ill.

2 Could be expected to go back on a promise to an individual who he or she had told could transfer back into previous department if he or she did not like the new one.

Ineffective 1 Could be expected to make promises to an individual about his or her salary being based on department sales even when he or she knew such a practice was against company policy.

a custom-tailored set of work goals while still working within the action context of organizational means–ends chains.

MBO is the most individualized of all the appraisal systems and tends to work well for counseling if the objectives go beyond simply desired outputs and focus on important activities as well. In comparing one employee with another, a key concern is the ease or difficulty of achieving the goals. If one person has an easier set of objectives to meet than another, then comparisons are unfair. Since MBO tends to rely less heavily on ratings than do other appraisal systems, rating errors are less likely to be a problem.

■ MEASUREMENT ERRORS IN PERFORMANCE APPRAISAL

To be meaningful, an appraisal system must be both *reliable*—provide consistent results each time it is used—and *valid*—actually measure people on relevant job content. A number of measurement errors can threaten the reliability or validity of performance appraisals.[24] Note the strong tie between these errors and Chapter 5, covering perception and attribution.

Halo Errors   A **halo error** results when one person rates another person on several different dimensions and gives a similar rating for each dimension. For example, a sales representative considered to be a "go-getter" and thus rated high on "dynamism" also would be rated high on dependability, tact, and whatever other performance dimensions were used. The rater fails to discriminate between the person's strong and weak points; a "halo" carries over from one dimension to the next. This effect can create a problem when each performance dimension is considered an important and relatively independent aspect of the job. A variation is the *single criterion error*, in which only one of several important performance aspects is considered at all.

Leniency/Strictness Errors   Just as some professors are known as "easy A's," some managers tend to give relatively high ratings to virtually everyone under their supervision. This is known as a **leniency error**. Sometimes the opposite occurs; some raters tend to give everyone a low rating. This is called a **strictness error**. The problem in both instances is the inadequate discrimination between good and poor performers. Leniency is likely to be a problem when peers assess one another, especially if they are asked to provide feedback to each other, because it is easier to discuss high ratings than low ones.

Central Tendency Errors   **Central tendency errors** occur when managers lump everyone together around the "average," or middle, category. This tendency gives the impression that there are no very good or very poor performers on the dimensions being rated. No true performance discrimination is made. Both leniency and central tendency errors are examples of raters who exhibit **low differentiation errors**. These raters simply restrict themselves to only a small part of the rating scale.

Recency Errors   A different kind of error, known as a **recency error**, occurs when a rater allows recent events to influence a performance rating over earlier events. Take, for example, the case of an employee who is usually on time but shows up one hour late for work the day before his or her performance rating. The employee is rated low on "promptness" because the one incident of tardiness overshadows his or her usual promptness.

Personal Bias Errors   Raters sometimes allow specific biases to enter into performance evaluations. When this happens, **personal bias errors** occur. For example, a rater may intentionally give higher ratings to white employees than to nonwhite employees. In this case, the performance appraisal reflects a racial bias. Bias toward members of other demographic categories, such as age, gender, and disability, also can occur, based on stereotypes the rater may have. Such bias appears to have been widespread at Monarch Paper Company, when a former vice president was demoted to a warehouse-maintenance job for not accepting an early retirement offer. A federal jury judged the firm guilty of age bias.[25] This example shows that raters must reflect carefully on their personal biases and guard against their interference with performance-based ratings of subordinates.

■ **Halo error** results when one person rates another person on several different dimensions and gives a similar rating for each one.

■ **Leniency error** is the tendency to give relatively high ratings to virtually everyone.

■ **Strictness error** occurs when a rater tends to give everyone a low rating.

■ **Central tendency error** occurs when managers lump everyone together around the average, or middle, category.

■ **Low differentiation error** occurs when raters restrict themselves to a small part of the rating scale.

■ **Recency error** is a biased rating that develops by allowing the individual's most recent behavior to speak for his or her overall performance on a particular dimension.

■ **Personal bias error** occurs when a rater allows specific biases, such as racial, age, or gender, to enter into performance appraisal.

■ IMPROVING PERFORMANCE APPRAISALS

As is true of most other issues in organizational behavior, managers must recognize certain tradeoffs in setting up and implementing any performance appraisal system. In addition to the pros and cons already mentioned for each method, some specific issues to keep in mind in order to reduce errors and improve appraisals include the following:[26]

Steps to improve performance appraisals

1. Train raters so that they understand the evaluation process rationale and can recognize the sources of measurement error.
2. Make sure that raters observe ratees on an ongoing, regular basis and that they do not try to limit all their evaluations to the formally designated evaluation period, for instance, every six months or every year.
3. Do not have the rater rate too many ratees. The ability to identify performance differences drops, and fatigue sets in when the evaluation of large numbers of people is involved.
4. Make sure that the performance dimensions and standards are stated clearly and that the standards are as noncontaminating and nondeficient as possible.
5. Avoid terms such as *average* because different evaluators tend to react differently to the terms.

Remember that appraisal systems cannot be used to discriminate against employees on the basis of age, gender, race, ethnicity, and so on. To help provide a legally defensible system in terms of governing legislation, the following recommendations are useful:[27]

Legal foundations of performance appraisals

- Appraisal must be based on an analysis of job requirements as reflected in performance standards.
- Appraisal is appropriate only where performance standards are clearly understood by employees.
- Clearly defined individual dimensions should be used rather than global measures.
- Dimensions should be behaviorally based and supported by observable evidence.
- If rating scales are used, abstract trait names, such as "loyalty," should be avoided unless they can be defined in terms of observable behaviors.
- Rating scale anchors should be brief and logically consistent.
- The system must be validated and psychometrically sound, as must the ratings given by individual evaluators.
- An appeal mechanism must be in place in the event the evaluator and the ratee disagree.

Technological advances now provide various PC programs designed to facilitate the rating process. Specifically, these allow for easier and more comprehensive scale construction, faster feedback, and the additional flexibility called for in today's new workplace.[28]

■ GROUP EVALUATION

As indicated earlier, the growing trend is toward group or team performance evaluations. Such an evaluation is consistent with self-managed teams and high performance organizations. Frequently, this emphasis is accompanied by a group-based compensation system such as discussed later in this chapter. Traditional individually oriented appraisal systems are no longer appropriate and need to be replaced with group systems such as suggested in The Effective Manager 7.2.

Rewards and Reward Systems

In addition to staffing, training, career planning and development, and performance appraisal, another key aspect of HR management is the design and implementation of reward systems. These reward systems emphasize a mix of extrinsic and intrinsic rewards. As we noted in Chapter 6, *extrinsic rewards* are positively valued work outcomes that are given to an individual or group by some other person or source in the work setting. In contrast, *intrinsic rewards* are positively valued work outcomes that the individual receives directly as a result of task performance; they do not require the participation of another person or source. A feeling of achievement after accomplishing a particularly challenging task is an example of an intrinsic reward. Managing intrinsic work rewards presents the additional challenge of designing a work setting so that employees can, in effect, reward themselves for a job well done. That is the topic of Chapter 8. In the remainder of this chapter, we emphasize the management of pay as an extrinsic reward.

■ PAY AS AN EXTRINSIC REWARD

Pay is an especially complex extrinsic reward. It can help organizations attract and retain highly capable workers, and it can help satisfy and motivate these workers to work hard to achieve high performance. But if there is dissatisfaction with the salary, pay can also lead to strikes, grievances, absenteeism, turnover, and sometimes even poor physical and mental health.

Edward Lawler, a management expert, has contributed greatly to our understanding of pay as an extrinsic reward. His research generally concludes that, for pay to serve as a source of work motivation, high levels of job performance must be viewed as the path through which high pay can be achieved.[29] **Merit pay** is defined as a compensation system that bases an individual's salary or wage increase on a measure of the person's performance accomplishments during a specified time period. That is, merit pay is an attempt to make pay contingent upon performance.

THE EFFECTIVE MANAGER 7.2

SUGGESTIONS FOR A GROUP PERFORMANCE EVALUATION SYSTEM

- Link the team's results to organizational goals.
- Start with the team's customers and the team work process needed to satisfy those needs:
  Customer requirements.
  Delivery and quality.
  Waste and cycle time.
- Evaluate team and each individual member's performance.
- Train the team to develop its own measures.

■ **Merit pay** is a compensation system that bases an individual's salary or wage increase on a measure of the person's performance accomplishments during a specific time period.

Although research supports the logic and theoretical benefits of merit pay, it also indicates that the implementation of merit pay plans is not as universal or as easy as we might expect. In fact, surveys over the past 30 years have found that as many as 80 percent of respondents felt that they were not rewarded for a job well done.[30] An effective merit pay system is one approach to dealing with this problem.

To work well, a merit pay plan should be based on realistic and accurate measures of individual work performance and create a belief among employees that the way to achieve high pay is to perform at high levels. In addition, merit pay should clearly discriminate between high and low performers in the amount of pay reward received. Finally, managers should avoid confusing "merit" aspects of a pay increase with "cost-of-living" adjustments.

■ CREATIVE PAY PRACTICES

Merit pay plans are just one attempt to enhance the positive value of pay as a work reward. But some argue that merit pay plans are not consistent with the demands of today's organizations, for they fail to recognize the high degree of task interdependence among employees, as illustrated particularly in high performance management organizations. Also, as we argued earlier, HR management strategies should be consistent with overall organization strategies. For example, the pay system of a firm with an emphasis on highly skilled individuals in short supply should emphasize employee retention rather than performance.[31]

With these points in mind, let us examine a variety of creative pay practices. These practices are becoming more common in organizations with increasingly diverse workforces and increased emphasis on TQM or similar setups.[32] They include skill-based pay, gain-sharing plans, profit-sharing plans, employee stock ownership plans, lump-sum pay increases, and flexible benefit plans.

■ **Skill-based pay** is a system that rewards people for acquiring and developing job-relevant skills in number and variety relevant to the organization's need.

Skill-Based Pay   **Skill-based pay** rewards people for acquiring and developing job-relevant skills. Pay systems of this sort pay people for the mix and depth of skills they possess, not for the particular job assignment they hold. An example is the cross-functional team approach at Monsanto-Benevia where each team member has developed quality, safety, administrator, maintenance coaching, and team leader skills. In most cases, these skills involve high-tech, automated equipment. Workers are paid for this "breadth" of capability and their willingness to use any of the skills needed by the company.

Skill-based pay is one of the fastest growing pay innovations in the United States. Among the better known firms using this plan is Polaroid.[33] Besides flexibility, some advantages of skill-based pay are employee cross-training—workers learn to do one another's job; fewer supervisors—workers can provide more of these functions themselves; and more individual control over compensation—workers know in advance what is required to receive a pay raise. One disadvantage is possible higher pay and training costs that are not offset by greater productivity. Another is that of deciding on appropriate monetary values for each skill.[34]

Gain-Sharing Plans   Cash bonuses, or extra pay for performance above standards or expectations, have been common practice in the compensation of managers and executives for a long time. Top managers in some industries earn annual bonuses of 50 percent or more of their base salaries. Attempts to extend such opportunities to all employees are growing in number and importance today. One popular plan is **gain sharing**, which links pay and performance by giving workers the opportunity to share in productivity gains through enhanced earnings.

The Scanlon Plan is probably the oldest and best known gain-sharing plan. Others you may have heard about are the Lincoln Electric Plan, the Rucker Plan™ or IMPROSHARE™. Gain-sharing plans possess some similarities to profit-sharing plans, but they are not the same. Typically, profit-sharing plans grant individuals or work groups a specified portion of any economic profits earned by an organization as a whole. Gain-sharing plans involve a specific measurement of productivity combined with a calculation of a bonus designed to offer workers a mutual share of any increase in total organizational productivity.

The intended benefits of gain-sharing plans include increased worker motivation because of the pay-for-performance incentives, and a greater sense of personal responsibility for making performance contributions to the organization. Because they can be highly participative in nature, gain-sharing plans also may encourage cooperation and teamwork in the workplace. Although more remains to be learned about gain sharing, the plans are receiving increasing attention from organizations.[35]

Profit-Sharing Plans   **Profit-sharing plans** possess some similarities to gain-sharing plans, but they are not identical. Profit-sharing plans reward employees based on the entire organization's performance. Unlike gain sharing, profit-sharing plans do not attempt to reward employees for productivity gains, and they reflect things, such as economic conditions, over which employees have no control. At the same time, gain-sharing plans generally use a "hard productivity" measure, while profit-sharing plans do not.

Profit sharing also tends to use a mechanistic formula for profit allocation and does not utilize employee participation. Most often, profit-sharing plans fund employee retirement and thus are considered benefits and not incentives.[36]

Employee Stock Ownership Plans (ESOPs)   Like profit sharing, **ESOPs** are based on the total organization's performance—but measured in terms of stock price. The stock may be given to employees, or employees may purchase it at a price below-market value. Organizations often use ESOPs as a low-cost retirement benefit for employees because they are nontaxable to the organization until the employees redeem the stock. Of course, like all stock investments, ESOPs involve risk.[37]

Lump-Sum Pay Increases   While most pay plans distribute increases as part of a regular pay check, an interesting alternative is the **lump-sum increase** program, by which individuals can elect to receive an increase in one or more lump-sum payments. The full increase may be taken at the beginning of the year and used for some valued purpose, for example, a down payment on a car or a sizable deposit in a savings account. Or a person may elect to take one-half of the raise early and get the rest at the start of the winter holiday season. In either case, the individual should be more motivated because of the larger doses or because it is attached to something highly valued.

A related, but more controversial, development in this area is the lump-sum payment, which differs from the lump-sum increase. The lump-sum payment is an attempt by employers to hold labor costs in line while still giving workers

■ **Gain sharing** is a pay system that links pay and performance by giving the workers the opportunity to share in productivity gains through increased earnings.

■ **Profit sharing plans** reward employees based on the entire organization's performance.

■ **ESOPs**, like profit sharing, are based on the total organization's performance—but measured in terms of stock price.

■ **Lump sum increases** is a pay system in which people elect to receive their wage or salary increase in one or more "lump-sum" payments.

more money, if corporate earnings allow. It involves giving workers a one-time lump-sum payment, often based on a gain-sharing formula, instead of a yearly percentage wage or salary increase. In this way, a person's base pay remains fixed, whereas overall monetary compensation varies according to the bonus added to this figure by the annual lump-sum payment. American labor unions typically are resistant to this approach since base pay does not increase and management determines the size of the bonus. However, survey's generally show that around two-thirds of the respondents have favorable reactions and think that the plans have a positive effect on performance.[38]

Flexible Benefit Plans   An employee's total compensation package includes not only direct pay but also any fringe benefits that are paid by the organization. These fringe benefits often add an equivalent of 10 to 40 percent to a person's salary. It is argued that organizations need to allow for individual differences when developing such benefit programs. Otherwise, the motivational value of this indirect form of pay incentive is lost. One approach is to let individuals choose their total pay package by selecting benefits, up to a certain dollar amount, from a range of options made available by the organization. These **flexible benefit plans** allow workers to select benefits according to needs. A single worker, for example, may prefer quite a different combination of insurance and retirement contributions than would a married person.[39]

■ **Flexible benefit plans** are pay systems that allow workers to select benefits according to their individual needs.

Chapter 7 Study Guide

Summary

What are the essentials of human resource strategy and practice?

■ HR planning is the process of providing capable and motivated people to carry out the organization's mission and strategy.

■ HR staffing involves job analysis, attracting individuals through recruitment, selecting those best qualified through screening and hiring, and socializing employees through initial orientation and followup over time.

What is training and career planning and development?

■ Training is a set of activities that provides the opportunity to acquire and improve job-related skills.

■ On-the-job training involves job instruction in the workplace and commonly utilizes internships, apprenticeships, and job rotation.

■ Off-the-job training takes place off the job and commonly involves lectures, videos, and simulations.

■ Career planning and development involves working with managers and HR experts on careers and involves the following: a five-stage planning framework; personal responsibilities for developing of a portfolio of skills to keep one marketable at any time; a balance sheet approach to evaluating each career opportunity; and recognition of the relationship between life and career stages and transitions.

What is performance appraisal?

■ Performance appraisal involves systematically evaluating performance and providing feedback on which performance adjustments can be made.

■ Performance appraisals serve the two general purposes of evaluation and feedback and development.

■ Performance appraisals traditionally are done by an individual's immediate superior but are moving toward 360-degree evaluations involving the full circle of contacts a person may have in job performance.

■ Performance appraisals use either or both output measures and activity measures.

■ Performance appraisal methods involve comparative methods and absolute methods.

■ There are at least half-a-dozen rater errors important in performance appraisal.

■ There are six steps that can be used to reduce errors and improve performance appraisals.

■ Group performance evaluation systems are being used increasingly.

What are rewards and reward systems?

- Rewards are another key aspect of HR management and involve the design and implementation of positively valued work outcomes.

- Reward systems emphasize a mix of extrinsic and intrinsic rewards.

How does one manage pay as an extrinsic reward?

- Pay as an extrinsic reward involves merit pay and creative pay practices.

- Creative pay practices include skill-based pay, gain-sharing plans, lump-sum pay increases, and flexible benefit plans.

How does one manage intrinsic rewards?

- Managing intrinsic rewards involves the challenge of designing a work setting so that employees can, in effect, reward themselves for a job well done.

Key Terms

Behaviorally anchored rating scale (BARS) (p. 140)
Career planning and development (p. 133)
Career plateau (p. 135)
Career stages (p. 135)
Central tendency error (p. 143)
Critical incident diary (p. 140)
ESOPs (p. 147)
Flexible benefit plans (p. 148)
Forced distribution (p. 140)

Gain sharing (p. 147)
Graphic rating scales (p. 140)
Halo error (p. 143)
Human resource strategic planning (p. 128)
Job analysis (p. 129)
Leniency error (p. 143)
Low differentiation error (p. 143)
Lump-sum increases (p. 147)
Management by objectives (MBO) (p. 141)
Merit pay (p. 145)

Paired comparison (p. 139)
Performance appraisal (p. 136)
Personal bias error (p. 143)
Profit sharing plans (p. 147)
Ranking (p. 139)
Recency error (p. 143)
Recruitment (p. 130)
Selection (p. 131)
Skill-based pay (p. 146)
Socialization (p. 132)
Strictness error (p. 143)
Training (p. 133)
360-degree evaluation (p. 137)

Self-Test 7

■ MULTIPLE CHOICE

1. HR staffing consists of all of the following except _____. (a) selection (b) socialization (c) recruitment (d) training

2. Job analysis is _____. (a) the same as job description (b) the same as job specification (c) involved with organizational tasks (d) the same as performance appraisal

3. Training _____. (a) is the same as socialization (b) is another name for career development (c) is a set of activities for improving job-related skills (d) precedes staffing

4. The notions of a career based within a single organization _____. (a) are truer than ever (b) are increasingly obsolete (c) were never really true (d) apply to some industries but not others

5. A career plateau is where _____. (a) a person is demoted (b) promotions decrease (c) promotions increase (d) promotions cease

6. Performance appraisal and job analysis are _____. (a) similar (b) unrelated (c) related such that the job analysis should be based on the performance appraisal (d) related such that the performance appraisal should be based on the job analysis

7. Performance appraisals have the two general purposes of _____. (a) rewards and punishments (b) evaluating and development decisions (c) rewards and evaluative decisions (d) feedback and job analysis decisions

8. Two kinds of awards are _____. (a) extrinsic and intrinsic (b) internal and external (c) strong and weak (d) higher level and lower level

9. Merit pay _____. (a) rewards people for increased job-related skills (b) is a form of gain sharing (c) is similar to a lump-sum pay increase (d) enhances the positive value of pay as a work reward

10. In a flexible benefit plan _____. (a) workers select benefits according to needs (b) there are high benefits early in a job and lower ones later (c) there are low benefits early in a job and higher ones later (d) rewards can be split between salary and nonsalary payouts

■ TRUE–FALSE

11. Staffing is narrower than recruitment.   T   F

12. Selection follows socialization.   T   F

13. Training can be on the job or off the job.   T   F

14. The career planning framework consists of five steps.   T   F

15. Adult transitions are linked to career stages.   T   F

16. Performance appraisals are best done by an immediate superior.   T   F

17. Performance appraisals can use output measures or activity measures.   T   F

18. Forced distribution is an absolute performance appraisal method.   T   F

19. Pay is an intrinsic reward.   T   F

20. Gain-sharing plans and profit-sharing plans are the same.   T   F

■ SHORT RESPONSE

21. Discuss the relationship between an organization's mission and HR strategic planning.

22. Discuss how training and career development relate to the organization–job requirements–individual characteristics match.

23. Discuss the linkage between adult and career stages and transitions.

24. Compare and contrast the evaluative and feedback and development aspects of performance appraisal.

■ APPLICATIONS ESSAY

25. Assume you belong to a student organization on campus. Making any necessary assumptions, discuss, in some detail, how the human-resource management concepts in this chapter could be applied at the local and/or national level of your student organization.

Explore application-oriented **Fast Company** articles, cases, experimental exercises, and self-assessments in the **OB Skills Workbook**

■ **Visit the Schermerhorn Web site to find the Interactive Self-Test and Internet exercises for this chapter.**

High Performance Job Designs

HOW TO BREW A GREAT WORKPLACE

www.peets.com

Workers at California-based Peet's Coffee and Tea take pride in being known as "Peetniks." There are over 1000 of them now employed by the company started over 30 years ago by Alfred Peet, a Dutch-born coffee roaster. Peet's has a large mail-order business, over 40 retail outlets, and more than $42 million in annual sales. Not bad for a company whose unique culture is built around the notion that having a paying job shouldn't be confused with having a career. Most Peetniks are what we might call hard-working and loyal part-timers. For the most part, they work to earn a living and pursue special talents in off-job time. Gina Hall is a cross-country mountain bike racer; Rich Avella is a guitarist with the group, Snowmen; Amie Bailey-Eismont is a *doula*, a Greek term describing someone who helps expectant parents; Kevin Brown is a pencil artist. Why work for Peet's? Bailey-Eismont says, "There's a mystique about it and the people who work here," adding, "The benefits sure don't hurt."

No doubt about it. The benefits are part of the key to Peet's low employee turnover rate in a high-turnover industry. The firm pays its workers relatively well and allows full benefits to those who work at least 21 hours a week. That includes medical/dental coverage, 401(k) plan, paid vacation and sick days, and more—even domestic partner benefits. Peetniks enjoy flexible hours, so that work can be scheduled around their "real" careers. And if Peet's is to your liking, the firm promotes from within. Says Avella: "I could probably find a profession that would pay me more money, but not one that would be as flexible or work as well with my lifestyle."

One has to wonder. Could Peet's formula for high performance be brewed in other workplaces?[1]

The same article that tells the story of Peet's also suggests that the kind of opportunities workers find in this organization are altogether too rare. This may be especially true with respect to part-time workers, but the implications extend as well into the work lives of full-time employees. Just talk to your family and friends. There are too many people still working today in jobs that do not provide substantial opportunities for personal growth, creative contribution, and job satisfaction. A student of ours, for example, passed along this comment that he had once heard: "Even the best day at work can never be as good as the worst day of golf."

This chapter on high performance job designs takes a more positive view. Our point is that jobs can and should be designed for both high performance and individual satisfaction. When a job is properly designed, when the tasks are clear, when the goals are challenging but attainable, and when the work schedules respect individual needs, both outcomes are possible. High performance and satisfaction can become the norms instead of exceptions to the rule. Simply put, good jobs facilitate performance, quality, and continuous improvement while also allowing for job satisfaction.

Study Questions

Chapter 8 introduces the essentials of job design, goal setting, and work scheduling as important strategies for developing high performance work settings. As you read the chapter, keep in mind these key questions.

- What are the alternative job design approaches?
- What are the keys to designing motivating jobs?
- How does technology influence job design?
- How can goal setting improve performance?
- What alternative work arrangements are used today?

Job Design Approaches

Job design is the planning and specification of job tasks and the work arrangements through which they are to be accomplished. Figure 8.1 shows how alternative job-design approaches differ in the way required tasks are defined and in the amount of intrinsic motivation provided for the worker. Obviously, the "best" job design is always one that meets organizational requirements for high performance, offers a good fit with individual skills and needs, and provides opportunities for job satisfaction.

> ■ **Job design** is the process of defining job tasks and the work arrangements to accomplish them.

■ SCIENTIFIC MANAGEMENT

The history of scholarly interest in job design can be traced in part to Frederick Taylor's work with *scientific management* in the early 1900s.[2] Taylor and his contemporaries sought to increase people's efficiency at work. Their approach was to study a job carefully, break it into its smallest components, establish exact time and motion requirements for each task to be done, and then train workers to do these tasks in the same way over and over again. These early efforts were forerunners of current industrial engineering approaches to job design that emphasize efficiency. Such approaches attempt to determine the best processes, methods, work-flow layouts, output standards, and person–machine interfaces for various jobs.

Today the term **job simplification** is used to describe the approach of standardizing work procedures and employing people in clearly defined and highly specialized tasks. The machine-paced automobile assembly line is a classic example of this job-design strategy. Why is it used? Typically, the answer is to increase operating efficiency by reducing the number of skills required to do a job, being able to hire low-cost labor, keeping the needs for job training to a minimum, and emphasizing the accomplishment of repetitive tasks. However, the very nature of such jobs creates potential disadvantages as well, especially loss of efficiency in the face of lower quality, high rates of absenteeism and turnover, and demand for higher wages to compensate for unappealing jobs.

> ■ **Job simplification** standardizes tasks and employs people in very routine jobs.

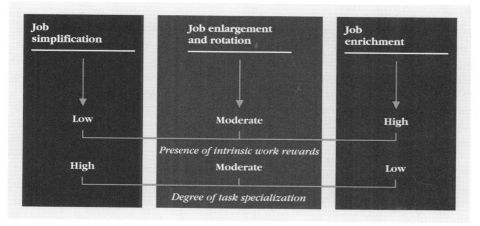

Figure 8.1
A continuum of job-design strategies.

www.volvo.com

⊕ **GLOBALIZATION**

When Ford Motor Company purchased Volvo it bought quality. At Volvo's Torslanda, Sweden, plant, the new S80 model is built with a unique combination of high technology and human contribution. The assembly line operates on a "platform" concept where large components come together in modules. It offers ergonomic advantages to the workers to facilitate movements and to keep reaching and stretching to a minimum. Teams with broad responsibilities for planning and building large sections of the car replace monotonous individual jobs. Workers check their own quality and make corrections. Says a company spokesperson: "Responsibility, expertise, and collaboration are the key words when it comes to car production."[3]

■ JOB ENLARGEMENT AND JOB ROTATION

■ Job enlargement increases task variety by adding new tasks of similar difficulty to a job.

■ Job rotation increases task variety by shifting workers among jobs involving tasks of similar difficulty.

In job simplification the number or variety of different tasks performed is limited. Although this makes the tasks easier to master, the repetitiveness can reduce motivation. Thus, a second set of job-design approaches has been created to add breadth to the variety of tasks performed. **Job enlargement** increases task variety by combining into one job two or more tasks that were previously assigned to separate workers. Sometimes called *horizontal loading*, this approach increases *job breadth* by having the worker perform more and different tasks, but all at the same level of responsibility and challenge. **Job rotation**, another horizontal loading approach, increases task variety by periodically shifting workers among jobs involving different tasks. Again, the responsibility level of the tasks stays the same. The rotation can be arranged according to almost any time schedule, such as hourly, daily, or weekly schedules. An important benefit of job rotation is training. It allows workers to become more familiar with different tasks and increases the flexibility with which they can be moved from one job to another.

■ JOB ENRICHMENT

■ Job enrichment increases job content by giving workers more responsibility for planning and evaluating duties.

Frederick Herzberg's two-factor theory of motivation (described in Chapter 6) suggests that high levels of motivation should not be expected from jobs designed on the basis of simplification, enlargement, or rotation.[4] "Why," asks Herzberg, "should a worker become motivated when one or more 'meaningless' tasks are added to previously existing ones or when work assignments are rotated among equally 'meaningless' tasks?" Instead of pursuing one of these job-design strategies, therefore, Herzberg recommends an alternative approach he calls "job enrichment."

In Herzberg's model, **job enrichment** is the practice of enhancing job content by building into it more motivating factors such as responsibility, achievement, recognition, and personal growth. This job-design strategy differs markedly from strategies previously discussed in that it adds to job content planning and evaluating duties that would otherwise be reserved for managers. These content changes (see The Effective Manager 8.1) involve what Herzberg calls *vertical loading* to increase *job depth*. Enriched jobs, he states, help to satisfy the higher-order needs that people bring with them to work and will therefore increase their motivation to achieve high levels of job performance.

Despite the inherent appeal of Herzberg's ideas, two common questions raise words of caution. *Is job enrichment expensive?* Job enrichment can be very costly, particularly when it requires major changes in work flows, facilities, or technology. *Will workers demand higher pay when moving into enriched jobs?* Herzberg argues that if employees are being paid a truly competitive wage or salary, then the intrinsic rewards of performing enriched tasks will be adequate compensation. Other researchers are more skeptical, advising that pay must be carefully considered.[5]

> **THE EFFECTIVE MANAGER 8.1**
>
> ### JOB ENRICHMENT ADVICE FROM FREDERICK HERZBERG
>
> - Allow workers to plan.
> - Allow workers to control.
> - Maximize job freedom.
> - Increase task difficulty.
> - Help workers become task experts.
> - Provide performance feedback.
> - Increase performance accountability.
> - Provide complete units of work.

Designing Jobs to Increase Motivation

OB scholars have been reluctant to recommend job enrichment as a universal solution to all job performance and satisfaction problems. The prior questions raise cost and pay concerns. Also, individual differences must be considered in answering the additional question: "Is job enrichment for everyone?" A diagnostic approach developed by Richard Hackman and Greg Oldham offers a broader and contingency-based framework for job design to increase motivation.[6] This model opens up many opportunities to individualize job designs.

■ JOB CHARACTERISTICS MODEL

Figure 8.2 presents a model of **job characteristics theory**. It identifies five core job characteristics that are particularly important to job designs. The higher a job scores on each characteristic, the more it is considered to be enriched. The core job characteristics are:

- *Skill variety:* The degree to which a job includes a variety of different activities and involves the use of a number of different skills and talents.

- *Task identity:* The degree to which the job requires completion of a "whole" and identifiable piece of work, one that involves doing a job from beginning to end with a visible outcome.

- *Task significance:* The degree to which the job is important and involves a meaningful contribution to the organization or society in general.

- *Autonomy:* The degree to which the job gives the employee substantial freedom, independence, and discretion in scheduling the work and determining the procedures used in carrying it out.

■ **Job characteristics theory** identifies five core job characteristics of special importance to job design—skill variety, task identity, task significance, autonomy, and feedback.

Core job characteristics

Figure 8.2
Job-design implications of job characteristics theory.

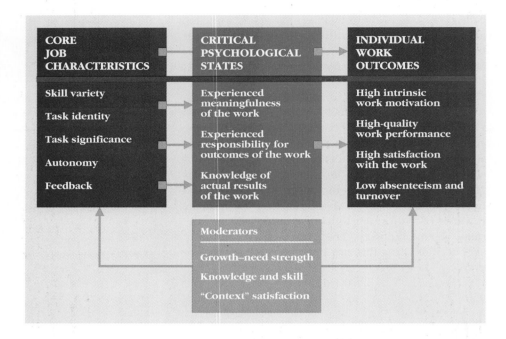

• *Job feedback:* The degree to which carrying out the work activities provides direct and clear information to the employee regarding how well the job has been done.

For those who want to use this model in an actual work situation, Hackman and Oldham recommend determining the current status of each job on each core characteristic.[7] Then, these characteristics can be changed systematically with the goal of enriching the job and increasing its motivational potential. Hackman and his colleagues have developed an instrument called the Job Diagnostic Survey, or JDS, that can be formally used for such an assessment (see the end-of-book experiential exercise, "Job Design"). Scores on the JDS are then combined to create a **motivating potential score**, which indicates the degree to which the job is capable of motivating people.

■ The **motivating potential score** describes the extent to which the core characteristics of a job create motivating conditions.

$$\text{MPS} = \frac{\text{Skill variety} + \text{Task identity} + \text{Task significance}}{3} \times \text{Autonomy} \times \text{Feedback}$$

A job's MPS can be raised by combining tasks to create larger jobs, opening feedback channels to enable workers to know how well they are doing, establishing client relationships to experience such feedback directly from customers, and employing vertical loading to create more planning and controlling responsibilities. When the core characteristics are enriched in these ways and the MPS for a job is raised as high as possible, they can be expected to influence three critical psychological states for the individual in a positive way. These are (1) experienced meaningfulness in the work; (2) experienced responsibility for the outcomes of the work; and (3) knowledge of actual results of the work activities. The positive psychological states, in turn, can be expected to create more positive work outcomes in respect to individual motivation, performance, and satisfaction.

Individual Difference Moderators   Job characteristics theory recognizes that the five core job characteristics do not affect all people in the same way. Rather than accept Herzberg's implication that enriched jobs should be good for everyone, this approach allows for individual differences. It accepts the idea that jobs should be designed to arrive at the best match of core characteristics and individual needs and talents. Specifically, the theory suggests that enriched jobs will lead to positive outcomes only for those persons who are a good match for them. When the fit between the person and an enriched job is poor, positive outcomes are less likely and problems may well result.

Figure 8.2 highlights three individual difference moderators that can influence individual preferences in how their jobs are designed. The first moderator is *growth-need strength*—the degree to which a person desires the opportunity for self-direction, learning, and personal accomplishment at work. It is similar to Abraham Maslow's esteem and self-actualization needs and Alderfer's growth needs, as discussed in Chapter 6. When applied here, the expectation is that people with high growth-need strengths at work will respond positively to enriched jobs, whereas people low in growth-need strengths will find enriched jobs a source of anxiety. The second moderator is *knowledge and skill*. People whose capabilities fit the demands of enriched jobs are predicted to feel good about them and perform well. Those who are inadequate or who feel inadequate in this regard are likely to experience difficulties. The third moderator is *context satisfaction*, or the extent to which an employee is satisfied with aspects of the work setting such as salary levels, quality of supervision, relationships with co-workers, and working conditions. In general, people more satisfied with job context are more likely than dissatisfied ones to support and do well with job enrichment.

Research Results   Considerable research has been done on the job characteristics approach in a variety of work settings, including banks, dentist offices, corrections departments, telephone companies, and manufacturing firms, as well as in government agencies. Experts generally agree that the job characteristics theory and its diagnostic approach are useful, but not yet perfect, guides to job design.[8] On the average, job characteristics do affect performance but not nearly as much as they do satisfaction. The research also emphasizes the importance of growth-need strength as a moderator of the job design–job performance/job satisfaction relationships. Positive job characteristics impact performance more strongly for high-growth need than low-growth need individuals. The relationship is about the same with job satisfaction. It is also clear that job enrichment can fail when job requirements are increased beyond the level of individual capabilities or interests. Finally, employee perceptions of job characteristics often differ from measures taken by managers and consultants. These perceptions are important and must be considered. After all, they will largely determine whether the workers view a job as high or low in the core characteristics, and consequently will affect work outcomes.

■ SOCIAL INFORMATION PROCESSING

Gerald Salancik and Jeffrey Pfeffer question whether or not jobs have stable and objective characteristics to which individuals respond predictably and consistently.[9] Instead, they view job design from the perspective of **social information processing theory**. This theory argues that individual needs, task percep-

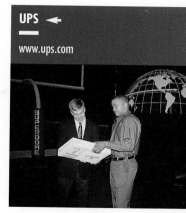

United Parcel Service (UPS) is well known for its operating efficiency and engineered job designs, including prescribed routes for drivers and clear delivery time guidelines. A new approach that empowers drivers to provide more input on their routes is improving customer satisfaction and productivity.

■ The **social information processing** approach believes that individual needs and task perceptions result from socially constructed realities.

Gap, Inc. ◀
www.gap.com

The Gap has gone virtual. Its popular Web site offers customers a great on-line opportunity—"Surf. Shop. Ship." This is made possible by a complex enterprise software system supporting the latest developments in electronic commerce.

tions, and reactions are a result of socially constructed realities. Social information in organizations influences the way people perceive their jobs and respond to them. The same holds true, for example, in the classroom. Suppose that several of your friends tell you that the instructor for a course is bad, the content is boring, and the requirements involve too much work. You may then think that the critical characteristics of the class are the instructor, the content, and the workload, and that they are all bad. All of this may substantially influence the way you perceive your instructor and the course and the way you deal with the class—regardless of the actual characteristics.

Research on social information processing indicates that both social information and core characteristics are important. Although social information processing does influence task perceptions and attitudes, the job characteristics discussed earlier are also important. Indeed, how someone perceives job characteristics is likely to be influenced by both the objective characteristics themselves and the social information present in the workplace.

■ MANAGERIAL AND GLOBAL IMPLICATIONS

A question and answer approach can again be used to summarize final points and implications worth remembering about job enrichment. *Should everyone's job be enriched?* The answer is clearly "No." The logic of individual differences suggests that not everyone will want an enriched job. Individuals most likely to have positive reactions to job enrichment are those who need achievement, who hold middle-class working values, or who are seeking higher-order growth-need satisfaction at work. Job enrichment also appears to be most advantageous when the job context is positive and when workers have the abilities needed to do the enriched job. Furthermore, costs, technological constraints, and work group or union opposition may make it difficult to enrich some jobs.[10] *Can job enrichment apply to groups?* The answer is "Yes." The application of job-design strategies at the group level is growing in many types of settings. In Part 3 we discuss creative work group designs, including cross-functional work teams and self-managing teams.

A final question extends the job enrichment context globally. *What is the impact of culture on job enrichment?* The answer is: "Substantial." Research conducted in Belgium, Israel, Japan, The Netherlands, the United States, and Germany found unique aspects of what constitutes work in each country.[11] Work was seen as a social requirement most strongly in Belgium and Japan and least so in Germany. Work was regarded as something done for money in all countries but Belgium. In most cases, however, work was regarded as having both an economic and a societal contribution component. These results, as well as differences in such national culture dimensions as power distance and individualism, reinforce a contingency approach to job enrichment, and further suggest that cultural differences should be given consideration in job design.

Technology and Job Design

■ **Sociotechnical systems** integrate people and technology into high performance work settings.

The concept of **sociotechnical systems** is used in organizational behavior to indicate the importance of integrating people and technology to create high performance work systems.[12] As computers and information technologies continue to dominate the modern workplace, this concept remains an important point of reference in incorporating new developments into job designs.

■ AUTOMATION AND ROBOTICS

As mentioned earlier, highly simplified jobs often cause problems because they offer little intrinsic motivation for the worker. Such tasks have been defined so narrowly that they lack challenge and lead to boredom when someone has to repeat them over and over again. Given the high technology now available, one way to tackle this problem is through complete **automation** where a machine is used to do the work previously accomplished by a human. This approach increasingly involves the use of robots, which are becoming ever more versatile and reliable. Also, robot prices are falling as the cost of human labor rises. Japan presently leads the world in robot use, with a ratio of one robot for every 36 people employed in manufacturing. The United States lags far behind, but its robot use is growing rapidly.[13] If you were to travel to Wolfsburg, Germany, you would find that Volkswagen's car plant is one of the world's largest and most highly automated. Robots do 80 percent of welding work and can be programmed to perform different tasks. Computers control the assembly line, adjusting production to fit schedules for different models and options.[14]

> ■ **Automation** allows machines to do work previously accomplished by people.

■ FLEXIBLE MANUFACTURING SYSTEMS

In **flexible manufacturing systems**, adaptive computer-based technologies and integrated job designs are used to shift work easily and quickly among alternative products. This approach is increasingly common, for example, in companies supporting the automobile industry with machined metal products, such as cylinder heads and gear boxes.[15] Here, a cellular manufacturing system contains a number of automated production machines that cut, shape, drill, and fasten together various metal components. The machines can be quickly changed from manufacturing one product to another.[16] Workers in flexible manufacturing cells perform few routine assembly-line tasks. Rather, they ensure that the operations are handled correctly, and they deal with the changeover from one product configuration to another. They develop expertise across a wide range of functions and the jobs are rich in potential for enriched core job characteristics.

> ■ **Flexible manufacturing systems** use adaptive technology and integrated job designs to easily shift production among alternative products.

■ ELECTRONIC OFFICES

Electronic office technology was the key when U.S. Healthcare, a large, private practice–based health maintenance organization (HMO), became interested in improving the quality of its health-care services. The company installed large electronic bulletin boards that monitored progress toward a range of performance goals. It also installed an E-mail system, put in robots to deliver the paper mail, and installed a computerized answering machine. Essentially, the company tried to automate as many tasks as possible to free people for more challenging work. Similarly, Mutual Benefit Life completely reorganized the way it serviced insurance application forms—once handled by as many as 19 people across five departments. Mutual created a new case manager position responsible for processing applications from their inception until policies were issued. Accompanying this radical change in job design were powerful PC-based workstations designed to assist decision making and connected to a variety of automated subsystems on a mainframe.[17]

Continuing developments in electronic offices offer job enrichment possibilities for those workers equipped to handle the technology. But those jobs can be stressful and difficult for those who do not have the necessary education or skills. One survey showed that even in highly developed countries like those in Europe, 54 percent of workers possessed inadequate skills to operate a computer; the proportion was about one-third in the United States.[18] People who work continuously with computers are also beginning to experience physical ailments associated with repetitive keyboarding and mouse movements. Clearly, the high technologies of the new workplace must be carefully integrated with the human factor.

WORK-FLOW AND PROCESS REENGINEERING

■ **Process reengineering** analyzes, streamlines, and reconfigures actions and tasks to achieve work goals.

One of the latest approaches for improving job designs and performance is based on the concept of **process reengineering**—the analysis, streamlining, and reconfiguration of actions and tasks required to reach a work goal.[19] The process design approach systematically breaks processes down into their specific components and subtasks, analyzes each for relevance and simplicity, and then does everything possible to reconfigure the process to eliminate wasted time, effort, and resources. A classic example might be the various steps required to gain approval for a purchase order to buy a new computer. The process reengineering approach looks at every step in the process, from searching for items and vendors to obtaining bids, completing necessary forms, securing required signatures and approvals, actually placing the order, and so on to the point at which the new computer arrives, is checked in, is placed into an equipment inventory, and then is finally delivered to the workplace. In all this, one simple question drives the reengineering approach: What is necessary and what can be eliminated?

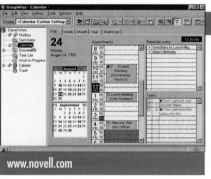

www.novell.com

💻 TECHNOLOGY

Novell Corporation, a leading software vendor for groups and networking environments, isn't letting the great potential of work-flow and business process reengineering pass unnoticed. The company offers GroupWise Workflow as a graphical tool for managing the decision processes involved in such reengineering approaches. The software focuses user attention first on roles—who does what in the process—and then on processes—when and how they do it and at what stage in the cycle. Novell believes that the software encourages people to work together in the reengineering process and supports the notion of worker empowerment for continuous organizational improvement.[20]

Goal Setting and Job Design

Goals are important aspects of any job design. Without proper goals, employees may suffer a direction problem. Some years ago, for example, a Minnesota

Vikings' defensive end gathered up an opponent's fumble. Then, with obvious effort and delight, he ran the ball into the wrong end zone. Clearly, the athlete did not lack motivation. Unfortunately, however, he failed to channel his energies toward the right goal. Similar problems are found in many work settings. They can be eliminated, or at least reduced, by the proper setting and clarification of task goals.

■ GOAL SETTING THEORY

Goals play an important part in high performance work environments. **Goal setting** is the process of developing, negotiating, and formalizing the targets or objectives that a person is responsible for accomplishing.[21] Over a number of years, Edwin Locke and his associates have developed a comprehensive framework linking goals to performance as shown in Figure 8.3. The model uses elements of expectancy theory from Chapter 6 to help clarify the implications of goal setting for performance while taking into account certain moderating conditions, such as ability and task complexity.

■ **Goal setting** is the process of developing and setting motivational performance objectives.

■ GOAL SETTING GUIDELINES

Research using and extending these predictions is now quite extensive. Indeed, more research has been done on goal setting than any other theory related to work motivation.[22] Nearly 400 studies have been conducted in several countries, including Australia, England, Germany, Japan, and the United States.[23] The basic precepts of goal-setting theory remain a most important source of advice for managing human behavior in the work setting.

Managerially speaking, the implications of the Locke and Latham model and related goal-setting research can be summarized as follows.[24] First, *difficult goals are more likely to lead to higher performance than are less difficult ones.* However, if the goals are seen as too difficult or impossible, the relationship with per-

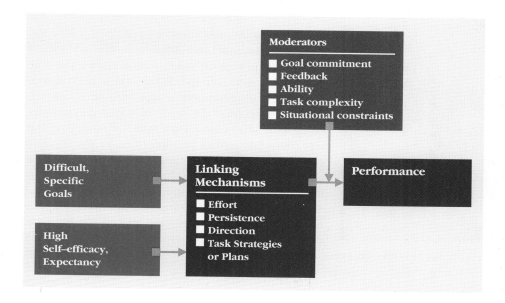

Figure 8.3
Essentials of the Locke and Latham goal-setting framework.

Xerox Corporation ◄

www.xerox.com

Xerox relies on good labor-management relations to help maintain its position as the largest document company in the world. The former director of corporate industrial relations, Joseph W. Laymon, worked with the union to develop and implement a training program on conflict resolution to achieve smoother negotiations. Laymon said: "You have to have an open mind and treat the union and your workers as a partner."

formance no longer holds. For example, you will likely perform better as a financial services agent if you have a goal of selling six annuities a week than if you have a goal of three. However, if your goal is 15 annuities a week, you may consider that as impossible to achieve, and your performance may well be lower than what it would be with a more realistic goal.

Second, *specific goals are more likely to lead to higher performance than are no goals or vague or very general ones.* All too often people work with very general goals such as the encouragement to "do your best." Research indicates that more specific goals, such as selling six computers a day, are much more motivational than a simple "do your best" goal.

Third, *task feedback, or knowledge of results, is likely to motivate people toward higher performance by encouraging the setting of higher performance goals.* Feedback lets people know where they stand and whether they are on course or off course in their efforts. For example, think about how eager you are to find out how well you did on an examination.

Fourth, *goals are most likely to lead to higher performance when people have the abilities and the feelings of self-efficacy required to accomplish them.* The individual must be able to accomplish the goals and feel confident in those abilities. To take the financial services example again, you may be able to do what's required to sell six annuities a week and feel confident that you can. If your goal is 15, however, you may believe that your abilities are insufficient to the task and thus lack the confidence to work hard enough to accomplish it.

Fifth, *goals are most likely to motivate people toward higher performance when they are accepted and there is commitment to them.* Participating in the goal-setting process helps build such acceptance and commitment. It helps create "ownership" of the goals. However, Locke and Latham report that goals assigned by someone else can be equally effective. The assigners are likely to be authority figures, and that can have an impact. The assignment also implies that the subordinate can actually reach the goal. Moreover, assigned goals often are a challenge and help define the standards people use to attain self-satisfaction with their performance. According to Locke and Latham, assigned goals lead to poor performance only when they are curtly or inadequately explained.

www.redhat.com

📈 ENTREPRENEURSHIP

Goals and motivation aren't a problem for the team at Red Hat Software, Inc. Dress codes aren't important either. Programmers may wear shorts one day and a black tailcoat the next, or parachute pants and sweatshirt. Who cares? They and the other Red Hatters share the goal of helping to make the software program Linux a major alternative to industry-dominant MicroSoft's products. Red Hat started developing its version of open-source Linux five years ago, and have since been refining and extending it almost non-stop. The days often start in late morning and extend past midnight. Says one, "You come in when you wake up, you go home when you are tired." In between, the work is challenging and fun, and the goal is highly motivating.[25]

■ GOAL SETTING AND MBO

When we speak of goal setting and its potential to influence individual performance at work, the concept of *management by objectives*, or MBO, immediately comes to mind. The essence of MBO is a process of joint goal setting between a supervisor and a subordinate.[26] It involves managers working with their subordinates to establish performance goals and plans that are consistent with higher level work unit and organizational objectives. When this process is followed throughout an organization, MBO helps clarify the hierarchy of objectives as a series of well-defined means–end chains.

Figure 8.4 shows a comprehensive view of MBO. The concept is consistent with the notion of goal setting and its associated principles discussed above. Notice how joint supervisor–subordinate discussions are designed to extend participation from the point of establishing initial goals to the point of evaluating results in terms of goal attainment. In addition to these goal-setting steps, a successful MBO system calls for careful implementation. Not only must workers have the freedom to carry out the required tasks, managers should be prepared to actively support their efforts to achieve the agreed-upon goals.

Although a fair amount of research based on case studies of MBO success is available, few rigorously controlled studies have been done. What there is reports mixed results.[27] In general, and as an application of goal-setting theory, MBO has much to offer. But it is by no means easy to start and keep going. Many firms have started and dropped the approach because of difficulties experienced early on. Among the specific problems it creates are too much paperwork documenting goals and accomplishments and too much emphasis on goal-oriented rewards and punishments, top-down goals, goals that are easily stated in objective terms, and individual instead of group goals. MBO also may need to be implemented organizationwide if it is to work well.

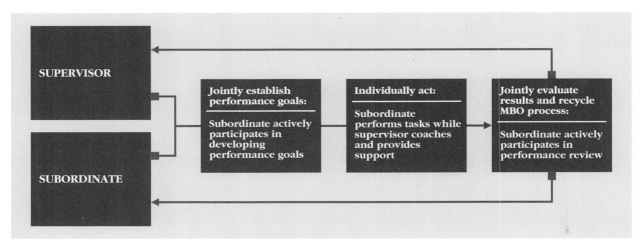

Figure 8.4
How the management by objectives process works.

Excite Inc. ←
www.excite.com

Work at this Internet firm is continuous, 7 days a week, 24 hours a day. And the competition for high-tech talent is extreme. But Excite offers telecommut-ing that makes it possible for many employees to work outside of the office and outside of normal working hours.

■ A **compressed work week** allows a full-time job to be completed in less than five full workdays.

Alternative Work Arrangements

Alternative ways of scheduling time are becoming increasingly common in the workplace. These arrangements are essentially reshaping the traditional 40-hour week, 9 to 5 schedules where work is done on the premises. Virtually all such plans are designed to influence employee satisfaction and to help employees balance the demands of their work and nonwork lives.[28] They are becoming more and more important in fast-changing societies where demands for "work-life balance" and more "family-friendly" employers are growing ever more apparent.[29] For example, dual-career families with children, part-time students, older workers (retired or near retirement age), and single parents are all candidates for alternative work arrangements.

■ COMPRESSED WORK WEEKS

A **compressed work week** is any scheduling of work that allows a full-time job to be completed in fewer than the standard five days. The most common form of compressed work week is the "4/40" or 40 hours of work accomplished in four 10-hour days.

This approach has many possible benefits. For the worker added time off is a major feature of this schedule. The individual often appreciates increased leisure time, three-day weekends, free weekdays to pursue personal business, and lower commuting costs. The organization can benefit, too, in terms of lower employee absenteeism, and improved recruiting of new employees. But, there are also potential disadvantages. Individuals can experience increased fatigue from the extended workday and family adjustment problems. The organization can experience work scheduling problems and customer complaints because of breaks in work coverage. Some organizations may face occasional union opposition and laws requiring payment of overtime for work exceeding eight hours of individual labor in any one day. Overall reactions to compressed work weeks are likely to be most favorable for employees allowed to participate in the decision to adopt the new work week, who have their jobs enriched as a result of the new schedule, and who have strong higher-order needs in Maslow's hierarchy.[30]

■ FLEXIBLE WORKING HOURS

■ **Flexible working hours** give employees some daily choice in scheduling arrival and departure times from work.

Another innovative work schedule, **flexible working hours** or flextime, gives individuals a daily choice in the timing of their work commitments. One such schedule requires employees to work four hours of "core" time but leaves them free to choose their remaining four hours of work from among flexible time blocks. One person, for example, may start early and leave early, whereas another may start later and leave later. This flexible work schedule is becoming increasingly popular and is a valuable alternative for structuring work to accommodate individual interests and needs.

Flextime increases individual autonomy in work scheduling and offers many opportunities and benefits (see The Effective Manager 8.2). It is a way for dual-career couples to handle children's schedules as well as their own; it is a way to meet the demands of caring for elderly parents or ill family members; it is even a way to better attend to such personal affairs as medical and dental appointments, home emergencies, banking needs, and so on. Proponents of this scheduling strategy argue that the discretion it allows workers in scheduling their own hours of work encourages them to develop positive attitudes and to increase commitment to the organization. A majority of American workplaces already have flextime programs, and the number is growing.[31] An Aetna manager, commenting on the firm's flexible working hours program, said: "We're not doing flexible work scheduling to be nice, but because it makes business sense."[32]

■ JOB SHARING

In **job sharing**, one full-time job is assigned to two or more persons who then divide the work according to agreed-upon hours. Often, each person works half a day, but job sharing can also be done on a weekly or monthly basis. Although it is practiced by only a relatively small percentage of employers, human-resource experts believe that job sharing is a valuable alternative work arrangement.[33]

Organizations benefit from job sharing when they can attract talented people who would otherwise be unable to work. An example is the qualified teacher who also is a parent. This person may be able to work only half a day. Through job sharing, two such persons can be employed to teach one class. Some job sharers report less burnout and claim that they feel recharged each time they report for work. The tricky part of this arrangement is finding two people who will work well with each other. When middle managers Sue Mannix and Charlotte Schutzman worked together at Bell Atlantic, for example, they faithfully coordinated each other's absences with Schutzman working Mondays, Tuesdays, and Wednesday mornings and Mannix working the rest of the work week.[34]

Job sharing should not be confused with a more controversial arrangement called *work sharing*. This occurs when workers agree to cut back on the number of hours they work in order to protect against layoffs. Workers may agree to voluntarily reduce 20 percent of hours worked and pay received, rather than have the employer cut 20 percent of the workforce during difficult economic times. Legal restrictions prohibit this practice in some settings.

■ WORK AT HOME AND THE VIRTUAL OFFICE

High technology is influencing yet another alternative work arrangement that is becoming increasingly visible in many employment sectors ranging from higher education to government and from manufacturing to services. **Telecommuting** describes work done at home or in a remote location via use of computers and advanced telecommunications linkages with a central office or other employment locations. This arrangement sometimes is called *flexiplace*. At IBM, Canada, flexiplace means working most of the time from a home office and coming into IBM corporate offices only for special meetings. In a practice known as *hoteling*, temporary offices are reserved for these workers during the times they visit the

---

THE EFFECTIVE MANAGER 8.2

FLEXTIME BENEFITS

For organizations:
Less absenteeism, tardiness, turnover
More commitment
Higher performance

For workers:
Shorter commuting time
More leisure time
More job satisfaction
Greater sense of responsibility

■ **Job sharing** allows one full-time job to be divided among two or more persons.

■ **Telecommuting** is work at home or in remote locations and using computer and telecommunication linkages with the office.

main office. Worldwide, some 20 percent of IBM's workforce of 270,000 employees spends two or more days a week working at home or visiting customers.[35]

The notion of telecommuting is more and more associated with the *virtual office*, where the individual works literally "from the road" and while traveling from place-to-place or customer-to-customer by car or airplane. In all cases, the worker remains linked electronically with the home office.[36] The number of workers who are telecommuting is growing daily; AT&T reports that some 55 percent of its managers telecommute, and Cisco Systems states that 66 percent of its workforce overall telecommutes.[37]

HIGH PERFORMANCE ORGANIZATION

At Cisco Systems in San Jose, California, productivity has risen as much as 25 percent through telecommuting. The firm estimates that it has saved over $1 million and improved retention rates for key employees. Telecommuters enjoy the freedom to set their own work schedules, avoid rush-hour traffic, and spend more time with their families, among other advantages. The firm benefits, too, in both commitment and hard work. Human-resource manager John Hotchkiss says, "It's surprising the number of engineers who will respond to a question at 11:00 PM on a Saturday night. We can solve a problem that would not have been solved until Monday morning."[38]

www.cisco.com

Telecommuting offers the individual the potential advantages of flexibility, the comforts of home, and choice of locations consistent with one's lifestyle. In terms of advantages to the organization, this alternative often produces cost savings and efficiency as well as employee satisfaction. On the negative side, telecommuters sometimes complain of isolation from co-workers, decreased identification with the work team, and technical difficulties with the computer linkages essential to their work arrangement. Yet overall, the practice continues to grow, with more organizations now offering special training in the *virtual management* of telecommuters. Increasingly too, managers are also telecommuting. At AT&T, for example, almost 30 percent of managers work at home at least one day per week.[39]

■ PART-TIME WORK

■ **Temporary part-time work** is temporary work of fewer hours than the standard week.

■ **Permanent part-time work** is permanent work of fewer hours than the standard week.

Part-time work has become an increasingly prominent and controversial work arrangement. In **temporary part-time work** an employee is classified as "temporary" and works less than the standard 40-hour work week. In **permanent part-time work** the person is considered a "permanent" member of the workforce but contributes fewer hours than the standard, typically 40-hour work week. In the chapter opening example of Peet's Coffee and Tea, many of the loyal and satisfied Peetniks fall into this category. By working at least 21 hours a week, they are considered permanent and gain access to important benefits otherwise denied to the temporary part-time workers.[40]

Usually, temporary part-timers are easily released and hired as needs dictate. Accordingly, many organizations use part-time work to hold down labor costs and to help smooth out peaks and valleys in the business cycle. Employers also may use part-time work to better manage what may be called "retention quality." These workers are highly skilled individuals committed to their careers who want to continue to develop professionally but who can only work part time. Part-time nurses, among others, fall in this category.[41]

The part-time work schedule can be a benefit to people who want to supplement other jobs or who want something less than a full work week for a variety of personal reasons. For someone who is holding two jobs, including at least one part time, the added burdens can be stressful and may affect performance in either one or both work settings. Furthermore, part-timers often fail to qualify for fringe benefits, such as health care, life insurance, and pensions, and they may be paid less than their full-time counterparts. Nevertheless, part-time work schedules are of growing practical importance because of the organizational advantages they offer.

OB Across Functions

BUSINESS LAW

New Hiring Practices Have Legal Implications

Flexibility is a watchword of the day in any consideration of work scheduling. The term applies not only to the needs of the workers who want more flexibility in their hours, but also to employers who want flexibility in expanding and contracting their workforces. It is here that the role of the part-time or temporary worker becomes important. When companies employ temporary workers on a regular basis, for at least a year or more, these workers are sometimes called "permatemps." New legal challenges in U.S. courts are raising important issues of labor law even as part-time and contingency workers become more integral to the human-resource strategies of many organizations. The question relates largely to the availability of benefits for permatemps, based on who is considered their true "employer." If the company is considered the employer, instead of the individual worker being considered an independent contractor, permatemps in effect become "common-law workers." As such, under federal pension laws they are eligible for the benefits available to other workers, unless they have been specifically excluded by policy. Benefits lawyers are watching current cases carefully, since the rulings could open the door for future lawsuits.

Chapter 8 Study Guide

What are the alternative job design approaches?

Summary

- Job design is the creation of tasks and work settings for specific jobs.

- Job design by scientific management or job simplification standardizes work and employs people in clearly defined and specialized tasks.

- Job enlargement increases task variety by combining two or more tasks previously assigned to separate workers.

- Job rotation increases task variety by periodically rotating workers among jobs involving different tasks.

- Job enrichment builds bigger and more responsible jobs by adding planning and evaluating duties.

What are the keys to designing motivating jobs?

- Job characteristics theory offers a diagnostic approach to job enrichment based on the analysis of five core job characteristics: skill variety, task identity, task significance, autonomy, and feedback.

- Job characteristics theory does not assume that everyone wants an enriched job; it indicates that job enrichment will be more successful for persons with high-growth needs, requisite job skills, and context satisfaction.

- The social information processing theory points out that information from co-workers and others in the workplace influences a worker's perceptions and responses to a job.

- Not everyone's job should be enriched; job enrichment can be done for groups as well as individuals; cultural factors may influence job enrichment success.

How does technology influence job design?

- Well-planned sociotechnical systems integrate people and technology for high performance.

- Robotics and complete automation are increasingly used to replace people to perform jobs that are highly simplified and repetitive.

- Workers in flexible manufacturing cells utilize the latest technology to produce high-quality products with short cycle times.

- The nature of office work is being changed by computer workstation technologies, networks, and various forms of electronic communication.

- Work-flow and business process reengineering analyzes all steps in work sequences to streamline activities and tasks, save costs, and improve performance.

How can goal setting improve job performance?

- Goal setting is the process of developing, negotiating, and formalizing performance targets or objectives.

- Research supports predictions that the most motivational goals are challenging and specific, allow for feedback on results, and create commitment and acceptance.

- The motivational impact of goals may be affected by individual difference moderators such as ability and self-efficacy.

- Management by objectives is a process of joint goal setting between a supervisor and worker.

- The management by objectives process is a good action framework for applying goal-setting theory on an organizationwide basis.

What alternative work arrangements are used today?

- Today's complex society is giving rise to a number of alternative work arrangements designed to balance the personal demands on workers with job responsibilities and opportunities.

- The compressed work week allows a full-time work week to be completed in under 5 days, typically offering four 10-hour days of work and 3 days free.

- Flexible working hours allow employees some daily choice in timing between work and nonwork activities.

■ Job sharing occurs when two or more people divide one full-time job according to agreements among themselves and the employer.

■ Telecommuting involves work at home or at a remote location while communicating with the home office as needed via computer and related technologies.

■ Part-time work requires less than a 40-hour work week and can be done on a schedule classifying the worker as temporary or permanent.

Key Terms

Automation (p. 161)
Compressed work week (p. 166)
Flexible manufacturing systems (p. 161)
Flexible working hours (p. 166)
Goal setting (p. 163)
Job characteristics theory (p. 157)

Job design (p. 155)
Job enlargement (p. 156)
Job enrichment (p. 156)
Job rotation (p. 156)
Job sharing (p. 167)
Job simplification (p. 155)
Motivating potential score (p. 158)
Permanent part-time work (p. 168)

Process reengineering (p. 162)
Social information processing (p. 159)
Sociotechnical systems (p. 160)
Telecommuting (p. 167)
Temporary part-time work (p. 168)

■ MULTIPLE CHOICE

Self-Test 8

1. Job simplification is closely associated with _____ as originally developed by Frederick Taylor. (a) vertical loading (b) horizontal loading (c) scientific management (d) self-efficacy

2. Job _____ increases job _____ by combining into one job several tasks of similar difficulty. (a) rotation; depth (b) enlargement; depth (c) rotation; breadth (d) enlargement; breadth

3. In job characteristics theory, _____ indicates the degree to which an individual is able to make decisions affecting his or her work. (a) task variety (b) task identity (c) task significance (d) autonomy

4. The basic logic of sociotechnical systems is that: (a) people must be integrated with technology. (b) technology is more important than people. (c) people are more important than technology. (d) technology alienates people.

5. Which goals tend to be more motivating? (a) challenging goals (b) easy goals (c) general goals (d) low-feedback goals

6. The MBO process emphasizes _____ as a way of building worker commitment to goal accomplishment. (a) authority (b) joint goal setting (c) infrequent feedback (d) general goals

7. _____ is one of the concerns sometimes raised about organizationwide MBO programs. (a) Too much paperwork (b) Too little paperwork (c) Too little emphasis on top-down goals (d) Too much emphasis on group instead of individual goals

8. The "4/40" is a type of _____ work arrangement. (a) compressed work week (b) flextime (c) job sharing (d) permanent part-time

9. The flexible working hours schedule allows workers to choose _____ (a) days of week to work (b) total hours to work in week (c) location of work (d) starting and ending times for work days

10. Today's society is creating a demand for more jobs that by design _____. (a) are easy to perform (b) minimize the need for employee skills (c) are family friendly (d) have low-performance goals

■ TRUE–FALSE

11. In some cases, job enrichment may be difficult to implement because of the expenses involved and/or union opposition.   T   F

12. The characteristic of task significance indicates the degree to which a job is meaningful to the organization or society.   T   F

13. According to job characteristics theory, everyone's job should be enriched.   T   F

14. The social information processing approach stresses the importance of objective job characteristics to motivation and performance.   T   F

15. Job enrichment is a management practice that is not universally applicable in all cultural settings.   T   F

16. One sure way to motivate through goal setting is to tell people simply to "do your best."   T   F

17. Goals are most likely to lead to higher performance for people high in feelings of self-efficacy.   T   F

18. Flextime is unique in that it offers advantages to the individual worker with no disadvantages for the employer.   T   F

19. Trends seem to indicate that telecommuting is of growing appeal to organizations.   T   F

20. The presence of more part-time work is a uniformly positive trend for a society at large.   T   F

■ SHORT RESPONSE

21. How can you create job enrichment by building job depth?

22. What role does growth-need strength play in job characteristics theory?

23. How can a manager increase employee commitment to stated task goals?

24. What is the difference between temporary part-time and permanent part-time work?

■ APPLICATIONS ESSAY

25. When Jean-Paul Latrec opened his first "Outfitter's Plus" store, he wanted to create a motivational work environment for his sales associates. He decided to implement MBO as a core management strategy. Over time he became well known in Quebec City for his success. If you were to visit his store to study Jean-Paul's MBO approach, what would you expect to find him doing to make the program work so well?

Explore application-oriented Fast Company articles, cases, experimental exercises, and self-assessments in the OB Skills Workbook

■ **Visit the Schermerhorn Web site to find the Interactive Self-Test and Internet exercises for this chapter.**

www.wiley.com/college/schermerhorn

The Nature of Groups

GROUPS CAN BRING OUT THE BEST

www.apple.com

Groups helped launch Apple Computer, Inc.'s, early success, and they are still playing an important role in the company's rebirth. The team that created Apple's original Macintosh computer was really "hot." The brainchild of Apple's co-founder Steve Jobs, it was composed of high-achieving members who were excited and turned on to their highly challenging task. They worked all hours and at an unrelenting pace. Housed in a separate building flying the "Jolly Roger," the MacIntosh team combined youthful enthusiasm with great expertise and commitment to an exciting goal. The result was a bench-mark computer produced in record time. Apple thrived.

Then came the computer wars. Intense competition in the ever-changing and fast-paced industry took its toll. Apple struggled against the likes of Compaq, Dell, Gateway, and even the renewed IBM. Given the chance to return as CEO to the company he founded, Steven Jobs built another team charged with reinvigorating of the company. This was the team "at the top." Building what he calls a "world-class" executive team, Jobs found an important key to corporate turnaround. On Apple's team were sales, hardware, software, services, inventory, and legal gurus. Together with Jobs they brought about major changes in such areas as human resources, manufacturing, and marketing. And what they created first was the iMac, a product *Fortune* described as follows: "The iMac is the first desktop computer to get the whole industry excited since…well, since the original MacIntosh."[1]

That, so to speak, is what groups in organizations can and should be all about!

T he new workplace places great value on change and adaptation. Organizations are continually under pressure to find new ways of operating in the quest for higher productivity, total quality and service, customer satisfaction, and better quality of working life. Among the many trends and developments we perceive today, none is more important than the attempts being made to tap the full potential of groups more creatively as critical organizational resources. Groups are increasingly becoming focal points as organizations seek the advantages of smaller size, flatter structures, cross-functional integration, and more flexible operations. To meet competitive demands in challenging environments, the best organizations mobilize groups and teams in many capacities in the quest to reach their full potential as high performance systems.

Study Questions

Groups can be important sources of performance, creativity, and enthusiasm for organizations. This chapter introduces you to the basic attributes of groups as they are found in today's progressive organizations. As you read Chapter 9, keep in mind these study questions:

- What is the nature of groups in organizations?
- What are the stages of group development?
- What are the input foundations of group effectiveness?
- What are group and intergroup dynamics?
- How do groups make decisions?

Groups in Organizations

■ **Groups** involve two or more people working together regularly to achieve common goals.

A **group** may be defined as a collection of two or more people who work with one another regularly to achieve common goals. In a true group, members are mutually dependent on one another to achieve common goals, and they interact with one another regularly to pursue those goals over a sustained period of time.[2] Groups are good for both organizations and their members, helping to accomplish important tasks and to maintain a high-quality workforce. Consultant and management scholar Harold J. Leavitt is a well-known advocate for the power and usefulness of groups.[3] Recently, he has described "hot groups" that thrive in conditions of crisis and competition and whose creativity and innovativeness generate extraordinary returns.[4] The original MacIntosh team featured in the chapter opener was a hot group; in many ways, Apple's current top management team is one, too.

■ WHAT IS AN EFFECTIVE GROUP?

An **effective group** is one that achieves high levels of task performance, member satisfaction and team viability.[5] With regard to *task performance*, this group achieves its performance goals—in the standard sense of quantity, quality, and timeliness of work results. For a permanent work group, such as a manufacturing team, this may mean meeting daily production targets. For a temporary group, such as a new policy task force, this may involve meeting a deadline for submitting a new organizational policy to the company president. With regard to *member satisfaction*, an effective group is one whose members believe that their participation and experiences are positive and meet important personal needs. They are satisfied with their tasks, accomplishments, and interpersonal relationships. With regard to *team viability*, the members are sufficiently satisfied to continue working well together on an ongoing basis and/or to look forward to working together again at some future point in time. The group in this way has all-important long-term performance potential.

■ **Effective groups** achieve high levels of task, performance, member satisfaction and team viability.

■ UNIQUE CONTRIBUTIONS OF GROUPS

Effective groups help organizations accomplish important tasks. In particular, they offer the potential for **synergy**—the creation of a whole that is greater than the sum of its parts. When synergy occurs, groups accomplish more than the total of their members' individual capabilities. Group synergy is necessary for organizations to become competitive and achieve long-term high performance in today's dynamic times.[6]

■ **Synergy** is the creation of a whole greater than the sum of its parts.

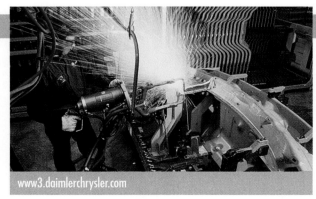

HIGH PERFORMANCE ORGANIZATION

Chrysler would probably never have been bought by the prestigious German auto maker Daimler Benz if it hadn't been known for consistently turning out fleet after fleet of best-selling cars. When asked how Chrysler does it, CEO Robert Eaton has a one-word answer—"empowerment." Here he's referring to a team-oriented approach to new model development. Workers from engineering, manufacturing, design, finance, marketing, and other areas come together in cross-functional teams. They work together to meet

www3.daimlerchrysler.com

vehicle design, performance, and cost goals sketched out by a top management group. Given that contract, says Eaton, team members "then go away and do it, and they don't get back to us unless they have a major problem."[7]

THE EFFECTIVE MANAGER 9.1

HOW GROUPS CAN HELP ORGANIZATIONS

- Groups are good for people.
- Groups can improve creativity.
- Groups can make better decisions.
- Groups can increase commitments to decisions.
- Groups help control their members.
- Groups help offset large organization size.

The Effective Manager 9.1 lists in general the benefits groups can bring to organizations. More specifically, groups often have three performance advantages over individuals acting alone.[8] First, when there is no clear "expert" in a particular task or problem, groups seem to make better judgments than does the average individual alone. Second, when problem solving can be handled by a division of labor and the sharing of information, groups are typically more successful than individuals. And third, because of their tendencies to make riskier decisions, groups can be more creative and innovative than individuals.

In addition, groups are important settings where people learn from one another and share job skills and knowledge.[11] The learning environment and the pool of experience within a group can be used to solve difficult and unique problems. This is especially helpful to newcomers who often need help in their jobs. When group members support and help each other in acquiring and improving job competencies, they may even make up for deficiencies in organizational training systems.

Groups are also able to satisfy the needs of members. They offer opportunities for social interaction and can provide individuals with a sense of security in available work assistance and technical advice. They can provide emotional support in times of special crisis or pressure, and allow for ego involvement in group goals and activities.

■ **Social loafing** occurs when people work less hard in groups than they would individually.

At the same time that they have enormous performance potential, groups can also have problems. One concern is **social loafing**, also known as the *Ringelmann effect*. It is the tendency of people to work less hard in a group than they would individually.[9] Max Ringlemann, a German psychologist, pinpointed the phenomenon by asking people to pull on a rope as hard as they could, first alone and then in a group.[10] He found that average productivity dropped as more people joined the rope-pulling task. He acknowledged two reasons why people may not work as hard in groups as they would individually: (1) their individual contribution is less noticeable in the context of the group, and (2) they prefer to see others carry the workload. Some considerations in dealing with social loafing or trying to prevent it from occurring include:

How to handle social loafing

- Define member roles and tasks to maximize individual interests
- Link individual rewards to performance contributions to the group
- Raise accountability by identifying individuals' performance contributions to the group

■ **Social facilitation** is the tendency for one's behavior to be influenced by the presence of others in a group.

Another issue in group work is **social facilitation**—the tendency for one's behavior to be influenced by the presence of others in a group or social setting.[11] In general, *social facilitation theory* indicates that working in the presence of others creates an emotional arousal or excitement that stimulates behavior and therefore affects performance. Arousal tends to work positively when one is proficient with the task. Here, the excitement leads to extra effort at doing something that already comes quite naturally. An example is the play of a world-class athlete in front of an enthusiastic "hometown" crowd. But the effect of social facilitation can be negative when the task is not well learned. You may know this best in the context of public speaking. When asked to speak in front of a class or larger audience, you may well stumble as you try hard in public to talk about an unfamiliar topic.

■ FORMAL GROUPS

There are many ways in the new workplace for groups to be used to great advantage. A **formal group** is officially designated to serve a specific organizational purpose. An example is the work unit headed by a manager and consisting of one or more direct reports. The organization creates such a group to perform a specific task, which typically involves the use of resources to create a product such as a report, decision, service, or commodity.[12] The head of a formal group is responsible for the group's performance accomplishments, but all members contribute the required work. Also, the head of the group plays a key "linking-pin" role that ties it horizontally and vertically with the rest of the organization.[13]

Formal groups may be permanent or temporary. *Permanent work groups*, or *command groups* in the vertical structure, often appear on organization charts as departments (e.g., market research department), divisions (e.g., consumer products division), or teams (e.g., product-assembly team). Such groups can vary in size from very small departments or teams of just a few people to large divisions employing a hundred or more people. In all cases, permanent work groups are officially created to perform a specific function on an ongoing basis. They continue to exist until a decision is made to change or reconfigure the organization for some reason.

In contrast, *temporary work groups* are *task groups* specifically created to solve a problem or perform a defined task. They often disband once the assigned purpose or task has been accomplished.[14] Examples are the many temporary committees and task forces that are important components of any organization. Indeed, today's organizations tend to make more use of *cross-functional teams* or *task forces* for special problem-solving efforts. The president of a company, for example, might convene a task force to examine the possibility of implementing flexible work hours for nonmanagerial employees. Usually, such temporary groups appoint chairpersons or heads who are held accountable for results, much as is the manager of a work unit. Another common form is the *project team* that is formed, often cross-functionally, to complete a specific task with a well-defined end point. Examples include installing a new E-mail system and introducing a new product modification.[15]

Information technology is bringing a new type of group into the workplace. This is the *virtual group*, a group whose members convene and work together

OB Across Functions
HUMAN RESOURCE MANAGEMENT

Stock Options Can Build the Companywide Team

The human-resources function in any organization is dedicated to the attraction and maintenance of a high-quality and talented workforce. As executives struggle today with the complex challenges of tight labor markets and social trends, they are rediscovering one of the foundations of teamwork in any setting—ownership. When workers take stock in their company, something happens. And mostly it's good—good for them and good for the organization. Take the case of MCI/WorldCom Advanced Networks. When the former CompuServe network division in Hilliard, Ohio, was bought by WorldCom, employees gained. They were able to buy WorldCom stock at a discounted price, with options to buy more. Says Mike Herron, health and fitness coordinator at the Hilliard operation: "A lot of people, myself included, continually check the stock price." The National Center for Employee Ownership (*www.nceo.org/*) estimates that at least 6 million workers received stock options from employers, and the number is rising each year. John Logue, director of the Ohio Employee Ownership Center at Kent State University, says: "The whole purpose of stock options is to get people to become owners and act like owners." This should mean more commitment to the job and a greater sense of teamwork around the company. After all, there's no greater bond among workers than a collective sense of ownership and shared responsibility for making their investments successful.

■ **Formal groups** are officially designated for a specific organizational purpose.

electronically via networked computers. In this new age of the Internet and intranets, and more, virtual groups will become increasingly common in organizations. Facilitated by ever-advancing team-oriented software, or groupware, members of virtual groups can do the same things as members of face-to-face groups. They can share information, make decisions, and complete tasks. The important role of virtual groups or teams in the high performance workplace is discussed in the next chapter.

www.ti.com

⇄ WORKPLACE DIVERSITY

Virtual teams are an everyday phenomenon at Texas Instruments, where physical distance doesn't stop people from working together. On any given day you can find computer designers working together from all over the world—linked via computers to pool ideas and create new products. Talented engineers in Bangalore, India, may work with other group members in Japan and Texas to develop a new chip. When the design is finished, it is sent via computer to Texas for fabrication, and then it goes back to Bangalore for any required "debugging." TI now has some 400 employees working on complex chip designs in Bangalore. Says a TI group vice president, "Problems that used to take three years now take a year."[16]

■ INFORMAL GROUPS

■ **Informal groups** are unofficial and emerge to serve special interests.

Informal groups emerge without being officially designated by the organization. They form spontaneously and are based on personal relationships or special interests, and not on any specific organizational endorsement. They are commonly found within most formal groups. *Friendship groups,* for example, consist of persons with natural affinities for one another. They tend to work together, sit together, take breaks together, and even do things together outside of the workplace. *Interest groups* consist of persons who share common interests. These may be job-related interests, such as an intense desire to learn more about computers, or nonwork interests, such as community service, sports, or religion.

Informal groups often help people get their jobs done. Through their network of interpersonal relationships, they have the potential to speed up the work flow as people assist each other in ways that formal lines of authority fail to provide. They also help individuals satisfy needs that are thwarted or otherwise left unmet in a formal group. In these and related ways, informal groups can provide their members with social satisfactions, security, and a sense of belonging.

Stages of Group Development

Whether one is part of a formal work unit, a temporary task force, or a virtual team, the group itself passes through different stages in its life cycle.[17] Furthermore, depending on the stage the group has reached, the leader and members can face very different challenges. Figure 9.1 describes five stages of group development: (1) forming, (2) storming, (3) norming, (4) performing, and (5) adjourning.[18]

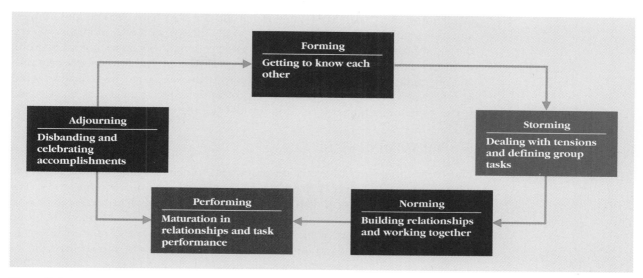

Figure 9.1
Five stages of group development.

■ FORMING STAGE

In the *forming stage* of group development, a primary concern is the initial entry of members to a group. During this stage, individuals ask a number of questions as they begin to identify with other group members and with the group itself. Their concerns may include: "What can the group offer me?" "What will I be asked to contribute?" "Can my needs be met at the same time I contribute to the group?" Members are interested in getting to know each other and discovering what is considered acceptable behavior, in determining the real task of the group, and in defining group rules.

■ STORMING STAGE

The *storming stage* of group development is a period of high emotionality and tension among the group members. During this stage, hostility and infighting may occur, and the group typically experiences many changes. Coalitions or cliques may form as individuals compete to impose their preferences on the group and to achieve a desired status position. Outside demands, including premature expectations for performance results, may create uncomfortable pressures. In the process, membership expectations tend to be clarified, and attention shifts toward obstacles standing in the way of group goals. Individuals begin to understand one another's interpersonal styles, and efforts are made to find ways to accomplish group goals while also satisfying individual needs.

■ NORMING STAGE

The *norming stage* of group development, sometimes called initial integration, is the point at which the group really begins to come together as a coordinated unit. The turmoil of the storming stage gives way to a precarious balancing of forces. With the pleasures of a new sense of harmony, group members will strive to

PeopleSoft ←
www.peoplesoft.com

In just four years the software maker PeopleSoft grew from 300 to over 7000 employees. The firm's director of global telecommunications credits use of Sony Videoconferencing technology for helping manage such explosive growth. He says: "It's simply better when you meet someone over video than the phone. It's much more like a live meeting."

maintain positive balance. Holding the group together may become more important to some than successfully working on the group's tasks. Minority viewpoints, deviations from group directions, and criticisms may be discouraged as group members experience a preliminary sense of closeness. Some members may mistakenly perceive this stage as one of ultimate maturity. In fact, a premature sense of accomplishment at this point needs to be carefully managed as a "stepping stone" to the next higher level of group development.

■ PERFORMING STAGE

The *performing stage* of group development, sometimes called total integration, marks the emergence of a mature, organized, and well-functioning group. The group is now able to deal with complex tasks and handle internal disagreements in creative ways. The structure is stable, and members are motivated by group goals and are generally satisfied. The primary challenges are continued efforts to improve relationships and performance. Group members should be able to adapt successfully as opportunities and demands change over time. A group that has achieved the level of total integration typically scores high on the criteria of group maturity shown in Figure 9.2.

■ ADJOURNING STAGE

A well-integrated group is able to disband, if required, when its work is accomplished. The *adjourning stage* of group development is especially important for the many temporary groups that are increasingly common in the new workplace,

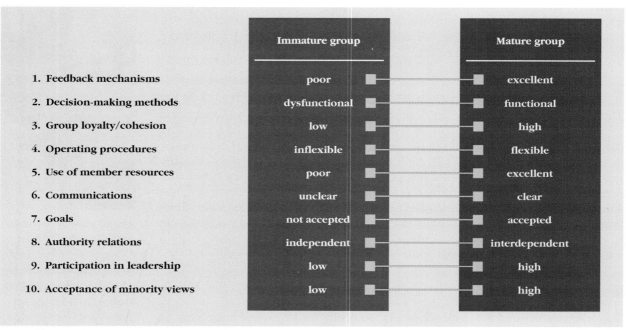

	Immature group	Mature group
1. Feedback mechanisms	poor	excellent
2. Decision-making methods	dysfunctional	functional
3. Group loyalty/cohesion	low	high
4. Operating procedures	inflexible	flexible
5. Use of member resources	poor	excellent
6. Communications	unclear	clear
7. Goals	not accepted	accepted
8. Authority relations	independent	interdependent
9. Participation in leadership	low	high
10. Acceptance of minority views	low	high

Figure 9.2
Ten criteria for measuring the maturity of a group.

including task forces, committees, project teams and the like. Members of these groups must be able to convene quickly, do their jobs on a tight schedule, and then adjourn—often to reconvene later if needed. The members' willingness to disband when the job is done and to work well together in future responsibilities, group or otherwise, is an important long-run test of group success.

Input Foundations of Group Effectiveness

An organization's success depends largely on the performance of its internal networks of formal and informal groups. Groups in this sense are an important component of the *human resources* and *intellectual capital* of organizations.[19] Like individuals, group contributions are essential if the organization is to prosper through high performance over the long run.

The systems model in Figure 9.3 shows how groups, like organizations, pursue effectiveness by interacting with their environments to transform resource inputs into product outputs.[20] The inputs are the initial "givens" in any group situation. They are the foundations for all consequent action. As a general rule-of-thumb, the stronger the input foundations the better the chances for long-term group effectiveness. Key group inputs include the nature of the task, goals, rewards, resources, technology, membership diversity, and group size.

■ TASKS

Tasks place different demands on groups, with varying implications for group effectiveness. The *technical demands* of a group's task include its routineness, difficulty, and information requirements. The *social demands* of a task involve relationships, ego involvement, controversies over ends and means, and the like. Tasks that are complex in technical demands require unique solutions and more information processing; those that are complex in social demands involve diffi-

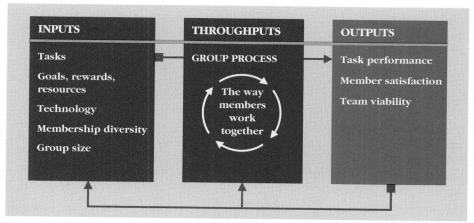

Figure 9.3
The work group as an open system transforming resource inputs into product outputs.

EDS ←
www.eds.com

High tech meeting facilities are to be expected at computer-services giant EDS. In the firm's Capture Labs teams have full access to the Internet and the company's Intranet in a fully integrated information network. Large-screen projections facilitate discussion.

■ The **diversity–consensus dilemma** is the tendency for diversity in groups to create process difficulties even as it offers improved potential for problem solving.

culties reaching agreement on goals or methods for accomplishing them. Naturally, group effectiveness is harder to achieve when the task is highly complex.[21] To master complexity, group members must apply and distribute their efforts broadly and actively cooperate to achieve desired results. When their efforts are successful at mastering complex tasks, however, group members tend to experience high levels of satisfaction with the group and its accomplishments.

■ GOALS, REWARDS, AND RESOURCES

Appropriate goals, well-designed reward systems, and adequate resources are all essential to support long-term performance accomplishments. A group's performance, much as an individual's performance, can suffer when goals are unclear, insufficiently challenging, or arbitrarily imposed. It can also suffer if goals and rewards are focused too much on individual instead of group outcomes. And it can suffer if adequate budgets, the right facilities, good work methods and procedures, and the best technologies are not available. By contrast, having the right goals, rewards, and resources can be a strong launching pad for group success.

■ TECHNOLOGY

Technology provides the means to get work accomplished. It is always necessary to have the right technology available for the task at hand. The nature of the work-flow technology can also influence the way group members interact with one another while performing their tasks. It is one thing to be part of a group that crafts products to specific customer requests; it is quite another to be part of a group whose members staff one section of a machine-paced assembly line. The former technology permits greater interaction among group members. It will probably create a closer knit group with a stronger sense of identity than the one formed around one small segment of an assembly line.

■ MEMBERSHIP CHARACTERISTICS

To achieve success a group must have the right skills and competencies available for group problem solving. Although talents alone cannot guarantee desired results, they establish an important baseline of performance potential. When the input competencies are insufficient, a group's performance limits will be difficult to overcome.

In *homogeneous groups* where members are very similar to one another, members may find it very easy to work together. But they may also suffer performance limitations if their collective skills, experiences and perspectives are not a good match for complex tasks. In *heterogeneous groups* whose members vary in age, gender, race, ethnicity, experience, culture, and the like, a wide pool of talent and viewpoints is available for problem-solving. But this diversity may also create difficulties as members try to define problems, share information, and handle interpersonal conflicts. These difficulties may be quite pronounced in the short run, but once members learn how to work together, the diversity can be turned into enhanced performance potential.[22]

Researchers identify what is called the **diversity–consensus dilemma**—the tendency for increasing diversity among group members to make it harder for group members to work together, even though the diversity itself expands the skills and perspectives available for problem solving.[23] The challenge to group effectiveness in a multinational team, for example, is to take advantage of the diversity without suffering process disadvantages.[24]

The mix of personalities is also important in a group or team. The **FIRO-B theory** (with "FIRO" standing for fundamental interpersonal orientation) helps to identify differences in how people relate to one another based on their needs to express and receive feelings of inclusion, control, and affection.[25] Developed by William Schutz, the theory points out that groups whose members are compatible on these needs are likely to be more effective than groups whose members are more incompatible on them. Symptoms of incompatibilities in a group include withdrawn members, open hostilities, struggles over control, and domination of the group by a few members. Schutz states the management implications of the FIRO-B theory this way: "If at the outset we can choose a group of people who can work together harmoniously, we shall go far toward avoiding situations where a group's efforts are wasted in interpersonal conflicts."[26]

Another source of diversity in group membership is *status*—a person's relative rank, prestige, or standing in a group. Status within a group can be based on any number of factors, including age, work seniority, occupation, education, performance, or standing in other groups. **Status congruence** occurs when a person's position within the group is equivalent to ones held outside of the group. Problems are to be expected when status incongruence is present and someone's position in the group does not reflect the outside status. In high-power distance cultures such as Malaysia, for example, the chair of a committee is expected to be the highest-ranking member of the group. When such status congruity is present, members can feel comfortable for the group to proceed with its work. If the senior member is not appointed to head the committee, discomfort will ensue and difficulties in group performance are likely. Similar problems might occur, for example, when a young college graduate is appointed to chair a project group composed of senior and more experienced workers.

■ **FIRO-B theory** examines differences in how people relate to one another based on their needs to express and receive feelings of inclusion, control, and affection.

■ **Status congruence** involves consistency between a person's status within and outside of a group.

■ GROUP SIZE

The size of a group, as measured by the number of its members, can make a difference in a group's effectiveness. As a group becomes larger, more people are available to divide up the work and accomplish needed tasks. This can boost performance and member satisfaction, but only up to a point. As a group continues to grow in size, communication and coordination problems often set in. Satisfaction may dip, and turnover, absenteeism, and social loafing may increase. Even logistical matters, such as finding time and locations for meetings, become more difficult for larger groups and can affect performance negatively.[27]

A good size for problem-solving groups is between five and seven members. A group with fewer than five may be too small to adequately share responsibilities. With more than seven, individuals may find it harder to participate and offer ideas. Larger groups are also more prone to possible domination by aggressive members and have tendencies to split into coalitions or subgroups.[28] Groups with an odd number of members find it easier to use majority voting rules to resolve disagreements. When speed is required, this form of conflict management is useful, and odd-numbered groups may be preferred. But when careful deliberations are required and the emphasis is more on consensus, such as in jury duty or very complex problem solving, even-numbered groups may be more effective unless an irreconcilable deadlock occurs.[29]

Group and Intergroup Dynamics

The effectiveness of any group, as previously depicted in Figure 9.3, requires more than the correct inputs. It always depends in part on how well members work together to utilize these inputs to produce the desired outputs. When we speak about people "working together" in groups, we are dealing with issues of **group dynamics**—the forces operating in groups that affect the way members relate to and work with one another. From the perspective of an open system, group dynamics are the *processes* through which inputs are transformed into outputs.

■ **Group dynamics** are the forces operating in groups that affect the ways members work together.

■ WHAT GOES ON WITHIN GROUPS

George Homans described a classic model of group dynamics involving two sets of behaviors—required and emergent. In a work group, *required behaviors* are those formally defined and expected by the organization.[30] For example, they may include such behaviors as punctuality, customer respect, and assistance to co-workers. *Emergent behaviors* are those that group members display in addition to what the organization asks of them. They derive not from outside expectations but from personal initiative. Emergent behaviors often include things that people do beyond formal job requirements and that help get the job done in the best ways possible. Rarely can required behaviors be specified so perfectly that they meet all the demands that arise in a work situation. This makes emergent behaviors so essential. An example might be someone taking the time to send an E-mail to an absent member to keep her informed about what happened during a group meeting. The concept of empowerment, often discussed in this book as essential to the high performance workplace, relies strongly on unlocking this positive aspect of emergent behaviors.

Homans' model of group dynamics also describes member relationships in terms of activities, interactions, and sentiments, all of which have their required and emergent forms. *Activities* are the things people do or the actions they take in groups while working on tasks. *Interactions* are interpersonal communications and contacts. *Sentiments* are the feelings, attitudes, beliefs, or values held by group members.

www.sandiegozoo.org

⚖ ETHICS AND SOCIAL RESPONSIBILITY

The San Diego Zoo is known for showing its animals in natural environments. Animals and plants from a particular region are housed together in cageless enclosures designed to resemble natural settings with appropriate bioclimatic zones. Each bioclimatic zone is managed by its own team, typically consisting of 7 to 10 employees. A typical team is likely to be made up of mammal specialists, bird experts, horticulturists, and maintenance and construction workers. Their jobs blend and merge, making it difficult sometimes to tell who does what. Gone is the "it's-not-my-job" syndrome. If something needs to be done, it is the job of the entire team. In learning to work well together, members let go of traditional practices and develop new skills matched to team concepts.[31]

■ WHAT GOES ON BETWEEN GROUPS

The term **intergroup dynamics** refers to the dynamics that take place between two or more groups. Organizations ideally operate as cooperative systems in which the various components support one another. In the real world, however, competition and intergroup problems often develop within an organization and have mixed consequences. On the negative side—such as when manufacturing and sales units don't get along, intergroup dynamics may divert energies as members focus more on their animosities toward the other group than on the performance of important tasks.[32] On the positive side, competition among groups can stimulate them to work harder, become more focused on key tasks, develop more internal loyalty and satisfaction, or achieve a higher level of creativity in problem solving. Japanese companies, for example, often use competitive themes to motivate their organization-wide workforces. At Sony, it has been said that the slogan "BMW" stands for "Beat Matsushita Whatsoever."[33]

Organizations and their managers go to great lengths to avoid the negative and achieve the positive aspects of intergroup dynamics. Groups engaged in destructive competition, for example, can be refocused on a common enemy or a common goal. Direct negotiations can be held among the groups, and members can be trained to work more cooperatively. It is important to avoid win–lose reward systems in which one group must lose something in order for the other to gain. Rewards can be refocused on contributions to the total organization and on how much groups help one another. Also, cooperation tends to increase as interaction between groups increases.

■ **Intergroup dynamics** are relationships between groups cooperating and competing with one another.

Decision Making in Groups

One of the most important activities engaged in by any group is *decision making*—discussed in detail in Chapter 17 as the process of choosing among alternative courses of action. Obviously, the quality and timeliness of decisions made and the processes through which they are arrived at can have an important impact on group effectiveness.

■ HOW GROUPS MAKE DECISIONS

Edgar Schein, a noted scholar and consultant, has worked extensively with groups to analyze and improve their decision-making processes.[34] He observes that groups may make decisions through any of the following six methods: lack of response, authority rule, minority rule, majority rule, consensus, or unanimity.

In *decision by lack of response*, one idea after another is suggested without any discussion taking place. When the group finally accepts an idea, all others have been bypassed and discarded by simple lack of response rather than by critical evaluation. In *decision by authority rule*, the chairperson, manager, or leader makes a decision for the group. This can be done with or without discussion and is very time efficient. Whether the decision is a good one or a bad one, however, depends on whether or not the authority figure has the necessary information and on how well other group members accept this approach. In *decision by minority rule*, two or three people are able to dominate or "railroad" the

W. L. Gore & Associates ←
www.gore.com

Teams are center stage at this maker of popular GORE-TEX® fabrics and other high-tech products, including GLIDE® dental floss. Employees, or associates, praise a "bossless" management style in which they are encouraged to make their own commitments. An associate stock ownership plan adds incentive to making good investment decisions.

THE EFFECTIVE MANAGER 9.2

GUIDELINES FOR GROUP CONSENSUS

1. Don't argue blindly; consider others' reactions to your points.
2. Don't change your mind just to reach quick agreement.
3. Avoid conflict reduction by voting, coin tossing, and bargaining.
4. Try to involve everyone in the decision process.
5. Allow disagreements to surface so that information and opinions can be deliberated.
6. Don't focus on winning versus losing; seek alternatives acceptable to all.
7. Discuss assumptions, listen carefully, and encourage participation by everyone.

■ **Consensus** is a group decision that has the expressed support of most members.

group into making a decision to which they agree. This is often done by providing a suggestion and then forcing quick agreement by challenging the group with such statements as: "Does anyone object?... No? Well, let's go ahead then."

One of the most common ways groups make decisions, especially when early signs of disagreement set in, is *decision by majority rule*. Here, formal voting may take place, or members may be polled to find the majority viewpoint. This method parallels the democratic political system and is often used without awareness of its potential problems. The very process of voting can create coalitions. That is, some people will be "winners," and others will be "losers" when the final vote is tallied. Those in the minority—the "losers," may feel left out or discarded without having had a fair say. As a result, they may be less enthusiastic about implementing the decision of the "winners." Lingering resentments may impair group effectiveness in the future.

Another alternative is *decision by consensus*. Formally defined, **consensus** is a state of affairs whereby discussion leads to one alternative being favored by most members and the other members agreeing to support it. When a consensus is reached, even those who may have opposed the chosen course of action know that they have been listened to and have had a fair chance to influence the outcome. Consensus, as suggested by the guidelines in The Effective Manager 9.2, does not require unanimity. What it does require is the opportunity for any dissenting members to feel they have been able to speak, and that their voices have been heard.[35]

A *decision by unanimity* may be the ideal state of affairs. Here, all group members agree totally on the course of action to be taken. This is a "logically perfect" group decision method that is extremely difficult to attain in actual practice. One reason that groups sometimes turn to authority decisions, majority voting, or even minority decisions is the difficulty of managing the group process to achieve consensus or unanimity.[36]

■ ASSETS AND LIABILITIES OF GROUP DECISION MAKING

The best groups don't limit themselves to just one decision-making method, using it over and over again regardless of circumstances. Instead, they change decision methods to best fit the problem and situation at hand. Indeed, an important group leadership skill is helping a group choose the "right" decision method—that is, the one providing for a timely and quality decision and to which the members are highly committed. This choice should be made with a full awareness of the assets and liabilities of group decision making. For example, the *potential advantages of group decision making* include:[37]

Advantages of group decision making

1. *Information*—more knowledge and expertise is applied to solve the problem.
2. *Alternatives*—a greater number of alternatives are examined, avoiding tunnel vision.

3. *Understanding and acceptance*—the final decision is better understood and accepted by all group members.

4. *Commitment*—there is more commitment among all group members to make the final decision work.

We also know that groups can experience problems when they are making decisions. The *potential disadvantages of group decision making* include:[38]

1 *Social pressure to conform*—individuals may feel compelled to go along with the apparent wishes of the group.

2. *Minority domination*—the group's decision may be forced or "railroaded" by one individual or a small coalition.

3. *Time demands*—with more people involved in the dialogue and discussion, group decisions usually take longer to make than individual decisions.

> **Disadvantages of group decision making**

■ GROUPTHINK

An important potential problem in group decision making, identified by social psychologist Irving Janis, is **groupthink**—the tendency of members in highly cohesive groups to lose their critical evaluative capabilities.[39] Janis believes that, because highly cohesive groups demand conformity, their members tend to become unwilling to criticize one another's ideas and suggestions. Desires to hold the group together and to avoid unpleasant disagreements lead to an overemphasis on agreement and an underemphasis on critical discussion. The possible result is a poor decision. Janis suggests that groupthink played a role in the lack of preparedness of U.S. forces at Pearl Harbor in World War II. It has also been linked to U.S. decision making during the Vietnam War and to the space shuttle *Challenger* disaster.

> ■ **Groupthink** is the tendency of cohesive group members to lose their critical evaluative capabilities.

Group leaders and members must be on guard to spot the symptoms of groupthink and take any necessary action to prevent its occurrence.[40] The Effective Manager 9.3 identifies steps that can be taken to avoid groupthink. Among them, for example, President Kennedy chose to absent himself from certain strategy discussions by his cabinet during the Cuban Missile crisis. Reportedly, this facilitated discussion and helped to improve decision making as the crisis was successfully resolved.

■ HOW TO IMPROVE GROUP DECISION MAKING

In order to take full advantage of the group as a decision-making resource, care must be taken to manage group dynamics to balance individual contributions and group operations.[41] A particular concern is with the process losses that often occur in free-flowing meetings, such as a committee deliberation or a staff meeting on a specific problem. In these settings the risk of social pressures to conformity, domination, time pressures, and even highly emotional de-

THE EFFECTIVE MANAGER 9.3

HOW TO AVOID GROUPTHINK

- Assign the role of critical evaluator to each group member.
- Have the leader avoid seeming partial to one course of action.
- Create subgroups to work on the same problem.
- Have group members discuss issues with outsiders and report back.
- Invite outside experts to observe and react to group processes.
- Assign someone to be a "devil's advocate" at each meeting.
- Write alternative scenarios for the intentions of competing groups.
- Hold "second-chance" meetings after consensus is apparently achieved.

bates may detract from the purpose at hand. They are also settings in which special group decision techniques may be used to advantage.[42]

Brainstorming   In **brainstorming**, group members actively generate as many ideas and alternatives as possible, and they do so relatively quickly and without inhibitions. Four rules typically govern the brainstorming process. First, *all criticism is ruled out*. No one is allowed to judge or evaluate any ideas until the idea-generation process has been completed. Second, *"freewheeling" is welcomed*. The emphasis is on creativity and imagination; the wilder or more radical the ideas, the better. Third, *quantity is wanted*. The emphasis is also on the number of ideas; the greater the number, the more likely a superior idea will appear. Fourth, *"piggy-backing" is good*. Everyone is encouraged to suggest how others' ideas can be turned into new ideas or how two or more ideas can be joined into still another new idea. Typical results include enthusiasm, involvement, and a free flow of ideas useful in creative problem solving.

■ **Brainstorming** involves generating ideas through "freewheeling" and without criticism.

Nominal Group Technique   In any group, there will be times when the opinions of members differ so much that antagonistic arguments will develop during free-wheeling discussions. At other times the group will be so large that open discussion and brainstorming are awkward to manage. In such cases, a form of structured group decision making called the **nominal group technique** may be helpful.[43] It puts people in small groups of six to seven members and asks everyone to respond individually and in writing to a "nominal question" such as: "What should be done to improve the effectiveness of this work team?" Everyone is encouraged to list as many alternatives or ideas as they can. Next, participants read aloud their responses to the nominal question in round-robin fashion. The recorder writes each response on large newsprint as it is offered. No criticism is allowed. The recorder asks for any questions that may clarify items on the newsprint. This is again done in round-robin fashion, and no evaluation is allowed. The goal is simply to make sure that everyone present fully understands each response. A structured voting procedure is then used to prioritize responses to the nominal question. The nominal group procedure allows ideas to be evaluated without risking the inhibitions, hostilities, and distortions that may occur in an open meeting.

■ The **nominal group technique** involves structured rules for generating and prioritizing ideas.

Delphi Technique   A third group decision approach, the **Delphi technique**, was developed by the Rand Corporation for use in situations where group members are unable to meet face to face. In this procedure, a series of questionnaires are distributed to a panel of decision makers, who submit initial responses to a decision coordinator. The coordinator summarizes the solutions and sends the summary back to the panel members, along with a followup questionnaire. Panel members again send in their responses, and the process is repeated until a consensus is reached and a clear decision emerges.

■ The **Delphi technique** involves generating decision-making alternatives through a series of survey questionnaires.

Computer-Mediated Decision Making   Today's information and computer technologies enable group decision making to take place across great distances with the support of group decision support systems. The growing use of *electronic brainstorming* is one example of the trend toward virtual meetings. Assisted by special software, participants use personal computers to enter ideas at will, either through simultaneous interaction or over a period of time. The software compiles and disseminates the results. Both the nominal group and Delphi techniques also lend themselves to computer mediation. Electronic approaches to group decision making can offer several advantages, including the benefits of anonymity, greater number of ideas generated, efficiency of recording and storing for later use, and ability to handle large groups with geographically dispersed members.[44]

Chapter 9 Study Guide

Summary

What is the nature of groups in organizations?

- A group is a collection of people who interact with one another regularly to attain common goals.

- Groups can help organizations by helping their members to improve task performance and experience more satisfaction from their work.

- One way to view organizations is as interlocking networks of groups, whose managers serve as leaders in one group and subordinates in another.

- Synergy occurs when groups are able to accomplish more than their members could by acting individually.

- Formal groups are designated by the organization to serve an official purpose; examples are work units, task forces, and committees; informal groups are unofficial and emerge spontaneously because of special interests.

What are the stages of group development?

- Groups pass through various stages in their life cycles, and each stage poses somewhat distinct management problems.

- In the forming stage, groups have problems managing individual entry.

- In the storming stage, groups have problems managing expectations and status.

- In the norming or initial integration stage, groups have problems managing member relations and task efforts.

- In the performing or total integration stage, groups have problems managing continuous improvement and self-renewal.

- In the adjourning stage, groups have problems managing task completion and the process of disbanding.

What are the input foundations of group effectiveness?

- An effective group is one that achieves high levels of task accomplishment and member satisfaction, and achieves viability to perform successfully over the long term.

- As open systems, groups must interact successfully with their environments to obtain resources that are transformed into outputs.

- Group input factors establish the core foundations for effectiveness, and include: goals, rewards, resources, technology, the task, membership characteristics, and group size, among other possibilities.

What are group and intergroup dynamics?

- Group dynamics are the way members work together to utilize inputs; they are another foundation of group effectiveness.

- Group dynamics are based on the interactions, activities, and sentiments of group members, and on the required and emergent ways in which members work together.

- Intergroup dynamics are the forces that operate between two or more groups.

- Although groups in organizations ideally cooperate with one another, they often become involved in dysfunctional conflicts and competition.

- The disadvantages of intergroup competition can be reduced through management strategies to direct, train, and reinforce groups to pursue cooperative instead of purely competitive actions.

How do groups make decisions?

- Groups can make decisions by lack of response, authority rule, minority rule, majority rule, consensus, and unanimity.

- The potential assets to more group decision making include having more information available and generating more understanding and commitment.

- The potential liabilities to more group decision making include social pressures to conform and greater time requirements.

- "Groupthink" is the tendency of some groups to lose critical evaluative capabilities.

- Techniques for improving creativity in group decision making include brainstorming, nominal group technique, and the Delphi method, including computer applications.

Key Terms

Brainstorming (p. 188)
Consensus (p. 186)
Delphi technique (p. 188)
Diversity–consensus dilemma (p. 182)
Effective groups (p. 175)
FIRO-B theory (p. 183)

Formal groups (p. 177)
Groups (p. 174)
Group dynamics (p. 184)
Groupthink (p. 187)
Informal group (p. 178)
Intergroup dynamics (p. 185)

Nominal group technique (p. 188)
Social loafing (p. 176)
Social facilitation (p. 176)
Status congruence (p. 183)
Synergy (p. 175)

Self-Test 9 ■ **MULTIPLE CHOICE**

1. The FIRO-B theory addresses _____ in groups. (a) membership compatabilities (b) social loafing (c) dominating members (d) conformity

2. It is during the _____ stage of group development that members begin to re-

ally come together as a coordinated unit. (a) storming (b) norming (c) performing (d) total integration

3. An effective group is defined as one that achieves high levels of task performance, member satisfaction, and _____. (a) coordination (b) harmony (c) creativity (d) team viability

4. Task characteristics, reward systems, and group size are all _____ that can make a difference in group effectiveness. (a) group processes (b) group dynamics (c) group inputs (d) human-resource maintenance factors

5. The best size for a problem-solving group is usually _____ members. (a) no more than 3 or 4 (b) 5 to 7 (c) 8 to 10 (d) around 12 to 13

6. When two groups are in competition with one another, within each group _____ may be expected. (a) more in-group loyalty (b) less reliance on the leader (c) less task focus (d) more conflict

7. The tendency of groups to lose their critical evaluative capabilities during decision making is a phenomenon called _____. (a) groupthink (b) the Ringlemann effect (c) decision congruence (d) group consensus

8. When a decision requires a high degree of commitment for its implementation, a/an _____ decision is generally preferred. (a) authority (b) majority vote (c) group consensus (d) groupthink

9. What does the Ringlemann effect describe in respect to group behavior? (a) tendency of groups to make risky decisions (b) social loafing (c) social facilitation (d) satisfaction of members' social needs

10. Members of a multinational task force in a large international business should be aware that _____ might initially slow the progress of the group in meeting its task objectives. (a) synergy (b) groupthink (c) diversity-consensus dilemma (d) intergroup dynamics

■ TRUE–FALSE

11. The creation of a whole that is greater than the sum of its parts defines synergy. T   F

12. Informal groups tend to hurt organizations and should not be tolerated by managers. T   F

13. Generally speaking, members of homogeneous groups are expected to work easily and well with one another.   T   F

14. Poor attitudes toward work are examples of sentiments that may exist in group dynamics.   T   F

15. Decision by majority voting is the only group decision method without any disadvantages.   T   F

16. The potential liabilities or disadvantages of group decision making include social pressures to conform.   T   F

17. When group members are not getting along well together, the brainstorming technique is a good approach for improving creativity in decision making.   T   F

18. Devil's advocate roles and second-chance meetings are good ways for members to avoid the dangers of groupthink.   T   F

19. Increasing interactions among members is one way of dealing with dysfunctional intergroup relationships.   T   F

20. Group decision making is always superior to individual decision making.   T   F

■ SHORT RESPONSE

21. How can groups be good for organizations?

22. What types of formal groups are found in organizations today?

23. What is the difference between required and emergent behaviors in group dynamics?

24. How can intergroup competition be bad for organizations?

■ APPLICATIONS ESSAY

25. Alejandro Puron recently encountered a dilemma in working with his quality circle (QC) team. One of the team members claims that the QC must always be unanimous in its recommendations. "Otherwise," she says, "we will not have a true consensus." Alejandro, the current QC leader, disagrees. He believes that unanimity is desirable but not always necessary to achieve consensus. You are a management consultant specializing in group utilization in organizations. Alejandro calls you for advice. What would you tell him and why?

Explore application-oriented Fast Company articles, cases, experimental exercises, and self-assessments in the OB Skills Workbook

■ **Visit the Schermerhorn Web site to find the Interactive Self-Test and Internet exercises for this chapter.**

www.wiley.com/college/schermerhorn

Teamwork and High Performance Teams

PUTTING CREATIVITY TO WORK

www.audible.com

The office building is nondescript; the location is nothing special. But the little company on the third floor is something else! It is the Internet start-up Audible.com, founded by entrepreneur Donald Katz, and it is out to change your life. How would you like to listen, anywhere and anytime you want, to an audible digest of *The Wall Street Journal* or a program from National Public Radio? Audible.com is developing the capability to deliver this type of on-demand audio to portable Web devices that can be used anywhere, in the car, at home, while outside working in the yard, or even jogging. Eventually, the product will be everything from audible books, to entertainment, news, advice, and corporate information and training programs.

What's behind this innovative firm? Well it takes entrepreneurship and vision—that's Donald Katz. A risk-taker, he decided to start Audible.com to tap both his background as a writer and the unlimited potential of the Internet. That's where technology comes in. Says Katz: "Audible seeks to wed the oldest of technologies, the spoken word, with the newest of technologies. We want to be the leader in teaching the Internet to talk." But successful companies are not built on good ideas alone. It takes a team to make them work.

Katz's team of 35 people is working hard to bring the corporate Web site to life. Stop by on a Friday afternoon and you're likely to find everyone gathered together for darts and refreshments. If an adage may be coined, "The staff that plays together wins together," the team at Audible.com is off to a running start. Whether the company makes the big time, only time will tell. Watch for it.[1]

"Who needs a boss?" once read the headline of a provocative *Fortune* magazine article. "Not the employees who work in self-managed teams," answers the first paragraph.[2] Since then the shift of focus from individual jobs to teams and teamwork is one of the most notable ways in which work is changing today.[3] In many situations teams and teamwork are considered major, even essential, keys to productivity and quality of working life improvements. But putting team concepts to work is a major challenge for people used to more traditional ways of working. As more and more jobs are turned over to teams, special problems relating to group and intergroup dynamics may occur. It is not enough for visionary entrepreneurs, leaders, and managers like Donald Katz to recognize the value of teams and implement creative work group designs. They must also carefully nurture and support people and relationships if the groups are to become confident and enduring high performance teams.

Study Questions

Highly motivated and successful teams are benchmarks of successful organizations today. This chapter introduces the essentials of teams and teamwork for high performance systems. As you read Chapter 10, keep in mind these questions:

- What is a high performance team...and what is teamwork?
- What is team building?
- What can be done to improve team processes?
- How do teams contribute to the high performance workplace?

High Performance Teams

When we think of the word "teams," a variety of popular sporting teams usually comes to mind. Work groups can also be considered as teams to the extent that they meet the demands of this definition. A **team** is a small group of people with complementary skills, who work actively together to achieve a common purpose for which they hold themselves collectively accountable.[4]

Teams are one of the major forces behind today's revolutionary changes in organizations. Management scholar Jay Conger calls the team-based organization

■ **Teams** are groups of people who work actively together to achieve a purpose for which they are all accountable.

194

the management system of the future, the business world's response to the need for speed in an ever more competitive environment.[5] He cites the example of an American jet engine manufacturer that switched to cross-functional teams instead of traditional functional work units. The firm cut the time required to design and produce new engines by 50 percent. Conger says: "Cross-functional teams are speed machines."[6] Clearly, we need to know more about such teams and teamwork in organizations.

■ TYPES OF TEAMS

A major challenge in any organization is to turn formal groups, as discussed in Chapter 9, into true high performance teams in any of the following settings.[7] First, there are *teams that recommend things*. Established to study specific problems and recommend solutions to them, these teams typically work with a target completion date and disband once their purpose has been fulfilled. They are temporary groups including task forces, ad hoc committees, project teams, and the like. Members of these teams must be able to learn quickly how to work well together, accomplish the assigned task, and make good action recommendations for followup work by other people.

Second, there are *teams that run things*. These management teams consist of people with the formal responsibility for leading other groups. These teams may exist at all levels of responsibility, from the individual work unit composed of a team leader and team members to the top management team composed of a CEO and other senior executives. Teams can add value to work processes at any level and offer special opportunities for dealing with complex problems and uncertain situations. Key issues addressed by top management teams, for example, include identifying overall organizational purposes, goals, and values, crafting strategies, and persuading others to support them.[8]

Third, there are *teams that make or do things*. These are functional groups and work units that perform ongoing tasks, such as marketing or manufacturing. Members of these teams must have good long-term working relationships with one another, solid operating systems, and the external support needed to achieve effectiveness over a sustained period of time. And they need energy to keep up the pace and meet the day-to-day challenges of sustained high performance.

HIGH PERFORMANCE ORGANIZATION

There's a lot of energy in Nancy Deibler's sales team in Sprint's small business sales division in Kansas City, Missouri. The work can be tedious as members work shifts and make a lot of cold calls. You might expect high turnover and burnout, but that's not so on Deibler's team. And it's "fun" that makes the difference. Deibler says: "Many of us really look forward to going to work because of the other people on the team. We relate to and get along with each other as friends." If you stop in to see them, don't be surprised if you find them taking off at 3:00 PM to go bowling, hold cookouts, or even share evenings at Karaoke. Says Deibler again: "It lifts productivity."[9]

www.sprint.com

■ THE NATURE OF TEAMWORK

All teams need members who believe in team goals and are motivated to work with others actively to accomplish important tasks—whether those tasks involve recommending things, making or doing things, or running things. Indeed, an essential criterion of a true team is that the members feel "collectively accountable" for what they accomplish.[10]

■ **Teamwork** occurs when group members work together in ways that utilize their skills well to accomplish a purpose.

This sense of collective accountability sets the stage for real **teamwork**, where team members actively working together in such a way that all their respective skills are well utilized to achieve a common purpose.[11] A commitment to teamwork is found in the willingness of every member to "listen and respond constructively to views expressed by others, give others the benefit of the doubt, provide support, and recognize the interests and achievements of others."[12] Teamwork of this type is the central foundation of any high performance team. But developing it is a challenging leadership task, regardless of the setting. It takes a lot more work to build a well-functioning team, than to simply assign members to the same group and then expect them to do a great job.[13] See for example, The Effective Manager 10.1.

High performance teams have specific characteristics that allow them to excel at teamwork and achieve special performance advantages. First, *high performance teams have strong core values* that help guide their attitudes and behaviors in directions consistent with the team's purpose. Such values act as an internal control system for a group or team and can substitute for much of the outside direction that a supervisor might otherwise provide. Second, *high performance teams turn a general sense of purpose into specific performance objectives.* Whereas a shared sense of purpose gives general direction to a team, commitment to specific performance results—such as reducing the time of getting the product to market by half, makes this purpose truly meaningful. Specific objectives provide a focus for solving problems and resolving conflicts, and they set standards for measuring results and obtaining performance feedback. They also help group members understand the need for "collective" versus purely individual efforts. Third, members of *high performance teams have the right mix of skills,* including technical skills, problem-solving and decision-making skills, and interpersonal skills. Finally, *high performance teams possess creativity.* In the new workplace, teams must use their creativity to assist organizations in continuous improvement of operations—including productivity and customer service—and in continuous development of new products, services, and markets.

THE EFFECTIVE MANAGER 10.1

HOW TO CREATE A HIGH-PERFORMING TEAM

- Communicate high-performance standards.
- Set the tone in the first team meeting.
- Create a sense of urgency.
- Make sure members have the right skills.
- Establish clear rules for team behavior.
- As a leader, model expected behaviors.
- Find ways to create early "successes."
- Continually introduce new facts and information.
- Make sure members spend a lot of time together.
- Give positive feedback and reward high performance.

■ DIVERSITY AND TEAM PERFORMANCE

In order to create and maintain high performance teams, all of the various elements of group effectiveness discussed in Chapter 9 must be addressed and successfully managed. Among them, membership diversity as an important input to group and team dynamics carries special significance in today's workplace.[14] When team members are homogeneous, that is, when members are alike in respect to such things as age, gender, race, ethnicity, experience, ethnicity and culture, there are certain potential benefits. It will probably be easy for them to quickly build social relationships and begin the interactions needed to work harmoniously together. On the other hand, the homogeneity may be limiting in terms of ideas, viewpoints, and creativity. With team diversity in terms of demography, experiences, and cultures, by contrast, comes a rich pool of information, talent, and varied perspectives that can help improve problem solving and increase creativity. These assets are especially valuable when the team is working on complex and very demanding tasks.

Research indicates that diversity among team members may create performance difficulties early in the team's life or stage of development. This occurs when interpersonal stresses and conflicts relating to diversity slow down group processes such as relationship building, problem definition, and information sharing.[15] But even though diverse teams may struggle in the short run to resolve these issues, they are also likely to develop enhanced performance potential once things are worked out.[16] Although it may take a bit more time and effort to create teamwork from foundations of diversity, longer-term gains in creativity and performance can make it all worthwhile. Teamwork rich in diversity is one of the great advantages of high performance organizations.

> ## OB Across Functions
> ### RESEARCH & DEVELOPMENT
> #### Working Together Across Cultures
> "Something magical happens," says John Thomas, project engineer in the Science and Technology's Process Modeling and Measurement Directorate, when Corning scientists from the Fontainebleau Research Center in France and those at Sullivan Park solve a problem together. This is not because they've entered some big melting pot where everyone thinks the same. No, that "something magical" comes from an environment that honors, and even demands, the different perspectives inherent in the two cultures. "Europeans are very creative thinkers, they take time to really reflect on a problem to come up with the very best theoretical solution," states Thomas. "Americans are more tactical and practical—we want to get down to developing a working solution as soon as possible." His partner at the Fontainebleau Research Center in France, Patrick Herveé, summarizes the difference this way: "The French are more focused on ideas and concepts. If we get blocked in the execution of those ideas, we give up. Not the Americans. They pay more attention to details, processes and time schedules. They make sure they are prepared and have involved everyone in the planning process so that they won't get blocked. But it's best if you mix the two approaches. In the end, you will achieve the best results."

Team Building

Teamwork doesn't always happen naturally in a group. It is something that team members and leaders must work hard to achieve. In the sports world, for example, coaches and managers focus on teamwork when building new teams at the start of each season. And as you are aware, even experienced teams often run into problems as a season progresses. Members slack off or become disgruntled; some have performance "slumps;" some are traded to other teams. Even world-champion teams have losing streaks, and the most talented players can lose motivation at times, quibble among themselves, and end up contributing little to team success. When these things happen, the owners, managers, and players are apt to examine their problems, take corrective action to rebuild the team, and restore the teamwork needed to achieve high performance results.

Work groups and teams have similar difficulties. When newly formed, they must master challenges in the early stages of group development. Even when they are mature, most work teams encounter problems of insufficient teamwork at different points in time. When difficulties occur, or as a means of preventing them from occurring, a systematic process of **team building** can help. This is a sequence of planned activities designed to gather and analyze data on the functioning of a group and to initiate changes designed to improve teamwork and increase group effectiveness.[17]

■ **Team building** is a collaborative way to gather and analyze data to improve teamwork.

■ HOW TEAM BUILDING WORKS

The action steps and continuous improvement theme highlighted in Figure 10.1 are typical of most team-building approaches. The process begins when someone notices that a problem exists or may develop with team effectiveness. Members then work together to gather data relating to the problem, analyze these data, plan for improvements, and implement the action plans. The entire team-building process is highly collaborative. Everyone is expected to participate actively as group operations are evaluated and decisions are made on what needs to be done to improve the team's functioning in the future. This process can and should become an ongoing part of any team's work agenda. It is an approach to continuous improvement that can be very beneficial to long-term team effectiveness.

Team-building is participatory, and it is data based. Whether the data are gathered by questionnaire, interview, nominal group meeting, or other creative methods, the goal is to get good answers to such questions as: "How well are we doing in terms of task accomplishment?"... "How satisfied are we as individual members with the group and the way it operates?" There are a variety of ways for such questions to be asked and answered in a collaborative and motivating manner.

■ APPROACHES TO TEAM BUILDING

In the *formal retreat approach*, team building takes place during an off-site "retreat." During this retreat, which may last from one to several days, group members work intensively on a variety of assessment and planning tasks. They are initiated by a review of team functioning using data gathered through survey, interviews, or other means. Formal retreats are often held with the assistance of a consultant, who is either hired from the outside or made available from in-house staff. Team-building retreats are quite common and offer opportunities for intense and concentrated efforts to examine group accomplishments and operations.

Not all team building is done in a formal retreat format or with the assistance of consultants. In a *continuous improvement approach*, the manager, team leader, or group members themselves take responsibility for regularly engaging in the team-building process. This method can be as simple as periodic meetings that implement the team-building steps; it can also include self-managed formal retreats. In all cases, the team members commit themselves to monitoring group development and accomplishments continuously and making the day-to-day changes needed to ensure team effectiveness. Such continuous improvement of teamwork is essential to the total quality and total service management themes so important to organizations today.

Charles Schwab & Co. ◄
www.schwab.com

The financial services giant and leader in on-line brokerage Charles Schwab & Co. is committed to making meetings better. In most meetings someone serves as "observer" and completes a Plus/Delta list of what went right and wrong. The lists are used company-wide to create agendas for change.

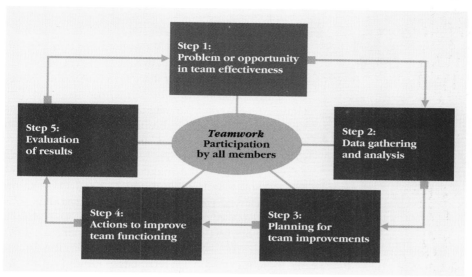

Figure 10.1
The team-building process.

In addition, the *outdoor experience approach* is an increasingly popular team-building activity that may be done on its own or in combination with other approaches. The outdoor experience places group members in a variety of physically challenging situations that must be mastered through teamwork, not individual work. By having to work together in the face of difficult obstacles, team members are supposed to experience increased self-confidence, more respect for others' capabilities, and a greater commitment to teamwork. A popular sponsor of team building through outdoor experience is the Outward Bound Leadership School, but many others exist. For a group that has never done team building before, outdoor experience can be an exciting way to begin; for groups familiar with team building, it can be a way of further enriching the experience.

Improving Team Processes

Like many changes in the new workplace, the increased emphasis on teams and teamwork is a major challenge for people used to more traditional ways of working. As more and more jobs are turned over to teams and as more and more traditional supervisors are asked to function as team leaders, special problems relating to team processes may arise. As teams become more integral to organizations, multiple and shifting memberships can cause complications. Team leaders and members alike must be prepared to deal positively with such issues as introducing new members, handling disagreements on goals and responsibilities, resolving delays and disputes when making decisions, and reducing friction and interpersonal conflicts. Given the complex nature of group dynamics, team building in a sense is never done. Something is always happening that creates the need for further leadership efforts to help improve team processes.

www.blackenterprise.com

📈 ENTREPRENEURSHIP

The team at the top is without doubt, a family affair. Earl G. Graves, Sr. is chairman & CEO of Earl G. Graves, Ltd., parent company of Earl G. Graves Publishing Company, publisher of *Black Enterprise* magazine. Earl Graves, Sr. founded the magazine in 1970 and remains Chairman, Editor and Publisher. Working with him in the executive suite is Earl, Jr., ("Butch") President & COO of Earl G. Graves Publishing Company. John C. Graves ("Johnny") the middle sibling, is President of Black Enterprise Unlimited and General Counsel for Earl G. Graves Ltd. Michael Graves, the youngest, is Unit Manager of Pepsi-Cola Washington, D.C., L.P., a franchise of The Pepsi Bottling Group. Until November 1998, Earl Graves was Chairman and CEO of the bottling operation, the largest minority-controlled Pepsi-Cola franchise in the United States. Running a family business as a family takes work. "Family businesses are doomed from the start if members don't share respect, love, and certainly, trust." says Earl, Jr. A common bond among this team is the pride they all share in the magazine. Earl Jr., says "*Black Enterprise* makes a positive contribution to the African-American Community," adding further, "I'd like to see my children carry it on in the spirit."

▪ NEW MEMBER PROBLEMS

Special difficulties are likely to occur when members first get together in a new group or work team, or when new members join an existing one. Problems often arise as new members try to understand what is expected of them while dealing with anxiety and discomfort in a new social setting. New members, for example, may worry about: *Participation*—"Will I be allowed to participate?" *Goals*—"Do I share the same goals as others?" *Control*—"Will I be able to influence what takes place?" *Relationships*—"How close do people get?" *Processes*—"Are conflicts likely to be upsetting?"

Edgar Schein points out that people may try to cope with individual entry problems in self-serving ways that may hinder group operations.[18] He identifies three behavior profiles that are common in such situations. The *tough battler* is frustrated by a lack of identity in the new group and may act aggressively or reject authority. This person wants answers to the question: "Who am I in this group?" The *friendly helper* is insecure, suffering uncertainties of intimacy and control. This person may show extraordinary support for others, behave in a dependent way, and seek alliances in subgroups or cliques. The friendly helper needs to know whether she or he will be liked. The *objective thinker* is anxious about how personal needs will be met in the group. This person may act in a passive, reflective, and even single-minded manner while struggling with the fit between individual goals and group directions.

▪ TASK AND MAINTENANCE LEADERSHIP

Research in social psychology suggests that the achievement of sustained high performance by groups requires that both "task needs" and "maintenance needs"

Figure 10.2
Task and maintenance leadership in group team dynamics.

be met.[19] Although anyone formally appointed as group leader should help fulfill these needs, all members should also contribute. This responsibility for **distributed leadership** in group dynamics is an important requirement of any high performance team.[20]

Figure 10.2 describes group **task activities** as the various things members do that directly contribute to the performance of important group tasks. They include activities such as initiating discussion, sharing information, asking information of others, clarifying something that has been said, and summarizing the status of a deliberation.[21] If these task activities are not adequate, the group will have difficulty accomplishing its objectives. By contrast, in an effective group, members contribute important task activities as needed and as building blocks for performance success.

Maintenance activities support the group's social and interpersonal relationships. They help the group stay intact and healthy as an ongoing social system. A member contributes maintenance leadership, for example, by encouraging the participation of others, trying to harmonize differences of opinion, praising the contributions of others, and agreeing to go along with a popular course of action. When maintenance leadership is poor, members become dissatisfied with one another and their group membership. This sets the stage for conflicts that can drain energies otherwise needed for task performance. In an effective group, by contrast, maintenance activities help sustain the relationships needed for group members to work well together over time.

In addition to helping meet a group's task and maintenance needs, group members share the additional responsibility of avoiding *disruptive behaviors*—behaviors that harm the group process. Full participation in distributed leadership means taking individual responsibility for avoiding the following types of behaviors, and helping others do the same:

1. Being overly aggressive toward other members.
2. Withdrawing and refusing to cooperate with others.
3. Horsing around when there is work to be done.
4. Using the group as a forum for self-confession.
5. Talking too much about irrelevant matters.
6. Trying to compete for attention and recognition.

■ ROLES AND ROLE DYNAMICS

In groups and teams, new and old members alike need to know what others expect of them and what they can expect from others. A **role** is a set of expecta-

■ **Distributed leadership** is the sharing of responsibility for meeting group task and maintenance needs.

■ **Task activities** directly contribute to the performance of important tasks.

■ **Maintenance activities** support the emotional life of the team as an ongoing social system.

Disruptive behaviors that harm teams

■ A **role** is a set of expectations for a team member or person in a job.

■ **Role ambiguity** occurs when someone is uncertain about what is expected of him or her.

■ **Role overload** occurs when too much work is expected of the individual.

■ **Role underload** occurs when too little work is expected of the individual.

■ **Role conflict** occurs when someone is unable to respond to role expectations that conflict with one another.

Forms of role conflict

tions associated with a job or position on a team. When roles are unclear or conflictive, performance problems can occur. Groups and work teams sometimes experience problems that are caused by difficulties in defining and managing the roles of members.

Role ambiguity occurs when a person is uncertain about his or her role. To do any job well, people need to know what is expected of them. In new group or team situations, role ambiguities may create problems as members find that their work efforts are wasted or unappreciated by others. Even on mature groups and teams, the failure of members to share expectations and listen to one another may at times create a similar lack of understanding. Being asked to do too much or too little can also create problems. **Role overload** occurs when too much is expected and the individual feels overwhelmed with work. **Role underload** occurs when too little is expected and the individual feels underutilized. Any group benefits from clear and realistic expectations regarding the contributions of each member.

Role conflict occurs when a person is unable to meet the expectations of others. The individual understands what needs to be done but for some reason cannot comply. The resulting tension can reduce job satisfaction and affect both work performance and relationships with other group members. Four common forms of role conflict are: (1) *Intrasender role conflict* occurs when the same person sends conflicting expectations. (2) *Intersender role conflict* occurs when different people send conflicting and mutually exclusive expectations. (3) *Person–role conflict* occurs when one's personal values and needs come into conflict with role expectations. (4) *Interrole conflict* occurs when the expectations of two or more roles held by the same individual become incompatible, such as the conflict between work and family demands.

One way of managing role dynamics in any group or work setting is by *role negotiation*. This is a process through which individuals negotiate to clarify the role expectations each holds for the other. Sample results from an actual role negotiation are shown in Figure 10.3. Note the "give and take" between negotiators.

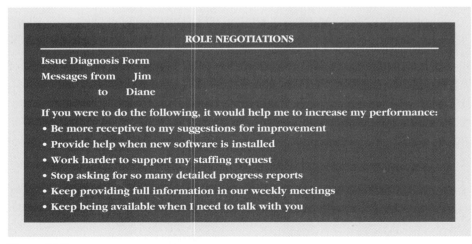

Figure 10.3
A sample role negotiations agreement.

■ POSITIVE NORMS

The **norms** of a group or team represent ideas or beliefs about how members are expected to behave. They can be considered as "rules" or "standards" of conduct.[22] Norms help clarify the expectations associated with a person's membership in a group. They allow members to structure their own behavior and to predict what others will do; they help members gain a common sense of direction; and they reinforce a desired group or team culture. When someone violates a group norm, other members typically respond in ways that are aimed at enforcing the norm. These responses may include direct criticisms, reprimands, expulsion, and social ostracism.

Managers, task force heads, committee chairs, and team leaders must all try to help their groups adopt positive norms that support organizational goals (see The Effective Manager 10.2). A key norm in any setting is the *performance norm*, which conveys expectations about how hard group members should work. Other norms are important too. In order for a task force or a committee to operate effectively, for example, norms regarding attendance at meetings, punctuality, preparedness, criticism, and social behaviors are needed. Groups also commonly have norms regarding how to deal with supervisors, colleagues, and customers, as well as norms establishing guidelines for honesty and ethical behaviors. The following list shows how everyday conversations can lend insight into the various types of norms that operate with positive and negative implications for groups and organizations.[23]

■ **Norms** are rules or standards for the behavior of group members.

> ### THE EFFECTIVE MANAGER 10.2
>
> #### SEVEN STEPS TO POSITIVE NORMS
>
> 1. Act as a positive role model.
> 2. Hold meetings to agree on goals.
> 3. Select members who can and will perform.
> 4. Provide support and training for members.
> 5. Reinforce and reward desired behaviors.
> 6. Hold meetings for feedback and performance review.
> 7. Hold meetings to plan for improvements.

- *Organizational and personal pride norms*—"It is a tradition around here for people to stand up for the company when others criticize it unfairly" (positive); "In our company, they are always trying to take advantage of us" (negative).

- *High-achievement norms*—"On our team, people always try to work hard" (positive); "There's no point in trying harder on our team, nobody else does" (negative).

- *Support and helpfulness norms*—"People on this committee are good listeners and actively seek out the ideas and opinions of others" (positive); "On this committee it's dog-eat-dog and save your own skin" (negative).

- *Improvement and change norms*—"In our department people are always looking for better ways of doing things" (positive); "Around here, people hang on to the old ways even after they have outlived their usefulness" (negative).

Types of group norms

■ TEAM COHESIVENESS

Group or team **cohesiveness** is the degree to which members are attracted to and motivated to remain part of it.[24] Cohesiveness tends to be high when members are similiar in age, attitudes, needs, and backgrounds. It is also high in groups of small size, where members respect one another's competencies, agree

■ **Cohesiveness** is the degree to which members are attracted to a group and motivated to remain a part of it.

on common goals, and work on interdependent tasks. Cohesiveness tends to increase when groups are physically isolated from others and when they experience performance success or crisis.

Persons in a highly cohesive group value their membership and strive to maintain positive relationships with other group members. In this sense, cohesive groups and teams are good for their members. In contrast to less cohesive groups, members of highly cohesive ones tend to be more energetic when working on group activities, less likely to be absent, and more likely to be happy about performance success and sad about failures. Cohesive groups generally have low turnover and satisfy a broad range of individual needs, often providing a source of loyalty, security, and esteem for their members.

Conformity to Norms   Even though cohesive groups are good for their members, they may or may not be good for the organization. Figure 10.4 demonstrates the performance implications for a basic *rule of conformity in group dynamics*: the more cohesive the group, the greater the conformity of members to group norms.

When the performance norms are positive in a highly cohesive work group or team, the resulting conformity to the norm should have a positive effect on task performance as well as member satisfaction. This is a "best-case" situation for everyone. When the performance norms are negative in a highly cohesive group, however, the same power of conformity can have undesirable results. As shown in the figure, this creates a "worst-case" situation for the organization. Although team members are highly motivated to support group norms, the organization suffers from poor performance results. In between these two extremes are mixed-case situations in which a lack of cohesion fails to rally strong conformity to the norm. With its strength reduced, the outcome of the norm is somewhat unpredictable and performance will most likely fall on the moderate or low side.

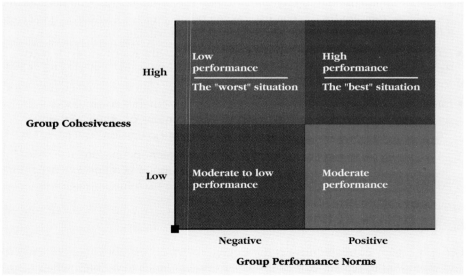

Figure 10.4
How cohesiveness and conformity to norms affect group performance.

Figure 10.5
**Ways to increase and
decrease group
cohesiveness.**

Influencing Cohesiveness   Team leaders and managers must be aware of the steps they can take to build cohesiveness, such as in a group that has positive norms but suffers from low cohesiveness. They must also be ready to deal with situations when cohesiveness adds to the problems of negative and hard-to-change performance norms. Figure 10.5 shows how group cohesiveness can be increased or decreased by making changes in group goals, membership composition, interactions, size, rewards, competition, location, and duration.

Teams and the High Performance Workplace

> When it was time to re-engineer its order-to-delivery process to eliminate an uncompetitive and costly 26-day cycle time, Hewlett-Packard turned to a team. In just nine months they slashed the time to eight days, improved service, and cut costs. How did they do it? Team leader Julie Anderson says: "We took things away: no supervisors, no hierarchy, no titles, no job descriptions…the idea was to create a sense of personal ownership." Says a team member: "…no individual is going to have the best idea, that's not the way it works—the best ideas come from the collective intelligence of the team."[25]

Just like this example from Hewlett-Packard, organizations everywhere in the new workplace are finding creative ways of using teams to solve problems and make changes to improve performance. The watchwords of these new approaches to teamwork are empowerment, participation, and involvement, and the setting is increasingly described as an organization that looks and acts much more "lateral" or "horizontal" than vertical.[26]

■ PROBLEM-SOLVING TEAMS

One way organizations can use teams is in creative problem solving. The term **employee involvement team** applies to a wide variety of teams whose mem-

■ Members of **employee involvement teams** meet regularly to examine work-related problems and opportunities.

bers meet regularly to collectively examine important workplace issues. They discuss ways to enhance quality, better satisfy customers, raise productivity, and improve the quality of work life. In this way, employee involvement teams mobilize the full extent of workers' know-how and gain the commitment needed to fully implement solutions.

A special type of employee involvement group is the **quality circle**, or QC for short. It is a small group of persons who meet periodically (e.g., an hour or so, once a week) to discuss and develop solutions for problems relating to quality, productivity, or cost.[27] QCs are popular in organizations around the world, but cannot be seen as panaceas for all of an organization's ills. To be successful, members of QCs should receive special training in group dynamics, information gathering, and problem analysis techniques. Leaders of quality circles should also be trained in participation and team building. Any solutions to problems should be jointly pursued by QC members and organizational management. QCs work best in organizations that place a clear emphasis on quality in their mission and goals, promote a culture that supports participation and empowerment, encourage trust and willingness to share important information, and develop a "team spirit."

■ Members of a **quality circle** meet regularly to find ways for continuous improvement of quality operations.

■ CROSS-FUNCTIONAL TEAMS

In today's organizations, teams are essential components in the achievement of more horizontal integration and better lateral relations. The **cross-functional team**, consisting of members representing different functional departments or work units, plays an important role in this regard. Traditionally, many organizations have suffered from what is often called the **functional silos problem**. This problem occurs when members of functional units stay focused on matters internal to the function and minimize their interactions with members of other functions. In this sense, the functional departments or work units create artificial boundaries or "silos" that discourage rather than encourage more integrative thinking and active coordination with other parts of the organization.

The new team-based organizations discussed in Chapter 11 are designed to help break down this problem and improve lateral communication.[28] Members of cross-functional teams can solve problems with a positive combination of functional expertise and integrative or total systems thinking. They do so with the great advantages of better information and more speed. Boeing, for example, used this concept to great advantage in designing and bringing to market the 777 passenger jet.[29] A complex network of cross-functional teams brought together design engineers, mechanics, pilots, suppliers, and even customers to manage the "design/build" processes.

■ **Cross-functional teams** bring together persons from different functions to work on a common task.

■ The **functional silos problem** is when persons working in different functions fail to communicate and interact with one another.

■ VIRTUAL TEAMS

Until recently, teamwork was confined in concept and practice to those circumstances in which members could meet face-to-face. Now, the advent of new technologies and sophisticated computer programs known as groupware have changed all that. **Virtual teams**, introduced in the last chapter as ones whose members meet at least part of the time electronically and with computer support, are a fact of life.[30] The real world of work in businesses and other organizations today involves a variety of electronic communications that allow people to work

■ A **virtual team** convenes and operates with members linked together electronically via networked computers.

together through computer mediation, and often separated by vast geographical space. *Groupware*, in popular forms such as Lotus Domino, Microsoft Exchange and Netscape SuiteSpot, allows for virtual meetings and group decision making in a variety of forms and situations.[31] This is further supported by advancements in conferencing and collaboration, including audio, data, and video conferencing alternatives.[32]

Virtual teams offer a number of potential advantages. They bring cost-effectiveness and speed to teamwork where members are unable to meet easily face-to-face. They also bring the power of the computer to bear on typical team needs for information processing and decision making.[33] With the computer as the "go-between" for virtual team members, however, group dynamics can emerge with a slightly different form than found in face-to-face settings.[34] Although technology can help to overcome great distance in making communication possible among a group of people, it may also create teams whose members do not share much, if any, direct "personal" contact. Whereas this may have an advantage of focusing interaction and decision making on facts and objective information rather than emotional considerations, it also may increase risks as decisions are made in a limited social context. Virtual teams may suffer from less social rapport and less direct interaction among members.

Just as with any form of teamwork, virtual teams rely on the efforts and contributions of their members as well as organizational support to achieve effectiveness. Teamwork in any form always takes work. The same stages of development, the same input considerations, and same process requirements are likely to apply in a virtual team as with any team. Where possible, the advantages of face-to-face and virtual teamwork should be combined for maximum benefit. The computer technology should also be appropriate and team members should be well trained in using it.[35]

■ SELF-MANAGING TEAMS

A high-involvement work group design that is increasingly well-established today is known as the **self-managing team**. These are small groups empowered to make the decisions needed to manage themselves on a day-to-day basis.[36] Although there are different variations of this theme, members of a true self-managing work team make decisions on scheduling work, allocating tasks, training for job skills, evaluating performance, selecting new team members, and controlling quality of work. Members are collectively held accountable for the team's overall performance results.

How Self-Managing Teams Work Self-managing teams, also called *self-directed teams* or *empowered teams*, are permanent and formal elements in the organizational structure. They replace the traditional work group headed by a supervisor. What differentiates self-managing teams from the more traditional work group is that the team members assume duties otherwise performed by a manager or first-line supervisor. The team members, not a supervisor, perform and are collectively accountable for such activities as planning and work scheduling, performance evaluation, and quality control.

A self-managing team should probably include between 5 and 15 members. The teams must be large enough to provide a good mix of skills and resources, but small enough to function efficiently.

MCI WorldCom ◄
www.mciworldcom.com

Better meetings are a business opportunity for MCI WorldCom. The firm reports a survey finding that one-third of responding professionals found their meetings unproductive. With the goal of "changing the way the world meets," MCI WorldCom is the fastest-growing conferencing company in the world.

■ **Self-managing teams** are empowered to make decisions about planning, doing, and evaluating their daily work.

■ **Multiskilling** occurs when team members are trained in skills to perform different jobs.

Members must have substantial discretion in determining work pace and in distributing tasks. This is made possible, in part, by **multiskilling**, whereby team members are trained in performing more than one job on the team. In self-managing teams, each person is expected to perform many different jobs—even all of the team's jobs, as needed. The more skills someone masters, the higher the base pay. Team members themselves conduct the job training and certify one another as having mastered the required skills.

www.ti.com

🌐 GLOBALIZATION

If you visit the Texas Instruments plant in Malaysia you will find many workers and no traditional supervisors. The plant uses self-managing teams that make decisions on quality and production issues, schedule work and work breaks, and keep track of work hours on the "honor system." When teams were first introduced, people were anxious. Management styles had to be changed, and rigid job descriptions were eliminated. But the changes increased productivity, improved product quality, and reduced staff absenteeism. Says a TI senior executive: "Teams bring about better sharing of ideas and learning. Better decisions are made and implementation of ideas takes less time."[37]

Operational Implications of Self-Managing Teams   The expected benefits of self-managing teams include productivity and quality improvements, production flexibility and faster response to technological change, reduced absenteeism and turnover, and improved work attitudes and quality of work life. But these results are not guaranteed. Like all organizational changes, the shift to self-managing teams can encounter difficulties. Structural changes in job classifications and management levels will have consequent implications for supervisors and others used to more traditional ways. Simply put, with a self-managing team you don't need the formal first-line supervisor anymore. The possible extent of this change is shown in Figure 10.6, where the first level of supervisory management has been eliminated and replaced by self-managing teams. Note also that many of the supervisor's traditional tasks are reallocated to the team.

For persons used to more traditional work, the new arrangement can be challenging; for managers learning to deal with self-managing teams rather than individual workers, the changeover can be difficult; for any supervisors displaced by self-managing teams, the implications are even more personal and threatening.

Given this situation, a question must be asked: *Should all work groups operate as self-managing teams?* The best answer is "No." Self-managing teams are probably not right for all organizations, work situations, and people. They have great potential, but they also require a proper setting and support. At a minimum, the essence of any self-managing team—high involvement, participation, and empowerment, must be consistent with the values and culture of the organization.

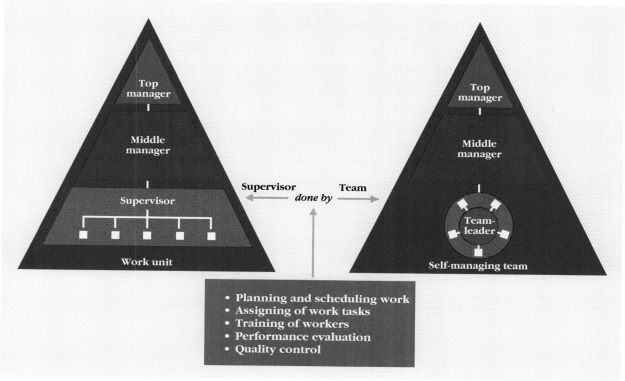

Figure 10.6
Organizational and management implications of self-managing teams.

Chapter 10   Study Guide

Summary

What is a high performance team...and what is teamwork?

- A team is a small group of people working together to achieve a common purpose for which they hold themselves collectively accountable.

- High performance teams have core values, clear performance objectives, the right mix of skills, and creativity.

- Teamwork occurs when members of a team work together so that their skills are well utilized to accomplish common goals.

What is team building?

- Team building is a data-based approach to analyzing group performance and taking steps to improve it in the future.

- Team building is participative and engages all group members in collaborative problem solving and action.

What can be done to improve team processes?

- Individual entry problems are common when new teams are formed and when new members join existing teams.

- Task leadership involves initiating and summarizing, making direct contributions to the group's task agenda; maintenance leadership involves gatekeeping and encouraging, helping to support the social fabric of the group over time.

- Role difficulties occur when expectations for group members are unclear, overwhelming, underwhelming, or conflicting.

- Norms, as rules or standards for what is considered appropriate behavior by group members, can have a significant impact on group processes and outcomes.

- Members of highly cohesive groups value their membership and are very loyal to the group; they also tend to conform to group norms.

How do teams contribute to the high performance workplace?

- An employee involvement team is one whose members meet regularly to address important work-related problems and opportunities.

- Members of a quality circle, a popular type of employee involvement group, meet regularly to deal with issues of quality improvement in work processes.

- Self-managing teams are small work groups that operate with empowerment and essentially manage themselves on a day-to-day basis.

- Members of self-managing teams typically plan, complete, and evaluate their own work, train and evaluate one another in job tasks, and share tasks and responsibilities.

- Self-managing teams have structural and management implications for organizations because they largely eliminate the first-line supervisors.

Key Terms

Cohesiveness (p. 203)
Cross-functional teams (p. 206)
Distributed leadership (p. 201)
Employee involvement group (p. 205)
Functional silos problem (p. 206)

Maintenance activities (p. 201)
Multiskilling (p. 208)
Norms (p. 203)
Quality circle (p. 206)
Role (p. 201)
Role ambiguity (p. 202)
Role conflict (p. 202)
Role overload (p. 202)

Role underload (p. 202)
Self-managing team (p. 207)
Task activities (p. 201)
Teams (p. 194)
Teamwork (p. 196)
Team building (p. 198)
Virtual team (p. 206)

Self-Test 10

■ MULTIPLE CHOICE

1. A group having difficulty becoming a high performance team might be hindered by _____. (a) specific performance objectives (b) high creativity (c) poor mix of membership skills (d) strong core values

2. The team-building process can best be described as _____. (a) participative (b) data based (c) action oriented (d) all of these

3. When a new team member is anxious about questions such as, "Will I be able to influence what takes place?" the underlying issue is one of _____. (a) relationships (b) goals (c) processes (d) control

4. A person facing an ethical dilemma involving differences between personal values and team expectations is experiencing _____ conflict. (a) person–role (b) intrasender role (c) intersender role (d) interrole

5. The statement "On our team, people always try to do their best" is an example of an _____ norm. (a) support and helpfulness (b) high-achievement (c) organizational pride (d) organizational improvement

6. Highly cohesive teams tend to _____. (a) be bad for organizations (b) be good for their members (c) have more social loafing among members (d) have greater membership turnover

7. To increase team cohesiveness, one would _____. (a) make the group bigger (b) increase membership diversity (c) isolate the group from others (d) relax performance pressures

8. Self-managing teams _____. (a) reduce the number of different job tasks members need to master (b) largely eliminate the need for a traditional supervisor (c) rely heavily on outside training to maintain job skills (d) add another management layer to overhead costs

9. Which statement about self-managing teams is correct? (a) They can improve performance but not satisfaction. (b) They should have limited decision-making authority. (c) They should operate without any team leaders. (d) They should let members plan work schedules.

10. A team member who does a good job at summarizing discussion, offering new ideas, and clarifying points made by others is contributing _____ activities to the group process. (a) required (b) disruptive (c) task (d) maintenance

■ TRUE–FALSE

11. Collective accountability for results is essential for a true team.   T   F

12. Team building should only be done in a formal retreat with the help of an outside consultant.   T   F

13. Team members work best with role ambiguity and unclear expectations.   T   F

14. Role overload is bad; role underload is good.   T   F

15. The only norm that is really important to team success is the performance norm.   T   F

16. A quality circle is an example of an employee involvement team.   T   F

17. Virtual teams are unique in that they work well for all tasks and in all situations.   T   F

18. Through multiskilling, members of self-managing teams are capable of switching job tasks.   T   F

19. Diversity in team membership can be a valuable performance asset.   T   F

20. In any team only the formal leader should engage in task leadership behaviors.   T   F

■ SHORT RESPONSE

21. What is the team-building process?

22. How can a team leader help build positive group norms?

23. How do cohesiveness and conformity to norms influence group performance?

24. What are members of self-managing teams typically expected to do?

■ APPLICATIONS ESSAY

25. While surfing the Internet, you encounter this note posted in your favorite discussion group. *Help. I have just been assigned to head a new product design team at my company. The division manager has high expectations for the team and me, but I have been a technical design engineer for four years since graduating from university. I have never "managed" anyone, let alone led a team. The manager keeps talking about her confidence that I will create a "high performance team." Does anyone out there have any tips to help me master this challenge? Help. /s/Galahad.* As a good citizen of the Internet you decide to answer. What message will you send out?

Explore application-oriented Fast Company articles, cases, experimental exercises, and self-assessments in the OB Skills Workbook

■ **Visit the Schermerhorn Web site to find the Interactive Self-Test and Internet exercises for this chapter.**

Basic Attributes of Organizations

INTEGRATING SYSTEMS FOR IMPROVED PROBLEM SOLVING

At First Community Financial, CEO Jim Adamany faced a conventional but vexing problem. First Community Financial is a modest-sized small business lender specializing in loans backed by the assets of small firms and factoring (loans based on invoices a firm has sent to clients who have yet to pay). Analyzing the creditworthiness for conventional loans and factoring call for different skills and are typically organized in separate departments. Small business clients rarely understand the use of loans or factoring, and they often don't see how a firm such as First Community can help them grow, even though the financial firm charges somewhat higher rates on its higher risk loans and factoring.

Jim's solution was simple and elegant. He organized the firm into three major groups: (1) marketing organized around client groups with a single business development officer for each client, (2) a finance division for loans in which employees analyze client creditworthiness and recommend approval for loans, and (3) a factoring division in which employees evaluate the account receivables of a client. The structure means that marketing will want to make loans and factoring agreements even to clients with very questionable credit ratings, whereas the finance and factoring managers want to approve only the highest quality loans. To minimize this problem, Jim relies extensively on personal methods of coordination across the three groups. Employees from all three groups work together with Jim to develop an acceptable tradeoff between risk and sales for each potential client. There are no easy answers, but Jim knows that his experienced staff realizes that solving this problem is a key to success.[1]

O
rganizations do things people can't do alone or in groups simply because they are organized to get people working together in a division of labor to achieve a common purpose. In this chapter, we will provide you with a working knowledge of organizational goals, the ways firms organize managers and departments, as well as some classic organization types used to reach toward success. Without a proper consideration of basic organizational attributes, even the largest and historically most successful firms can start to stumble.

Study Questions

The basic attributes of organizations create the setting for individual and group action in the workplace. This setting may both liberate and constrain individuals as they pursue their careers. As you read Chapter 11, keep in mind these study questions:

- What types of contributions do organizations make, and what types of goals do they adopt?
- What is the formal structure of the organization, and what is meant by the term *division of labor*?
- How is vertical specialization used to allocate formal authority within the organization?
- How does an organization control the actions of its members?
- What different patterns of horizontal specialization can be used in the organization?
- Which personal and impersonal coordination techniques should the organization use?
- What are bureaucracies and what are the common types?

Contributions and Goals of Organizations

Without organizations, our modern societies would cease to function. Economies would collapse, governments would evaporate, religion would fade, and education would all but come to a halt. We would need to revert to older forms of social organization based on royalty, clans, and tribes. Thus, our world is one of organizations from the time we are born.[2] They are so pervasive and so commonplace that it is sometimes easy to forget that organizations may be viewed as entities with specific goals—goals that will be pursued even when members appear disinterested in the organization's progress.

Jim Adamany of First Community Financial knows the basics and recognizes that there are many different ways to improve his corporation. He is aware that often the goals he emphasizes are multifaceted and conflict with one another. He also recognizes that corporate goals are common to individuals within the organization only to the extent that an individual's interests can be partially served by the organization. In this section, we examine the multiple goals of firms such as First Community Financial starting with how the organization intends to serve society. We then examine the types of goals organizations adopt in their attempts to survive.

■ SOCIETAL CONTRIBUTIONS OF ORGANIZATIONS

Organizations do not operate in a social vacuum but reflect the needs and desires of the societies in which they operate. **Societal goals** reflect an organization's intended contributions to the broader society.[3] Organizations normally serve a specific societal function or an enduring need of the society. Astute top-level managers build on the professed societal contribution of the organization by relating specific organizational tasks and activities to higher purposes. **Mission statements**—written statements of organizational purpose—may include these corporate ideas of service to the society. Weaving a mission statement together with an emphasis on implementation to provide direction and motivation is an executive order of the first magnitude. A good mission statement says whom the firm will serve and how it will go about accomplishing its societal purpose.[4]

> ■ **Societal goals** are goals reflecting the intended contributions of an organization to the broader society.
>
> ■ **Mission statements** are written statements of organizational purpose.

A sense of mission in a political party may be linked to generating and allocating power for the betterment of citizens. Universities profess to both develop and disseminate knowledge. Churches intend to instill values and protect the spiritual well-being of all. Courts are expected to integrate the interests and activities of citizens. Finally, business firms are expected to provide economic sustenance and material well-being to society.

By claiming to provide specific types of societal contributions, an organization can make legitimate claims over resources, individuals, markets, and products. For instance, would you not want more money to work for a tobacco firm than a health food store? Tobacco firms are also very heavily taxed and under increasing pressure for regulation simply because their societal contribution is highly questionable.

Organizations that can more effectively translate the positive character of their societal contribution into a favorable image have an advantage over firms that neglect this sense of purpose. More astute executives who link their firm to a desirable mission can lay claim to important motivational tools that are based on a shared sense of noble purpose.

■ PRIMARY BENEFICIARIES

Most organizations refine their societal contributions in order to target their efforts toward a particular group.[5] In the United States, for example, it is generally expected that the primary beneficiary of business firms is the stockholder. Interestingly, in Japan employees are much more important, and stockholders are considered as important as banks and other financial institutions.

Although each organization may have a primary beneficiary, its mission statement may also recognize the interests of many other parties. Thus, business mission statements often include service to customers, the organization's obligations to employees, and its intention to support the community.

■ OUTPUT GOALS

■ Output goals are the goals that define the type of business an organization is in.

Many larger organizations have found it useful to state very carefully which business they are in.[6] This statement can form the basis for long-term planning and may help prevent huge organizations from diverting too many resources to peripheral areas. For some corporations, answering the question of which business they are in may yield a more detailed statement concerning their products and services. These product and service goals provide an important basis for judging the firm. **Output goals** define the type of business an organization is in and provide some substance to the more general aspects of mission statements. For instance, First Community Federal's output goals would center around loans and factoring to small businesses.

■ SYSTEMS GOALS AND ORGANIZATIONAL SURVIVAL

Fewer than 10 percent of the businesses founded in a typical year can be expected to survive to their twentieth birthday.[7] The survival rate for public organizations is not much better. Even in organizations for which survival is not an immediate problem, managers seek specific types of conditions within their firms that minimize the risk of demise and promote survival. These conditions are positively stated as systems goals.

■ Systems goals are goals concerned with conditions within the organization that are expected to increase its survival potential.

Systems goals are concerned with the conditions within the organization that are expected to increase the organization's survival potential. The list of systems goals is almost endless, since each manager and researcher links today's conditions to tomorrow's existence in a different way. For many organizations, however, the list includes growth, productivity, stability, harmony, flexibility, prestige, and human-resource maintenance. In some businesses, analysts consider market share and current profitability important systems goals. Other recent studies suggest that innovation and quality are also considered important.[8] In a very practical sense, systems goals represent short-term organizational characteristics that higher level managers wish to promote. Systems goals must often be balanced against one another. For instance, a productivity and efficiency drive, if taken too far, may reduce the flexibility of an organization.

Different parts of the organization are often asked to pursue different types of systems goals. For example, higher level managers may expect to see their production operations strive for efficiency while pressing for innovation from their R&D lab and promoting stability in their financial affairs. In the case of First Community Federal, Jim Adamany recognizes the tension between the marketing group and its desire for loan and factoring volume and the other group's concern with the quality of these loans and factoring agreements.

The relative importance of different systems goals can vary substantially across various types of organizations. Although we may expect the University of British Columbia or the University of New South Wales to emphasize prestige and innovation, few expect such businesses as Pepsi or AT&T to subordinate growth and profitability to prestige.

ETHICS AND SOCIAL RESPONSIBILITY ⚖️

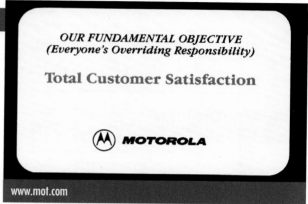

OUR FUNDAMENTAL OBJECTIVE
(Everyone's Overriding Responsibility)

Total Customer Satisfaction

Ⓜ **MOTOROLA**

www.mot.com

At Motorola, executives are asked to carry a card on them at all times showing the corporation's central focus on customers and its commitment to key beliefs, goals, and initiatives. On the front, in bold letters, the card says, "OUR FUNDAMENTAL OBJECTIVE (Everyone's Overriding Responsibility), TOTAL CUSTOMER SATISFACTION." On the back, it lists key beliefs on how executives will act. The two listed are constant respect for people and uncompromising integrity. To match these beliefs, it provides the following goals: increased global market share and best in class (people, marketing, technology, product, manufacturing, service). It then provides some key mechanisms Motorola will use in the jargon of the firm: Six Sigma Quality, Total Cycle Time Reduction, Product and Manufacturing Leadership, Profit Improvement, and Participative Management Within and Cooperation Between Organizations.

Systems goals are important to firms because they provide a road map that helps them link together various units of their organization to assure survival. Well-defined systems goals are practical and easy to understand; they focus the manager's attention on what needs to be done. Accurately stated systems goals also offer managers flexibility in devising ways to meet important targets. They can be used to balance the demands, constraints, and opportunities facing the firm. In addition, they can form a basis for dividing the work of the firm—a basis for developing a formal structure.

Formal Structures and the Division of Labor

To help accomplish their goals, managers develop an intended formal structure that shows the general, planned configuration of positions, job duties, and the lines of authority among different parts of the enterprise. Traditionally, the formal structure of the firm has also been called the division of labor. Some still use this term to separate issues concerning the formal structure of the firm from related questions, such as those concerning the division of markets, the choice of businesses, or the selection of a technology. The formal structure is important because it provides the foundations for managerial action. It outlines the job to be done, the person(s) (in terms of position) who are to perform specific activities, and the ways the total task of the organization is to be accomplished. In other words, it is the skeleton of the organization.

Organization charts are diagrams that depict the formal structures of organizations. A typical chart shows the various positions, the position holders, and the lines of authority that link them to one another. Figure 11.1 presents a partial organization chart for a large university. The total chart allows university em-

■ **Organization charts** are diagrams that depict the formal structures of organizations.

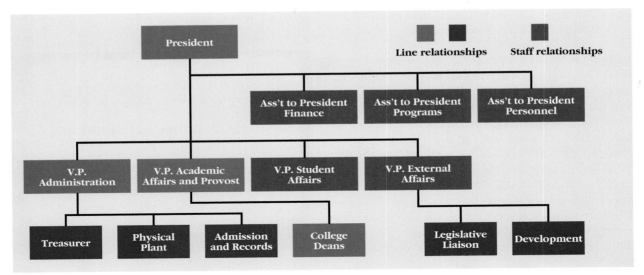

Figure 11.1
A partial organization chart for a state university.

ployees to locate their positions in the structure and to identify the lines of authority linking them with others in the organization. For instance, in this figure, the treasurer reports to the vice president of administration, who, in turn, reports to the president of the university.

Vertical Specialization

■ **Vertical specialization** is a hierarchical division of labor that distributes formal authority.

In larger organizations, there is a clear separation of authority and duties by hierarchical rank. This separation represents **vertical specialization**, a hierarchical division of labor that distributes formal authority and establishes where and how critical decisions are to be made. This division creates a hierarchy of authority—an arrangement of work positions in order of increasing authority.

In the United States, the distribution of formal authority is evident in the responsibilities typical of managers. Top managers or senior executives plan the overall strategy of the organization and plot its long-term future.[9] They also act as final judges for internal disputes and certify promotions, reorganizations, and the like.

Middle managers guide the daily operations of the organization, help formulate policy, and translate top-management decisions into more specific guidelines for action. Lower level managers supervise the actions of subordinates to ensure implementation of the strategies authorized by top management and compliance with the related policies established by middle management. Managers in Japan often have different responsibilities than their counterparts in the typical U.S. firm. Japanese top managers do not develop and decide the overall strategy of the firm. Instead, they manage a process involving middle managers. The process involves extensive dialogue about actions the firm needs to take. Lower level managers are also expected to act as advocates for the ideas and suggestions of their subordinates. The strategy of the firm emerges from dialogue and discussion, and implementation proceeds according to the ideas and suggestions of lower managers and nonmanagers.

In many European firms, the senior managers are highly trained in the core of their business. For example, it is not unusual for the head of a manufacturing firm to have a Ph.D. in engineering. Thus, many European executives become more centrally involved in plotting the technical future of their firm. In contrast, few U.S. or Japanese executives have the necessary technical background to tackle this responsibility. Despite the differences in managerial responsibilities across Japan, Europe, and North America, all organizations have vertical specialization.

■ CHAIN OF COMMAND AND THE SPAN OF CONTROL

Executives, managers, and supervisors are hierarchically connected through the *chain of command*—a listing of who reports to whom up and down the firm. Individuals are expected to follow their supervisor's decisions in the areas of responsibility outlined in the organization chart. Traditional management theory suggests that each individual should have one boss and each unit one leader. Under the circumstances, there is a "unity of command." Unity of command is considered necessary to avoid confusion, to assign accountability to specific individuals, and to provide clear channels of communication up and down the organization. Under traditional management, with unity of command, the number of individuals a manager can supervise directly is obviously limited.

The number of individuals reporting to a supervisor is called the **span of control**. Narrower spans of control are expected when tasks are complex, when subordinates are inexperienced or poorly trained, or when tasks call for team effort. Unfortunately, narrow spans of control yield many organizational levels. The excessive number of levels is not only expensive, but it also makes the organization unresponsive to necessary change. Communications in such firms often become less effective because they are successively screened and modified so that subtle but important changes get ignored. Furthermore, with many levels, managers are removed from the action and become isolated.

New information technologies, discussed in the next chapter, now allow organizations to broaden the span of control, flatten their formal structures, and still maintain control of complex operations.[10] At Nucor, for instance, senior managers pioneered the development of "minimills" for making steel and developed what they call "lean" management. At the same time, management has expanded the span of control with extensive employee education and training backed by sophisticated information systems. The result: Nucor has four levels of management from the bottom to the top.

■ LINE AND STAFF UNITS

A very useful way to examine the vertical division of labor is to separate line and staff units. **Line units** and personnel conduct the major business of the organization. The production and marketing functions are two examples. In contrast, **staff units** and personnel assist the line units by providing specialized expertise and services, such as accounting and public relations. For example, the vice president of administration in a university (Figure 11.1) heads a staff unit, as

■ **Span of control** refers to the number of individuals reporting to a supervisor.

■ **Line units** are work groups that conduct the major business of the organization.

■ **Staff units** are groups that assist the line units by performing specialized services to the organization.

does the vice president of student affairs. All academic departments are line units since they constitute the basic production function of the university.

Two useful distinctions are often made in firms. One distinction is the nature of the relationship of a unit in the chain of command. A staff department, such as the office of the V.P for External Affairs in Figure 11.1, may be divided into subordinate units, such as Legislative Liaison and Development (again see Figure 11.1). Although all units reporting to a higher level staff unit are considered staff from an organizational perspective, some subordinate staff units are charged with conducting the major business of the higher unit—they have a line relationship up the chain of command. In Figure 11.1 both Legislative Liaison and Development are staff units with a line relationship to the unit immediately above them in the chain of command—the V.P. for External Affairs. Why the apparent confusion? It is a matter of history with the notion of line and staff originally coming from the military with its emphasis on command. In a military sense the V.P. for External Affairs is the commander of this staff effort—the individual responsible for this activity and the one held accountable.

A second useful distinction to be made for both line and staff units concerns the amount and types of contacts each maintains with outsiders to the organization. Some units are mainly internal in orientation; others are more external in focus. In general, internal line units (e.g., production) focus on transforming raw materials and information into products and services, whereas external line units (e.g., marketing) focus on maintaining linkages to suppliers, distributors, and customers. Internal staff units (e.g., accounting) assist the line units in performing their function. Normally, they specialize in specific technical or financial areas. External staff units (e.g., public relations) also assist the line units, but the focus of their actions is on linking the firm to its environment and buffering internal operations. To recapitulate, the Legislative Liaison unit is external staff with a line relationship to the office of the V.P. for External Affairs.

■ WHAT TO DO WITH THE STAFF

Staff, particularly internal staff, contribute indirectly to corporate goals by using their specialized knowledge and talents. Traditionally, someone needed to keep the books, hire and train the personnel, and conduct the research and development. Figure 11.2 shows how the placement of staff alters the appearance of the firm. Staff units can be assigned predominantly to senior, middle, or lower level managers. When staff is assigned predominantly to senior management, the capability of senior management to develop alternatives and make decisions is expanded. When staff is at the top, senior executives can directly develop information and alternatives and check on the implementation of their decisions. Here, the degree of vertical specialization in the firm is comparatively lower because senior managers plan, decide, and control via their centralized staff. With new information technologies, fewer and fewer firms are placing most staff at the top. They are replacing internal staff with information systems and placing talented individuals further down the hierarchy. For instance, executives at Owens-Illinois have shifted staff from top management to middle management. When staff are removed to the middle of the organization, middle managers see more delegation. They now have the specialized help necessary to expand their role.

Many firms are also beginning to ask whether certain staff should be a permanent part of the organization at all. Some are outsourcing many of their staff

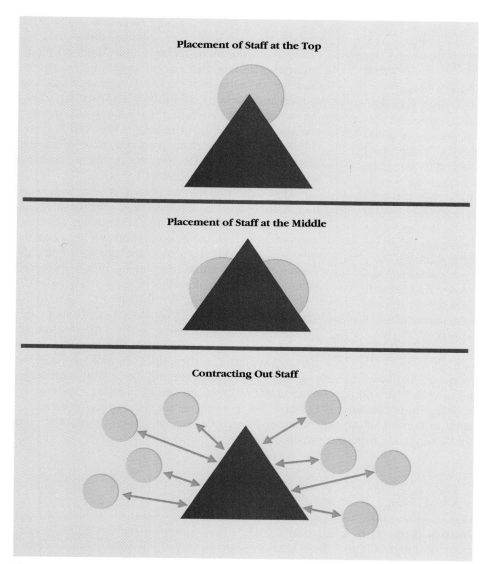

Placement of Staff at the Top

Placement of Staff at the Middle

Contracting Out Staff

Figure 11.2
How the placement of staff alters the look of an organization.

functions. Manufacturing firms are spinning off much of their accounting, personnel, and public relations activities to small, specialized firms.[11] Outsourcing by large firms has been a boon for smaller corporations. Figure 11.2 illustrates the use of staff via "contracting out."

■ INFORMATION SYSTEMS AND MANAGERIAL TECHNIQUES

One of the foremost trends in management involves using information technology to streamline operations and reduce staff in order to lower costs and raise productivity.[12] One way to facilitate these actions is to provide line managers and employees with information and managerial techniques designed to expand on their

High Finance at the Click of a Button

Facing a highly volatile global stock market, Curtis Pope, senior vice president and portfolio manager of Salomon-Smith Barney, has an information advantage. He can tap into the extensive Salomon-Smith Barney global information system called NEXTGEN. NEXTGEN contains his firm's reports on trends and stocks listed on the American, New York, and NASDAQ exchanges. Using NEXTGEN, Curtis can instantly access a firm's projected, current, and past records and trends for earnings and stock prices, the risk rating for the stock, the number of shares traded and outstanding, the number of shares sold daily and weekly, biographies of the senior executives, and national news reports on the firm as well as a host of related information. Furthermore, with just a few keystrokes, Curtis can buy or sell virtually any stock and respond to an automatic warning if the price fluctuates. It's all in a day's work....

analytical and decision-making capabilities—that is, to replace internal staff. For instance, those studying financial management recognize the importance of financial planning models (in detecting problems), financial decision aids, such as capital budgeting models and discounted cash-flow analyses (for selecting among alternatives), and budgets (to monitor progress and ensure that managers stay within financial limits). With computer programs, each of these is now accessible to all levels of management and is no longer restricted to financial staff.[13]

Although a great variety of managerial techniques have been available to managers for decades, only with the widespread use of computers have the costs of these techniques been reduced. Most organizations use a combination of line and staff units, alliances with specialized providers, plus managerial techniques to specialize the division of labor vertically (e.g., to distribute formal authority). The most appropriate pattern of vertical specialization depends on the environment of the organization, its size, its technology, and its goals. For instance, as organizations grow, vertical specialization typically increases just to keep up with the volume of work. We will return to this theme in the next chapter and pay special attention to information technology and its role in changing organizations. For now, let us turn our attention to those issues relating to control of the organization simply because the issue of control should not be separated from the division of labor.

Control

■ **Control** is the set of mechanisms used to keep actions and outputs within predetermined limits.

Control is the set of mechanisms used to keep action or outputs within predetermined limits. Control deals with setting standards, measuring results versus standards, and instituting corrective action. Although all organizations need controls, just a few controls may go a long way. Astute managers need to be aware of the danger of too much control in the organization.

■ OUTPUT CONTROLS

Earlier in this chapter, we suggested that systems goals could be used as a road map to tie together the various units of the organization toward achieving a practical objective. Developing targets or standards, measuring results against these targets, and taking corrective action are all steps involved in developing output controls.[14] **Output controls** focus on desired targets and allow managers to use their own methods to reach defined targets. Most modern organizations use output controls as part of an overall method of managing by exception.

■ **Output controls** are controls that focus on desired targets and allow managers to use their own methods for reaching defined targets.

Output controls are popular because they promote flexibility and creativity as well as facilitate dialogue concerning corrective action. Reliance on outcome controls separates what is to be accomplished from how it is to be accomplished. Thus, the discussion of goals is separated from the dialogue concerning methods. This separation can facilitate the movement of power down the organization, as senior managers are reassured that individuals at all levels will be working toward the goals senior management believes are important, even as lower level managers innovate and introduce new ways to accomplish these goals.

■ PROCESS CONTROLS

Few organizations run on outcome controls alone. Once a solution to a problem is found and successfully implemented, managers do not want the problem to recur, so they institute process controls. **Process controls** attempt to specify the manner in which tasks are accomplished. There are many types of process controls, but three groups have received considerable attention: (1) policies, procedures, and rules; (2) formalization and standardization; and (3) total quality management controls.

■ **Process controls** are controls that attempt to specify the manner in which tasks are to be accomplished.

Policies, Procedures, and Rules   Most organizations implement a variety of policies, procedures, and rules to help specify how goals are to be accomplished. Usually, we think of a *policy* as a guideline for action that outlines important objectives and broadly indicates how an activity is to be performed. A policy allows for individual discretion and minor adjustments without direct clearance by a higher level manager. *Procedures* indicate the best method for performing a task, show which aspects of a task are the most important, or outline how an individual is to be rewarded.

Many firms link *rules and procedures*. Rules are more specific, rigid, and impersonal than policies. They typically describe in detail how a task or a series of tasks is to be performed, or they indicate what cannot be done. They are designed to apply to all individuals, under specified conditions. For example, most car dealers have detailed instruction manuals for repairing a new car under warranty, and they must follow very strict procedures to obtain reimbursement from the manufacturer for warranty work.

Rules, procedures, and policies are often employed as substitutes for direct managerial supervision. Under the guidance of written rules and procedures, the organization can specifically direct the activities of many individuals. It can ensure virtually identical treatment across even distant work locations. For example, a McDonald's hamburger and fries taste much the same whether they are purchased in Hong Kong, Indianapolis, London, or Toronto simply because the ingredients and the cooking methods follow written rules and procedures.

Formalization and Standardization   **Formalization** refers to the written documentation of rules, procedures, and policies to guide behavior and decision making. Beyond substituting for direct management supervision, formalization is often used to simplify jobs. Written instructions allow individuals with less training to perform comparatively sophisticated tasks. Written procedures may also be available to ensure that a proper sequence of tasks is executed, even if this sequence is performed only occasionally.

■ **Formalization** is the written documentation of work rules, policies, and procedures.

Most organizations have developed additional methods for dealing with recurring problems or situations. **Standardization** is the degree to which the range of allowable actions in a job or series of jobs is limited. It involves the

■ **Standardization** is the degree to which the range of actions in a job or series of jobs is limited.

creation of guidelines so that similar work activities are repeatedly performed in a similar fashion. Such standardized methods may come from years of experience in dealing with typical situations, or they may come from outside training. For instance, if you are late in paying your credit card, the bank will automatically send you a notification and start an internal process of monitoring your account.

Total Quality Management   The process controls discussed so far—policies, procedures, rules, formalization, and standardization—represent the lessons of experience within an organization. That is, managers institute these process controls based on past experience typically one at a time. Often there is no overall philosophy for using control to improve the overall operations of the company. Another way to institute process controls is to establish a total quality management process within the firm.

The late W. Edwards Deming is the modern-day founder of the total quality management movement. When Deming's ideas were not generally accepted in the United States, he found an audience in Japan. Thus, to some managers, Deming's ideas appear in the form of the best Japanese business practices.

The heart of Deming's approach is to institute a process approach to continual improvement based on statistical analyses of the firm's operations. Around this core idea, Deming built a series of 14 points for managers to implement.[15] As you look at these points, note the emphasis on both managers and employees working together using statistical controls to continually improve. Deming's 14 points are:

Deming's 14 points

- Create a consistency of purpose in the company to
  a. innovate.
  b. put resources into research and education.
  c. put resources into maintaining equipment and new production aids.
- Learn a new philosophy of quality to improve every system.
- Require statistical evidence of process control and eliminate financial controls on production.
- Require statistical evidence of control in purchasing parts; this will mean dealing with fewer suppliers.
- Use statistical methods to isolate the sources of trouble.
- Institute modern on-the-job training.
- Improve supervision to develop inspired leaders.
- Drive out fear and instill learning.
- Break down barriers between departments.
- Eliminate numerical goals and slogans.
- Constantly revamp work methods.
- Institute massive training programs for employees in statistical methods.
- Retrain people in new skills.
- Create a structure that will push, every day, on the above 13 points.

All levels of management are to be involved in the quality program. Managers are to improve supervision, train employees, retrain employees in new skills, and create a structure that pushes the quality program. Where the properties of the firm's outcomes are well defined, as in most manufacturing operations, Deming's system and emphasis on quality appears to work well when it is implemented in conjunction with empowerment and participative management.[16] For instance, Electroglas—a small high-tech manufacturer of software and hardware for measuring the quality of computer chips—has long married the Deming philosophy with a heavy emphasis on empowerment and participation for each and every one of its employees. This has allowed it to survive the recent disastrous decline in the semiconductor equipment supply business and still improve quality.

HIGH PERFORMANCE ORGANIZATION

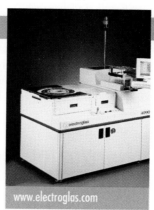

www.electroglas.com

ISO (International Organization for Standardization)—a worldwide federation of national standards bodies from some 100 countries, has a mission to promote quality. It has established rigorous quality process standards in part based on Deming's work. Firms seeking ISO certification must obtain a third-party assessment and undergo periodic audits to ensure they meet the standards set forth in the ISO 9000 series. Very few small firms based in the United States have an ISO 9000 certification. Semiconductor equipment manufacturer Electroglas was one of the very first in its business to receive certification. Electroglas produces "wafer probers"—a sophisticated piece of equipment to check on the quality of the semiconductors produced in chip plants. CEO Curt Wozniak says of the ISO designation, "Improvements in quality…have already had a measurable impact on defect rates, reliability and cycle times, delivering added value to our worldwide customer base."

■ ALLOCATING FORMAL AUTHORITY: CENTRALIZATION AND DECENTRALIZATION

Different firms use very different mixes of vertical specialization, output controls, process controls, and managerial techniques to allocate the authority or discretion to act. The farther up the hierarchy of authority the discretion to spend money, to hire people, and to make similar decisions is moved, the greater the degree of **centralization**. The more such decisions are delegated, or moved down the hierarchy of authority, the greater the degree of **decentralization**. Greater centralization is often adopted when the firm faces a single major threat to its survival. Thus, it is little wonder that armies tend to be centralized and that firms facing bankruptcy increase centralization.

Generally speaking, greater decentralization provides higher subordinate satisfaction and a quicker response to a diverse series of unrelated problems. Decentralization also assists in the on-the-job training of subordinates for higher level positions. Decentralization is now a popular approach in many industries. For instance, Union Carbide is pushing responsibility down the chain of command, as are General Motors, Ford, and Daimler/Chrysler.[17] In each case, the senior managers hope to improve both performance quality and organizational responsiveness. Closely related to decentralization is the notion of participation. Many people want to be involved in making decisions that affect their work. Participation results when a manager delegates some authority for such decision

■ **Centralization** is the degree to which the authority to make decisions is restricted to higher levels of management.

■ **Decentralization** is the degree to which the authority to make decisions is given to lower levels in an organization's hierarchy.

making to subordinates in order to include them in the choice process. Employees may want a say both in what the unit objectives should be and in how they may be achieved.[18]

Especially in recent years, even conservative firms are experimenting with new ways to decentralize parts of their operations and are encouraging managers to increase participation. Firms, such as Intel Corporation, Eli Lilly, Dow Chemical, Ford Motor Company, and Hoffman-LaRoche, have all experimented by moving decisions down the chain of command and increasing participation. These firms found that just cutting the number of organizational levels was insufficient. They also needed to alter their controls toward quality, to stress constant improvement, and to change other basic features of the organization. As these firms changed their degree of vertical specialization, they also changed the division of work among units or the firm's horizontal specialization.

Horizontal Specialization

■ **Horizontal specialization** is a division of labor through the formation of work units or groups within an organization.

Vertical specialization and control are only half the picture. Managers must also divide the total task into separate duties and group similar people and resources together.[19] **Horizontal specialization** is a division of labor that establishes specific work units or groups within an organization; it is often referred to as the process of departmentation. There are a variety of pure forms of departmentation.

■ **Functional departmentation** is grouping individuals by skill, knowledge, and action yields.

■ DEPARTMENTATION BY FUNCTION

Grouping individuals by skill, knowledge, and action yields a pattern of **functional departmentation**. Recall Figure 11.1 shows the partial organization chart for a large university in which each department has a technical specialty. Marketing, finance, production, and personnel are important functions in business. In many small firms, this functional pattern dominates. However, even large firms use this pattern in technically demanding areas. For instance, Boeing uses this pattern in its engineering areas. Figure 11.3 summarizes the advantages of the

Major Advantages and Disadvantages of Functional Specialization	
Advantages	**Disadvantages**
1. Yields very clear task assignments, consistent with an individual's training.	1. May reinforce the narrow training of individuals.
2. Individuals within a department can easily build on one another's knowledge, training, and experience.	2. May yield narrow, boring, and routine jobs.
3. Provides an excellent training ground for new managers.	3. Communication across technical area is complex and difficult.
4. It is easy to explain.	4. "Top management overload" with too much attention to cross-functional problems.
	5. Individuals may look up the organizational hierarchy for direction and reinforcement rather than focus attention on products, services, or clients.

Figure 11.3
Major Advantages and Disadvantages of Functional Specialization.

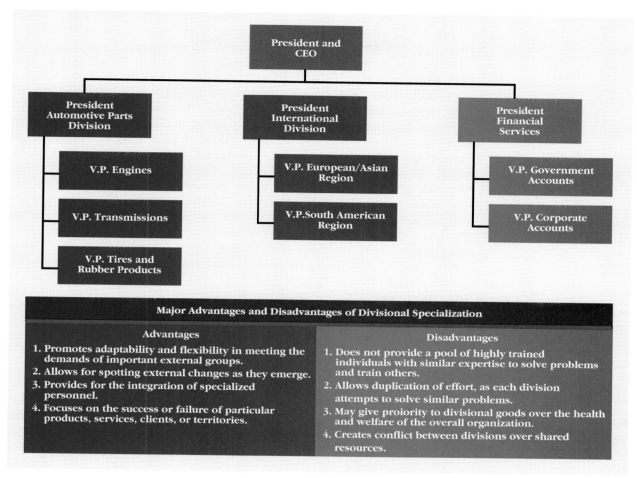

Figure 11.4
A divisional pattern of departmentation.

functional pattern. With all these advantages, it is not surprising that the functional form is extremely popular. It is used in most organizations, particularly toward the bottom of the hierarchy. Functional specialization also has some disadvantages, which are summarized in Figure 11.3. Organizations that rely heavily on functional specialization may expect the following tendencies to emerge over time: an emphasis on quality from a technical standpoint, rigidity to change, and difficulty in coordinating the actions of different functional areas.

■ DEPARTMENTATION BY DIVISION

Divisional departmentation groups individuals and resources by products, territories, services, clients, or legal entities.[20] Figure 11.4 shows a divisional pattern of organization grouped around products, regions, and customers for three divisions of a conglomerate. This pattern is often used to meet diverse external threats and opportunities. As shown in Figure 11.4, the major advantages of the

■ **Divisional departmentation** groups individuals and resources by products, territories, services, clients, or legal entities.

divisional pattern are its flexibility in meeting external demands, spotting external changes, integrating of specialized individuals deep within the organization, and focusing on the delivery of specific products to specific customers. Among its disadvantages are duplication of effort by function, the tendency for divisional goals to be placed above corporate interests, and conflict among divisions. It is also not the structure most desired for training individuals in technical areas, and firms relying on this pattern may fall behind competitors with a functional pattern.

Many larger, geographically dispersed organizations that sell to national and international markets may rely on departmentation by geography. The savings in time, effort, and travel can be substantial, and each territory can adjust to regional differences. Organizations that rely on a few major customers may organize their people and resources by client. Here, the idea is to focus attention on the needs of the individual customer.[21] To the extent that customer needs are unique, departmentation by customer can also reduce confusion and increase synergy. Organizations expanding internationally may also form divisions to meet the demands of complex host country ownership requirements. For example, NEC, Sony, Nissan, and many other Japanese corporations have developed U.S. divisional subsidiaries to service their customers in the U.S. market. Some huge European-based corporations such as Philips and Nestlé have also adopted a divisional structure in their expansion to the United States. Similarly, most of the internationalized U.S.-based firms, such as IBM, GE, and DuPont, have incorporated the divisional structure as part of their internalization programs.

■ DEPARTMENTATION BY MATRIX

■ **Matrix departmentation** is a combination of functional and divisional patterns wherein an individual is assigned to more than one type of unit.

Originally from the aerospace industry, a third unique form of departmentation was developed and is now becoming more popular; it is now called **matrix departmentation**.[22] In aerospace efforts, projects are technically very complex, involving hundreds of subcontractors located throughout the world. Precise integration and control are needed across many sophisticated functional specialties and corporations. This is often more than a functional or divisional structure can provide, for many firms do not want to trade the responsiveness of the divisional form for the technical emphasis provided by the functional form. Thus, matrix departmentation uses both the functional and divisional forms simultaneously. Figure 11.5 shows the basic matrix arrangement for an aerospace program. Note the functional departments on one side and the project efforts on the other. Workers and supervisors in the middle of the matrix have two bosses—one functional and one project.

The major advantages and disadvantages of the matrix form of departmentation are also summarized in Figure 11.5. The key disadvantage of the matrix method is the loss of unity of command. Individuals can be unsure as to what their jobs are, whom they report to for specific activities, and how various managers are to administer the effort. It can also be a very expensive method because it relies on individual managers to coordinate efforts deep within the firm. In Figure 11.5, note that the number of managers in a matrix structure almost doubles compared to either a functional or a divisional structure. Despite these limitations, the matrix structure provides a balance between functional and divisional concerns. Many problems can be resolved at the working level, where the balance among technical, cost, customer, and organizational concerns can be dealt with. In the case of Ford, Jac Nasser was relentless in simultaneously sell-

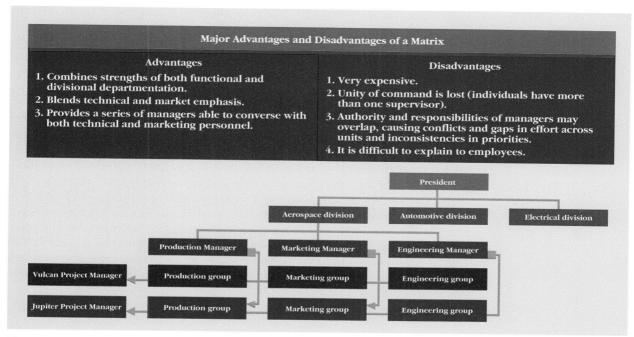

Major Advantages and Disadvantages of a Matrix

Advantages	Disadvantages
1. Combines strengths of both functional and divisional departmentation.	1. Very expensive.
2. Blends technical and market emphasis.	2. Unity of command is lost (individuals have more than one supervisor).
3. Provides a series of managers able to converse with both technical and marketing personnel.	3. Authority and responsibilities of managers may overlap, causing conflicts and gaps in effort across units and inconsistencies in priorities.
	4. It is difficult to explain to employees.

Figure 11.5
A matrix pattern of departmentation in an aerospace division.

ing empowerment, participation, cost reduction, and communication to provide the incentive for managers to reach out across its new matrix.

 GLOBALIZATION

www.ford.com

Alex Trotman, the retiring CEO, rested much of his reputation as Ford Motor Company's CEO on Ford 2000—a worldwide reorganization of engineering operations from a functional structure to a global matrix across its North American and European operations. Once all engineers reported to a single function boss, such as in departments for engines and transmissions. Now many engineers report to two bosses—their old functional boss and a new supervisor in one of the so-called platform groups. One of the platform groups for small cars is European-based, with engineers in both North America and Western Europe reporting to supervisors in Germany. Although Alex Trotman initiated the structural change, it was up to Jack Nassau to implement it. Jack also bet his future and won—he is the new CEO. The new matrix arrangement not only speeds product development but also helped make Ford more responsive to its global customers. Said Alex Trotman, "As Ford 2000 has taken root, it has given us a glimpse of what we can accomplish for our customers and shareholders. We have exciting new products and are continuing to improve quality and lower our total costs."

Many organizations also use elements of the matrix structure without officially using the term *matrix*. For example, special project teams, coordinating committees, and task forces can be the beginnings of a matrix. Yet, these temporary structures can be used within a predominantly functional or divisional form and without upsetting the unity of command or hiring additional managers.

■ MIXED FORMS OF DEPARTMENTATION

Which form of departmentation should be used? As the matrix concept suggests, it is possible to departmentalize by two different methods at the same time. Actually, organizations often use a mixture of departmentation forms. It is often desirable to divide the effort (group people and resources) by two methods at the same time in order to balance the advantages and disadvantages of each. To continue the example of Ford Motor Company, it did not include its assembly and parts plants in the matrix for Ford 2000. Instead it adopted a unique divisional form creating a separate unit called Visteon for its parts operations. It also kept Visteon distinct from its assembly plants as a separate company so that it could sell parts to other manufacturers. Within the assembly plants, the functional form is the dominant.

Coordination

■ **Coordination** is the set of mechanisms used in an organization to link the actions of its subunits into a consistent pattern.

Whatever is divided up horizontally must also be integrated.[23] **Coordination** is the set of mechanisms that an organization uses to link the actions of its units into a consistent pattern. Much of the coordination within a unit is handled by its manager. Smaller organizations may rely on their management hierarchy to provide the necessary consistency and integration. As the organization grows, however, managers become overloaded. The organization then needs to develop more efficient and effective ways of linking work units to one another.

■ PERSONAL METHODS OF COORDINATION

Personal methods of coordination produce synergy by promoting dialogue, discussion, innovation, creativity, and learning, both within and across organizational units. Personal methods allow the organization to address the particular needs of distinct units and individuals simultaneously. There are a wide variety of personal methods of coordination.[24] Perhaps the most popular is direct contact between and among organizational members. As new information technologies have moved into practice, the potential for developing and maintaining effective contact networks has expanded. For example, many executives use E-mail, Lotus Notes, and other computer-based links to supplement direct personal communication. Direct personal contact is also associated with the ever-present "grapevine." Although the grapevine is notoriously inaccurate in its role as the corporate rumor mill, it is often both accurate enough and quick enough that managers cannot ignore it. Instead, managers need to work with and supplement the rumor mill with accurate information.

Managers are also often assigned to numerous committees to improve coordination across departments. Even though committees are generally expensive and have a very poor reputation, they can become an effective personal mechanism for mutual adjustment across unit heads. Committees can be effective in communicating complex qualitative information and in helping managers whose units must work together to adjust schedules, workloads, and work assignments to increase productivity. As more organizations develop flatter structures with greater delegation, they are finding that task forces can be quite useful. Whereas committees tend to be long lasting, task forces are typically formed with a more limited agenda. Individuals from different parts of the organization are assembled into a task force to identify and solve problems that cut across different departments.

No magic is involved in selecting the appropriate mix of personal coordination methods and tailoring them to the individual skills, abilities, and experience of subordinates. Managers need to know the individuals involved, their preferences, and the accepted approaches in different organizational units. Different personal methods can be tailored to match different individuals. Personal methods are only one important part of coordination. The manager may also establish a series of impersonal mechanisms (see The Effective Manager 11.1).

THE EFFECTIVE MANAGER 11.1

ADJUSTING COORDINATION EFFORTS

The astute manager should recognize some individuals and/or units:

1. Have their own views of how best to move toward organizational goals.
2. Emphasize immediate problems and quick solutions; others stress underlying problems and longer-term solutions.
3. Have their own unique vocabulary and standard way of communicating.
4. Have pronounced preferences for formality or informality.

■ IMPERSONAL METHODS OF COORDINATION

Impersonal methods of coordination produce synergy by stressing consistency and standardization so that individual pieces fit together. Impersonal coordination methods are often refinements and extensions of process controls with an emphasis on formalization and standardization. Most larger organizations have written policies and procedures, such as schedules, budgets, and plans that are designed to mesh the operations of several units into a whole by providing predictability and consistency.

The most highly developed form of impersonal coordination comes with the adoption of a matrix form of departmentation. As noted earlier, this form of departmentation is expressly designed to coordinate the efforts of diverse functional units. Although a few organizations rely exclusively on a matrix structure, many firms are using cross-functional task forces. These task forces are replacing specialized staff units that once dealt mainly with ensuring coordination.

The final example of impersonal coordination mechanisms is undergoing radical change in many modern organizations. Originally, management information systems were developed and designed so that senior managers could coordinate and control the operations of diverse subordinate units. These systems were intended to be computerized substitutes for schedules, budgets, and the like. In some firms, the management information system still operates as a combined process control and impersonal coordination mechanism. In the hands of astute managers, the management information system becomes an electronic network, linking individuals throughout the organization. Using decentralized communication systems, supplemented with the phone, fax machine, and E-mail, a once centrally controlled system becomes a supplement to personal coordination.

The fundamental change ongoing in most larger organizations is the realization of the potential offered by information technologies. This fundamental change is so important and so pervasive that it is altering the way firms put together their specialization of labor, control, and coordination. This will be shown in the next chapter. For now it is important to understand basic combinations of specialization control and coordination.

The Bureaucracy

■ **Bureaucracy** is an ideal form of organization, the characteristics of which were defined by the German sociologist Max Weber.

In the developed world, most firms are bureaucracies. In OB this term has a very special meaning, beyond its negative connotation. The famous German sociologist Max Weber suggested that organizations would thrive if they became **bureaucracies** by emphasizing legal authority, logic, and order.[25] Bureaucracies rely on a division of labor, hierarchical control, promotion by merit with career opportunities for employees, and administration by rule. He argued that the rational and logical idea of bureaucracy was superior to building the firm on the basis of charisma or cultural tradition. The "charismatic" ideal-type organization was overreliant on the talents of one individual and would likely fail when the leader left. Too much reliance on cultural traditions blocked innovation, stifled efficiency, and was often unfair. Since the bureaucracy prizes efficiency, order and logic, Weber hoped that it could also be fair to employees and provide more freedom for individual expression than is allowed when tradition dominates. Although far from perfect, Weber predicted that the bureaucracy, or some variation of this ideal form, would dominate modern society. And it has. While charismatic leadership and cultural traditions are still important today, it is the rational, legal, and efficiency aspects of the firm that characterize modern corporations.

THE EFFECTIVE MANAGER 11.2

THE NATURAL DYSFUNCTIONAL TENDENCIES OF A BUREAUCRACY

1. Overspecialization and failure to mitigate the resulting conflicts of interest resulting from specialization.
2. Overuse of the formal hierarchy and emphasis on adherence to official channels rather than problem solving.
3. Reification of senior mangers as superior performers on all tasks and as rulers of a political system rather than as individuals who should help others reach goals.
4. Overemphasis on insignificant conformity that limits individual growth.
5. Treatment of rules as ends in and of themselves rather than as poor mechanisms for control and coordination.

■ TYPES OF BUREAUCRACIES

The notion of a bureaucracy has evolved over time. Figure 11.6 illustrates three popular basic types of bureaucracies: the mechanistic, the organic, and the divisionalized approaches. And it shows how some huge corporations are collections of very different firms called conglomerates. Each is a different mix of the basic elements discussed in this chapter, and each mix yields firms with a slightly different blend of capabilities and natural tendencies.

The Mechanistic Type The **mechanistic type** emphasizes vertical specialization and control.[26] Organizations of this type stress rules, policies, and procedures; specify techniques for decision making; and emphasize developing well-documented control systems backed by a strong middle management and supported by a centralized staff. There is often ex-

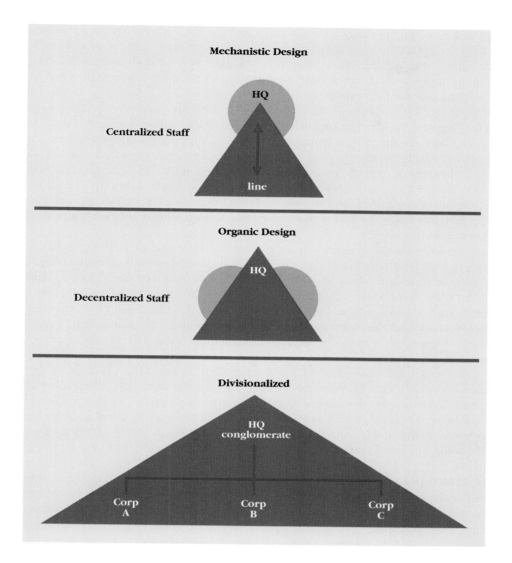

Figure 11.6
Different basic overall bureaucratic patterns.

tensive use of the functional pattern of departmentation throughout the firm. Henry Mintzberg uses the term *machine bureaucracy* to describe an organization that is entirely structured in this manner.[27]

The mechanistic design results in a management emphasis on routine for efficiency. Until the implementation of new information systems, most large-scale firms in basic industries were machine bureaucracies. Included in this long list were all the auto firms, banks, insurance companies, steel mills, large retail establishments, and government offices. Efficiency was achieved through extensive vertical and horizontal specialization tied together with elaborate controls and informal coordination mechanisms.

There are, however, limits to the benefits of specialization backed by rigid controls. Employees do not like rigid designs, and so motivation becomes a problem. Unions further solidify narrow job descriptions by demanding fixed work rules and regulations to protect employees from the extensive vertical con-

■ **Mechanistic type** or machine bureaucracy emphasizes vertical specialization and control with impersonal coordination and a heavy reliance on standardization, formalization, rules, policies, and procedures.

trols. Key employees may leave. In short, using a machine bureaucracy can hinder an organization's capacity to adjust to subtle external changes or new technologies. You are already familiar with this tendency toward stagnation—your high school was probably a machine bureaucracy with the assistant principal as the chief enforcement officer.

■ **Organic type** or professional bureaucracy emphasizes horizontal specialization, extensive use of personal coordination, and loose rules, policies, and procedures.

The Organic Type   The **organic type** is much less vertically oriented than its mechanistic counterpart; it emphasizes horizontal specialization. Procedures are minimal, and those that do exist are not as formalized. The organization relies on the judgments of experts and personal means of coordination. When controls are used, they tend to back up professional socialization, training, and individual reinforcement. Staff units tend to be placed toward the middle of the organization. Because this is a popular design in professional firms, Mintzberg calls it a professional bureaucracy.[28]

Your university is probably a professional bureaucracy that looks like a broad, flat pyramid with a large bulge in the center for the professional staff. Power in this ideal type rests with knowledge. Furthermore, the elaborate staff historically helped the line managers and often had very little formal power, other than to block action. Control is enhanced by the standardization of professional skills and the adoption of professional routines, standards, and procedures. Other examples of organic types include most hospitals, libraries, and social service agencies.

Although not as efficient as the machine bureaucracy, the professional bureaucracy is better for problem solving and for serving individual customer needs. Since lateral relations and coordination are emphasized, centralized direction by senior management is less intense. Thus, this type is good at detecting external changes and adjusting to new technologies, but at the sacrifice of responding to central management direction.[29]

Hybrid Types   Many very large firms found that neither the mechanistic nor the organic approach was suitable for all their operations. Adopting a machine bureaucracy would overload senior management and yield too many levels of management. Yet, adopting an organic type would mean losing control and becoming too inefficient. Senior managers may opt for one of a number of hybrid types.

Two hybrid types we have already introduced. One is an extension of the divisional pattern of departmentation, so that different divisions can be more or less organic or mechanistic. Here the divisions may be treated as separate businesses, even though they share a similar mission and output and systems goals.[30]

■ **Conglomerates** are firms that own several different unrelated businesses.

A second hybrid is the true conglomerate. A **conglomerate** is a single corporation that contains a number of unrelated businesses. On the surface, these firms look like divisionalized firms, but when the various businesses of the divisions are unrelated, the term conglomerate is applied.[31]   For instance, General Electric is a conglomerate that has divisions in quite unrelated businesses and industries, ranging from producing light bulbs, to designing and servicing nuclear reactors, to building jet engines, to operating the National Broadcasting Company. RJR-Nabisco was created through a series of financial maneuvers that brought together a food company and a tobacco firm. Many state and federal entities are also, by necessity, conglomerates. For instance, a state governor is the chief executive officer of those units concerned with higher education, welfare, prisons, highway construction and maintenance, police, and the like.

The conglomerate type also simultaneously illustrates two important points that will be the highlight of the next chapter. (1) All structures are combinations of the basic elements. (2) There is no one best structure—it all depends on a number of factors such as the size of the firm, its environment, its technology, and its strategy.

Chapter 11 Study Guide

Summary

What types of contributions do organizations make, and what types of goals do they adopt?

- Organizations make specific contributions to society.

- Firms often concentrate on primary beneficiaries and specify output goals (specific products and services).

- A societal contribution focused on a primary beneficiary may be represented in the firm's mission statement.

- Corporations have systems goals to show the conditions managers believe will yield survival and success.

What is the formal structure of the organization, and what is meant by the term *division of labor*?

- The formal structure defines the intended configuration of positions, job duties, and lines of authority among different parts of the enterprise.

- The formal structure is also known as the firm's division of labor.

How is vertical specialization used to allocate formal authority within the organization?

- Vertical specialization is the hierarchical division of labor that specifies where formal authority is located.

- Typically, a chain of command exists to link lower level workers with senior managers.

- The distinction between line and staff units also indicates how authority is distributed, with line units conducting the major business of the firm and staff providing support.

- Managerial techniques, such as decision support and expert computer systems, are used to expand the analytical reach and decision-making capacity of managers to minimize staff.

How does an organization control the actions of its members?

- Control is the set of mechanisms the organization uses to keep action or outputs within predetermined levels.

- Output controls focus on desired targets and allow managers to use their own methods for reaching these targets.

- Process controls specify the manner in which tasks are to be accomplished through (1) policies, rules, and procedures; (2) formalization and standardization; and (3) total quality management processes.

- Firms are learning that decentralization often provides substantial benefits.

What different patterns of horizontal specialization can be used in the organization?

- Horizontal specialization is the division of labor that results in various work units and departments in the organization.

- Three main types or patterns of departmentation are observed: functional, divisional, and matrix. Each pattern has a mix of advantages and disadvantages.

- Organizations may successfully use any type, or a mixture, as long as the strengths of the structure match the needs of the organization.

Which personal and impersonal coordination techniques should the organization use?

- Coordination is the set of mechanisms an organization uses to link the actions of separate units into a consistent pattern.

- Personal methods of coordination produce synergy by promoting dialogue, discussion, innovation, creativity, and learning.

- Impersonal methods of control produce synergy by stressing consistency and standardization so that individual pieces fit together.

Why are bureaucracies, and what are the common types?

- The bureaucracy is an ideal form based on legal authority, logic, and order that provides superior efficiency and effectiveness.

- Mechanistic, organic, and hybrids are common types of bureaucracies.

- Hybrid types include the divisionalized firm and the conglomerate. No one type is always superior to the others.

Key Terms

Bureaucracy (p. 232)
Centralization (p. 225)
Conglomerates (p. 234)
Control (p. 222)
Coordination (p. 230)
Decentralization (p. 225)
Divisional departmentation (p. 226)
Formalization (p. 223)
Functional departmentation (p. 226)

Horizontal specialization (p. 226)
Line units (p. 219)
Mechanistic type (p. 233)
Mission statements (p. 215)
Matrix departmentation (p. 228)
Organic type (p. 234)
Organization charts (p. 217)
Output controls (p. 222)

Output goals (p. 216)
Process controls (p. 223)
Societal goals (p. 215)
Span of control (p. 219)
Staff units (p. 219)
Standardization (p. 223)
Systems goals (p. 216)
Vertical specialization (p. 218)

■ MULTIPLE CHOICE

Self-Test 11

1. The formal structures of organizations may be shown in a(n) _____. (a) environmental diagram (b) organization chart (c) horizontal diagram (d) matrix depiction (e) labor assignment chart

2. A major distinction between line and staff units concerns _____. (a) the amount of resources each is allowed to utilize (b) linkage of their jobs to the goals of the firm (c) amount of education or training they possess (d) their use of computer information systems (e) their linkage to the outside world

3. The division of labor by grouping people and material resources deals with _____. (a) specialization (b) coordination (c) divisionalization (d) vertical specialization (e) goal setting

4. Control involves all but _____. (a) measuring results (b) establishing goals (c) taking corrective action (d) comparing results with goals (e) selecting manpower

5. Grouping individuals and resources in the organization around products, services, clients, territories, or legal entities is an example of _____ specialization. (a) divisional (b) functional (c) matrix (d) mixed form (e) outsourced specialization

6. Grouping resources into departments by skill, knowledge, and action is the _____ pattern. (a) functional (b) divisional (c) vertical (d) means-end chains (e) matrix

7. A matrix structure _____. (a) reinforces unity of command (b) is inexpensive (c) is easy to explain to employees (d) gives some employees two bosses (e) yields a minimum of organizational politics

8. Formalization _____. (a) groups individuals and resources by product, service, client, territory, or legal entity (b) groups individuals and resources by skill, knowledge, and action (c) groups individuals and resources by the goals of an organization (d) provides written documentation of work rules, policies, and procedures (e) yields the combination of knowledge and technology that creates a product or service output for an organization

9. _____ is the concern for proper communication enabling the units to understand one another's activities. (a) Control (b) Coordination (c) Specialization (d) Departmentation (e) Division of labor

10. Compared to the machine bureaucracy (mechanistic type), the professional bureaucracy (organic type) _____. (a) is more efficient for routine operations (b) has more vertical specialization and control (c) is larger (d) has more horizontal specialization and coordination mechanism (e) is smaller

■ TRUE–FALSE

11. Mission statements are written statements of organizational purpose.   T   F

12. A specific group, such as a political campaign, is an example of a primary beneficiary.   T   F

13. The configuration of positions, job duties, and lines of authority among the component parts of an organization is called its structure.   T   F

14. The hierarchy of authority is the process of breaking work into small components that serve the organization's purpose.   T   F

15. Specialization and coordination are two core issues in the concept of organizational structure. T F

16. The span of control distributes formal authority and establishes where and how critical decisions are to be made. T F

17. Grouping people together by skill, knowledge, and action yields a divisional pattern of departmentation. T F

18. Line units and personnel in an organization provide specialized expertise and services to staff units and personnel. T F

19. One of the advantages of a matrix structure is that it helps provide a blending of technical and market emphases in organizations operating in exceedingly complex environments. T F

20. As opposed to committees, task forces are typically formed with a limited agenda to identify and solve problems that cut across different departments. T F

■ SHORT RESPONSE

21. Compare and contrast output goals with systems goals.

22. Describe the types of controls that are typically used in organizations.

23. What are the major advantages and disadvantages of functional departmentation?

24. What are the major advantages and disadvantages of matrix departmentation ?

■ APPLICATIONS ESSAY

25. Describe some of the side effects of organizational controls in a large mechanistically structured organization, such as the United States Postal Service.

Explore application-oriented Fast Company articles, cases, experimental exercises, and self-assessments in the OB Skills Workbook

■ **Visit the Schermerhorn Web site to find the Interactive Self-Test and Internet exercises for this chapter.**

Information Technology and Organizational Design

INFORMATION AND TECHNOLOGY FUEL A NEW SPIRIT

www.gm.com

For generations, General Motors set the standard by which other corporations were measured. Its size alone was the clearest indicator of the firm's strength and success. Then GM became known as "generous motors" for all the executive perks it gave to its top managers even as its share of the U.S. market dropped from almost 50 percent to less than 33 percent. Now under John (Jack) F. Smith there is a new spirit. The focus has shifted from size to speed and the capability to adapt and change rapidly. Technology in general and information technology in particular are seen as not only important but vital as GM reinvents the people-to-people processes to propel it again to set the standard for other corporations. CEO Smith has clear priorities to (1) increase commonality in the processes, parts, and vehicle platforms worldwide to save time, confusion, and money, (2) think lean and run fast by streamlining the organization for learning and quicker response from idea generation to implementation, (3) compete on a global basis by increasing international production capacity, and (4) reestablish GM as a growth company.[1]

We all recognize that a GM auto assembly plant and the musical group Golden Smog are quite different but they have something in common. Auto assembly plants are organized to emphasize routine, efficient production, whereas the musical group is loose, experimental, and devoted to artistic expression. Yet, both must also use the most recent and competitive information technologies. For Golden Smog it may be computerized logistics for travel, movement of the equipment, and ticket sales. For GM it includes an extensive and sophisticated internal information system for learning. In this chapter, we discuss how managers adjust the basic elements of organizational structure to fit the scale of the operation and the ways in which senior management intends to compete. In the last decade, the range of organizational design options has changed dramatically. Even for the small firm, information technology has started to revolutionize the way it manages.

Study Questions

As you read Chapter 12, keep in mind these study questions.

■ What is organizational design, and how do the designs of small and large firms differ?
■ Does the operations and information technology of the firm influence its organizational design?
■ What is the relationship between environmental conditions and organizational design?
■ What is strategy, and how do organizational learning and information technology influence strategic competency?

Organizational Design and Size

■ **Organizational design** is the process of choosing and implementing a structural configuration for an organization.

Organizational design is the process of choosing and implementing a structural configuration.[2] The choice of an appropriate organizational design is contingent upon several factors, including the size of the firm, its operations and information technology, its environment, and the strategy it selects for growth and survival.

240

For many reasons, large organizations cannot be just bigger versions of their smaller counterparts. As the number of individuals in a firm increases arithmetically, the number of possible interconnections among them increases geometrically. In other words, the direct interpersonal contact among all members in a large organization must be managed. The design of small firms is directly influenced by its core operations technology, whereas larger firms have many core operations technologies in a wide variety of much more specialized units. In large organizations, a key to success is efficiency by economies of scale—production of products and services efficiently through repetition. Specialization of labor, equipment, and departments is one way of capturing the potential economies of scale. Increasing specialization calls for increased control and coordination to ensure that actions are directed toward common goals and linked together in a meaningful way. In short, larger organizations are often more complex than smaller firms. This additional complexity calls for a more sophisticated organizational design. Yet even very large organizations also rely on simple design elements.

■ THE SIMPLE DESIGN FOR SMALLER UNITS AND FIRMS

The **simple design** is a configuration involving one or two ways of specializing individuals and units. That is, vertical specialization and control typically emphasize levels of supervision without elaborate formal mechanisms (e.g., rule books, policy manuals), and the majority of the control resides in the manager. Thus, the simple design tends to minimize the bureaucratic aspects and rest more heavily on the leadership of the manager.

The simple design is appropriate for many small firms, such as family businesses, retail stores, and small manufacturing firms.[3] The strengths of the simple design are simplicity, flexibility, and responsiveness to the desires of a central manager—in many cases, the owner. Because a simple design relies heavily on the manager's personal leadership, however, this configuration is only as effective as is the senior manager.[4]

■ **Simple design** is a configuration involving one or two ways of specializing individuals and units.

ENTREPRENEURSHIP 📈

www.bandatravel.com

B&A Travel is a comparatively small travel agency run by Helen Druse. Reporting to Helen are two staff members—Jane Bloom for accounting and finance, and Ken Wiener for training and market development. The operations arm is headed by Joan Wiland, who supervises 10 lead travel agents. Whereas each of the lead travel agents specializes in a geographical area, all but Sue Connely and Bart Merve take client requests for all types of trips. Sue is in charge of three major business accounts, and Bart heads a tour group. Each of the 10 lead agents heads a group of 5 to 7 associates. Coordination is achieved through their dedicated intranet connections and weekly meetings as well as a lot of personal contact by Helen and Joan. Control is enhanced by the computerized reservation system they all use. Helen makes sure each agent has a monthly sales target, and she routinely chats with important clients about their level of service. She realizes that developing participation from even the newest associate is an important tool in maintaining a "fun" atmosphere.

Operations Technology and Organizational Design

Although the design of an organization should reflect its size, it must also be adjusted to fit technological opportunities and requirements.[5] That is, successful organizations are said to arrange their internal structures to meet the dictates of their dominant "technologies" or work flows and, more recently, information technology opportunities.[6] **Operations technology** is the combination of resources, knowledge, and techniques that creates a product or service output for an organization.[7] **Information technology** is the combination of machines, artifacts, procedures, and systems used to gather, store, analyze, and disseminate information for translating it into knowledge.[8]

For over 30 years, researchers in OB have chartered the links between operations technology and organizational design. For operations technology, two common classifications have received considerable attention: Thompson's and Woodward's classifications.

■ **Operations technology** is the combination of resources, knowledge, and techniques that creates a product or service output for an organization.

■ **Information technology** is the combination of machines, artifacts, procedures, and systems used to gather, store, analyze, and disseminate information for translating it into knowledge.

▩ THOMPSON'S VIEW OF TECHNOLOGY

James ·D. Thompson classified technologies based on the degree to which the technology could be specified and the degree of interdependence among the work activities with categories called intensive, mediating, and long linked.[9] Under *intensive technology*, there is uncertainty as to how to produce desired outcomes. A group of specialists must be brought together interactively to use a variety of techniques to solve problems. Examples are found in a hospital emergency room or a research and development laboratory. Coordination and knowledge exchange are of critical importance with this kind of technology.

Mediating technology links parties that want to become interdependent. For example, banks link creditors and depositors and store money and information to facilitate such exchanges. Whereas all depositors and creditors are indirectly interdependent, the reliance is pooled through the bank. The degree of coordination among the individual tasks with pooled technology is substantially reduced, and information management becomes more important than coordinated knowledge application.

Under *long-linked technology*, also called mass production or industrial technology, the way to produce the desired outcomes is known. The task is broken down into a number of sequential steps. A classic example is the automobile assembly line. Control is critical, and coordination is restricted to making the sequential linkages work in harmony.

▩ WOODWARD'S VIEW OF TECHNOLOGY

Joan Woodward also divides technology into three categories: small-batch, mass production, and continuous-process manufacturing.[10] In units of *small-batch production*, a variety of custom products are tailor-made to fit customer specifications, such as tailor-made suits. The machinery and equipment used are generally not very elaborate, but considerable craftsmanship is often needed. In *mass pro-*

duction, the organization produces one or a few products through an assembly-line system. The work of one group is highly dependent on that of another; the equipment is typically sophisticated; and the workers are given very detailed instructions. Automobiles and refrigerators are produced in this way. Organizations using *continuous-process technology* produce a few products using considerable automation. Classic examples are automated chemical plants and oil refineries.

From her studies, Woodward concluded that the combination of structure and technology was critical to the success of the organizations. When technology and organizational design were properly matched, a firm was more successful. Specifically, successful small-batch and continuous-process plants had flexible structures with small work groups at the bottom; more rigidly structured plants were less successful. In contrast, successful mass production operations were rigidly structured and had large work groups at the bottom. Since Woodward's studies, this technological imperative has been supported by various other investigations. Yet, today we recognize that technology is just one factor involved in the success of an organization.[11]

■ WHERE OPERATIONS TECHNOLOGY DOMINATES: THE ADHOCRACY

The influence of operations technological is most clearly seen in small organizations and in specific departments within large ones. In some instances, managers and employees simply do not know the appropriate way to service a client or to produce a particular product. This is the extreme of Thompson's intensive type of technology, and it may be found in some small-batch processes where a team of individuals must develop a unique product for a particular client.

Mintzberg suggests that at these technological extremes, the "adhocracy" may be an appropriate design.[12] An **adhocracy** is characterized by few rules, policies, and procedures; substantial decentralization; shared decision making among members; extreme horizontal specialization (as each member of the unit may be a distinct specialist); few levels of management; and virtually no formal controls.

The adhocracy is particularly useful when an aspect of the firm's operations technology presents two sticky problems: (1) the tasks facing the firm vary considerably and provide many exceptions, as in a hospital, or (2) problems are difficult to define and resolve.[13] The adhocracy places a premium on professionalism and coordination in problem solving.[14] Large firms may use temporary task forces, form special committees, and even contract consulting firms to provide the creative problem identification and problem solving that the adhocracy promotes. For instance, Microsoft creates new autonomous departments to encourage talented employees to develop new software programs. Allied Chemical and 3M also set up quasi-autonomous groups to work through new ideas.

■ **Adhocracy** is an organizational structure that emphasizes shared, decentralized decision making; extreme horizontal specialization; few levels of management; the virtual absence of formal controls; and few rules, policies, and procedures.

Information Technology and Organizational Design

Today, information technology (IT) and the computer are virtually inseparable.[15] Some even suggest that IT only refers to computer-based systems used in the management of the enterprise.[16] Certainly, the computer and extensions of the personal computer are a major force in most corporations. However, substantial collateral advances have also been made in telecommunication options. Furthermore, advances in the computer as a machine are much less profound than how information technology is transforming how firms manage.

It is important to understand just what IT does from an organizational standpoint—not from the view of the PC user.[17] From an organizational standpoint IT can be used, among other things, as (1) a partial substitute for some operations as well as some process controls and impersonal methods of coordination, (2) a capability for transforming information to knowledge for learning, and (3) a strategic capability.

■ INFORMATION TECHNOLOGY AS A SUBSTITUTE

Old bureaucracies prospered and dominated other forms, in part, because they provided more efficient production through specialization and their approach to dealing with information. Where the organization used mediating technology or long-linked technology, the machine bureaucracy ran rampant. In these firms rules, policies, and procedures, as well as many other process controls, could be rigidly enforced based on very scant information.[18] Such was the case for the post office: postal clerks even had rules telling them how to hold their hands when sorting mail.

In many organizations, the initial implementation of IT would displace the most routine, highly specified, and repetitive jobs.[19] The clerical tasks in bookkeeping, writing checks for payroll, and keeping track of sales were some of the first targets of computerization. Here IT was often initiated in the form of a large centralized mainframe computer. For instance, mainframe computers were still the major business for IBM well into the 1990s. Initial implementation did not alter the fundamental character or design of the organization. To continue the example of the post office, initial computerization focused mainly on replacing the hand tracking of mail. Then IT was infused into automated reading machines to help sort mail. This called for implementation of the ZIP code.

A second wave of substitution replaced process controls and informal coordination mechanisms. Rules, policies, and procedures could be replaced with a decision support system (DSS). In the case of a DSS, repetitive routine choices could be programmed into a computer-based system. For instance, if you applied for a credit card, a computer program would check your credit history and other financial information. If your application passed several preset tests, you would be issued a credit card. If your application failed any of the tests, it would either be rejected or sent to an individual for further analysis.

The second wave of implementation brought some marginal changes in organizational design. Specifically, the firm often needed fewer levels of

OB Across Functions

MARKETING

Will Salespeople and Distributors Be the New Clerical Casualties of the Web?

In just a few years the stock market value of amazon.com has surpassed that of industry leader Barnes and Noble, even though Amazon has no retail stores and sells fewer books. Firms in other industries are reexamining their channels of distribution and their reliance on internal sales units. Direct sales via the Web undercut the need for traditional dealers and provide direct access for consumers. At the same time, salespeople establish valuable relationships with customers. Yet, as amazon.com illustrates, many customers may want direct access. Now most corporate Web sites serve as window dressing for corporate images rather than marketing tools. But as Amazon exemplifies, that role is changing...and quickly.

management and fewer internal staff. A small number of firms also recognized that they could outsource some internal staff operations. For instance, in many firms independent organizations actually do all of their employee payroll.

The emphasis on direct substitution was still the norm in many organizations well into the 1990s, and in smaller firms it continues today. This is much as one would expect with the implementation of a new-to-the-world technology. It takes decades to move from the lab to full implementation, and the first applications are often in the form of substitutes for existing solutions. For instance, autos were once just substitutes for the horse and buggy. Both computer technology and the auto took about 20 years to enter the mass market. However, IT, just as the auto, has transformed our society because it added new capability.

■ INFORMATION TECHNOLOGY AS A CAPABILITY FOR LEARNING

IT has also long been recognized for its potential to add capability.[20] For over 20 years, scholars have talked of using IT to improve the efficiency, speed of responsiveness, and effectiveness of operations. Married to machines, IT became advanced manufacturing technology when computer-aided design (CAD) was combined with computer-aided manufacturing (CAM) to yield the automated manufacturing cell. More complex decision support systems have provided middle and lower level managers programs to aid in analyzing complex problems rather than just ratify routine choices. Computer-generated reports now give even senior executives the opportunity to track the individual sales performance of the lowliest salesperson.

Now instead of substituting for existing operations, or process controls, IT provides individuals deep within the organization the information they need to plan, make choices, coordinate with others, and control their own operations.

Although simple substitution could proceed one application at a time, the real impact of adding IT capability could not come until it was broadly available to nearly everyone.[21] To use the auto analogy again, the real impact of the auto was felt only after Henry Ford sold hundreds of thousands of his Model T and new roads were constructed. For IT to have a similar impact on organizational design, the seamless use of computerized information across the organization was needed. The extremely powerful mainframe of the 1970s and 1980s was not up to the task simply because the information individuals required to do their jobs more quickly and better was often unique to them. They now needed a common technology with the capability for uniqueness. And nearly everyone would have to have it and use it in cooperation with others.

Enter WINTEL—that is, Microsoft Windows in combination with an Intel microprocessing chip. This combination provided a relatively cheap, easy-to-use personal computer with an almost standardized technology that could be individually tailored at a comparatively modest cost. WINTEL was the PC equivalent of the tin lizzie—Henry Ford's Model T designed for the masses.

With the adoption of WINTEL, three important changes occurred. First, IT applications for tasks found across many organizations were quickly developed and received board acceptance. Thus, the era of the spreadsheet and the word processing program began and displaced the old mainframes. Individuals could develop and transfer information to others with some assurance that the other party could read their output and duplicate their processes. Second, WINTEL expanded to incorporate existing telecommunications systems such as the Internet.[22] Thus, the era of connectivity also emerged. Married to parallel developments in telecommunications, a whole world of electronic commerce, teleconferencing—with combinations of data, pictures, and sound—and cell phones emerged. Third, IT was transformed from a substitute to a mechanism for learning.[23] For example, we now ask you to learn from the Internet connections and Web exercises at the end of each chapter.

Collectively, the impact of IT organizational design was and remains profound. The changes can often occur from the bottom up. New IT systems empower individuals, expanding their jobs and making them both interesting and challenging. The emphasis on narrowly defined jobs replete with process controls imposed by middle management can be transformed to broadly envisioned, interesting jobs based on IT-embedded processes with output controls. A new series of coordination devices based on IT can displace the memo and the coordinating department as firms constitute temporary teams and task forces using "virtual meetings"—meetings via E-mail to solve cross-departmental problems.[24] The whole world of staff units has changed as bureaucratic professionals have adjusted to the new world of IT. And many middle managers replete with their staff assistants are no longer needed.

For the production segments of firms using long-linked technology such as in auto assembly plants and canneries, IT can be linked to total quality management (TQM) programs and be embedded in the machinery. Here data on operations can be transformed into knowledge of operations and used to systematically improve quality and efficiency. This also has meant that firms have had to rethink their view of employees as brainless robots. To make TQM work with IT all employees must plan, do, and control. Thus, we have taken special care to talk about job enrichment and job design in Chapter 8, for combining IT and TQM with empowerment and participation is fundamental for success. For instance, in the mid-1990s two computer equipment manufacturers embarked on improvement programs combining IT and TQM. One manufacturer imposed the program on all employees. There was some initial success, but ultimately this program failed. The second combined the IT-TQM program with extensive empowerment and participation. Although implementation was slower, today the combination has produced a constantly improving learning environment.[25]

■ INFORMATION TECHNOLOGY AS A STRATEGIC CAPABILITY

A whole new series of firms has arisen in which IT is the business of the firm or the firm would not exist without sophisticated IT.[26] The whole computer and semiconductor business is the most obvious example. Where IT dominates, the firm is often designed as an adhocracy.

Perhaps IT's most profound effect can be seen in firms that rely on a mediating technology; banks, finance companies, dating services, and employment agencies are some examples. The job of the firm, as we know, is to facilitate exchange by matching types of individuals. In the case of banks, individuals who want to borrow are matched with those who want to lend by placing individual interests into categories. So those who have a savings account are put in a category of precisely that type of savings account and are pooled with others. IT can revolutionize the categorization process that underlies the matching by helping to create much more sophisticated categories and link these categories in new and novel ways. For example, IT lies behind the multibillion dollar secondary market for home mortgages. Until recent years, a bank or savings and loan (S&L) provided the funds for the mortgage from its depositors and would hold the mortgage until it was paid off. You would apply to a local bank or S&L for a mortgage. If they granted you a mortgage, you would pay the bank or the S&L that sold it to you. Much the same was the case for student loans. Now with IT, the bank or S&L can sell the mortgage to others, and normally does, so that it can recoup new funds to sell additional mortgages. It may even sell the right to "service" the loan so that you no longer send your money to the originating bank but to someone else. This change in information technology now allows all types of financial institutions to participate in lending money for mortgages. The job of the old banker or S&L manger has fundamentally changed. Now you can get a mortgage, a credit card, or use the ATM machine without ever contacting an individual.

TECHNOLOGY 🖥

www.chasemanhattan.com

More firms are recognizing the strategic value of information technology and using IT as a basis for global operations. In an annual report, Chase states that the "effective use of information technology is allowing Chase to successfully pursue a consumer services strategy different from that of many competitors. Its consumer businesses, while fully nationwide, are less dependent upon physical presence, relying more and more on alternative distribution channels. For example, in auto finance, where Chase is the leading bank lender, more than 1,000 car dealerships across the country provide the channel, many tied directly to Chase by computer for instantaneous credit decisions. In mortgage banking loan officers with laptops are the channel."

Some financial firms could not exist without IT, which has become the basis for whole new industries. For instance, IT is the foundation for multitrillion dollar markets in international finance in which new exotic products are available which were nonexistent 15 years ago. A small handful of individuals in Connecticut working for a firm called Long Term Capital used sophisticated IT systems to bet several billion dollars on the interest spread between different kinds of bonds. Although they made several hundred million dollars in the mid 1990s, in 1998 their losses threatened the whole U.S. financial system to the point that the Federal Reserve (a quasigovernment agency) had to orchestrate a rescue. Long Term Capital had become too big to fail in an aspect of the global financial markets that barely existed in the 1980s. Few existing financial managers or regulatory agencies had the understanding of IT to develop effective controls for the global derivatives markets. Of course, IT has not developed in a vacuum, and its effective implementation often rests on others adopting common IT standards and operations. Just because IT presents a potential capability does not automatically mean the firm should adopt it or change its design to facilitate its use.

The appropriate design also rests on external factors and the strategy of the firm. We turn to these issues now.

Environment and Organizational Design

An effective organizational design also reflects powerful external forces as well as size and technological factors. Organizations, as open systems, need to receive inputs from the environment and in turn to sell outputs to their environment. Therefore, understanding the environment has become important.[27]

The *general environment* is the set of cultural, economic, legal-political, and educational conditions found in the areas in which the organization operates. Much of Chapter 3 on international concerns dealt with the influences of the general environment, and throughout this volume we have shown examples of globalization. The owners, suppliers, distributors, government agencies, and competitors with which an organization must interact to grow and survive constitute its *specific environment*. A firm typically has much more choice in the composition of its specific environment than its general environment. It can develop policies and strategies that will alter the mix of owners, suppliers, distributors, and competitors with which it interacts. Although it is often convenient to separate the general and specific environmental influences on the firm, designers need to recognize the combined impact of both. Choosing some businesses, for instance, means entering global competition with advanced technologies.

■ ENVIRONMENTAL COMPLEXITY

■ **Environmental complexity** is the magnitude of the problems and opportunities in the organization's environment as evidenced by the degree of richness, interdependence, and uncertainty.

A basic concern that must be addressed in analyzing the environment of the organization is its complexity. A more complex environment provides an organization with more opportunities and more problems. **Environmental complexity** refers to the magnitude of the problems and opportunities in the organization's environment, as evidenced by three main factors: the degree of richness, the degree of interdependence, and the degree of uncertainty stemming from both the general and the specific environment.

Environmental Richness Overall, the environment is richer when the economy is growing, when individuals are improving their education, and when those on whom the organization relies are prospering. For businesses, a richer environment means that economic conditions are improving, customers are spending more money, and suppliers (especially banks) are willing to invest in the organization's future. In a rich environment, more organizations survive, even if they have poorly functioning organizational designs. A richer environment is also filled with more opportunities and dynamism—the potential for change. The organizational design must allow the company to recognize these opportunities and capitalize on them.

The opposite of richness is decline. For business firms, a general recession is a good example of a leaner environment. Whereas corporate reactions vary, it is instructive to examine three typical responses to decline. In Japan, core manufacturing firms are reluctant to lay off core workers. Instead, they cut the hours of women employees, move some individuals to long-term suppliers, and initiate training for the remaining workers to prepare for a recovery. Since economic problems in Japan have lasted more than five years, however, these typical responses are starting to change. Japanese firms are looking more like their U.S. counterparts as they are giving employees early retirement options, cutting staff, and outsourcing more of their operations.

In the United States, firms have traditionally reacted to decline first by issuing layoffs to nonsupervisory workers and then by moving up the organizational ladder as the environment becomes leaner. As global competition has increased and new IT options have become more widely available, firms have also started to alter their organizational designs by cutting staff units and the number of organizational levels. This downsizing, though traumatic, can be minimized.

Many European firms find it very difficult to cut full-time employees legally when the economy deteriorates. In sustained periods of decline, many firms have therefore turned to national governments for help. Much like U.S.-based firms, European-based firms view changes in organizational design as a last but increasingly necessary resort as they must now compete with Asian and North American rivals.

Environmental Interdependence   The link between external interdependence and organizational design is often subtle and indirect. The organization may coopt powerful outsiders by including them. For instance, many large corporations have financial representatives from banks and insurance companies on their boards of directors. The organization may also adjust its overall design strategy to absorb or buffer the demands of a more powerful external element. Perhaps the most common adjustment is the development of a centralized staff department to handle an important external group. For instance, few large U.S. corporations do not have some type of governmental relations group at the top. Where service to a few large customers is considered critical, the organization's departmentation is likely to switch from a functional to a divisionalized form.[28]

Uncertainty and Volatility   Environmental uncertainty and volatility can be particularly damaging to large bureaucracies. In times of change, investments quickly become outmoded, and internal operations no longer work as expected. The obvious organizational design response to uncertainty and volatility is to opt for a more organic form. At the extremes, movement toward an adhocracy may be important. However, these pressures may run counter to those that come from large size and operations technology. In these cases, it may be too hard or too time consuming for some organizations to make the design adjustments. Thus, the organization may continue to struggle while adjusting its design just a little bit at a time.

■ USING ALLIANCES WHERE ENVIRONMENTAL FACTORS DOMINATE

In high-tech areas and businesses dominated by IT, such as robotics, semiconductors, advanced materials (ceramics and carbon fibers), and advanced information systems, a single company often does not have all the knowledge necessary to bring new products to the market. Often, the firms with the knowledge are not even in the same country. The organizational design must therefore go beyond

Procter and Gamble ←

www.pg.com

When Procter and Gamble entered the European market, its organization centered around country locations. Then its emphasis became regional. Today, it is centered around focused product lines, such as laundry detergent or soap. It has a matrix linkage between the old national and regional units and the new product ones. The European market is now responsible for about one-third of P&G's total sales.

■ **Interfirm alliances** are announced cooperative agreements or joint ventures between two independent firms.

the boundaries of the organization into **interfirm alliances**—announced cooperative agreements or joint ventures between two independent firms. Often, these agreements involve corporations that are headquartered in different nations.[29]

Alliances are quite common in such high-technology industries, because they seek not only to develop technology but to ensure that their solutions become standardized across regions of the world. In some cases, the fight for a dominant design pits one nation against another. For instance, Zenith joined forces with AT&T to develop one high-definition television (HDTV) system, and Toshiba, Sony, and some 30 other Japanese firms formed a strategic network to develop their own system. After a bitter contest the winner in the United States included the Zenith and AT&T group, who are likely get the lion's share of the estimated $20 billion HDTV market in North America.

Firms may also develop alliances to explore potentials for future collaboration. One of the largest and potentially most influential strategic alliances is the cooperation between West Germany's Daimler-Chrysler and Japan's Mitsubishi. The two companies agreed to share technology and to develop joint ventures, market-based cooperations, or high-tech consortia, as the need arises. Yet some alliances to share technology date to the turn of the twentieth century.

www.warner-lambert.com

⊕ GLOBALIZATION

There is a myth that international alliances, particularly in high-tech areas, are short-lived. But that is not always the case. The alliance between Warner-Lambert (best known as a U.S.-based pharmaceutical firm) and Japan's Sankyo (one of Japan's most successful pharmaceutical firms) dates to 1902 when Parke-Davis, now a division of Warner-Lambert, selected Sankyo as a distributor for one of its drugs and again after World War II to market Parke-Davis antibiotics. As Warner-Lambert states in its annual report, "Our relationship has flourished like a great tree." The latest fruit from this relationship is REZULIN, a new medication to treat diabetes. First discovered by Sankyo, the drug was developed, perfected, and marketed via the alliance. It is one of the most successful new drugs in the United States. As Maurice Renshaw, president of Parke-Davis, states, "We believe that when our business allies win, we win as well."

In more developed industries, interfirm alliances are also quite popular, but they are often known by other names. In Europe, for example, they are called *informal combines* or *cartels*: Competitors work cooperatively to share the market in order to decrease uncertainty and improve favorability for all. Except in rare cases, these arrangements are often illegal in the United States.

In Japan, the network of relationships among well-established firms in many industries is called a *keiretsu*. There are two common forms. The first is a bank-centered keiretsu, in which firms are linked to one another directly through cross ownership and historical ties to one bank. The Mitsubishi group is a good example. In the second type, a vertical keiretsu, a key manufacturer is at the hub of a network of supplier firms or distributor firms. The manufacturer typically has both long-term supply contracts with members and cross-ownership ties.

These arrangements help isolate Japanese firms from stockholders and provide a mechanism for sharing and developing technology. Toyota is an example of a firm at the center of a vertical keiretsu.

The network organization is beginning to evolve in the United States as well. Here, the central firm specializes in a core activity, such as design and assembly, and works with a comparatively small number of participating suppliers on a long-term basis for both component development and manufacturing efficiency. Nike is a leader in the development of these relationships.

More extreme variations of this network design are also emerging to meet apparently conflicting environmental, size, and technological demands simultaneously. Firms are spinning off staff functions to reduce their overall size and take advantage of new IT options. With these new environmental challenges and technological opportunities, firms must choose and not just react blindly.

Strategy and Organizational Design

For many firms, size, technology, and environment provide too many challenges and opportunities. Organizational design scholars recommend that the design follow the strategy of the firm and that the strategy take advantage of a combination of advantages offered by size, technology, and the environment.

Organizational strategy is the process of positioning the organization in its competitive environment and implementing actions to compete successfully.[30] The study of linking strategy, organizational design, and firm performance has a long tradition in organizational analysis. In the 1960s, Alfred Chandler studied the evolution of major U.S. firms and concluded that structure follows from the strategy established predominantly by senior management. More recent work suggests that the formula for success is much more complicated.[31] A winning strategy is more likely when the firm recognizes both the importance of a focus and the unique skills and abilities within the firm. Forming a strategy is an interactive process. Senior managers select those systems goals they believe should define corporate success, form these goals into a vision, select a target position within the general and specific environments, and develop a design to accomplish the vision.

■ **Organizational strategy** is the process of positioning the organization in the competitive environment and implementing actions to compete successfully.

■ COMPETENCY-BASED STRATEGIES

Once executives were told to develop a successful strategy by emphasizing one of a limited number economic advantages.[32] Today many strategists are emphasizing the skills and abilities the firms need to have to compete effectively; just saying you want your firm to be a technical leader and instituting an adhocracy does not get the job done.[33] Over time, the firm may develop specific administrative and technical competencies. As middle and lower level managers institute minor modifications and adjustments to solve specific problems and capitalize on specific opportunities, they and their firms may learn new skills. These skills may be recognized by senior management and give them the opportunity to adjust, modify, and build a so-called competency strategy.

The organization needs to build on and refine its unique experience and competencies. In this process, the firm may shift products and markets by rely-

Kodak Camera ◀

www.kodak.com

After a significant restructuring under Gord Wilson, Kodak Canada is entering into alliances to improve its technical competence in electronic imaging. These moves go beyond personal empowerment or employee participation in implementing the reorganization. Employees and middle managers are building a unique strategy based on their skills and abilities. The emphasis is on learning.

■ **Organizational learning** is the process of knowledge acquisition, information distribution, information interpretation, and organizational retention.

■ **Mimicry** is the copying of the successful practices of others.

ing on the creativity, innovation, and skills of all its employees. IBM was once known as a successful second-to-market imitator with the best service for its mainframe computers. It was not the technical leader, but it developed the standard for others, provided excellent service, and offered a wide array of mainframe products and services. Now IBM, or "Big Blue," is on the move. It has turned to flexible manufacturing for its personal computers to increase efficiency, accompanied by fewer levels of management and substantially greater participation. It is also reaching out to become the hub in a network of high-tech computer firms to service the expanding network computer market. IBM is fighting a long history of traditional management as it seeks to cut levels of management, reduce staff, stress innovation, and infuse itself with unique competencies.

Senior executives at such firms as Ford, AT&T, and Dow are now recognizing that an effective strategy builds on the competence of employees. Technical skills combined with astute management in an organizational design that reinforces employee contributions are fundamental to organizational success. This emphasis on individuals has also brought attention to the important topic of organizational learning. Executives now recognize that their firms must learn or die.

Strategic Competency Through Learning

Organizational learning is the process of knowledge acquisition, information distribution, information interpretation, and organizational retention in adapting successfully to changing circumstances.[34] In simpler terms, organizational learning involves the adjustment of the organization's and individual's actions based on its experience and that of others. The challenge is doing to learn and learning to do.

■ KNOWLEDGE ACQUISITION

All firms learn by obtaining information in a variety of ways and at different rates during their histories. Perhaps the most important information is obtained from sources outside the firm at the time of its founding. During the firm's initial years, its managers copy, or mimic, what they believe are the successful practices of others.[35] As they mature, however, firms can also acquire knowledge through experience and systematic search.

Mimicry   *Mimicry* is important to the new firm because (1) it provides workable, if not ideal, solutions to many problems; (2) it reduces the number of decisions that need to be analyzed separately, allowing managers to concentrate on more critical issues; and (3) it establishes legitimacy or acceptance by employees, suppliers, and customers and narrows the choices calling for detailed explanation.

One of the key factors involved in examining mimicry is the extent to which managers attempt to isolate cause-effect relationships. Simply copying others without attempting to understand the issues involved often leads to failure. The literature is filled with examples of firms that have tried to implement quality circles, empowerment, and decentralization simply because others have used them successfully. Too many firms have abandoned these techniques because managers failed to understand why and under what conditions they worked for other firms. When mimicking others, managers need to adjust for the unique circumstances of their corporation.

Experience   A primary way to acquire knowledge is through experience. All organizations and managers can learn in this manner. Besides learning by doing, managers can also systematically embark on structured programs to capture the lessons to be learned from failure and success. For instance, a well-designed research and development program allows managers to learn as much through failure as through success.

Learning by doing in an intelligent way is at the heart of many Japanese corporations, with their emphasis on statistical quality control, quality circles, and other such practices. Many firms have discovered that numerous small improvements can cumulatively add up to a major improvement in both quality and efficiency. The major problem with emphasizing learning by doing is the inability to forecast precisely what will change and how it will change. Managers need to believe that improvements can be made, listen to suggestions, and actually implement the changes. It is much more difficult to do than to say, however.

Vicarious Learning   Vicarious learning involves capturing the lessons of others' experiences. At the individual level, managers are building on individualized "social learning" and using it to help transform their potential for organizational improvement.

Individual Social Learning   *Social learning* is learning that is achieved through the reciprocal interactions among people, behavior, and environment. Figure 12.1 illustrates and elaborates on this individualized view of learning drawn from the work of Albert Bandura.[36] According to the figure, the individual uses modeling or vicarious learning to acquire behavior by observing and imitating others. The person then attempts to acquire these behaviors by modeling them through practice. In a work situation, the model may be a manager or

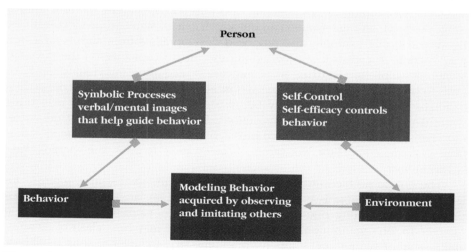

Figure 12.1
Social learning model.

co-worker who demonstrates desired behaviors. Mentors or senior workers who befriend younger and more inexperienced protégés can also be important models. Indeed, some have argued that a shortage of mentors for women in management is a major constraint to their progression up the career ladder.[37]

The symbolic processes depicted in Figure 12.1 are also important in social learning. Words and symbols used by managers and others in the workplace can help communicate values, beliefs, and goals and thus serve as guides to the individual's behavior. For example, a "thumbs up" or a symbol from the boss lets you know your behavior is appropriate. At the same time, the person's self-control is important in influencing his or her own behavior. *Self-efficacy*—the person's belief that he or she can perform adequately in a situation—is an important part of such self-control. People with self-efficacy believe that they have the necessary ability for a given job; that they are capable of the effort required; and that no outside events will hinder them from attaining their desired performance level.[38] In contrast, people with low self-efficacy believe that no matter how hard they try, they cannot manage their environment well enough to be successful. For example, if you feel self-efficacious as a student, a low grade on one test is likely to encourage you to study harder, talk to the instructor, or do other things to enable you to do well the next time. In contrast, a person low in self-efficacy would probably drop the course or give up studying. Of course, even people who are high in self-efficacy do not control their environment entirely.

Much of the learning in corporations is less systematic than that depicted in Figure 12.1. Some firms have learned that the process of searching for new information may not always be structured or planned in conjunction with an identified problem or opportunity. Managers may embark upon learning in less systematic ways, including scanning, grafting, and contracting out.

■ **Scanning** is looking outside the firm and bringing back useful solutions to problems.

Scanning involves looking outside the firm and bringing back useful solutions. At times, these solutions may be applied to recognized problems. More often, these solutions float around management until they are needed to solve a problem.[39] Astute managers can contribute to organizational learning by scanning external sources, such as competitors, suppliers, industry consultants, customers, and leading firms. For instance, by reverse engineering the competitor's products (developing the engineering drawings and specifications from the existing product), an organization can quickly match all standard product features. By systematically exploring the proposed developments from suppliers, a firm may become a lead user and be among the first to capitalize on the developments of suppliers. **Grafting** is the process of acquiring individuals, units, or firms to bring in useful knowledge. Almost all firms seek to hire experienced individuals from other firms simply because experienced individuals may bring with them a whole new series of solutions. For instance, at Dayton-Hudson senior management hired a new vice president for one of their department stores from a leading competitor, Nordstrom's. They wanted to know the winning ways of this industry leader.

■ **Grafting** is the process of acquiring individuals, units, and/or firms to bring in useful knowledge to the organization.

The critical problem in grafting is much the same as that in scanning: Obtaining the knowledge is not enough; it must be translated into action. A key problem with grafting one unit onto an existing organization is discussed in Chapter 13, on organizational culture. That is, there may be a clash of cultures, and instead of getting new solutions, both units may experience substantial conflict. Contracting out or outsourcing is the reverse of grafting and involves asking outsiders to perform a particular function. Whereas all organizations contract out and outsource, the key question for managers is often what to keep. As we have already noted, firms often outsource peripheral or staff functions.

■ INFORMATION DISTRIBUTION

Once information is obtained, managers must establish mechanisms to distribute relevant information to the individuals who may need it. A primary challenge in larger firms is to locate quickly who has the appropriate information and who needs specific types of information. A partial solution is the development of disbursed IT networks that connect related organizational units.

Although data collection is helpful, it is not enough. Data is not information; the information must be interpreted.

■ INFORMATION INTERPRETATION

Information within organizations is a collective understanding of the firm's goals and of how the data relate to one of the firm's stated or unstated objectives within the current setting. Unfortunately, the process of developing multiple interpretations is often thwarted by a number of common problems.[40]

Self-Serving Interpretations   A manager's ability to interpret events, conditions, and history to his or her own advantage is almost universal. Managers and employees alike often see what they have seen in the past or see what they want to see. Rarely do they see what is or can be.

Managerial Scripts   A *managerial script* is a series of well-known routines for problem identification and alternative generation and analysis common to managers within a firm.[41] Different organizations have different scripts, often based on what has worked in the past. In a way, the script is a ritual that reflects what the "memory banks" of the corporation hold. Managers become bound by what they have seen. The danger is that they may not be open to what actually is occurring. They may be unable to unlearn.

The script may be elaborate enough to provide an apparently well-tested series of solutions based on the firm's experience. Larger, older firms are rarely structured for learning; rather, they are structured for efficiency. That is, the organizational design emphasizes repetition, volume processing, and routine. In order to learn, the organization needs to be able to unlearn, switch routines to obtain information quickly, and provide various interpretations of events rather than just tap into external archives.[42]

Few managers question a successful script. Consequently, they start solving today's problems with yesterday's solutions. Managers have been trained, both in the classroom and on the job, to initiate corrective action within the historically shared view of the world. That is, managers often initiate small, incremental improvements based on existing solutions instead of creating new approaches to identify the underlying problems.

Common Myths   An **organizational myth** is a commonly held cause-effect relationship or assertion that cannot be empirically supported.[43] Even though myths cannot be substantiated, both managers and workers may base their inter-

Ben and Jerry's ←

www.benjerry.com

Ben and Jerry's, the premium ice-cream maker with the social conscience has invested over $140,000 in videoconferencing systems. The dedicated TV hookups allow teams of 10 to 15 employees from different locations to work together on common total quality management issues.

■ An **organizational myth** is a commonly held cause-effect relationship or assertion that cannot be empirically supported.

pretations of problems and opportunities on the potentially faulty views. Three common myths often block the development of multiple interpretations.

The first common myth is the presumption that *there is a single organizational truth*. This myth is often expressed as, "Although others may be biased, I am able to define problems and develop solutions objectively." We are all subject to bias in varying degrees and in varying ways. The more complex the issue, the stronger the likelihood of many different supportable interpretations.

A second common myth is the *presumption of competence*. Managers at all levels are subject to believing that their part of the firm is okay and just needs minor improvements in implementation. As we have documented throughout this book, such is rarely the case. We are in the middle of a managerial revolution in which all managers need to reassess their general approach to managing organizational behavior.

A third common myth is the *denial of tradeoffs*. Most managers believe that their group, unit, or firm can avoid making undesirable tradeoffs and simultaneously please nearly every constituency. Whereas the denial of tradeoff is common, it can be a dangerous myth in some firms. For instance, when complex, dangerous technologies are involved, safe operations may come at some sacrifice to efficiency. Yet, some firms claim that "an efficient operation is a safe one" and aggressively move to improve efficiency. Although managers are stressing efficiency, they may fail to work on improving safety. The result may be a serious accident.[44]

■ INFORMATIONAL RETENTION

Organizations contain a variety of mechanisms that can be used to retain useful information.[45] Seven important mechanisms are: individuals, culture, transformation procedures, formal structures, ecology, external archives, and internal information technologies.

Individuals are the most important storehouses of information for organizations. Organizations that retain a large and comparatively stable group of experienced individuals are expected to have a higher capacity to acquire, retain, and retrieve information. Collectively, the organizational *culture* is an important repository of the shared experiences of corporate members. The culture often maintains the organizational memory via rich, vivid, and meaningful stories that outlive those who experienced the event.

Documents, rule books, written procedures, and even standard but unwritten methods of operation are all *transformation mechanisms* used to store accumulated information. In cases where operations are extremely complex but rarely needed, written sources of information are often invaluable. Pacific Gas and Electric, for example, maintains an extensive library for its Diablo Canyon nuclear power plant. In the library, one can find the complete engineering drawings for the whole plant as well as the changes made since the plant opened, together with a step-by-step plan for almost every possible accident scenario.

The organization's *formal structure* and the positions in an organization are less obvious but equally important mechanisms for storing information. When an aircraft lands on the deck of a U.S. Navy aircraft carrier, there are typically dozens of individuals on the deck, apparently watching the aircraft land. Each person on the deck is there for a specific purpose. Each can often trace his or her position to a specific accident that would not have occurred had some individual originally been assigned that position.

Physical structures (or *ecology*, in the language of learning theorists) are potentially important but often neglected mechanisms used to store information. For example, a traditional way of ordering parts and subcomponents in a factory is known as the "two-bin" system. One bin is always kept in reserve. Once an individual opens the reserve bin, he or she automatically orders replacements. In this way, the plant never runs out of components.

External archives can be tapped to provide valuable information on most larger organizations. Former employees, stock market analysts, suppliers, distributors, and the media can be important sources of valuable information. These external archives are important because they may provide a view of events quite different from that held in the organization.

Finally, the IT system of the organization, its *internal information technology,* can provide a powerful and individually tailored mechanism for storing information. All too often, however, managers are not using their IT systems strategically and are not tapping into them as mechanisms for retention.

Strategic Organizational Learning Cycles

Throughout the 1990s, a common headline running in the business press was: "Major Corporation Downsizes." Whether the corporation was AT&T, General Motors, or IBM, the message appeared to be the same: major U.S.-based corporations were in trouble. They were finally adjusting to a new competitive reality—on the backs of their workers and managers. As we have noted in this chapter, today the message from these firms is quite different. All are emphasizing competency via individual development and empowerment to learn and to make the needed incremental changes and decisions along the way. All are trying to avoid the past mistakes where they engaged in massive attempts to redirect themselves when it was apparent to all that change was overdue (see The Effective Manager 12.1). Some recent work on learning cycles helps explain why many organizations apparently fail to learn, while others appear to improve rapidly.[46]

■ A **deficit cycle** is a pattern of deteriorating performance that is followed by even further deterioration.

■ DEFICIT CYCLES

A **deficit cycle** is a pattern of deteriorating performance that is followed by even further deterioration. Firms that are continually downsizing, such as Boeing Aircraft, are examples of firms in a deficit cycle. The same problems keep reoccurring, and the firm fails to develop adequate mechanisms for learning. The firm often has problems in one or more phases of the learning process. The past inability to adjust yields more problems and fewer resources available to solve the next wave of problems, and the firm continues to deteriorate.

Major factors associated with deficit cycles are still being uncovered, but three are obvious from

THE EFFECTIVE MANAGER 12.1

AVOIDING MORE PROBLEMS WITH DOWNSIZING

When downsizing, firms should keep in mind that they must:

1. Accurately identify the causes of the decline.
2. Avoid grandiose attempts to reverse past history.
3. Avoid the tendency to increase centralization and rigidity and to reduce participation.
4. Target cuts and retrain employees wherever possible.
5. Keep employees informed to alleviate fear.
6. Systematically work to rebuild morale and emphasize more participation.

current research.[47] One is *organizational inertia*. It is very difficult to change organizations, and the larger the organization, the more inertia it often has. A second is *hubris*. Too few senior executives are willing to challenge their own actions or those of their firms because they see a history of success. They fail to recognize that yesterday's successful innovations are today's outmoded practices. A third is the issue of *detachment*. Executives often believe they can manage far-flung, diverse operations through analysis of reports and financial records. They lose touch and fail to make the needed unique and special adaptations required of all firms. One consultant has made millions advising executives to focus on improvement and to practice management by walking around the office to avoid detachment.

■ BENEFIT CYCLES

■ A **benefit cycle** is a pattern of successful adjustment followed by further improvements.

Inertia, hubris, and detachment are common maladies, but they are not the automatic fate of all corporations. As we have repeatedly demonstrated, managers are trying to reinvent their firms each and every day. They hope to initiate a **benefit cycle**—a pattern of successful adjustment followed by further improvements. Microsoft is an example of a firm experiencing a benefit cycle. In this cycle, the same problems do not keep reoccurring as the firm develops adequate mechanisms for learning. The firm has a few major difficulties with the learning process, and managers continually attempt to improve knowledge acquisition, information distribution, information interpretation, and organizational memory.

Organizations that successfully adapt can ride the benefit cycle. Inertia can work for managers if they do not become overconfident and if they can stay directly involved with the key operations of the firm. The need to keep involved and maintain a benefit cycle may be leading to a new type of organizational design—the cellular form.

Cellular Form: A Design for the Future

In discussing IT, we noted that new information technologies could be used strategically, but we said relatively little about how. Now that we have discussed the environmental and strategic influences on design and noted the importance of consistent learning, it is time to project into the future.

■ The **cellular form** is an organizational structure that emphasizes quasi-independent clusters of self-organizing components.

In a global setting where the firm has well-developed information technology and faces a consistent pressure to learn or die, executives may well adopt aspects of the cellular form. The **cellular form** is an organizational structure that emphasizes quasi-independent clusters of self-organizing components. Each quasi-independent cluster is expected to collaboratively invest in the firm's know-how, products, and services to innovate for all markets where clusters have created and developed a business.[48] Control is exercised through personnel selection and the market, whereas coordination is effected predominantly through integrated information systems. The underlying strategy is to learn profitably. If a cell cannot meet the market test, executives will replace it or at least its key managers. If a cell becomes too large and begins to become too bureaucratic, it can be divided.

Do any firms have a cellular form? We do not know of any pure examples, but several firms are using elements of this design. Stan Shih created Acer as a global computer company and built it around his vision of a federation of firms. When Acer wanted a stylish, affordable PC for the North American market, it developed the Acer Aspire via cellular cooperation inside and outside the corporation. Frog, an independent firm, did the industrial design, while "cells" within Acer in the United States and Singapore manufactured and marketed the Aspire. Other Acer cells were free to use and modify the design for other customers and regions.

Chapter 12   Study Guide

Summary

What is organizational design, and how do the designs of small and large firms differ?

- Organizational design is the process of choosing and implementing a structural configuration for an organization.

- Smaller firms often adopt a simple structure, whereas larger firms often adopt a bureaucratic form.

How does the operations and information technology of the firm influence its organizational design?

- Operations technology and organizational design are interrelated.

- In highly intensive and small-batch technologies, organizational designs may tend toward the adhocracy, a very decentralized form of operation.

- Information technology and organizational design can be interrelated.

- IT provides an opportunity to change the design by substitution, for learning, and to capture strategic advantages.

What is the relationship between environmental conditions and organizational design?

- Environmental and organizational design are interrelated.

- In analyzing environments, both the general (background conditions) and specific (key actors and organizations) environments are important.

- The more complex the environment, the greater the demands on the organization, and firms should respond with more complex designs, such as the use of interfirm alliances.

What is strategy, and how do organizational learning and information technology influence strategic competency?

- Strategy and organizational design are interrelated. The organizational design must support the strategy if it is to prove successful.

- Effective managers are able to build on competency-based strategies to modify and extend their differential advantage over competitors.

What is organizational learning?

- Organizational learning is the process of knowledge acquisition, information distribution, information interpretation, and organizational memory used to adapt successfully to changing circumstances.

How are organizational learning cycles helpful in understanding organizational behavior?

- Organizational learning cycles help us understand how some organizations continually decline while others appear to be rising stars.

Key Terms

Adhocracy (p. 243)
Benefit cycle (p. 258)
Cellular form (p. 258)
Deficit cycle (p. 257)
Environmental complexity (p. 248)
Grafting (p. 254)

Information technology (p. 242)
Interfirm alliances (p. 250)
Operations technology (p. 242)
Organizational design (p. 240)

Organizational learning (p. 252)
Organizational myth (p. 255)
Organizational strategy (p. 251)
Scanning (p. 254)
Simple design (p. 241)

Self-Test 12

■ MULTIPLE CHOICE

1. The design of the organization needs to be adjusted to all but _____. (a) the environment of the firm (b) the strategy of the firm (c) the size of the firm (d) the operations and information technology of the firm (e) the personnel to be hired by the firm

2. _____ is the combination of resources, knowledge, and techniques that creates a product or service output for an organization: (a) Information technology (b) Strategy (c) Organizational learning (c) Operations technology (d) The general environment (e) The benefit cycle.

3. _____ is the combination of machines, artifacts, procedures, and systems used to gather, store, analyze, and disseminate information for translating it into knowledge: (a) The specific environment (b) Strategy (c) Operations technology (d) Information technology (e) Organizational decline

4. Which of the following is an accurate statement about an adhocracy? (a) The design facilitates information exchange and learning. (b) There are many rules and policies. (c) Use of IT is always minimal. (d) It handles routine problems efficiently. (e) It is quite common in older industries.

5. The set of cultural, economic, legal-political, and educational conditions in the areas in which a firm operates is called the _____. (a) task environment (b) specific environment (c) industry of the firm (d) environmental complexity (e) general environment

6. The segment of the environment that refers to the other organizations with which an organization must interact in order to obtain inputs and dispose of outputs is called (a) the general environment (b) the strategic environment (c) the learning environment (d) the technological setting (e) the specific environment.

7. _____ are announced cooperative agreements or joint ventures between two independent firms: (a) Mergers (b) Acquisitions (c) Interfirm alliances (d) Adhocracies (e) Strategic configurations

8. The process of acquiring knowledge, organizational retention, and distributing and interpreting information is called _____. (a) vicarious learning (b) experience (c) organizational learning (d) an organizational myth (e) a self-serving interpretation

9. Three methods of vicarious learning are _____. (a) scanning, grafting, and contracting out (b) grafting, contracting out, and mimicry (c) maladaptive specialization, scanning, and grafting (d) scanning, grafting, and mimicry (e) experience, mimicry, and scanning

10. Three important factors that block information interpretation are _____. (a) detachment, scanning, and common myths (b) self-serving interpretations, detachment, and common myths (c) managerial scripts, maladaptive specialization, and common myths (d) contracting out, common myths, and detachment (e) common myths, managerial scripts, and self-serving interpretations

■ TRUE–FALSE

11. The organizational design for a small and a large firm are almost the same.   T   F

12. Organizations with well-defined and stable operations technologies have more opportunity to substitute managerial techniques for managerial judgment than do firms relying on more variable operations technologies.   T   F

13. Adhocracies tend to favor vertical specialization and control.   T   F

14. With extensive use of IT, more staff are typically added.   T   F

15. The general environment of organizations includes other organizations with which an organization must interact in order to obtain inputs and dispose of outputs.   T   F

16. The specific environment of the organization includes other organizations with which an organization must interact in order to obtain inputs and dispose of outputs.   T   F

17. An organizational alliance is an extreme example of an adhocracy.   T   F

18. Mimicry is the copying of the successful practices of others.   T   F

19. The key to effective organizational learning is manipulation.   T   F

20. A deficit cycle is a pattern of deteriorating performance that is followed by further deterioration.   T   F

■ SHORT RESPONSE

21. Explain why a large firm could not use a simple structure.

22. Explain the deployment of IT and its uses in organizations.

23. Describe the effect operations technology has on an organization from both Thompson's and Woodward's point of view.

24. What are the three primary determinants of environmental complexity?

■ APPLICATIONS ESSAY

25. Why would Ford Motors want to shift to a matrix design organization for the design and development of cars and trucks but not do so in its manufacturing and assembly operations?

Explore application-oriented Fast Company articles, cases, experimental exercises, and self-assessments in the OB Skills Workbook

■ **Visit the Schermerhorn Web site to find the Interactive Self-Test and Internet exercises for this chapter.**

High Performance Organizational Cultures

THE INTERNET CHANGES EVERYTHING

www.cisco.com

"What people have not grasped is that the Internet will change everything," says Cisco chairman John Chambers. The press lists Cisco as the most important American company no one has ever heard of, and we think it is a good example of a high performance company. Cisco is becoming a most important player in the global market of the World Wide Web. It ranks in Fortune's 100 Best Companies, and it is or will be looking for a few thousand new employees to join its unique culture. Cisco makes the equipment that makes the WEB go and provides the services to help firms tap into the expanding world of WEB commerce. Forget Amazon.com. Cisco is the network giant. They give two sets of reasons for joining them (in addition to good salaries, bonuses, stock options, and other incentives). Their Web site says, "First there is the technology. It works. It's everywhere.... The second reason for joining Cisco is the unique atmosphere. Our culture has been created by the people who work here and is rather undefinable. Suffice it to say, Cisco is an exciting, enjoyable workplace." We would add, get ready to work long hours, learn rapidly, and adjust to a diverse expanding workforce. If you are not a systems engineer, a few foreign languages and a willingness to relocate anywhere in the world would not hurt. Check the jobs in Australia.[1]

I n Chapter 12 we noted the transformations occurring in many organizations ranging from the giant auto manufacturers to the small software design firms. At all levels of operations, people are striving for productivity using a wide variety of new information technologies. Quality, innovation, and value are replacing the drive toward short-term efficiency. Managers are recognizing the need to build high performance organizations that stand for something. They are rediscovering the critical importance of human resources. The old methods of command and control are being replaced by new methods of participation and involvement.[2] Managers are becoming facilitators, helpers, guides, and coaches. In our terminology, they are changing their organization's culture.

Study Questions

The not-so-hidden advantage of many leading high performance organizations is their corporate culture. As you read Chapter 13, keep in mind these questions:

- What is organizational culture?
- What are the observable aspects of organizational culture?
- How do values and assumptions influence organizational cultures?
- How can the organizational culture be "managed," "nurtured" and "guided"?
- How can the process of organization development enhance organizational culture?

■ **Organizational or corporate culture** is the system of shared actions, values, and beliefs that develops within an organization and guides the behavior of its members.

The Concept of Organizational Culture

Organizational or corporate culture is the system of shared actions, values, and beliefs that develops within an organization and guides the behavior of its members.[3] In the business setting, this system is often referred to as the *corporate culture*. Just as no two individual personalities are the same, no two organizational cultures are identical. Most significantly, management scholars and consultants increasingly believe that cultural differences can have a major impact on the performance of organizations and the quality of work life experienced by their members.

■ FUNCTIONS AND COMPONENTS OF ORGANIZATIONAL CULTURE

Through their collective experience, members of an organization solve two extremely important survival issues.[4] The first is the question of external adaptation: What precisely needs to be accomplished, and how can it be done? The second is the question of internal integration: How do members resolve the daily problems associated with living and working together?

External Adaptation   **External adaptation** involves reaching goals and dealing with outsiders. The issues concerned are tasks to be accomplished, methods used to achieve the goals, and methods of coping with success and failure.

Through their shared experiences, members may develop common views that help guide their day-to-day activities. Organizational members need to know the real mission of the organization, not just the pronouncements to key constituencies, such as stockholders. Members will naturally develop an understanding of how they contribute to the mission via interaction. This view may emphasize the importance of human resources, the role of employees as cogs in a machine, or a cost to be reduced.

Closely related to the organization's mission and view of its contribution are the questions of responsibility, goals, and methods. For instance, at 3M, employees believe that it is their responsibility to innovate and contribute creatively. They see these responsibilities reflected in achieving the goal of developing new and improved products and processes.

Each collection of individuals in an organization also tends to (1) separate more important from less important external forces; (2) develop ways to measure their accomplishments; and (3) create explanations for why goals are not always met. Daimler-Chrysler's managers, for example, have moved away from judging their progress against specific targets to estimating the degree to which they are moving a development process forward. Instead of blaming a poor economy or upper level managers for the firm's failure to reach a goal, Daimler-Chrysler managers have set hard goals that are difficult to reach and have redoubled their efforts to improve participation and commitment.[5]

The final issues in external adaptation deal with two important, but often neglected, aspects of coping with external reality. First, individuals need to develop acceptable ways of telling outsiders just how good they really are. At 3M, for example, employees talk about the quality of their products and the many new, useful products they have brought to the market. Second, individuals must collectively know when to admit defeat. At 3M, the answer is easy for new projects: At the beginning of the development process, members establish "drop" points at which to quit the development effort and redirect it.[6]

In sum, external adaptation involves answering important instrumental or goal-related questions concerning coping with reality: What is the real mission? How do we contribute? What are our goals? How do we reach our goals? What external forces are important? How do we measure results? What do we do if specific targets are not met? How do we tell others how good we are? When do we quit?

Internal integration   The corporate culture also provides answers to the problems of internal integration. *Internal integration* deals with the creation of a collective identity and with finding ways of matching methods of working and living together.

The process of internal integration often begins with the establishment of a unique identity; that is, each collection of individuals and each subculture within the organization develops some type of unique definition of itself. Through dialogue and interaction, members begin to characterize their world. They may see it as malleable or fixed, filled with opportunity or threatening. Real progress toward innovation can begin when group members collectively believe that they can change important parts of the world around them and that what appears to be a threat is actually an opportunity for change.[7]

Three important aspects of working together are (1) deciding who is a member and who is not; (2) developing an informal understanding of acceptable and unacceptable behavior; and (3) separating friends from enemies. Effective total quality management holds that subgroups in the organization need to view their immediate supervisors as members of the group who are expected to represent them to friendly higher managers.

To work together effectively, individuals need to decide collectively how to allocate power, status, and authority. They need to establish a shared understanding of who will get rewards and sanctions for specific types of actions. Too often, managers fail to recognize these important aspects of internal integration. For example, a manager may fail to explain the basis for a promotion and to show why this reward, the status associated with it, and the power given to the newly promoted individual are consistent with commonly shared beliefs.

⧉ WORKPLACE DIVERSITY

The leather coat was black with soot as Gloria Johnson pulled it from the sealed container as owner Fred Fernandez looked on. Was there any question that the blackened coat could not be saved and restored? Not really. A long visit in the Venus Cleaners' Ozone Room and two cleanings later, it looked like new. It was almost as routine as individuals driving 50 and 60 miles into the heart of Detroit to drop off their cleaning. This is no ordinary cleaners. Fred Fernandez, its president and CEO, has welded a diverse staff of immigrants and long-time Detroit residents into a cohesive, highly skilled, dedicated group. They believe they can clean most anything, and often they do. Although just a small business, Venus is the largest fire restoration cleaning facility in the state. Insurance companies throughout southeast Michigan bring in clothes from fires and natural disasters for their unique services. Customers return because of the quality. And employees stay because Fred knows how to knit diverse individuals together so that they take pride in their work and enjoy working with each other.

Collections of individuals need to work out acceptable ways to communicate and to develop guidelines for friendships. Although these aspects of internal integration may appear esoteric, they are vital. To function effectively as a team, individuals must recognize that some members will be closer than others; friendships are inevitable. However, the basis for friendships can be inappropriately restricted. At the U.S. Department of Interior, for example, recent budget cuts may have had a beneficial effect. At one time, the political appointees could be found eating together in their own executive dining room. Now, all employees eat at the Interior Department lunchroom, and even the political appointees are making new friends with the career civil servants.

In sum, internal integration involves answers to important questions associated with living together. What is our unique identity? How do we view the world? Who is a member? How do we allocate power, status, and authority? How do we communicate? What is the basis for friendship? Answering these questions is important to organizational members because the organization is more than a place to work; it is a place where individuals spend much of their adult life.[8]

■ DOMINANT CULTURE, SUBCULTURES, AND COUNTERCULTURES

Smaller firms often have a single dominant culture with a unitary set of shared actions, values, and beliefs. Most larger organizations contain several subcultures as well as one or more countercultures.[9] **Subcultures** are groups of individuals with a unique pattern of values and philosophy that is not inconsistent with the organization's dominant values and philosophy.[10] Interestingly, strong subcultures are often found in high performance task forces, teams, and special project groups in organizations. The culture emerges to bind individuals working intensely together to accomplish a specific task. For example, there are strong subcultures of stress engineers and liaison engineers in the Boeing Renton plant. These highly specialized groups must solve knotty technical issues to ensure that Boeing planes are safe. Though distinct, these groups of engineers share in the dominant values of Boeing.

> ■ **Subcultures** are unique patterns of values and philosophies within a group that are consistent with the dominant culture of the larger organization or social system.

In contrast, **countercultures** have a pattern of values and a philosophy that reject the surrounding culture.[11] When Stephen Jobs reentered Apple computer as its interim CEO, he quickly formed a counterculture within Apple. Over the next 18 months, numerous clashes occurred as the followers of the old CEO (Gil Amelio) fought to maintain their place. Jobs won and Apple won. His counterculture became dominant.

> ■ **Countercultures** are the patterns of values and philosophies that outwardly reject those of the larger organization or social system.

Within an organization, mergers and acquisitions may produce countercultures. Employers and managers of an acquired firm may hold values and assumptions that are quite inconsistent with those of the acquiring firm. This is known as the "clash of corporate cultures."[12] When Coca-Cola bought Columbia Pictures, the soft-drink company found out too late that the picture business was quite different from selling beverages. It sold Columbia, with its unique corporate culture, to Sony rather than fight a protracted clash of cultures.[13]

Importing Subcultures Every large organization imports potentially important subcultural groupings when it hires employees from the larger society. In North America, for instance, subcultures and countercultures may naturally form based on ethnic, racial, gender, generational, or locational similarities. In Japanese organizations, subcultures often form based on the date of graduation from a university, gender, or geographic location. In European firms, ethnicity and language play an important part in developing subcultures, as does gender. In many less developed nations, language, education, religion, or family social status are often grounds for forming societally popular subcultures and countercultures.

The difficulty with importing groupings from the larger societies lies in the relevance these subgroups have to the organization as a whole. At the one extreme, senior managers can merely accept these divisions and work within the confines of the larger culture. There are three primary difficulties with this approach. First, subordinated groups, such as members of a specific religion or ethnic group, are likely to form into a counterculture and to work more diligently to change their status than to better the firm. Second, the firm may find it extremely difficult to cope with broader cultural changes. For instance, in the United States the expected treatment of women, ethnic minorities, and the disabled has changed dramatically over the last 20 years. Firms that merely accept old customs and prejudices have experienced a greater loss of key personnel and increased communication difficulties, as well as greater interpersonal conflict, than have their more progressive counterparts. Third, firms that accept and build on natural divisions from the larger culture may find it extremely difficult to develop sound international operations. For example, many Japanese firms have had substantial difficulty adjusting to the equal treatment of women in their U.S. operations.[14]

Valuing Cultural Diversity   Managers can work to eradicate all naturally occurring subcultures and countercultures. Firms are groping to develop what Taylor Cox calls the multicultural organization. The multicultural organization is a firm that values diversity but systematically works to block the transfer of societally based subcultures into the fabric of the organization.[15] Because Cox focuses on some problems unique to the United States, his prescription for change may not apply to organizations located in other countries with much more homogeneous populations.

Cox suggests a five-step program for developing the multicultural organization. First, the organization should develop pluralism with the objective of multibased socialization. To accomplish this objective, members of different naturally occurring groups need to school one another to increase knowledge and information and to eliminate stereotyping. Second, the firm should fully integrate its structure so that there is no direct relationship between a naturally occurring group and any particular job—for instance, there are no distinct male or female jobs. Third, the firm must integrate the informal networks by eliminating barriers and increasing participation. That is, it must break down existing societally based informal groups. Fourth, the organization should break the linkage between naturally occurring group identity and the identity of the firm. In other words, the firm should not be just for the young, old, men, women, and so on. Fifth, the organization must actively work to eliminate interpersonal conflict based on either the group identity or the natural backlash of the largest societally based grouping.

The key problems associated with fully implementing Cox's program are separating the firm from the larger culture in which it must operate and eliminating some societally based groupings that are relevant for achieving the firm's goals. For instance, the U.S. military is barred from fully implementing Cox's recommendations simply because it is not currently legal to put women into all combat roles. The issue of generational groupings provides another example. Implementing Cox's recommendations would call for 20 year olds to be represented proportionally in the senior management ranks; most corporations want and need the judgment honed by experience. However, astute senior managers are recognizing that they may be out of touch with younger employees. For example, Robert Hausman, chairman of Coventry Industries of Boca Raton, Florida routinely meets young employees once a month over pizza.[16]

■ LEVELS OF CULTURAL ANALYSIS

Three important levels of cultural analysis in organizations are: observable culture, shared values, and common assumptions.[17] These levels may be envisioned as layers. The deeper one gets, the more difficult it is to discover the culture.

The first level concerns *observable culture*, or "the way we do things around here." These are the methods the group has developed and teaches to new members. The observable culture includes the unique stories, ceremonies, and corporate rituals that make up the history of a successful work group.

The second level of analysis recognizes that *shared values* can play a critical part in linking people together and can provide a powerful motivational mechanism for members of the culture. Many consultants suggest that organizations should develop a "dominant and coherent set of shared values."[18] The term *shared* in cultural analysis implies that the group is a whole. Every member may not agree with the shared values, but they have all been exposed to them and have often been told they are important. At Hewlett-Packard, for example, "quality" is part of everyone's vocabulary. The firm was founded on the belief that everyone could make a creative contribution to developing quality products.

At the deepest level of cultural analysis are common assumptions, or the taken-for-granted truths that collections of corporate members share as a result of their joint experience. It is often extremely difficult to isolate these patterns, but doing so helps explain why culture invades every aspect of organizational life.

OB Across Functions

MARKETING

Marketing at a High Performance Organization: Hewlett-Packard

A corporation with nearly 125,000 employees and with sales approaching $50 billion, Hewlett-Packard (HP) is a leader in many information technology fields. Throughout its international product line advertising there is a constant repetition of an HP core value—quality. For instance, in 1999 HP launched its first advertising campaign on behalf of its European channel partners to support the Connect Programme—a program designed to bring better account management, increased business opportunities, and higher profitability to some of HP's international marketing partners. To qualify, retailers and resellers must meet a number of quality criteria for both their technical and sales staff. Then they become members of the Connect Programme group. The theme of the marketing campaign—"Connect with our family of skilled resellers"—urges European, Middle Eastern, and African IT executives to trust in HP dealers.

Observable Aspects of Organizational Culture

Important parts of an organization's culture emerge from the collective experience of its members. These emergent aspects of the culture help make it unique and may well provide a competitive advantage for the organization. Some of these aspects may be directly observed in day-to-day practices. Others may have to be discovered—for example, by asking members to tell stories of important incidents in the history of the organization. We often learn about the unique aspects of the organizational culture through descriptions of specific events.[19] By observing employee actions, listening to stories, and asking members to interpret what is going on, one can begin to understand the organization's culture.

■ STORIES, RITES, RITUALS, AND SYMBOLS

Organizations are rich with stories of winners and losers, successes and failures. Perhaps one of the most important stories concerns the founding of the organization. The founding story often contains the lessons learned from the heroic efforts of an embattled entrepreneur, whose vision may still guide the firm. The story of the founding may be so embellished that it becomes a **saga**—a heroic account of accomplishments.[20] Sagas are important because they are used to tell new members the real mission of the organization, how the organization operates, and how individuals can fit into the company. Rarely is the founding story totally accurate, and it often glosses over some of the more negative aspects of the founders. Such is the case with Nike.

■ **Sagas** are embellished heroic accounts of the story of the founding of an organization.

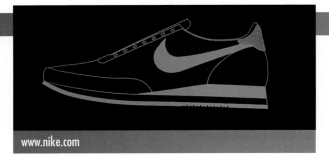

www.nike.com

📈 ENTREPRENEURSHIP

When Phil Knight, CEO of Nike, entered the athletic shoe business, he envisioned owning a company that produced inexpensive, high-quality running shows for serious athletes. Knight's true love, however, was the research and development of shoes. In its early years, the company did not have the resources to purchase a factory or employ large numbers of workers. Since labor was cheap in the Far East, Knight negotiated deals with a number of Asian suppliers to sell him set numbers of shoes. As a result, the cost of producing a pair of Nikes was far less than that of the company's primary competition, Adidas, which made its shoes in labor-extensive Germany. By focusing on its competencies and outsourcing production, Nike is now one of the largest and most successful firms in the shoe business.

If you have job experience, you may well have heard stories concerning the following questions: How will the boss react to a mistake? Can someone move from the bottom to the top of the company? What will get me fired? These are common story topics in many organizations.[21] Often, the stories provide valuable hidden information about who is more equal than others, whether jobs are secure, and how things are really controlled. In essence, the stories begin to suggest how organizational members view the world and live together. Some of the most obvious aspects of organizational culture are rites and rituals. **Rites** are standardized and recurring activities that are used at special times to influence the behaviors and understanding of organizational members; **rituals** are systems of rites. It is common, for example, for Japanese workers and managers to start their workdays together with group exercises and singing of the "company song." Separately, the exercises and song are rites. Together, they form part of a ritual. In other settings, such as the Mary Kay Cosmetics company, scheduled ceremonies reminiscent of the Miss America pageant (a ritual) are used regularly to spotlight positive work achievements and reinforce high performance expectations with awards, including gold and diamond pins and fur stoles.

Rituals and rites may be unique to particular groups within the organization. Subcultures often arise from the type of technology deployed by the unit, the specific function being performed, and the specific collection of specialists in the unit. The boundaries of the subculture may well be maintained by a unique language.

■ **Rites** are standardized and recurring activities used at special times to influence the behaviors and understanding of organizational members.

■ **Rituals** are systems of rites.

Often, the language of a subculture, and its rituals and rites, emerge from the group as a form of jargon. In some cases, the special language starts to move outside the firm and begins to enter the larger society. For instance, an ad for a Hewlett-Packard hand-held computer read: "All the features you need are built right in. MS-DOS, Lotus 1-2-3…and a 512 K RAM version of the HP 95LX." Not everyone found this a user-friendly ad, but it did appeal to knowledgeable individuals.[22]

Another observable aspect of corporate culture centers on the symbols found in organizations. A **cultural symbol** is any object, act, or event that serves to transmit cultural meaning. Good examples are the corporate uniforms worn by UPS and Federal Express delivery personnel. Although many such symbols are quite visible, their importance and meaning may not be.

■ A **cultural symbol** is any object, act, or event that serves to transmit cultural meaning.

■ CULTURAL RULES AND ROLES

Organizational culture often specifies when various types of actions are appropriate and where individual members stand in the social system. These cultural rules and roles are part of the normative controls of the organization and emerge from its daily routines.[23] For instance, the timing, presentation, and methods of communicating authoritative directives are often quite specific to each organization. In one firm, meetings may be forums for dialogue and discussion, where managers set agendas and then let others offer new ideas, critically examine alternatives, and fully participate. In another firm, the "rules" may be quite different: The manager goes into the meeting with fixed expectations. Any new ideas, critical examinations, and the like are expected to be worked out in private before the meeting takes place. The meeting is a forum for letting others know what is being done and for passing out orders on what to do in the future.

■ THE EVOLUTION OF SHARED MEANINGS FROM OBSERVABLE CULTURE

What you see as an outside observer may or may not be what organizational members see. You may see NASA personnel on television filling the tanks of a booster rocket for the space shuttle. If you could ask the workers directly what they are doing, you might be surprised by the answer. They are not just filling booster tanks; they are assisting with an important part of exploring space. Through interaction with one another, and as reinforced by the rest of the organization, the workers have infused a larger shared meaning—or sense of broader purpose—into their tasks. In this sense, organizational culture is a "shared" set of meanings and perceptions that are created and learned by organizational members in the course of interactions.[24] This set of shared meanings may be accompanied by shared values.

Values and Organizational Culture

To describe more fully the culture of an organization, it is necessary to go deeper than the observable aspects. To many researchers and managers, shared common values lie at the very heart of organization culture. Shared values help turn routine activities into valuable, important actions, tie the corporation to the important values of society, and may provide a very distinctive source of com-

At Mills College the board of trustees voted to admit men to the all-women's school to avert bankruptcy. They claimed that changing to coeducation was an economic necessity. The board retreated, however, when students, alumnae, and administrators demonstrated the educational importance and unique contributions of an all-women's liberal arts college. These often separate constituencies united to develop a new plan to save the tradition and philosophy that they all believed to be fundamental to Mills.

■ **Management philosophy** is a philosophy that links key goal-related issues with key collaboration issues to come up with general ways by which the firm will manage its affairs.

petitive advantage. In organizations, what works for one person is often taught to new members as the correct way to think and feel. Important values are then attributed to these solutions to everyday problems. By linking values and actions, the organization taps into some of the strongest and deepest realms of the individual. The tasks a person performs are given not only meaning but value; what one does is not only workable but correct, right, and important.

Some successful organizations share some common cultural characteristics.[25] Organizations with "strong cultures" possess a broadly and deeply shared value system. Unique, shared values can provide a strong corporate identity, enhance collective commitment, provide a stable social system, and reduce the need for formal and bureaucratic controls. A strong culture can be a double-edged sword, however. A strong culture and value system can reinforce a singular view of the organization and its environment. If dramatic changes are needed, it may be very difficult to change the organization. General Motors may have a "strong" culture, for example, but the firm faces enormous difficulty in its attempts to adapt its ways to a dynamic and highly competitive environment.

In many corporate cultures, one finds a series of common assumptions known to most everyone in the corporation: "We are different." "We are better at…." "We have unrecognized talents." Cisco Systems at the opening of this chapter provides an excellent example. Senior managers often share common assumptions, such as, "We are good stewards." "We are competent managers." "We are practical innovators." Like values, such assumptions become reflected in the organizational culture.

■ MANAGEMENT PHILOSOPHY

A **management philosophy** links key goal-related issues with key collaboration issues and comes up with a series of general ways by which the firm will manage its affairs.[26] A well-developed management philosophy is important because (1) it establishes generally understood boundaries on all members of the firm; (2) it provides a consistent way of approaching new and novel situations; and (3) it helps hold individuals together by assuring them of a known path toward success. Wal-Mart has a clearly identified management philosophy linking growth and profitability with customer service and individual employee commitment. Each manager runs "a store within a store," supported by more senior management and corporate buyers. This concept both liberates individuals to try new initiatives and binds their efforts within managerial constraints and purchasing realities. Once, the homespun comments of legendary CEO Sam Walton helped to help bind individuals together; now managers evoke his memory. The philosophy is expressed in some old-fashioned values, such as customer service, frugality, hard work, and service toward employees.

Elements of the management philosophy may be formally documented in a corporate plan, a statement of business philosophy, or a series of goals (see The Effective Manager 13.1). Yet, it is the unstated but well-understood fundamentals these written documents signify that form the heart of a well-developed management philosophy.

■ ORGANIZATIONAL MYTHS

In many firms, the management philosophy is supported by a series of organizational myths. **Organizational myths** are unproven and often unstated beliefs

■ An **organizational myth** is an unproven and often unstated belief that is accepted uncritically.

that are accepted uncritically. In a study of safety in nuclear power plants, senior managers were asked whether they felt there was a tradeoff between safeness and efficiency. The response was clear: A safe plant is an efficient plant. Yet, most of these executives had seen data showing that measures of safeness and efficiency were quite independent. To admit there was a tradeoff raised the issue of making choices between efficiency and safety. All wanted to believe that to do one was to promote the other.[27]

Whereas some may scoff at these organizational myths and want to see rational, hard-nosed analysis replace mythology, each firm needs a series of managerial myths.[28] Myths allow executives to redefine impossible problems into more manageable components. Myths can facilitate experimentation and creativity, and they allow managers to govern. For instance, senior executives are not just decision makers or rational allocators of resources. All organization members hope these individuals will also be fair, just, and compassionate.

■ NATIONAL CULTURE INFLUENCES

Widely held common assumptions may often be traced to the larger culture of the corporation's host society.[29] The difference between Sony's corporate emphasis on group achievements and Zenith's emphasis on individual engineering excellence, for example, can be traced to the Japanese emphasis on collective action versus the U.S. emphasis on individualism.

National cultural values may also become embedded in the expectations of important organizational constituencies and in generally accepted solutions to problems. When moving across national cultures, managers need to be sensitive to national cultural differences so that their actions do not violate common assumptions in the underlying national culture. In Japan and Western Europe, for example, executives are expected to work cooperatively with government officials on an informal basis. Informal business-government relations that are perfectly acceptable in these countries are considered influence peddling in the United States. Whereas some South American executives expect to pay directly for some government services, in the United States such payments are considered bribes.

Inappropriate actions that violate common assumptions drawn from national culture can have an important impact on performance and may alienate organizational members, even if managers have the best intentions. To improve morale at General Electric's new French subsidiary, Chi. Generale de Radiologie, American managers invited all the European managers to a "get acquainted" meeting near Paris. The Americans gave out colorful T-shirts with the GE slogan, "Go for One," a typical maneuver in many American training programs. The French resented the T-shirts. One outspoken individual said, "It was like Hitler was back, forcing us to wear uniforms. It was humiliating."

THE EFFECTIVE MANAGER 13.1

ELEMENTS OF STRONG CORPORATE CULTURES

- A widely shared real understanding of what the firm stands for, often embodied in slogans.
- A concern for individuals over rules, policies, procedures, and adherence to job duties.
- A recognition of heroes whose actions illustrate the company's shared philosophy and concerns.
- A belief in ritual and ceremony as important to members and to building a common identity.
- A well-understood sense of the informal rules and expectations so that employees and managers understand what is expected of them.
- A belief that what employees and managers do is important and that it is important to share information and ideas.

Managing Organizational Culture

The culture should be considered as critical as structure and strategy in establishing the organizational foundations of high performance. Good managers are able to reinforce and support an existing strong culture; good managers are also able to help build resilient cultures in situations where they are absent. For instance, CEO Mike Walsh of Union Pacific has brought a new and fresh approach to the firm with what *Fortune* Magazine called an "introverted corporate culture." Cultural changes under Walsh's leadership included the empowerment of managers at all levels. A typical response: "We were so elated the company was willing to give new authority that we wanted it to work."

Two broad strategies for managing the corporate culture have received considerable attention in the OB literature. One strategy calls for managers to help modify observable culture, shared values, and common assumptions directly. A second strategy involves the use of organizational development techniques to modify specific elements of the culture.

www.disney.com

🌐 GLOBALIZATION

All new Disney employees are told the story of Walt Disney. He was said to have emphasized the idea that everyone is a child at heart and that every individual in the Disney theme parks is a performer. This emphasis is commonly attributed to his founding philosophy. Actually, Walt Disney was a perfectionist. A harder boss would be difficult to find, and several times Disney bet the entire firm on the success of one picture. The emphasis on "everyone is a performer" did not come from a philosophy but from hard-won experience. In fact, the initial opening of Disneyland Park in California was not a success until the firm eliminated much of the staff whose experience was limited to county fairs. They were replaced by an inexperienced crew of young employees trained by Disney. In France, Disneyland Paris Resort took almost five years to answer the question of how to match European culture and Disney's created culture. The Disney challenge now is what to do with CapCities/ABC. Instead of just Disney, the corporation now includes well-known entities such as ABC, ESPN, as well as a host of lesser known daily newspapers, 50 trade publications, a host of feature film companies, and even a portion of a baseball team. It is a challenge of managing a corporate culture within the framework of a conglomerate.

■ BUILDING, REINFORCING, AND CHANGING CULTURE

Managers can modify the visible aspects of culture, such as the language, stories, rites, rituals, and sagas. They can change the lessons to be drawn from common stories and even encourage individuals to see the reality they see. Because of their positions, senior managers can interpret situations in new ways and can adjust the meanings attached to important corporate events. They can create new rites and rituals. This takes time and enormous energy, but the long-run benefits can also be great.

Top managers, in particular, can set the tone for a culture and for cultural change. Managers at Aetna Life and Casualty Insurance built on its humanistic traditions to provide basic skills to highly motivated but underqualified individuals. Even in the highly cost-competitive steel industry, Chairperson F. Kenneth Iverson of Nucor built on basic entrepreneurial values in U.S. society to reduce the number of management levels by half. And at Procter and Gamble, Richard Nicolosi evoked the shared values for greater participation in decision making dramatically to improve creativity and innovation.

Each of these examples illustrates how managers can help foster a culture that provides answers to important questions concerning external adaptation and internal integration. Recent work on the linkages among corporate culture and financial performance reaffirms the importance of an emphasis on helping employees adjust to the environment. It also suggests that this emphasis alone is not sufficient. Neither is an emphasis solely on stockholders or customers associated with long-term economic performance. Instead, managers must work to emphasize all three issues simultaneously. This emphasis on customers, stockholders, and employees comes at a cost of emphasizing management. Large offices, multimillion-dollar salaries, golden parachutes (protections for executives if the firm is bought by others), as well as the executive plane, dining room, and country club are out.

Early research on culture and culture change often emphasized direct attempts to alter the values and assumptions of individuals by resocializing them—that is, trying to change their hearts so that their minds and actions would follow.[30] The goal was to establish a clear, consistent organizationwide consensus. More recent work suggests that this unified approach of working through values may not be either possible or desirable.

Trying to change people's values from the top down without also changing how the organization operates and recognizing the importance of individuals does not work very well. Take a look at the example of Cisco Systems. Here managers realize that keeping a dynamic, change-oriented and fun culture is a mix of managerial actions, decisions about technology, and initiatives from all employees. The values are not set and imposed from someone on high. The shared values emerge, and they are not identical across all of Cisco's operating sites. Subtle but important differences emerge across their operations in Silicon Valley, the North Carolina operation, and the Australian setting.

It is also a mistake for managers to attempt to revitalize an organization by dictating major changes and ignoring shared values. Although things may change a bit on the surface, a deeper look often shows whole departments resisting change and many key people unwilling to learn new ways. Such responses may indicate that the managers responsible are insensitive to the effects of their proposed changes on shared values. They fail to ask whether the changes are contrary to the important values of participants within the firm, a challenge to historically important corporatewide assumptions, and inconsistent with important common assumptions derived from the national culture, outside the firm. Note the example of Stephen Jobs at Apple earlier in this chapter. He did not make all the changes. Rather, he worked with others to make changes in strategy, structure, products, and marketing and to build on deep-seated common assumptions that long-term employees shared.

IBM Japan ←
www.ibm.com

Newly hired Japanese workers at IBM Japan were shocked when an American executive indicated that the goal of the firm was to maximize stockholder wealth. In Japan, stockholders are a less important corporate stakeholder than are core employees.

THE EFFECTIVE MANAGER 13.2

PICKING A FIRM BY ITS CULTURE

One study suggests that there are four dominant types of corporate cultures:

1. Academies—individuals are carefully moved through training programs for career development.
2. Fortresses—individuals are asked to engage in a turnaround and a fight for corporate survival.
3. Clubs—seniority, loyalty, status, commitment, and "fitting in" are most important.
4. Baseball teams—talent and performance are considered critical.

■ **Organization development (OD)** is the application of behavioral science knowledge in a long-range effort to improve an organization's ability to cope with change in its external environment and increase its problem-solving capabilities.

Few executives are able to reshape common assumptions or "the taken-for-granted truths" in a firm without taking drastic, radical action. Roger Smith of General Motors realized this challenge and established a new division to produce the Saturn.

At Harley Davidson, a new senior management team had to replace virtually all of the company's middle managers in order to establish a new, unique, and competitive culture. All too often, however, executives are unable to realize that they, too, can be captured by the broadly held common assumptions within their firms. Just as executives in Eastern European firms must reexamine the philosophical foundation of their firms as their countries adopt market economies, so must managers in the United States and other Western nations, as they anticipate the exciting challenges of a new century.

■ CONTINUOUS CULTURAL DEVELOPMENT

To keep the culture fresh and competitive, the challenge today is to engage in a process of continuous self-assessment and planned change in order to stay abreast of problems and opportunities in a complex and demanding environment. **Organization development (OD)** is a comprehensive approach to planned change that is designed to improve the overall effectiveness of organizations. Formally defined, OD is the application of behavioral science knowledge in a long-range effort to improve an organization's ability to cope with change in its external environment and to increase its internal problem-solving capabilities.[31]

Organization development is used to improve performance in organizations of many types, sizes, and settings. It includes a set of tools with which any manager who is concerned about achieving and maintaining high levels of productivity will want to be familiar. Because of its comprehensive nature and scientific foundations, OD was frequently implemented with the aid of an external consultant. As OD techniques have been combined with a better understanding of organizational culture, its basic concepts can and should be used routinely by all managers.

Organizational Development Processes and Applications

Organizational development provides a set of well-proven methods for developing and changing what cultural analyses call *external adaptation* and *internal integration*. Importantly, OD seeks to achieve change in such a way that the organization's members become more active and confident in taking similar steps to maintain the culture and longer run organization effectiveness. A large part of any OD program's success in this regard rests with its asumptions, values and action research foundations.

■ UNDERLYING ASSUMPTIONS OF OD

The organizational development foundations for achieving change are rooted in underlying assumptions about individuals, groups, and organizations. At the individual level, OD is guided by principles that reflect an underlying respect for people and their capabilities. It assumes that individual needs for growth and development are most likely to be satisfied in a supportive and challenging work environment. It also assumes that most people are capable of taking responsibility for their own actions and of making positive contributions to organizational performance.

At the *group level*, OD is guided by principles that reflect a belief that groups can be good for both people and organizations. It assumes that groups help their members satisfy important individual needs and can also be helpful in supporting organizational objectives. And it assumes that effective groups can be created by people working in collaboration to meet individual and organizational needs.

At the *organizational level*, OD is guided by principles that show a respect for the complexity of an organization as a system of interdependent parts. It assumes that changes in one part of the organization will affect other parts as well. And it assumes that organizational structures and jobs can be designed to meet the needs of individuals and groups as well as those of the organization.

■ SHARED VALUES AND PRINCIPLES UNDERLYING OD

Organizational development offers a systematic approach to planned change in organizations which addresses two main goals: outcome goals (mainly issues of external adaptation) and process goals (mainly issues of internal integration). Outcome goals include achieving improvements in task performance by improving external adaptation capabilities. In OD, these goals focus on what is actually accomplished through individual and group efforts. Process goals include achieving improvements in such things as communication, interaction, and decision making among an organization's members. These goals focus on how well people work together, and they stress improving internal integration.

In pursuit of these goals, OD is intended to help organizations and their members by (1) creating an open problem-solving climate throughout an organization, (2) supplementing formal authority with that of knowledge and competence, (3) moving decision making to points where relevant information is available, (4) building trust and maximizing collaboration among individuals and groups, (5) increasing the sense of organizational "ownership" among members, and (6) allowing people to exercise self-direction and self-control at work.[32] Thus, using OD implicitly involves these values. That is, organization development is designed to improve the contributions of individual members in achieving the organizational goals, and it seeks to do so in ways that respect the organization's members as mature adults who need and deserve high-quality experiences in their working lives.

■ ACTION RESEARCH FOUNDATIONS OF OD

Organizational development practitioners refer to **action research** as the process of systematically collecting data on an organization, feeding it back to the members for action planning, and evaluating results by collecting and reflecting on more data after the planned actions have been taken. This is a data-based

■ **Action research** is the process of systematically collecting data on an organization, feeding it back for action planning, and evaluating results by collecting and reflecting on more data.

and collaborative approach to problem solving and organizational assessment. When used in the OD process, action research helps identify action directions that may enhance an organization's effectiveness. In a typical action-research sequence depicted in Figure 13.1, the sequence is initiated when someone senses a performance gap and decides to analyze the situation systematically for the problems and opportunities it represents. The process continues through the following steps: data gathering, data feedback, data analysis, and action planning. It continues to the point at which action is taken and results are evaluated. The evaluation or reassessment stage may or may not generate another performance gap. If it does, the action-research cycle begins anew.

Figure 13.2 identifies one set of frameworks that can assist OD practitioners in accomplishing the required diagnoses. These foundations apply the open systems framework and OB concepts with which you are already familiar from earlier parts of this book. At the organizational level, the figure indicates that effectiveness must be understood with respect to forces in the external environment and major organizational aspects, such as strategy, technology, structure, culture, and management systems. At the group level, effectiveness is viewed in a context of forces in the internal environment of the organization and major group aspects, such as tasks, membership, norms, cohesiveness, and group processes.

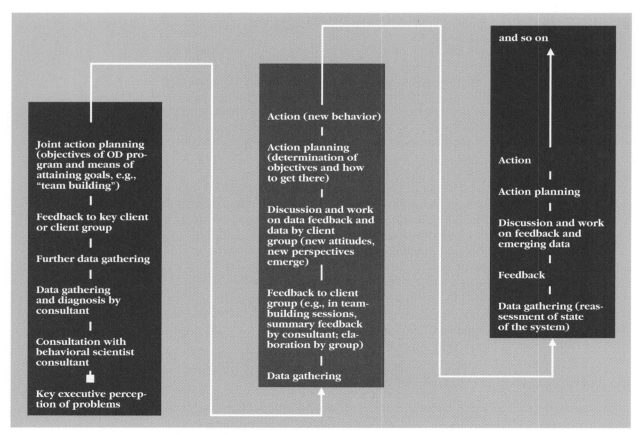

Figure 13.1
An action-research model for organization development.

At the individual level, effectiveness is considered in relationship to the internal environment of the work group and individual aspects, such as tasks, goals, needs, and interpersonal relationships.

ORGANIZATIONAL DEVELOPMENT INTERVENTIONS

The action research process should engage members of an organization in activities designed to accomplish the required diagnoses and to develop and implement plans for constructive change. Action research, data collection, and the diagnostic foundations should come together through the choice and use of OD "interventions." **Organizational development interventions** are activities initiated by the consultant to facilitate planned change and to assist the client system in developing its own problem-solving capabilities. With less formality, many of these techniques are also now being used by managers to help understand and improve their own operations. Major OD interventions can be categorized with respect to their major impact at the organizational, group, and individual levels of action.[33]

■ **Organization development interventions** are activities initiated to support planned change and improve work effectiveness.

Organizationwide Interventions An effective organization is one that achieves its major performance objectives while maintaining a high quality of work life for

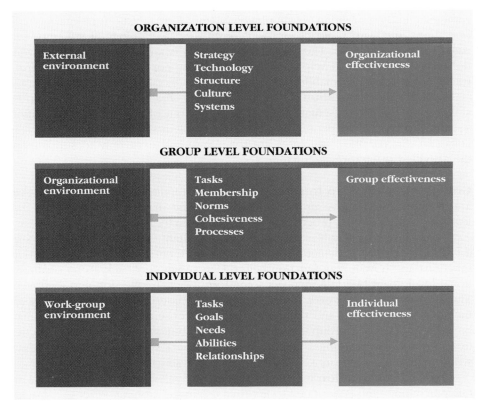

Figure 13.2
Diagnostic foundations of organization development and OD techniques: concerns for individual, group, and organizational effectiveness.

its members. OD interventions designed for systemwide application include the following.

■ **Survey feedback** begins with the collection of data via questionnaires from organization members or a representative sample of them.

Survey feedback begins with the collection of data via questionnaire responses from organization members, or a representative sample of such responses. The data are then presented, or fed back, to the members. They subsequently engage in a collaborative process to interpret the data and to develop action plans in response.

■ A **confrontation meeting** helps determine how an organization may be improved and start action toward improvement.

Confrontation meetings are designed to help determine quickly how an organization may be improved and to take initial actions to better the situation.[34] The intervention involves a one-day meeting conducted by an OD facilitator for a representative sample of organizational members, including top management. In a structured format, the consultant asks participants to make individual lists of what they feel can be done to improve things. Then, through a series of small-group work sessions and sharing of results, these ideas are refined into a tentative set of actions that top management then endorses for immediate implementation. The major trick here is to get senior managers to propose changing their part of the firm. Confrontation meetings fail if all the proposed changes call for adjustments by subordinates without any alterations by the top managers.

■ **Structural redesign** involves realigning the structure of the organization or major subsystem in order to improve performance.

Structural redesign involves realigning the structure of the organization or major subsystems to improve performance. It includes examining the best fit between structure, technology, and environment. In today's highly dynamic environments, in light of the increasing involvement of organizations in international operations and with rapid changes in information technology, a structure can easily grow out of date. Thus, structural redesign is an important OD intervention that can be used to help maintain the best fit between organizational structures and situational demands.

■ **Collateral organization** involves a representative set of members in periodic small-group, problem-solving sessions.

Collateral organization is designed to make creative problem solving possible by pulling a representative set of members out of the formal organization structure to engage in periodic small-group problem-solving sessions.[35] These collateral, or "parallel," structures are temporary and exist only to supplement the activities of the formal structure.

Group and Intergroup Interventions OD interventions at the group level are designed to improve group effectiveness. The major interventions at this level are team building, process consultation, and intergroup team building.

■ **Team building** is designed to gather and analyze data on the functioning of a group and implement changes to increase its operating effectiveness.

Team building involves a manager or consultant engaging the members of a group in a series of activities designed to help them examine how the group functions and how it may function better. Like survey feedback at the organizational level, team building involves some form of data collection and feedback. The key elements, however, are a collaborative assessment of the data by all members of the group and the achievement of consensus regarding what may be done to improve group effectiveness. Team building is often done at "retreats" or off-site meetings, where group members spend two to three days working intensely together on this reflection–analysis–planning process.

■ **Process consultation** helps a group improve on such things as norms, cohesiveness, decision-making methods, communication, conflict, and task and maintenance activities.

Process consultation involves structured activities that are facilitated by an OD practitioner and is designed to improve group functioning. Process consultation has a more specific focus than does team building, however; its attention is directed toward the key "processes" through which members of a group work with one another. The process consultant is concerned with helping a group function better on such things as norms, cohesiveness, decision-making methods, communication, conflict, and task and maintenance activities.

Intergroup team building is a special form of team building. It is designed to help two or more groups improve their working relationships with one another and, it is hoped, to experience improved group effectiveness as a result. Here, the OD practitioner engages the groups or their representatives in activities that increase awareness of how each group perceives the other. Given this understanding, collaborative problem solving can improve coordination between the groups and encourage more mutual support of one another as important components in the total organization.

> ■ **Intergroup team building** helps groups improve their working relationships with one another and experience improved group effectiveness.

Individual Interventions   Task performance and job satisfaction are important concerns with respect to improving individual effectiveness in the workplace. OD interventions at this level of attention range from those that address personal issues to those that deal more with specific job and career considerations. Individual-level OD interventions include the following.

Role negotiation is a means of clarifying what individuals expect to give and receive of one another in their working relationship. Because roles and personnel change over time, role negotiation can be an important way to maintain task understandings among individuals in an organization. This kind of understanding is quite easily accomplished by helping people who work together clarify what they need from one another to do their jobs well.

> ■ **Role negotiation** is a process through which individuals clarify expectations about what each should be giving and receiving as group members.

Job redesign is the process of creating long-term congruence between individual goals and organizational career opportunities. A good example is the Hackman and Oldham diagnostic approach to job enrichment discussed in Chapter 8.[36] Recall that this approach involves (1) analyzing the core characteristics of a job or group of jobs, (2) analyzing the needs and capabilities of workers in those jobs, and (3) taking action to adjust the core job characteristics either to enrich or to simplify the jobs to best match individual preferences.

> ■ **Job redesign** creates long-term congruence between individual goals and organizational career opportunities.

Career planning takes the form of structured opportunities for individuals to work with their managers or staff experts from the personnel or human resources department on career issues. They may map career goals, assess personal development needs, and actively plan short-term and long-term career moves. Increasingly, career planning is becoming a major part of the support that highly progressive organizations provide for their members.

> ■ **Career planning** creates long-term congruence between individual goals and organizational career opportunities.

OD and the Continuous Cultural Evolution   Today, a new wave of successful high-tech firms exemplifies the use of organization development assumptions, values, and techniques without using the term OD. It is not that such firms as Cisco Systems or Starbucks are trying to force change on their employees. Rather, the managers in these systems take a very practical approach to managing culture. They realize that both external adaptation and internal integration are important for a variety of subcultures within their firms. They use OD intervention techniques to improve both. They do not dictate values or set common assumptions in isolation but with their fellow employees. They are working with others to help nurture and guide the continual evolution of organizational culture from day to day.

Chapter 13 Study Guide

Summary

What is the concept of organizational culture?

- Organizational or corporate culture is the system of shared actions, values, and beliefs that develops within an organization and guides the behavior of its members.

- Corporate culture can assist in responding to both external adaptation and internal integration issues.

- Most organizations contain a variety of subcultures, and a few have countercultures that can become the source of potentially harmful conflicts.

- Organizational cultures may be analyzed in terms of observable actions, shared values, and common assumptions (the taken-for-granted truths).

What are the observable aspects of organizational culture?

- Observable aspects of culture include the stories, rites, rituals, and symbols that are shared by organization members.

- Cultural rules and roles specify when various types of actions are appropriate and where individual members stand in the social system.

- Shared meanings and understandings help everyone know how to act and expect others to act in various circumstances.

How do values and assumptions influence organizational cultures?

- Common assumptions are the taken-for-granted truths that are shared by collections of corporate members.

- Some organizations express these truths in a management philosophy that links key goal-related issues with key collaboration issues into a series of general ways in which the firm will manage its affairs.

- The management philosophy is supported by a series of corporate myths.

How can the organizational culture be "managed," "nurtured" and "guided"?

- Executives may manage many aspects of the observable culture directly.

- Nurturing shared values among the membership is a major challenge for executives.

- Adjusting actions to common understandings limits the decision scope of even the CEO.

How can the process of organization development enhance organizational culture?

- All managers may use organization development (OD) techniques in their attempts to manage, nurture, and guide cultural change.

- OD is a special application of knowledge gained from behavioral science to create a comprehensive effort to improve organizational effectiveness.

- OD has both outcome goals, with respect to improved task accomplishments, and process goals, with respect to improvements in the way organization members work together.

■ With a strong commitment to collaborative efforts and human values, OD utilizes basic behavioral science principles with respect to individuals, groups, and organizations.

■ Organizationwide interventions include survey feedback, confrontation meetings, structural redesign, and collateral organization.

■ Group and intergroup interventions include team building, process consultation, and intergroup team building.

■ Individual interventions include sensitivity training, role negotiation, job redesign, and career planning.

Key Terms

Action research (p. 279)
Career planning (p. 282)
Collateral organization (p. 281)
Confrontation meeting (p. 280)
Countercultures (p. 267)
Cultural symbol (p. 271)
External adaptation (p. 265)
Intergroup team building (p. 281)

Job redesign (p. 282)
Management philosophy (p. 272)
Organizational or corporate culture (p. 264)
Organizational myth (p. 273)
Organization development (OD) (p. 276)
Organization development interventions (p. 279)

Process consultation (p. 281)
Rites (p. 270)
Rituals (p. 270)
Role negotiation (p. 282)
Sagas (p. 270)
Structural redesign (p. 281)
Subcultures (p. 267)
Survey feedback (p. 280)
Team building (p. 281)

Self-Test 13

■ MULTIPLE CHOICE

1. Culture concerns all of the following except _____. (a) the collective concepts shared by members of a firm (b) acquired capabilities (c) the personality of the leader (d) the beliefs of members (e) members' view of their collective personality

2. The three levels of cultural analysis highlighted in the text concern _____. (a) observable culture, shared values, and common assumptions (b) stories, rites, and rituals (c) symbols, myths, and stories (d) manifest culture, latent culture, and observable artifacts (e) cultural symbols, myths, and sagas

3. External adaptation concerns _____. (a) the unproven beliefs of senior executives (b) the process of coping with outside forces (c) the vision of the founder (d) the processes working together (e) standard recurring activities that are used at special times

4. Internal integration concerns _____. (a) the process of deciding the collective identity and how members will live together (b) the totality of the daily life of members . as they see and describe it (c) expressed unproven beliefs that are accepted uncritically and used to justify current actions (d) groups of individuals with a pattern of values that rejects those of the larger society (e) the process of coping with outside forces

5. When Japanese workers start each day with the company song, this is an example of a(n) _____. (a) symbol (b) myth (c) underlying assumption (d) ritual (e) saga

6. _____ is a sense of broader purpose that workers infuse into their tasks as a result of interaction with one another. (a) A rite (b) A cultural symbol (c) A foundation myth (d) A shared meaning (e) An internal integration

7. The story of a corporate turnaround attributed to the efforts of a visionary manager is an example of a(n) _____. (a) saga (b) foundation myth (c) internal integration (d) latent cultural artifact (e) common assumption

8. OD is designed primarily to improve _____. (a) the overall effectiveness of an organization (b) intergroup relations (c) synergy (d) the planned change process (e) group dynamics

9. The three stages in the OD process are _____. (a) data collection, intervention, and evaluation (b) diagnosis, intervention, and reinforcement (c) intervention, application, and innovation (d) diagnosis, intervention, and evaluation (e) planning, implementing, and evaluating

10. OD is planned change plus _____. (a) evaluation (b) intervention (c) ability for self-renewal (d) any future changes that may occur (e) reinforcement

■ TRUE–FALSE

11. The system of shared beliefs and values that develops within an organization is called organizational culture. T F

12. The belief that senior managers can manage all levels of the corporate culture is a myth. T F

13. External adaptation concerns such issues as the real mission of the firm, its goals, and how goals are reached. T F

14. Who gets rewards and punishments is part of external adaptation. T F

15. Rites and rituals often emerge from a subculture. T F

16. A ritual is a standardized activity used to manage anxiety. T F

17. Any object, art, or event that serves to transmit cultural meaning is called a rite. T F

18. The organizationwide OD interventions are survey feedback, confrontation meeting, structural redesign, management by objectives, and collateral organization. T F

19. The confrontation meeting is an OD intervention used to handle conflicts. T F

20. MBO is an organizationwide OD intervention. T F

■ SHORT RESPONSE

21. Describe the five steps Taylor Cox suggests need to be developed to help generate a multicultural organization or pluralistic company culture.

22. List the three aspects that help individuals and groups work together effectively and illustrate them through practical examples.

23. Give an example of how cultural rules and roles affect the atmosphere in a college classroom. Provide specific examples from your own perspective.

24. What are the major elements of a strong corporate culture?

■ APPLICATIONS ESSAY

25. Discuss the process of OD and provide an overview of its diagnostic foundations in a small business such as Venus Cleaners.

Explore application-oriented Fast Company articles, cases, experimental exercises, and self-assessments in the OB Skills Workbook

■ **Visit the Schermerhorn Web site to find the Interactive Self-Test and Internet exercises for this chapter.**

High Performance Leadership

WHERE SPEED CREATES THE DIFFERENCE

www.autopro.com

Peter Lewis's Progressive Corporation, a $4.6 billion revenue auto insurance maverick is built around speed, service, and software. He is pushing for claim inspections in nine hours or less and settlements within seven days. With this goal, he not only has built an increasingly prosperous and fast-growing company, but may also transform the struggling, slow-moving auto insurance industry. All this is done with rapid, on-the-spot claims inspections (and sometimes settlements), 24 hours a day, 7 days a week, using two-way radios, laptop computers with custom-designed intelligent software, rapid-moving omnipresent sports utility vehicle, and the power to make on-the-spot-decisions. Indeed, Progressive prides itself on settling claims before other companies even know an accident has occurred. All these activities take place with a maze of terminals operated by informally dressed claims representatives who interview customers involved in accidents, enter data into the mainframe computer, and initiate an immediate response—all in just minutes. Progressive also uses unconventional approaches in selling its insurance, where it shares with customers information about exact pricing not only on its policies, but on the identical policy from other competitors.

Progressive employees describe both the firm and Peter Lewis as "intense," "aggressive," and "unconventional." He also has been described as 65 going on 24 and has been Progressive's CEO for the past 33 years. Says Lewis: "We're not in the business of auto insurance. We're in the business of reducing the human trauma and economic costs of automobile accidents—in effective and profitable ways that delight customers."

For many, Peter Lewis captures the essence of leadership: the vision to seize the day and make a difference. Although most people probably agree that leadership makes a difference, some argue that it isn't important. For them, leaders are so bound by constraints that they just don't have much impact. Some also see leadership as so mystical that they can't define it but know it when they see it. In this chapter, we address these views and more in examining how leadership fits in organizations in general, and especially high performance organizations.

Study Questions

As you read Chapter 14, keep in mind these key questions.

- What is leadership, and how does it differ from management?
- What are the trait or behavioral leadership perspectives?
- What are the situational or contingency leadership approaches?
- How does attribution theory relate to leadership?
- What new leadership perspectives are evident in high performance organizations?

Leadership and Management

In the chapters in Part 1, we talked about managers and management functions, roles, activities, and skills. The question to ask now is how are leaders and leadership linked to all this?

Currently, controversy has arisen over whether leaders are different from managers or whether management is different from leadership and, if so, how. One way of making these differentiations is to argue that the role of *management* is to promote stability or to enable the organization to run smoothly, whereas the role of *leadership* is to promote adaptive or useful changes.[1] Persons in managerial positions could be involved with both management and leadership activities, or they could emphasize one activity at the expense of the other. Both management and leadership are needed, however, and if managers don't assume responsibility for both, then they should ensure that someone else handles the neglected activity.

For our purpose, we treat **leadership** as a special case of interpersonal influence that gets an individual or group to do what the leader or manager wants done. The broader influence notions, of which leadership is a part, are dealt with in Chapter 15. Leadership appears in two forms: (1) *formal leadership*, which is exerted by persons appointed to or elected to positions of formal authority in organizations; and (2) *informal leadership*, which is exerted by persons who become influential because they have special skills that meet the resource needs of others. Although both types are important in organizations, this chapter will emphasize formal leadership.

■ **Leadership** is a special case of interpersonal influence that gets an individual or group to do what the leader wants done.

The leadership literature is vast—upwards of 10,000 studies—and consists of numerous approaches.[2] It is convenient to organize these studies and their implications in terms of transitions from traditional leadership perspectives—including trait, behavioral and situational or contingency theories, to new leadership perspectives—including attribution theory, charismatic approaches and transformational leadership. These leadership transitions are especially relevant to the high performance context of organizational behavior today. As you will see, all are important for a leader.

Trait and Behavioral Theories Perspectives

■ TRAIT THEORIES

Trait perspectives assume that traits play a central role in differentiating between leaders and nonleaders (leaders must have the "right stuff")[3] or in predicting leader or organizational outcomes. The *great person–trait approach* reflects this leader and nonleader difference and is the earliest approach in studying leadership, having been introduced more than a century ago. What traits differentiated "great persons" from the masses? (E.g., How did Catherine the Great differ from her subjects?)[4] Later studies examined both leader/nonleader differences and trait predictions of outcomes. For various reasons, including inadequate theorizing and trait measurement, the studies were not successful enough to provide consistent findings.[5]

■ **Trait perspectives** assume that traits play a central role in differentiating between leaders and nonleaders.

More recent work has yielded more promising results. A number of traits have been identified that help identify important leadership strengths (see Figure 14.1). As it turns out, most of these traits also tend to predict leadership outcomes.

Leaders tend to be energetic and to operate on an even keel. They crave power not as an end in itself but as a means to achieving a vision or desired goals. Leaders also are very ambitious and have a high need for achievement. At the same time, they have to be emotionally mature enough to recognize their own strengths and weaknesses, and they are oriented toward self-improvement. Furthermore, as shown by HealthSouth's Richard Scrushy, to be trusted they must have integrity; without trust, they cannot hope to maintain the loyalty of their followers. Leaders also must not be easily discouraged. They need to stick to a chosen course of action and to push toward goal accomplishment. At the same time, they must be cognitively sharp enough to deal well with the large amount of information they receive. However, they do not need to be brilliant;

Figure 14.1
Traits with positive implications for successful leadership.

> **Energy and adjustment or stress tolerance:** Physical vitality and emotional resilience.
>
> **Prosocial power motivation:** A high need for power exercised primarily for the benefit of others.
>
> **Achievement orientation:** Need for achievement, desire to excel, drive to success, willingness to assume responsibility, concern for task objectives.
>
> **Emotional maturity:** Well adjusted, does not suffer from severe psychological disorders.
>
> **Self-confidence:** General confidence in self and in the ability to perform the job of a leader.
>
> **Integrity:** Behavior consistent with espoused values; honest, ethical, trustworthy.
>
> **Perseverance or tenacity:** Ability to overcome obstacles; strength of will.
>
> **Cognitive ability, intelligence, social intelligence:** Ability to gather, integrate, and interpret information; intelligence; understanding of social setting.
>
> **Task-relevant knowledge:** Knowledge about the company, industry, and technical aspects.
>
> **Flexibility:** Ability to respond appropriately to changes in the setting.

they just need to show above-average intelligence. In addition, leaders must have a good understanding of their social setting. Finally, they must possess lots of specific knowledge concerning their industry, firm, and job.

www.healthsouth.com

⚖️ ETHICS AND SOCIAL RESPONSIBILITY

"Our goal is not just to be the best-managed health-care company in America...but to be one of the best-managed companies [in any industry] if not the best-managed companies in America, one of the categories needs to be philanthropy." So says Richard Scrushy, CEO of health-care giant HealthSouth, which he started in 1984. Convinced of the "doing well by doing good" adage, Scrusley and Health-South will shell out $10 million over the next decade to support its HealthSouth Go for It Roadshow which is designed to reach millions of children with the likes of star athletes Michael Jordan and Emmitt Smith. The Roadshow figures remind children to stay off drugs, stay in school, and stay healthy. Scrushy also uses philanthropy as a measuring rod for evaluating his managers and provides rewards to those facilities most successful in raising money for charity.

■ BEHAVIORAL THEORIES

■ **Behavioral perspective** assumes that leadership is central to performance and other outcomes.

Like the trait perspective covered above, the **behavioral perspective** assumes that leadership is central to performance and other outcomes. In this case, however, instead of dealing with underlying traits, behaviors are considered. Two classic research programs—at the University of Michigan and Ohio State University—provide useful insights into leadership behaviors.

Michigan Studies   In the late 1940s, researchers at the University of Michigan introduced a research program on leadership behavior. They sought to identify the leadership pattern that results in effective performance. From interviews of high- and low-performing groups in different organizations, the researchers derived two basic forms of leader behaviors: employee centered and production centered. *Employee-centered supervisors* are those who place strong emphasis on their subordinates' welfare. In contrast, *production-centered supervisors* are more concerned with getting the work done. In general, employee-centered supervisors were found to have more productive work groups than did the production-centered supervisors.[6]

These behaviors may be viewed on a continuum, with employee-centered supervisors at one end and production-centered supervisors at the other. Sometimes, the more general terms *human relations oriented* and *task oriented* are used to describe these alternative leader behaviors.

Ohio State Studies At about the same time as the Michigan studies, an important leadership research program was started at Ohio State University. A questionnaire was administered in both industrial and military settings to measure subordinates' perceptions of their superiors' leadership behavior. The researchers identified two dimensions similar to those found in the Michigan studies: **consideration** and **initiating structure**.[7] A highly considerate leader is sensitive to people's feelings and, much like the employee-centered leader, tries to make things pleasant for his or her followers. In contrast, a leader high in initiating structure is more concerned with defining task requirements and other aspects of the work agenda; he or she might be seen as similar to a production-centered supervisor. These dimensions are related to what people sometimes refer to as socioemotional and task leadership, respectively.

At first, the Ohio State researchers believed that a leader high on consideration, or socioemotional warmth, would have more highly satisfied or better performing subordinates. Later results indicated that leaders should be high on both consideration and initiating structure behaviors, however. This dual emphasis is reflected in the leadership grid approach.

■ **Consideration** is a highly considerate leader is sensitive to people's feelings and tries to make things pleasant for the followers.

■ **Initiating structure** This kind of leader is concerned with spelling out the task requirements and clarifying other aspects of the work agenda.

The Leadership Grid Robert Blake and Jane Mouton have developed the leadership grid approach. Results are plotted on a nine-position grid that places concern for people on the vertical axis and concern for production on the horizontal axis. As an example, a person with a 9/1 concern for people/concern for production is termed a "country club manager." A 1/1 position is an "impoverished manager style," and a 1/9 position is a "task management style." A 5/5 position is "middle of the road" and a 9/9 "team manager," high on both dimensions, is considered ideal.

Graen's Leader–Member Exchange Theory Another perspective that emphasizes the centrality of leadership on outcomes is Graen's Leader–Member Exchange (LMX) approach. However, in contrast to the perspectives just described, which emphasize the influence of the leader's behavior on follower outcomes, LMX theory focuses on the quality of the working relationship between leaders and followers. The LMX 7 scale assesses the degree to which leaders and followers have mutual respect for each other's capabilities, feel a deepening sense of mutual trust, and have a strong sense of obligation to one another. Taken together, these dimensions determine the extent to which followers will be part of the leader's "in group" or "out group."[8]

In-group followers tend to function as assistants, lieutenants, or advisers and to have higher quality personalized exchanges with the leader than do out-group

Lovelace Institutes ◀
www.lhiweb.com

More than 50 years old Lovelace Institutes, a biomedical research firm in Albuquerque, New Mexico, had lost sight of its mission. To deal with this problem, Robert Rubin was hired as the new CEO because of his sense of leadership vision and management skills to carry out a necessary reorganization.

followers. The out-group followers tend to emphasize more formalized job requirements, and a relatively low level of mutual influence exists between leaders and out-group followers. The more personalized in-group exchanges typically involve a leader's emphasis on assignments to interesting tasks, delegation of important responsibilities, information sharing, and participation in the leader's decisions, as well as special benefits, such as personal support and approval and favorable work schedules.

Research suggests that high-quality LMX is associated with increased follower satisfaction and productivity, decreased turnover, increased salaries, and faster promotion rates. These findings are encouraging, and the approach continues to receive increasing emphasis in the literature. Of course, many questions remain, such as: What happens in the event of too much disparity in the treatment of in-group and out-group members? Will out-group members become resentful and sabotage team efforts? In addition, more needs to be learned about how the in-group/out-group exchange starts in the first place and how these relations change over time.[9]

Cross Cultural Implications   It is important to consider how well the kinds of behavioral dimensions discussed earlier transfer internationally. Some work in the United States, Britain, Hong Kong, and Japan shows that the behaviors must be carried out in different ways in alternative cultures. For instance, British leaders are seen as considerate if they show subordinates how to use equipment, whereas in Japan the highly considerate leader helps subordinates with personal problems.[10] Similarly, LMX theory has been shown to operate in Japan.[11]

Situational Contingency Theories

The trait and behavioral perspectives assume that leadership, by itself, would have a strong impact on outcomes. Another development in leadership thinking recognized, however, that leader traits and behaviors can act in conjunction with *situational contingencies*—other important aspects of the leadership situation—to predict outcomes.

House and Aditya argue that the effects of traits are enhanced by their relevance to the leader's situational contingencies.[12] For example, achievement motivation should be most effective for challenging tasks that require initiative and require assumption of personal responsibility for success. Leader flexibility should be most predictive in unstable environments or when leaders lead different people over time. Prosocial power motivation is likely to be most important in complex organizations where decision implementation requires lots of persuasion and social influence. "Strong" or "weak" situations also make a difference. An example of a strong situation is a highly formal organization with lots of rules, procedures, and so forth. Here, traits will have less impact than in a weaker, more unstructured situation (e.g., I can't show my dynamism as much when the organization restricts me). Traits sometimes have a direct relationship to outcomes or to leaders versus nonleaders. They may also make themselves felt by influencing leader behaviors (e.g., a leader high in energy engages in directive, take-charge behaviors).[13]

■ FIEDLER'S LEADERSHIP CONTINGENCY THEORY

Fred Fiedler's work began the situational contingency era in the mid-1960s.[14] His theory holds that group effectiveness depends on an appropriate match between a leader's style (essentially a trait measure) and the demands of the situation. Specifically, Fiedler considers **situational control**—the extent to which a leader can determine what his or her group is going to do as well as the outcomes of the group's actions and decisions.

Fiedler uses an instrument called the **least preferred co-worker (LPC) scale** to measure a person's leadership style. Respondents are asked to describe the person with whom they have been able to work least well—their least preferred co-worker, or LPC—using a series of adjectives such as the following two:

Unfriendly ___ ___ ___ ___ ___ ___ ___ ___ Friendly
         1   2   3   4   5   6   7   8

Pleasant ___ ___ ___ ___ ___ ___ ___ ___ Unpleasant
         1   2   3   4   5   6   7   8

Fiedler argues that high-LPC leaders (those describing their LPC very positively) have a relationship-motivated style, whereas low-LPC leaders have a task-motivated style. He considers this task or relationship motivation to be a trait that leads to either directive or nondirective behavior, depending on whether the leader has high, moderate, or low situational control. In other words, a task-motivated leader tends to be nondirective in high-control situations and directive in moderate- and low-control situations. A relationship-motivated leader tends to be the opposite.

Figure 14.2 shows the task-oriented leader as having greater group effectiveness under high and low situational control, whereas the relationship-oriented leader has a more effective group under a moderate control situation.

■ **Situational control** is the extent to which leaders can determine what their group is going to do and what the outcomes of their actions and decisions are going to be.

■ **Least preferred co-worker (LPC) scale** is a measure of a person's leadership style based on a description of the person with whom respondents have been able to work least well.

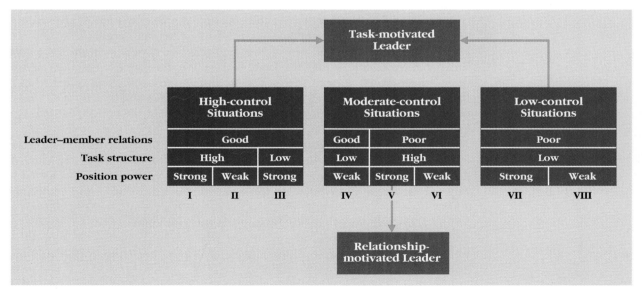

Figure 14.2
Predictions from Fiedler's contingency theory of leadership.

The figure also shows that Fiedler measures high, moderate, and low control with the following three variables arranged in the situational combinations indicated:

Fiedler's three situational control variables

- *Leader–member relations* (good/poor)—Membership support for the leader.
- *Task structure* (high/low)—Spelling out the leader's task goals, procedures, and guidelines in the group.
- *Position power* (strong/weak)—The leader's task expertise and reward or punishment authority.

Consider an experienced and well-trained supervisor of a group manufacturing a part for a personal computer. The leader is highly supported by his group members and can grant raises and make hiring and firing decisions. This supervisor has very high situational control and is operating in situation I in Figure 14.2. Those leaders operating in situations II and III would have high situational control, though lower than our production supervisor. For these high-control situations, a task-oriented leader behaving directively would have the most effective group.

Now consider the chair of a student council committee of volunteers (the chair's position power is weak) who are unhappy about this person being the chair and who have the low-structured task of organizing a Parents' Day program to improve university–parent relations. This low-control situation VIII calls for a task-motivated leader who needs to behave directively to keep the group together and focus on the ambiguous task; in fact, the situation demands it. Finally, consider a well-liked academic department chair with tenured faculty. This is a cell IV moderate-control situation with good leader–member relations, low task structure, and weak position power, calling for a relationship-motivated leader. The leader should emphasize nondirective and considerate relationships with the faculty.

Fiedler's Cognitive Resource Theory   Fiedler recently moved beyond his contingency theory by developing the cognitive resource theory.[15] Cognitive resources are abilities or competencies. According to this approach, whether a leader should use directive or nondirective behavior depends on the following situational contingencies: (1) the leader's or subordinate group members' ability or competency, (2) stress, (3) experience, and (4) group support of the leader. Basically, cognitive resource theory is most useful because it directs us to leader or subordinate group-member ability, an aspect not typically considered in other leadership approaches.

The theory views directiveness as most helpful for performance when the leader is competent, relaxed, and supported. In this case, the group is ready, and directiveness is the clearest means of communication. When the leader feels stressed, he or she is diverted. In this case, experience is more important than ability. If support is low, then the group is less receptive, and the leader has less impact. Group-member ability becomes most important when the leader is nondirective and receives strong support from group members. If support is weak, then task difficulty or other factors have more impact than do either the leader or the subordinates.

Evaluation and Application   The roots of Fiedler's contingency approach date back to the 1960s and have elicited both positive and negative reactions.

The biggest controversy concerns exactly what Fiedler's LPC instrument measures. Some question Fiedler's behavioral interpretation, whereby the specific behaviors of high- and low-LPC leaders change, depending on the amount of situational control. Furthermore, the approach makes the most accurate predictions in situations I and VIII and IV and V; results are less consistent in the other situations.[16] Tests of cognitive resource theory have shown mixed results.[17]

In terms of application, Fiedler has developed **leader match training**, which Sears Roebuck and other organizations have used. Leaders are trained to diagnose the situation to match their high and low LPC scores with situational control, as measured by leader–member relations, task structure, and leader position power, following the general ideas shown in Figure 14.2. In cases with no match, the training shows how each of these situational control variables can be changed to obtain a match. Alternatively, another way of getting a match is through leader selection or placement based on LPC scores.[18] For example, a high-LPC leader would be selected for a position with high situational control, as in our earlier example of the manufacturing supervisor. As in the case of Fiedler's contingency theory, a number of studies have been designed to test leader match. Although they are not uniformly supportive, more than a dozen such tests have found increases in group effectiveness following the training.[19]

We conclude that although there are still unanswered questions concerning Fiedler's contingency theory, especially concerning the meaning of LPC, the theory and the leader match program have relatively strong support.[20] The approach and training program are also especially useful in encouraging situational contingency thinking.

■ HOUSE'S PATH–GOAL THEORY OF LEADERSHIP

Another well-known approach to situational contingencies is one developed by Robert House based on the earlier work of others.[21] This theory has its roots in the expectancy model of motivation discussed in Chapter 6. The term **path–goal** is used because of its emphasis on how a leader influences subordinates' perceptions of both work goals and personal goals and the links, or paths, found between these two sets of goals.

The theory assumes that a leader's key function is to adjust his or her behaviors to complement situational contingencies, such as those found in the work setting. House argues that when the leader is able to compensate for things lacking in the setting, subordinates are likely to be satisfied with the leader. For example, the leader could help remove job ambiguity or show how good performance could lead to more pay. Performance should improve as the paths by which (1) effort leads to performance—expectancy—and (2) performance leads to valued rewards—instrumentality—become clarified.

House's approach is summarized in Figure 14.3. The figure shows four types of leader behavior—directive, supportive, achievement oriented, and participative—and two categories of situational contingency variables—subordinate attributes and work-setting attributes. The leader behaviors are adjusted to complement the situational contingency variables in order to influence subordinate satisfaction, acceptance of the leader, and motivation for task performance.

Directive leadership has to do with spelling out the what and how of subordinates' tasks; it is much like the initiating structure mentioned earlier. **Supportive leadership** focuses on subordinate needs and well-being and promoting

■ In **leader match training** leaders are trained to diagnose the situation to match their high and low LPC scores with situational control.

■ **House's path-goal theory of leadership** assumes that a leader's key function is to adjust his or her behaviors to complement situational contingencies.

■ **Directive leadership** spells out the what and how of subordinates' tasks.

■ **Supportive leadership** focuses on subordinate needs, well-being, and promotion of a friendly work climate.

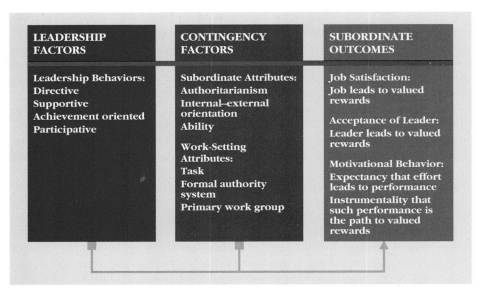

Figure 14.3
Summary of major path–goal relationships in House's leadership approach.

■ **Achievement-oriented leadership** emphasizes setting challenging goals, stressing excellence in performance, and showing confidence in people's ability to achieve high standards of performance.

■ **Participative leadership** focuses on consulting with subordinates and seeking and taking their suggestions into account before making decisions.

a friendly work climate; it is similar to consideration. **Achievement-oriented leadership** emphasizes setting challenging goals, stressing excellence in performance, and showing confidence in the group members' ability to achieve high standards of performance. **Participative leadership** focuses on consulting with subordinates and seeking and taking their suggestions into account before making decisions.

Important subordinate characteristics are *authoritarianism* (close-mindedness, rigidity), *internal–external orientation* (e.g., locus of control), and *ability*. The key work-setting factors are the nature of the subordinates' tasks (task structure), the *formal authority system*, and the *primary work group*.

Predictions from Path–Goal Theory   Directive leadership is predicted to have a positive impact on subordinates when the task is ambiguous; it is predicted to have just the opposite effect for clear tasks. In addition, the theory predicts that when ambiguous tasks are being performed by highly authoritarian and close-minded subordinates, even more directive leadership is called for.

Supportive leadership is predicted to increase the satisfaction of subordinates who work on highly repetitive tasks or on tasks considered to be unpleasant, stressful, or frustrating; the leader's supportive behavior helps compensate for these adverse conditions. For example, many would consider traditional assembly-line auto worker jobs to be highly repetitive, perhaps even unpleasant and frustrating. A supportive supervisor could help make these jobs more pleasant. Achievement-oriented leadership is predicted to encourage subordinates to strive for higher performance standards and to have more confidence in their ability to meet challenging goals. For subordinates in ambiguous, nonrepetitive jobs, achievement-oriented leadership should increase their expectancies that effort leads to desired performance.

Participative leadership is predicted to promote satisfaction on nonrepetitive tasks that allow for the ego involvement of subordinates. For example, on a challenging research project, participation allows employees to feel good about dealing with the challenge of the project on their own. On repetitive tasks, open-minded or nonauthoritarian subordinates will also be satisfied with a participative leader. On a task where employees screw nuts on bolts hour after hour, for example, those who are nonauthoritarian will appreciate having a leader who allows them to get involved in ways that may help break the monotony.

Evaluation and Application   House's path–goal approach has now been with us for nearly 30 years. Early work provided some support for the theory in general and for the particular predictions discussed earlier.[22] However, current assessments by well-known scholars have pointed out that many aspects have not been tested adequately, and there is very little recent research concerning the theory.[23] House himself recently revised and extended path–goal theory into the Theory of Work Unit Leadership. It's beyond our scope to discuss details of this new theory, but as a base, the new theory expands the list of leader behaviors beyond those in path–goal theory, including aspects of both traditional and new leadership.[24] It remains to be seen how much research it will generate.

In terms of application, there is enough support for original path–goal theory to suggest two possibilities. First, training could be used to change leadership behavior to fit the situational contingencies. Second, the leader could be taught to diagnose the situation and to learn how to try to change the contingencies, as in leader match.

Hersey and Blanchard's Situational Leadership Model   Like other situational contingency approaches, the situational leadership model developed by Paul Hersey and Kenneth Blanchard posits that there is no single best way to lead.[25] Hersey and Blanchard focus on the situational contingency of maturity, or "readiness," of followers, in particular. Readiness is the extent to which people have the ability and willingness to accomplish a specific task. Hersey and Blanchard argue that "situational" leadership requires adjusting the leader's emphasis on task behaviors, for instance, giving guidance and direction, and relationship behaviors, for example, providing socioemotional support, according to the readiness of followers to perform their tasks. Figure 14.4 identifies four leadership styles: delegating, participating, selling, and telling. Each emphasizes a different combination of task and relationship behaviors by the leader. The figure also suggests the following situational matches as the best choice of leadership style for followers at each of four readiness levels.

A *"telling" style is best for low follower readiness*. The direction provided by this style defines roles for people who are unable and unwilling to take responsibility themselves; it eliminates any insecurity about the task that must be done.

A *"selling" style is best for low to moderate follower readiness*. This style offers both task direction and support for people who are unable but willing to take task responsibility; it involves combining a directive approach with explanation and reinforcement in order to maintain enthusiasm.

A *"participating" style is best for moderate to high follower readiness*. Able but unwilling followers require supportive behavior in order to increase their

**Figure 14.4
Hersey and Blanchard
model of situational
leadership.**

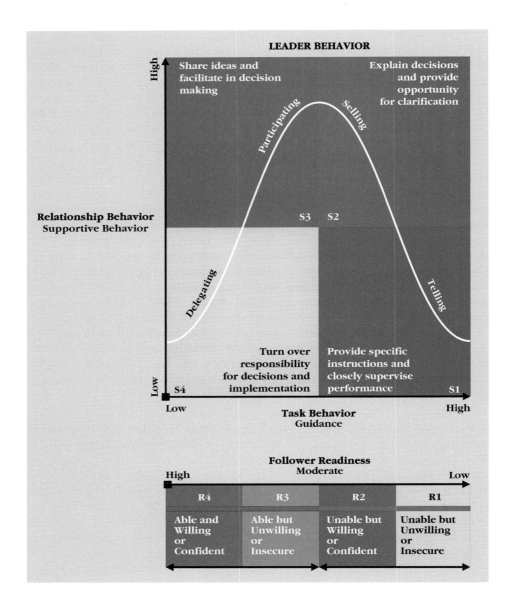

motivation; by allowing followers to share in decision making, this style helps enhance the desire to perform a task.

- *A "delegating" style is best for high readiness.* This style provides little in terms of direction and support for the task at hand; it allows able and willing followers to take responsibility for what needs to be done.

This situational leadership approach requires the leader to develop the capability to diagnose the demands of situations and then to choose and implement the appropriate leadership response. The model gives specific attention to followers and their feelings about the task at hand and suggests that an effective leader focus especially on emerging changes in the level of readiness of the people involved in the work.

In spite of its considerable history and incorporation into training programs by a large number of firms, the situational leadership approach has only recently begun to receive systematic research attention.[26]

■ SUBSTITUTES FOR LEADERSHIP

In contrast to the previous traditional leadership approaches, the substitutes for leadership theory argues that sometimes hierarchical leadership makes essentially no difference. John Jermier and others contend that certain individual, job, and organizational variables can either serve as substitutes for leadership or neutralize a leader's impact on subordinates.[27] Some examples of these variables are shown in Figure 14.5.

Substitutes for leadership make a leader's influence either unnecessary or redundant in that they replace a leader's influence. For example, in Figure 14.5, it will be unnecessary and perhaps not even possible for a leader to provide the kind of task-oriented direction already available from an experienced, talented, and well-trained subordinate. In contrast, neutralizers prevent a leader from behaving in a certain way or nullify the effects of a leader's actions. If a leader has little formal authority or is physically separated, for example, his or her leadership may be nullified even though task supportiveness may still be needed.

■ **Substitutes for leadership** make a leader's influence both unnecessary and redundant in that they replace a leader's influence.

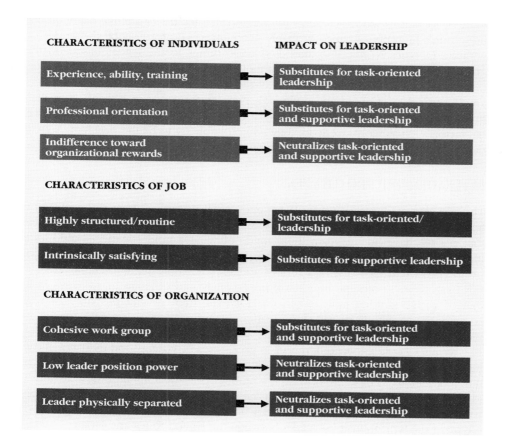

Figure 14.5
Some example leadership substitutes and neutralizers.

Some research comparing Mexican and U.S. workers, as well as workers in Japan, suggests both similarities and differences between various substitutes in the countries examined. More generally, a review of 17 studies in the United States as well as other countries found mixed results for the substitutes theory. Among other things, the authors argued that the kinds of characteristics and leader behaviors should be broadened and that the approach appeared to be especially important for high-performance work teams.[28] With regard to these work teams, for example, in place of a hierarchical leader specifying standards and ways of achieving goals (task-oriented behaviors), the team might set its own standards and substitute those for the leader's.

Attribution Theory and Leadership

The traditional leadership theories discussed so far have all assumed that leadership and its substantive effects can be identified and measured objectively. This is not always the case, however. Attribution theory addresses this very point—that of individuals trying to understand causes, to assess responsibilities, and to evaluate personal qualities, as all of these are involved with certain events. Attribution theory is particularly important in understanding leadership.

For openers, think about a work group or student group that you see as performing really well. Now assume that you are asked to describe the leader on one of the leadership scales discussed earlier in the chapter. If you are like many others, the group's high performance probably encouraged you to describe the leader favorably; in other words, you attributed good things to the leader based on the group's performance. Similarly, leaders themselves make attributions about subordinate performance and react differently depending on those attributions. For example, if leaders attribute an employee's poor performance to lack of effort they may issue a reprimand, whereas if they attribute the poor performance to an external factor, such as work overload, they will probably try to fix the problem. A great deal of evidence supports these attributional views of subordinates and leaders.[29]

■ LEADERSHIP PROTOTYPES

■ **Leadership prototype** is an image people have in their minds of what a model leader should look like.

There is also evidence that people have a mental picture of what makes a "good leader" or ways in which "real leaders" would act in a given situation. The view that people have an image in their minds of what a model leader should look like is sometimes called a **leadership prototype**.[30] These implicit theories or prototypes usually consist of a mix of specific and more general characteristics. For example, a prototype of a bank president would differ in many ways from that of a high-ranking military officer. However, there would probably also be some core characteristics reflecting leaders in our society in general—for example, integrity and self-efficacy.

We also would expect differences in prototypes by country and by national culture.[31] As an example of such country differences, a study asked people from eight different nations to describe how well a number of leadership attributes previously identified described their image of a business leader. In each country, five attributes were identified as most prototypical of such a leader. Note the difference in the prototype of the typical business leader between the United States and Japan.

U.S.: determined, goal-oriented, verbally skilled, industrious, persistent.

Japan: responsible, educated, trustworthy, intelligent, disciplined.

Similar differences exist across other countries, although there is some overlap as well.

The closer the behavior of a leader is to the implicit theories of his or her followers, the more favorable the leader's relations and key outcomes tend to be.[32] Both of the attributional treatments above emphasize leadership as something that is largely symbolic or resides in the eye of the beholder. This general notion has also carried over to a related set of research directions. Ironically, the first of these directions argues that leadership makes little or no real difference in organizational effectiveness. The second tends to attribute greatly exaggerated importance to leadership and ultimately leads us into charisma and other aspects of the new leadership.

■ EXAGGERATION OF THE LEADERSHIP DIFFERENCE

Jeffrey Pfeffer has looked at what happens when leaders at the top of the organization are changed. Pfeffer is among those contending that even CEOs of large corporations have little leadership impact on profits and effectiveness compared to environmental and industry forces, such as cutbacks in the federal defense budget. Furthermore, these leaders are typically accountable to so many groups of people for the resources they use that their leadership impact is greatly constrained. Pfeffer argues that in light of such forces and constraints, much of the impact a top leader does have is symbolic; leaders and others develop explanations to legitimize the actions they take.[33]

This exaggeration or attribution occurs particularly when performance is either extremely high or extremely low or when the situation is such that many people could have been responsible for the performance. James Meindl and his colleagues call this phenomenon the **romance of leadership**, whereby people attribute romantic, almost magical, qualities to leadership.[34] Consider the firing of a baseball manager or football coach whose team doesn't perform well. Neither the owner nor anyone else is really sure why this occurred. But the owner can't fire all the players, so a new team manager is brought in to symbolize "new leadership" that is "sure to turn the team around."

TD Industries, a large commercial air conditioning and plumbing company in Dallas, Texas, was just ranked number 2 on *Fortune* magazine's list of 100 best companies to work for. Jack Lowe, Jr., who is seen as both savvy and down to earth, is an ideal match for the good leader prototype among his blue-collar employees.

■ **Romance of leadership**
People attribute romantic, almost magical qualities to leadership.

Leadership Transitions for High Performance Organizations

The focus on leadership attributions and symbolic aspects moves us away from traditional leadership and into the new leadership. The **new leadership** emphasizes charismatic and transformational approaches and various aspects of vision related to them. The new leadership is considered especially important in changing and transforming individuals and organizations with a commitment to high performance.[35]

■ **New leadership**
emphasizes charismatic and transformational approaches and various aspects of vision related to them.

■ CHARISMATIC APPROACHES

Robert House and his associates have done a lot of work recently based on extensions of an earlier charismatic theory House developed. (Do not confuse this with House's path–goal theory or its extension, discussed earlier in the chapter.)[36] Of special interest is the fact that House's theory uses both trait and behavior combinations.

■ **Charismatic leaders** are those who, by force of their personal abilities, are capable of having a profound and extraordinary effect on followers.

House's **charismatic leaders** are leaders who, by force of their personal abilities, are capable of having a profound and extraordinary effect on followers. These leaders are high in need for power and have high feelings of self-efficacy and conviction in the moral rightness of their beliefs. That is, the need for power motivates these people to want to be leaders. This need is then reinforced by their conviction of the moral rightness of their beliefs. The feeling of self-efficacy, in turn, makes these people feel that they are capable of being leaders. These traits then influence such charismatic behaviors as role modeling, image building, articulating goals (focusing on simple and dramatic goals), emphasizing high expectations, showing confidence, and arousing follower motives.

Some of the more interesting and important work based on aspects of House's charismatic theory involves a study of U.S. presidents.[37] The research showed that behavioral charisma was substantially related to presidential performance and that the kind of personality traits in House's theory, along with response to crisis, among other things, predicted behavioral charisma for the sample of presidents. Related presidential work by others also shows that voters who saw Bill Clinton as charismatic followed through by voting for him.[38]

House and his colleagues summarize other work that partially supports the theory. Some of the more interesting related work has shown that negative, or "dark-side," charismatic leaders emphasize personalized power—focus on themselves—whereas positive, or "bright-side," charismatics emphasize socialized power that tends to empower their followers. This helps explain differences between such dark-side leaders as Adolf Hitler and David Koresh, and a bright-side Martin Luther King, Jr.[39]

Delphi ◄
www.delphiauto.com

Delphi Packard Electric Systems, a former General Motors subsidiary, is the world's leading supplier of automotive power and signal distribution systems. Its Brookhaven, Mississippi facility emphasizes self-led work teams to achieve world-class stature. The team leader is responsible for ten tasks ranging from conducting meetings to training his or her replacement.

Jay Conger and Rabindra Kanungo have developed a three-stage charismatic leadership model.[40] In the initial stage, the leader critically evaluates the status quo. Deficiencies in the status quo lead to formulations of future goals. Before developing these goals, the leader assesses available resources and constraints that stand in the way of the goals. The leader also assesses follower abilities, needs, and satisfaction levels. In the second stage, the leader formulates and articulates the goals along with an idealized future vision. Here the leader emphasizes articulation and impression management skills. Then in the third stage, the leader shows how these goals and the vision can be achieved. The leader emphasizes innovative and unusual means to achieve the vision. Martin Luther King, Jr. illustrated these three stages in his nonviolent civil rights approach, where he changed race relations in this country.

Conger and Kanungo have argued that if leaders use behaviors such as vision articulation, environmental sensitivity, and unconventional behavior, rather than maintaining the status quo, followers will attribute charismatic leadership to them. Such leaders are also seen as behaving quite differently from those labeled "noncharismatic."[41]

Finally, an especially important question about charismatic leadership is whether it is described in the same way for close-up or at-a-distance leaders. Boas Shamir recently examined this issue in Israel.[42] He found that descriptions

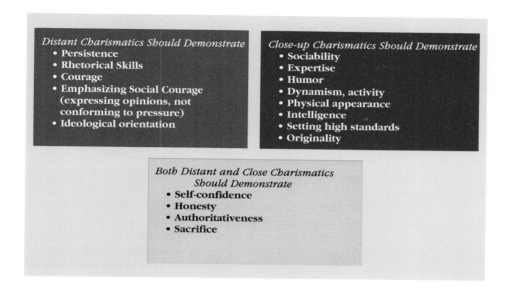

**Figure 14.6
Descriptions of
characteristics of
distant and close-up
charismatics.**

of distant charismatics, for instance, former Israeli prime minister Golda Meir, and close-up charismatics, for instance, a specific teacher, were generally more different than they were similar. Figure 14.6 shows the high points of his findings. Clearly, leaders with whom followers have close contact and those with whom they seldom, if ever, have direct contact are both described as charismatic but possess quite different traits and behaviors.

■ TRANSFORMATIONAL VERSUS TRANSACTIONAL APPROACHES

Building on notions originated by James MacGregor Burns, as well as ideas from House's work, Bernard Bass has developed an approach that focuses on both transformational and transactional leadership.[43]

Transactional leadership involves leader-follower exchanges necessary for achieving routine performance agreed upon between leaders and followers. These exchanges involve four dimensions as shown in The Effective Manager 14.1.

Transformational leadership goes beyond this routine accomplishment, however. For Bass, **transformational leadership** occurs when leaders broaden and elevate their follower's interests, when they generate awareness and acceptance of the group's purposes and mission, and when they stir their followers to look beyond their own self-interests for the good of others.

Dimensions of Transformational Leadership
Transformational leadership has four dimensions: charisma, inspiration, intellectual stimulation, and individualized consideration. *Charisma* provides vision and a sense of mission, and it instills pride, along

■ **Transactional leadership** involves leader-follower exchanges necessary for achieving routine performance agreed upon between leaders and followers.

■ **Transformational leadership** occurs when leaders broaden and elevate followers' interests and stir followers to look beyond their own interests for the good of others.

THE EFFECTIVE MANAGER 14.1

FOUR DIMENSIONS OF TRANSACTIONAL LEADERSHIP

- Contingent rewards: Providing various kinds of rewards in exchange for mutually agreed upon goal accomplishment.
- Active management by exception: Watching for deviations from rules and standards and taking corrective action.
- Passive management by exception: Intervening only if standards are not met.
- Laissez-faire: Abdicating responsibilities and avoiding decisions.

with follower respect and trust. For example, Steve Jobs, who founded Apple Computer, showed charisma by emphasizing the importance of creating the Macintosh as a radical new computer. Inspiration communicates high expectations, uses symbols to focus efforts, and expresses important purposes in simple ways. For example, in the movie *Patton*, George C. Scott stood on a stage in front of his troops with a wall-sized American flag in the background and pearl-handled revolvers in holsters at his side. *Intellectual stimulation* promotes intelligence, rationality, and careful problem solving. For instance, your boss encourages you to look at a very difficult problem in a new way. *Individualized consideration* provides personal attention, treats each employee individually, and coaches and advises. For example, your boss drops by and makes remarks reinforcing your worth as a person.

Bass concludes that transformational leadership is likely to be strongest at the top-management level, where there is the greatest opportunity for proposing and communicating a vision. However, it is not *restricted* to the top level; it is found throughout the organization. Furthermore, transformational leadership operates *in combination with* transactional leadership. Transactional leadership is similar to most of the traditional leadership approaches mentioned earlier. Leaders need both transformational and transactional leadership in order to be successful, just as they need both leadership and management.[44]

www.dell.com

💻 TECHNOLOGY

In the 15 years since Michael Dell began selling computers from his University of Texas dorm room, his company has grown to an $18 billion-a-year business. Dell's driving vision has been to eliminate the middleman and sell PCs directly to customers. "Our only religion is the direct model," says Kevin Rollins, vice-chair of the board. Being direct has allowed Dell to crack the huge Chinese government market. Michael Dell expects that eventually 50 percent of the firm's sales will be on the Internet and that Internet technology "is the ultimate direct model."

Evaluation and Application Some of extensive reviews have summarized a large number of studies using Bass's approach. These reviews report significant favorable relationships between Bass's leadership dimensions and various aspects of performance and satisfaction, as well as extra effort, burnout and stress, and predispositions to act as innovation champions on the part of followers. The strongest relationships tend to be associated with charisma or inspirational leadership, although, in most cases, the other dimensions are also important. These findings are consistent with those reported elsewhere.[45] They broaden leadership outcomes beyond those cited in traditional leadership studies.

■ LEADERSHIP IN HIGH PERFORMANCE WORK TEAMS

The leadership approaches discussed in this chapter apply to all organizations as appropriate.[46] However, given our emphasis on high performance organizations, we must specifically examine how such leadership operates in self-directing or self-leading work teams. As we have shown in earlier chapters, the workers in these self-directing work teams manage or lead the team themselves. The question then is, do they have a leader from outside? The answer is yes, but what the leader does is quite different from what a traditional supervisor does. Indeed, even the title is different—a widely used one is "coordinator," although "facilitator" is not uncommon.

Among the key leadership behaviors by coordinators are those in Figure 14.7. These behaviors focus on coordinator encouragements, and the team activities show the specific actions involved in meeting the coordinator's expectations. Even if team members do carry out the team activities encouraged by the coordinator, how much difference does it make? One study showed that perceived coordinator encouragement of the team self-leadership activities was positively related to coordinator effectiveness. Another study showed that coordinator leader behavior predicted positive team performance and various aspects of satisfaction.[47] So these leader behaviors do seem to be important.

Take another look at the figure. Notice that while these behaviors are important, they focus on self-leadership activities. They do not examine other leader-

COORDINATOR BEHAVIOR	ACTIVITIES INVOLVED IN COORDINATOR TEAM ENCOURAGEMENTS*
Encourages rehearsal Work team goes over an activity and "thinks it through" before actually performing the activity	• Go over activity • Practice new task • Go over new task • Think about how to do a job
Encourages self-goal setting Work team sets performance goals	• Define team goals • Define own goals • Establish task goals • Set team perfomance goals
Encourages self-criticism Work team self-critical of low team performance	• Be critical of ourselves • Be tough on ourselves • Be self-critical • Be critical when we do poorly
Encourages self-reinforcement Work team self-reinforcing of high team performance	• Praise each other • Feel positive about ourselves • Praise each other for a good job • Feel good about ourselves
Encourages self-expectation Work team has high expectations for team performance	• Think we can do very well • Expect high performance • Expect a lot from ourselves
Encourages self-observation/evaluation Work team monitors, is aware of, and evaluates levels of performance	• Be aware of performance level • Know how our performance stands • Judge how well we are performing

*These activities were specifically described in a questionnaire, and some of the questions were designed to be very similar to increase the reliability of the questionnaire.

Figure 14.7
Sample leader behaviors for high performance work teams.

OB Across Functions

PRODUCTION

Production Module Leaders Handle Shop Floor Complexity

John Deere and Company, the world's largest maker of farm machinery, produces seed planters in 45 models, with 1.7 million options. Dealing with this complexity involved instituting a process flow, moving machines closer together, and reorganizing the work into 12 modules, each responsible for building particular subassemblies and attaching them to planter frames. To help leaders and workers cope with the immensely complex tasks involved, Deere provides them with information on everything from assembly schedules to quality control. As much as possible, Deere distributes authority to where information and incentives currently reside. Module leaders thus have the information needed to control their own budgets, including staffing, overtime, maintenance, and other functions. Therefore, module leaders and team members can plan ahead and deal with the many issues in their own module and elsewhere on the line. For example, if there is a quality problem as a planter rolls past an assembler's module, the assembler fixes it or finds the person responsible, regardless of the person's job and gets it fixed. *www.Deere.com*

ship functions such as managing resources and boundary spanning with other units. In other words, they emphasize the social system and not the technical system. Indeed, Manz and Sims[48] suggest that the coordinator, outside the group, has the fundamental responsibility to get the team to lead itself and thus emphasizes various team self-leadership behaviors. In contrast, these authors argue that the team leader within the team serves as an additional member who facilitates the team's organizing itself, coordinating job assignments and making sure resources are available. A second set of authors points out that even though coordinator self-leadership encouragement was related to team effectiveness and satisfaction, the relationship probably would have been much stronger if these other kinds of leadership dimensions had been included, in addition to the self-leadership ones.[49]

To conclude, note two other considerations. First, these self-leadership activities from the team members themselves can be considered a partial substitute for hierarchical leadership, even though the coordinator encourages them. For example, members praise each other rather than looking to the coordinator for praise. As we have shown previously, such behaviors are becoming increasingly important in high-performance organizations.

Second, although these behaviors provide a lot of participation from team members, they do not appear to be particularly charismatic. They should work best when combined with the kinds of resource and coordination behaviors mentioned above and when reinforced by new leadership from bright-side leaders higher up in the organization.

■ NEW LEADERSHIP ISSUES

In addition to contrasting the core themes of traditional and new leadership in high performance environments, it is important to examine a number of issues concerning the role of new leadership in the workplace. First, *can people be trained in new leadership?* According to research in this area, the answer is yes. Bass and his colleagues have put a lot of work into such training efforts. For example, they have created a workshop where leaders are given initial feedback on their scores on Bass's measures. The leaders then devise improvement programs to strengthen their weaknesses and work with the trainers to develop their leadership skills. Bass and Bass and Avolio report findings that demonstrate the beneficial effects of this training. They also report team training and programs tailored to individual firms' needs.[50] Similarly, Conger and Kanungo propose training to develop the kinds of behaviors summarized in their model as suggested in The Effective Manager 14.2.[51]

Approaches with special emphasis on vision often emphasize training. Kouzas and Posner report results of a week-long training program at AT&T. The program involved training leaders on five dimensions oriented around developing, communicating, and reinforcing a shared vision. According to Kouzas and Posner, leaders showed an average 15 percent increase in these visionary behaviors 10 months after participating in the program.[52] Similarly, Sashkin has developed a leadership approach that emphasizes various aspects of vision and organizational culture change. Sashkin discusses a number of ways to train leaders to be more visionary and to enhance the culture change.[53] All of the new leadership training programs involve a heavy hands-on workshop emphasis so that leaders do more than just read about vision.

A second issue involves the question—*is new leadership always good?* As we pointed out earlier, dark-side charismatics, such as Adolf Hitler, can have negative effects on the population of followers. Similarly, new leadership is not always needed. Sometimes emphasis on a vision diverts energy from more important day-to-day activities. It is also important to note that new leadership by itself is not sufficient. New leadership needs to be used in conjunction with traditional leadership. Finally, new leadership is not important only at the top. A number of experts argue that it applies at all levels of organizational leadership.

THE EFFECTIVE MANAGER 14.2

FIVE CHARISMATIC SKILLS

- Sensitivity to most appropriate contexts for charisma—Emphasis on critical evaluation and problem detection
- Visioning—Emphasis on creative thinking to learn and think about profound change
- Communication—Working with oral and written linguistic aspects
- Impression management—Emphasis on modeling, appearance, body language, and verbal skills
- Empowering—Emphasis on communicating high performance expectations, improving participation in decision making, loosening up bureaucratic constraints, setting meaningful goals, and establishing appropriate reward systems

---

Chapter 14 Study Guide

Summary

What is leadership, and how does it differ from management?

- Leadership is a special case of interpersonal influence that gets an individual or group to do what the leader wants done.

- Leadership and management differ in that management is designed to promote stability or to make the organization run smoothly, whereas the role of leadership is to promote adaptive change.

What are the trait and behavioral leadership perspectives?

- Trait, or great person, approaches argue that leader traits have a major impact on differentiating between leaders and nonleaders and predicting leadership outcomes.

- Traits are considered relatively innate and hard to change.

- Similar to trait approaches, behavioral theories argue that leader behaviors have a major impact on outcomes.

- The Michigan, Ohio State, and Graen's Leader–Member Exchange (LMX) approaches are particularly important leader behavior theories.

- Leader behavior theories are especially suitable for leadership training.

What are the situational or contingency leadership approaches?

- Leader situational contingency approaches argue that leadership, in combination with various situational contingency variables, can have a major impact on outcomes.

- The effects of traits are enhanced to the extent of their relevance to the situational contingencies faced by the leader.

- Strong or weak situational contingencies influence the impact of leadership traits.

- Fiedler's contingency theory, House's path–goal theory, Hersey and Blanchard's situational leadership theory, and Kerr and Jermier's substitutes for leadership theory are particularly important, specific situational contingency approaches.

- Sometimes, as in the case of the substitutes for leadership approach, the role of the situational contingencies replaces that of leadership so that leadership has little or no impact in itself.

How does attribution theory relate to leadership?

- Attribution theory extends traditional leadership approaches by recognizing that substantive effects cannot always be objectively identified and measured.

- Leaders form attributions about why their employees perform well or poorly and respond accordingly.

- Leaders and followers often infer that there is good leadership when their group performs well.

- Leaders and followers often have in mind a good leader prototype, compare the leader against such a prototype, and conclude that the closer the fit the better the leadership.

- Some contend that leadership makes no real difference and is largely symbolic; others, following the "romance of leadership" notion, embrace this symbolic emphasis and attribute almost magical qualities to leadership.

What new leadership perspectives are evident in high performance organizations?

- The new leadership consists of charismatic, visionary, transformational, and related perspectives, according to which followers tend to attribute extraordinary leadership abilities to a leader when they observe certain behaviors.

- These attributions then help transform followers to achieve goals that transcend their own self-interests and help transform the organization.

- Particularly important new leadership perspectives are Bass's transformational theory and House's and Conger and Kanungo's charismatic approaches.

- Transformational approaches are broader than charismatic ones and often include charisma as one of their dimensions.

- Leadership in self-leading teams, involved in high performing organizations, changes the external leadership role by making it a facilitative one to encourage team members to lead themselves.

- Behaviors of team coordinators are assumed to work best when reinforced by leaders who provide empowerment and stress various aspects of the new leadership.

- The new leadership, in general, is important because it goes beyond traditional leadership in facilitating change in the increasingly fast-moving and high performance workplace.

Key Terms

Achievement-oriented leadership (p. 293)

Behavioral perspective (p. 288)

Charismatic leaders (p. 300)

Consideration (p. 289)

Directive leadership (p. 293)

House's path-goal theory of leadership (p. 293)

Initiating structure (p. 289)

Leader match training (p. 293)

Leadership (p. 286)

Leadership prototype (p. 298)

Least preferred co-worker (LPC) scale (p. 291)

New leadership (p. 299)

Participative leadership (p. 294)

Romance of leadership (p. 299)

Situational control (p. 291)

Substitutes for leadership (p. 297)

Supportive leadership (p. 293)

Trait perspectives (p. 287)

Transactional leadership (p. 301)

Transformational leadership (p. 301)

■ MULTIPLE CHOICE

Self Test 14

1. "Leadership is central, and other variables are less important," best describes _____ theories. (a) trait and behavioral (b) attribution (c) situational contingency (d) substitutes for leadership

2. Leader trait and behavioral approaches assume that traits and behaviors are _____. (a) equally important with other variables (b) more important than other variables (c) caused by other variables (d) symbolic of leadership

3. In comparing leadership and management, _____. (a) leadership promotes stability, management promotes change (b) leadership promotes change, management promotes stability (c) leaders are born but managers are developed (d) the two are pretty much the same

4. The earliest theory of leadership stated that individuals become leaders by _____. (a) the behavior of those they lead (b) the traits they possess (c) the particular situation in which they find themselves (d) being very tall

5. In Fiedler's contingency theory, the three situational control variables are leader–member relations, task structure, and _____. (a) command power (b) position power (c) discretionary power (d) complexity

6. Which leadership theory argues that a leader's key function is to act in ways that complement the work setting? (a) trait (b) behavioral (c) path-goal (d) multiple influence

7. A leadership prototype _____. (a) is useful primarily for selection and training (b) uses LPC as an important component (c) depicts the image of a model leader (d) emphasizes leadership skills

8. Conger and Kanungo's model emphasizes all of the following except _____. (a) active management by exception (b) vision articulation (c) environmental sensitivity (d) unconventional behavior

9. Leadership of self-leading teams _____. (a) emphasizes charisma (b) emphasizes team-member empowerment (c) emphasizes leader traits (d) has been replaced by technology

10. Leadership of high performing organizations _____. (a) uses traditional, new and self-leading perspectives (b) uses only a self-leading perspective (c) has largely been replaced (d) is very autocratic

■ TRUE–FALSE

11. The earliest studies of leadership tended to focus on leader behaviors.   T   F

12. Leadership and management usually are considered the same.   T   F

13. The University of Michigan studies concluded that employee-centered leaders tended to have more productive work groups.   T   F

14. Hersey and Blanchard's situational leadership theory focuses on the maturity or readiness of the followers.   T   F

15. Neutralizers prevent a leader from behaving in a certain way or nullify the effects of a leader's actions.   T   F

16. In the romance of leadership, it is argued that leaders are unimportant.   T   F

17. Transformational leadership acts in combination with transactional leadership.   T   F

18. Charismatic and transformational leadership are part of the "new leadership."   T   F

19. Team coordinators and team leaders each perform the same functions.   T   F

20. Leadership of self-leading teams emphasizes charisma in the team.   T   F

■ SHORT RESPONSE

21. Define leadership and contrast it with management.

22. Discuss the role of leader trait and behavior approaches in leadership.

23. Discuss the role of situational contingency approaches in leadership.

24. Compare and contrast traditional leadership and the new leadership.

■ APPLICATION ESSAY

25. You have just been called in as a consultant to analyze the role of leadership in the corporation in the chapter opener and suggest ways to develop it further. Making any necessary assumptions, discuss how you would handle this assignment.

Explore application-oriented Fast Company articles, cases, experimental exercises, and self-assessments in the OB Skills Workbook

■ **Visit the Schermerhorn Web site to find the Interactive Self-Test and Internet exercises for this chapter.**

Power and Politics

THE ADVANTAGES OF EMPOWERMENT

www.microsoft.com

Microsoft founder and billionaire Bill Gates has been continuously able to build the sales and profitability of his company through practical empowerment and coalition development with other firms.[1] Perhaps Bill has done too well. Microsoft's DOS operating system was used in 95 percent of the personal computers built in the 1980s. Developed in conjunction with Intel's computer chips, the combination was so successful it has been called Wintel. In the 1990s and again with Intel, Microsoft's Windows was a smash hit. With other new innovative products, Microsoft's growth seemed unstoppable. Gates is and has been able to empower his researchers and product managers by arranging them in small task-oriented groups.

Microsoft's leadership has found that by eliminating bureaucracy, new products can make it from concep-tion to production much more quickly. As a result, Microsoft is now able to develop its products significantly faster than can its competitors. According to Gates, "Big groups of programmers often create bad software more slowly than small ones who make good software."

In 1998, however, the U.S. government, and a few competitors for a program that allowed users to reach the Internet (called a browser) accused Microsoft of anticompetitive practices. In addition to quick quality development, they accused Microsoft of using its dominant position in the market to force PC makers to adopt the Microsoft browser rather than one made by Netscape. Until Microsoft linked its browser to the Windows operating system, Netscape had dominated the market. With the incorporation of the browser, Netscape sales dropped in the face of Microsoft's power.[1]

ndividuals rarely join a corporation simply to work for the organization's stated goals. They join for their own reasons to meet their own goals. As individuals vie for their own interests in a hierarchical setting, analyses of power and politics are a key to understanding the behavior of individuals within organizations. Yet, managers find there are never enough resources, either money, people, time, or authority to get things done. They see a power gap.[2] As discussed throughout this chapter, power and politics have two sides. On the one hand, power and politics represent the seamy side of management, since organizations are not democracies composed of individuals with equal influence. On the other hand, power and politics are important organizational tools that managers must use to get the job done. In effective organizations, power is delicately developed, nurtured, and managed by astute individuals. Politics is always infused into the organization. Yet it is possible to isolate many instances where individual and organizational interests are compatible. The astute manager knows how to find these opportunities.[3]

Study Questions

Analysis of power and politics is crucial to understanding the roles of individuals in organizations. As you read Chapter 15 keep in mind these study questions.

- What is power?
- How do managers acquire the power needed for leadership?
- What is empowerment, and how can managers empower others?
- What are organizational politics?
- How does organizational politics affect managers and management?

Power

In OB, **power** is defined as the ability to get someone to do something you want done or the ability to make things happen in the way you want them to. In Chapter 14 we examined leadership as a key power mechanism to make things happen. Now it is time to discusses other ways. The essence of power is control over the behavior of others.[4] Power is the force you use to make things happen in an intended way, whereas **influence** is what you have when you exercise power, and it is expressed by others' behavioral response to your exercise of power. Managers derive power from both organizational and individual sources. These sources are called *position power* and *personal power*, respectively.[5]

■ POSITION POWER

Three bases of power are available to a manager solely as a result of his or her position in the organization: reward, coercive, and legitimate power.

Reward power is the extent to which a manager can use extrinsic and intrinsic rewards to control other people. Examples of such rewards include money, promotions, compliments, or enriched jobs. Although all managers have some access to rewards, success in accessing and utilizing rewards to achieve influence varies according to the skills of the manager.

Power can also be founded on punishment instead of reward. For example, a manager may threaten to withhold a pay raise, or to transfer, demote, or even recommend the firing of a subordinate who does not act as desired. Such **coercive power** is the extent to which a manager can deny desired rewards or administer punishments to control other people. The availability of coercive power also varies from one organization and manager to another. The presence of unions and organizational policies on employee treatment can weaken this power base considerably.

The third base of "position" power is **legitimate power**, or formal authority. It stems from the extent to which a manager can use subordinates' internalized values or beliefs that the "boss" has a "right of command" to control their behavior. For example, the boss may have the formal authority to approve or deny such employee requests as job transfers, equipment purchases, personal time off, or overtime work. Legitimate power represents a special kind of power a manager has because subordinates believe it is legitimate for a person occupying the managerial position to have the right to command. If this legitimacy is lost, authority will not be accepted by subordinates. Since legitimate power is multifaceted and much of it may be "latent," some additional discussion is required.

One of the most important aspects of legitimacy is the access to and control of information. Indeed, some observers believe that information power should be listed as a separate source of power. In most organizations, the "right" to know and use information is restricted and confined by a series of rules and regulations. For instance, in most firms an individual's pay is not broadly known, nor are engineering drawings typically allowed outside engineering. Marketing plans may be "top secret," as is the latest evaluation of the boss. The nominal reason for controlling information is to protect the firm. The real reason is often to allow information holders to increase their power.

■ **Power** is the ability to get someone else to do something you want done or the ability to make things happen or get things done the way you want.

■ **Influence** is a behavioral response to the exercise of power.

■ **Reward power** is the extent to which a manager can use extrinsic and intrinsic rewards to control other people.

■ **Coercive power** is the extent to which a manager can deny desired rewards or administer punishment to control other people.

■ **Legitimate power** or formal authority is the extent to which a manager can use the "right of command" to control other people.

Underpinning legitimacy in most organizations is an implicit moral and technical order. As we will note later in this chapter, from the crib to the school to the corporation to retirement, individuals in our society are taught to obey "higher authority." In U.S. firms, "higher authority" means those close to the top of the corporate pyramid. In other societies, "higher authority" does not have a bureaucratic or organizational reference but consists of those with moral authority such as tribal chiefs, religious leaders, and the like. In firms, the legitimacy of those at the top increasingly derives from their positions as representatives for various constituencies. This is a technical or instrumental role, but many senior executives evoke social causes in their role as authority figures.

■ PERSONAL POWER

Personal power resides in the individual and is independent of that individual's position. Personal power is important in many well-managed firms. Three bases of personal power are expertise, rational persuasion, and reference.

Expert power is the ability to control another person's behavior through the possession of knowledge, experience, or judgment that the other person does not have but needs. A subordinate obeys a supervisor possessing expert power because the boss ordinarily knows more about what is to be done or how it is to be done than does the subordinate. Expert power is relative, not absolute.

Rational persuasion is the ability to control another's behavior because through the individual's efforts, the person accepts the desirability of an offered goal and a reasonable way of achieving it. Much of what a supervisor does day to day involves rational persuasion up, down, and across the organization. Rational persuasion involves both explaining the desirability of expected outcomes and showing how specific actions will achieve these outcomes.

Referent power is the ability to control another's behavior because the person wants to identify with the power source. In this case, a subordinate obeys the boss because he or she wants to behave, perceive, or believe as the boss does. This obedience may occur, for example, because the subordinate likes the boss personally and therefore tries to do things the way the boss wants them done. In a sense, the subordinate attempts to avoid doing anything that would interfere with the pleasing boss–subordinate relationship. A person's referent power can be enhanced when the individual taps into the moral order or shows a clearer long-term path to a morally desirable end. In common language, individuals with the ability to tap into these more esoteric aspects of corporate life have "charisma" and "the vision thing." Followership is not based on what the subordinate will get for specific actions or specific levels of performance, but on what the individual represents—a path toward a loftier future.

■ ACQUIRING AND USING POWER AND INFLUENCE

A considerable portion of any manager's time is directed toward what is called *power-oriented behavior*. Power-oriented behavior is action directed primarily at developing or using relationships in which other people are to some degree willing to defer to one's wishes.[6] Figure 15.1 shows three basic dimensions of power and influence with which a manager will become involved in this regard: downward, upward, and lateral. Also shown in the figure are some preliminary ideas for achieving success along each of these dimensions.

Margin notes

■ **Expert power** is the ability to control another's behavior because of the possession of knowledge, experience, or judgment that the other person does not have but needs.

■ **Rational persuasion** is the ability to control another's behavior because through the individual's efforts, the person accepts the desirability of an offered goal and a reasonable way of achieving it.

■ **Referent power** is the ability to control another's behavior because of the individual's desire to identify with the power source.

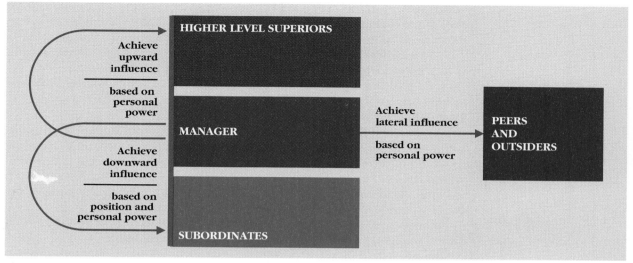

Figure 15.1
Three dimensions of managerial power and influence.

The effective manager is one who succeeds in building and maintaining high levels of both position and personal power over time. Only then is sufficient power of the right types available when the manager needs to exercise influence on downward, lateral, and upward dimensions.

Building Position Power Position power can be enhanced when managers are able to demonstrate to others that their work units are highly relevant to organizational goals and are able to respond to urgent organizational needs. To increase centrality and criticality in the organization, managers may seek to acquire a more central role in the work flow by having information filtered through them, making at least part of their job responsibilities unique, expanding their network of communication contacts, and occupying an office convenient to main traffic flows.

Managers may also attempt to increase the relevance of their tasks and those of their unit to the organization. There are many ways to do this. Executives may attempt to become an internal coordinator within the firm or external representative. They may suggest their subordinates take on these roles, particularly when the firm is downsizing. When the firm is in a dynamic setting of changing technology, the executive may also move to provide unique services and information to other units. This is particularly effective if the executive moves his unit into becoming involved with decisions central to the organization's top-priority goals. To expand their position, managers may also delegate routine activities, expand the task variety and novelty for subordinates, initiate new ideas, and get involved in new projects. We will have more to say about this matter when discussing empowerment.

There are also ways managers attempt to build influence that may or may not have a positive effect on the organization. Managers may attempt to define tasks so that they are difficult to evaluate, such as by creating an ambiguous job description or developing a unique language for their work.

Building Personal Power   Personal power arises from the personal characteristics of the manager rather than from the location and other characteristics of his or her position in the organization's hierarchy of authority.

Three personal characteristics, expertise, political savvy, and likability, have special potential for enhancing personal power in an organization. The most obvious is *building expertise*. Additional expertise may be gained by advanced training and education, participation in professional associations, and involvement in the early stages of projects.

A somewhat less obvious way to increase personal power is to learn *political savvy*—better ways to negotiate, persuade individuals, and understand the goals and means they are most willing to accept. The novice believes that most individuals are very much the same, see the same goals, and will accept much the same paths toward these goals. The more astute individual recognizes important individual differences.

A manager's reference power is increased by characteristics that enhance his or her "*likability*" and create personal attraction in relationships with other people. These include pleasant personality characteristics, agreeable behavior patterns, and attractive personal appearance. The demonstration of sincere hard work on behalf of task performance can also increase personal power by enhancing both expertise and reference. A person who is perceived to try hard may be expected to know more about the job and thus be sought out for advice. A person who tries hard is also likely to be respected for the attempt and may even be depended on by others to maintain that effort.

www.cybex.com

⊕ GLOBALIZATION

Doyle Weeks has a new position at Cybex Computer Products Corporation. Cybex manufactures and markets products for computers that boost, split, or switch the signals between the CPU (central processing units) and the keyboard, video monitor, and mouse for IBM and compatible computers, the Apple Macintosh, and related equipment. For instance, using Cybex equipment, individuals on hooked-up computers can examine each other's screens without special software or expensive licenses. Stephen F. Thronton, CEO, in announcing the promotion of Doyle C. Weeks to the newly created position of Executive Vice President, Group Operations and Business Development, cited Doyle's critical role in "directing our international expansion." Unsaid, but recognized by both market analysts and key individuals within the firm, was the five-year average growth of 42 percent for the firm, much of it outside the United States.

Combined Building of Position and Personal Power   From a purely analytical standpoint, most sources of power can be traced to position power or personal power. However, many of the influential actions and behaviors are combinations of position and personal power.

Most managers attempt to increase the visibility of their job performance by (1) expanding the number of contacts they have with senior people, (2) making oral presentations of written work, (3) participating in problem-solving task forces, (4) sending out notices of accomplishment, and (5) generally seeking additional opportunities to increase personal name recognition. Most managers also recognize that, between superiors and subordinates, access to or control over information is an important element. A boss may appear to expand his or her expert power over a subordinate by not allowing the individual access to critical information. Although the denial may appear to enhance the boss's expert power, it may reduce the subordinate's effectiveness. In a similar manner a supervisor may also control access to key organizational decision makers. An individual's ability to contact key persons informally can offset some of this disadvantage. Furthermore, astute senior executives routinely develop "back channels" to lower-level individuals deep within the firm to offset the tendency of bosses to control information and access.

Expert power is often relational and embedded within the organizational context. Many important decisions are made outside formal channels and are substantially influenced by key individuals with the requisite knowledge. By developing and using coalitions and networks, an individual may build on their expert power. Though coalitions and networks, an individual may alter the flow of information and the context for analysis. By developing coalitions and networks, executives also expand their access to information and their opportunities for participation.

Executives also attempt to control, or at least influence, decision premises. A decision premise is a basis for defining the problem and for selecting among alternatives. By defining a problem in a manner that fits the executive's expertise, it is natural for that executive to be in charge of solving it. Thus, the executive subtly shifts his or her position power.

Executives who want to increase their power often make their goals and needs clear and bargain effectively to show that their preferred goals and needs are best. They do not show their power base directly but instead provide clear "rational persuasion" for their preferences. So the astute executive does not threaten or attempt to evoke sanctions to build power. Instead, he or she combines personal power with the position of the unit to enhance total power. As the organizational context changes, different personal sources of power may become more important alone and in combination with the individual's position power. So there is an art to building power.

■ TURNING POWER INTO RELATIONAL INFLUENCE

Using position and personal power well to achieve the desired influence over other people is a challenge for most managers. Practically speaking, there are many useful ways of exercising relational influence. The most common strategies involve the following:[7]

Reason	Using facts and data to support a logical argument.
Friendliness	Using flattery, goodwill, and favorable impressions.
Coalition	Using relationships with other people for support.
Bargaining	Using the exchange of benefits as a basis for negotiation.
Assertiveness	Using a direct and forceful personal approach.
Higher authority	Gaining higher level support for one's requests.
Sanctions	Using organizationally derived rewards and punishments.

Strategies for exercising influence

Research on these strategies suggests that reason is the most popular strategy overall.[8] In addition, friendliness, assertiveness, bargaining, and higher authority are used more frequently to influence subordinates than to influence supervisors. This pattern of influence attempts is consistent with our earlier contention that downward influence generally includes mobilization of both position and personal power sources, whereas upward influence is more likely to draw on personal power.

Little research is available on the subject of upward influence in organizations. This is unfortunate, since truly effective managers are able to influence their bosses as well as their subordinates. One study reports that both supervisors and subordinates view reason, or the logical presentation of ideas, as the most frequently used strategy of upward influence.[9] When queried on reasons for success and failure, however, the viewpoints of the two groups show both similarities and differences. The perceived causes of success in upward influence are similar for both supervisors and subordinates and involve the favorable content of the influence attempt, a favorable manner of its presentation, and the competence of the subordinate.[10] The two groups disagree on the causes of failure, however. Subordinates attribute failure in upward influence to the close-mindedness of the supervisor, unfavorable content of the influence attempt, and unfavorable interpersonal relationships with the supervisor. In contrast, supervisors attribute failure to the unfavorable content of the attempt, the unfavorable manner in which it was presented, and the subordinate's lack of competence.

■ POWER, FORMAL AUTHORITY, AND OBEDIENCE

As we have shown, power is the potential to control the behavior of others, and formal authority is the potential to exert such control through the legitimacy of a managerial position. Yet, we also know that people who seem to have power don't always get their way. Why do some people obey directives and others do not? More specifically, why should subordinates respond to a manager's authority, or "right to command," in the first place? Furthermore, given that subordinates are willing to obey, what determines the limits of obedience?

The Milgram Experiments The mythology of American independence and unbridled individualism is so strong we need to spend some time explaining how most of us are really quite obedient. So we turn to the seminal studies of Stanley Milgram on obedience.[11] Milgram designed experiments to determine the extent to which people obey the commands of an authority figure, even if they believe they are endangering the life of another person. Subjects, ranging in age from 20 to 50 and representing a diverse set of occupations (engineers, salespeople, schoolteachers, laborers, and others), were paid a nominal fee for participation in the project.

The subjects were falsely told that the purpose of the study was to determine the effects of punishment on learning. The subjects were to be the "teachers." The "learner" was a confederate of Milgram's, who was strapped to a chair in an adjoining room with an electrode attached to his wrist. The "experimenter," another confederate of Milgram's, was dressed in a gray laboratory coat. Appearing impassive and somewhat stern, the experimenter instructed the "teacher" to read a series of word pairs to the "learner" and then to reread the first word along with four other terms. The learner was supposed to indicate which of the four terms was in the original pair by pressing a switch that caused a light to flash on a response panel in front of the teacher.

The teacher was instructed to administer a shock to the learner each time a wrong answer was given. This shock was to be increased one level of intensity each time the learner made a mistake. The teacher controlled switches that ostensibly administered shocks ranging from 15 to 450 volts. In reality, there was no electric current in the apparatus, but the learners purposely "erred" often and responded to each level of "shock" in progressively distressing ways. If a "teacher" (subject) proved unwilling to administer a shock, the experimenter used the following sequential prods to get him or her to perform as requested: (1) "Please continue" or "Please go on"; (2) "The experiment requires that you continue"; (3) "It is absolutely essential that you continue"; and (4) "You have no choice, you must go on." Only when the "teacher" refused to go on after the fourth prod would the experiment be stopped. When would you expect the "teachers" to refuse to go on?

Milgram asked some of his students and colleagues the same question. Most felt that few, if any, of the subjects would go beyond the "very strong shock" level. Actually, 26 subjects (65 percent) continued to the end of the experiment and shocked the "learners" to the maximum. None stopped before 300 volts, the point at which the learner pounded on the wall. The remaining 14 subjects refused to obey the experimenter at various intermediate points.

Most people are surprised by these results, as was Milgram. The question is why other people would have a tendency to accept or comply with authoritative commands under such extreme conditions. Milgram conducted further experiments to try to answer this question. The subjects' tendencies toward compliance were somewhat reduced (1) when experimentation took place in a rundown office (rather than a university lab), (2) when the victim was closer, (3) when the experimenter was farther away, and (4) when the subject could observe other subjects. However, the level of compliance was still much higher than most of us would expect.

What does this mean for empowerment? Note the tendency for individuals to comply and be obedient—to switch off and merely do exactly what they are told to do. In many firms, employees are hired to be obedient; they are rewarded for being so, and they feel alienated when others seek to "empower them."

Obedience and the Acceptance of Authority

Direct defiance within organizational settings is quite rare, as is the individual who institutes new and different ways to get the job done. If the tendency to follow instructions is great and defiance is rare, then why do so many organizations appear to drift into apparent chaos?

The answer to this question can be found in work by the famous management writer Chester Barnard.[12] Barnard's argument focused on the "consent of the governed" rather than on the rights derived from ownership. He argued that subordinates accepted or followed a directive from the boss only under special circumstances.

All four of these circumstances must be met: (1) the subordinate can and must understand the directive; (2) the subordinate must feel mentally and physi-

cally capable of carrying out the directive; (3) the subordinate must believe that the directive is not inconsistent with the purpose of the organization; and (4) the subordinate must believe that the directive is not inconsistent with his or her personal interests.

These four conditions are very carefully stated. For instance, to accept and follow an order, the subordinate does not need to understand how the proposed action will help the organization. He or she only needs to believe that the requested action is not inconsistent with the purpose of the firm. The astute manager will not take these guidelines for granted. In giving directives, the astute manager recognizes that the acceptance of the request is not assured. When seeking empowerment, two of the biggest problems are embodied in Barnard's work. First, few employees understand what they are to do when a boss says they are empowered. They just do not understand what is to be done or what is to be accomplished. Second, many employees are deeply suspicious of management and need to know why empowerment is better for them or at least not inconsistent with their own interests. Continual lauding of the importance of empowerment for the firm does not satisfy this important factor.

Obedience and the Zone of Indifference   Most people seek a balance between what they put into an organization (contributions) and what they get from an organization in return (inducements). Within the boundaries of the psychological contract, therefore, employees will agree to do many things in and for the organization because they think they should. In exchange for certain inducements, subordinates recognize the authority of the organization and its managers to direct their behavior in certain ways. Based on his acceptance view of authority, Chester Barnard calls this area in which directions are obeyed the "zone of indifference."[13]

A **zone of indifference** is the range of authoritative requests to which a subordinate is willing to respond without subjecting the directives to critical evaluation or judgment. Directives falling within the zone are obeyed. Requests or orders falling outside the zone of indifference are not considered legitimate under terms of the psychological contract. Such "extraordinary" directives may or may not be obeyed. This link between the zone of indifference and the psychological contract is shown in Figure 15.2.

The zone of indifference is not fixed. There may be times when a boss would like a subordinate to do things falling outside the zone. In this case, the manager must enlarge the zone to accommodate additional behaviors. In these attempts, a manager most likely will have to use more incentives than pure position power. In some instances, no power base may be capable of accomplishing the desired result. Consider your own zone of indifference and tendency to obey. When will you say "No" to your boss? When should you be willing to say "No"? At times, the situation may involve ethical dilemmas, where you may be asked to do things that are illegal, unethical, or both.

Research on ethical managerial behavior shows that supervisors can become sources of pressure for subordinates to do such things as support incorrect viewpoints, sign false documents, overlook the supervisor's wrongdoing, and do business with the supervisor's friends.[14] Most of us will occasionally face such ethical dilemmas during our careers. For now, we must simply remember that saying "No" or "refusing to keep quiet" can be difficult and potentially costly.

■ A **zone of indifference** is the range of authoritative requests to which a subordinate is willing to respond without subjecting the directives to critical evaluation or judgment.

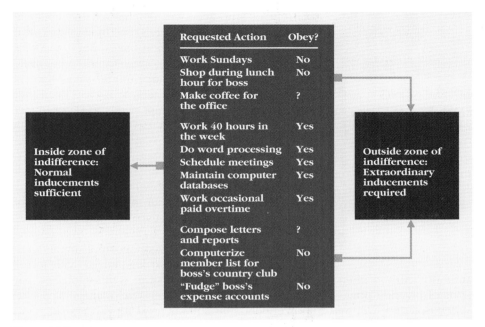

Requested Action	Obey?
Work Sundays	No
Shop during lunch hour for boss	No
Make coffee for the office	?
Work 40 hours in the week	Yes
Do word processing	Yes
Schedule meetings	Yes
Maintain computer databases	Yes
Work occasional paid overtime	Yes
Compose letters and reports	?
Computerize member list for boss's country club	No
"Fudge" boss's expense accounts	No

Inside zone of indifference: Normal inducements sufficient

Outside zone of indifference: Extraordinary inducements required

Figure 15.2
Hypothetical psychological contract for a secretary.

Empowerment

Empowerment is the process by which managers help others to acquire and use the power needed to make decisions affecting themselves and their work. More than ever before, managers in progressive organizations are expected to be good at (and highly comfortable with) empowering the people with whom they work. Rather than considering power to be something to be held only at higher levels in the traditional "pyramid" of organizations, this view considers power to be something that can be shared by everyone working in flatter and more collegial structures.

The concept of empowerment is part of the sweeping change being witnessed in today's corporations. Corporate staff is being cut back; layers of management are being eliminated; the number of employees is being reduced as the volume of work increases. What is left is a leaner and trimmer organization staffed by fewer managers who must share more power as they go about their daily tasks. Indeed, empowerment is a key foundation of the increasingly popular self-managing work teams and other creative worker involvement groups.

■ THE POWER KEYS TO EMPOWERMENT

One of the bases for empowerment is a radically different view of power itself. So far, our discussion has focused on power that is exerted over other individuals. In this traditional view, power is relational in terms of individuals. In contrast, the

■ **Empowerment** is the process by which managers help others to acquire and use the power needed to make decisions affecting themselves and their work.

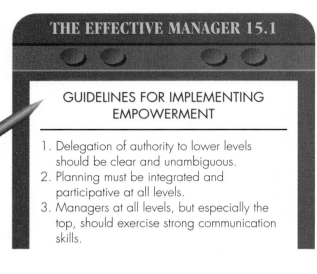

GUIDELINES FOR IMPLEMENTING EMPOWERMENT

1. Delegation of authority to lower levels should be clear and unambiguous.
2. Planning must be integrated and participative at all levels.
3. Managers at all levels, but especially the top, should exercise strong communication skills.

concept of empowerment emphasizes the ability to make things happen. Power is still relational, but in terms of problems and opportunities, not individuals. Cutting through all the corporate rhetoric on empowerment is quite difficult, since the term has become quite fashionable in management circles. Each individual empowerment attempt needs to be examined in light of how power in the organization will be changed (see The Effective Manager 15.1).

Changing Position Power   When an organization attempts to move power down the hierarchy, it must also alter the existing pattern of position power. Changing this pattern raises some important questions. Can "empowered" individuals give rewards and sanctions based on task accomplishment? Has their new right to act been legitimized with formal authority? All too often, attempts at empowerment disrupt well-established patterns of position power and threaten middle and lower level managers. As one supervisor said, "All this empowerment stuff sounds great for top management. They don't have to run around trying to get the necessary clearances to implement the suggestions from my group. They never gave me the authority to make the changes, only the new job of asking for permission."

Expanding the Zone of Indifference   When embarking on an empowerment program, management needs to recognize the current zone of indifference and systematically move to expand it. All too often, management assumes that its directive for empowerment will be followed; management may fail to show precisely how empowerment will benefit the individuals involved, however. Management at Montgomery Ward, for example, told salesclerks that they were "empowered" to accept merchandise returns. At the same time, management cut full-time staff, hired more part-time salespeople at minimum wage, and refused to consider offering full benefits to part-time workers. Although management wanted salesclerks to do more work, they cut their staff's zone of indifference by reducing the level of inducements. Now, in many Montgomery Ward stores, all merchandise returns are processed in one central location under the direct supervision of the store manager.

■ POWER AS AN EXPANDING PIE

Along with empowerment, employees need to be trained to expand their power and their new influence potential. This is the most difficult task for managers and a difficult challenge for employees, for it often changes the dynamic between supervisors and subordinates. The key is to change the concept of power within the organization from a view that stresses power over others to one that emphasizes the use of power to get things done. Under the new definition of power, all employees can be more powerful.

A clearer definition of roles and responsibilities may help managers empower others. For instance, senior managers may choose to concentrate on long-term, large-scale adjustments to a variety of challenging and strategic forces in the external environment. If top management tends to concentrate on the long term and downplay quarterly mileposts, others throughout the organization must be ready and willing to make critical operating decisions to maintain current profitability. By providing opportunities for creative problem solving coupled with the discretion to act, real empowerment increases the total power available in an organization. In other words, the top levels don't have to give up power in order for the lower levels to gain it. Note that senior managers must give up the illusion of control—the false belief that they can direct the actions of employees five or six levels of management below them.

The same basic arguments hold true in any manager–subordinate relationship. Empowerment means that all managers need to emphasize different ways of exercising influence. Appeals to higher authority and sanctions need to be replaced by appeals to reason. Friendliness must replace coercion, and bargaining must replace orders for compliance.

Given the all too familiar history of an emphasis on coercion and compliance within firms, special support may be needed for individuals so that they become comfortable in developing their own power over events and activities. What executives fear, and all too often find, is that employees passively resist empowerment by seeking directives they can obey or reject. The fault lies with the executives and the middle managers who need to rethink what they mean by power and rethink their use of traditional position and personal power sources. The key is to lead, not push; reward, not sanction; build, not destroy; and expand, not shrink. To expand the zone of indifference also calls for expanding the inducements for thinking and acting, not just for obeying.

Organizational Politics

Any study of power and influence inevitably leads to the subject of "politics." For many, this word may conjure up thoughts of illicit deals, favors, and special personal relationships. Perhaps this image of shrewd, often dishonest, practices of obtaining one's way is reinforced by Machiavelli's classic fifteenth-century work *The Prince*, which outlines how to obtain and hold power via political action. It is important, however, to adopt a perspective that allows politics in organizations to function in a much broader capacity.[15]

■ THE TWO TRADITIONS OF ORGANIZATIONAL POLITICS

There are two quite different traditions in the analysis of organizational politics. One tradition builds on Machiavelli's philosophy and *defines politics in terms of self-interest and the use of nonsanctioned means*. In this tradition, **organizational politics** may be formally defined as the management of influence to obtain ends not sanctioned by the organization or to obtain sanctioned ends through nonsanctioned influence means.[16] Managers are often considered political when they seek their own goals or use means that are not currently authorized by the organization or that push legal limits. Where there is uncertainty or ambiguity, it is often extremely difficult to tell whether a manager is being political in this self-serving sense.[17] For instance, was John Meriwether a great innovator when he established Long Term Capital Management (LTCM) as a hedge

■ **Organizational politics** is the management of influence to obtain ends not sanctioned by the organization or to obtain sanctioned ends through nonsanctioned means and the art of creative compromise among competing interests.

Visit the Internet site for America's Job Bank and find access to a million or more jobs—available from Maine to California and Florida to Washington State. This Web site includes job market information and search tips, and also features America's Talent Bank and America's Career Infonet.

fund to bet on interest rate spreads?[18] At one time, the firm included 2 Nobel laureates and some 25 Ph.D.s. Or was he the consummate insider when he got the U.S. Federal Reserve to orchestrate a bailout when it looked like he would either go broke or lose control to a rich investor? Or as often happens in the world of corporate politics, could both of these statements be partially true?

The second tradition *treats politics as a necessary function resulting from differences in the self-interests of individuals.* Here, organizational politics is viewed as the art of creative compromise among competing interests. In the case of John Meriwether and LTCM, when it went bankrupt the country's financial leaders were concerned that it could cause a panic in the markets and so hurt everyone. So the Federal Reserve stepped in. That Meriwether did not lose everything was merely a byproduct of saving the whole financial system. In a heterogeneous society, individuals will disagree as to whose self-interests are most valuable and whose concerns should therefore be bounded by collective interests. Politics arise because individuals need to develop compromises, avoid confrontation, and live together. The same holds true in organizations, where individuals join, work, and stay together because their self-interests are served. Furthermore, it is important to remember that the goals of the organization and the acceptable means are established by organizationally powerful individuals in negotiation with others. Thus, organizational politics is also the use of power to develop socially acceptable ends and means that balance individual and collective interests.

■ THE DOUBLE-EDGED SWORD OF ORGANIZATIONAL POLITICS

The two different traditions of organizational politics are reflected in the ways executives describe their effects on managers and their organizations. In one survey, some 53 percent of those interviewed indicated that organizational politics enhanced the achievement of organizational goals and survival.[19] Yet, some 44 percent suggested that it distracted individuals from organizational goals. In this same survey, 60 percent of respondents suggested that organizational politics was good for career advancement; 39 percent reported that it led to a loss of power, position, and credibility.

Organizational politics is not automatically good or bad. It can serve a number of important functions, including overcoming personnel inadequacies, coping with change, and substituting for formal authority.

Even in the best managed firms, mismatches arise among managers who are learning, burned out, lacking in needed training and skills, overqualified, or lacking the resources needed to accomplish their assigned duties. Organizational politics provides a mechanism for circumventing these inadequacies and getting the job done. Organizational politics can facilitate adaptation to changes in the environment and technology of an organization.

Organizational politics can help identify such problems and move ambitious, problem-solving managers into the breach. It is quicker than restructuring. It allows the firm to meet unanticipated problems with people and resources quickly, before small headaches become major problems. Finally, when a person's formal authority breaks down or fails to apply to a particular situation, political actions can be used to prevent a loss of influence. Managers may use political behavior to maintain operations and to achieve task continuity in circumstances where the failure of formal authority may otherwise cause problems.

■ ORGANIZATIONAL POLITICS AND SELF-PROTECTION

Whereas organizational politics may be helpful to the organization as a whole, it is probably more commonly known and better understood in terms of self-protection.[20] Whether or not management likes it, all employees recognize that in any organization they must watch out for themselves first. In too many organizations, if the employee doesn't protect himself or herself, no one else will.

Individuals can employ three common strategies to protect themselves. They can (1) avoid action and risk taking, (2) redirect accountability and responsibility, or (3) defend their turf.

Avoidance   *Avoidance* is quite common in controversial areas where the employee must risk being wrong or where actions may yield a sanction. Perhaps the most common reaction is to "work to the rules." That is, employees are protected when they adhere strictly to all the rules, policies, and procedures or do not allow deviations or exceptions. Perhaps one of the most frustrating but effective techniques is to "play dumb." We all do this at some time or another. When was the last time you said, "Officer, I didn't know the speed limit was 35. I couldn't have been going 52."

Although working to the rules and playing dumb are common techniques, experienced employees often practice somewhat more subtle techniques of self-protection. These include depersonalization and stalling. Depersonalization involves treating individuals, such as customers, clients, or subordinates, as numbers, things, or objects. Senior managers don't fire long-term employees; the organization is merely "downsized" or "delayered." Routine stalling involves slowing down the pace of work to expand the task so that the individuals look as if they are working hard. With creative stalling, the employees may spend the time supporting the organization's ideology, position, or program and delaying implementation.

Redirecting Responsibility   Politically sensitive individuals will always protect themselves from accepting blame for the negative consequences of their actions. Again, a variety of well-worn techniques may be used for *redirecting responsibility.* "Passing the buck" is a common method employees and managers use. The trick here is to define the task in such a way that it becomes someone else's formal responsibility. The ingenious ways individuals can redefine an issue to avoid action and transfer responsibility are often amazing.

Both employees and managers may avoid responsibility by *buffing,* or *rigorous documentation.* Here, individuals take action only when all the paperwork is in place and it is clear that they are merely following procedure. Closely related to rigorous documentation is the "blind memo," which explains an objection to an action implemented by the individual. Here, the required action is taken, but the blind memo is prepared should the action come into question. Politicians are particularly good at this technique. They will meet with a lobbyist and then send a memo to the files confirming the meeting. Any relationship between what was discussed in the meeting and the memo is accidental.

As the last example suggests, a convenient method some managers use to avoid responsibility is merely to *rewrite history.* If a program is successful, the manager claims to have been an early supporter. If a program fails, the manager was the one who expressed serious reservations in the first place. Whereas a memo in the files is often nice to have to show one's early support or objections,

Little Caesars

www.littlecaesars.com

Marian Ilitch, co-founder of Little Caesars Pizza, has helped put her stamp on the corporate philosophy of Little Caesars by making it one of the best places for working women. The firm also has a long and distinguished record of supporting local charities and is headquartered in downtown Detroit. Marian recently made a million-dollar contribution to establish a hospice in Detroit.

some executives don't bother with such niceties. They merely start a meeting by recapping what has happened in such a way that makes them look good.

For the really devious, there are three other techniques for redirecting responsibility. One technique is to blame the problem on someone or some group that has difficulty defending themselves. Fired employees, outsiders, and opponents are often targets of such scapegoating. Closely related to scapegoating is blaming the problem on uncontrollable events. The really astute manager goes far beyond the old "the-dog-ate-my-homework" routine. A perennial favorite is, "Given the unexpected severe decline in the overall economy, firm profitability was only somewhat below reasonable expectations." Meaning, the firm lost a bundle.

Should these techniques fail, there is always another possibility: Facing apparent defeat, the manager can escalate commitment to a losing cause of action. That is, when all appears lost, assert your confidence in the original action, blame the problems on not spending enough money to implement the plan fully, and embark on actions that call for increased effort. The hope is that you will be promoted or retired by the time the negative consequences are recognized.

Defending Turf   Defending turf is a time-honored tradition in most large organizations. As noted earlier in the chapter, managers seeking to improve their power attempt to expand the jobs their groups perform. Defending turf also results from the coalitional nature of organizations. That is, the organization may be seen as a collection of competing interests held by various departments and groups. As each group attempts to expand its influence, it starts to encroach on the activities of other groups. Turf protection can be seen more easily in the following analysis of political action and the manager.

Political Action and the Manager

Managers may gain a better understanding of political behavior by placing themselves in the positions of other persons involved in critical decisions or events. Each action and decision can be seen as having benefits for and costs to all parties concerned. Where the costs exceed the benefits, the manager may act to protect his or her position.

Figure 15.3 shows a sample payoff table for two managers, Lee and Leslie, in a problem situation involving a decision as to whether or not to allocate resources to a special project. If both managers authorize the resources, the project gets completed on time, and their company keeps a valuable client. Unfortunately, if they do this, both Lee and Leslie overspend their budgets. Taken on its own, a budget overrun would be bad for the managers' performance records. Assume that the overruns are acceptable only if the client is kept. Thus, if both managers act, both they and the company win, as depicted in the upper left block of the figure. Obviously, this is the most desirable outcome for all parties concerned.

Assume that Leslie acts, but Lee does not. In this case, the company loses the client, Leslie overspends the budget in a futile effort, but Lee ends up within budget. While the company and Leslie lose, Lee wins. This scenario is illustrated

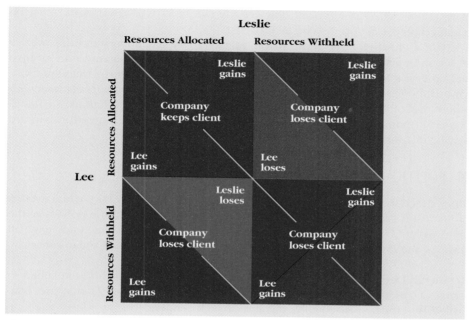

Figure 15.3
Political payoff matrix for the allocation of resources on a sample project.

in the lower left block of the figure. The upper right block shows the reverse situation, where Lee acts but Leslie does not. In this case, Leslie wins, while the company and Lee lose. Finally, if both Lee and Leslie fail to act, each stays within the budget and therefore gains, but the company loses the client.

The company clearly wants both Lee and Leslie to act. But will they? Would you take the risk of overspending the budget, knowing that your colleague may refuse? The question of trust is critical here, but building trust among co-managers and other workers takes time and can be difficult. The involvement of higher level managers may be needed to set the stage better. Yet, in many organizations both Lee and Leslie would fail to act because the "climate" or "culture" too often encourages people to maximize their self-interest at minimal risks.

■ POLITICAL ACTION AND SUBUNIT POWER

Political action links managers more formally to one another as representatives of their work units. Five of the more typical lateral, intergroup relations in which you may engage as a manager are work flow, service, advisory, auditing, and approval.[21] Work-flow linkages involve contacts with units that precede or follow in a sequential production chain. Service ties involve contacts with units established to help with problems. For instance, an assembly-line manager may develop a service link by asking the maintenance manager to fix an important piece of equipment on a priority basis. In contrast, advisory connections involve formal staff units having special expertise, such as a manager seeking the advice of the personnel department on evaluating subordinates. Auditing linkages involve units that have the right to evaluate the actions of others after action has been taken, whereas approval linkages involve units whose approval must be obtained before action may be taken.

To be effective in political action, managers should understand the politics of subunit relations. Line units are typically more powerful than are staff groups, and units toward the top of the hierarchy are often more powerful than are those toward the bottom. In general, units gain power as more of their relations with others are of the approval and auditing types. Work-flow relations are more powerful than are advisory associations, and both are more powerful than are service relations.

■ POLITICAL ACTION IN THE CHIEF EXECUTIVE SUITE

From descriptions of the 1890s' robber barons such as Jay Gould to the actions of Microsoft's Bill Gates, Americans have been fascinated with the politics of the chief executive suite. An analytical view of executive suite dynamics may lift some of the mystery behind the political veil at the top levels in organizations.

Resource Dependencies   Executive behavior can sometimes be explained in terms of resource dependencies—the firm's need for resources that are controlled by others.[22] Essentially, the resource dependence of an organization increases as (1) needed resources become more scarce, (2) outsiders have more control over needed resources, and (3) there are fewer substitutes for a particular type of resource controlled by a limited number of outsiders. Thus, one political role of the chief executive is to develop workable compromises among the competing resource dependencies facing the organization—compromises that enhance the executive's power. To create such compromises, executives need to diagnose the relative power of outsiders and to craft strategies that respond differently to various external resource suppliers.

For larger organizations, many strategies may center on altering the firm's degree of resource dependence. Through mergers and acquisitions, a firm may bring key resources within its control. By changing the "rules of the game," a firm may also find protection from particularly powerful outsiders. In the opening case, for instance, Netscape was seeking relief from the onslaught of Microsoft by appealing to the U.S. government. Markets may also be protected by trade barriers, or labor unions may be put in check by "right to work" laws. Yet, there are limits on the ability of even our largest and most powerful organizations to control all important external contingencies.

International competition has narrowed the range of options for chief executives; they can no longer ignore the rest of the world. Some may need to redefine fundamentally how they expect to conduct business. For instance, once U.S. firms could go it alone without the assistance of foreign corporations. Now, chief executives are increasingly leading them in the direction of more joint ventures and strategic alliances with foreign partners from around the globe. Such "combinations" provide access to scarce resources and technologies among partners, as well as new markets and shared production costs.

On the seamier side, there is a new wrinkle in the discussion of resource dependencies—executive pay. Traditionally, U.S. CEOs made about 30 times the pay of the average worker. This was similar to CEO pay scales in Europe and Japan.[23] Today many U.S. CEOs are making 3000 times the average pay of workers. How did they get so rich? CEOs may tie themselves to the short-term interests of powerful stockholders. Their pay may be directly linked to short-term stock price increases, even though CEOs are most often expected to focus on the long-term health of the firm. When a CEO downsizes, embarks on a merger campaign, or cuts such benefits as worker health care, short-term profits may jump dramatically and lift the stock price. Although the long-term health of the firm may be put in jeopardy, few U.S. CEOs seem able to resist the temptation. It is little wonder that there is renewed interest in how U.S. firms are governed.

Organizational Governance   **Organizational governance** refers to the pattern of authority, influence, and acceptable managerial behavior established at the top of the organization. This system establishes what is important, how issues will be defined, who should and should not be involved in key choices, and the boundaries for acceptable implementation.

Students of organizational governance suggest that a "dominant coalition" comprised of powerful organizational actors is a key to understanding a firm's governance.[24] Although one expects many top officers within the organization to be members of this coalition, the dominant coalition occasionally includes outsiders with access to key resources. Thus, analysis of organizational governance builds on the resource dependence perspective by highlighting the effective control of key resources by members of a dominant coalition.

■ **Organizational governance** is the pattern of authority, influence, and acceptable managerial behavior established at the top of the organization.

TECHNOLOGY 🖳

www.catalinamktg.com

On a fine spring day, CEO George W. Off announced the promotion of Daniel D. Geringer to president and chief operating officer, Catalina Marketing Corporation. Dan was also elected to its board of directors. Catalina Marketing markets core electronic marketing programs, advertising through customized newsletters to pharmacy customers and distribution via the WWW for secure store coupons. Dan is now a member of the dominant coalition and will help establish the management philosophy for the firm. In his new job Dan will help establish the firm's strategy, deal with key external groups, and run the day-to-day affairs of the firm.

This view of the executive suite recognizes that the daily practice of organizational governance is the development and resolution of issues. Through the governance system, the dominant coalition attempts to define reality. See the tasks given Dan Geringer of Catalina Marketing. By accepting or rejecting proposals from subordinates, by directing questions toward the interests of powerful outsiders, and by selecting individuals who appear to espouse particular values and qualities, the pattern of governance is slowly established within the organization. Furthermore, this pattern rests, at least in part, on very political foundations.

Whereas organizational governance was an internal and a rather private matter in the past, it is now becoming more public and openly controversial. This was evidenced to some extent in the many well-publicized hostile takeovers of the 1980s and 1990s. Whereas some argue that senior managers don't represent shareholder interests well enough, others are concerned that they give too little attention to broader constituencies.

It has been estimated that the *Fortune* 500 corporations have cut some 8 million positions over the last 15 years of downsizing.[25] Managers and employees of these firms once felt confident that the management philosophy of their firm included their interests. In the new millennium, only a few employees seem to share this confidence. For instance, Boeing announced record production, near-record profits, and a merger with McDonnell-Douglas at the same time that it eliminated some 20,000 engineers from its home Seattle operations. Boeing eliminated almost all of the engineers hired in the last two years. As one critic caustically noted, "They ate their young to get executive bonuses." Obviously, Boeing is not a high performance organization.

Public concerns about U.S. corporations, especially those organizations with high-risk technologies such as chemical processing, medical technology, and integrated oil refineries, appear on the rise. For instance, Dow-Corning's survival is questionable because it has been accused of selling breast implants that cause immune system problems. Dow-Corning cites the lack of scientific evidence linking their product with such problems, but jury after jury is awarding damages to women who have had Dow-Corning implants and immune system problems. Without doubt juries are holding Dow-Corning management accountable.

Imbalanced organizational governance by some U.S. corporations may limit their ability to manage global operations effectively. Although U.S. senior managers may blame such externalities as unfavorable trade laws for their inability to compete in Japan or other Asian competitors, their critics suggest that it's just a lack of global operating savvy that limits the corporations these managers are supposed to be leading. Organizational governance is too closely tied to the short-term interests of stockholders and the pay of the CEO.

On a more positive note, there are bright spots suggesting that the governance of U.S. firms is extending well beyond the limited interests of the owners to include employees and into communities.

Cavanagh, Moberg, and Velasquez argue that organizational governance should have an ethical base.[26] They suggest that from the CEO to the lowest employee, a person's behavior must satisfy the following criteria to be considered ethical. First, the behavior must result in optimizing the satisfaction of people both inside and outside the organization to produce the greatest good for the greatest number of people. Second, the behavior must respect the rights of all affected parties, including the human rights of free consent, free speech, freedom of conscience, privacy, and due process. Third, the behavior must respect the rules of justice by treating people equitably and fairly, as opposed to arbitrarily.

There may be times when a behavior is unable to fulfill these criteria but can still be considered ethical in the given situation. This special case must satisfy the criterion of overwhelming factors, in which the special nature of the situation results in (1) conflicts among criteria (e.g., a behavior results in some good and some bad being done), (2) conflicts within criteria (e.g., a behavior uses questionable means to achieve a positive end), or (3) incapacity to employ the criteria (e.g., a person's behavior is based on inaccurate or incomplete information).

Choosing to be ethical often involves considerable personal sacrifice, and, at all corporate levels, it involves avoiding common rationalizations. CEOs and employees alike may justify unethical actions by suggesting that (1) the behavior is not really illegal and so could be moral; (2) the action appears to be in the firm's best interests; (3) the action is unlikely ever to be detected; and (4) it appears that the action demonstrates loyalty to the boss, the firm, or short-term stockholder interests. Whereas these rationalizations may appear compelling at the moment of action, each deserves close scrutiny if the firm's organizational governance system is to avoid falling into being dominated by the more unsavory side of organizational politics.

Chapter 15 Study Guide

What is power?

Summary

- Power is the ability to get someone else to do what you want him or her to do.

- Power vested in managerial positions derives from three sources: rewards, punishments, and legitimacy (formal authority).

How do managers acquire the power needed for leadership?

- Formal authority is based on the manager's position in the hierarchy of authority, whereas personal power is based on one's expertise and referent capabilities.

- Managers can pursue various ways of acquiring both position and personal power.

- They can also become skilled at using various tactics, such as reason, friendliness, ingratiation, and bargaining, to influence superiors, peers, and subordinates.

- People may have a tendency to obey directives coming from others who appear powerful and authoritative.

- The zone of indifference defines the boundaries within which people in organizations let others influence their behavior.

- Ultimately, power and authority work only if the individual "accepts" them.

What is empowerment, and how can managers empower others?

- Empowerment is the process through which managers help others acquire and use the power needed to make decisions that affect themselves and their work.

- Empowerment emphasizes power as the ability to get things done rather than the ability to get others to do what you want.

- Clear delegation of authority, integrated planning, and the involvement of senior management are all important to implementing empowerment.

What are organizational politics?

- Organizational politics are inevitable.

- Politics involves the use of power to obtain ends not officially sanctioned and the use of power to find ways of balancing individual and collective interests in otherwise difficult circumstances.

How do organizational politics affect managers and management?

- For the manager, politics often occurs in decision situations where the interests of another manager or individual must be reconciled with one's own.

- For managers, politics also involves subunits that jockey for power and advantageous positions vis-à-vis one another.

- For chief executives, politics come into play as resource dependencies with external environmental elements must be strategically managed.

- Organizational governance is the pattern of authority, influence, and acceptable managerial behavior established at the top of the organization.

- CEOs and managers can develop an ethical organizational governance system that is free from rationalizations.

Key Terms

Coercive power (p. 311)
Empowerment (p. 316)
Expert power (p. 312)
Influence (p. 311)
Legitimate power (p. 311)

Organizational governance (p. 327)
Organizational politics (p. 321)
Power (p. 311)

Rational persuasion (p. 312)
Referent power (p. 312)
Reward power (p. 311)
Zone of indifference (p. 318)

Self-Test 15

■ MULTIPLE CHOICE

1. The three bases of position power are _____. (a) reward, expertise, and coercive power (b) legitimate, experience, and judgment power (c) knowledge, experience, and judgment power (d) reward, coercive, and knowledge power (e) reward, coercive, and legitimate power

2. _____ is the ability to control another's behavior because, through the individual's efforts, the person accepts the desirability of an offered goal and a reasonable way of achieving it. (a) Rational persuasion (b) Legitimate (c) Reward (d) Coercive power (e) Charismatic power

3. A worker who behaves in a certain manner to ensure an effective boss–subordinate relationship shows _____ power. (a) expert (b) reward (c) coercive (d) approval (e) referent

4. One guideline for implementing a successful empowerment strategy is that _____. (a) delegation of authority should be left ambiguous and open to individual interpretation (b) managers should refrain from communicating effectively to

subordinates (c) planning should be separated according to the level of empower-ment (d) it can be assumed that any empowering directives from management will be automatically followed (e) the authority delegated to lower levels should be clear and precise

5. The major lesson of the Milgram experiments is that _____. (a) Americans are very independent and unwilling to obey (b) individuals are willing to obey as long as it does not hurt another person (c) individuals will obey an authority figure even if it does appear to hurt someone else (d) individuals will always obey an authority figure (e) individuals will hardly ever obey unless repeatedly directed to do so by an au-thority figure

6. The range of authoritative requests to which a subordinate is willing to respond with-out subjecting the directives to critical evaluation or judgment is called the _____. (a) psychological contract (b) zone of indifference (c) Milgram experi-ments (d) functional level of organizational politics (e) power vector

7. The three basic power relationships to ensure success are _____. (a) upward, downward, and lateral (b) upward, downward, and oblique (c) downward, lateral, and oblique (d) downward, lateral, and external (e) internal, external, and oblique

8. In which dimension of power and influence would a manager find the use of both position power and personal power most advantageous? (a) upward (b) lateral (c) downward (d) work flow (e) advisory

9. Reason, coalition, bargaining, and assertiveness are strategies for _____. (a) enhancing personal power (b) enhancing position power (c) exercising referent power (d) exercising influence (e) enhancing coercive power

10. Negotiating the interpretation of a union contract is an example of _____. (a) organizational politics (b) lateral relations (c) an approval relationship (d) an auditing linkage (e) unethical behavior

■ TRUE–FALSE

11. Coercion is a behavioral response to the exercise of power.   T   F

12. Reference is an example of power derived from personal, as opposed to organiza-tional, sources.   T   F

13. Position power includes the ability to control another's behavior through an appeal to reason.   T   F

14. Legitimate power and formal authority are one and the same.   T   F

15. Reward power is the extent to which a manager can use extrinsic and intrinsic re-wards to control other people.   T   F

16. The acceptance theory of authority indicates that subordinates will always accept the orders of their superiors in organizations.   T   F

17. The Milgram experiments demonstrate that persons are generally unwilling to obey the commands of authoritative persons.   T   F

18. The process by which managers help others acquire and use the power needed to make decisions is called organizational politics.   T   F

19. A resource dependence perspective suggests that one of the key roles played by top management is to develop and allocate power.   T   F

20. Increasing knowledge and attractiveness are ways to increase position power.   T   F

■ SHORT RESPONSE

21. Explain how the various bases of position and personal power do or do not apply to the classroom relationship between instructor and student. What sources of power do students have over their instructors?

22. Identify and explain at least three guidelines for the acquisition of (a) position power and (b) personal power by managers.

23. Identify and explain at least four strategies of managerial influence. Give examples of how each strategy may or may not work when exercising influence (a) downward and (b) upward in organizations.

24. Define "organizational politics" and give an example of how it operates in both functional and dysfunctional ways.

■ APPLICATIONS ESSAY

25. What explanations for mergers and acquisitions would you offer if it were found that they rarely produce positive financial gains for the shareholders?

Explore application-oriented Fast Company articles, cases, experimental exercises, and self-assessments in the OB Skills Workbook

■ **Visit the Schermerhorn Web site to find the Interactive Self-Test and Internet exercises for this chapter.**

Information and Communication

HOW TO MAKE COMMUNICATION COUNT

www.sun.com

Scott G. McNealy, CEO of Sun Microsystems, Inc., has made his mark in corporate America. With an MBA from Stanford University, he is well known in the technology world for a unique vision of the future—one that emphasizes the power of networking rather than desktop PCs. Known for its focus on network computing and building Java, which allows programs as well as data to be transferred over networks, Sun keeps marching forward as a bold alternative in the technology industry. As to the future, McNealy says: "The PC is just a blip. It's a big, bright blip, but just a blip. Fifty years from now, people are going to look back and say: 'Did you really have a computer on your desk? How weird.'"

But it's not just computers that drive the system at Sun; people count too. Like many enlightened executives, McNealy supports a comprehensive organizational communication program that includes an emphasis on employee surveys. Sun uses E-mail questionnaires or polls to gather information on a regular basis regarding employee perceptions of such elements as "performance inhibitors"—things that made it hard for them to do a good job in the past month. The results are used to create an "employee quality index" that rates Sun as a place to work. Jim Lynch, Sun's director of corporate quality, sees a direct link between Sun's quality as a workplace and the likelihood that customers will be attracted to it.

With good employee communication, information about workplace problems can be identified and used to correct situations to the benefit of the employees and in the context of a broader corporate commitment to quality. At Sun, management recognizes information and communication as keys to continued organizational development.[1]

E veryone knows that "communication" is vital to an organization. But it takes hard work and true commitment to create the type of information-rich environment that has just been described at Sun Microsystems. This is especially true in an age where speed is of utmost importance to organizations and where Microsoft's chairman Bill Gates says: "Only managers who master the digital universe will gain competitive advantage."[2] Using information and technology for the high performance advantage, however, requires an extraordinary willingness to open up communication linkages and opportunities among people in organizations, and between them and their customers. It also requires a culture of trust throughout the organization, a culture that encourages a free flow of ideas and suggestions up and down the hierarchy as well as among peers and colleagues. The payoffs for the enlightened organizations are found in both organizational performance and member satisfaction.

Study Questions

Chapter 16 examines the process of communication, with special attention to its interpersonal and organizational challenges as well as the opportunities of new developments in information technology. As you read this chapter, keep in mind these questions:

- What is the nature of the communication process?
- What are the essentials of interpersonal communication?
- What barriers interfere with effective communication?
- What is organizational communication?
- What forces influence communication in the high performance workplace?

The Nature of Communication

Lucent Technologies, one of the major technology companies of our day, opened a recent annual report with these words: "There is a revolution going on in the communications industry." The report went on to note that over 900 million voice-mail messages are now exchanged every day, 2.7 trillion E-mails are sent in a year—some 5 million per minute—100 million Internet users come online in a year, and Internet traffic doubles every 100 days.[3] The figures are amazing, and the implications are clear. Appetites for information are growing by leaps and bounds, and the future of organizations is increasingly depending on their abilities to harness information and information technology for competitive advantage. At the center of all this stands the great demands and opportunities of the process we know as "communication."

■ THE COMMUNICATION PROCESS

It is useful to think of **communication** as a process of sending and receiving messages with attached meanings. The key elements in the communication process are illustrated in Figure 16.1. They include a *source*, who encodes an intended meaning into a message, and a *receiver*, who decodes the message into a perceived meaning.[4] The receiver may or may not give feedback to the source. Although this process may appear to be very elementary, it is not quite as simple as it looks. **Noise** is the term used to describe any disturbance that disrupts it and interferes with the transference of messages within the communication process.

The information source is a person or group trying to communicate with someone else. The source seeks to communicate, in part, to change the atti-

■ **Communication** is the process of sending and receiving symbols with attached meanings.

■ **Noise** is anything that interferes with the effectiveness of communication.

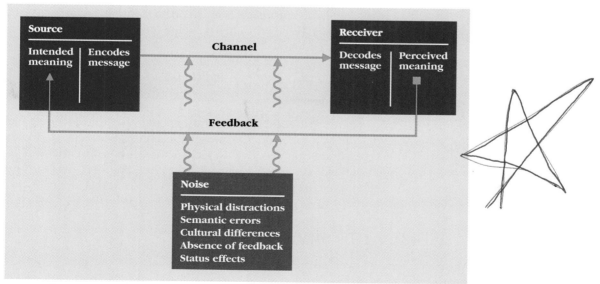

Figure 16.1
The communication process and possible sources of "noise."

tudes, knowledge, or behavior of the receiver. A team leader, for example, may want to communicate with a division manager in order to explain why the team needs more time or resources to finish an assigned project. This involves *encoding*—the process of translating an idea or thought into a message consisting of verbal, written, or nonverbal symbols (such as gestures), or some combination of them. Such messages are transmitted through various **communication channels**, such as face-to-face meetings, electronic mail and other forms, written letters or memorandums, and telephone communications or voice-mail, among others. The choice of channel can have an important impact on the communication process. Some people are better at using certain channels over others, and some messages are better handled by specific channels. In the earlier case of the team leader communicating with the division manager, for example, it can make quite a difference whether the message is sent face to face, in a written memo, by voice-mail, or by E-mail.

■ **Communication channels** are the pathways through which messages are communicated.

www.cp.net

ENTREPRENEURSHIP

One of the hot and entrepreneurial new companies of the digital age is Critical Path. Founded by Wayne Correia and David Hayden in 1997, the mission of the company is straightforward and timely: "To handle the world's E-mail." Systems engineer Correia built the computer network to support the mission. What's the result? The firm is rapidly expanding in corporate customers as the leading outsourcer of E-mail services. The business of E-mail outsourcing is considered a growth prospect and some analysts put the potential market as high as 65% of U.S. businesses by 2001. The entrepreneurial vision of Correia and Hayden has put Critical Path on top of the curve in information and communication technologies in the new business revolution.[5]

The communication process is not completed just because a message is sent. The receiver is the individual or group of individuals to whom a message is directed. In order for meaning to be assigned to any received message, its contents must be interpreted through *decoding*. This process of translation is complicated by many factors, including the knowledge and experience of the receiver and his or her relationship with the sender. A message may also be interpreted with the added influence of other points of view, such as those offered by friends, co-workers, or organizational superiors. Ultimately, the decoding may result in the receiver interpreting a message in a way that is different from that originally intended by the source.

■ FEEDBACK AND COMMUNICATION

■ **Feedback** communicates how one feels about something another person has done or said.

Most receivers are well aware of the potential gap between the intended message of the source and the perceived meaning assigned to it by the recipient. One way in which these gaps are identified is through **feedback**, the process through which the receiver communicates with the sender by returning another message. The exchange of information through feedback can be very helpful in improving the communication process, and the popular advice to always "keep the feedback channels open" is good to remember.

In practice, giving "feedback" is often associated with one person communicating an evaluation of what another person has said or done. There is an art to giving this special type of feedback so that the receiver accepts it and uses it constructively (see The Effective Manager 16.1). Words that are intended to be polite and helpful can easily end up being perceived as unpleasant and even hostile. This risk is particularly evident in the performance appraisal process. A manager or team leader must be able to do more than just complete a written appraisal to document another person's performance for the record. To serve the person's developmental needs, feedback regarding the results of the appraisal—both the praise and the criticism, must be well communicated.[6]

THE EFFECTIVE MANAGER 16.1

HOW TO GIVE CONSTRUCTIVE FEEDBACK

- Give directly and in a spirit of mutual trust.
- Be specific not general; use clear examples.
- Give when receiver is most ready to accept.
- Be accurate; check validity with others.
- Focus on things the receiver can control.
- Limit how much receiver gets at one time.

Essentials of Interpersonal Communication

Organizations today are information rich. They are also increasingly "high-tech." But, we always need to remember that people still drive the system. And if people are to work together well and commit their mutual talents and energies to create high performance organizations, they must excel at interpersonal communication.

■ EFFECTIVE AND EFFICIENT COMMUNICATION

When people communicate with one another, at least two important things are at issue. One is the accuracy of the communication—an issue of effectiveness; the other is its cost—an issue of efficiency.

Effective communication occurs when the intended meaning of the source and the perceived meaning of the receiver are virtually the same.[7] Although this should be the goal in any communication, it is not always achieved. Even now, we worry about whether or not you are interpreting these written words exactly as we intend. Our confidence would be higher if we were face to face in class together and you could ask clarifying questions. Opportunities to offer feedback and ask questions are important ways of increasing the effectiveness of communication.

Efficient communication occurs at minimum cost in terms of resources expended. Time, for example, is an important resource. Picture your instructor taking the time to communicate individually with each student in your class about the course subject matter. It would be virtually impossible to do so. Even if it were possible, it would be very costly in terms of time. People at work often choose not to visit one another personally to communicate messages. Instead, they rely on the efficiency of written memos, posted bulletins, group meetings, E-mail, or voice-mail.

■ **Effective communication** is when the intended meaning equals the perceived meaning.

■ **Efficient communication** is low cost in its use of resources.

As efficient as these forms of communication may be, they are not always effective. A change in policy posted by efficient E-mail may save time for the sender, but it may not achieve the desired interpretations and responses. Similarly, an effective communication may not be efficient. For a business manager to visit each employee and explain a new change in procedures may guarantee that everyone understands the change, but it may also be prohibitively expensive in terms of the required time expenditure.

■ NONVERBAL COMMUNICATION

■ **Nonverbal communication** occurs by facial expressions, body motions, eye contact, and other physical gestures.

We all know that people communicate in ways other than the spoken or written word. Indeed, **nonverbal communication** that takes place through facial expressions, body position, eye contact, and other physical gestures is important both to understand and master. It is basically the act of speaking without using words. *Kinesics*, the study of gestures and body postures, has achieved a rightful place in communication theory and research.[8] The nonverbal side to communication can often hold the key to what someone is really thinking or meaning. It can also affect the impressions we make on others. Interviewers, for example, tend to respond more favorably to job candidates whose nonverbal cues, such as eye contact and erect posture, are positive than to those displaying negative nonverbal cues, such as looking down or slouching. The art of impression management during interviews and in other situations requires careful attention to both verbal and nonverbal aspects of communication, including one's dress, timeliness, and demeanor.

Nonverbal communication can also take place through the physical arrangement of space, such as that found in various office layouts. *Proxemics*, the study of the way space is utilized, is important to communication.[9] Figure 16.2 shows three different office arrangements and the messages they may communicate to visitors. Check the diagrams against the furniture arrangement in your office or that of your instructor or a person with whom you are familiar. What are you/they saying to visitors by the choice of furniture placement?[10]

"I am the boss!"   "I am the boss, but let's talk."   "Forget I'm the boss, let's talk."

Figure 16.2
Furniture placement and nonverbal communication in the office.

■ ACTIVE LISTENING

The ability to listen well is a distinct asset to anyone whose job involves a large proportion of time spent "communicating" with other people. After all, there are always two sides to the communication process: (1) sending a message, or "telling," and (2) receiving a message, or "listening." There is legitimate concern that too many people emphasize the telling and neglect the listening.[11] Everyone in the new workplace should develop good skills in **active listening**—the ability to help the source of a message say what he or she really means. The concept comes from the work of counselors and therapists, who are trained to help people express themselves and talk about things that are important to them.[12] Take a moment to more thoroughly consider the guidelines for active listening shown in The Effective Manager 16.2. Then read the conversations below. One involves active listening on the part of the branch manager; the other does not. How would you feel as the group leader in each case?[13]

THE EFFECTIVE MANAGER 16.2

GUIDELINES FOR ACTIVE LISTENING

1. Listen for content—try to hear exactly what is being said.
2. Listen for feelings—try to identify how the source feels about things.
3. Respond to feelings—let the source know that his or her feelings are recognized.
4. Note all cues—be sensitive to both verbal and nonverbal expressions.
5. Reflect back—repeat in your own words what you think you are hearing.

■ **Active listening** encourages people to say what they really mean.

Example 1

Group leader: Hey, Sal, I don't get this work order. We can't handle this today. What do they think we are?

Branch manager: But that's the order. So get it out as soon as you can. We're under terrific pressure this week.

Group Leader: Don't they know we're behind schedule already because of that software problem?

Branch manager: Look, I don't decide what goes on upstairs. I just have to see that the work gets out, and that's what I'm going to do.

Group leader: The team won't like this.

Branch manager: That's something you'll have to work out with them, not me.

Example 2

Group leader: Hey, Kelley, I don't get this work order. We can't handle this today. What do they think we are?

Branch manager: Sounds like you're pretty sore about it.

Group leader: I sure am. We're just about getting back to schedule while fighting that software breakdown. Now this comes along.

Branch manager: As if you didn't have enough work to do?

Group leader: Right, I don't know how to tell the team about this. They're under a real strain today. Seems like everything we do around here is rush, rush, rush.

Branch manager: I guess you feel like it's unfair to load anything more on them.

Group leader: Well, yes. But I know there must be plenty of pressure on everybody up the line. If that's the way it is, I'll get the word to them.

Branch manager: Thanks. If you'll give it a try, I'll do my best to hold with the schedule in the future.

The branch manager in Example 2 possesses active listening skills. She responded to the group leader's communication in a way that increased the flow of information. The manager learned more about the situation. The group leader felt better after having been able to really say what she thought, and after being heard!

Communication Barriers

It is important to understand six sources of noise that are common to most interpersonal exchanges: physical distractions, semantic problems, mixed messages, cultural differences, absence of feedback, and status effects. They were shown earlier in Figure 16.1 as potential threats to the communication process.

■ PHYSICAL DISTRACTIONS

Any number of physical distractions can interfere with the effectiveness of a communication attempt. Some of these distractions are evident in the following conversation between an employee, George, and his manager.[14]

> Okay, George, let's hear your problem (phone rings, boss picks it up, promises to deliver the report, "just as soon as I can get it done"). Uh, now, where were we—oh, you're having a problem with marketing. They (the manager's secretary brings in some papers that need immediate signatures; he scribbles his name and the secretary leaves)...you say they're not cooperative? I tell you what, George, why don't you (phone rings again, lunch partner drops by)...uh, take a stab at handling it yourself. I've got to go now.

Besides what may have been poor intentions in the first place, George's manager allowed physical distractions to create information overload. As a result, the communication with George suffered. This mistake can be eliminated by setting priorities and planning. If George has something to say, his manager should set aside adequate time for the meeting. In addition, interruptions such as telephone calls, drop-in visitors, and the like, should be prevented. At a minimum, George's manager could start by closing the door to the office and instructing his secretary not to disturb them.

■ SEMANTIC PROBLEMS

Semantic barriers to communication involve a poor choice or use of words and mixed messages. The following illustrations of the "bafflegab" that once tried to pass as actual "executive communication" are a case in point.[15]

A. "We solicit any recommendations that you wish to make, and you may be assured that any such recommendations will be given our careful consideration."

B. "Consumer elements are continuing to stress the fundamental necessity of a stabilization of the price structure at a lower level than exists at the present time."

Mechanical Man

At his Laguna Hills, California, repair shop Mechanical Man, owner Duane Delp isn't afraid to ask for help from those who know best—the ones doing the work. "I do a lot of management by wandering around," he says. New employees are asked to carry notepads and write down things that concern them or things that they believe might be changed.

One has to wonder why these messages weren't stated more simply as: (A) "Send us your recommendations. They will be carefully considered," and (B) "Consumers want lower prices." In this regard, the popular **KISS principle** of communication is always worth remembering: "Keep it short and simple."

■ The **KISS principle** stands for "keep it short and simple."

■ MIXED MESSAGES

Mixed messages occur when a person's words communicate one thing while actions or "body language" communicate another. They are important to spot since nonverbals can add important insight into what is really being said in face-to-face communication.[16] For instance, someone may voice a cautious "Yes" during a business meeting at the same time that her facial expression shows stress and she begins to lean back in her chair. The body language in this case may suggest the existence of important reservations, even though the words indicate agreement.

■ **Mixed messages** occur when words say one thing while nonverbal cues say something else.

■ CULTURAL DIFFERENCES

People must always exercise caution when they are involved in cross-cultural communication—whether between persons of different geographical or ethnic groupings within one country, or between persons of different national cultures. A common problem is *ethnocentrism*, first defined in Chapter 3 as the tendency to believe one's culture and its values are superior to those of others. It is often accompanied by an unwillingness to try to understand alternative points of view and to take the values they represent seriously. This mindset can easily create communication problems among people of diverse backgrounds.

The difficulties with cross-cultural communication are perhaps most obvious in respect to language differences. Advertising messages, for example, may work well in one country but encounter difficulty when translated into the language of another. Problems may accompany with the introduction of Ford's European model, the "Ka," in Japan. In Japanese, *Ka* means mosquito and analysts wonder if a car that is named for a disease-carrying pest can ever sell well.[17] Gestures may also be used quite differently in the various cultures of the world. For example, crossed legs in the United Kingdom are quite acceptable, but are rude in Saudia Arabia if the sole of the foot is directed toward someone. Pointing at someone to get their attention may be acceptable in Canada, but in Asia it is considered inappropriate.[18]

Monsanto ←

www.monsanto.com

"Box buddies" are in at Monsanto's headquarters in St. Louis, Missouri. Scientists and functional specialists in adjoining work cubicles jointly run important projects. The goal is improved communication, creativity and speed. Says a team member: "Our diversity of experience really makes us more effective because we can look at problems from different perspectives."

■ ABSENCE OF FEEDBACK

One-way communication flows from sender to receiver only, as in the case of a written memo or a voice-mail message. There is no direct and immediate feedback from the recipient. Two-way communication, by contrast, goes from sender to receiver and back again. It is characterized by the normal interactive conversations in our daily experiences. Research indicates that two-way communication is more accurate and effective than is one-way communication, even though it is also more costly and time consuming. Because of their efficiency, however, one-way forms of communication—memos, letters, E-mail, voice-mail, and the like are frequently used in work settings. One-way messages are easy for the sender but often frustrating for the receiver, who may be left unsure of just what the sender means or wants done.

■ STATUS EFFECTS

Status differences in organizations create potential communication barriers between persons of higher and lower ranks. On the one hand, given the authority of their positions, managers may be inclined to do a lot of "telling" but not much "listening." On the other hand, we know that communication is frequently biased when flowing upward in organizational hierarchies.[19] Subordinates may *filter* information and tell their superiors only what they think the boss wants to hear. Whether the reason is a fear of retribution for bringing bad news, an unwillingness to identify personal mistakes, or just a general desire to please, the result is the same: The higher level decision maker may end up taking the wrong actions because of biased and inaccurate information supplied from below. This is sometimes called the **MUM effect** in reference to tendencies to sometimes keep "mum" from a desire to be polite and a reluctance to transmit bad news.[20]

■ The **MUM effect** occurs when people are reluctant to communicate bad news.

To avoid such problems, managers and group leaders must develop trust in their working relationships with subordinates and team members, and take advantage of all opportunities for face-to-face communications. *Management by wandering around*, or **MBWA** for short, is now popularly acclaimed as one way to achieve this trust.[21] It simply means getting out of the office and talking to people regularly as they do their jobs. Managers who spend time walking around can greatly reduce the perceived "distance" between themselves and their subordinates. It helps to create an atmosphere of open and free-flowing communication between the ranks. As a result, more and better information is available for decision making, and the relevance of decisions to the needs of operating workers increases.

■ **MBWA** involves getting out of the office to directly communicate with others.

Organizational Communication

Communication among members of an organization, as well as between them and external customers, suppliers, distributors, alliance partners, and a host of outsiders, provides vital information for the enterprise. **Organizational communication** is the specific process through which information moves and is exchanged throughout an organization.[22] Information flows through both formal and informal structures, and it flows downward, upward, and laterally.

■ **Organizational communication** is the process by which information is exchanged in the organizational setting.

Today, more than ever before, computer technology plays a major role in how information is shared and utilized in organizations. Research in the area of *channel richness*, the capacity of a channel to convey information effectively, lends insight into how various channel alternatives may be used depending on the type of message to be conveyed. In general, the richest channels are face to face. Next are telephone, E-mail, written memos and letters. The leanest channels are posted notices and bulletins. When messages get more complex and open ended, richer channels are necessary to achieve effective communication; leaner channels work well for more routine and straightforward messages, such as announcing the location of a previously scheduled meeting.

■ FORMAL AND INFORMAL CHANNELS

■ **Formal channels** follow the official chain of command.

Information flows in organizations through both formal and informal channels of communication. **Formal channels** follow the chain of command established by an organization's hierarchy of authority. For example, an organization chart indicates the proper routing for official messages passing from one level or part of the hierarchy to another. Because formal channels are recognized as authoritative, it is typical for communication of policies, procedures, and other official announcements to adhere to them. On the other hand, much "networking" takes place through the use of **informal channels** that do not adhere to the organization's hierarchy of authority.[23] They coexist with the formal channels but frequently diverge from them by skipping levels in the hierarchy or cutting across vertical chains of command. Informal channels help to create open communications in organizations and ensure that the right people are in contact with one another."[24]

■ **Informal channels** do not follow the chain of command.

HIGH PERFORMANCE ORGANIZATION

www.carramerica.com

At CarrAmerica, a national commercial real estate company headquartered in Washington, D.C., the opportunities for information communication are encouraged and used to advantage. When designing its new offices, management opted for a modern workplace that improved communication among employees. A coffee bar located near meeting rooms and work spaces encourages informal communication. Says vice president of corporate communications, Karen Widemayer: "We don't ask 'Why aren't you at your desk?' We encourage movement through the office and an open exchange of ideas, and believe our space design supports this."[25]

One familiar informal channel is the **grapevine** or network of friendships and acquaintances through which rumors and other unofficial information are passed from person to person. Grapevines have the advantage of being able to transmit information quickly and efficiently. Grapevines also help fulfill the needs of people involved in them. Being part of a grapevine can provide a sense of security from "being in the know" when important things are going on. It also provides social satisfaction as information is exchanged interpersonally. The primary disadvantage of grapevines occurs when they transmit incorrect or untimely information. Rumors can be very dysfunctional, to both people and organizations. One of the best ways to avoid them is to make sure that key persons in a grapevine get the right information to begin with.

■ A **grapevine** transfers information through networks of friendships and acquaintances.

■ COMMUNICATION FLOWS AND DIRECTIONS

As shown in Figure 16.3, *downward communication* follows the chain of command top to bottom. One of its major functions is to inform. Lower level personnel need to know what higher levels are doing and to be regularly reminded of key policies, strategies, objectives, and technical developments. Of special importance is feedback and information on performance results. Sharing such information helps minimize the spread of rumors and inaccuracies regarding higher level intentions. It also helps create a sense of security and involvement among receivers, who feel they know the whole story. Unfortunately, a lack of adequate downward communication is often cited as a management failure. On the issue of corporate

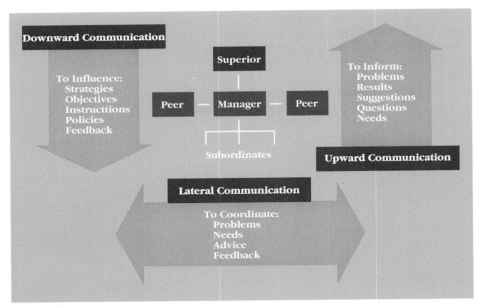

Figure 16.3
Directions for information flows in organizations.

downsizing, for example, one sample showed that 64 percent of employees did not believe what management said, 61 percent felt uninformed about company plans, and 54 percent complained that decisions were not well explained.[26]

The flow of messages from lower to higher levels is *upward communication*. As shown in Figure 16.3, it serves several purposes. Upward communication keeps higher levels informed about what lower level workers are doing, what their problems are, what suggestions they have for improvements, and how they feel about the organization and their jobs. The employee surveys used by Sun Microsystems and mentioned in the chapter opener are examples. But, as you should recall, status effects can potentially interfere with the effectiveness of upward communication.

The importance of *lateral communication* in the new workplace has been a recurrent theme in this book. Today's customer-sensitive organizations need timely and accurate feedback and product information. To serve customer needs they must get the right information—and get it fast enough—into the hands of workers. Furthermore, inside the organization, people must be willing and able to communicate across departmental or functional boundaries and to listen to one another's needs as "internal customers." New organization designs are emphasizing lateral communication in the form of cross-departmental committees, teams, or task forces and the matrix organization. Among the developments is growing attention to *organizational ecology*—the study of how building design may influence communication and productivity by improving lateral communications.

■ COMMUNICATION NETWORKS

Figure 16.4 depicts three interaction patterns and communication networks that are common within organizations.[27] Having the right interaction pattern and

On any given day, outsiders wander around this Missouri-based company to learn about "open book management." CEO Jack Stack trains employees to understand financial data and shares it with them. Given the numbers and their implications, he finds people work better and with greater satisfaction.

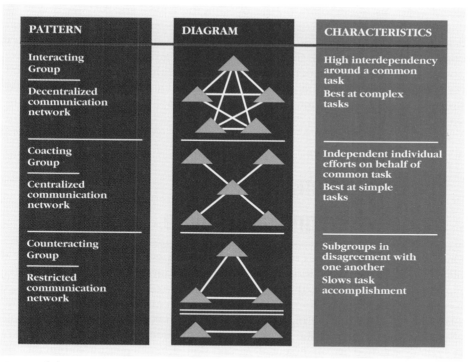

Figure 16.4
Interaction patterns and communication networks in groups.

communication network can make a big difference in the way groups function and in the performance results they achieve.

Some work arrangements involve *interacting groups* whose members work closely together on tasks and in which close coordination of activities takes place. Information flows to everyone. This interaction pattern results in a **decentralized communication network** in which all group members communicate directly and share information with one another. Sometimes these are also referred to as all-channel or star communication networks.[28] They work best for complex and non-routine tasks. They also tend to create high levels of member satisfaction.

Other work arrangements involve *coacting groups* whose members work on tasks independently, while linked through some form of central coordination. The required work is divided up and then largely completed by individuals working alone. Each individual's activities are coordinated and results pooled by a central control point. Information flows to a central person and is redistributed. This creates a **centralized communication network**, with the central person serving as the "hub." Sometimes these are called wheel or chain communication networks. They work best when tasks are easily routinized or subdivided. In these groups, it is usually the central or "hub" person who experiences this satisfaction. After all, he or she alone is most involved in all aspects of group information processing.

Counteracting groups exist when subgroups disagree on some aspect of workplace operations. The subgroups may experience issue-specific disagree-

■ **Decentralized communication networks** link all group members directly with one another.

■ **Centralized communication networks** link group members through a central control point.

ments—such as a temporary debate over the best means to achieve a goal, or the disagreements may be of longer-term duration—such as labor–management disputes. In either case, the resulting interaction pattern involves a **restricted communication network** in which polarized subgroups contest one another's positions and maintain sometimes antagonistic relations. As would be expected, communication between the groups is often limited and biased. Problems of destructive competition in intergroup dynamics are likely under such circumstances.

■ **Restricted communication networks** link subgroups that disagree with one another's positions.

Communication and the High Performance Workplace

One of the greatest changes in organizations and in everyday life in recent years has been the great explosion in new communication technologies. We have moved from the world of the telephone, mail, photocopying, and face-to-face meetings into one of voice-mail, E-mail, facsimile transmission, computer-mediated conferencing, and use of the Internet and Intranets. The ability to participate effectively in all forms of the electronic office and communications environment is well established as an essential career skill. The increasing importance of E-commerce is also transforming the very nature of business in modern society.[29] Given the pace and extensiveness of these dynamics, everyone must keep themselves up to date with the full range of information technologies and emerging issues in organizational communication.

■ CHANGING TECHNOLOGIES

The impact of the new technologies is discussed throughout this book with respect to job design and the growth of telecommuting, organizational design and the growth of network organizations, and teamwork and the availability of software for electronic meetings and decision making, among many other applications. Advances in information technology are allowing organizations to. (1) distribute information much faster than before; (2) make more information available than ever before; (3) allow broader and more immediate access to this information; (4) encourage participation in the sharing and use of information; and, (5) integrate systems and functions, and use information to link with environments in unprecedented ways.

The potential disadvantages of electronic communications must also be recognized. To begin, the technologies are largely impersonal; people interact with machines, not with one another. Electronics also removes nonverbal communications from the situation—aspects that may otherwise add important context to an interaction. In addition, the electronic medium can influence the emotional aspects of communication. Some argue, for example, that it is far easier to be blunt, overly critical, and insensitive when conveying messages electronically rather than face-to-face. The term "flaming" is sometimes used to describe rudeness in electronic communication. In this sense, the use of computer mediation may make people less inhibited and more impatient in what they say.[30]

American Express ◄
www.americanexpress.com

Kenneth Chenault is not only one of the few African Americans to head a multinational corporation, he's also considered one of the best COOs in the business. At American Express he is known for an open office door, engaging personality, luncheons with rank-and-file employees, and his role as mentor to junior managers.

Another risk of the new communication technologies is information overload. In some cases, too much information may find its way into the communication networks and E-mail systems and basically overload the systems—both organizational and individual. Individual users may have difficulty sorting the useful from the trivial and may become impatient while doing so.

In all this, one point remains undeniable: New communication technologies will continue to keep changing the nature of work and of office work in particular. The once-conventional office is fast giving way to new forms such as telecommuting and the use of electronic networks. Workers in the future will benefit as new technologies allow them to spend more time out of the traditional office and more time working with customers on terms that best fit individual needs.

■ COMPLEX SOCIAL CONTEXT

There are any number of issues affecting communication in the complex social context of organizations today. Of continuing interest, for example, is the study of male and female communication styles. In her book *Talking 9 to 5*, Deborah Tannen argues that men and women learn or are socialized into different styles and as a result often end up having difficulties communicating with one another.[31] She sees women more oriented toward relationship building in communication, for example, while men are more prone to seek status through communications.[32] Because people tend to surround themselves with those whose communication styles fit with their own, a further implication is that either women or men may dominate communications in situations where they are in the majority.[33]

More and more people are asking a question related to the prior discussion: "Are women better communicators than men?" A study by the consulting firm Lawrence A. Pfaff and Associates suggests they may well be.[34] The survey shows that supervisors rank women managers higher than men managers on communication, approachability, evaluations, and empowering others; their subordinates also rank women higher on these same items. A possible explanation is that early socialization and training better prepare women for the skills involved in communication and may make them more sensitive in interpersonal relationships. In contrast, men may be more socialized in ways that cause communication problems—such as aggression, competitiveness, and individualism.[35] In considering such possibilities, however, it is important to avoid gender stereotyping and to focus instead on the point of ultimate importance—how communication in organizations can be made most effective.[36]

OB Across Functions
MANAGEMENT INFORMATION SYSTEMS

Enterprise Resource Planning Builds the E-Corporation

Total enterprise integration is one of the big pushes these days. The emergence of the new "E-corporation" is a major competitive challenge in many industries. Consider the example of VF Corporation, which manufactures some $2 billion of jeans each year for major brands including Lee, Wrangler, Britannia, and Rustler. When Mackey McDonald took over as the firm's CEO his vision was to create a computer-savvy company that would use the latest in technologies to continually identify customer demographics, point-of-sale, and other relevant information to drive its production and distribution systems. In short, information and technology were to be used for competitive advantage. VF's integrated information systems begin with SAP software, which addresses resource planning at the corporate level and for the entire organization. SAP serves as the information systems hub and communicates with special software programs that individually deal with such needs as product development, micromarketing, forecasting, capacity and raw materials planning, manufacturing control, and warehouse control. It's all sophisticated and integrated, and with a purpose. The investment costs over $100 million, and VF is still working to get all the software systems in place. However, the goals of speed to market and cost efficiency are within reach. McDonald is confident that the returns will be high. After all, he began the process by involving employees from all levels of the firm in planning and identifying systems needs. He says: "Our people designed the products and the processes. That's why I think we can have success."

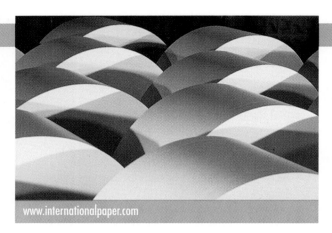

www.internationalpaper.com

WORKPLACE DIVERSITY

At International Paper's Memphis, Tennessee, office, P. J. Smoot serves as a learning and development leader. She has realized that the traditional concept of the boss passing judgment on the subordinate just doesn't work. It is difficult to give performance reviews that end up motivating subordinates and improving their performance. At International Paper she has reversed the traditional top-down process and started a new program that builds the reviews from the bottom up—beginning with the employee's self-evaluation. Smoot believes the manager's job is to listen and learn about employees and their needs and then to help guide them to meet agreed-upon performance plans. Her advice is: "Listen for understanding and then react honestly and constructively. Focus on the business goals, not the personality."[37]

Among the controversies in organizational communication today is the issue of *privacy*. An example is concern for eavesdropping by employers on employee use of electronic messaging in corporate facilities. Progressive organizations are developing internal policies regarding the privacy of employee communications, and the issue is gaining attention from legislators. A state law in Illinois now makes it legal for bosses to listen in on employees' telephone calls. But the law leaves the boundaries of appropriateness unclear. Such eavesdropping is common in some service areas such as airlines reservations, where union concerns are sometimes expressed in the context of "Big brother is watching you!"[38] The privacy issue is likely to remain controversial as communication technologies continue to make it easier for employers to electronically monitor the performance and communications of their workers.

Our society also struggles with the *political correctness* of communications in the workplace. The vocabulary of work is changing, and people are ever more on guard not to let their choice of words offend another individual or group. We now hear references to "people of color," the "physically challenged," and "seniors;" not too long ago these references may have been different, and they may be different again in the future. Organizations are taking notice of this issue and are offering more training to their members to help eliminate in any communications possible overtones of intolerance and insensitivity.

Chapter 16 Study Guide

Summary

What is the nature of the communication process?

- Communication is the process of sending and receiving messages with attached meanings.

- The communication process involves encoding an intended meaning into a message, sending the message through a channel, and receiving and decoding the message into perceived meaning.

- Noise is anything that interferes with the communication process.

- Feedback is a return message from the original recipient back to the sender.

- To be constructive, feedback must be direct, specific, and given at an appropriate time.

What are the essentials of interpersonal communication?

- Communication is effective when both sender and receiver interpret a message in the same way.

- Communication is efficient when messages are transferred at a low cost.

- Nonverbal communication occurs through facial expressions, body position, eye contact, and other physical gestures.

- Active listening encourages a free and complete flow of communication from the sender to the receiver; it is nonjudgmental and encouraging.

- Communication in organizations uses a variety of formal and informal channels; the richness of the channel, or its capacity to convey information, must be adequate for the message.

What barriers interfere with effective communication?

- The possible barriers to communication include physical distractions, semantic problems, and cultural differences.

- Mixed messages that give confused or conflicting verbal and nonverbal cues may interfere with communications.

- The absence of feedback can make it difficult to know whether or not an intended message has been accurately received.

- Status effects in organizations may result in restricted and filtered information exchanges between subordinates and their superiors.

What is organizational communication?

- Organizational communication is the specific process through which information moves and is exchanged within an organization.

- Organizations depend on complex flows of information, upward, downward, and laterally, to operate effectively.

- Groups in organizations work with different interaction patterns and use different communication networks.

- Interacting groups with decentralized networks tend to perform well on complex tasks; coacting groups with centralized networks may do well at simple tasks.

- Restricted communication networks are common in counteracting groups involving subgroup disagreements.

What forces influence communication in the high performance workplace?

- As new electronic communication technologies change the workplace, they bring many advantages of rapid and greater information processing capability.

- These same technologies have the potential to bring disadvantages in the form of a loss of emotion and personality in the communication process.

- Researchers are interested in possible differences in communication styles among men and women and in the relative effectiveness of these styles for conditions in the new workplace.

- Current controversies in organizational communication also include both issues of privacy and political correctness in workplace communications.

Key Terms

Active listening (p. 339)
Centralized communication networks (p. 345)
Communication (p. 335)
Communication channels (p. 336)
Decentralized communication networks (p. 345)
Effective communication (p. 337)

Efficient communication (p. 337)
Feedback (p. 336)
Formal channels (p. 342)
Grapevine (p. 343)
Informal channels (p. 343)
KISS principle (p. 341)
MBWA (p. 342)
Mixed messages (p. 341)
MUM effect (p. 342)

Noise (p. 335)
Nonverbal communication (p. 338)
Organizational communication (p. 342)
Restricted communication networks (p. 346)

Self-Test 16

■ MULTIPLE CHOICE

1. When criticism is given to someone, it should be _____. (a) general and non-specific (b) given when the sender feels the need (c) tied to things the recipient can do something about (d) given all at once to get everything over with

2. In _____ communication the cost is low, whereas in _____ communication the intended message is fully received. (a) effective, electronic (b) efficient, electronic (c) electronic, face-to-face (d) efficient, effective

3. Which channel is more appropriate for sending a complex and open-ended message? (a) Face-to-face. (b) Written memorandum. (c) E-mail. (d) Telephone call.

4. When someone's words convey one meaning and his body posture conveys some-

thing else, a(n) _____ is occurring. (a) ethnocentric message (b) mixed message (c) semantic problem (d) status effect

5. Management by wandering around is a technique that can help to overcome the limitations of _____ in the communication process. (a) status effects (b) semantics (c) physical distractions (d) proxemics

6. A coacting group is most likely to use a(n) _____ communication network. (a) interacting (b) decentralized (c) centralized (d) restricted

7. A complex problem is best dealt with by a group using a(n) _____ communication network. (a) all-channel (b) wheel (c) chain (d) linear

8. Although new communication technologies have the advantage of handling large amounts of information, they may also make organizational communication _____. (a) less accessible (b) less immediate (c) more impersonal (d) more personal

9. The physical arrangement of office furniture and its impact on communication is an issue of _____. (a) kinesics (b) proxemics (c) semantics (d) status

10. In _____ communication the sender is likely to be most comfortable, whereas in _____ communication the receiver is likely to feel more informed. (a) one-way, two-way (b) top-down, bottom-up (c) bottom-up, top-down (d) two-way, one-way

■ TRUE–FALSE

11. Encoding in the communication process translates an intended message into perceived meaning.   T   F

12. Proxemics is the study of mixed messages in organizations.   T   F

13. A rule of active listening is to avoid reflecting back or paraphrasing what the other person has said.   T   F

14. Grapevines can have a positive impact on communication in organizations.   T   F

15. Poor downward communication is a common management failure.   T   F

16. New trends in organizational design emphasize more lateral communications.   T   F

17. Developments in organizational ecology recognize the importance of informal communication.   T   F

18. Members in a coacting group tend to interact frequently and share information directly with one another.   T   F

19. A tendency toward "flaming" to express intense anger is a possible drawback of electronic communication.   T   F

20. There is little concern for the political correctness of communications in organizations today.   T   F

■ SHORT RESPONSE

21. Why is channel richness a useful concept for managers?

22. What place do informal communication channels have in organizations today?

23. Why are communications between lower and higher organizational levels sometimes filtered?

24. Is there a gender difference in communication styles?

■ APPLICATIONS ESSAY

25. "People in this organization don't talk to one another anymore. Everything is E-mail, E-mail, E-mail. If you are mad at someone, you can just say it and then hide behind your computer." With these words, Wesley expressed his frustrations with Delta General's operations. Xiaomei echoed his concerns, responding, "I agree, but surely the managing director should be able to improve organizational communication without losing the advantages of E-mail." As a consultant overhearing this conversation, how would you suggest the managing director respond to Xiaomei's challenge?

Explore application-oriented Fast Company articles, cases, experimental exercises, and self-assessments in the OB Skills Workbook

■ **Visit the Schermerhorn Web site to find the Interactive Self-Test and Internet exercises for this chapter.**

Decision Making

17

BREAK THROUGH WITH PERSEVERENCE AND CREATIVITY

www.freshexpress.com

The local supermarket's produce counter has it; sales run over $450 million per year for Steve Taylor's Fresh International Corporation. What's the product? It's Fresh Express's freshly packaged salad also known as salad-in-a-bag. Fresh Express is the originator and the world leader of the fast growing national retail packaged salad category. It offers everything from a traditional garden salad to fancy greens to convenient salad kits with all the accoutrements—fresh and ready to eat, all in a patented keep crisp bag. Getting salads to stay fresh in a bag, however, hasn't been an easy process. It took perseverance and creativity. The idea originated with Steve Taylor's father, who was trying to find a way to reduce the risks associated with his family's commodity lettuce business. He had the gut feeling that serving-size packaged salads would sell, but the problem was that lettuce and green vegetables turned brown in a bag. They just wouldn't stay fresh long enough. But Taylor didn't give in; he kept pushing to find a way to make his idea work. The eventual breakthrough came with the development and patenting of a new breathable film. As it turns out, the principal cause of decay in lettuce is the overabsorption of oxygen and a self-induced rapid rate of decomposition. Taylor's scientists eventually created a film that allowed more carbon dioxide to escape and less oxygen to enter; they also injected the bag with nitrogen. The result is a green salad made from thoroughly washed greens that can stay fresh for weeks—inside a bag.[1] No preservatives are needed or used.

O
rganizations depend for their success on day-to-day decisions made by their members. The quality of these decisions influences both the long-term performance of an organization and its day-to-day "character"—in the eyes of employees, customers, and society at large. Today's challenging environments, moreover, demand ever more rigor and creativity in the decision-making process. New products, such as the salad-in-a-bag, and new manufacturing and service processes all come from ideas. Organizations must provide for decision making that encourages the free flow of new ideas and supports the efforts of people who want to make their ideas work. And just as with organizations themselves, the success of our individual careers depends on the quality of the decisions we make regarding our jobs and employment situations.

Study Questions

Chapter 17 examines the many aspects of decision making in organizations. As you read the chapter, keep in mind these key questions.

- How are decisions made in organizations?
- What are the useful decision making models?
- How do intuition, judgment, and creativity affect decision making?
- How can the decision-making process be managed?
- How do technology, culture and ethics influence decision making?

Decision Making Process

■ **Decision making** is choosing a course of action to deal with a problem.

Formally defined, **decision making** is the process of choosing a course of action for dealing with a problem or opportunity.[2] The five basic steps involved in systematic decision making are:

Five steps in decision making

1. Recognize and define the problem or opportunity.
2. Identify and analyze alternative courses of action, and estimate their effects on the problem or opportunity.

3. Choose a preferred course of action.

4. Implement the preferred course of action.

5. Evaluate the results and follow up as necessary.

We must also recognize that in settings where substantial change and many new technologies prevail, this step-by-step approach may not be followed. Occasionally, a nontraditional sequence works and yields superior performance over the traditional view. We also think it is important to consider the ethical consequences of decision making. To understand when and where to use the traditional or novel decision techniques calls for a further understanding of decision environments and the types of decisions to be made.

■ DECISION ENVIRONMENTS

Problem-solving decisions in organizations are typically made under three different conditions or environments: certainty, risk, and uncertainty.[3] **Certain environments** exist when information is sufficient to predict the results of each alternative in advance of implementation. When a person invests money in a savings account, for example, absolute certainty exists about the interest that will be earned on that money in a given period of time. Certainty is an ideal condition for managerial problem solving and decision making. The challenge is simply to locate the alternative offering the best or ideal solution. Unfortunately, certainty is the exception instead of the rule in decision environments.

Risk environments exist when decision makers lack complete certainty regarding the outcomes of various courses of action, but they are aware of the probabilities associated with their occurrence. A *probability*, in turn, is the degree of likelihood of an event's occurrence. Probabilities can be assigned through objective statistical procedures or through personal intuition. For instance, managers can make statistical estimates of quality rejects in production runs, or a senior production manager can make similar estimates based on past experience. Risk is a common decision environment in today's organizations.

Uncertain environments exist when managers have so little information on hand that they cannot even assign probabilities to various alternatives and their possible outcomes. This is the most difficult of the three decision environments. Uncertainty forces decision makers to rely heavily on individual and group creativity to succeed in problem solving. It requires unique, novel, and often totally innovative alternatives to existing patterns of behavior. Responses to uncertainty are often heavily influenced by intuition, educated guesses, and hunches. Furthermore, an uncertain decision environment may also be characterized as a rapidly changing organizational setting in terms of (a) external conditions, (b) the information technology requirements called for to analyze and make decisions, and (c) the personnel influencing problem and choice definitions. This has been called an **organized anarchy**, a firm or division in a firm in a transition characterized by very rapid change and lack of a legitimate hierarchy and collegiality. Although this was once a very unique setting, many high-tech firms and those with expanding global operations share many of the characteristics of an organized anarchy.

■ **Certain environments** provide full information on the expected results for decision-making alternatives.

■ **Risk environments** provide probabilities regarding expected results for decision-making alternatives.

■ **Uncertain environments** provide no information to predict expected results for decision-making alternatives.

■ **Organized anarchy** is a firm or division in a firm in a transition characterized by very rapid change and lack of a legitimate hierarchy.

■ TYPES OF DECISIONS

■ **Programmed decisions**
are determined by past
experience as appropriate for
a problem at hand.

The many routine and nonroutine problems in the modern workplace call for different types of decisions. Routine problems arise on a regular basis and can be addressed through standard responses, called **programmed decisions**. These decisions simply implement solutions that have already been determined by past experience as appropriate for the problem at hand. Examples of programmed decisions are reordering inventory automatically when stock falls below a predetermined level and issuing a written reprimand to someone who violates a certain personnel procedure.

■ **Nonprogrammed
decisions** are created to
deal uniquely with a
problem at hand.

Nonroutine problems are unique and new, having never been encountered before. Because standard responses are not available, these circumstances call for creative problem solving. These **nonprogrammed decisions** are specifically crafted or tailored to the situation at hand. Higher level managers generally spend a greater proportion of their decision-making time on nonroutine problems. An example is a senior marketing manager who has to respond to the introduction of a new product by a foreign competitor. Although past experience may help deal with this competitive threat, the immediate decision requires a creative solution based on the unique characteristics of the present market situation.

■ **Associative choices** are
decisions that can be loosely
linked to nagging continual
problems but that were not
specifically developed to
solve the problem.

For firms in or characterized by "organized anarchy," we also suggest there is a third class of decisions called associative choices. **Associative choices** are decisions that can be loosely linked to nagging continual problems but that were not specifically developed to solve the problem. Given the chaotic nature of the setting, the necessity to take action as opposed to waiting, and the ability of employees to make nearly any "decision" work, a stream of associative choices may be used to improve the setting, even though the problems are not solved.

Decision Making Models

The field of organizational behavior historically emphasizes two alternative approaches to decision making—classical and behavioral (see Figure 17.1).[4] **Classical decision theory** models view the manager as acting in a world of complete certainty. **Behavioral decision theory** models accept the notion of bounded rationality and suggests that people act only in terms of what they perceive about a given situation.

■ **Classical decision
theory** views decision
makers as acting in a world
of complete certainty.

■ **Behavioral decision
theory** views decision
makers as acting only in
terms of what they perceive
about a given situation.

■ CLASSICAL AND BEHAVIORAL DECISION THEORY

Ideally, the manager faces a clearly defined problem, knows all possible action alternatives and their consequences, and then chooses the alternative that offers the best, or "optimum," solution to the problem. This optimizing style is an ideal way to make decisions. This classical approach is normative and prescriptive, and is often used as a model for how managers should make decisions.

TECHNOLOGY

For Saiyid T. Naqvi, president and CEO of PNC Mortgage, the installation of LINKS was a simple decision to use advanced technology to help employees make better decisions. As he suggested, "This is one more example of how we are maximizing the use of technology." What is it? It is a corporate intranet for better decision making called LINKS. The goals of LINKS, which uses Lotus Notes, is to (a) support an empowered working environment by sharing of timely information, (b) provide faster access to company data, (c) reduce paper work, and (d) establish a basis for better information flow in the future.

www.pncbank.com

Behavioral scientists are cautious about applying classical decision theory to many decision situations. They recognize that the human mind is a wonderful creation, capable of infinite achievements. But they also recognize that human beings have *cognitive limitations* that restrict their information-processing capabilities. Information deficiencies and overload compromise the ability of decision makers to achieve complete certainty and otherwise operate according to the classical model. Human decision makers also operate with *bounded rationality*.[5] Bounded rationality is a short-hand term suggesting that, while individuals are reasoned and logical, humans have their limits. Individuals interpret and make sense of things within the context of their personal situation. They engage in decision making "within the box" of a simplified view of a more complex reality. This makes it difficult to realize the ideal of classical decision making. As a result, the classical model does not give a full and accurate description of how most decisions are made in organizations.[6]

Classical decision theory does not appear to fit today's chaotic world of globalizing high-tech organizations, yet it would be a mistake to dismiss it and the

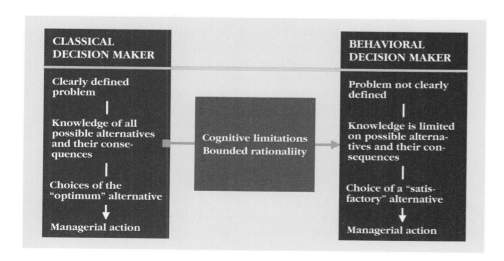

CLASSICAL DECISION MAKER		BEHAVIORAL DECISION MAKER
Clearly defined problem		Problem not clearly defined
Knowledge of all possible alternatives and their consequences	Cognitive limitations Bounded rationaliity	Knowledge is limited on possible alternatives and their consequences
Choices of the "optimum" alternative		Choice of a "satisfactory" alternative
Managerial action		Managerial action

Figure 17.1
Decision making viewed from the classical and behavioral perspectives.

types of progress that can be made with classical models. Classical models can be used toward the bottom of many firms. For instance, even the most high-tech firm faces many clearly defined problems with known alternatives where firms have already selected an optimal solution. That a firm's managers don't know the answer may make it appear nonclassical when, in fact, it should not be.

As noted above, **behavioral decision theory** models accept the notion of bounded rationality and suggest that people act only in terms of what they perceive about a given situation. Because these perceptions are frequently imperfect, most organizational decision making does not take place in a world of complete certainty. Rather, the behavioral decision maker is viewed as acting most often under uncertain conditions and with limited information. Organizational decision makers face problems that are often ambiguous, and they have only partial knowledge of the available action alternatives and their consequences. This leads to a phenomenon which Herbert Simon has described as **satisficing**—decision makers choose the first alternative that appears to give an acceptable or a satisfactory resolution of the problem. As Simon states: "Most human decision making, whether individual or organizational, is concerned with the discovery and selection of satisfactory alternatives; only in exceptional cases is it concerned with the discovery and selection of optimal decisions."[7]

■ **Satisficing** is choosing the first alternative that appears to give an acceptable or satisfactory resolution of the problem.

■ THE GARBAGE CAN MODEL

■ **Garbage can model** views the main components of the choice process— problems, solutions, participants, and choice situations—as all mixed up together in the garbage can of the organization.

A third view of decision making stems from the so-called **garbage can model**.[8] In this view, the main components of the choice process—problems, solutions, participants, and choice situations—are all mixed up together in the "garbage can" of the organization. In many organizations where the setting is stable and the technology is well known and fixed, tradition, strategy, and the administrative structure help order the contents of the garbage can. Specific problems can be matched to specific solutions, an orderly process can be maintained, and the behavior view of decision making may be appropriate.

But when the setting is dynamic, the technology is changing, demands are conflicting or the goals are unclear, things can get mixed up. More action than thinking can take place. Solutions emerge as "potential capabilities"—capabilities independent of problems or opportunities. Solutions often emerge not to solve specific problems but as lessons learned from the experience of other organizations. These new solution/capabilities may be in the form of new employees, new technical experts, consultants, or reports on best practices. Many solutions might well be implemented even if they cannot be tied to a specific problem. Solutions may also be implemented when no other solution has solved a persistent, chronic problem. Although implemented solutions change the organization, they are unlikely to solve specific problems.

The garbage can model highlights an important feature of decision making in many large organizations. Choice making and implementation may be done by quite different individuals. Often, the job of subordinates is to make the decisions of senior managers work. They must interpret the intentions of their bosses as well as solve local problems. Implementation becomes an opportunity to instill many changes related to the choice of more senior executives. So what is chosen gets implemented along with many other changes. The link between choice and implementation may become even weaker when senior managers are vague or do not vigorously follow up on implementation. The net result from those actually implementing the decision is the appearance that what was chosen does not exactly match what is implemented.

There is a final aspect of the garbage can view. Many problems go unsolved. That is, all organizations have chronic, persistent deficiencies that never seem to get much better. In a garbage can view, this is because decision makers cannot agree to match these problems with solutions, make a choice, and implement it on a timely and consistent basis; nor do they know how to resolve chronic problems. It is only when a problem and a solution "bump into one another" under a decision maker willing to implement a choice that problems, solutions, and choice come together as expected under other views. Thus, one key job challenge for the astute manager is to make the appropriate linkages among problems and solutions.

■ DECISION MAKING REALITIES

All three of these models highlight specific features of the complex choice processes managers must engage in as professionals. A key difference between a manager's ability to make an optimum decision in the classical style and the manager's tendency to make a satisfying decision in the behavioral style is the availability of information. The organizational realities of bounded rationality and cognitive limitations affect the way people define problems, identify action alternatives, and choose preferred courses of action. By necessity, most decision making in organizations involves more than the linear and step-by-step rational choice that models often suggest. The process may not be as chaotic as the garbage can models; yet it is often not as rational as even a behavioral view suggests. In real organizations, decisions must be made under risk and uncertainty. Decisions must be made to solve nonroutine problems. And decisions must be made under the pressures of time and information limitations.

> **OB Across Functions**
>
> **MARKETING**
>
> **The Making of a Good Banker:
> From Marketing to President**
>
> The president of PNC Bank–Northwest, Marlene D. Mosco, did not major in accounting or finance in school, and she did not work her way up the bank through the operations or loan sections, the typical path to be a bank president. Rather, Marlene graduated from Mercyhurst College and systematically climbed the ladder rung by rung from training director, to marketing officer, to PR director, to VP of marketing, to senior VP and manager of retail banking (the number-two slot) before becoming president. The key to her success? Marlene learned how to make good decisions and to help others make good decisions. Even outside the bank, people noticed as she was chosen one of Pennsylvania's Best 50 Women in Business.

Intuition, Judgment, and Creativity

Choices always bear the unique imprint of the individuals who make them, the politics within the organization, and the challenges facing its decision makers. In reality, intuition, judgment, and creativity are as critical as understanding how decisions can be made.

A key element in decision making under risk and uncertainty is intuition. **Intuition** is the ability to know or recognize quickly and readily the possibilities of a given situation.[9] Intuition adds elements of personality and spontaneity to decision making. As a result, it offers potential for creativity and innovation.

In an earlier time, scholars carried on a vigorous debate regarding how managers should plan and make decisions.[10] On one side of the issue were those who believed that planning could be accomplished in a systematic step-by-step

■ **Intuition** is the ability to know or recognize quickly the possibilities of a situation.

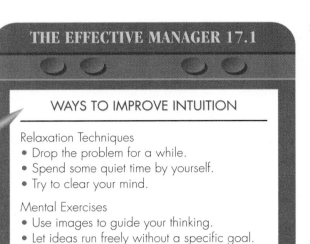

THE EFFECTIVE MANAGER 17.1

WAYS TO IMPROVE INTUITION

Relaxation Techniques
• Drop the problem for a while.
• Spend some quiet time by yourself.
• Try to clear your mind.

Mental Exercises
• Use images to guide your thinking.
• Let ideas run freely without a specific goal.

fashion. On the other side were those who believed that the very nature of managerial work made this hard to achieve in actual practice. We now know that managers favor verbal communication. Thus, they are more likely to gather data and to make decisions in a relational or interactive way than in a systematic step-by-step fashion.[11] Managers often deal with impressions. Thus, they are more likely to synthesize than to analyze data as they search for the "big picture" in order to redefine problems and link problems with a variety of solutions. Managers work fast, do a variety of things, and are frequently interrupted. Thus, they do not have a lot of quiet time alone to think, plan, or make decisions systematically (see The Effective Manager 17.1).

Are managers correct when they favor the more intuitive and less systematic approach? The more chaotic environments and technologies of many of today's organizations press for this emphasis on intuition. Unfortunately, many business firms are better at implementing the common solutions of others than uniquely solving their problems. Since managers do work in chaotic settings, this reality should be accepted and decision makers should be confident in using their intuitive skills. However, they should combine analytical and intuitive approaches to create new and novel solutions to complex problems.

www.nokia.com

🌐 GLOBALIZATION

Nokia, initially a Finnish Corporation, is the world's second largest mobile phone manufacturer and a leading supplier of digital and fixed networks. Its ability to maintain its leadership position in the fastest growing telecommunications segments is based squarely on its employees and the way they make decisions. It is not just a Finnish way—it is a Nokia way. The choice-making process is characterized by an emphasis on technology development and goals attainment, not bureaucracy, so that Nokia can quickly apply and refine the newest technologies. The decision-making process is supported by four Nokia values—customer satisfaction, respect for the individual, achievement, and continuous learning. Moreover, Nokia managers recognize that the application and emphasis on these values as well as their incorporation into the decision-making process will vary substantially across different cultures.

■ JUDGMENTAL HEURISTICS

Judgment, or the use of one's intellect, is important in all aspects of decision making. When we question the ethics of a decision, for example, we are questioning the "judgment" of the person making it. Research shows that people are prone to mistakes using biases that often interfere with the quality of decision making.[12] These can be traced to the use of **heuristics**—simplifying strategies or "rules of thumb" used to make decisions. Heuristics serve a useful purpose in making it easier to deal with uncertainty and limited information in problem situations. But they can also lead to systematic errors that affect the quality, and perhaps the ethical implications, of any decisions made. It is helpful to understand the common judgmental heuristics of availability, representativeness, and anchoring and adjustment.[13]

The **availability heuristic** involves assessing a current event based on past occurrences that are easily available in one's memory. An example is the product development specialist who bases a decision not to launch a new product on her recent failure with another product offering. In this case, the existence of a past product failure has negatively, and perhaps inappropriately, biased the decision maker's judgment of how to best handle the new product.

The **representativeness heuristic** involves assessing the likelihood that an event will occur based on its similarity to one's stereotypes of similar occurrences. An example is the team leader who selects a new member not because of any special qualities of the person, but only because the individual comes from a department known to have produced high performers in the past. In this case, it is the individual's current place of employment—and not his or her job qualifications—that is the basis for the selection decision.

The **anchoring and adjustment heuristic** involves assessing an event by taking an initial value from historical precedent or an outside source, and then incrementally adjusting this value to make a current assessment. An example is the executive who makes salary increase recommendations for key personnel by simply adjusting their current base salaries by a percentage amount. In this case, the existing base salary becomes an "anchor" that drives subsequent salary increases. In some situations this anchor may be inappropriate, such as the case of an individual whose market value has become substantially higher than is reflected by the base salary plus increment.

In addition to using the common judgmental heuristics, decision makers are also prone to more general biases in decision making. One bias is the **confirmation trap**, whereby the decision maker seeks confirmation for what is already thought to be true and neglects opportunities to acknowledge or find disconfirming information. A form of selective perception, this bias involves seeking only those cues in a situation that support a preexisting opinion. A second bias is the **hindsight trap**, whereby the decision maker overestimates the degree to which he or she could have predicted an event that has already taken place. One risk of hindsight is that it may foster feelings of inadequacy or insecurity in dealing with future decision situations.

■ CREATIVITY FACTORS

Creativity in decision making involves the development of unique and novel responses to problems and opportunities. In a dynamic environment full of nonroutine problems, creativity in crafting decisions often determines how well people and organizations do in response to complex challenges.[14]

In Part 3 of this book, we examined the group as an important resource for improving creativity in decision making. Indeed, making good use of such traditional techniques as brainstorming, nominal groups, and the Delphi method can greatly expand the creative potential of people and organizations. The addition

■ **Heuristics** are simplifying strategies or "rules of thumb" used to make decisions.

■ The **availability heuristic** bases a decision on recent events relating to the situation at hand.

■ The **representativeness heuristic** bases a decision on similarities between the situation at hand and stereotypes of similar occurrences.

■ The **anchoring and adjustment heuristic** bases a decision on incremental adjustments to an initial value determined by historical precedent or some reference point.

■ The **confirmation trap** is the tendency to seek confirmation for what is already thought to be true and to not search for disconfirming information.

■ The **hindsight trap** is a tendency to overestimate the degree to which an event that has already taken place could have been predicted.

■ **Creativity** generates unique and novel responses to problems. Individual decisions are made by one individual on behalf of a group.

Greg Steltenpohl didn't want to just start a business, he wanted one that "…didn't wreak havoc on the environment." The result was Odwalla, Inc., the nation's leading ready-to-serve fresh squeezed and nutritionally fortified juice and smoothie company. Its all-natural and no-preservative beverages, and now food bars, are proving popular with consumers across the country.

of new computer-based group meeting and decision-making techniques extends this great potential even further.

Creative thinking may unfold in a series of five stages. First is *preparation*.[15] Here people engage in the active learning and day-to-day sensing required to deal successfully with complex environments. The second stage is *concentration*, whereby actual problems are defined and framed so that alternatives can be considered for dealing with them. In the third stage, *incubation*, people look at the problems in diverse ways that permit the consideration of unusual alternatives, avoiding tendencies toward purely linear and systematic problem solving. The fourth stage is *illumination* in which people respond to flashes of insight and recognize when all pieces to the puzzle suddenly fit into place. The fifth and final stage is *verification*, which proceeds with logical analysis to confirm that good problem-solving decisions have really been made.[16]

All of these stages of creativity need support and encouragement in the organizational environment. However, creative thinking in decision making can be limited by a number of factors. Judgmental heuristics like those just reviewed can limit the search for alternatives. When attractive options are left unconsidered, creativity can be limited. Cultural and environmental blocks can also limit creativity. This occurs when people are discouraged from considering alternatives viewed as inappropriate by cultural standards or inconsistent with prevailing norms.

Managing the Decision-Making Process

As suggested by our discussion of creativity, people working at all levels, in all areas, and in all types and sizes of organizations are not supposed to simply make decisions. They must make *good* decisions—the right decisions in the right way at the right time.[17] Managing the decision-making process involves choices itself. Critical choices include which "problems" to work on, who to involve and how to involve them as well as when to quit.

■ CHOOSING PROBLEMS TO ADDRESS

Most people are too busy and have too many valuable things to do with their time to personally make the decisions on every problem or opportunity that comes their way. The effective manager and team leader knows when to delegate decisions to others, how to set priorities, and when to abstain from acting altogether. When faced with the dilemma of whether or not to deal with a specific problem, asking and answering the following questions can sometimes help.[18]

Is the problem easy to deal with? Small and less significant problems should not get the same time and attention as bigger ones. Even if a mistake is made, the cost of decision error on small problems is also small. *Might the problem resolve itself?* Putting problems in rank order leaves the less significant for last. Surprisingly, many of these less important problems resolve themselves or are solved by others before you get to them. One less problem to solve leaves decision-making time and energy for other uses. *Is this my decision to make?* Many problems can be handled by other persons. They should be delegated to people who are best prepared to deal with them; ideally, they should be delegated to people whose work they most affect. Finally, *is this a solvable problem within the context of the organization?* The astute decision maker recognizes the difference between problems that realistically can be solved and those that are simply not solvable for all practical purposes.

■ DECIDING WHO SHOULD PARTICIPATE

A mistake commonly made by many new managers and team leaders is presuming that they must solve every problem by making every decision themselves. In practice, good organizational decisions are made by individuals acting alone, by individuals consulting with others, and by groups of people working together.

When individual decisions, also called **authority decisions**, are made, the manager or team leader uses information that he or she possesses and decides what to do without involving others. This decision method often reflects the prerogatives of a person's position of formal authority in the organization. For instance, in deciding a rotation for lunch hours in a retail store, the manager may post a schedule. In **consultative decisions**, by contrast, inputs on the problem are solicited from other persons. Based on this information and its interpretation, the decision maker arrives at a final choice. To continue the example, the manager may tell subordinates that a lunch schedule is needed and ask them when they would like to schedule their lunch and why before making the decision. In other cases, true **group decisions** can be made by both consulting with others and allowing them to help make the final choice. To complete the example, the manager may hold a meeting to get everyone's agreement on a lunch schedule or a system for deciding how to make the schedule.

Victor Vroom, Phillip Yetton, and Arthur Jago have developed a framework for helping managers choose which of these decision-making methods is most appropriate for various problem situations.[19] (See Figure 17.2.) The central proposition in their model is that the decision-making method used should always be appropriate to the problem being solved. The challenge is to know when and how to implement each of the possible methods as the situation demands. They further clarify individual, consultative, and group decision options as follows.

- **AI** (*first variant on the authority decision*): The manager solves the problem or makes the decision alone, using information available at that time.

- **AII** (*second variant on the authority decision*): The manager obtains the necessary information from subordinate(s) or other group members and then decides on the problem solution. The manager may or may not tell subordinates what the problem is before obtaining the information from them. The subordinates provide the necessary information but do not generate or evaluate alternatives.

- **CI** (*first variant on the consultative decision*): The manager shares the problem with relevant subordinates or other group members individually, getting their ideas and suggestions without bringing them together as a group. The manager then makes a decision that may or may not reflect the subordinates' input.

■ **Authority decisions** are made by the manager or team leader without involving others using information that he or she possesses.

■ **Consultative decisions** are made by one individual after seeking input from or consulting with members of a group.

■ **Group decisions** are made by all members of the group.

Decision-making methods

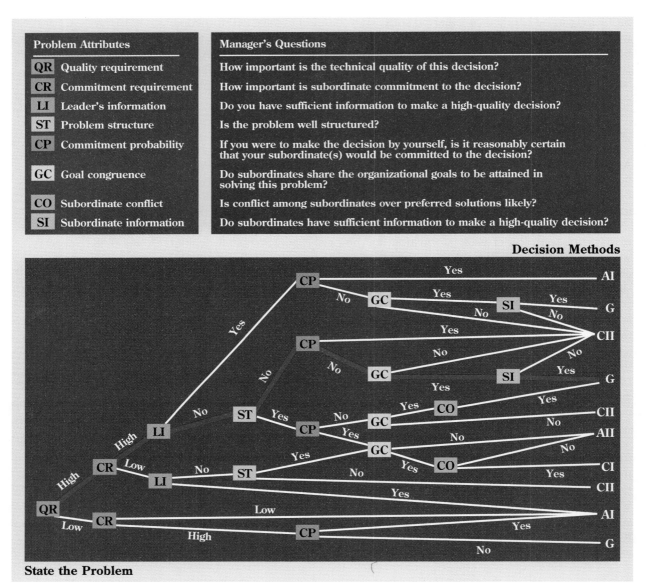

Figure 17.2
Selecting alternative decision-making methods: The Vroom and Jago decision process flowchart.

- **CII** (*second variant on the consultative decision*): The manager shares the problem with subordinates or other group members, collectively obtaining their ideas and suggestions. The manager then makes a decision that may or may not reflect the subordinates' input.

- **G** (*the group or consensus decision*): The manager shares the problem with the subordinates as a total group and engages the group in consensus seeking to arrive at a final decision.

In the most recent version of this decision-making framework, Vroom and Jago use the flowchart shown in Figure 17.2 to help managers analyze problem situations and choose the most appropriate decision-making methods. Key issues involve the quality requirements of a decision, the availability and location of the relevant information, the commitments needed to fully implement the decision, and the amount of time available. Although this model appears complex and cumbersome, its underlying logic offers a useful decision-making discipline. Try it by working through Figure 17.2 for an organizational problem with which you are familiar. The analysis forces you to recognize how time, quality requirements, information availability, and subordinate acceptance issues can affect decision outcomes. It also reminds you that all of the decision methods are important and useful. The key to effectively managing participation in decision making is first knowing when to use each decision method and then knowing how to implement each of them well.

■ KNOWING WHEN TO QUIT— ELIMINATING ESCALATING COMMITMENTS

The organization's natural desire to continue on a selected course of action reinforces some natural tendencies among decision makers.[20] Once the agonizing process of making a choice is apparently completed, executives make public commitments to implementation, and implementation begins, managers are often reluctant to change their minds and admit a mistake. Instead of backing off, the tendency is to press on to victory. This is called **escalating commitment**— continuation and renewed efforts on a previously chosen course of action, even though it is not working. Escalating commitment is reflected in the popular adage, "If at first you don't succeed, try, try, again."

In beginning Finance courses, students learn about the fallacy of sunk costs. Money committed and spent is gone. The decision to continue is just that—a decision. It needs to be based on what investment is needed and the returns on that investment. This is one of the most difficult aspects of decision making to convey to executives simply because so many of these executives rose to their positions by turning apparently losing courses of action into winners.[21] The tendency to escalate commitments often outweighs the willingness to disengage from them. Decision makers may rationalize negative feedback as a temporary condition, protect their egos by not admitting that the original decision was a mistake, or characterize any negative results as a "learning experience" that can be overcome with added future effort.[22]

The self-discipline required to admit mistakes and change direction, however, is sometimes difficult to achieve. Escalating commitments are a form of decision entrapment that leads people to do things that the facts of a situation do not justify. We should be proactive in spotting "failures" and more open to reversing decisions or dropping plans that do not appear to be working.[23] But again, this is easier said than done. Good decision makers know when to call it quits. They are willing to reverse previous decisions and stop investing time and other resources in unsuccessful courses of action. As the late W. C. Fields is said to have muttered, "If at first you don't succeed, try, try, again. Then quit."

■ **Escalating commitment** is the tendency to continue a previously chosen course of action even when feedback suggests that it is failing.

Technology, Culture, and Ethics in Decision Making

In today's environments, the problems facing organizational decision makers seem to get ever more complex. For example, consider the following workplace trends:[24]

Key workplace trends

- Businesses are becoming smaller in size; they are doing more outsourcing and employing fewer full-time workers.
- New, more flexible, and adaptable organizational forms are replacing the traditional pyramid structures.
- Multifunctional understanding is increasingly important as organizations emphasize lateral coordination.
- Workers with both technical knowledge and team skills are becoming increasingly sought after.
- The nature of "work" is in flux as jobs change fast, require continuous learning, and are less bound by the "9 to 5" tradition.

Each of these trends is changing who, when, where, and how decision making is accomplished. We face difficult stresses and strains as the quest for higher and higher productivity challenges the needs, talents, and opportunities of people at work. Complexities in the decision making process include issues of information technology, culture and ethics.

■ INFORMATION TECHNOLOGY AND DECISION MAKING

■ **Artificial intelligence** is the study of how computers can be programmed to think like the human brain.

As we have discussed throughout this book, today's organizations are becoming ever more sophisticated in applying information technologies. Eventually, developments in the field of **artificial intelligence** (AI), the study of how computers can be programmed to think like the human brain, will allow computers to displace many decision makers.[25] Nobel Laureate and decision scientist Herbert Simon is convinced that computers will someday be more intelligent than humans.

Already, the applications of AI to organizational decision making are significant. We have access to decision-making support from expert systems that reason like human experts and follow "either-or" rules to make deductions. For example, if you call an advertised 800 number to apply for a home equity loan, you will not get a human but a computer program to take all the necessary information and provide confirmation of a loan. On the factory floor, decision support systems schedule machines and people for maximum production efficiencies.

In the very near future, fuzzy logic that reasons beyond either-or choices and neural networks that reason inductively by simulating the brain's parallel processing capabilities will become operational realities to move beyond simple programmed decisions. Uses for such systems may be found everywhere from hospitals where they will check on medical diagnoses to investment houses where they will analyze potential investment portfolios to a wide and growing variety of other settings.[26]

Computer support for group decision making, including developments with the Internet and with intranets, has broken the decision-making meeting out of the confines of face-to-face interactions. With the software now available, problems can be defined and decisions can be made through virtual teamwork by people in geographically dispersed locations. We know that group decision software can be especially useful for generating ideas, such as in electronic brainstorming, and for improving the time efficiency of decisions. People working under electronically mediated conditions tend to stay focused on tasks and avoid the interpersonal conflicts and other problems common in face-to-face deliberations. On the negative side, decisions made by "electronic groups" carry some risks of being impersonal and perhaps less compelling in terms of commitments to implementation and follow-through. There is evidence, moreover, that use of computer technology for decision making is better accepted by today's college students than by persons who are already advanced in their organizational careers.[27]

What new information technology will not do is deal with the issues raised by the garbage can model. The information technologies promise a more orderly world where the process of choosing conforms more to the traditional models with an extension of the normal boundaries of rationality. For us, what is still on the information technology horizon are the most important decisions that come before the classical and standard approaches. These are pre-decision choices that are heavily influenced by cultural factors and ethics.

TECHNOLOGY

At Analog Devices the TigerSharc is now on top, and Analog is leading the charge in the development of DSP chips. TigerSharc is the name given to one of Analog's digital signal processing chips (DSPs). DSPs are the latest in a series of specialized computer chips to transform analog signals, such as speech or radio waves, into the digital zeros and ones of most chips and to make this conversion at amazing speed. In other terms, these chips can begin to mimic human senses for the computer. For some the dream has always been a computer that would obey spoken commands, as in Star Trek; for others it was the dream of artificial computer-driven limbs as in the *Bionic Woman* TV series. With the DSP chips able to process speech and transform it so that other chips can use it in the more conventional digital manner, we are on the threshold of substituting a computer chip to make quick, certain choices based on verbal commands. Want an optimal TV program for the evening? Just talk to the TV. Based on your preferences, it will pick the best program available.

www.analog.com

■ CULTURAL FACTORS AND DECISION MAKING

Fons Trompenaars notes that culture is "the way in which a group of people solves problems."[28] It is only reasonable to expect that as cultures vary so too will choices concerning what is to be solved and how. For example, there are historical cultural preferences for solving problems. The approach favored in this

Advanced Telecom Research Laboratory

Hugo de Varis dreams of the day when a computer possesses brainpower equal to that of all humans that have ever lived. At Advanced Telecom Research Laboratory in Japan, he is part of a brain-builder team creating computer chips that act like the human brain and central nervous system. Artificial intelligence, or AI, studies how computers can be made to think like the human brain.

chapter emphasizes the North American view stressing decisiveness, speed, and individual selection of alternatives. This view speaks more to choice and less to implementation. Yet, the garbage can view suggests that implementation can proceed almost separately from other aspects of decision making.

Other cultures place less emphasis on individual choice than on developing implementations that work. They start with what is workable and better rather than with the classical and behavioral comparison of current conditions with some ideal.[29] If a change can improve the current situation, even if it is not apparently directed toward a problem identified by senior management, subordinate managers may work together to implement it. And then senior management may be informed of the success of the change. To emphasize the importance of smooth implementation over grand decision making, corporations may adopt systems similar to the Japanese ringi system where lower-levels indicate their written approval of proposals prior to formal implementation. Written approval is an issue not of whether the change should be done but whether it is feasible for the group to implement.[30]

The more important role of culture in decision making concerns not how problems are solved but which concerns are elevated to the status of problems solvable within the firm. For instance, the very fact that a procedure is old may make it more suspect in the United States than in France.[31] Far too many of our views maybe dictated by Western bureaucratic thinking.[32] Not all cultures are as pluralistic, bluntly competitive, or impersonal as that of the United States. In other parts of the world, personal loyalties may drive decisions, and preserving harmony may be considered more important than achieving a bit more efficiency. In short, problems may be more person centered and socially defined than bureaucratically proscribed.

■ ETHICAL ISSUES AND DECISION MAKING

The subject of ethical behavior in the workplace cannot be overemphasized, and it is worth reviewing once again the framework for ethical decision making first introduced in Chapter 1. An *ethical dilemma* was defined as a situation in which a person must decide whether or not to do something that, although personally or organizationally beneficial, may be considered unethical and perhaps illegal. Often, ethical dilemmas are associated with risk and uncertainty, and with nonroutine problem situations. Just how decisions are handled under these circumstances, ones that will inevitably appear during your career, may well be the ultimate test of your personal ethical framework.

An Effective Manager feature in Chapter 1 introduced a useful decision-making checklist for resolving ethical dilemmas. Before any decision is made the checklist tests the preliminary decision with stiff questions.[33] First, it would have you ask: "Is my action legal? Is it right? Is it beneficial?" Second, it would have you ask: "How would I feel if my family found out about this? How would I feel if my decision were printed in the local newspaper?" Only after these questions are asked and satisfactorily answered, does the model suggest you should take action.

When it comes to the ethics of decision making, the criteria individuals use to define problems and the values that underlie these criteria must be considered.[34] Moral conduct is involved in choosing problems, deciding who should be involved, estimating the impacts of alternatives, and selecting an alternative for implementation.

Moral conduct does not arise from after-the-fact embarrassment. As Fineman suggests, "If people are unable to anticipate shame or guilt before they act in particular ways, then moral codes are invalid.... Decisions may involve lying, deceit, fraud, evasion of negligence—disapproved of in many cultures. But ethical monitoring and control go beyond just the pragmatics of harm."[35] In other words, when you are the decision maker, decision making is not just a choice process followed by implementation for the good of the organization. It involves your values and your morality whether or not you think it should. Thus, effective implemented choices need to not only solve a problem or capitalize on choices but also match your values and help others. It is little wonder, then, that decision making will likely be the biggest challenge of your organizational career.[36]

Chapter 17 Study Guide

Summary

How are decisions made in organizations?

■ Decision making is a process of identifying problems and opportunities and choosing among alternative courses of action for dealing successfully with them.

■ Organizational decisions are often made in risky and uncertain environments, where situations are ambiguous and information is limited.

■ Routine and repetitive problems can be dealt with through programmed decisions; nonroutine or novel problems require nonprogrammed decisions that are crafted to fit the situation at hand.

What are the useful decision making models?

■ According to classical decision theory, optimum decisions are made after carefully analyzing all possible alternatives and their known consequences.

■ According to behavioral decision theory, most organizational decisions are made with limited information and by satisficing—choosing the first acceptable or satisfactory solutions to problems.

■ According to the garbage can model, the main components of the choice process— problems, solutions, participants, choice situations—are all mixed up together in the garbage can of the organization.

How do intuition, judgment, and creativity affect decision making?

■ Intuition is the ability to recognize quickly the action possibilities for resolving a problem situation.

■ Both systematic decision making and intuitive decision making are important in today's complex work environments.

■ The use of judgmental heuristics, or simplifying rules of thumb, is common in decision making but can lead to biased results.

■ Common heuristics include availability decisions based on recent events; representativeness decisions based on similar events; and anchoring and adjustment decisions based on historical precedents.

■ Creativity in finding unique and novel solutions to problems can be enhanced through both individual and group problem-solving strategies.

How can the decision-making process be managed?

■ Good managers know that not every problem requires an immediate decision; they also know how and when to delegate decision-making responsibilities.

■ A common mistake is for a manager or team leader to make all decisions alone; instead, a full range of individual, consultative, and group decision-making methods should be utilized.

■ The Vroom–Yetton/Jago model offers a way of matching problems with appropriate decision methods, based on quality requirements, information availability, and time constraints.

■ Tendencies toward escalating commitment, continuing previously chosen courses of action even when they are not working, should be recognized in work settings.

How do technology, culture and ethics influence decision making?

■ Technological developments are continuing to change the nature of organizational decision making.

■ Culture counts; differences in culture alter who, how, when, and why decisions are made.

■ Ethics is involved in each stage of the decision-making process, and effective decision making includes individual moral criteria and values.

Key Terms

Anchoring and adjustment heuristic (p. 361)
Artificial intelligence (p. 366)
Associative choices (p. 356)
Authority decisions (p. 363)
Availability heuristic (p. 361)
Behavioral decision theory (p. 356)
Certain environments (p. 355)
Classical decision theory (p. 356)

Confirmation trap (p. 361)
Consultative decisions (p. 363)
Creativity (p. 361)
Decision making (p. 354)
Escalating commitment (p. 365)
Garbage can model (p. 358)
Group decisions (p. 363)
Heuristics (p. 361)
Hindsight trap (p. 361)
Intuition (p. 360)

Nonprogrammed decisions (p. 356)
Organized anarchy (p. 355)
Programmed decisions (p. 356)
Representativeness heuristic (p. 361)
Risk environments (p. 355)
Satisficing (p. 358)
Uncertain environment (p. 355)

Self-Test 17   ■ MULTIPLE CHOICE

1. After a preferred course of action has been implemented, the next step in the decision-making process is to _____. (a) recycle the process (b) look for addi-

tional problems or opportunities (c) evaluate results (d) document the reasons for the decision

2. In which environment does the decision maker deal with probabilities regarding possible courses of action and their consequences? (a) certain (b) risk (c) organized anarchy (d) uncertain

3. In which characterizations of the decision environment is associative choice most likely to occur? (a) organized anarchy (b) certainty (c) risk (d) satisficing setting

4. A manager who must deal with limited information and substantial risk is most likely to make decisions based on _____. (a) optimizing (b) classical decision theory (c) behavioral decision theory (d) escalation

5. A team leader who makes a decision not to launch a new product because the last new product launch failed is falling prey to the _____ heuristic. (a) anchoring (b) availability (c) adjustment (d) representativeness

6. The five steps in the creativity process are preparation, _____, illumination, _____, and verification. (a) extension, evaluation (b) reduction, concentration (c) adaptation, extension (d) concentration, incubation

7. In Vroom's decision-making model, the choice among individual and group decision methods is based on criteria that include quality requirements, availability of information, and _____. (a) need for implementation commitments (b) size of organization (c) number of people involved (d) position power of leader

8. The saying "If at first you don't succeed, try and try again" is most associated with a decision-making tendency called _____. (a) groupthink (b) the confirmation trap (c) escalating commitment (d) associative choice

9. Among the developments with artificial intelligence, _____ attempt to have computers reason inductively in solving problems. (a) neural networks (b) expert systems (c) fuzzy logics (d) electronic brainstorms

10. Preferences for who makes decisions (a) vary slightly across cultures (b) characterize individualistic cultures (c) are important only in high power distance (d) vary substantially across cultures.

■ TRUE–FALSE

11. Most managerial decisions take place in certain environments.   T   F

12. Nonprogrammed decisions fit best with routine and repetitive problems.   T   F

13. Systematic decision making is always preferred to intuitive decision making.   T   F

14. Managers do not have to solve all the problems that come their way.   T   F

15. Escalating commitments is a way of improving implementation of group decisions.   T   F

16. A good way to resolve a nagging problem is to implement some of the new information technology solutions.   T   F

17. The ringi system is a Japanese approach to gaining lower-level agreement and making sure that decisions can be implemented.   T   F

18. Group consensus is always preferred to the authority decision.   T   F

19. Impersonality in relationships is one possible disadvantage of electronic group decision making.   T   F

20. In the final analysis, the turbulence in today's work environments makes decision making impossible.   T   F

■ SHORT RESPONSE

21. What are heuristics, and how can they affect individual decision making?

22. What are the main differences among individual, consultative, and group decisions?

23. What is escalating commitment, and why is it important to recognize in decision making?

24. What questions might a manager or team leader ask to help determine which problems to deal with and with what priorities?

■ APPLICATIONS ESSAY

25. Your friends know you are taking OB courses and constantly show you Dilbert cartoons in which managers are implementing decisions that are unrelated to problems. What insight can you share with them to understand Dilbert better?

Explore application-oriented Fast Company articles, cases, experimental exercises, and self-assessments in the OB Skills Workbook

■ **Visit the Schermerhorn Web site to find the Interactive Self-Test and Internet exercises for this chapter.**

Conflict and Negotiation

TAKING MATTERS INTO YOUR OWN HANDS

www.nawbo.org

When Whitney Johns couldn't get sufficient investment capital to expand her consulting firm for small and mid-sized businesses, she took matters into her own hands. A member of the board for the National Association of Women Business Owners, she founded an investment firm, Capital Across America, specifically to serve women-owned businesses. The firm provides capital to companies that need at least $300,000 to expand. Over 8 million business owners in the United States are women, and they employ one in four American corporate workers. But it is often hard for women to break into the world of substantial investment capital, as Johns well knew from her own experience in trying to establish her investment firm. She says: "I had to go outside of my existing network and talk to people who didn't really understand the dynamic women-business-owner market. We talked to a lot of people that had blank looks on their faces."

Most of the capital funds that Johns dealt with were managed by men, who seemed more comfortable dealing with men. Johns believes that women and men have somewhat different approaches to business. According to her, women often underestimate themselves and consequently don't ask for enough money during negotiations to accomplish their business goals. Men, by contrast, "shoot for the moon" and ask for more than they typically need. But women have a great capacity to develop extensive networks and relationships—with customers, suppliers, and others. These are great resources that can be rallied to help a business in economic difficulties. As a final reminder in dealing with the venture capitalists, however, Johns tells women to remember the basics when entering the negotiation: "Have an excellent business plan." [1]

The daily work of people in organizations is intensely based on communication and interpersonal relationships. Managers must therefore have the interpersonal skills to work well with others in order to implement action agendas in situations that are often complicated and stressful. [2] The exchange of information in the workplace is typically purposeful and intentionally persuasive, as was the case in the opening vignette of Whitney Johns and her quest for venture business capital. At the same time, communication in interpersonal relationships frequently opens the door for differences and disagreements that can create difficulties. Success in today's high performance organizations increasingly requires a good understanding of the fundamentals of conflict and negotiation.

Study Questions

This chapter introduces you to conflict and negotiation as key processes of organizational behavior that can have a substantial impact on the performance and satisfaction of people at work. As you read Chapter 18, keep in mind these study questions.

- What is conflict?
- How can conflict be managed successfully?
- What is negotiation?
- What are the different strategies involved in negotiation?

Conflict

■ **Conflict** occurs when parties disagree over substantive issues or when emotional antagonisms create friction between them.

Conflict occurs whenever disagreements exist in a social situation over issues of substance or whenever emotional antagonisms create frictions between individuals or groups. [3] Managers and team leaders can spend considerable time dealing with conflict, including conflicts in which the manager or leader is directly involved as one of the principal actors. [4] In other situations, the manager or leader may act as a mediator, or third party, whose job it is to resolve conflicts between other people. In all cases, a manager and team leader must be comfortable with the interpersonal conflict. This includes being able to recognize situations that have the potential for conflict and to deal with these situations in ways that will best serve the needs of both the organization and the people involved. [5]

■ TYPES OF CONFLICT

Conflict as it is experienced in the daily workplace involves at least two basic forms. **Substantive conflict** is a fundamental disagreement over ends or goals to be pursued and the means for their accomplishment. [6] A dispute with one's boss over a plan of action to be followed, such as the marketing strategy for a new product, is an example of substantive conflict. When people work together day in and day out, it is only normal that different viewpoints on a variety of substantive workplace issues will arise. At times people will disagree over such things as group and organizational goals, the allocation of resources, the distribution of rewards, policies and procedures, and task assignments. Dealing with such conflicts successfully is an everyday challenge for most managers.

By contrast, **emotional conflict** involves interpersonal difficulties that arise over feelings of anger, mistrust, dislike, fear, resentment, and the like. [7] This conflict is commonly known as a "clash of personalities." Emotional conflicts can drain the energies of people and distract them from important work priorities. They can emerge from a wide variety of settings and are common among co-workers as well as in superior–subordinate relationships. The latter form of emotional conflict is perhaps the most upsetting organizational conflict for any person to experience. Unfortunately, competitive pressures in today's business environment and the resulting emphasis on downsizing and restructuring have created more situations in which the decisions of a "tough" boss can create emotional conflict.

> ■ **Substantive conflict** involves fundamental disagreement over ends or goals to be pursued and the means for their accomplishment.

> ■ **Emotional conflict** involves interpersonal difficulties that arise over feelings of anger, mistrust, dislike, fear, resentment, and the like.

■ LEVELS OF CONFLICT

When dealing personally with conflicts in the workplace, the relevant question becomes: "How well prepared are you to encounter and deal successfully with conflicts of various types?" People at work may encounter conflict at the intrapersonal level (conflict within the individual), the interpersonal level (individual-to-individual conflict), the intergroup level, or the interorganizational level.

Some conflicts that affect behavior in organizations involve the individual alone. These **intrapersonal conflicts** often involve actual or perceived pressures from incompatible goals or expectations of the following types: *Approach–approach conflict* occurs when a person must choose between two positive and equally attractive alternatives. An example is having to choose between a valued promotion in the organization or a desirable new job with another firm. *Avoidance–avoidance conflict* occurs when a person must choose between two negative and equally unattractive alternatives. An example is being asked either to accept a job transfer to another town in an undesirable location or to have one's employment with an organization terminated. *Approach–avoidance conflict* occurs when a person must decide to do something that has both positive and negative consequences. An example is being offered a higher paying job whose responsibilities entail unwanted demands on one's personal time.

Interpersonal conflict occurs between two or more individuals who are in opposition to one another. It may be substantive or emotional or both. Two persons debating each other aggressively on the merits of hiring a job applicant is

> ■ **Intrapersonal conflict** occurs within the individual because of actual or perceived pressures from incompatible goals or expectations.

> ■ **Interpersonal conflict** occurs between two or more individuals in opposition to each other.

an example of a substantive interpersonal conflict. Two persons continually in disagreement over each other's choice of work attire is an example of an emotional interpersonal conflict.

Intergroup conflict that occurs among members of different teams or groups can also have substantive and/or emotional underpinnings. Intergroup conflict is quite common in organizations, and it can make the coordination and integration of task activities very difficult.[8] The classic example is conflict among functional groups or departments, such as marketing and manufacturing, in organizations. The growing use of cross-functional teams and task forces is one way of trying to minimize such conflicts and promote more creative and efficient operations.

Interorganizational conflict is most commonly thought of in terms of the competition and rivalry that characterizes firms operating in the same markets. A good example is the continuing battle between U.S. businesses and their global rivals. But interorganizational conflict is a much broader issue than that represented by market competition alone. Consider, for example, disagreements between unions and the organizations employing their members; between government regulatory agencies and the organizations subject to their surveillance; between organizations and those who supply them with raw materials.

> ■ **Intergroup conflict** occurs among groups in an organization.

> ■ **Interorganizational conflict** occurs between organizations.

www.starbucks.com

⚖️ ETHICS AND SOCIAL RESPONSIBILITY

Watch for the new insulated cup when you have your next cup of Starbuck's Coffee. After three years in the making, a new cup is now ready to replace "double-cupping" or the use of an extra corrugated sleeve. Both practices have been criticized by environmental groups as wasteful. The new cup was created to keep coffee hot, protect the drinker's hands from heat, and meet customer demands for less packaging. It was designed with input from the Alliance for Environmental Innovation, a nonprofit group that supports the environment. The new cup will make its mark. Starbucks serves some eight million customers each week.[9]

■ FUNCTIONAL AND DYSFUNCTIONAL CONFLICTS

Conflict in organizations can be upsetting both to the individuals directly involved and to others affected by its occurrence. It can be quite uncomfortable, for example, to work in an environment in which two co-workers are continually hostile toward each other. In OB, however, the two sides to conflict shown in Figure 18.1 are recognized—the functional or constructive side, and the dysfunctional or destructive side.

Functional conflict, alternatively called *constructive conflict*, results in positive benefits to individuals, the group, or the organization. On the positive side, conflict can bring important problems to the surface so that they can be addressed. It can cause decisions to be considered carefully and perhaps reconsidered to ensure that the right path of action is being followed. It can increase the amount of information used for decision making. And it can offer opportunities

> ■ **Functional conflict** results in positive benefits to the group.

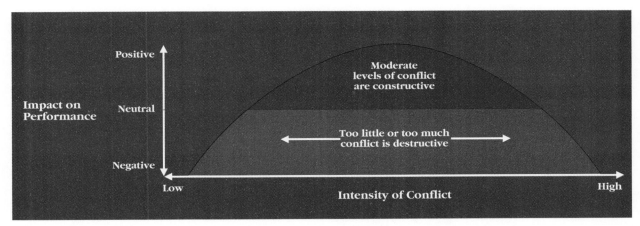

Figure 18.1
The two faces of conflict: functional conflict and dysfunctional conflict.

for creativity that can improve individual, team, or organizational performance. Indeed, an effective manager is able to stimulate constructive conflict in situations in which satisfaction with the status quo inhibits needed change and development.

Dysfunctional conflict, or *destructive conflict*, works to the individual's, group's, or organization's disadvantage. It diverts energies, hurts group cohesion, promotes interpersonal hostilities, and overall creates a negative environment for workers. This occurs, for example, when two employees are unable to work together because of interpersonal differences (a destructive emotional conflict) or when the members of a committee fail to act because they cannot agree on group goals (a destructive substantive conflict). Destructive conflicts of these types can decrease work productivity and job satisfaction and contribute to absenteeism and job turnover. Managers must be alert to destructive conflicts and be quick to take action to prevent or eliminate them or at least minimize their disadvantages.

■ **Dysfunctional conflict** works to the group's or organization's disadvantage.

■ CULTURE AND CONFLICT

Society today shows many signs of wear and tear in social relationships. We experience dificulties born of racial tensions, homophobia, gender gaps, and more. All trace in some way to tensions among people who are different in some ways from one another. They are also a reminder that culture and cultural differences must be considered for their conflict potential.

Among the popular dimensions of culture discussed in Chapter 3, for example, substantial differences may be noted in time orientation. When persons from short-term cultures such as the United States try to work with persons from long-term cultures such as Japan, the likelihood of conflict developing is high. The same holds true when individualists work with collectivists and when persons from high-power distance work with those from low-power distance cultures. [10] In each case, individuals who are not able to recognize and respect the impact of culture on behavior may contribute to the emergence of dysfunctional situations. On the other hand, by approaching a cross-cultural work situation with sensitivity and respect, one can find ways to work together without great difficulty and even with the advantages that constructive conflict may offer.

www.ibm.com

WORKPLACE DIVERSITY

High performance organizations like IBM have to capitalize on diversity. They must take full advantage of the talents and potential in a multicultural workforce and workplace. As cultures vary around the world, the way business is conducted varies also. The best firms and their managers are culturally aware and they understand and respect diversity. J.T. Childs, Jr., vice president for Global Diversity at IBM, says: "Workforce diversity is the bridge between the workplace and the marketplace. And, it is anchored on ideals that guide how you treat citizens of all countries as potential customers."

Managing Conflict

■ **Conflict resolution**

occurs when the reasons for a conflict are eliminated.

Conflict can be addressed in many ways, but the important goal is to achieve or set the stage for true **conflict resolution**—a situation in which the underlying reasons for a given destructive conflict are eliminated. The process begins with a good understanding of causes and recognition of the stage to which conflict has developed.

■ STAGES OF CONFLICT

Most conflicts develop in stages, as shown in Figure 18.2. Managers should recognize that unresolved prior conflicts help set the stage for future conflicts of the same or related sort. Rather than try to deny the existence of conflict or settle on a temporary resolution, it is always best to deal with important conflicts so that they are completely resolved.[11] *Conflict antecedents* establish the conditions from which conflicts are likely to develop. When the antecedent conditions become the basis for substantive or emotional differences between people or groups, the stage of *perceived conflict* exists. Of course, this perception may be held by only one of the conflicting parties. It is important to distinguish between perceived and *felt conflict*. When conflict is felt, it is experienced as tension that motivates the person to take action to reduce feelings of discomfort. For conflict to be resolved, all parties should both perceive it and feel the need to do something about it.

When conflict is expressed openly in behavior, it is said to be manifest. A state of *manifest conflict* may be resolved by removing or correcting its antecedents. It can also be suppressed. With suppression, no change in antecedent conditions occurs; the manifest conflict behaviors are controlled. For example, one or both parties may choose to ignore the conflict in their dealings with one another. *Suppression* is a superficial and often temporary form of conflict resolution. Indeed, we have already noted that unresolved and suppressed conflict fall into

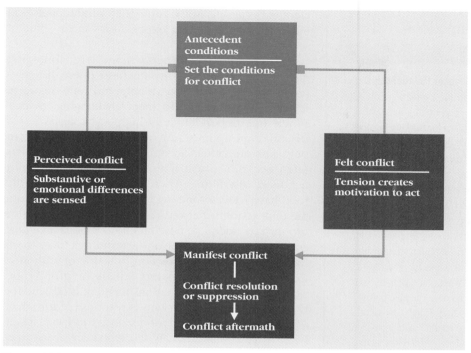

Figure 18.2
The stages of conflict.

this category. Both may continue to fester and cause future conflicts over similar issues. For the short run, however, they may represent the best a manager can achieve until antecedent conditions can be changed.

Unresolved substantive conflicts can result in sustained emotional discomfort and escalate into dysfunctional emotional conflict between individuals. In contrast, truly resolved conflicts may establish conditions that reduce the potential for future conflicts or make it easier to deal with them. Thus, any manager should be sensitive to the influence of *conflict aftermath* on future conflict episodes.

■ CAUSES OF CONFLICT

The process of dealing successfully with conflict begins with a recognition of several types of conflict situations. *Vertical conflict* occurs between hierarchical levels. It commonly involves supervisor–subordinate disagreements over resources, goals, deadlines, or performance results. *Horizontal conflict* occurs between persons or groups at the same hierarchical level. These disputes commonly involve goal incompatibilities, resource scarcities, or purely interpersonal factors. A common variation of horizontal conflict is *line–staff conflict*. It often involves disagreements over who has authority and control over certain matters such as personnel selection and termination practices.

Also common to work situations are *role conflicts* that occur when the communication of task expectations proves inadequate or upsetting. As discussed in respect to teamwork in Chapter 9, this often involves unclear communication of work expectations, excessive expectations in the form of job overloads, insuffi-

Human Resource Management News

www.shrm.org/hrnews

The 360-degree performance review is used by 90% of America's top 1000 companies, say Kris Oser, editor of *Human Resource Management News*. The approach reduces conflict and creates a sense of fairness by opening performance appraisal to a range of people, not just the boss.

OB Across Functions

PURCHASING

Conflict Management in Supplier Relationships

Suppliers and manufacturers in the United States have often experienced conflict over price, quality, and service. By contrast, the Japanese are known for working together creatively to turn this potentially destructive relationship into constructive conflict. Recently, U.S. firms are attempting much the same to maintain global competitiveness. In fact, you certainly know that Chrysler was bought by Germany's Daimler Benz and the combined firm is highly regarded in a very competitive industry. What you may not know is that part of the foundation for Chrysler's success was set in the supplier relationships developed by the firm's vice president for purchasing, Thomas T. Stallkamp. He says: "When you start to see your suppliers as experts, then they become valuable partners instead of a switchable commodity." Under Stallkamp's leadership, Chrysler eliminated competitive bidding to gain supplier contracts. Instead, Chrysler gave suppliers detailed specifications and asked them to meet the specifications and cut costs. In return, the firm agreed to share the savings with the suppliers and to give long-term purchase contracts. Part of Chrysler's overall TQM approach, this cooperative approach to supplier relationships called SCORE—Supplier Cost Reduction Effort, has been credited with over 4600 cost-saving ideas and actual savings of some $235 million.

cient expectations in the form of job underloads, and incompatibilities among expectations from different sources.

Work-flow interdependencies are breeding grounds for conflicts. Disputes and open disagreements may erupt among people and units who are required to cooperate to meet challenging goals.[12] When interdependence is high—that is, when a person or group must rely on task contributions from one or more others to achieve its goals—conflicts often occur. You will notice this, for example, in a fast-food restaurant, when the people serving the food have to wait too long for it to be delivered from the cooks. Conflict also escalates when individuals or groups lack adequate task direction or goals. *Domain ambiguities* involve misunderstandings over such things as customer jurisdiction or scope of authority. Conflict is likely when individuals or groups are placed in ambiguous situations where it is difficult for them to understand just who is responsible for what.

Actual or perceived *resource scarcity* can foster destructive competition. When resources are scarce, working relationships are likely to suffer. This is especially true in organizations that are experiencing downsizing or financial difficulties. As cutbacks occur, various individuals or groups try to position themselves to gain or retain maximum shares of the shrinking resource pool. They are also likely to try to resist resource redistribution, or to employ countermeasures to defend their resources from redistribution to others.

Finally, *power or value asymmetries* in work relationships can create conflict. They exist when interdependent people or groups differ substantially from one another in status and influence or in values. Conflict resulting from asymmetry is prone to occur, for example, when a low-power person needs the help of a high-power person, who does not respond; when people who hold dramatically different values are forced to work together on a task; or when a high-status person is required to interact with and perhaps be dependent on someone of lower status.

■ INDIRECT CONFLICT MANAGEMENT APPROACHES

Indirect conflict management approaches share the common ground of avoiding direct dealings with personalities. They include reduced interdependence, appeals to common goals, hierarchical referral, and alterations in the use of mythology and scripts.

Reduced Interdependence   When work-flow conflicts exist, managers can adjust the level of interdependency among units or individuals.[13] One simple option is *decoupling*, or taking action to eliminate or reduce the required contact between conflict parties. In some cases, the units' tasks can be adjusted to reduce the number of required points of coordination. The conflicting units can then be separated from one another, and each can be provided separate access to valued resources. Although decoupling may reduce conflict, it may also result in duplication and a poor allocation of valued resources.

Buffering is another approach that can be used when the inputs of one group are the outputs of another group. The classic buffering technique is to build an inventory, or buffer, between the two groups so that any output slowdown or excess is absorbed by the inventory and does not directly pressure the target group. Although it reduces conflict, this technique is increasingly out of favor because it increases inventory costs. This consequence is contrary to the elements of "just-in-time" delivery that is now valued in operations management.

Conflict management can be facilitated by assigning people to serve as formal *linking pins* between groups that are prone to conflict.[14] Persons in linking-pin roles, such as project liaison, are expected to understand the operations, members, needs, and norms of their host group. They are supposed to use this knowledge to help their group work better with other groups in order to accomplish mutual tasks. Though expensive, this technique is often used when different specialized groups, such as engineering and sales, must closely coordinate their efforts on complex and long-term projects.

Appeals to Common Goals   An *appeal to common goals* can focus the attention of potentially conflicting parties on one mutually desirable conclusion. By elevating the potential dispute to a common framework wherein the parties recognize their mutual interdependence in achieving common goals, petty disputes can be put in perspective. However, this can be difficult to achieve when prior performance is poor and individuals or groups disagree over how to improve performance. In this negative situation, the manager needs to remember the attributional tendency of individuals to blame poor performance on others or on external conditions. In this case, conflict resolution begins by making sure that the parties take personal responsibility for improving the situation.

HIGH PERFORMANCE ORGANIZATIONS

Common goals drive the system when Ford managers meet in cross-functional teams to work on special "100-day projects." An initiative spearheaded by Ford's CEO Jacques Nasser, the project teams are part of his attempt to move the firm's culture toward speed and flexibility in meeting customer needs. One way to do this is to communicate common goals in terms like "shareholder value" and then turn the teams lose to find ways to improve upon it. A team in England found ways to cut travel costs for engineers working on new factory startups; another team in Michigan relocated a metal brace on pick-up trucks to eliminate a noise problem. Nasser leads by example, participating in training sessions and showing his commitment to the new corporate culture.[15]

www.ford.com

Hierarchical Referral *Hierarchical referral* makes use of the chain of command for conflict resolution. Here, problems are simply referred up the hierarchy for more senior managers to reconcile. Whereas hierarchical referral can be definitive in a given case, it also has limitations. If conflict is severe and recurring, the continual use of hierarchical referral may not result in true conflict resolution. Managers removed from day-to-day affairs may fail to diagnose the real causes of a conflict, and conflict resolution may be superficial. Busy managers may tend to consider most conflicts as results of poor interpersonal relations and may act quickly to replace a person with a perceived "personality" problem.[16]

Altering Scripts and Myths In some situations, conflict is superficially managed by *scripts*, or behavioral routines that become part of the organization's culture.[17] The scripts become rituals that allow the conflicting parties to vent their frustrations and to recognize that they are mutually dependent on one another via the larger corporation. An example is a monthly meeting of "department heads," held presumably for purposes of coordination and problem solving but that actually becomes just a polite forum for superficial agreement.[18] Managers in such cases know their scripts and accept the difficulty of truly resolving any major conflicts. By sticking with the script, expressing only low-key disagreement and then quickly acting as if everything has been resolved, for instance, the managers publicly act as if problems are being addressed. Such scripts can be altered to allow and encourage active confrontation of issues and disagreements.

■ DIRECT CONFLICT MANAGEMENT APPROACHES

Figure 18.3 describes the five approaches to conflict management from the perspective of their relative emphasis on cooperativeness and assertiveness in the relationship. Consultants and academics generally agree that true conflict resolution can occur only when the underlying substantive and emotional reasons for the conflict are identified and dealt with through a solution that allows all conflicting parties to "win."[19] (See The Effective Manager 18.1.) This important issue of "Who wins?" can be addressed from the perspective of each conflicting party.

Lose–Lose Conflict *Lose–lose conflict* occurs when nobody really gets what he or she wants. The underlying reasons for the conflict remain unaffected and a similar conflict is likely to occur in the future. Lose–lose conflicts often result when there is little or no assertiveness and conflict management takes these forms. **Avoidance** is an extreme form of inattention; everyone simply pretends that the conflict does not really exist and hopes that it will go away. **Accommodation**, or **smoothing** as it is sometimes called, involves playing down differences among the conflicting parties and highlighting similarities and

---

THE EFFECTIVE MANAGER 18.1

WHEN TO USE CONFLICT MANAGEMENT STYLES

- Collaboration and problem solving is preferred to gain true conflict resolution when time and cost permit.
- Avoidance may be used when an issue is trivial or more important issues are pressing, or when people need to cool down temporarily and regain perspective.
- Authoritative command may be used when quick and decisive action is vital or when unpopular actions must be taken.
- Accommodation may be used when issues are more important to others than to yourself or when you want to build "credits" for use in later issues.
- Compromise may be used for temporary settlements to complex issues or to arrive at expedient solutions when time is limited.

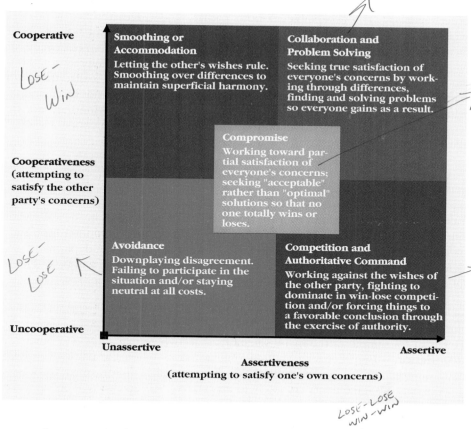

Figure 18.3
Five ways to manage conflict.

[Handwritten annotations on figure: "Win-Win", "Win-Lose / Lose-Win", "Lose-Win", "Lose-Lose", "Win-Lose", "Lose-Lose / Win-Win"]

Cooperative

Cooperativeness (attempting to satisfy the other party's concerns)

Uncooperative

Smoothing or Accommodation
Letting the other's wishes rule. Smoothing over differences to maintain superficial harmony.

Collaboration and Problem Solving
Seeking true satisfaction of everyone's concerns by working through differences, finding and solving problems so everyone gains as a result.

Compromise
Working toward partial satisfaction of everyone's concerns; seeking "acceptable" rather than "optimal" solutions so that no one totally wins or loses.

Avoidance
Downplaying disagreement. Failing to participate in the situation and/or staying neutral at all costs.

Competition and Authoritative Command
Working against the wishes of the other party, fighting to dominate in win-lose competition and/or forcing things to a favorable conclusion through the exercise of authority.

Unassertive — **Assertive**

Assertiveness (attempting to satisfy one's own concerns)

areas of agreement. This peaceful coexistence ignores the real essence of a given conflict and often creates frustration and resentment. **Compromise** occurs when each party gives up something of value to the other. As a result of no one getting its full desires, the antecedent conditions for future conflicts are established.

Win–Lose Conflict   In *win–lose conflict*, one party achieves its desires at the expense and to the exclusion of the other party's desires. This is a high-assertiveness and low-cooperativeness situation. It may result from outright **competition** in which a victory is achieved through force, superior skill, or domination by one party. It may also occur as a result of **authoritative command**, whereby a formal authority simply dictates a solution and specifies what is gained and what is lost by whom. Win–lose strategies fail to address the root causes of the conflict and tend to suppress the desires of at least one of the conflicting parties. As a result, future conflicts over the same issues are likely to occur.

Win–Win Conflict   *Win–win conflict* is achieved by a blend of both high cooperativeness and high assertiveness.[20] **Collaboration** or **problem solving** involves a recognition by all conflicting parties that something is wrong and needs attention. It stresses gathering and evaluating information in solving disputes and making choices. Win–win conditions eliminate the reasons for continuing or resurrecting the conflict since nothing has been avoided or suppressed. All relevant issues are raised and openly discussed. The ultimate test for a win–win solution is whether or not the conflicting parties see that the solution (1) achieves each

■ **Avoidance** involves pretending a conflict does not really exist.

■ **Accommodation** or **smoothing** involves playing down differences and finding areas of agreement.

■ **Compromise** occurs when each party gives up something of value to the other.

■ **Competition** seeks victory by force, superior skill, or domination.

■ **Authoritative command** uses formal authority to end conflict.

■ **Collaboration** involves recognition that something is wrong and needs attention through problem solving.

■ **Problem solving** uses information to resolve disputes.

other's goals, (2) is acceptable to both parties, and (3) establishes a process whereby all parties involved see a responsibility to be open and honest about facts and feelings. When success is achieved, true conflict resolution has occurred.

Although collaboration and problem solving are generally favored, one limitation is the time and energy it requires. It is also important to realize that both parties to the conflict need to be assertive and cooperative in order to develop a win–win joint solution. Finally, collaboration and problem solving may not be feasible if the firm's dominant culture does not place a value on cooperation.[21]

Negotiation

Talk about conflict! Picture yourself trying to make a decision in the following situation: You have ordered a new state-of-the-art notebook computer for a staff member in your department. At about the same time another department ordered a different brand. Your boss indicates that only one brand will be ordered. Of course, you believe the one chosen by your department is the best.

■ WHAT IS NEGOTIATION?

This is just a sample of the many situations that involve managers and others in **negotiation**—the process of making joint decisions when the parties involved have different preferences.[22] Negotiation has special significance in work settings, where disagreements are likely to arise over such diverse matters as wage rates, task objectives, performance evaluations, job assignments, work schedules, work locations, and more.

■ **Negotiation** is the process of making joint decisions when the parties involved have different preferences.

■ NEGOTIATION GOALS AND OUTCOMES

In negotiation two important goals must be considered: substance and relationship goals. *Substance goals* deal with outcomes that relate to the "content" issues under negotiation. The dollar amount of a wage agreement in a collective bargaining situation is one example. *Relationship goals* deal with outcomes that relate to how well people involved in the negotiation and any constituencies they may represent are able to work with one another once the process is concluded. An example is the ability of union members and management representatives to work together effectively after a contract dispute has been settled.

Unfortunately, many negotiations result in damaged relationships because the negotiating parties become preoccupied with substance goals and self-interests. In contrast, *effective negotiation* occurs when substance issues are resolved and working relationships are maintained or even improved. It results in overlapping interests and joint decisions that are "for the better" of all parties. Three criteria for effective negotiation are described in The Effective Manager 18.2.

■ ETHICAL ASPECTS OF NEGOTIATION

To maintain good working relationships in negotiations, managers and other involved parties should strive for high ethical standards. This goal may be side tracked by an over emphasis on self-interests. The motivation to behave ethically in negotiations is put to the test by each party's desire to "get more" than the other from the negotiation, and/or with a belief that there are insufficient resources to satisfy all parties.[23] After the heat of negotiations dies down, the parties involved often try to rationalize or explain away questionable ethics as unavoidable, harmless, or justified. Such after-the-fact rationalizations may be offset by long-run negative consequences, such as not being able to achieve one's wishes again the next time. At the very least, the unethical party may be the target of revenge tactics by those who were disadvantaged. Furthermore, once some people have behaved unethically in one situation, they may become entrapped by such behavior and prone to display it again in the future.[24]

■ **ORGANIZATIONAL SETTINGS FOR NEGOTIATION**

Managers and team leaders should be prepared to participate in at least four major action settings for negotiations. In *two-party negotiation* the manager negotiates directly with one other person. In *group negotiation* the manager is part of a team or group whose members are negotiating to arrive at a common decision. In *intergroup negotiation* the manager is part of a group that is negotiating with another group to arrive at a decision regarding a problem or situation affecting both. And in *constituency negotiation* the manager is involved in negotiation with other persons, with each party representing a broader constituency. A common example of constituency negotiation involves representatives of management and labor negotiating a collective bargaining agreement.

■ **CULTURE AND NEGOTIATION**

The existence of cultural differences in time orientation, individualism-collectivism, and power distance can have a substantial impact on negotiation. For example, when American businesses try to negotiate quickly with Chinese counterparts, they often do so with the goal of getting definitive agreements that will govern a working relationship. Culture isn't always on their side. A typical Chinese approach to negotiation might move much more slowly, require the development of good interpersonal relationships prior to reaching any agreement, display reluctance to commit everything to writing, and anticipate that any agreement reached will be subject to modification as future circumstances may require.[25] All this is quite the opposite of the typical expectations of negotiators used to the individualist and short-term American culture.

Negotiation Strategies

Managers and other workers frequently negotiate with one another over access to scarce organizational resources. These resources may be money, time, people,

---

THE EFFECTIVE MANAGER 18.2

CRITERIA OF AN EFFECTIVE NEGOTIATION

1. *Quality*—The negotiation results offer a "quality" agreement that is wise and satisfactory to all sides.
2. *Harmony*—The negotiation is "harmonious" and fosters rather than inhibits good interpersonal relations.
3. *Efficiency*—The negotiation is "efficient" and no more time consuming or costly than absolutely necessary.

Deloitte & Touche
www.us.deloitte.com

At Deloitte & Touche the conflict problems of work-life balance are being addressed. A policy curbs some consultants' travels so that they spend only three nights and four days on the road. Says Malva Rabinowitz, a managing director: "You can plan your life and be home for a real weekend."

■ **Distributive negotiation** focuses on positions staked out or declared by the parties involved who are each trying to claim certain portions of the available pie.

■ **Integrative negotiation** focuses on the merits of the issues, and the parties involved try to enlarge the available pie rather than stake claims to certain portions of it.

facilities, equipment, and so on. In all such cases, the general approach to or strategy for the negotiation can have a major influence on its outcomes. In **distributive negotiation**, the focus is on "positions" staked out or declared by conflicting parties. Each party is trying to claim certain portions of the available "pie." In **integrative negotiation**, sometimes called *principled negotiation*, the focus is on the "merits" of the issues. Everyone involved tries to enlarge the available pie rather than stake claims to certain portions of it.[26]

■ DISTRIBUTIVE NEGOTIATION

In distributive bargaining approaches, the participants would each ask the question: "Who is going to get this resource?" This question, and the way in which it frames subsequent behavior, will have a major impact on the negotiation process and outcomes. A case of distributive negotiation usually unfolds in one of two directions, neither of which yields optimal results. *"Hard" distributive negotiation* takes place when each party holds out to get its own way. This leads to competition, whereby each party seeks dominance over the other and tries to maximize self-interests. The hard approach may lead to a win–lose outcome in which one party dominates and gains. Or it can lead to an impasse.

"Soft" distributive negotiation, by contrast, takes place when one party is willing to make concessions to the other to get things over with. In this case, one party tries to find ways to meet the other's desires. A soft approach leads to accommodation in which one party gives in to the other, or to compromise in which each party gives up something of value in order to reach agreement. In either case at least some latent dissatisfaction is likely to develop. Even when the soft approach results in compromise (e.g., splitting the difference between the initial positions equally), dissatisfaction may exist since each party is still deprived of what it originally wanted.

Figure 18.4 introduces the case of the graduating senior negotiating a job offer with a corporate recruiter.[27] The example illustrates the basic elements of classic two-party negotiation in distributive contexts. To begin, look at the situation from the graduate's perspective. She has told the recruiter that she would like a salary of $45,000; this is her initial offer. But she also has in mind a minimum reservation point of $35,000—the lowest salary that she will accept for this job. Thus, she communicates a salary request of $45,000 but is willing to accept one as low as $35,000. The situation is somewhat reversed from the recruiter's perspective. His initial offer to the graduate is $30,000, and his maximum reservation point is $40,000; this is the most he is prepared to pay.

■ The **bargaining zone** is the zone between one party's minimum reservation point and the other party's maximum reservation point in a negotiating situation.

The **bargaining zone** is defined as the range between one party's minimum reservation point and the other party's maximum reservation point. In Figure 18.4, the bargaining zone is $40,000–$45,000. This is a positive bargaining zone since the reservation points of the two parties overlap. Whenever a positive bargaining zone exists, bargaining has room to unfold. Had the graduate's minimum reservation point been greater than the recruiter's maximum reservation point (for example, $42,000), no room would have existed for bargaining. Classic two-party bargaining always involves the delicate tasks of first discovering the respective reservation points (one's own and the other's) and then working toward an agreement that lies somewhere within the resulting bargaining zone and is acceptable to each party.

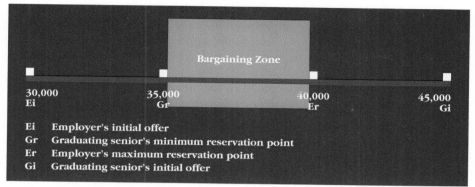

Ei   Employer's initial offer
Gr   Graduating senior's minimum reservation point
Er   Employer's maximum reservation point
Gi   Graduating senior's initial offer

Figure 18.4
An example of the bargaining zone in classic two-party negotiation.

■ INTEGRATIVE NEGOTIATION

In the integrative approach to negotiation, participants would ask: "How can the resource best be utilized?" Notice that this question is very different from the one described for distributive negotiation. It is much less confrontational, and it permits a broader range of alternatives to be considered in the process. From the outset there is much more of a "win–win" orientation.

At one extreme, integrative negotiation may involve selective avoidance, in which both parties realize that there are more important things on which to focus their time and attention. The time, energy, and effort needed to negotiate may not be worth the rewards. Compromise can also play a role in the integrative approach, but it must have an enduring basis. This is most likely to occur when the compromise involves each party giving up something of perceived lesser personal value to gain something of greater value. For instance, in the classic two-party bargaining case over salary, both the graduate and the recruiter could expand the negotiation to include the starting date of the job. Since it will be a year before the candidate's first vacation, she may be willing to take a little less money if she can start a few weeks later. Finally, integrative negotiation may involve true collaboration. In this case, the negotiating parties engage in problem solving to arrive at a mutual agreement that maximizes benefits to each.

■ HOW TO GAIN INTEGRATIVE AGREEMENTS

Underlying the integrative or principled approach is negotiation based on the merits of the situation. The foundations for gaining truly integrative agreements rest in supportive attitudes, constructive behaviors, and good information.[28]

Attitudinal Foundations   There are three attitudinal foundations of integrative agreements. First, each party must approach the negotiation with a *willingness to trust* the other party. This is a reason why ethics and maintaining relationships are so important in negotiations. Second, each party must convey a *willingness to share information* with the other party. Without shared information, effective problem solving is unlikely to occur. Third, each party must show a *willingness to ask concrete questions* of the other party. This further facilitates information sharing.

Equal Employment Opportunity Commission ◄

www.eeoc.gov

The EEOC handles some 20,000 cases annually of complaints filed by employees against their employers under the Age Discrimination in Employment Act. Under the act, workers who are 40 or over are a protected class. In a 1998 survey one in five companies had faced age discrimination claims in the past five years.

Behavioral Foundations During a negotiation, all behavior is important for both its actual impact and the impressions it leaves behind. Accordingly, the following behavioral foundations of integrative agreements must be carefully considered and included in any negotiator's repertoire of skills and capabilities:

Behavioral foundations of integrative agreements

- The ability to separate the people from the problem to avoid allowing emotional considerations to affect the negotiation.
- The ability to focus on interests rather than positions.
- The ability to avoid making premature judgments.
- The ability to keep the acts of alternative creation separate from their evaluation.
- The ability to judge possible agreements on an objective set of criteria or standards.

Information Foundations The information foundations of integrative agreements are substantial. They involve each party becoming familiar with the BATNA, or "best alternative to a negotiated agreement." That is, each party must know what he or she will do if an agreement can't be reached. This requires that both negotiating parties identify and understand their personal interests in the situation. They must know what is really important to them in the case at hand, and they must come to understand the relative importance of the other party's interests. As difficult as it may seem, each party must achieve an understanding of what the other party values, even to the point of determining its BATNA.

■ COMMON NEGOTIATION PITFALLS

The negotiation process is admittedly complex on cultural and many other grounds. It is further characterized by all the possible confusions of sometimes volatile interpersonal and group dynamics. Accordingly, negotiators need to guard against some common negotiation pitfalls.[29]

First, is the tendency in negotiation to stake out your position based on the assumption that in order to gain your way, something must be subtracted from the other party's way. This *myth of the fixed pie* is a purely distributive approach to negotiation. The whole concept of integrative negotiation is based on the premise that the pie can sometimes be expanded or utilized to the maximum advantage of all parties, not just one.

Second, because parties to negotiations often begin by stating extreme demands, the possibility of *escalating commitment* is high. That is, once demands have been stated, people become committed to them and are reluctant to back down. Concerns for protecting one's ego and saving face may lead to nonrational escalation of conflict. Self-discipline is needed to spot this tendency in one's own behavior as well as in others.

Third, negotiators often develop *overconfidence* that their positions are the only correct ones. This can lead them to ignore the other party's needs. In some cases, negotiators completely fail to see merits in the other party's position—merits that an outside observer would be sure to spot. Such overconfidence makes it harder to reach a positive common agreement.

Fourth, communication problems can cause difficulties during a negotiation. It has been said that "negotiation is the process of communicating back and forth for the purpose of reaching a joint decision."[30] This process can break down because of a *telling problem*—the parties don't really talk to one another, at least not in the sense of making themselves truly understood. It can also be damaged by a *hearing problem*—the parties are unable or unwilling to listen well enough to understand what each other is saying. Indeed, positive negotiation is most likely when each party engages in active listening and frequently asks questions to clarify what the other is saying. Each party occasionally needs to "stand in the other party's shoes" and to view the situation from their perspective.[31]

■ THIRD-PARTY ROLES IN NEGOTIATION

Negotiation may sometimes be accomplished through the intervention of third parties, such as when stalemates occur and matters appear unresolvable under current circumstances. In **arbitration**, such as the salary arbitration now common in professional sports, this third party acts as the "judge" and has the power to issue a decision that is binding on all parties. This ruling takes place after the arbitrator listens to the positions advanced by the parties involved in a dispute. In **mediation** a neutral third party tries to engage the parties in a negotiated solution through persuasion and rational argument. This is a common approach in labor–management negotiations, where trained mediators acceptable to each side are called in to help resolve bargaining impasses. Unlike arbitrator, the mediator is not able to dictate a solution.

■ In **arbitration** a neutral third party acts as judge with the power to issue a decision binding on all parties.

■ In **mediation** a neutral third party tries to engage the parties in a negotiated solution through persuasion and rational argument.

Chapter 18   Study Guide

What is conflict?

Summary

- Conflict appears in a social situation as any disagreement over issues of substance or emotional antagonisms that create friction between individuals or groups.

- Conflict can be either emotional—based on personal feelings—or substantive—based on work goals.

- When kept within tolerable limits, conflict can be a source of creativity and performance enhancement; it becomes destructive when these limits are exceeded.

- Conflict situations in organizations occur in vertical and lateral working relations and in line–staff relations.

- Most typically, conflict develops through a series of stages, beginning with antecedent conditions and progressing into manifest conflict.

- Unresolved prior conflicts set the stage for future conflicts of a similar nature.

How can conflict be managed successfully?

- Indirect forms of conflict management include appeals to common goals, hierarchical referral, organizational redesign, and the use of mythology and scripts.

- Direct conflict management proceeds with different combinations of assertiveness and cooperativeness by conflicting parties.

- Win–win conflict resolution is preferred; it is achieved through collaboration and problem solving.

- Win–lose conflict resolution should be avoided; it is associated with competition and authoritative command.

What is negotiation?

- Negotiation occurs whenever two or more people with different preferences must make joint decisions.

- Managers may find themselves involved in various types of negotiation situations, including two-party, group, intergroup, and constituency negotiation.

- Effective negotiation occurs when issues of substance are resolved and human relationships are maintained, or even improved, in the process.

- Ethical conduct is important to successful negotiations.

What are the different strategies involved in negotiation?

- In distributive negotiation, the focus of each party is on staking out positions in the attempt to claim desired portions of a "fixed pie."

- In integrative negotiation, sometimes called principled negotiation, the focus is on determining the merits of the issues and finding ways to satisfy one another's needs.

- The success of the strategies depends on avoiding common negotiating pitfalls and building good communications.

Key Terms

Accommodation or
smoothing (p. 383)
Arbitration (p. 389)
Authoritative command
(p. 383)
Avoidance (p. 383)
Bargaining zone (p. 386)
Collaboration (p. 383)
Competition (p. 383)
Compromise (p. 383)
Conflict (p. 374)
Conflict resolution (p. 378)

Distributive negotiation
(p. 386)
Dysfunctional conflict
(p. 377)
Emotional conflict (p. 375)
Functional conflict (p. 376)
Integrative negotiation
(p. 386)
Intergroup conflict
(p. 376))
Interpersonal conflict
(p. 375)

Interorganizational conflict
(p. 376)
Intrapersonal conflict
(p. 375)
Mediation (p. 389)
Negotiation (p. 384)
Problem solving (p. 383)
Substantive conflict
(p. 375)

Self-Test 18   ■ MULTIPLE CHOICE

1. A conflict that occurs in the form of a fundamental disagreement over ends or goals to be pursued and the means for accomplishment is known specifically as a(n) _____ conflict. (a) relationship (b) emotional (c) substantive (d) procedural

2. The indirect conflict management approach that uses chain of command for conflict resolution is known as _____. (a) hierarchical referral (b) avoidance (c) organizational redesign (d) appeals to common goals

3. Which of the following is not a way in which conflict can be positive for a group or organization? (a) It can help identify otherwise neglected problems. (b) It can enhance creativity. (c) It can broaden the bargaining zone. (d) It can improve performance.

4. Lose–lose conflicts typically arise from each of the following except _____. (a) competition (b) compromise (c) accommodation (d) avoidance

5. When might a manager most effectively use accommodation? (a) When quick and decisive action is vital. (b) When she or he wants to build "credit" for use in later issues. (c) To let people cool down and gain perspective. (d) For temporary settlement of complex issues.

6. According to the conflict management grid, the _____ conflict management style is highly cooperative and assertive. (a) competition (b) compromise (c) accommodation (d) collaboration

7. The criteria for effective negotiation are _____. (a) harmony, efficiency, and quality (b) efficiency and effectiveness (c) ethical, practical, and cost effective (d) quality, practical, and productive

8. _____ are two goals that should be considered in any negotiation. (a) Performance and evaluation (b) Task and substance (c) Substance and relationship (d) Task and performance

9. Which of the following statements is true? (a) Principled negotiation leads to accommodation. (b) Hard distributive negotiation leads to collaboration (c) Soft distributive negotiation leads to accommodation or compromise. (d) Hard distributive negotiation leads to win–win conflicts.

10. Each of the following is a common negotiator pitfall, as identified by the text, except _____. (a) falling prey to the myth of the "fixed pie" (b) rational escalation to conflict (c) overconfidence (d) listening to other's needs (e) unethical behavior

■ TRUE–FALSE

11. Intergroup conflict typically facilitates the coordination of task activities.   T   F

12. Interpersonal conflicts can be substantive, emotional, or both.   T   F

13. Moderate levels of conflict are constructive.   T   F

14. When work-flow interdependency is high, conflicts often occur.   T   F

15. The conflict management grid classifies management style along two dimensions: cooperativeness and assertiveness.   T   F

16. Two goals are at stake in any negotiation: distributive and integrative.   T   F

17. The most preferred approach to negotiation is distributive.   T   F

18. In integrative negotiations, everyone tries to enlarge the "pie."   T   F

19. BATNA requires that each party know what will be done if an agreement can't be reached.   T   F

20. Two types of communication difficulties are common in negotiations: telling and hearing.   T   F

▪ SHORT RESPONSE

21. List and discuss three conflict situations faced by managers.

22. List and discuss the major indirect conflict management approaches.

23. Under what conditions might a manager use avoidance or accommodation?

24. Compare and contrast distributive and integrative negotiation. Which is more desirable? Why?

▪ APPLICATIONS ESSAY

25. Discuss the common pitfalls you would expect to encounter in negotiating your salary for your first job, and explain how you would try to best deal with them.

Explore application-oriented Fast Company articles, cases, experimental exercises, and self-assessments in the OB Skills Workbook

▪ **Visit the Schermerhorn Web site to find the Interactive Self-Test and Internet exercises for this chapter.**

Change, Innovation, and Stress

THE ORGANIZATION OF THE FUTURE

www.greatplains.com

The best organizations in our new workplace respect talented people. The best of the best build high performance work settings in which everyone uses their talents to greatest advantage. People are never taken for granted. Today people have more choices than ever before about where to work, who to work for, and the conditions under which they put their talents to use. Organizations must work hard to be preferred employers. They must do all they can to attract and retain talented people—all of which requires a commitment to continuous learning and ongoing change and development.

Great Plains Software, a Fargo, North Dakota, maker of financial software, is among those progressive firms gaining reputations as great places to work. Great Plains is known for a commitment to work–life balance based upon respect for diversity and a commitment to flexibility. The firm seeks to hire the best people and then give them freedom to do their work the best way they can. For Tami Reller, a graduate of Moorehead State University, this has meant the ability to telecommute, pursue an MBA part-time, and take time off after having her first child. CEO Doug Burgum is proud of the way his company is continually evolving in ways that keep talented people like Reller happy and productive. He says: "There has to be a deeper level of satisfaction, a sense that things are all right. If you can help people find that level, they tend to stick around." Under Burgum's leadership, Great Plains seems poised for a continual evolution as a "preferred employer" even as people and environments continue to change.[1]

"Turbulence" is a term often used to describe the current environment of business and management. The global economy is full of problems and opportunities, and is constantly springing new surprises on even the most experienced business executives. Workplaces like Great Plains Software deal with these forces positively. As the environment changes, they change too—not just in the quest for customers in highly competitive markets, but also in the quest for the best in employee talents. Flexibility is a rule of the day. People in the new workplace must be comfortable dealing with adaptation and continuous change.[2] Amidst the calls for greater productivity, willingness to learn from the successes of others, total quality, and continuous improvement, everyone is being called upon to achieve success while pursuing change and innovation and experiencing inevitable stress. In the words of management consultant Tom Peters: "The turbulent marketplace demands that we make innovation a way of life for everyone. We must learn—individually and as organizations—to welcome change and innovation as vigorously as we have fought it in the past."[3]

Study Questions

This chapter addresses the important issues of change, innovation, and stress as they relate to developments in the modern workplace. As you read Chapter 19, keep in mind these questions.

- What is organizational change?
- What change strategies are used in organizations?
- What can be done about resistance to change?
- How do organizations innovate?
- How does stress affect people at work?

Change in Organizations

"Change" is the watchword of the day for many, if not most, organizations. Some of this change may be described as *radical change*, or frame-breaking change.[4] This is change that results in a major overhaul of the organization or its component systems. In today's business environments, such radical changes are often initiated by a critical event, such as a new CEO, a new ownership brought about by merger or takeover, or a dramatic failure in operating results. When it occurs in the life cycle of an organization, radical change is intense and all-encompassing.

Another common form of organizational change is *incremental change*, or frame-bending change. This type of change, being part of an organization's natural evolution, is frequent and less traumatic. Typical changes of this type include the introduction of new products, new technologies, and new systems and processes. Although the nature of the organization remains relatively the same, incremental change builds on the existing ways of operating to enhance or extend them in new directions. The capability of improving continuously through incremental change is an important asset in today's demanding environments.

The success of both radical and incremental change in organizations depends in part on **change agents** who lead and support the change processes. These are individuals and groups who take responsibility for changing the existing behavior patterns of another person or social system. Although change agents sometimes are hired as consultants from outside the organization, any manager or leader in today's dynamic times is expected to act in a change agent capacity. Indeed, this responsibility is increasingly defined even more specifically as essential to the leadership role. Simply put, being an effective change agent means being a great "change leader."[5]

■ **Change agents** are people who take action to change the behavior of people and systems.

ENTREPRENEURSHIP

He started by launching a student magazine, moved on to start a record company and ended up being the brains and the drive behind the $4 billion global conglomerate Virgin Group. We're talking about Richard Branson of course, named England's best business leader by his peers. Branson believes in starting companies rather than buying them. Says he: "We start from scratch each time as a way of making sure it's really ours." Change is part of the culture. "We split our ventures into smaller units when they get too big, so that each will become the swiftest at

www.virgin.com

what it does best," says Branson. The Virgin brand is dedicated to service and value for customers, and to an organizational culture focused on satisfaction, creativity, irreverence and fun. Branson fits the image with an ever-present smile, open-necked shirt and eye toward the future.[6]

■ PLANNED AND UNPLANNED CHANGE

Not all change in organizations is the result of a change agent's direction. **Unplanned changes** occur spontaneously or randomly. They may be disruptive,

■ **Unplanned change** occurs spontaneously and without a change agent's direction.

such as a wildcat strike that ends in a plant closure, or beneficial, such as an interpersonal conflict that results in a new procedure designed to smooth the flow of work between two departments. When the forces of unplanned change begin to appear, the appropriate goal is to act quickly to minimize any negative consequences and maximize any possible benefits. In many cases, unplanned changes can be turned into good advantage.

■ **Planned change** is intentional and occurs with a change agent's direction.

In contrast, **planned change** is the result of specific efforts by a change agent. It is a direct response to someone's perception of a *performance gap*—a discrepancy between the desired and actual state of affairs. Performance gaps may represent problems to be resolved or opportunities to be explored. Most planned changes may be regarded as efforts intended to deal with performance gaps in ways that benefit an organization and its members. The processes of continuous improvement require constant vigilance to spot performance gaps—both problems and opportunities—and to take action to resolve them.

■ ORGANIZATIONAL FORCES AND TARGETS FOR CHANGE

The forces for change driving organizations of all types and sizes are ever present in and around today's dynamic work settings.[7] They are found in the *organization–environment relationship*, with mergers, strategic alliances, and divestitures among the examples of organizational attempts to redefine their relationships with challenging social and political environments. They are found in the *organizational life cycle*, with changes in culture and structure among the examples of how organizations must adapt as they evolve from birth through growth and toward maturity. They are found in the *political nature of organizations*, with changes in internal control structures, including benefits and reward systems, that attempt to deal with shifting political currents.

Planned change based on any of these forces can be internally directed toward a wide variety of organizational components, most of which have already been discussed in this book. As shown in Figure 19.1, these targets include organizational purpose, strategy, structure, and people, as well as objectives, culture, tasks, and technology. When considering these targets, however, it must be recognized that they are highly intertwined in the workplace. Changes in any one are likely to require or involve changes in others. For example, a change in the basic *tasks*—what it is that people do, is almost inevitably accompanied by a change in *technology*—the way in which tasks are accomplished. Changes in tasks and technology usually require alterations in structures, including changes in the patterns of authority and

OB Across Functions

OPERATIONS

Building Support for Organizational Transformations

Change doesn't come easy in most circumstances, and the larger the organization the more difficult the process often becomes. At Royal Dutch/Shell you'll find some 100,000+ employees and operations spread worldwide. When Steve Miller took over as group managing director, he found that a two-year-old effort to transform the company was bogged down. It was designed to start at the top and progress throughout the firm level by level. Miller decided to tackle the resistant bureaucracy by actively involving employees from the front line. Through "grassroots" leadership, he set out to work as directly as possible with a cross section of Shell employees from over 25 countries. The response was quick and positive. Miller and his management team found that the employees were willing to participate. Their energies spread to the levels above, and the change processes were reinvigorated. Through communication, empowerment, and respect for ideas and experience, Miller tapped what may be an organization's most important change asset—its people. But you don't get the advantages if you aren't willing to step out of the executive office, meet the people doing all types of jobs on the front line, and then ask the right questions. Sincerity and trust, of course, add the final ingredients to grassroots change leadership.

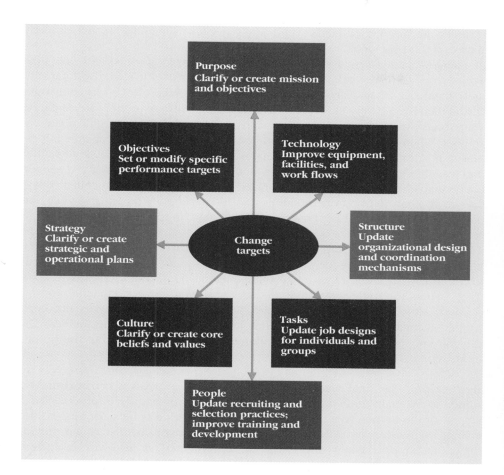

Figure 19.1
Organizational targets for planned change.

General Motors
Corporation ←

www.gm.com

When GM planned its joint venture manufacturing plant in Shanghai, China, it was going to build Buicks. But as Asian economies changed and the situation in China evolved, the firm stayed flexible. It is working to adapt the plant to produce as well a compact car more suited to the current markets.

communication as well as in the roles of workers. These technological and structural changes can, in turn, necessitate changes in the knowledge, skills, and behaviors of *people*—the members of the organization.[8] In all cases, of course, tendencies to accept easy-to-implement, but questionable, "quick fixes" to problems should be avoided.[9]

■ PHASES OF PLANNED CHANGE

Psychologist Kurt Lewin recommends that any change effort be viewed as a process with three distinct phases—unfreezing, changing, and refreezing, all of which must be well handled for a change to be successful.[10] He also suggests that we may become easily preoccupied with the changing phase and neglect the importance of the unfreezing and refreezing stages.

Unfreezing In Lewin's model, **unfreezing** is the managerial responsibility of preparing a situation for change. It involves disconfirming existing attitudes and behaviors to create a felt need for something new. Unfreezing is facilitated by environmental pressures, declining performance, recognition of a problem, or awareness that someone else has found a better way, among other things. Many

■ **Unfreezing** is the stage at which a situation is prepared for change.

changes are never tried or they fail simply because situations are not properly unfrozen to begin with.

Large systems seem particularly susceptible to what is sometimes called the *boiled frog phenomenon*.[11] This refers to the notion that a live frog will immediately jump out when placed in a pan of hot water. When placed in cold water that is then heated very slowly, however, the frog will stay in the water until the water boils the frog to death. Organizations, too, can fall victim to similar circumstances. When managers fail to monitor their environments, recognize the important trends, or sense the need to change, their organizations may slowly suffer and lose their competitive edge. Although the signals that change may be needed are available, they aren't noticed or given any special attention—until it is too late. In contrast, the best organizations are led by people who are always on the alert and understand the importance of "unfreezing" in the change process.

■ **Changing** is the stage in which specific actions are taken to create change.

Changing The **changing** stage involves taking action to modify a situation by changing things, such as the people, tasks, structure, or technology of the organization. Lewin believes that many change agents are prone to an activity trap. They bypass the unfreezing stage and start changing things prematurely or too quickly. Although their intentions may be correct, the situation has not been properly prepared for change. This often leads to failure. Changing something is difficult enough in any situation, let alone having to do so without the proper foundations.

■ **Refreezing** is the stage in which changes are reinforced and stabilized.

Refreezing The final stage in the planned change process is **refreezing**. Designed to maintain the momentum of a change and eventually institutionalize it as part of the normal routine, refreezing secures the full benefits of long-lasting change. Refreezing involves positively reinforcing desired outcomes and providing extra support when difficulties are encountered. It involves evaluating progress and results, and assessing the costs and benefits of the change. And it allows for modifications to be made in the change to increase its success over time. When all of this is not done and refreezing is neglected, changes are often abandoned after a short time or incompletely implemented.

Planned Change Strategies

Managers and other change agents use various means for mobilizing power, exerting influence over others, and getting people to support planned change efforts. As described in Figure 19.2, each of these strategies builds from the various bases of social power discussed in Chapter 15. Note in particular that each power source has somewhat different implications for the planned change process.[12]

■ FORCE–COERCION

■ A **force–coercion strategy** uses authority, rewards, and punishments to create change.

A **force–coercion strategy** uses legitimacy, rewards, or punishments as primary inducements to change. That is, the change agent acts unilaterally to "command" change through the formal authority of his or her position, to induce change via an offer of special rewards, or to bring about change via threats of punishment. People respond to this strategy mainly out of the fear of being pun-

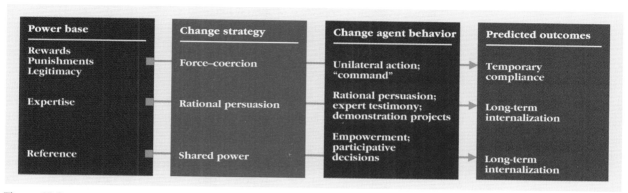

Figure 19.2
Power bases, change strategies, and predicted change outcomes.

ished if they do not comply with a change directive or out of the desire to gain a reward if they do. Compliance is usually temporary and continues only as long as the change agent and his or her legitimate authority are visible, or as long as the opportunities for rewards and punishments remain obvious.

Your actions as a change agent using the force–coercion strategy might match the following profile.

> You believe that people who run things are basically motivated by self-interest and by what the situation offers in terms of potential personal gains or losses. Since you feel that people change only in response to such motives, you try to find out where their vested interests lie and then put the pressure on. If you have formal authority, you use it. If not, you resort to whatever possible rewards and punishments you have access to and do not hesitate to threaten others with these weapons. Once you find a weakness, you exploit it and are always wise to work "politically" by building supporting alliances wherever possible.[13]

■ RATIONAL PERSUASION

Change agents using a **rational persuasion strategy** attempt to bring about change through the use of special knowledge, empirical support, or rational arguments. This strategy assumes that rational people will be guided by reason and self-interest in deciding whether or not to support a change. Expert power is mobilized to convince others that the change will leave them better off than before. It is sometimes referred to as an *empirical-rational strategy* of planned change. When successful, this strategy results in a longer lasting, more internalized change than does force–coercion.

As a change agent taking the rational persuasion approach to a change situation, you might behave as follows.

> You believe that people are inherently rational and are guided by reason in their actions and decision making. Once a specific course of action is demonstrated to be in a person's self-interest, you assume that reason and rationality will cause the person to adopt it. Thus, you approach change with the objective of communicating—through information and facts—the essential "desirability" of

■ A **rational persuasion strategy** uses facts, special knowledge, and rational argument to create change.

change from the perspective of the person whose behavior you seek to influence. If this logic is effectively communicated, you are sure of the person's adopting the proposed change.[14]

■ SHARED POWER

■ A **shared-power strategy** uses participatory methods and emphasizes common values to create change.

A **shared-power strategy** actively and sincerely involves the people who will be affected by a change in planning and making key decisions relating to this change. Sometimes called a *normative-reeducative approach*, this strategy tries to develop directions and support for change through involvement and empowerment. It builds essential foundations, such as personal values, group norms, and shared goals, so that support for a proposed change emerges naturally. Managers using normative-reeducative approaches draw upon the power of personal reference and also share power by allowing others to participate in planning and implementing the change. Given this high level of involvement, the strategy is likely to result in a longer lasting and internalized change.

As a change agent who shares power and adopts a normative-reeducative approach to change, you are likely to fit this profile:

> You believe that people have complex motivations. You feel that people behave as they do as a result of sociocultural norms and commitments to these norms. You also recognize that changes in these orientations involve changes in attitudes, values, skills, and significant relationships, not just changes in knowledge, information, or intellectual rationales for action and practice. Thus, when seeking to change others, you are sensitive to the supporting or inhibiting effects of group pressures and norms. In working with people, you try to find out their side of things and to identify their feelings and expectations.[15]

Resistance to Change

■ **Resistance to change** is an attitude or behavior that shows unwillingness to make or support a change.

In organizations, **resistance to change** is any attitude or behavior that indicates unwillingness to make or support a desired change. Change agents often view any such resistance as something that must be "overcome" in order for change to be successful. This is not always the case, however. It is helpful to view resistance to change as feedback that the change agent can use to facilitate gaining change objectives.[16] The essence of this constructive approach to resistance is to recognize that when people resist change, they are defending something important and that appears threatened by the change attempt.

■ WHY PEOPLE RESIST CHANGE

People have many reasons to resist change. The Effective Manager 19.1 identifies fear of the unknown, insecurity, lack of a felt need to change, threat to vested interests, contrasting interpretations, and lack of resources, among other possibilities. A work team's members, for example, may resist the introduction of advanced workstation computers because they have never used the operating system and are apprehensive. They may wonder whether the new computers will eventually be used as justification for "getting rid" of some of them; or they may believe that they have been doing their jobs just fine and do not need the new computers to improve things. These and other viewpoints often create resistance to even the best and most well-intended planned changes.

Resistance to the Change Itself Sometimes a change agent experiences resistance to the change itself. People may reject a change because they believe it is not worth their time, effort, or attention. To minimize resistance in such cases, the change agent should make sure that everyone who may be affected by a change knows specifically how it satisfies the following criteria.[17]

- *Benefit*—The change should have a clear relative advantage for the people being asked to change; it should be perceived as "a better way."

- *Compatibility*—The change should be as compatible as possible with the existing values and experiences of the people being asked to change.

- *Complexity*—The change should be no more complex than necessary; it must be as easy as possible for people to understand and use.

- *Triability*—The change should be something that people can try on a step-by-step basis and make adjustments as things progress.

Resistance to the Change Strategy Change agents must also be prepared to deal with resistance to the change strategy. Someone who attempts to bring about change via force–coercion, for example, may create resistance among individuals who resent management by "command" or the use of threatened punishment. People may resist a rational persuasion strategy in which the data are suspect or the expertise of advocates is not clear. They may resist a shared-power strategy that appears manipulative and insincere.

Resistance to the Change Agent Resistance to the change agent is directed at the person implementing the change and often involves personality and other differences. Change agents who are isolated and aloof from other persons in the change situation, who appear self-serving, or who have a high emotional involvement in the changes are especially prone to such problems. Research also indicates that change agents who differ from other persons in the change situation on such dimensions as age, education, and socioeconomic factors may encounter greater resistance to change.[18]

■ HOW TO DEAL WITH RESISTANCE

An informed change agent has many options available for dealing positively with resistance to change, in any of its forms.[19] The first approach is through *education and communication.* The objective is to educate people about a change before it is implemented and to help them understand the logic of the change. Education and communication seem to work best when resistance is based on

---

THE EFFECTIVE MANAGER 19.1

EIGHT REASONS FOR RESISTING CHANGE

1. Fear of the unknown
2. Lack of good information
3. Fear for loss of security
4. No reasons to change
5. Fear for loss of power
6. Lack of resources
7. Bad timing
8. Habit

Criteria for successful changes

Lonnie Johnson

You may not know Lonnie Johnson's name but you likely know his product. The former NASA engineer holds the patent for the Super Soaker water gun along with Larami Limited. After discovering that a special pump he developed was perfect for squirt guns, Johnson built a prototype and eventually took it to Larami. The rest is history, with over 250 million sold to date.

inaccurate or incomplete information. A second way is the use of *participation and involvement.* With the goal of allowing others to help design and implement the changes, this approach asks people to contribute ideas and advice or to work on task forces or committees that may be leading the change. This is especially useful when the change agent does not have all the information needed to successfully handle a problem situation.

Facilitation and support involves providing assistance—both emotional and material, for people experiencing the hardships of change. A manager using this approach actively listens to problems and complaints, provides training in the new ways, and helps others to overcome performance pressures. Facilitation and support is highly recommended when people are frustrated by work constraints and difficulties encountered in the change process. A *negotiation and agreement* approach offers incentives to actual or potential change resistors. Tradeoffs are arranged to provide special benefits in exchange for assurances that the change will not be blocked. It is most useful when dealing with a person or group that will lose something of value as a result of the planned change.

Manipulation and cooptation makes use of covert attempts to influence others, selectively providing information and consciously structuring events so that the desired change occurs. In some cases, leaders of the resistance may be "bought off" with special side deals to gain their support. Manipulation and cooptation are common when other tactics do not work or are too expensive. Finally, *explicit or implicit coercion* employs the force of authority to get people to accept change. Often, resistors are threatened with a variety of undesirable consequences if they do not go along as planned. This may be done, for example, in crisis situations when speed is of the essence.

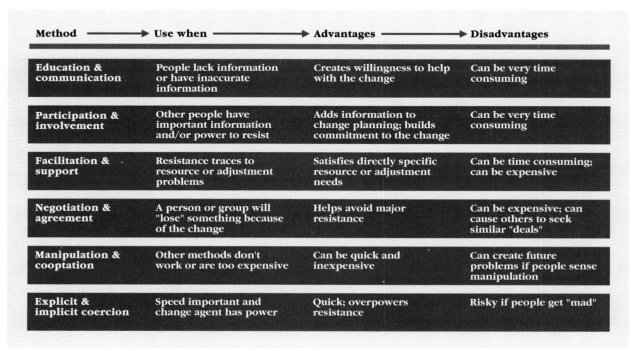

Method →	Use when →	Advantages →	Disadvantages
Education & communication	People lack information or have inaccurate information	Creates willingness to help with the change	Can be very time consuming
Participation & involvement	Other people have important information and/or power to resist	Adds information to change planning; builds commitment to the change	Can be very time consuming
Facilitation & support	Resistance traces to resource or adjustment problems	Satisfies directly specific resource or adjustment needs	Can be time consuming; can be expensive
Negotiation & agreement	A person or group will "lose" something because of the change	Helps avoid major resistance	Can be expensive; can cause others to seek similar "deals"
Manipulation & cooptation	Other methods don't work or are too expensive	Can be quick and inexpensive	Can create future problems if people sense manipulation
Explicit & implicit coercion	Speed important and change agent has power	Quick; overpowers resistance	Risky if people get "mad"

Figure 19.3
Methods for dealing with resistance to change.

Figure 19.3 summarizes additional insights into how and when each of these methods may be used to deal with resistance to change. Regardless of the chosen strategy, it is always best to remember that the presence of resistance typically suggests that something can be done to achieve a better fit among the change, the situation, and the people affected. A good change agent deals with resistance to change by listening to feedback and acting accordingly.

Innovation in Organizations

The best organizations don't stagnate; they innovate.[20] And they are able to innovate on an ongoing basis—they value and expect "innovation," and it becomes a normal part of everyday operations. **Innovation** is the process of creating new ideas and putting them into practice.[21] It is the means by which creative ideas find their way into everyday practices, ideally practices that contribute to improved customer service or organizational productivity. **Product innovations** result in the introduction of new or improved goods or services to better meet customer needs. **Process innovations** result in the introduction of new and better work methods and operations.

■ **Innovation** is the process of creating new ideas and putting them into practice.

■ **Product innovations** introduce new goods or services to better meet customer needs.

■ **Process innovations** introduce into operations new and better ways of doing things.

▓ THE INNOVATION PROCESS

The basic steps in a typical process of organizational innovation are shown in Figure 19.4. They include:

1. *Idea creation*—to create an idea through spontaneous creativity, ingenuity, and information processing.

2. *Initial experimentation*—to establish the idea's potential value and application.

3. *Feasibility determination*—to identify anticipated costs and benefits.

4. *Final application*—to produce and market a new product or service, or to implement a new approach to operations.

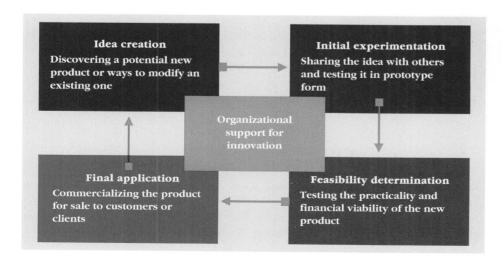

**Figure 19.4
The innovation process: a case of new product development.**

The innovation process is not complete until final application has been achieved. A new idea—even a great one—is not enough. In any organization, the idea must pass through all stages of innovation and reach the point of final application before its value can be realized.

■ FEATURES OF INNOVATIVE ORGANIZATIONS

The new workplace is placing great demands on organizations and their members to be continuously innovative. When we examine the characteristics of high-performing and innovative organizations, we observe certain common features. Highly innovative organizations have *strategies and cultures* that are built around a commitment to innovation. This includes tolerance for mistakes and respect for well-intentioned ideas that just do not work. Highly innovative organizations have *structures* that support innovation. They emphasize creativity through teamwork and cross-functional integration. They also utilize decentralization and empowerment to overcome the limitations of great size. In highly innovative organizations, *staffing* is done with a clear commitment to innovation. Special attention is given to critical innovation roles of idea generators, information gatekeepers, product champions, and project leaders. Finally, innovative organizations benefit from *top-management support*. Senior managers provide good examples for others, eliminate obstacles to innovation, and try to get things done that make innovation easier. Former Johnson & Johnson CEO James Burke, for example, once said, "I try to give people the feeling that it's okay to fail," while Quad Graphics founder Harry V. Quadrucci practiced what has been dubbed "management by walking away." The implication in both approaches is that employees know what needs to be done, and management's job is to trust and help them to do their best.[22]

www.pitneybowes.com

✦✦ HIGH PERFORMANCE ORGANIZATIONS

The interior office space of Pitney Bowes Credit Corp. in Shelton, Connecticut, looks like an indoor park. Amidst the cobblestone-style carpets, metallic street signs, and even an ornate clock, you'll find a French-style café and a 1950s-type diner. Why? All this is part of the firm's reinvention by new CEO Matthew Kissner. He calls the setting his "idea factory," and he says it fits his goal of creativity with "no straight lines" and "no linear thinking." According to Kissner: "The place wasn't broken, but we knew we could make it better. I'm a builder. I thrive on creating environments where people can excel."[23]

Dynamics of Stress

■ **Stress** is tension from extraordinary demands, constraints, or opportunities.

The processes of change and innovation often create new and increased pressures on the people involved. **Stress** must be understood as a state of tension experienced by individuals facing extraordinary demands, constraints, or opportunities.[24]

■ SOURCES OF STRESS

Any look toward your career future in today's dynamic times must include an awareness that stress is something you, as well as others, are sure to encounter.[25] **Stressors** are the wide variety of things that cause stress for individuals. Some stressors can be traced directly to what people experience in the workplace, whereas others derive from nonwork and personal factors.

Work-Related Stressors   Without doubt work can be stressful, and job demands can disrupt one's work-life balance. A study of two-career couples, for example, found some 43 percent of men and 34 percent of women reporting that they worked more hours than they wanted to.[26] We know that work-related stress can come from many sources—from excessively high or low task demands, role conflicts or ambiguities, poor interpersonal relations, or career progress that is either too slow or too fast. A list of common stressors includes the following:

- *Task demands*—being asked to do too much or being asked to do too little.

- *Role ambiguities*—not knowing what one is expected to do or how work performance is evaluated.

- *Role conflicts*—feeling unable to satisfy multiple, possibly conflicting, performance expectations.

- *Ethical dilemmas*—being asked to do things that violate the law or personal values.

- *Interpersonal problems*—experiencing bad relationships or working with others who do not get along.

- *Career developments*—moving too fast and feeling stretched; moving too slowly and feeling plateaued.

- *Physical setting*—being bothered by noise, lack of privacy, pollution, or other unpleasant working conditions.

Nonwork and Personal Stressors   A less obvious, though important, source of stress for people at work is the "spillover" effect from forces in their nonwork lives. Family events (e.g., the birth of a new child), economic difficulties (e.g., the sudden loss of a big investment), and personal affairs (e.g., a separation or divorce) can all be extremely stressful. Since it is often difficult to completely separate work and nonwork lives, stress of this nonwork sort can affect the way people feel and behave on the job as well as away from it.

Another set of stressors includes personal factors, such as individual needs, capabilities, and personality. Stress can reach a destructive state more quickly for example, when experienced by highly emotional people or by those with low self-esteem. People who perceive a good fit between job requirements and personal skills seem to have a higher tolerance for stress than do those who feel less competent as a result of a person–job mismatch.[27] Basic aspects of personality are also important. The achievement orientation, impatience, and perfectionism of individuals with Type A personalities, for example, often create stress for them in work settings that others find relatively stress-free.[28]

■ **Stressors** are things that cause stress.

Possible work-related stressors

Red Roof Inns
www.redroof.com

At Red Roof Inns employees are entitled to one hour and 15 minutes of exercise three times each week in the firm's corporate health clubs. Spokeswoman Mari Jazyk takes pride in Red Roof Inn's commitment to its employees and healthy living. She says: "That's been a real strong philosophy of the company from the beginning."

▪ STRESS AND PERFORMANCE

▪ **Constructive stress** has a positive impact on both attitudes and performance.

Stress isn't always negative as an influence on our lives. It has two faces—one positive and one negative.[29] **Constructive stress**, or *eustress*, acts in a positive way. Moderate levels of stress by prompting increased work effort, stimulating creativity, and encouraging greater diligence. You may know such stress as the tension that causes you to study hard before exams, pay attention, and complete assignments on time in a difficult class. **Destructive stress**, or *distress*, is dysfunctional for both the individual and the organization. Too much stress can overload and break down a person's physical and mental systems resulting in absenteeism, turnover, errors, accidents, dissatisfaction, reduced performance, unethical behavior and even illness. Stanford scholar and consultant Jeffrey Pfeffer, for example, criticizes organizations that suffer from such excessive practices for creating *toxic workplaces*.[30] A toxic company implicitly says to its employees: "We're going to put you in an environment where you have to work in a style and at a pace that is not sustainable. We want you to come in here and burn yourself out. Then you can leave."[31]

▪ **Destructive stress** has a negative impact on both attitudes and performance.

www.josephsoninstitute.com

⚖ ETHICS AND SOCIAL RESPONSIBILITY

The Josephson Institute of Ethics is a public-benefit nonprofit membership organization dedicated to improving the ethical quality of society. The Institute is an advocate of principled reasoning and ethical decision making. One of its concerns centers on the risks of employers pushing people too hard. One result of "overtasking"—asking employees to pursue unrealistic goals—can be unethical behavior or cheating. Impossible performance standards may cause people to falsify their "numbers" or engage in other questionable practices to make their performance look good.[32]

▪ STRESS AND HEALTH

As is well known, stress can impact a person's health. It is a potential source of both anxiety and frustration, which can harm the body's physiological and psychological well-being over time.[33] Health problems associated with stress include heart attack, stroke, hypertension, migraine headache, ulcers, substance abuse, overeating, depression, and muscle aches. As noted in The Effective Manager 19.2, managers and team leaders should be alert to signs of excessive stress in themselves and their co-workers. Key symptoms to look for are changes from normal patterns—changes from regular attendance to absenteeism, from punctuality to tardiness, from diligent work to careless work, from a positive attitude to a negative attitude, from openness to change to resistance to change, or from cooperation to hostility.

▪ STRESS MANAGEMENT

▪ **Stress prevention** involves minimizing the potential for stress to occur.

Stress prevention is the best first-line strategy in the battle against stress. It involves taking action to keep stress from reaching destructive levels in the first place. Personal and nonwork stressors must be recognized so that action can be taken to prevent them from adverse impact. Persons with Type A personalities, for example, may exercise self-discipline; supervisors of Type A employees may try to model a lower key, more relaxed approach to work. Family problems may be partially relieved by a change of work schedule; the anxiety caused by pressing family concerns may be reduced by simply knowing that your supervisor understands.

Once stress has reached a destructive point, special techniques of **stress management** can be implemented. This process begins with the recognition of stress symptoms and continues with actions to maintain a positive performance edge. The term **wellness** is increasingly used these days. Personal wellness involves the pursuit of one's physical and mental potential through a personal health promotion program.[34] The concept recognizes individual responsibility to enhance and maintain wellness through a disciplined approach to physical and mental health. It requires attention to such factors as smoking, weight, diet, alcohol use, and physical fitness. Organizations can benefit from commitments to support personal wellness. A University of Michigan study indicates that firms have saved up to $600 per year per employee by helping them to cut the risk of significant health problems.[35] Arnold Coleman, CEO of Healthy Outlook Worldwide, a health fitness consulting firm, states: "If I can save companies 5 to 20 percent a year in medical costs, they'll listen. In the end you have a well company and that's where the word 'wellness' comes from."[36]

Organizations that build positive work environments and make significant investments in their employees are best positioned to realize the benefits of their full talents and work potential. As Pfeffer says: "All that separates you from your competitors are the skills, knowledge, commitment, and abilities of the people who work for you." Organizations that treat people right will get high returns...."[37] That, in essence, is what the study of organizational behavior is all about.

THE EFFECTIVE MANAGER 19.2

SIGNS OF EXCESSIVE STRESS

- Change in eating habits
- Change in alcohol consumption or smoking
- Unhealthy feelings—aches and pains, upset stomach
- Restlessness, inability to concentrate, sleeping problems
- Tense, uptight, fidgety, nervous feelings
- Disoriented, overwhelmed, depressed, irritable feelings

■ **Stress management** takes an active approach to deal with stress that is influencing behavior.

■ **Wellness** involves maintaining physical and mental health to better deal with stress when it occurs.

Chapter 19 Study Guide

What is organizational change?

Summary

- Planned change takes place because change agents, individuals and groups, make it happen to resolve performance problems or realize performance opportunities.

- Organizational targets for planned change include purpose, strategy, culture, structure, people, tasks, and technology.

- The planned change process requires attention to the three phases—unfreezing, changing, and refreezing.

What change strategies are used in organizations?

- Change strategies are the means change agents use to bring about desired change in people and systems.

- Force–coercion change strategies use position power to bring about change through direct command or through rewards and punishments.

- Rational persuasion change strategies use logical arguments and appeals to knowledge and facts to convince people to change.

- Shared-power change strategies involve other persons in planning and implementing change.

What can be done about resistance to change?

- Resistance to change should be expected and not feared; it is a source of feedback that can be used to improve a change effort.

- People usually resist change because they are defending something of value; they may focus their resistance on the change itself, the change strategy, or the change agent as a person.

- Strategies for dealing with resistance to change include education and communication, participation and involvement, facilitation and support, negotiation and agreement, manipulation and cooptation, and explicit or implicit coercion.

How do organizations innovate?

- Innovation is the process of creating new ideas and then implementing them in practical applications.

- Product innovations result in improved goods or services; process innovations result in improved work methods and operations.

- Steps in the innovation process normally include idea generation, initial experimentation, feasibility determination, and final application.

- Common features of highly innovative organizations include supportive strategies, cultures, structures, staffing, and senior leadership.

How does stress affect people at work?

- Stress emerges when people experience tensions caused by extraordinary demands, constraints, or opportunities in their jobs.

- Work-related stressors arise from such things as excessive task demands, interpersonal problems, unclear roles, ethical dilemmas, and career disappointments.

- Nonwork stress can spill over to affect people at work; nonwork stressors may be traced to family situations, economic difficulties, and personal problems.

- Personal stressors derive from personality type, needs, and values, and can influence how stressful different situations become for different people.

■ Stress can be managed by prevention—such as making adjustments in work and nonwork factors; it can also be dealt with through personal wellness—taking steps to maintain a healthy body and mind capable of better withstanding stressful situations.

Key Terms

Change agents (p. 395)
Changing (p. 398)
Constructive stress (p. 406)
Destructive stress (p. 406)
Force–coercion strategy
    (p. 398)
Innovation (p. 402)
Planned change (p. 396)
Process innovations
    (p. 402)

Product innovations
    (p. 402)
Rational persuasion strategy (p. 399)
Refreezing (p. 398)
Resistance to change
    (p. 400)
Shared-power strategy
    (p. 400)
Stress (p. 404)

Stress management (p. 407)
Stress prevention (p. 406)
Stressors (p. 405)
Unfreezing (p. 397)
Unplanned change (p. 395)
Wellness (p. 407)

Self-Test 19

■ MULTIPLE CHOICE

1. Performance gaps creating change situations include both problems to be resolved and _____ (a) costs to be avoided (b) people to be terminated (c) structures to be changed (d) opportunities to be explored

2. The presence or absence of a felt need for change is an issue in the _____ phase of planned change. (a) diagnostic (b) evaluative (c) unfreezing (d) changing

3. Which change strategy uses empirical data and expert power? (a) Force–coercion. (b) Rational persuasion. (c) Shared power. (d) Authoritative command.

4. Which change strategy often creates only temporary compliance? (a) Force–coercion. (b) Rational persuasion. (c) Shared power. (d) Normative reeducation.

5. A good change agent _____ resistance to change in order to best achieve change objectives. (a) eliminates (b) ignores (c) listens to (d) retreats from

6. According to the criterion of _____, a good change is clearly perceived as a better way of doing things. (a) benefit (b) triability (c) complexity (d) compatibility

7. Training in use of a new computer technology is an example of managing resistance to change through _____. (a) participation and involvement (b) facilitation and support (c) negotiation and agreement (d) education and communication

8. The innovation process is not complete until _____ has occurred. (a) idea creation (b) invention (c) feasibility determination (d) final application

9. Task demands and ethical dilemmas are examples of _____ stressors, while a Type A personality is a _____ stressors. (a) work-related, personal (b) work-related, nonwork (c) nonpersonal, personal (d) real, imagined

10. Which is an example of stress management by the personal wellness strategy? (a) role negotiation (b) empowerment (c) regular physical exercise (d) flexible hours

■ TRUE–FALSE

11. The only significant change for today's organizations is radical or frame-breaking change.   T   F

12. Change agents, formally defined, are outside consultants hired to help managers change their organizations.   T   F

13. Changes in tasks, people, technology, and structures are often interrelated.   T   F

14. Positive reinforcement of desired behaviors is part of the refreezing phase of planned change.   T   F

15. The personality and style of the change agent may cause resistance to change.   T   F

16. The shared-power change strategy is the same as the rational persuasion.   T   F

17. A process innovation results in the creation of a new good or service.   T   F

18. Product champions and information gatekeepers play important innovation roles in organizations.   T   F

19. The only real way to deal with stress is to prevent its occurrence.   T   F

20. Stress from nonwork factors can spill over to affect a person's work activities.   T   F

■ SHORT RESPONSE

21. What should a manager do when forces for unplanned change appear?

22. What internal and external forces push for change in organizations?

23. What does the "boiled frog phenomenon" tell us about organizational change?

24. How might stress influence individual performance?

■ APPLICATIONS ESSAY

25. When Jorge Maldanado became general manager of the local civic recreation center, he realized that many changes would be necessary to make the facility a true community resource. Having the benefit of a new bond issue, the center had the funds for new equipment and expanded programming. All he needed to do now was get the staff committed to new initiatives. Unfortunately, his first efforts to raise performance have been met with considerable resistance to change. A typical staff comment is, "Why do all these extras? Everything is fine as it is." How may Jorge use the strategies for dealing with resistance to change, as discussed in the chapter, to move the change process along?

Explore application-oriented Fast Company articles, cases, experimental exercises, and self-assessments in the OB Skills Workbook

■ **Visit the Schermerhorn Web site to find the Interactive Self-Test and Internet exercises for this chapter.**

Research Foundations of Organizational Behavior

This book is full of findings and conclusions about organizational behavior as a field of study. These findings and conclusions rely heavily on research foundations. For example, the different motivational approaches and recommendations discussed in Chapter 5 are based on such research foundations. Thus, one key reason that research foundations are so important to you is that they provide the base for the content of this course. A second reason is that you can use them to evaluate not only the findings in your text and course but also everyday findings that are reported. For example, you are likely to see arguments presented in the media concerning leadership, motivation, and many other OB topics. Those of you who become managers will encounter even more information about management and OB topics. Not all of this information has been developed systematically using research foundations and a scientific approach, however. This module will help you evaluate the strengths and weaknesses of the OB information you receive. For example, your boss may ask you to respond to a new article she has just read regarding improving work group performance. The information here can help you provide a knowledgeable response.

Finally, OB research foundations are important because they can guide you, as a manager, in asking the right questions and obtaining the right information to deal systematically with managerial and OB problems. For example, you may want to see whether the application of one of the leadership approaches in Chapter 15 works as predicted. This module can guide you in examining that question. The module alone will not make a scientist or an OB expert out of you, but it will help you think scientifically and use appropriate research foundations to deal with problems of concern to you.

The Scientific Method

A key part of OB research foundations is the **scientific method**, which involves four steps. First, a *research question* or *problem* is specified. Then one or more

■ The **scientific method** is a key part of the OB research foundations, which involves four steps: the research question or problem, hypothesis generation or formulation, the research design, and data gathering, analysis, and interpretation.

hypotheses or explanations of what the research parties expect to find are formulated. These may come from many sources, including previous experience and careful review of the literature covering the problem area. The next step is the creation of a *research design*—an overall plan or strategy for conducting the research to test the hypothesis(es). Finally, *data gathering, analysis,* and *interpretation* are carried out.[1]

■ THE VOCABULARY OF RESEARCH

The previous discussion conveyed a quick summary of the scientific method. It's important to go beyond that summation and further develop a number of aspects of the scientific method. Before doing that, we consider the vocabulary of research. Knowing that vocabulary can help you feel comfortable with several terms used in OB research as well as help in our later discussion.[2]

Variable   A **variable** is a measure used to describe a real-world phenomenon. For example, a researcher may count the number of parts produced by workers in a week's time as a measure of the workers' individual productivity.

Hypothesis   Building on our earlier use of the term, we can define a **hypothesis** as a tentative explanation about the relationship between two or more variables. For example, OB researchers have hypothesized that an increase in the number of rest pauses allowed workers in a workday will increase productivity. Hypotheses are "predictive" statements. Once supported through empirical research, a hypothesis can be a source of direct action implications. Confirmation of the above hypothesis would lead to the following implication: If you want to increase individual productivity in a work unit, give the subordinates more frequent rest pauses.

Dependent Variable   The **dependent variable** is the event or occurrence expressed in a hypothesis that indicates what the researcher is interested in explaining. In OB research, for example, individual performance is often the dependent variable of interest; that is, researchers try to determine what factors appear to predict increases in performance. One hypothesized relationship is that increased rest periods predict increased performance.

Independent Variable   An **independent variable** is the event or occurrence that is presumed by a hypothesis to affect one or more other events or occurrences as dependent variables. In the OB study on individual performance, increased rest periods is the independent variable.

Intervening Variable   An **intervening variable** is an event or occurrence that provides the linkage through which an independent variable is presumed to affect a dependent variable. It has been hypothesized, for instance, that participative supervisory practices—independent variable—improve worker satisfaction—intervening variable—and therefore increase performance—dependent variable.

Moderator Variable   A **moderator variable** is an event or occurrence that, when systematically varied, changes the relationship between an independent

Sidebar definitions:

■ A **variable** is a measure used to describe a real-world phenomenon.

■ A **hypothesis** is a tentative explanation about the relationship between two or more variables.

■ A **dependent variable** is the event or occurrence expressed in a hypothesis that indicates what the researcher is interested in explaining.

■ An **independent variable** is the event or occurrence that is presumed by a hypothesis to affect one or more other events or occurrences as dependent variables.

■ An **intervening variable** is an event or occurrence that provides the linkage through which an independent variable is presumed to affect a dependent variable.

■ A **moderator variable** is an event or occurrence that, when systematically varied, changes the relationship between an independent variable and a dependent variable.

variable and a dependent variable. The relationship between these two variables differs depending on the level, for instance, high/low, young/old, male/female, of the moderator variable.[3] To illustrate, the previous example of individual performance hypothesizes that participative supervision leads to increased productivity. It may well be that this relationship holds true only when the employees feel that their participation is real and legitimate—a moderator variable. Likewise, it may be that participative supervision leads to increased performance for Canadian workers but not those from Brazil—here, country is a moderator variable.

Theory   A **theory** is a set of systematically interrelated concepts, definitions, and hypotheses that are advanced to explain and predict phenomena.[4] Theories tend to be abstract and to involve multiple variables. They usually include a number of hypotheses, each of which is based on clearly articulated arguments and definitions. Most, if not all, of the kinds of variables previously discussed would probably be involved in a theory. We should also note that many things we call "theories" in OB do not strictly meet the above definition. Rather, they represent viewpoints, explanations, or perspectives that have logical merit and that are in the process of being scientifically varified.

■ A **theory** is a set of systematically interrelated concepts, definitions, and hypotheses that are advanced to explain and predict phenomena.

Validity   **Validity** is concerned with the degree of confidence one can have in the results of a research study. It is focused on limiting research errors so that results are accurate and usable.[5] There are two key types of validity: internal and external. *Internal validity* is the degree to which the results of a study can be relied upon to be correct. It is strongest when alternative interpretations of the study's findings can be ruled out.[6] To illustrate, if performance improves with more participative supervisory practices, these results have a higher degree of internal validity if we can rule out the effects of differences in old and new machines.

■ **Validity** is the degree of confidence one can have in the results of a research study.

External validity is the degree to which the study's results can be generalized across the entire population of people, settings, and other similar conditions.[7] We cannot have external validity unless we first have internal validity; that is, we must have confidence that the results are caused by what the study says they are before we can generalize to a broader context.

Reliability   **Reliability** is the consistency and stability of a score from a measurement scale. There must be reliability for there to be validity or accuracy. Think of shooting at a bull's eye. If the shots land all over the target, there is neither reliability (consistency) or validity (accuracy). If the shots are clustered close together but outside the outer ring of the target, they are reliable but not valid. If they are grouped together within the bull's eye, they are both reliable and valid.[8]

■ **Reliability** is the consistency and stability of a score from a measurement scale.

Causality   **Causality** is the assumption that change in the independent variable caused change in the dependent variable. This assumption is very difficult to prove in OB research. Three types of evidence are necessary to demonstrate causality: (1) the variables must show a linkage or association; (2) one variable must precede the other in time; and (3) there must be an absence of other causal factors.[9] For example, say we note that participation and performance increase together—there is an association. If we can then show that an increase in participation has preceded an increase in performance and that other factors, such as

■ **Causality** is the assumption that change in the independent variable has caused change in the dependent variable.

new machinery, haven't been responsible for the increased performance, we can say that participation probably has caused performance.

Research Designs

■ A **research design** is an overall plan or strategy for conducting research to test a hypothesis.

As noted earlier, a **research design** is an overall plan or strategy for conducting the research to test the hypothesis(es). Four of the most popular research designs are laboratory experiments, field experiments, case studies, and field surveys.[10]

■ LABORATORY EXPERIMENTS

■ A **laboratory experiment** is conducted in an artificial setting in which the researcher intervenes and manipulates one or more independent variables in a highly controlled situation.

Laboratory experiments are conducted in an artificial setting in which the researcher intervenes and manipulates one or more independent variables in a highly controlled situation. Although there is a high degree of control, which, in turn, encourages internal validity, since these studies are done in an artificial setting, they may suffer from external validity.

To illustrate, assume we are interested in the impact of three different incentive systems on employee absenteeism: (1) a lottery with a monetary reward; (2) a lottery with a compensatory time off reward; and (3) a lottery with a large prize, such as a car. The researcher randomly selects individuals in an organization to come to an office to take part in the study. This randomization is important because it means that variables that are not measured are randomly distributed across the subjects so that unknown variables shouldn't be causing whatever is found. However, it often is not possible to obtain subjects randomly in organizations since they may be needed elsewhere by management.

The researcher is next able to select randomly each worker to one of the three incentive systems as well as a control group with no incentive system. The employees report to work in their new work stations under highly artificial but controlled conditions, and their absenteeism is measured both at the beginning and end of the experiment. Statistical comparisons are made across each group, considering before and after measures.

Ultimately, the researcher develops hypotheses about the effects of each of the lottery treatments on absenteeism. Given support for these hypotheses, the researcher could feel with a high degree of confidence that a given incentive condition caused less absenteeism than did the others since randomized subjects, pre- and posttest measures, and a comparison with a control group were used. However, since the work stations were artificial and the lottery conditions were highly simplified to provide control, external validity could be questioned. Ideally, the researcher would conduct a follow-up study with another design to check for external validity.

■ FIELD EXPERIMENTS

■ A **field experiment** is a research study that is conducted in a realistic setting, whereby the researcher intervenes and manipulates one or more independent variables and controls the situation as carefully as the situation permits.

Field experiments are research studies that are conducted in a realistic setting. Here, the researcher intervenes and manipulates one or more independent variables and controls the situation as carefully as the situation permits.

Applying the same research question as before, the researcher obtains management permission to assign one incentive treatment to each of three similar organizational departments, similar in terms of the various characteristics of people. A fourth control department keeps the current payment plan. The rest of the experiment is similar to the laboratory study except that the lottery treatments are more realistic but also less controlled. Also, it may be particularly difficult to obtain random assignment in this case since it may disrupt day-to-day work schedules, etc. When random assignment is not possible, the other manipulations may still be possible. An experimental research design without any randomization is called a *quasi-experimental design* and does not control for unmeasured variables as well as a randomized design.

■ CASE STUDIES

Case studies are in-depth analyses of one or a small number of settings. Case studies often are used when little is known about a phenomenon and the researcher wants to examine relevant concepts intensely and thoroughly. They can sometimes be used to help develop theory that can then be tested with one of the other research designs. Returning to the incentive and absenteeism example, one might look at one or more organizations and intensely study organizational success or failure in designing or implementing the system(s). This information could provide insights to be investigated further with additional case studies or other research designs.

> ■ A **case study** is an in-depth analysis of one or a small number of settings.

A major strength of case studies is their realism and the richness of data and insights they can provide. Some disadvantages are their lack of control by the researcher, the difficulty of interpreting the results because of their richness, and the large amount of time and cost that may be involved.

■ FIELD SURVEYS

Field surveys typically depend on the use of some form of questionnaire for the primary purpose of describing and/or predicting some phenomenon. Typically, they utilize a sample drawn from some large population. A key objective of field surveys is to look for relationships between or among variables. Two major advantages are their ability to examine and describe large populations quickly and inexpensively and their flexibility. They can be used to do many kinds of OB research, such as testing hypotheses and theories and evaluating programs. Field surveys assume that the researcher has enough knowledge of the problem area to know the kinds of questions to ask; sometimes, earlier case studies help provide this knowledge.

> ■ A **field survey** is a research design that relies on the use of some form of questionnaire for the primary purpose of describing and/or predicting some phenomenon.

In terms of our incentive and absenteeism problem, assume the researcher knows about organizations that have used different kinds of incentive systems to reduce absenteeism and reviews the appropriate literature on the topic. The investigator then constructs a questionnaire and sends it to firms that have implemented such incentive systems. The goal here is to describe characteristics of those organizations and incentive systems that have been successful in reducing absenteeism.

A key disadvantage of this kind of study is the lack of control. The researcher does not manipulate variables; even such things as who completes the surveys and their timing may not be under the researcher's control. Another disadvantage is the lack of depth of the standardized responses; thus, sometimes the data obtained are superficial.

Data Gathering, Analysis, and Interpretation

Once the research design has been established, we are ready for data gathering, analysis, and interpretation—the final step in the scientific method. Four common OB data-gathering approaches are interviews, observation, questionnaires, and nonreactive measures.[11]

■ INTERVIEWS

■ An **interview** involves face-to-face, telephone, or computer-assisted interactions to ask respondents questions of interest.

Interviews involve face-to-face, telephone, or computer-assisted interactions to ask respondents questions of interest. Structured interviews ask the respondents the same questions in the same sequence. Unstructured interviews are more spontaneous and do not require the same format. Often a mixture of structured and unstructured formats is used. Interviews allow for in-depth responses and probing. They are generally time consuming, however, and require increasing amounts of training and skill, depending on their depth and amount of structure.

■ OBSERVATION

■ **Observation** involves watching an event, object, or person and recording what is seen.

Observation involves watching an event, object, or person and recording what is seen. Sometimes, the observer is separate from the participants and events and functions as an outside researcher. In other cases, the observer participates in the events as a member of a work unit. In the latter case, observations are summarized in some kind of diary or log. Sometimes, the observer is hidden and records observations behind one-way glass or by using hidden cameras and the like.

Two advantages of observation are that (1) behavior is observed as it occurs rather than being obtained by asking people after the fact, and (2) the observer can often obtain data that subjects can't or won't provide themselves. A couple of disadvantages are cost and the possible fallibility of observers who sometimes do not provide complete and accurate data.

■ QUESTIONNAIRES

■ **Questionnaires** ask respondents for their opinions, attitudes, perceptions, and/or descriptions of work-related matters.

Questionnaires ask respondents for their opinions, attitudes, perceptions, and/or descriptions of work-related matters. They usually are based on previously developed instruments. Typically, a respondent completes the questionnaire and returns it to the researcher. Questions may be open ended, or they may be structured with true–false or multiple-choice responses.

Advantages of questionnaires include the relatively low cost and the fact that the anonymity that often accompanies them may lead to more open and truthful responses. Some disadvantages are the low response rates, which may threaten the generalizability of the results, and the lack of depth of the responses.

■ NONREACTIVE MEASURES

■ **Nonreactive measures** are used to obtain data without disturbing the setting.

Nonreactive measures are used to obtain data without disturbing the setting being studied. Sometimes, these are termed *unobtrusive measures* since they are designed not to intrude in a research situation. Nonreactive measures can focus on such things as physical traces, archives, and hidden observation. A kind of physical trace occurred when John Fry at 3M distributed test batches of Post-It Notes to 3M employees and discovered that they were using them at higher rates than 3M's leading adhesive product—Scotch Tape.[12] Archives are records that an organization keeps as a part of its day-to-day activities, for example, minutes, daily production counts.

A major advantage of nonreactive measures is that they don't disturb the research setting and so avoid the reaction of a respondent to a researcher. One possible disadvantage is their indirectness; incorrect inferences may be drawn from nonreactive measures. They work best in combination with more direct measures.

■ DATA ANALYSIS AND INTERPRETATION

Once the data have been gathered, they need to be *analyzed*. The most common means of analysis involves some kind of statistical approach, ranging from simple counting and categorizing to sophisticated multivariate statistical techniques.[13] It's beyond our scope to discuss this area beyond simply emphasizing its importance. However, various statistical tests often are used to examine support for hypotheses, to check for the reliability of various data-gathering approaches, and to provide information on causality and many other aspects of analysis.

After systematic analysis has been performed, the researcher *interprets* the results and prepares a report.[14] Sometimes, the report is used in-house by management; other times, the results are reported at various conferences and published in journals. Ultimately, many of the results in the OB area appear in textbooks like this one.

Ethical Considerations in Research

Given our emphasis on ethical considerations throughout this book, it is appropriate to end our discussion of OB research with a look at its ethical considerations. These ethical considerations involve rights of four broad parties involved in research in general and in OB research in particular: society, subjects, clients, and researchers.[15]

In terms of *societal rights*—those of the broadest of the parties involved in OB research—three key areas exist: the right to be informed, the right to expect objective results, and the right to privacy or to be left alone. Subjects of research also have rights: the right to choose (to participate or not), to safety, and to be informed. The rights of the client involve two primary concerns: the right to expect high-quality research and the right of confidentiality. Finally, two rights of the researcher stand out: the right to expect ethical client behavior and the right to expect ethical subject behavior.

All of these rights need to be communicated and adhered to by all parties. Indeed, various organizations conducting research are increasingly endorsing codes of ethics to codify such rights. Two particular organizations that have codes of ethics for research covering OB and related areas are the American Psychological Association and the Academy of Management.[16]

THE OB SKILLS WORKBOOK

SUGGESTED APPLICATIONS OF WORKBOOK MATERIALS

FAST COMPANY I. The FAST COMPANY Collection

Article	Suggested Part	Overview
1. *The Company of the Future*	Parts 1, 2, 4, 5	Written by Harvard University professor and former Secretary of Labor Robert Reich—focuses on high performance organizations, talented workers, loyalty and organizational commitment, progressive management practices, emerging workforce values, changing nature of organizations.
2. *Life In the Fast Lane*	Parts 1, 3, 5	Interview with Ray Everingham of Hendricks Motorsports and NASCAR crew chief—focuses on high performance teams, team leadership, competitive pressures, member talents, decision making, continuous improvement, and performance under pressure.
3. *Danger: Toxic Company*	Parts 1, 2, 4, 5	Interview with Stanford University professor Jeffrey Pfeffer—focuses on what is wrong about organizational work environments and what can be done to improve them, talented workers, importance of putting people first, training and development, and high performance organizations.
4. *Learning for a Change*	Parts 1, 4, 5	Interview with MIT professor and consultant Peter Senge—focuses on the origins and development of the "learning organization" concept, with emphasis on leadership, organizations as living systems, organizational cultures and change, and high performance organizations.

II. Cases for Critical Thinking

Case	Suggested Chapter	Cross-References and Integration
1. *Drexler's Bar-B-Que*	1 Organizational Behavior Today	organizational structure; design and culture; organizational change and innovation; decision making; leadership
2. *Sun Microsystems*	2 The High Performance Organization	human resource management; organizational cultures; innovation; information technology; leadership
3. *Crossing Borders*	3 Global Dimensions of Organizational Behavior	diversity and individual differences; perception and attribution; performance management; job design; communication; conflict decision making
4. *Never on a Sunday*	4 Diversity and Individual Differences	ethics and diversity; organizational structure, design, and culture; decision making; organizational change
5. *Magrec, Inc.*	5 Perception and Attribution	ethics and diversity; organizational structure, design, and culture; decision making; organizational change
6. *It isn't Fair*	6 Motivation and Reinforcement	perception and attribution; performance management and rewards; communication; ethics and decision making
7. *Amoco's Global Human Resource Systems*	7 Human Resource Management Systems	organizational cultures; globalization; communication; decision making

Case	Suggested Chapter	Cross-References and Integration
8. *I'm Not in Kansas Anymore*	8 High Performance Job Designs	organizational design; motivation; performance management and rewards
9. *The Forgotten Group Member*	9 The Nature of Groups	teamwork; motivation; diversity and individual differences; perception and attribution; performance management and rewards; communication; conflict; leadership
10. *NASCAR's Racing Teams*	10 Teamwork and High Performance Teams	organizational cultures; leadership; motivation and reinforcement; communication
11. *First Community Financial*	11 Basic Attributes of Organizations	organizational structure, designs and culture; performance management and rewards
12. *Mission Management and Trust*	12 Information Technology and Organizational Design	organizational structure, designs and culture; performance management and rewards
13. *Motorola*	13 High Performance Organizational Culture	innovation; conflict and negotiation; leadership; change and stress
14. *Perot Systems*	14 High Performance Leadership	organizational cultrues; group dynamics and teamwork; motivation and reinforcement
15. *Power or Empowerment at GM?*	15 Power and Politics	communication; conflict; decision making; organizational change; job design
16. *The Poorly Informed Walrus*	16 Information and Communication	diversity and individual differences; perception and attribution
17. *Johnson & Johnson*	17 Decision Making	organizational structure; organizational cultures; change and innovation; group dynamics and teamwork; diversity and individual differences
18. *American Airlines*	18 Conflict and Negotiation	change, innovation and stress; job designs; communication; power and politics
19. *The New Vice President*	19 Change, Innovation, and Stress	leadership; performance management and rewards; diversity and individual differences; communication; conflict and negotiation; power and influence

III. Cross-Functional Integrating Case

Case	Overview
Trilogy Software: High Performance Company of the Future?	Cross-functional integrating case on the launch and development of a highly innovative software company—focus on high performance organizations, competitive environment, innovation, talented workforce, motivation and rewards, organizational culture, technology and change

Note: This case appears on the Schermerhorn Web Site at www.wiley.com/college/schermerhorn

IV. Experiential Exercises

Exercise	Suggested Chapter	Cross-References and Integration
1. *My Best Manager*	1 Organizational Behavior Today	leadership

Exercise	Suggested Chapter	Cross-References and Integration
2. *Graffiti Needs*	1 Organizational Behavior Today	human resource management; communication
3. *My Best Job*	2 The High Performance Organization	motivation; job design; organizational cultures
4. *What Do You Value in Work?*	2 The High Performance Organization	diversity and individual differences; performance management and rewards; motivation; job design; decision making
5. *My Asset Base*	2 The High Performance Organization	perception and attribution; diversity and individual differences; groups and teamwork; decision making
6. *Expatriate Assignments*	3 Global Dimensions of Organizational Behavior	perception and attribution; diversity and individual differences; decision making
7. *Cultural Cues*	3 Global Dimensions of Organizational Behavior	perception and attribution; diversity and individual differences; decision making; communication; conflict; groups and teamwork
8. *Prejudice in Our Lives*	4 Diversity and Individual Differences	perception and attribution; decision making; conflict; groups and teamwork
9. *How We View Differences*	5 Perception and Attribution	culture; international; diversity and individual differences; decision making; communication; conflict; groups and teamwork
10. *Alligator River Story*	5 Perception and Attribution	diversity and individual differences; decision making; communication; conflict; groups and teamwork
11. *Teamwork & Motivation*	6 Motivation and Reinforcement	performance management and rewards; groups and teamwork
12. *The Downside of Punishment*	6 Motivation and Reinforcement	motivation; perception and attribution; performance management and rewards
13. *Annual Pay Raises*	7 Human Resource Management Systems	motivation; learning and reinforcement perception and attribution; decision making; groups and teamwork
14. *Tinker Toys*	8 High Performance Job Design	organizational structure; design and culture; groups and teamwork
15. *Job Design Preferences*	8 High Performance Job Design	motivation; organizational design; change
16. *My Fantasy Job*	8 High Performance Job Design	motivation; individual differences; organizational design; change
17. *Eggsperiential Exercise*	9 The Nature of Groups	group dynamics and teamwork; diversity and individual differences; communication
18. *Scavenger Hunt—Team Building*	10 Teamwork and High Performance Teams	groups; leadership; diversity and individual differences; communication; leadership
19. *Work Team Dynamics*	10 Teamwork and High Performance Teams	groups; motivation; decision making; conflict; communication
20. *Identifying Group Norms*	10 Teamwork and High Performance Teams	groups; communication; perception and attribution
21. *Workgroup Culture*	10 Teamwork and High Performance Teams	groups; communication; perception and attribution; job design; organizational culture
22. *The Hot Seat*	10 Teamwork and High Performance Teams	groups; communication; conflict and negotiation; power and politics

Exercise	Suggested Chapter	Cross-References and Integration
23. *Organizations Alive!*	11 Basic Attributes of Organizations	organizational design and culture; performance management and rewards
24. *Fast Food Technology*	12 Information Technology Organizational Design	organizational design; organizational culture; job design
25. *Alien Invasion*	13 High Performance Organizational Culture	organizational structure and design; international; diversity and individual differences; perception and attribution
26. *Interview a Leader*	14 High Performance Leadership	performance management and rewards; group and teamwork; new workplace; organizational change and stress
27. *Leadership Skills Inventories*	14 High Performance Leadership	individual differences; perception and attribution; decision making
28. *Leadership and Participation in Decision Making*	14 High Performance Leadership	decision making; communication; motivation; groups; teamwork
29. *My Best Manager: Revisited*	15 Power and Politics	diversity and individual differences; perception and attribution
30. *Active Listening*	16 Information and Communication	group dynamics and teamwork; perception and attribution
31. *Upward Appraisal*	16 Information and Communication	perception and attribution; performance management and rewards
32. *"360" Feedback*	17 Decision Making	communication; perception and attribution; performance management and rewards
33. *Role Analysis Negotiation*	17 Decision Making	communication; group dynamics and teamwork; perception and attribution; communication; decision making
34. *Lost at Sea*	17 Decision Making	communication; group dynamics and teamwork; conflict and negotiation
35. *Entering the Unknown*	17 Decision Making	communication; group dynamics and teamwork; perception and attribution
36. *Vacation Puzzle*	18 Conflict and Negotiation	conflict and negotiation; communication; power; leadership
37. *The Ugli Orange*	18 Conflict and Negotiation	communication; decision making
38. *Force-Field Analysis*	19 Change, Innovation, and Stress	decision making; organization structures, designs, cultures

 ## V. Self-Assessment Inventories

Assessment	Suggested Chapter	Cross-References and Integration
1. *Managerial Assumptions*	1 Organizational Behavior Today	leadership
2. *A 21st-Century Manager*	1 Organizational Behavior Today 2 The High Performance Organization	leadership; decision making; globalization

Assessment	Suggested Chapter	Cross-References and Integration
3. Turbulence Tolerance Test	1 Organizational Behavior Today 2 The High Performance Organization	perception; individual differences; organizational change and stress
4. Global Readiness Index	3 Global Dimensions of Organizational Behavior	diversity, culture, leading, perception, management skills, career readiness
5. Personal Values	4 Diversity and Individual Differences	perception; diversity and individual differences; leadership
6. Intolerance for Ambiguity	5 Perception and Attribution	perception; leadership
7. Two-Factor Profile	6 Motivation and Reinforcement	job design, perception, culture, human resource management
8. Are You Cosmopolitan?	7 Human Resource Management Systems 8 High Performance Job Design	diversity and individual differences; organizational culture
9. Group Effectiveness	9 The Nature of Groups 10 Teamwork and High Performance Teams	organizational designs and cultures; leadership
10. Organizational Design Preference	11 Basic Attributes of Organization 12 Information Technology and Organizational Design	job design; diversity and individual differences
11. Which Culture Fits You?	13 High Performance Organizational Culture	perception; diversity and individual differences
12. Least Preferred Coworker Scale	14 High Performance Leadership	diversity and individual differences; perception; group dynamics and teamwork
13. Leadership Style	14 High Performance Leadership	diversity and individual differences; perception; group dynamics and teamwork
14. "TT" Leadership Style	14 High Performance Leadership 16 Information and Communication	diversity and individual differences; perception; group dynamics and teamwork
15. Empowering Others	15 Power and Politics 16 Information and Communication	leadership; perception and attribution
16. Machiavellianism	15 Power and Politics	leadership; diversity and individual differences
17. Personal Power Profile	15 Power and Politics	leadership; diversity and individual differences
18. Your Intuitive Ability	17 Decision Making	diversity and individual differences
19. Decision-Making Biases	17 Decision Making	teams and teamwork, communication, perception
20. Conflict Management Styles	18 Conflict and Negotiation	diversity and individual differences; communication
21. Your Personality Type	19 Change, Innovation, and Stress	diversity and individual differences; job design
22. Time Management Profile	19 Change, Innovation, and Stress	diversity and individual differences

THE FAST COMPANY COLLECTION

ARTICLE 1

The Company of the Future

by Robert B. Reich

It is a revolutionary notion: Talented people are joining up with fast companies to create "social glue"—the essence of both a winning business and a humane workplace.

Danielle Rios, 28, has it all—a BS degree in computer science from Stanford, a great track record as a software developer for IBM, and the energy and savvy to market herself. With all that going for her, Rios could be a free-agent winner in the new economy, adding value by juggling different projects with different firms. Or she could have her pick of well-established corporate launch pads for her career.

But for the last three years, Rios has worked with Trilogy Software Inc., a small, rapidly growing software firm based in Austin, Texas. Trilogy is on the cutting edge of sales-and-marketing software, and Rios is part of a team that shows potential customers how the software can work for them.

Joe Liemandt, 30, founded Trilogy in 1989, after dropping out of Stanford only a few months before graduation. To finance the startup, Liemandt charged up 22 credit cards. If Trilogy were to go public today, analysts say, it would be valued at more than $1 billion. Four years

ago, Trilogy had 100 employees; today it has almost 1,000—and plans to add another 1,000 before the summer of 1999. But to call Trilogy workers "employees" misses the point. They're all shareholders. They're all managers. They're all partners. That's how Liemandt, Trilogy's CEO, has chosen to run his company—and that's what makes it successful.

Liemandt knows that Trilogy depends on talented people. He also knows that people can go anywhere. Which means that his biggest competitive headache isn't companies like SAP AG, Baan Co., and PeopleSoft Inc.—businesses he has to face down in the marketplace. His biggest worry is holding onto people like Rios. "There's nothing more important than recruiting and growing people," he says. "That's my number-one job."

It's a seller's market for talent. People with the right combination of savvy and ambition can afford to shop for the right boss, the right colleagues, the right environment. In the old economy, it was a buyer's market: Companies had their pick of the crop, and the question they asked was "Why hire?" Now the question is "Why join up?"

As a result, the economy is fostering new kinds of organizations with new kinds of practices and operating rules for pulling people together. These companies offer many of the advantages of free agency: flexibility in how,

First appeared: Fast Company issue 19 page 124
Reprinted with permission from Fast Company Magazine.

425

when, and where you work; compensation linked to what you contribute; freedom to move from project to project. But they also offer the advantages of belonging to an organization in which mutual commitment builds continuity. They are the enterprises of the future.

What makes them so different? Consider again Danielle Rios and Joe Liemandt at Trilogy. In the old economy, Rios and Liemandt would have been on opposite sides of the table: employee and employer. They'd be there for years, locked in their conflicting roles. Liemandt would want steady, reliable work from Rios. Rios would want a fair wage from Liemandt and an opportunity to move up the company ladder. In the new economy, Rios and Liemandt sit on the same side of the table. And they've joined together—for a time—to create new value.

Ask leaders what their biggest challenge is, and you get the same answer: finding, attracting, and keeping talented people. Ask talented people what their biggest career challenge is, and you'll hear the same refrain: finding good people to work with—and to work for.

For Liemandt and Rios, and for everyone in the new enterprises of the free-agent economy, the crucial questions are: What leads them to work together in the first place, and what keeps them together? Here are the six "social glues" of the company of the future.

Money Makes It Mutual

The world is awash in money. Venture capitalists are pouring funds into startups at a ferocious rate. In 1997, for example, venture-capital firms raised $10 billion. That same year, 629 companies went public, with a total valuation of more than $39 billion. The stock market has softened in recent months, but it's still way up there—making possible a previously unthinkable market for acquisitions and IPOs.

All of this money has had an unavoidable impact on the job market, where money is a powerful motivator. Freshly minted MBAs from leading business schools are commanding a premium from blue-chip consulting firms: Signing bonuses and first-year salaries often run higher than $120,000. And the pay packages that large, successful companies are putting in front of their most talented executives are critical in the rapidly escalating war to keep talent—or to steal it away. Not long ago, in the kind of deal that one usually reads about only in the sports pages, one of Wall Street's premier stock analysts landed a one-year, $25 million contract—a $15 million increase over his 1997 pay package.

But for most people who are trying to decide which company to join, the name of the game today is stock options. Chalk it up as another legacy of Microsoft and that company's now-legendary cadre of millionaires: Across the landscape of the new economy, young, well-educated, talented businesspeople are joining up to get a piece of the action. They're willing to forgo larger salaries at bigger and better-established firms in favor of stock options in upstarts that may be worth a great deal down the road. The result: Even small, little-known enterprises can compete for top talent. In fact, startups promising high risk and huge gain are winning.

"Obviously, it's not just compensation that motivates people to come to work here," says David Stewart, 30, head of human resources at Tripod, a Web company (http://www.tripod.com) based in Williamstown, Massachusetts. "But stock options are a big motivator." Founded in 1992 by Bo Peabody, then a 19-year-old Williams College student, Tripod launched its site in April 1995. Today the company employs 60 people, produces one of the 10 most heavily trafficked sites on the Web, and boasts more than 2 million members. To keep ahead of the competition, Tripod depends on talent.

Stewart doesn't have a classic high-tech background. Before coming to western Massachusetts, he was a lawyer in Montreal. He had worked his way through law school in Toronto by doing stand-up comedy at night. In January 1996, his wife, Margaret Gould Stewart, was offered a job as creative director at Tripod. (Now 27, she has risen to become Tripod's vice president of media and community development.) Stewart recalls that he pulled out a map and tried to locate Williamstown on it. He couldn't.

His wife accepted Tripod's offer, and Stewart followed her to Massachusetts. He joined a small law firm in North Adams, about 10 minutes from Tripod. Almost inevitably, Tripod became one of his clients; Stewart saw huge possibilities in the startup, and he wanted in. "Because there was a lot of buzz around the company, people thought, 'Hey, this stock could be worth something someday,'" Stewart recalls. In August 1997, he decided to take a job in Tripod's human-resources department—a big career change. The salary at Tripod was a little lower than what he'd been making at the law firm. But the company included a "decent-sized grant package." If it weren't for the options, he might not have made the switch. Now, says Stewart, "when you combine salary and options, I make more than I did at the law firm."

Money played a similar role in bringing Kara Berklich to Tripod as the company's director of communications. Berklich, now 26, graduated from Williams College in 1994, worked as a consultant in Cleveland for six months, and then returned to Williamstown to join

Tripod. She knew Bo Peabody from her college days and would have joined up right after graduation—but at that point, Tripod not only couldn't offer options; it couldn't even offer a livable salary. When Tripod was able to put together a package that included options, says Berklich, the company suddenly became much more attractive. "You think that eventually those options will become publicly traded stocks, whether through an IPO or through a buyout by a public company," she says.

Stewart and Berklich bet right. Last February, Tripod was bought by Lycos, one of the contending search engines-cum-Web portals, for $58 million. After the acquisition, Lycos stock rose by some 25 points and reached a high of 107. About six months after the acquisition, Lycos's stock split. Stewart and Berklich have had their Tripod options converted into Lycos options—an arrangement that will nevertheless bind them to Tripod for some time. "I continue to receive options in the company that continue to vest," says Berklich. "Lycos remains a really terrific financial opportunity."

Of course, underlying the popularity of stock options are three simple propositions about the nature of competition today. First, the real competition is over talent. Second, if you want to attract and keep talent, you have to pay for it. And third, if you want talent to work for your organization with the enthusiasm that comes with ownership, then you have to trade equity for it. These days, money does more than just talk. It creates glue.

Mission Makes a Difference

Xerox Parc guru John Seely Brown said it best: "The job of leadership today is not just to make money. It's to make meaning." When it comes to attracting, keeping, and making teams out of talented people, money alone won't do it. Talented people want to be part of something that they can believe in, something that confers meaning on their work and on their lives—something that involves a mission. And they don't want that mission to turn into the kind of predictable "mission statement" that plasters many a corporate-boardroom wall. Rather, they want spiritual goals that energize an organization by resonating with the personal values of the people who work there—the kind of mission that offers people a chance to do work that makes a difference. Along with the traditional bottom line, great enterprises have a second bottom line: a return on human investment that advances a larger purpose. A powerful mission is both a magnet and a motivator.

Meet David Bellshaw, 37, who six years ago joined Isaacson, Miller, a Boston-based boutique head-hunting firm. Isaacson, Miller has undertaken various head-hunt-ing tasks—including, for example, placing Dave Olson as CEO for Patagonia Inc. But the firm has carved out a special niche for itself by advancing women and minorities into executive positions and by finding leaders for a wide range of civic organizations and not-for-profit enterprises.

Bellshaw launched his career at the California office of Heidrick and Struggles, one of the leading head-hunting firms in the United States. When his wife, Ava, got into the Tufts University School of Medicine in Boston, Bellshaw considered several jobs with big firms in that city. But tiny Isaacson, Miller—smaller then than its 50-person staff today—stood out. A major reason why he joined up was "the company's unique mission," he says. "We are vicariously saving the world through our clients. That's a very, very strong pull for me."

Isaacson, Miller isn't just a head-hunting firm—it also helps its clients understand their own unique missions. The firm applies a mixture of psychological counseling and missionary zeal, while being attentive to the practical realities of good management.

Bellshaw comes to this calling naturally: His father was a Baptist minister, and so was his grandfather. "I rebelled against my background, and I still do—very actively," Bellshaw says. "But in some funny way, given my genes and upbringing, my work is a secular way of doing what my family has done. Two generations of ministers, and I broke the mold. Yet there remains a mission-driven theme in my life."

In his six years with Isaacson, Miller, Bellshaw has matched some high-powered people with some great organizations. One assignment: to find a new dean for New York University's Wagner School of Public Service—a place that trains the very sorts of civic leaders whom Isaacson, Miller recruits. The assignment wasn't easy. The school needed someone who combined administrative skills, a deep knowledge of both the public and the not-for-profit worlds, and an ability to define the future challenges of civic leadership, especially in the New York City area, where most of the school's graduates work.

How did Bellshaw begin? By sending an 11-page "Invitation to Apply" to 100 potential candidates. Among those who are rumored to have responded were former Colorado representative Pat Schroeder and former Ohio governor Dick Celeste. After an intensive search, Bellshaw selected Jo Ivey Boufford, then a high-ranking official in the U.S. Department of Health and Human Services and the U.S. representative on the executive board of the World Health Organization. Why choose Boufford from a list of such prestigious candidates? According to Bellshaw, not only did she have a proven track record as a manager, but she also had both a demonstrable interest in public service and the "New York-style gutsiness" needed for the position.

Another assignment: to find a new head for the Lovelace Institutes, a biomedical-research institute based in Albuquerque, New Mexico. Founded more than 50 years ago, Lovelace had seen its mission lose focus, and it needed a leader with the vision to set a new course and the management skills to implement the necessary reorganization. Bellshaw's pick to lead the institute: Robert Rubin, who had been the vice president of research at the University of Miami, where he had a reputation for taking risks and for demanding results. Soon after joining Lovelace in the fall of 1996, Rubin devised a solution to its problems: Completely reorganize the institute, rename it the Lovelace Respiratory Research Institute, and turn it into a national respiratory-research center. He plans to make Lovelace the leading authority on every aspect of research into respiratory disease.

How deep is David Bellshaw's commitment to Isaacson, Miller? Last May, when his wife accepted a medical residency at the University of California at San Francisco, Bellshaw had to make another decision: Would he leave the firm for a larger, more traditional head-hunting outfit in California—one that could pay him a lot of money? Or would he strike out on his own? In the end, Bellshaw says, the power of Isaacson, Miller's mission won out. He came up with a third option: He opened a new, West Coast office of the firm.

"It was a chance to do something that was interesting on a moral dimension, as well as an opportunity to build an office," he says. "The result is a blend of mission and market. With this job, I have all the mission of the best not-for-profits, and I also have all the rigors of the corporate world."

Learning Makes You Grow

In a knowledge-based economy, the new coin of the realm is learning. Want to build a business that can outlive its first good idea? Create a culture that values learning. Want to build a career that allows you to grow into new responsibilities? Maintain your hunger to learn—and join an organization where you'll be given the chance to learn continuously.

It's a proposition that fast companies have already figured out: Talented people join up in order to learn. Of course, part of the lure of learning goes back to the first "glue"—money. Learn more now, earn more in the future. But again, money is only part of the story. Talented people also want intellectual challenge: They like being explorers on the frontiers of the knowledge economy. And as apprentices have known for centuries, it's easiest to learn on the job—by working directly with people who can teach you and who are committed to the same goals you are.

Consider John Jordan, 40, director of electronic-commerce research at Ernst & Young LLP's Center for Business Innovation in Cambridge, Massachusetts. The center, which houses 35 people on two floors in an office designed with the ultramodern look-and-feel of a learning laboratory, functions as an in-house research and brainstorming facility for the 82,000-person, $9.1 billion global accounting and consulting firm.

If learning is a core competency, then Jordan already possesses it. Consider his degrees: a BA from Duke in political science and history, an MA from Yale in ethics, an MA and a PhD from the University of Michigan in American studies. But all of that education left Jordan hungry for something else: an understanding of the real business world. He could have opted for independence—freelancing for several clients—or he could have chosen to pursue various consulting roles. At the center, Jordan found the perfect blend of intellectual stimulation and real-world application, and an environment that keeps him glued to interesting people.

Part of the learning comes from contact with super-charged experts. "Working here has given me a rich Rolodex," Jordan says. "I'm invited to participate in a lot of stimulating conversations that I wouldn't take part in otherwise." The center taps various fields to bring in visiting fellows: a neuroscientist, a science-fiction writer, a provocative business-school professor, a magazine editor. "It's a group that I could never assemble on my own," says Jordan.

Being part of a high-powered think tank hasn't deprived Jordan of his autonomy. He largely designs his own goals, and he works to achieve them at a comfortable pace. And he's enlarged the scope of his work. "The brand called John Jordan has limited viability," he admits. His new brand has a much wider appeal.

Another part of the learning comes from the quality of the problems that cross Jordan's desk every day. The center acts as a kind of filter—screening out trivial issues and letting through only the hardest conceptual challenges. "The institutional affiliation gives you the leverage to do things you couldn't do on your own," he says. "The learning curve is so steep—I'm learning too much here to make going out on my own an attractive option."

Jordan's boss is Chris Meyer, who is himself an accomplished learner: Meyer, 50, graduated from Brandeis University, studied economics for two years at the University of Pennsylvania in its PhD program, and earned an MBA from Harvard Business School. As the director of the Center for Business Innovation, Meyer recruits people who want to learn from one another—a process that makes Ernst & Young a desirable place to work. "People are attracted to the company because working here helps them become better than they could be otherwise," says Meyer.

Through its cutting-edge innovations, the center also offers its people a window onto the future. "By coming here, you're learning not just how to identify the issues of the future but also how to do the work of the future," Meyer says. "Working in the knowledge economy requires the ability to recognize patterns, to share ideas with people inside and outside your organization, to maintain relationships with people who have common interests, and to pull value out of those relationships." Learning how to master those skills may be the most important kind of learning there is.

Fun Makes It Fresh

When people work as long and as hard as they do in today's competitive companies, when the line between huge financial success and total economic failure looks as thin as it does today, there's only one thing that can keep the energy in a workplace flowing: fun. Very simply, if work isn't fun, it won't attract the best talent. The lesson is so obvious that it's easily forgotten: Friendship and camaraderie are basic adhesives of the human spirit.

When David Stewart made the decision to abandon his legal career, one of the things that attracted him to Tripod was its convivial atmosphere. "We're in this little town," Stewart says, referring to quaint Williamstown. "We have a really cool office space on the top floor of a big mill, with a lot of people who wear shorts and T-shirts all the time. It's very relaxed."

Look at other high-tech upstarts, and you're likely to see the same thing: hard work harnessed to shared enjoyment. And you don't need to be in high-tech for this glue to work. Nancy Deibler, 50, manages Sprint's small-business-sales division in Kansas City, Missouri. There, more than 150 people sell telecommunications services to smaller businesses. It can be tedious work: The salespeople work eight-hour shifts, making cold calls—the kind of job that can turn into a grind, resulting in high employee turnover and a lot of customer dissatisfaction.

But Deibler and her crew have found a way to counteract the tedium. They've created a strong rapport within the team by building fun into their work—and as a result, Deibler has been able to attract and keep top performers. "Many of us really look forward to going to work because of the other people on the team," Deibler says. "We relate to and get along with each other as friends."

Making fun a legitimate part of work isn't all that difficult, Deibler says. For example, Deibler's team might leave work at 3 P.M. to go bowling. "After doing something like that," she says, "the difference that it makes is measurable and it lasts for weeks." Add baseball games, cookouts, goofy hats, evenings of karaoke, mock casinos, zany sports, dressing up staffers in costumes to deliver morning coffee to salespeople—a host of ways to introduce positive energy and a spirit of playfulness into the all-too-often all-too-serious work world. Deibler knows that all of this may seem hokey to some people—and she doesn't care. "It lifts productivity," she says.

But if you want to see what fun looks like both as a way of working and as a business, visit Playfair Inc., a Berkeley, California-based international consulting firm that devises innovative team-building and stress-reduction programs. Its distinctive business model: Celebrate wackiness, incorporate zaniness into the work process—and in short, have fun. Playfair's clients include FedEx, Dupont, AT&T, Charles Schwab, and the Young Presidents' Organization—not exactly the kinds of places where you'd expect to find a lot of blue jeans-wearing, pizza-eating, fun-loving business types playing a game for laughs. Yet since its founding in 1975, Playfair has proven that there's real bottom-line value in putting fun into the workplace: Fun attracts talent, and it improves productivity.

Terry Sand is Playfair's "senior vice empress"—an intentionally irreverent title for an exceptionally talented woman. Sand, who is in her forties, has a master's degree in modern dance and theater from UCLA, and began her career performing in films and commercials. A founding member of several improv-comedy groups, she won San Francisco's All-Pro Comedy Award in 1984 and went on to become a popular local-TV personality.

Then, in 1986, Sand was diagnosed with systemic lupus, a painful arthritic condition. "TV is very stressful," Sand says. "I love it, and I still do it for fun sometimes, but having it be your career—basing your life on ratings—is extremly high-stress. I couldn't do that and also do the healing I needed to do." Still, Sand noticed that whenever she had the opportunity to conduct a comedy class or workshop, her condition would improve. "To stay alive, I had to figure out how to make a living and have fun," she says.

Playfair provided the answer. Sand joined the firm's small roster of keynote speakers and trainers in 1989, and now she uses comedy and performance to convey Playfair's insights about the power of fun to improve teamwork and productivity. Meanwhile, the opportunity to perform and practice her comedy has served as important therapy for Sand: Her disease is in remission, and she's had no significant relapse in seven years. "My relationship with Playfair lets me be more of who I can be," Sand says.

Playfulness is almost always purposeful, the people at Playfair argue. A great company will harness people's natural spirit of fun and focus that spirit where it can do the most good. "Like children, adults play to learn—and learn through play," says Sand. "There's a profound purpose to it."

Pride Makes It Special

Why choose to work for this company rather than that one? Why attend one college rather than another? Why root for this team rather than that other team? The answer is elemental: We all like to be affiliated with an organization that feeds our sense of pride.

It could be because the place is hip: Talk to the staff people at any House of Blues club, and you'll hear about the pride they take in their company's way of doing business. Or it could be because the place is proper and precise: Talk to the concierge at any Four Seasons hotel, and she'll tell you how proud she is to work for an organization that delivers world-class service. "The few, the proud, the Marines" could be rewritten as a recruiting slogan for any great enterprise that uses its prestige strategically to attract and keep great people—the kind of people who will build on that sense of pride and enhance that sense of prestige.

Pride was a key factor in bringing Kevin Perry, 28, to Red Storm Entertainment Inc. 15 months ago. Red Storm, a Morrisville, North Carolina-based software-development house that creates and markets multimedia entertainment products, including interactive computer games and board games, has already scored a number of accolades in the game industry. Last summer, Red Storm released Rainbow Six, an action-strategy game that was the genesis for the novelist Tom Clancy's recent book of the same name—the first time that a book has been derived from a game. (The book, published this year by Putnam, has topped both the *New York Times* and *USA Today* best-seller lists.) Red Storm will release three new games by the end of 1998, and eight more games are incubating for 1999.

Amid all of this creative energy, Perry enjoys a plum assignment: He leads a team charged with creating a new interactive computer game, ruthless.com, which should be out this season. The game, says Perry, replicates the big-money world of modern corporate raiding, blending high-stakes strategy with low-down ruthlessness: "It

combines the crushing grip of business expansion with rapier-like strikes of deceit, dirty tricks, and outright crime," he says.

But fast action isn't the only thing that makes Perry proud to be part of Red Storm. He had his choice of firms—including the choice not to commit to any one shop. What made Perry choose to join this company was the fact that Tom Clancy not only works with Red Storm—he also founded the company and chairs its board. "This is a cool place to work," Perry says. And Clancy's involvement "really helps us make a splash. People know that Red Storm is not some flash in the pan run by a 16-year-old out of his garage. Tom's association with the company really opens a lot of doors."

Red Storm Entertainment is quickly gaining a reputation not just for its bread-and-butter Tom Clancy military-strategy games but also as a top-notch developer of other kinds of computer games. The company is riding a virtuous circle: As Red Storm's reputation rises, it attracts more talent (like Perry)—and the more talent it taps, the more its reputation will continue to rise.

A different kind of pride attracts talented people to venerable institutions like Goldman Sachs, Yale University, General Electric, and Covington and Burling, a prestigious law firm in Washington, DC. What these institutions lack in hipness, they more than make up for in old-fashioned prestige. Membership in these enterprises confers status—and status is a form of capital.

But beware: The cycle can shift into reverse if an organization's prestige degenerates, leaving a once-proud brand in its place. Unless a firm continues to add real financial value—or is grounded in a strong ethical mission, in mutual learning, or in fun and excitement—what's "hot" or prestigious today can become unfashionable tomorrow. Status can turn stagnant, and no one wants to be affiliated with an organization that has lost its vital energy. When that happens, talented people can be as easy to lure away as they were to lure in—and the best people are usually the first to go.

Balance Makes It Sustainable

Talk to almost anyone in any company at any level, and you'll hear the same words: "I love what I'm doing, but I'm way too busy to get a life." Equal parts boast and complaint, that is the most pervasive refrain of the new economy. The problem is balance—or, more simply, sanity. And it's the last, but perhaps most important, adhesive that companies are using to lure and keep talented people. The best enterprises know this and are winning talented people by offering balanced work.

Easy to say it, easy to promise it. What distinguishes

the best companies, however, is not that they recognize how important balance is to attracting talent—it's how they create such balance in their organizations. Not long ago, any decent listing of "great places to work" would identify companies large and small that offered a preset "Chinese menu" of programs for balancing work and life: maternity and paternity leave, company-sponsored day care and elder care, regular retreats and periodic sabbaticals, flextime and even flexplace. In the new economy, the kind of balance that attracts people isn't a set of programs. Rather, it's a way of doing business. Balance is deeply embedded in the company's core—a compelling part of its corporate DNA.

Consider Great Plains Software, a leading vendor of financial-management software for midsize companies. Great Plains is headquartered in Fargo, North Dakota, in a two-story office building wedged between corn fields and a bingo parlor—not exactly a hip location. But Great Plains has attracted, developed, and retained some of the most talented people in its line of business. With 850 employees, the company has a turnover rate of 7% a year, which is almost unheard-of the famously volatile software industry. Great Plains also has a robust revenue stream—bringing in almost $86 million in fiscal 1998, up 50% over 1997—and a roster of loyal customers, including Adidas, the Detroit Lions, Cinnabon Bakeries, and the Girl Scouts of America.

What's the secret? Great Plains not only offers a balanced life—it lives one. Tami Reller, 34, has been with Great Plains since she graduated from Moorhead State University in Moorhead, Minnesota, in the spring of 1987. Her career with the company, where she began as an intern, is one long testament to the value of flexibility. "I was amazed at the company's level of commitment to helping interns succeed and stay with the company," Reller says. Her first assignment was in the company's finance operation at its headquarters in Fargo. Then she moved to San Francisco to train in sales. After seven years there, Reller felt ready for a move into the rank of corporate management—but she didn't want to leave California. No problem: Great Plains didn't want her to leave the company either, so it gave her a senior position in corporate marketing and allowed her to telecommute to Fargo—and, by the way, to finish an MBA while working part-time for three months.

That arrangement lasted until 1996, when, for family reasons, Reller moved to Minneapolis. Still no problem: Now she directs finance and investor relations from there. The next development: In a few months, Reller will give birth to her first child. Is she worried about balance? Not a bit—Great Plains lets its people take voluntary time off while keeping benefits.

"For me, balance means having the flexibility to choose what to accomplish and how I want to accomplish it—in my career, my job, my personal life," Reller says. "It's not simply an issue of not working 8-to-5. It's the ability to accomplish the big things in life—like finishing an MBA or having a child."

The Great Plains approach is to hire the best people it can find and then to give them maximum freedom to get their work done—however, whenever, and wherever they choose to work. "We have really smart people who know what they need to accomplish," Reller says. "You find a way to get the work done in the hours that you need. Sometimes that's 30 hours a week; sometimes it's 70 hours a week."

Doug Burgum, 42, Great Plains's chairman and CEO, explains how the system works. "We put people through a vigorous hiring process and through a lot of interviews. Once they're part of the team, we say, 'We trust you.' From day one, you get a key to the building. You get a laptop. You become an equal member of our community, and we trust that you're going to pull your weight."

None of that happens by accident. When Burgum began with the company in 1983, he understood that it needed something more than good software to become competitive. Great Plains's edge would be in the quality of its people—in their ability to provide first-class customer support and to develop strong relationships with suppliers and vendors. How do you attract the best people when your headquarters is in Fargo, North Dakota? By recruiting carefully, selectively, and rigorously—and then by giving those you hire the power to organize their work by themselves.

"Balance is not about taking off the day when your kid gets sick," Burgum says. Any company can give employees that sort of flexibility. "Balance is what's needed when your kids are playing in a softball tournament, and they really want you to be there. We want parents to be able to say yes to their kids. There's a huge amount of value in giving people the opportunity to say yes to things that are important to them but that may conflict with their regular working hours."

For Burgum, the idea of balance goes deeper than simply juggling tasks and appointments. "It's important to have flexibility over a life span or a career span," he says. "There has to be a deeper level of personal satisfaction, a sense that things are all right. If you can help people find that level, they tend to stick around." Burgum is proud of Great Plain's extraordinarily low turnover. "That's no small accomplishment in an industry where so much of a company's assets are linked to individual employees' knowledge," he says.

The 21st-Century Company

What do all of these new enterprises have in common? They are only as good as their most talented people. And they don't take the loyalty of those people for granted. They understand that talented people have never had more options. So these companies have developed strategies to recruit and keep people from whom they want total commitment.

What do the joiners have in common? They could have gone anywhere. They had their pick of the best. Many could have successful careers as free agents. They've chosen to join up—to commit themselves, at least for a time—because the mix of social glue in one organization was overwhelmingly strong.

The big change today, then, is not the absolute demise of loyalty in the workplace. Nor is it the evolution of free agency into the only way that people can work. The basic facts of work life are the same as they've always been: Everybody works for somebody or something—be it a board of directors, a pension fund, a venture capitalist, or a traditional boss. Sooner or later, you're going to have to decide whom you want to work for. And everybody works with someone else. The linkage may be tight, or it may be loose. But you've got to decide who to work with, as well as how strong the bonds of mutual commitment will be.

The big change is in the amount of choice and the variety of experiences available in today's workplace: Talented people are actively shopping for colleagues and bosses who meet their needs and match their values. The market for talent—the sellers of it, the buyers of it—is the most vital market in the modern economy. To attract and keep talented people, companies today are not just experimenting with how they approach the competitive markeplace of goods and services. They're also experimenting with how they approach the competitive marketplace of talent. Companies are testing the attractiveness of various combinations of social glue, and they are recognizing that unusual benefits attract unusual people—and that what works in one industry, or at one time, may not work in another industry, or at another time. Deployed carefully, these social glues become stronger through use: Each can attract talent in a way that makes an enterprise even more attractive to the same kind of talent in the future.

More fundamentally, companies are experimenting with a new operating system for the employer-employee relationship—one to replace the old set of practices that put employers and employees on opposite sides of the table. The model for the organization of the future aims to create tangible and intangible value that both sides can share and enjoy. It accepts as a core reality—rather than as a pleasant fantasy—the old saw that a company's people are its most important asset. And it builds on that reality to create a way of working that is profoundly human and fundamentally humane.

It is a revolutionary notion: Collaboration and mutual advantage are the essence of the organization. They can create flexibility, resiliency, speed, and creativity—the fundamental qualities of the company of the 21st century.

ARTICLE 2

Life In The Fast Lane

by Chuck Salter

To finish first, you have to work fast. Ray Evernham—NASCAR's top crew chief and the man behind race-car champ Jeff Gordon—offers lessons from the pit on teamwork, surprise, and the pursuit of perfection.

Business is more demanding than ever, more perilous than ever—and faster than ever. Every company is rushing to launch the next great product, to seal the next big deal. No company knows what's waiting around the next corner.

It Sounds a Lot Like Auto Racing

Ray Evernham knows a little something about business. He's a key player in an enterprise that generates millions of dollars in annual revenues, and he's lectured audi-

First appeared: Fast Company issue 18 page 175
Reprinted with permission from Fast Company Magazine

ences of business executives from DuPont, Digital, and Ingersoll-Rand. But Evernham knows even more about racing. He's widely considered to be the premier crew chief in NASCAR, the National Association for Stock Car Auto Racing. Over the past five years, he and his team have steered the DuPont-sponsored No. 24 car and its celebrated driver, Jeff Goron, from anonymity to unprecedented success in the Winston Cup Series—the big leagues of stock-car racing.

Evernham and Gordon burst onto the Winston Cup scene in 1993, when Gordon walked away with the Cup's Rookie of the Year honors. In 1994, Evernham was named Crew Chief of the Year. And in 1995, Gordon and Evernham hit the jackpot when Gordon won the Winston Cup Championship, the culmination of a grueling race for points that stretches from February to November. Gordon, then just 24, was the Winston Cup's youngest-ever champion. After garnering 10 wins in 1996 (good for second place that year), he and Evernham teamed up for another Winston Cup Championship in 1997. Their $4.2 million in prize money set a new record for total regular-season earnings in one year of racing. During their six years as a team, Evernham and Gordon have celebrated 37 victories, including wins in NASCAR's major races—the Daytona 500, the Coca-Cola 600 (three times), and the Brickyard 400 (twice).

Gordon's sudden dominance, combined with his youth, charisma, and leading-man looks, has made him the hottest commodity in the fastest-growing sport around. He's everywhere: on Leno and Letterman, on *People* magazine's 50 Most Beautiful People list. And on many Sundays, he's in victory lane. He gives much of the credit for his success to Evernham and to the pit crew know as the Rainbow Warriors. (Crew members wear rainbow-striped jumpsuits.)

Gordon is the star attraction, to be sure. But it's Evernham, 41, who pulls the whole act together. It's Evernham, an indefatigable perfectionist, who ensures that the No. 24 car—a 700-horsepower Chevrolet Monte Carlo—is the fastest on the track; who leads the daring pit stop that takes place with 20 laps to go; who pushes the Rainbow Warriors to be the best crew in the business, week after week.

Fast Company visited Evernham at the Hendrick Motorsports complex in Harrisburg, North Carolina, just north of Charlotte. In between signing autographs, speaking at a sponsor's lunch, and fine-tuning the No. 24 car, Evernham took time out to reflect on what it takes to finish first: painstaking preparation, egoless teamwork, and thoroughly original strategizing—principles that apply to any company that understands the need for speed.

New Teams Should Do Things in New Ways

One reason we got off to such a fast start when the Rainbow Warrior team was assembled five years ago was that, right from the beginning, we dared to be different. I didn't hire anybody for the team who had Winston Cup experience. Racing is racing; the right people can figure it out. I wanted people who had the desire and the intelligence needed to excel.

When you have a team with different kinds of people, you get a chance to do things differently. We came up with innovative ideas about the mechanics of the car—about things like suspension components and shock absorbers—partly because we didn't know any better. And we hired a separate crew to work solely in the pits. Traditionally, the same mechanics who worked on the car all week also suited up on Sunday to work as the pit crew. The car was the number-one priority: People relied on horsepower and driving talent to win the day. But I believe that the crew should be as important as the car.

We were also the first team to hire a coach specifically to train and rehearse the pit crew. People laughed at the way we trained: rope climbing, wind sprints, guys carrying each other on their backs. People said, "What in the world are you guys doing?" I'm sure that it all looked funny, but it worked. Typically, we pit in 17 seconds or less—about a second faster than other teams do. In one second, a car going 200 mph travels nearly 300 feet. So right there, we gain 300 feet on the competition.

You Win as a Team

When you coach and support a superstar like Jeff Gordon, you give him the best equipment possible, you give him the information he needs, and then you get out of the way. But racing is a team sport. Everyone who races pretty much has the same car and the same equipment. What sets us apart is our people. I like to talk about our "team IQ"—because none of us is as smart as all of us.

I think a lot about people, management, and psychology: Specifically, how can I motivate my guys and make them gel as a team? I surround them with ideas about teamwork. I read every leadership book I can get my hands on. One thing that I took from my reading is the idea of a "circle of strength." When the Rainbow Warriors meet, we always put our chairs in a circle. That's a way of saying that we're stronger as a team than we are on our own.

I also base rewards on team performance rather than individual performance. When our car wins, everybody shares in the prize money. And everybody gets a cut of what I make. I put a percentage of my bonus into the team account. When I sign a personal-service contract and I get paid to sign autographs or to give a talk, everybody shares in what I earn. I wouldn't be in a position to earn that income if it weren't for the team. Everyone should feel as if his signature is on the finished product.

Push for Perfection—but Accept Imperfection

This sport is so competitive that you must never stop trying to improve. Even when the car is running well, I make Jeff find something wrong with it. A lot of people who hear him talking to me on the radio think that he's complaining. He's not. I've got a series of questions that I ask him over and over. I'm pumping him for information. I'm trying to find out exactly how Jeff feels in that car. The only time when we stop working on our setup is when it's time to race.

We always try to make the car perfect. But the car doesn't have to be perfect to win; it just has to be less imperfect than everyone else's car. Last year, on the very first pit stop at the Coca-Cola 600, we dropped the car off the jack and banged up the front end, leaving the car aerodynamically flawed. It took us three or four pit stops to straighten the fender. But we still won. After all, we had hundreds of laps in which to recover from that mistake.

Take risks, but don't gamble. When we're going into a race, we always have a clear strategy. But we can't predict exactly what's going to happen. Change is part of racing. Sometimes during a race, it looks as if I'm making a daring call. Well, I may be taking a risk, but I'm not gambling. I've calculated everything beforehand. I'm constantly looking at four or five possible scenarios: At the next pit stop, are we going to put in all of the gas or only half of it? Are we going to add air to the tires or let some out? Are we going to raise or lower the track bar to adjust the "roll center"—which alters the steering? There are so many variables to consider, and the slightest adjustment can make a huge difference in the car's performance. A race may come down to whether we change two tires or four. I need to make the right call.

[*Editor's Note:* Two days after this interview, the Coca-Cola 600 came down to just such a decision about tires. With 21 laps to go and with Gordon trailing the leaders, a caution flag went up. While the other cars changed two tires, Evernham opted to take longer in the pit and to change all four. When the green flag came out, Gordon easily sped past the others—and on to victory.]

To Speed Up, Slow Down

I still have to prove this principle to Jeff sometimes, I'll say, "Go out and bust me a lap." He'll drive the car hard, really work it. He'll mash the pedal on a straightaway, drive down into a corner, jam the brakes, turn the corner, and mash the pedal again. Then I'll say, "Now take it easy, and drive a smooth lap." And by letting the car do the work, he actually improves his time.

The same principle applies to a pit stop. Watch Mike Trower, my best tire changer, at work, and you'll swear that the guy next to him will be done first. You'll be thinking, "I wish Mike would hurry up." But nobody can beat him. He just looks as if he's going slow. It's all the choreography. If you watch Mike change a tire, you'll see how efficient he is: He's so deliberate that he never has to hit a lug nut twice. It's "zzzt–zzzt–zzzt." Nice and smooth.

Don't Strut Your Stuff

There aren't many secrets in the Winston Cup, so you've got to protect as much information as you can. We want to have the fastest car on the track, but we don't want everybody else to know how fast we are. We don't show our hand until it's time to race or to qualify.

We also try to mix things up on race day. We don't want to fall into patterns or to tip off the competition about our next pit stop. Since everybody can hear us on the scanners, we might use a code word to signal whether we're changing two tires or four. Sometimes, when the car is running well, Jeff might get on the radio and complain to me that the steering's tight, even though he's about to pass another driver. And that driver's crew chief will fall for it: "Yeah, Gordon can't pass you right now, because he's tight." The driver will leave a little opening and—boom—we're past him.

To Win the Race, Drive by Different Rules

We attack certain race tracks differently from how everybody else does. If conventional wisdom says, "This corner is the best place to pass," we practice on the other end of the track, because nobody's expecting to get passed there. If you can hold your own where others plan to pass, and then sneak up and get by the others on another part of the track, you can gain an advantage.

We've done this at Darlington Raceway. Traditionally, at Darlington, you pass when you come off turn number two, because you can carry more speed into that turn than elsewhere. We worked hard at being good there, so we could avoid getting passed and so we could pass if we had to. But we also worked at being better around the rest of the track than most cars are. That extra work helped us win the Mountain Dew Southern 500 last year.

Face Down Your Toughest Competitor: Success

I have a saying posted in the shop: "Success is a ruthless competitor for it flatters and nourishes our weakness and lulls us into complacency." When you win, if you're not careful—if you don't pay attention to how your team is handling success—you'll stop doing the things that put you on top. You've got to be very critical of what you do. Remember, the other teams are looking at how you beat them last Sunday, and they're trying to figure out how to beat you next Sunday. You can't let up.

ARTICLE 3
Danger: Toxic Company

by Alan M. Webber

The problem isn't that loyalty is dead or that careers are history. The real problem, argues Stanford's Jeffrey Pfeffer, is that so many companies are toxic—and that they get exactly what they deserve.

According to Jeffrey Pfeffer, when it comes to the link between people and profits, companies get exactly what they deserve. Companies that treat their people right get enormous dividends: high rates of productivity, low rates of turnover. Companies that treat their people poorly experience the opposite—and end up complaining about the death of loyalty and the dearth of talent. These are "toxic workplaces," according to Pfeffer, 52, the Thomas D. Dee Professor of Organizational Behavior at the Stanford Graduate School of Business and the author of *The Human Equation: Building Profits by Putting People First* (Harvard Business School Press, 1998).

Pfeffer disputes much of the conventional wisdom in the current conversation about work and business. Loyalty isn't dead, he insists—but toxic companies are driving people away. There isn't a scarcity of talent—but there is a growing unwillingness to work for toxic organizations. Pfeffer also disputes the idea of the end of the career. "I don't believe that people are looking to go flitting from one job to the next," he says. "People are looking for the opportunity to have variety in their work and to tackle challenging assignments. The best companies are figuring out how their employees can have both opportunities—without leaving." When Fast Company interviewed the plain-talking, provocative Pfeffer in his Palo Alto office, he offered the following observations about the primacy of people in the new economy and about how you can detoxify your workplace.

The One Guaranteed Way to Get a 30% to 40% Productivity Gain

It mystifies me that so many companies think they can get a cheap competitive advantage by purchasing something on the open market! Anything that you can purchase on the open market is also available to your competitors. So the question is, How can you distinguish yourself in a world in which your competitors can copy everything you do?

The answer is, all that separates you from your competitors are the skills, knowledge, commitment, and abilities of the people who work for you. There is a very compelling business case for this idea: Companies that manage people right will outperform companies that don't by 30% to 40%. This principle even applies to the current IPO market: IPO firms that value their people have a much higher five-year survival rate than those that don't. Similar studies of the steel industry, the oil-refining industry, the apparel industry, and the semiconductor industry all demonstrate the enormous productivity benefits that come with implementing high-performance, high-involvement management practices.

Most people immediately understand this point. It's not as though I've discovered some mysterious black magic. There is conclusive evidence that holds for all industries, regardless of their type, size, or age. The results are the same. If you don't believe me, look at the numbers.

First appeared: Fast Company issue 19 page 152
Reprinted with permission from Fast Company Magazine

"Welcome to the Toxic Workplace! We Fire at Will!"

There is a lot of turnover in Silicon Valley, because there are so many toxic workplaces in Silicon Valley. These are companies that create the conditions that they deplore. Companies say to me, "Nobody who comes to work for us stays for any length of time. Loyalty is dead." Let's accept that premise for a moment—even though it's wrong. But if we do accept that premise, the question becomes, If loyalty is dead, who killed it?

Companies killed loyalty—by becoming toxic places to work! Start with the interviewing and recruiting process. What happens on a new employee's first day? The company asks the employee to sign an at-will employment contract that gives the company the right to fire the person at any time and for any reason. The document was prepared by a lawyer; the company tells the employee to have it reviewed by a lawyer before signing it.

Think about it: It's your first day on the job, and I've already told you that you don't have a permanent employment relationship with me, that your job is based on a contractual relationship—and then I wonder why, on your second day, you're not approaching me with a long-term perspective and a feeling of trust!

A Place Where People Come to Work to Get Rich Enough to Quit

Here's another example of a practice that creates the conditions that companies deplore: stock options. David Russo, the head of human resources for SAS Institute, gave a talk to my class. My students were dumbfounded to learn that this successful software-development company doesn't offer its people stock options. David said, "You must know lots of people who have gotten stock options. Why do they want them? Explain the logic."

Finally, one of my students raised his hand and said, "I can tell you the logic. For most people, stock options are like the lottery. People are hoping to strike it rich and then quit." David smiled and said, "What an interesting thing! We've built an organization in which your motivation for coming to work is to make a lot of money—so that you can get the hell out of the organization."

To me, that's an operational definition of a toxic workplace: It's a place where people come to work so they can make enough money so they can leave. Dennis Bakke, of Applied Energy Services Corp. (AES), likes to point to a photo of the top 20 people at his company. The photo was taken more than a decade ago, and today 17 of those 20 people are still there. They're all plenty wealthy—because AES has grown tremendously. They

all could have quit. The fact that they didn't says a lot about that company.

Toxic Flextime: "Work any 18 Hours You Want."

Another sign that a company is toxic: It requires people to choose between having a life and having a career. A toxic company says to people, "We want to own you." There's an old joke that they used to tell about working at Microsoft: "We offer flexible time—you can work any 18 hours you want."

A toxic company says, "We're going to put you in a situation where you have to work in a style and on a pace that is not sustainable. We want you to come in here and burn yourself out—and then you can leave." That's one thing that SAS manages brilliantly: When you take a job there, you don't have to ask yourself, "Am I going to be a successful and effective SAS employee, or am I going to know the names of my children?"

What's the Difference Between a Factor of Production and a Human Being?

Another sign of a toxic workplace is that the company treats its people as if they were a factor of production. At a toxic workplace, the managers can reel off all of the various economic factors: "We've got capital that we invest, we've got raw material that we use, we've got the waste from the manufacturing process that we recycle—and, in the same category, we've got our people." It's a workplace that doesn't see people as people, but rather sees them as factors of production. And that's ironic, because what we celebrate as a competitive, capitalistic practice actually reflects a Marxist orientation: People are seen as a factor of production, from which a company has to extract an economic "surplus."

There is a huge difference between that perspective and the way AES, for example, looks at its people. Dennis Bakke even objects to the term "human resources." Dennis says that fuel is a resource—but that people aren't. Underlying this difference in language is a difference in philosophy that guides much of what a company does. If a company looks at you merely as a factor of production, then every day it must calculate whether your marginal revenue exceeds your marginal cost. That's how it decides whether or not to keep you.

If Your Company Is So Great, Why Doesn't Anyone Want to Work There?

You hear a lot about the shortage of talent. The thing to remember is that, for great workplaces, there is no short-

age of talent. Companies that are short on talent probably deserve to be! Anyone who is smart enough to work in a high-tech company is too smart to work in a toxic workplace. And if they do work in one, as soon as they have a choice, they choose to leave.

For example, according to David Russo, SAS Institute had a 3% voluntary-turnover rate in 1997. SAS almost never loses one of its people to a competitor, he says. When it does lose people, it's usually because of a lifestyle change or because someone at the company has to move to a place where there is no SAS facility.

That kind of thing is happening across the economy. Hewlett-Packard has lower turnover than many of its competitors. The Men's Wearhouse has lower turnover than many other companies in the retail industry. Starbucks has comparatively lower turnover than other companies in the fast-food business. Of course, none of these companies is perfect. But a company that says, "We want to create a place that attracts people, that makes them want to stay," will have lower turnover than places that say, "We don't care about our people's well-being or about whether they stay." And then, when these toxic companies conduct themselves in this way, they wonder why people leave.

Which Is Better Business—Paying Signing Bonuses or Treating People Right?

High turnover costs big money. First of all, it costs money to go out and replace all of the people you've lost. If the companies in Silicon Valley that are losing people would stop paying $50,000 signing bonuses and instead do what's necessary to keep the people they've got, they would be much better off economically. Along with incurring replacement costs, when you lose people, you lose knowledge, you lose experience, and you lose customer relationships. Every time a customer interacts with your company, he or she sees a different person. I like to go to my branch bank because I know that I'll always make a new friend there: The turnover is so high, I'm always meeting new people!

There is nothing soft and sentimental about this part of the argument. This is simple economics. David Russo did a calculation in my class one day: A student asked him why SAS does so much family-friendly stuff. He said, "We have something like 5,000 employees. Our turnover rate last year was 3%. What's the industry average?" Somebody said 20%. Russo replied, "Actually, 20% is low, but I don't care. We'll use 20%. The difference between 20% and 3% is 17%. Multiply 17% by 5,000 people, and that's 850 people. What does turnover cost per person? Calculate it in terms of salary." The students estimated

that the cost is one year's salary and that the average salary is $60,000. Russo said, "Both of those figures are low, but that doesn't matter. I'll use them. Multiply $60,000 by 850 people, and that's more than $50 million in savings."

That's how Russo pays for the SAS gymnasium, for on-site medical care, for all of the company's other family-friendly items. "Plus," he said. "I've got tons of money left over." If you can save $50 million a year in reduced turnover, you're talking about real financial savings. This is not tree-huggery. This is money in the bank.

When You Look at Your People, What Do You See—Expenses or Assets?

You've got to ask a question that gets back to an old cliche: Do you walk the talk? It's easy for a company to say, "We invest in people. We believe in training. We believe in mutual commitments between the managers and the workforce. We believe in sharing information widely with our people."

Many organizations say those things—but in their heart of hearts, they don't believe them. Most managers, if they're being honest with themselves, will admit it: When they look at their people, they see costs, they see salaries, they see benefits, they see overhead. Very few companies look at their people and see assets.

In part, it's because of the financial-reporting systems that we've got. The fact is, your salary is an expense. If I buy a computer to replace you, I can capitalize the computer and then depreciate its useful life over many years. If I hire you, I take on an expense.

But there are other things that companies can measure. Whole Foods Market Inc. and AES, for instance, not only do employee surveys; they also take them seriously. I know of managers at Hewlett-Packard who were fired because they received such poor reviews from their employees.

Why Nothing Changes #1: Wishing Doesn't Make It So

Everybody knows what to do, but nobody does it. For example, a lot of companies confuse talk with action. They believe that, because they've said it, it's actually happened. One of my students did a research project on the internship program at a large Wall Street securities company. Under the program, the firm hired interns right out of college; then, after a few years, the interns would go back to business school. But the program was catastrophic. The firm treated the interns like dog doo, and that had two bad consequences. First, the interns didn't go back to work for the firm after business school, so the two or three years that the firm had invested in them were wasted. Second, and even worse, when the interns arrived at Harvard, Stanford, Chicago, or Northwestern, they would tell all of the other business-school students that the firm was horse manure—which made its recruiting difficult, to say the least. At some level, people at the firm understood these problems. So the senior leadership asked my student, who had interned there, to help the firm fix its program.

After she had done a bunch of interviews, she told them, "You have a model that says you're going to treat people with respect and dignity. Let me tell you the 30 things—and that's a low number—that you do to your interns that violate your model."

When the top people at the firm heard her report, they said, "This can't be. The core values of this firm are respect for the individual, treating the individual with dignity, and teamwork. We believe in these values." In effect, they were saying, "Because we believe it, it must be happening." These were not bad people. They just thought that their wishes had become reality.

Why Nothing Changes #2: Memory Is No Substitute for Thinking

There's another reason why companies don't do what they know they should: They fall prey to the power of precedents. They do something once, and then they get trapped by their own history: This is the way we do it because this is the way we've always done it. They substitute memory ("We did it this way before") for thinking ("Is this a sensible way to do it?").

Not long ago, I went to a large, fancy San Francisco law firm—where they treat their associates like dog doo and where the turnover is very high. I asked the managing partner about the turnover rate. He said, "A few years ago, it was 25%, and we're now up to 30%." I asked him how the firm had responded to that trend. He said, "We increased our recruiting." So I asked him, "What kind of doctor would you be if your patient was bleeding faster and faster, and your only response was to increase the speed of the transfusion?"

But what this law firm knew how to do was recruit. Over the preceding five years, it had created 162 partners—and it had lost 163 people in the same period. It preferred undertaking lavish recruitment efforts to dealing with the root causes of the turnover. People do what they know how to do. This law firm knows how to recruit—so it steps up recruiting. But what it hasn't thought about for five seconds is how to solve the underlying problem.

How to Make Something Change: Start with You

Where do you start? You start with a philosophy, and the rest follows from that. If you believe in training and developing people, you don't necessarily need a huge training budget. You begin by imparting knowledge in various ways—by holding meetings, by talking to people, by coaching them, by mentoring them. If you believe in reciprocal commitments, you start by building those commitments with the people you work with. If you believe in information sharing, you share information with the people you have the most contact with. In other words, you begin in your immediate sphere of influence. You start with your own behavior.

ARTICLE 4
Learning for a Change

by Alan M. Webber

Ten years ago, Peter Senge introduced the idea of the "learning organization." Now he says that for big companies to change, we need to stop thinking like mechanics and to start acting like gardeners.

It's been almost 10 years since Peter Senge, 51, pub-

First appeared: Fast Company issue 24 page 178

lished *The Fifth Discipline: The Art & Practice of the Learning Organization* (Doubleday/Currency, 1990). The book was more than a business best-seller; it was a breakthrough. It propelled Senge into the front ranks of management thinkers; it created a language of change that people in all kinds of companies could embrace; and it offered a vision of workplaces that were humane and

of companies that were built around learning. Along the way, the book sold more than 650,000 copies, spawned a sequel—*The Discipline Fieldbook: Strategies and Tools for Building a Learning Organization* (Doubleday/Currency, 1994)—and gave birth to a worldwide movement.

But that movement hit a few speed bumps. People who adopted the themes and practices of *The Fifth Discipline* sometimes found themselves frustrated by the challenge of bringing about effective change—and sometimes found themselves out of work for trying. Now Senge and his colleagues have published *The Dance of Change: The Challenges to Sustaining Momentum in Learning Organizations* (Doubleday/Currency, March 1999). According to Senge, who is a senior lecturer at the Massachusetts Institute of Technology and a member of the Society for Organizational Learning (SoL)—a global consortium of companies and researchers who are examining learning and change—the new book presents "what we've learned about learning." The book begins with two key lessons: First, initiating and sustaining change is more daunting than the optimistic presentation that was offered in *The Fifth Discipline* had suggested. And second, the task of making change happen requires businesspeople to change the way they think about organizations: "We need to think less like managers and more like biologists," Senge argues.

To learn more about the evolving landscape of organizational learning, Fast Company interviewed Peter Senge in his office on the campus of MIT, in Cambridge, Massachusetts.

What's Your Assessment of the Performance of Large-Scale Change Efforts over the Past Decade?

Most leadership strategies are doomed to failure from the outset. As people have been noting for years, the majority of strategic initiatives that are driven from the top are marginally effective—at best. Corporate reorganizations are even more common than new strategies, but how many reorganizations actually produce companies that are dramatically more effective than they were before? Throw in mergers and acquisitions: Look at all of those that have failed. The traditional model of change—change that is led from the top—has a less-than-impressive track record.

And that's just the public track record. My own experience at MIT and at SoL has mostly been with big companies. How much change have they actually accomplished? If I stand back a considerable distance and ask, "What's the score?" I have to conclude that inertia is winning by a large margin. Of course, there have been enough exceptions to that conclusion to indicate that change is possible. I can identify 20 to 30 examples of significant sustained change efforts in the SoL community. On the other side of the ledger, there are many organizations that haven't gotten to first base when it comes to real change, and many others that have given up trying.

When I look at efforts to create change in big companies over the past 10 years, I have to say that there's enough evidence of success to say that change is possible—and enough evidence of failure to say that it isn't likely. Both of those lessons are important.

Why Haven't There Been More Successful Change Efforts?

If it were simply a matter of more resources, people would have figured out how to get more resources. If it were a matter of more time, more money, more consultants, or just more effort, we probably would have been able to fill those needs by now. Or if the problem were intelligence—and you could simply assert that most bosses are pretty dumb or that most CEOs are just not very bright—then presumably the intelligent ones would succeed, their companies would rise to the top, and that would solve the problem. The marketplace would reward the bright ones who could change, and it would punish the dumb ones who couldn't.

But it doesn't seem as if any of those things are happening—which suggests that it's not a matter of resources or intelligence. In fact, I can tell you from firsthand experience that a lot of very competent executives fail at producing and sustaining momentum around change. That suggests to me that something more universal is at work here.

So What Is the Deeper Explanation for the Failure of Corporate Change Efforts?

At the deepest level, I think that we're witnessing the shift from one age to another. The most universal challenge that we face is the transition from seeing our human institutions as machines to seeing them as embodiments of nature. I've been thinking about this shift for 25 years or more: We need to realize that we're a part of nature, rather than separate from nature.

Think about any environmental problem that we face, from global climate and resource issues to population crises. Or look at the problems that seem to afflict people in organizations: Why are contemporary institutions so inhumane? And somewhere in the middle, between environmental issues and personal issues, there are institutional issues: Why do we view our organizations as rigid hierarchies rather than as communities of practice?

Whether you're talking at the macro, the personal, or the institutional level, the questions all point in the same direction: The real character of an age is evident in how it conditions us to think, and how it conditions us to think determines how it conditions us to act. The thinking and acting of the past 200 years—nurtured in Europe, accelerated in the United States, diffused throughout the world today—is a machine mind-set. That mind-set directly affects how we see organizations—and, therefore, how we think about creating change in those organizations.

What Implications Does a Machine Mind-Set Have for Companies that Seek to Undergo Change?

In the Machine Age, the company itself became a machine—a machine for making money. That's a key point in Arie de Geus's book, *The Living Company* (Harvard Business School Press, 1997). Ironically, the word "company" couldn't be more at odds with the idea of a machine. "Company" has roots that go back long before the Industrial Age. In fact, it has the same root as the word "companion": It means "the sharing of bread."

Somehow, during the course of the Industrial Revolution, this very humane sense of "company" changed, and the company became more and more machinelike. For the most part, seeing the company as a machine has worked. There are people who design this machine: They put it together and get it up and working. They are founders. There are people who operate or control the machine: We call them managers. The machine also has owners, and when it operates correctly, it produces income for those owners. It's all about control: A good machine is one that its operators can control—in the service of its owners' objectives.

The company-as-a-machine model fits how people think about and operate conventional companies. And, of course, it fits how people think about changing conventional companies: You have a broken company, and you need to change it, to fix it. You hire a mechanic, who trades out old parts that are broken and brings in new parts that are going to fix the machine. That's why we need "change agents" and leaders who can "drive change."

But go back and consider all of the evidence that says that most change efforts aren't very successful. Here is our first plausible explanation: Companies are actually living organisms, not machines. That might explain why it's so difficult for us to succeed in our efforts to produce change. Perhaps treating companies like machines keeps them from changing, or makes changing them much more difficult. We keep bringing in mechanics—when

what we need are gardeners. We keep trying to drive change—when what we need to do is cultivate change. Surprisingly, this mechanical mind-set can afflict those who seek "humane" changes through "learning organizations" just as much as it can afflict those who drive more traditional changes, such as mergers and reorganizations.

Where, Specifically, Does the Mechanical Approach Go Wrong in Effecting Change?

The easiest way to see this is to look at our interpersonal relationships. In our ordinary experiences with other people, we know that approaching each other in a machine-like way gets us into trouble. We know that the process of changing a relationship is a lot more complicated than the process of changing a flat tire on your car. It requires a willingness to change. It requires a sense of openness, a sense of reciprocity, even a kind of vulnerability. You must be willing to be influenced by another person. You don't have to be willing to be influenced by your damn car! A relationship with a machine is fundamentally a different kind of relationship: It is perfectly appropriate to feel that if it doesn't work, you should fix it. But we get into real trouble whenever we try to "fix" people.

We know how to create and nurture close friendships or family relationships. But when we enter the realm of the organization, we're not sure which domain to invoke. Should we evoke the domain of the machine? After all, much of our daily life is about interacting with computers, tape recorders, automobiles, and ATMs. Or should we evoke the domain of living systems—because a lot of our daily life is about interacting with family, friends, and colleagues?

There are those who come down firmly on the people side: They tend to be HR professionals and line managers—people who understand that relationships, teamwork, and trust are essential to effective operations. But high-level executives are frequently separated from the day-to-day stuff of the enterprise: They look at the organization from the perspective of numbers, financial statements, and prospective deals. Their number-one variable is the company stock price. That outlook distances them substantially from the living, human aspects of the enterprise. You end up with organizational schizophrenia. Some people operate the company as if it were a machine, and some treat it as part of the messy, living world.

What Happens When You See a Company as a Part of Nature?

It shifts profoundly how you think about leadership and change. If you use a machine lens, you get leaders who

are trying to drive change through formal change programs. If you use a living-systems lens, you get leaders who approach change as if they were growing something, rather than just "changing" something. Even on a large scale, nature doesn't change things mechanically: You don't just pull out the old and replace it with the new. Something new grows, and it eventually supplants the old.

You see the same thing at the level of behaviors: If new behaviors are more effective than old behaviors, then the new behaviors win out. That insight gives us a doorway into a different way to think about how enterprises might change: What if we thought of organizational change as the interplay among the various forces that are involved in growing something new?

Looking at nature, we see that nothing that grows starts large; it always starts small. No one is "in charge," making the growth occur. Instead, growth occurs as a result of the interplay of diverse forces. And these forces fall into two broad categories: self-reinforcing processes, which generate growth, and limiting processes, which can impede growth or stop it altogether. The pattern of growth that occurs unfolds from the interplay of these two types of forces.

Looking at organizations, we find that one of the first things that changes is how we define the term "structure." *The Fifth Discipline* proposed a definition borrowed from system dynamics—which looks at structure in terms of feedback interactions within a system. Our new definition of that term is "a pattern of interdependency that we enact." Again, think about the relationships within a family rather than those within a company: People come to relate to each other in predictable ways, which form a pattern that then defines the structure of relationships—norms, expectations, taken-for-granted habits of communicating. Those patterns aren't fixed; they can change. And, more to the point, those patterns aren't given. Ultimately, the structures that come into play in our families are the result of the choices that we've made all along the way. We "enact" our families.

All of this applies directly to our ideas about leadership and, in particular, to the cult of the CEO-as-hero. In fact, that cult is one pattern that makes it easier for us to maintain change-averse institutions. When we enact the pattern of the CEO as hero, we infantalize the organization: That kind of behavior keeps everyone else in the company at a stage of development in which they can't accept their own possibilities for creating change. Moreover, it keeps executives from doing things that would genuinely contribute to creating significant change. The cult of the hero-leader only creates a need for more hero-leaders.

How Does Challenging the Idea of the Hero-Leader Promote Change?

Deep change comes only through real personal growth—through learning and unlearning. This is the kind of generative work that most executives are precluded from doing by the mechanical mind-set and by the cult of the hero-leader: The hero-leader is the one with "the answers." Most of the other people in the organization can't make deep changes, because they're operating out of compliance rather than out of commitment. Commitment comes about only when people determine that you are asking them to do something that they really care about. For that reason, if you create compliance-oriented change, you'll get change—but you'll preclude the deeper processes that lead to commitment, and you'll prevent the emergence of self-generated change.

Again, you end up creating a kind of addiction: People change as long as they're being commanded to change—or as long as they can be forced to change. But, as a result, they become still more dependent on change that's driven from the top.

If the Idea of the Hero-Leader Takes Us in the Wrong Direction, What's the Right Direction?

The first problem with all of the stuff that's out there about leadership is that we haven't got a clue about what we're talking about. We use the word "leader" to mean "executive": The leader is the person at the top. That definition says that leadership is synonymous with a position. And if leadership is synonymous with a position, then it doesn't matter what a leader does. All that matters is where the leader sits. If you define a "leader" as an "executive," then you absolutely deny everyone else in an organization the opportunity to be a leader.

But when we studied leaders inside the companies that are involved in the SoL consortium, that's not what we saw. We had several companies that were able to sustain significant momentum over many years, and there were no executives involved at all. In case after case, the most compelling lesson we learned was that if you want real, significant, sustainable change, you need talented, committed local line leaders. Find the people who are at the heart of the value-generating process—who design, produce, and sell products; who provide services; who talk to customers. Those value-generating activities are the province of the line manager, and if the line manager is not innovating, then innovation is not going to occur.

The next thing we noticed was that, in some organizations, the first round of change activities somehow led to second-order efforts. The original group would spawn a second group, and gradually new practices would spread throughout the organization. How did that happen? We identified people who were "seed carriers." They were internal networkers who knew how to get people talking to one another and how to build informal communities. In effect, they were creating communities of practice. These networkers represent a second type of leadership. Of course, we also found executives who were providing leadership by doing activities that were more mature and more profound than simply offering themselves as heroes. These were executives who focus on acting as a coach or as a mentor.

Out of these observations, we developed our own definition of "leadership." To me, the simplest definition of that word is "the ability to produce change": "We used to operate that way; now we operate this way." Then, using what we saw inside companies, we identified three leadership communities: local line leaders, internal networkers or community builders, and executive leaders. For significant change to take place, you need to create an interplay among those three communities. One community can't be substituted for another. Each community represents part of a necessary set.

What's the Best Way to Begin Creating Change?

I have never seen a successful organizational-learning program rolled out from the top. Not a single one. Conversely, every change process that I've seen that was sustained and that spread has started small. Usually these programs start with just one team. That team can be any team, including an executive team. At Shell, the critical generative work was done in a top team. Then, in a matter of a year or so, it spread to the top 150 managers, who percolated ideas among themselves—and they, in turn, formed new clusters of teams. At Ford, two teams started working almost in parallel. In case after case, the change effort begins small, and as it takes hold, networks form that carry change into wider groups.

Just as nothing in nature starts big, so the way to start creating change is with a pilot group—a growth seed. As you think about a pilot group, there are certain choices that you have to make in order to make the group work. The first choice goes back to the issue of compliance versus commitment: Will the change effort be driven by authority or by learning? To make that decision is to choose a central path. Then there are reinforcing elements: new guiding ideas; innovations in the infrastructure; theories, methods, and tools.

After a Pilot Group Forms, What Are the Next Steps?

Thinking about nature as the model again leads you to ask, "What are the self-reinforcing processes whereby the seed begins to realize its potential to grow? And what are the limiting processes that come into play as the seed interacts with the soil?"

There are a number of self-reinforcing factors that help a pilot program to take root. People develop a personal stake in it. People see that their colleagues take it seriously, and they want to be part of a network of committed people. There's also a pragmatic factor: It works. There are real business results—so it's worthwhile to become engaged. But the most fundamental reinforcer of a pilot program is hearing people say that they've found a better way of working. Most people would rather work with a group of people who trust one another. Most people would rather walk out of a meeting with the belief that they've just solved an important problem. Most people would rather have fun at work. It may be obvious, but what we've observed again and again is that personal enthusiasm is the initial energizer of any change process. And that enthusiasm feeds on itself. People don't necessarily want to "have a vision" at work or to "conduct dialogue." They want to be part of a team that's fun to work with and that produces results they are proud of.

But even if the pilot has potential to grow, there is no guarantee that growth will occur. All pilot groups encounter "challenges to initiating"—initial limiting processes that can keep growth from ever really starting. For example, it doesn't matter how promising a team is if its members don't have time to commit to the change effort, if they can't reorganize their schedules to accommodate weekly meetings, if they don't have time during which they can get together to reflect. Learning takes time. Invariably, you will get that time back—and then some—because most teams today waste lots of time, and therefore better learning capabilities will make them much more productive than they were before. But first you have to be able to make an investment of time.

Another example of an important potential limiting factor: A change effort has to have some relevance to people. It has to have some connection to them. It has to matter. Why should an engineer need to learn how to conduct a dialogue? Why should she care about that skill? The answer may be that the organization trips over certain technical issues that aren't really technical issues; rather, they're problems with internal conversations that lead to fights instead of creative resolutions. The point isn't to learn how to conduct a dialogue. The point is to invest some time and to get some help to change how people work together.

In Your New Book, You Identify the 10 Challenges of Change. Why Focus on Challenges?

The short answer: to produce effective leadership. In a natural system, the way to sustain growth is by paying attention to the interplay between reinforcing processes and limiting processes—and by paying special attention to the limiting processes. The limiting processes represent 90% to 98% of the real leverage in sustaining deep change. These 10 challenges are the limiting processes that we've seen again and again. They include processes that operate from the outset of a pilot—such as time and relevance—and they include processes that come into play once a pilot begins to succeed. After an initial success, things tend to get harder, not easier. So, if we want to have effective leadership, if we want to have humane communities that can sustain significant change, we need to learn how to focus on these types of challenges.

Are these the only 10 challenges? This is just the first cut; undoubtedly there are others. But if the discourse about change starts to focus on challenges and on strategies for dealing with those challenges, we may be able to build a body of knowledge that will allow for effective leadership and sustainable change.

Back to the First Question: A Decade after *The Fifth Discipline* Appeared, Do You Think that Big Companies Can Change?

Ultimately, organizational learning is about growing something new. Where does new growth take place? Often it happens in the midst of the old. Indeed, often the new grows out of the old. How will the old react? The only realistic expectation is that the traditional system of management, as [W. Edwards] Deming used to label it, will work harder and harder to maintain itself. But growing something new doesn't have to be a battle against the old. It doesn't need to be a fight between believers and nonbelievers. In any case, our Industrial Age management, our Industrial Age organization, and our Industrial Age way of living will not continue. The Industrial Age is not sustainable. It's not sustainable in ecological terms, and it's not sustainable in human terms.

It will change. The only question is how. Once we get out of our machine mind-set, we may discover new aptitudes for growth and change. Until then, change won't come easily.

Sidebar: Chronology of Learning Organization Concepts

1938 In his book *Experience and Education,* John Dewey publicizes the concept of experiential learning as an ongoing cycle of activity.

1940s The Macy Conferences—featuring Margaret Mead, Gregory Bateson, and Lawrence Kubie—bring "systems thinking" to the awareness of a cross-disciplinary group of intellectuals.

1940s Scottish psychologist Kenneth Craik coins the term "mental models," which later makes its way to MIT through Marvin Minsky and Seymour Papert.

1946 Kurt Lewin, founding theorist of National Training Laboratories, proposes the idea of a "creative tension" between personal vision and a sense of reality.

1956 Edgar Schein's research on brainwashing in Korea paves the way for an understanding of "process consultation."

1960 *The Human Side of Enterprise,* by Douglas McGregor, is published.

1961 Jay Forrester publishes *Industrial Dynamics.* This book, the first major application of system dynamics to corporations, describes the turbulence within a typical appliance value chain.

1970 Chris Argyris and Donald Schön begin work on "action science," the study of how espoused values clash with the values that underlie real actions.

1972 *The Limits to Growth: A Report for the Club of Rome's Project on the Predicament of Mankind,* by Donella Meadows and Dennis Meadows, is published. The book draws on Forrester's theories about system dynamics.

1971 to 1979 Erhard Seminars Training (EST) demonstrate the kind of powerful attitude shifts that can occur during a seminar that lasts several days.

1979 Consultant Charlie Kiefer, Forrester student Peter Senge, and researcher-artist Robert Fritz design the "Leadership and Mastery" seminar, which becomes the focal point of their new consulting firm, Innovation Associates.

1984 to 1985 Pierre Wack, scenario planner at Royal Dutch/Shell, spends a sabbatical at Harvard Business School and writes two articles about scenario planning as a learning activity.

1982 Senge, Arie de Geus, Hanover Insurance CEO Bill O'Brien, Analog Devices CEO Ray Stata, and other executive leaders form a learning-organization study group, which meets regularly at MIT.

1987 Peter Schwartz, Stewart Brand, Napier Collyns, Jay Ogilvy, and Lawrence Wilkinson form the Global Business Network, with a charter to foster organizational learning through scenario planning.

1989 Oxford University management scholar Bill Isaacs, an associate of quantum physicist David Bohm, introduces Senge to the concept of dialogue as a process for building team capability.

1989 *The Age of Unreason,* by Charles Handy, is published.

1989 The Center for Organizational Learning is formed at MIT, with Senge as director and with Ed Schein, Chris Argyris, Arie de Geus, Ray Stata, and Bill O'Brien as key advisers. The staff of the "learning center," as it's called, includes Bill Isaacs, Daniel Kim (whose research involves linking the learning organization work to the quality movement), and research director George Roth.

1990 *The Fifth Discipline* is published. The book draws on many influences: system dynamics, "personal mastery" (based on Fritz's work and the concept of creative tension), mental models (based on Wack's and Argyris's work), shared vision (based on work done at Innovation Associates), and team learning (based on David Bohm's concepts).

1990 Daniel Kim founds the "Systems Thinker," a newsletter devoted to "fifth discipline" issues. The following year, the newsletter's parent organization, Pegasus Communications, launches an annual conference series called Systems Thinking in Action.

1993 Harvard University professor David Garvin publishes an article on organizational learning in the *Harvard Business Review,* arguing that only learning that can be measured will be useful to managers.

1994 *The Fifth Discipline Fieldbook* is published. Authors of the book, which Senge edited, include Charlotte Roberts, Rick Ross, and Bryan Smith (president of Innovation Associates of Canada), and Art Kleiner (who serves as editorial director). The *Fieldbook* becomes a new management-book genre.

1994 The use of "learning histories" as a method of assessment begins at the Center for Organizational Learning.

1994 The first major Organizational Learning Center projects reach completion. Many of them have produced remarkable results. But a few have resulted in disappointing career prospects for some of the line leaders who were involved in them.

1995 Working with Dee Hock, the Organizational Learning Center begins a two-year process of building an ambitious international consortium called the Society for Organizational Learning, with Peter Senge as chairman.

1996 *The Age of Heretics,* by Art Kleiner, and *Synchronicity: The Inner Path of Leadership,* by Joseph Jaworski, are published.

1997 *The Living Company,* by Arie de Geus, is published.

1999 *The Dance of Change* is published.

CASE 1
Drexler's Bar-B-Que
. . . .

Developed by Forrest F. Aven, Jr., University of Houston—Downtown, and V. Jean Ramsey, Texas Southern University

Change seems to be a fact of life, yet in Texas some things remain the same—people's love for Texas-style barbecue. As you drive from Houston to Waco, for example, you will see many roadside stands asking you to stop by and sample different forms of bbq or bar b q (the tastes vary as much as the spellings, and both are often inspired). In the cities, there are many restaurants, several of them large chains, that compete with smaller, neighborhood businesses for the barbecue portion of individuals' dining out budgets.

Survival can sometimes depend on the restaurant's ability to identify and capitalize on "windows of opportunity." Small businesses are presumed to be more flexible, having the ability to react more quickly to changes when they occur—but the risk is also greater for them than for large organizations, which can more easily absorb losses. But although there may be differences in scale, an important question for *all* organizations is whether they have the willingness and the ability to take advantage of opportunities as they arise. On February 14, 1995, Drexler's Bar-B-Que, a small "neighborhood" restaurant in Houston, the fourth largest city in the United States, had an opportunity to test whether it had what it took.

Drexler's Bar-B-Que is located at 2020 Dowling Street in an area of Houston called the Third Ward—an economically disadvantaged neighborhood not far from downtown—and has been in the family "almost forever." The more recent history, however, begins in the late 1940s, when a great uncle of the present owners operated the establishment as Burney's BBQ. He died in the late 1950s, and an uncle of the present owners took the restaurant over and, because of a leasing arrangement with another popular barbeque restaurant in Southwest Houston, changed the name of the restaurant to Green's Barbecue. In the 1970s, James Drexler, 12 years old, began working with his uncle and learned the secrets of the old family recipes for the barbecue beef, chicken, and sausage. He learned the business "from the ground up." In 1982, when his uncle died, James and his mother took over the business, ended the leasing arrangement, and, in 1985, renamed it Drexler's Bar-B-Que. To this day, it continues to be a "family affair," but there has been increased specialization in tasks as business has grown. James Drexler continues to do all the meat preparation, his mother, Mrs. Eunice Scott, handles the other food preparation (the "standard fare" is potato salad, cole slaw, barbeque beans, and slices of white bread), and his sister, Virginia Scott, manages the "front operations"—customer orders and the cash register. There are only two or three other full-time employees, although sometimes during the summer a couple of nephews work part time.

Drexler's is a family business with strong underlying values. It is in the neighborhood and is *of* the neighborhood. Despite the success of the business and the increased patronage of individuals from other parts of the city (many of whom previously had few occasions to do more than drive through the Third Ward), the Drexlers have never considered moving from their original location. The culture of the organization, and the values underpinning it, are influenced by the current head of the family, Mrs. Scott. Her values of honesty, hard work, and treating people fairly and with respect—and her faith in God—permeate the atmosphere and operations of Drexler's. She moves through the restaurant inquiring about individual needs—equally for long-time customers and new ones—and always with a smile and warm greeting for all. She is there every day the restaurant is open and holds the same set of high standards for herself as she does for others who work in the restaurant.

Values also get played out in the way in which Drexler's Bar-B-Que "gives back to" the surrounding African-American community. Drexler's has, for many years, sponsored a softball team and a local Boy Scout troop. Youths from the neighborhood have opportunities to go camping and visit a local amusement park because the family believes that a business should not just involve itself in the community but has the

obligation to seek out aggressively opportunities to help others.

In some ways it would appear that Drexler's is not very flexible or adaptable. The restaurant is always closed at 6:00 P.M. and on Sundays and Mondays. The menu has remained the same for many years. Drexler's has always been well known in Houston's African-American community, especially that in the southwest portion of the city. Regular customers have frequented the restaurant for many years, and a successful side business of catering social functions has also developed. Business has improved every year. During the early 1990s, the business had grown to a point where the small, somewhat ramshackle, restaurant could no longer service the demand—there simply were not enough tables or space. So the decision was made in 1994 to close the business for six months, completely raze the building, and rebuild a new and modern restaurant (with additional space attached for future expansion into related, and unrelated, businesses by other family members). It was a good decision—upon reopening, business doubled. But the biggest test of the restaurant's ability to adapt to changes came on February 14, 1995.

Mrs. Scott has two sons, James and Clyde Drexler. James is the co-owner of the restaurant, and Clyde is an NBA basketball player. In 1994, Clyde Drexler appeared at the restaurant to generate publicity for the reopening. But on February 14, 1995, he was traded from the Portland Trailblazers to the local NBA franchise, the Houston Rockets. Clyde had played his collegiate ball at the local university and was popular in the city of Houston. He and Hakeem Olajuwon, the "star" of the Rockets team, had played together in college and were part of the team known as the Phi Slamma

Jamma. Clyde had been a very successful member of the Portland team; he had been selected to play on several all-star teams, had played for two NBA championships, and was a member of the original Dream Team that sent NBA players to the 1992 Summer Olympics.

The Houston Rockets, the defending NBA champions, were struggling during that winter of 1995. The acquisition of Clyde Drexler was seen as a "blockbuster" one and a key to helping the team repeat as NBA champions. The city was overjoyed with the idea that a local hero was returning home to assist the team in once more winning the championship.

The initial news of the trade brought many new customers to the restaurant. As the Rockets progressed through the playoffs during the spring of 1995, even more customers came. Some days, the restaurant had to close early because it ran out of food. During the semifinals with San Antonio and the finals with Orlando, there appeared to be as many newspaper articles and television reports originating from the restaurant as from the basketball arena. A radio station staged an event outside the restaurant for fans to earn tickets to the game. A major local newspaper gave the restaurant a favorable review in the food section. Many Rockets fans saw frequenting the restaurant as a way to "connect" to the ball team and came to hug Mrs. Scott or chat with her about her son, Clyde, or both. When the Rockets clinched their second NBA championship, everyone in the city knew about the Rockets, and many now knew of Drexler's Bar-B-Que.

The restaurant has since become the hub of several businesses located side by side. In addition to her two sons, Mrs. Scott has four daughters. Virginia Scott, who is heavily involved in the restaurant, is

• •

also co-owner of a beauty salon, with another sister, Charlotte Drexler. A bakery is owned and operated by a cousin, Barbara Wiltz. A bookstore with a sports emphasis is leased to a nonfamily member. In January 1996, a new addition was made to the building, and a significantly expanded catering business was begun. Meanwhile, the restaurant has increased its neighborhood involvement by offering free Thanksgiving and Christmas dinners to neighborhood residents in a neighborhood park.

Review Questions

1. Use the open systems model decribed in this chapter to show how Drexler's Bar-B-Que should operate as a learning organization.
2. How do the "values" of Drexler's Bar-B-Que relate to the ethics and social responsibility issues raised in this chapter?
3. What challenges of organization and managerial leadership face Drexler's in its current movement toward expansion? ■

CASE 2
Sun Microsystems: "We're the dot in .com"

Developed by David S. Chappell, Ohio University

What does it take to foster a computer revolution? Bill Gates's Microsoft model, based on distributed personal computers with software (largely Microsoft's) loaded on each individual machine, may be slowly giving way to a networked system long championed by McNealy's Sun Microsystems. In fact, McNealy has been one of the few computer industry leaders to take on Microsoft directly with a zeal and tenacity that is legendary. Steven M. Milunovich, an analyst with Merrill Lynch and Company, argues that "If you want to know where the computer industry is going, ask Sun."[1]

Sun Microsystems

Sun Microsystems was founded by Andreas Bechtolsheim, Bill Joy, Vinod Khosla, and Scott McNealy in 1982. The first Sun system, the Sun-1, was a high performance computer based on readily available, inexpensive components and the Unix operating system largely developed by Joy while in graduate school at the University of California-Berkeley.

Note: The blue underscored words/phrases in this case indicate Internet links provided in the online version. See the *Organizational Behavior, Seventh Edition* Web Site at http://www.wiley.com/college/schermerhorn.

From the very start, Sun resisted the so-called Microsoft Windows/Intel (Wintel) model and concentrated on high-end workstations, suitable for engineering, designers, Wall Street traders, and CAD/CAM applications.

Scott McNealy took over as president of Sun in 1984 and since then has waged a constant war with Bill Gates and Microsoft. At first, Sun's market niche of high-end workstations kept it from competing directly with personal computers. However, over time PCs acquired more and more computing power, putting them in more direct competition with workstations. As a conse-

quence, Sun has branched out into other computer areas, with an emphasis on the Internet.

Sun is the only major company that builds an entire line of computers based exclusively on its own designs, its own chips, dubbed Sparc, and its own software, a version of the Unix operating system known as Solaris. As such, Sun stands alone as the "pure" alternative to the Wintel world.[2] This strategy is not without its detractors, who point out that Sun handicaps itself by requiring huge R&D expenses compared to those firms relying on Windows and Intel. Sun spends 10.4% of its sales on R&D, compared to 4.5% at Compaq and 1.6% at Dell, who rely on Intel and Microsoft for much of their research.[3]

McNealy boasts that "there are three technology companies left in the computer world. Intel, Microsoft and Sun."[4] "They [Sun] are beginning to be viewed as much more credible as an end-to-end solution provider," says Joe Ferlazzo, an analyst at Technology Business Research. Sun offers an attractive alternative with the same operating system on everything from a $2500 workstation with a single Sparc chip to a $1 million server with 64 parallel chips delivering as much computing power as an IBM mainframe. "That's what's needed in the ISP environment and in corporate computing" he adds. In the opposite camp, Susan Whitney of IBM argues that "To believe that a single architecture will address all the business requirements is not a sound strategy."[5]

Undeterred, McNealy stays convinced of his mission, which is no less than to overthrow the personal computer. "The PC is just a blip. It's a big, bright blip," says McNealy. "Fifty years from now, people are going to look back and say: 'Did you really have a computer on your desk? How weird.'"[6] Analyst C. B. Lee of Sutro and Company and a former Sun manager argues that "McNealy shoots off his mouth too much. At some point, you've gotta be more mature."[7]

Offsetting McNealy's brashness is Ed Zander, chief operating officer for Sun, who exhibits a more conservative aura. "I think McNealy and Zander are kind of like yin and yang," says Milunovich from Merrill Lynch. "McNealy is the high priest of the religion. Ed is much more pragmatic. Having both is very good for Sun."[8]

One thing McNealy has been able to accomplish is the constant reinvention of Sun as times and external conditions change. Starting with workstations and their various components, he has now positioned the firm to offer top-of-the-line servers that power the Internet. With the development of Java and Jini, Sun is evolving into a powerful software machine that serves to drive the Internet and future "information appliances."

To do this, Sun recognizes the need for talented people. Many observers rate Sun's employees among the most talented in Silicon Valley. To keep them in a competitive marketplace, Sun emphasizes perks:

Family care: Adoptive parents receive financial assistance of up to $2000. Lactation rooms help new mothers return to work. In the San Francisco Bay Area, parents can take sick children to a special day-care center that cares for children with minor illnesses. Sun also offers a dependent-care spending account, a consultation and referral program, and an employee-assistance program providing short-term professional counseling.

Private workspace: When Sun designed its Menlo Park, California campus, the company asked employees for suggestions—and found that engineers prefer private offices over Dilbert-like cubicles. The engineers got the space they demanded for quiet development time.

Respecting employee time: Flexible hours and telecommuting help accommodate busy schedules and keep employees from wasting time on California freeways. Train travelers can catch a special shuttle to Sun facilities, and the company reimburses some commuting costs.[9]

Hard to Find Where the Sun Don't Shine

As early as 1987, Sun coined the phrase, "The network is the computer."[10] But it has only been recently, with the full advent of the Internet coupled with Sun's Java programming language, that all the pieces may actually be falling into place to make this vision a reality. "Microsoft's vision was to put a mainframe on everybody's desktop," claims McNealy. "We want to provide dial tone for the Internet. We couldn't have more different visions."[11]

In 1995, Java was introduced as the first universal software designed from the ground up for Internet and corporate intranet developers to write applications that run on any computer, regardless of the processor or operating system.[12] Most recently Sun has introduced Jini, a promising technology that lets computers and appliances connect to a network as simply as a telephone plugs into the wall.[13] Sun's objective is to make access to the Internet and computing as simple as picking up a phone and hearing a "Webtone".

Even Microsoft yielded to Java's appeal, licensing a version to develop its own line of software. Java's appeal is its ability to lower companies' IT costs because it runs unchanged on any device with a computer chip, enabling everything from wallet-sized cards to trucks to communicate over a network. However, Microsoft and Sun immediately got into a battle when Microsoft made a proprietary version of Java to run only on Windows programs. Sun sued and has won an initial ruling against Microsoft.

Sun claims that network computing will herald a shift away from personal computers to more friendly appliances such as phones, digital assistants, and televisions. It hopes Java will provide the link to its powerful network servers with these new network devices.[14] Microsoft prefers its Windows CE operating system to provide this link. In addition, it views Web appliances as "companions" rather than replacements to today's PCs.

The allure of a host of Internet devices is their ability to bring in more users. Their convenience and ease-of-use promotes a more ubiquitous presence for the Web and the information located there. Java goes after this "embedded" software market by powering the programs that run everything from phone switches to factory automation equipment.

Java-Powered Net "Appliances"

Network Computers
Stripped-down desktop computers run programs downloaded from the Internet.

TVs and Cable Set-Top Boxes
TCI will distribute 20 million Java-equipped set-top boxes to encourage communication over cable.

Screenphones
Simple devices for straightforward services such as grocery ordering.

Cellular phones and pagers
Cellular phone manufacturers plan to use Java to offer new services through their cellular devices.

Smart Cards
Java smart cards program routine processes, such as airline ticket purchases directly on the cards.

Cars
Navigation and diagnostic systems powered by Java programs.

Keys
Java-powered rings and pass cards.[15]

McNealy billed Java as the killer of Microsoft Windows. Sun claims Java is ideally suited for the "network computer" (NC) — a low-cost machine that has no hard drive, relying instead on a network that would supply it with small Java programs. Plummeting personal computer prices have stalled the takeoff of the NC, but McNealy and Sun remain committed to the idea. "Every day, 27,000 people (at Sun) get up and do one thing: network computing," claims Ed Zander. "That's a very, very powerful story."[16]

Sun-AOL-Netscape

In perhaps its greatest coup to date, on November 24, 1998, Sun signed an alliance agreement with America Online in association with its $4.2 billion purchase of Netscape Communications. Access to Netscape's e-commerce software allows Sun to hawk its servers and attract customers that want a more complete package.[17] In addition, Sun has access to one of the three largest portals on the Web. In exchange for providing $350 million in licensing, marketing, and advertising fees for the deal, AOL agrees to buy $500 million in Sun servers over the next three years.

Open system advocates were originally concerned about AOL's involvement in the deal. They felt that AOL might hinder the free distribution of Netscape's browser. However, Stephen Case, AOL founder, assures doubters that the partnership will continue to allow free access to Netscape's browser technology. He intends to depend on Sun Microsystems to develop systems to provide Internet access over next-generation devices.

As a partner with AOL and Netscape, Sun is now in position to challenge IBM, Hewlett-Packard, and others in developing the systems that will let corporations rebuild their businesses in cyberspace. The challenge for Sun CEO Scott G. McNealy will be to behave like the top-tier industry leader that this deal may finally make him. And he'll need to make sure that Sun not only talks like a good partner but behaves like one, too.[18]

A major factor in Sun's favor is a world in which companies will choose to outsource anything that's not a demonstrably clear competitive advantage. Things such as human resources, financials, e-mail, and Web hosting all will clearly follow in the steps of payroll and facility security — that is, they'll be outsourced. Sun's been saying that the network is the computer for at least a decade. Oracle has been talking the talk for about three years. SAP was founded on the principle of centralized control in the early 1970s. But so far, no vendor has been able to convince any company that it should put its technological assets into someone else's hands. This is starting to change.[19]

The firm most strategically positioned to take advantage of this shift is Sun or possibly IBM Global Services. Scott McNealy has stated several times that companies should never think about purchasing another server again. He means that companies should leave the costs of maintaining scalability and reliability of fundamental systems to someone that specializes in the technology.[20]

Even so, the Internet must continue to evolve in order for Sun to realize its vision. John McFarlane, head of Solaris software, puts it plainly. "We depend upon extreme reliability, availability and scalability as a market differentiator. . . . I know from my seventeen years as a Nortel employee how much it hurts when there's a service failure of any kind, and how great it feels when the network would take a licking and keep on ticking. The same ethic applies at Sun. We run our own company systems on Sun, and our average downtime is about 22 minutes per-employee-per-year. Another way to put it is we experience about 99.96% uptime for every company user. We won a contract with the New York Stock Exchange because of our ability to deliver their required 99.99% uptime — and so far we're at 100%. If the Internet is truly to succeed as the next great communication medium for mainstream users, and the WebTone is to truly represent the same level of connectivity as the dialtone, then that level of reliability must be our model for all users. We call it the utility model of computing."[21]

With all these changes going on, how does a company cope? McNealy sums up his strategy by arguing, "If everybody thought that what we were doing was the right thing, everybody would do what we are doing. If you are controversial and you are wrong, you've got a big problem. You have to be very controversial and very right to make lots of money."[22]

THE OB SKILLS WORKBOOK **449**

Review Questions

1. Discuss the authors' definition of high performance organizations. Is there anything you would add or delete?
2. Analyze Sun Microsystems based on the authors' five key characteristics of HPOs.
3. Does Sun represent a Greenfield or Redesign HPO?

References

1. Hof, Robert; Hamm, Steve; and Sager, Ira. "Is the Center of the Computing Universe Shifting?," *Business Week,* January 19, 1999, pp. 64–72.
2. Helft, Miguel. "Sun Succeeds with Market Savvy, Pragmatism," *San Jose Mercury News,* December 6, 1998.
3. Hof, Hamm, and Sager, op. cit.
4. Ibid.
5. Ibid.
6. Ibid.
7. Ibid.
8. Helft, op. cit.
9. Merrick, Amy. "Companies Go the Extra Mile to Retain Employees," *R&D,* September 1998, p. S3.
10. Hof, Hamm, and Sager, op. cit.
11. Ibid.
12. "Sun Microsystems Homepage—History," http://www.sun.com/corporate overview/who/html_history. html, April 20, 1999.
13. Hof, Hamm, and Sager, op. cit.
14. Helft, op. cit.
15. Hof, op. cit.
16. Helft, op. cit.
17. Hof, op. cit.
18. Sager, Ira; Yang, Catherine; Himelstein, Linda; and Gross, Neil. "Power-Play: AOL-Netscape-Sun," *Business Week,* December 7, 1998.
19. Taschek, John. "This Just In: The World Revolves Around Sun," *PC Week,* January 4, 1999, p. 48.
20. Ibid.
21. McFarlane, John. "Whose WebTone Is It, Anyway?," http://www.sun.com/corporate overview/news/webtone.html, May, 1998.
22. Helft, op. cit. ∎

CASE 3
Crossing Borders
....

Developed by Bernardo M. Ferdman, California School of Professional Psychology, San Diego, CA and Plácida I. Gallegos, Southwest Communication Resources, Inc. and The Kaleel Jamison Consulting Group, Inc.

This case study is based on the experiences of Angelica Garza, a woman of Mexican-American heritage who worked for 10 years in the Human Resource (HR) function of a multinational medical products company. This maquiladora plant was in Tijuana, Baja California, a large city directly across the U.S.-Mexican border from San Diego, California. Maquiladoras are manufacturing plants owned by foreign capital in the regions of Mexico bordering the United States, which have been set up to take advantage of favorable laws and cheap labor.

The Tijuana plant was one of a number of operations for USMed. Six other U.S. facilities were located in the Northeast, the Midwest, and Florida. In addition to her work in the manufacturing plant, where Angelica spent most of her time, she was also responsible for human resources for the small, primarily administrative facility in Chula Vista, on the U.S. side of the border. Eventually, there were 34 Americans—12 on the Mexican side and 22 on the United States side—and approximately 1100 Mexican nationals on the payroll.

There was little connection between Angelica and the HR managers at the other USMed plants, either in the United States or abroad. Angelica reported that USMed had no overall policy or strategy for dealing with human resources generally and diversity specifically.

The transition in Mexico was not a smooth one for Angelica. Nothing in her U.S. experience had prepared her for what she encountered in Mexico. Her Anglo colleagues had only vague knowledge about the operation in Tijuana and had little interest in understanding or relating to the Mexican workforce. Given her Hispanic upbringing in the United States, Angelica had some understanding of the culture and values of the Mexican employees. Her Spanish-speaking skills also enabled her to understand and relate to the workers. Although she had some understanding of the workers, however, the assumption on the part of U.S. management that her knowledge and connection to the Mexican workers was seamless was false. There were many aspects of cultural differences between herself and the Mexican employees that

Source: This is an abridged version of a case appearing in the Field Guide of E. E. Kossek and S. Cobel, *Managing Diversity: Human Resource Strategies for Transforming the Workplace* (Oxford, England: Blackwell, 1996).

the Anglo managers were unaware of:

In retrospect now, I can look back and [I'm] just amazed at what I was involved in at the time. I mean, I didn't have a clue. One of the things you find is that [people assume that Mexican Americans are most suited to work with Mexicans.] I guess just because I was of Mexican-American descent, it was like I would just know how to mingle with this total[ly] different culture.

As a result, Angelica experienced a great deal of frustration and misunderstanding. Her attempts to intercede between the management in Mexico and that in the United States often led to her disenfranchisement from her American colleagues, who did not value or appreciate her ideas or suggestions. Further complicating her experience in Mexico was the mixed reactions she engendered from the Mexican nationals. Because of her American status, Angelica was misunderstood and sometimes resented by Mexican employees and, at the same time, she lacked support from the U.S. organization.

I found that the Mexican women who were there [two women in accounting who were Mexican nationals, and had been there for about 5 years] were resentful. My saving grace was that I was an American because the Mexican women there looked at the Americans as being like a step above or whatever. And there was resentment of me coming in and taking away jobs. They perceived it as: They weren't doing a good job and we were coming in and taking responsibilities away from them. So me being a woman coming in, I was scrutinized by the two women who had been there. I couldn't get information from them. They gave me the least information or help they could and would be critical of anything I did once I took it from them.

You know, I look back and it was probably pretty frightening for them [the Mexican nationals] too, because we all came in and we knew what we had to do;

[USMed was] very straightforward about, you know, you fail to do this and you can lose your job and you've got to do that or you could lose your job, so getting them to follow these protocols and these operating procedures was very difficult. Change is difficult anyway but getting them to follow some of those rules [was] real challenging.

Angelica understood the employees' approach to the work as stemming from local conditions and from Mexican cultural styles. The great expansion of maquiladoras brought a number of changes, including new expectations and different cultural styles on the part of the managers. At first, potential employees were unfamiliar with these new expectations; the employers needed to train the workers if they were to meet these expectations. This was happening in the context of the meeting of two cultures. In her role, Angelica saw herself as more American than Mexican, yet also as different from her Anglo colleagues. She saw herself as bringing American training, expectations, and styles:

Well, see I'm American. I mean I was an American manager, and that's where I was coming from. But I was forced to come up with systems that would eliminate future misunderstandings or problems. Being a Mexican American I thought it would be easier working in Mexico because I had some exposure to the culture, but it was a real culture shock for me. It was a different group of people socioeconomically. A lot of those people came from ranchitos, [from] out in the sticks, where there were no restrooms or showers. There weren't infrastructures in Tijuana at all. It's pretty good now compared to what it was 10 years ago. We used to go to work through people's backyards and dirt roads. Dead dogs were marks for how to get there! And I think now, that if you go to Tijuana now—it's been 10 years of maquiladoras there—you can find more qualified Mexican managers or supervi-

sors or clerical people. [Finding] bilingual secretaries and engineers [was like] getting needles in a haystack back then.

I found myself being the only woman in an old-boy-network environment, and that was pretty tough. And it was also tough working in the Mexican environment. Because the Mexican men that I would deal with would look down on me because I was a woman. Again, my saving grace was because I was an American woman. If I had been a Mexican national woman, then I would have really had probably more problems. [For example] I had to work a lot, real close with the Mexican accounting manager, who was a male. And he would come to me and tell me how I had screwed up my numbers, or you didn't do this right, and stuff like that. I would go over the numbers and it was just a difference in terms of how things were calculated. Specifically, calculating an annual salary. He would do it by using 365 days, when I would do it by 52 weeks and you'd take your daily rate, it was different, it would always be off a little bit. But, I reported them the way the Americans would be expecting to see them.

Review Questions

1. What competencies are appropriate to ensure greater effectiveness of U.S. employees operating in a maquiladora or other non-U.S. organization?

2. What are some of the costs of not understanding diversity? What could the organization have gained by approaching the plant with greater cultural understanding?

3. From the HR perspective, what were the unique challenges that Angelica faced at various points in her work for USMed?

4. Angelica worked in a plant outside the United States. What do her experiences and perspectives tell us that applies to domestic operations? ■

CASE 4
Never on a Sunday

Developed by Anne C. Cowden, California State University, Sacramento

McCoy's Building Supply Centers of San Marcos, Texas, have been in continuous successful operation for almost 70 years in an increasingly competitive retail business. McCoy's is one of the nation's largest family-owned and -managed building-supply companies, with sales topping $400 million. The company serves 10 million customers a year in a regional area currently covering New Mexico, Texas, Oklahoma, Arkansas, Mississippi, and Louisiana in 103 stores employing 1600 employees. McCoy's strategy has been to occupy a niche in the market of small and medium-sized cities. McCoy's was originally a roofing business started by Frank McCoy in 1923; roofing remained the company's primary business until the 1960s, when it began to expand under the management of son, Emmett McCoy.

McCoy's grounding principle is acquiring and selling the finest quality products that can be found and providing quality service to customers. As an operations-oriented company, McCoy's has always managed without many layers of management. Managers are asked to concentrate on service-related issues in their stores: get the merchandise on the floor, price it, sell it, and help the customer carry it out. The majority of administrative workload is handled through headquarters so that store employees can concentrate on customer service. The top management team (Emmett McCoy and his two sons, Brian and Mike, who serve as co-presidents) has established 11 teams of managers drawn from the different regions McCoy's stores cover. The teams meet regularly to discuss new products, better ways for product delivery, and a host of items integral to maintaining customer satisfaction. Team leadership is rotated among the managers.

McCoy's has a workforce of 70 percent full-time and 30 percent part-time employees. McCoy's philosophy values loyal, adaptable, skilled employees as the most essential element of its overall success. To operationalize this philosophy, the company offers extensive on-the-job training. The path to management involves starting at the store level and learning all facets of operations before advancing into a management program. All management trainees are required to relocate to a number of stores. Most promotions come from within. Managers are rarely recruited from the outside. This may begin to change as the business implements more technology requiring greater reliance on college-educated personnel.

Permeating all that McCoy's does is a strong religious belief, including a strong commitment to community. In 1961 Emmett McCoy decided, in the wake of a devastating hurricane, to offer McCoy's goods to customers at everyday prices rather than charging what the market would bear. This decision helped establish McCoy's long-standing reputation of fair dealing, a source of pride for all employees, and allowed the company to begin its current expansion perspective. In 1989 McCoy's became a drug-free company. McCoy's takes part in the annual National Red Ribbon Campaign, "Choose to Be Drug Free." McCoy's also supports Habitat for Humanity in the United States and has provided support for low-income housing in Mexico.

Many McCoy family members are Evangelical Christians who believe in their faith through letting their "feet do it"—that is, showing their commitment to God through action, not just talk. Although their beliefs and values permeate the company's culture in countless ways, one very concrete way is reflected in the title of this case: Never on a Sunday. Even though Sundays are busy business days for retailers, all 103 McCoy's stores are closed on Sunday.

Review Questions

1. How do the beliefs of the McCoy family form the culture of this company?
2. Can a retailer guided by such strong beliefs compete and survive in the era of gigantic retailers such as Home Depot? If so, how?
3. Is such a strong commitment to social responsibility and ethical standards a help or a hindrance in managing a company?
4. How does a family-owned and -managed company differ from companies managed by outside professionals? ■

CASE 5
MAGREC, Inc.
....

Developed by Mary McGarry, Empire State College
and Barry R. Armandi, SUNY-Old Westbury

Background

MagRec, Incorporated was started in the late 1960s by Mr. Leed, a brilliant engineer (he has several engineering patents), who was a group manager at Fairchild Republic. The company's product was magnetic recording heads, a crucial device used for reading, writing, and erasing data on tapes and disks. Need for the product and its future potential was great. The computer industry was in its embryonic stage, and MagRec had virtually no serious competition. In fact, almost all magnetic head manufacturers today use methods, techniques, processes, and so on, that were developed and pioneered by MagRec.

Like any other startup, MagRec had a humble beginning. It struggled during the early years, facing cash-flow and technical problems. After a slow start, it began growing rapidly. In the mid-1970s it had captured 35 percent of the tape head market, making it the second largest supplier of MegaComputer computer tape heads in North America. Financially, the company suffered heavily in the early 1980s because of price erosions caused by Far East competition. Unlike all its competitors, the company resisted and never moved its manufacturing operations offshore. By the mid-1980s, the company had accumulated losses to a point of bankruptcy. Finally, plagued by a no-win situation, the company entered a major international joint venture, in which foreign governments agreed to participate as minority owners (20% equity). The company received blanket sales orders from Japanese firms (GME, Victor Data, Fijitsu, etc.). Things looked good once again. But . . .

Pat's Dilemma

When Fred Marsh promoted me to Sales Manager, I was in seventh heaven. Now, six months later, I feel I am in hell. This is the first time in my life that I am really on my own. I have been working with other people all my life. I tried my best and what I could not solve, I took upstairs. Now it's different because I am the boss (or am I?). Fred has taught me a lot. He was my mentor and gave me this job when he became vice-president. I have always respected him and listened to his judgment. Now thinking back I wonder whether I should have listened to him at all on this problem.

It started one late Friday evening. I had planned to call my West Coast customer, Partco, to discuss certain contract clauses. I wanted to nail this one fast (Partco had just been acquired by Volks, Inc.). Partco was an old customer, in fact—through good and bad it had always stayed with us. It was also a *major* customer. I was about to call Partco when Dinah Coates walked in clutching a file. I had worked with Dinah for three years. She was good. I knew that my call to Partco would have to wait. Dinah had been cleaning out old files and came across a report about design and manufacturing defects in Partco heads. The report had been written

nine years ago. The cover memo read as follows:

To: Ken Smith, Director of Marketing
From: Rich Grillo, V.P. Operations
Sub: Partco Head Schedule

This is to inform you that due to pole-depth problems in design, the Partco heads (all 514 in test) have failed. They can't reliably meet the reading requirements.* The problem is basically a design error in calculations. It can be corrected. However, the fix will take at least six months. Meanwhile Ron Scott in production informs me that the entire 5,000 heads (the year's production) have aready been pole-slotted, thus they face the same problem.

Ken, I don't have to tell you how serious this is, but how can we o.k. and ship them to Partco knowing that they'll cause read error problems in the field? My engineering and manufacturing people realize this is the number one priority. By pushing the Systems Tech job back we will be back on track in less than six months. In the interim I can modify Global Widgets heads. This will enable us to at least continue shipping some product to Partco. As a possible alternate I would like to get six Partco drives. Michaels and his team feel that with quick and easy changes in the drives tape path they can get the head to work. If this is true we should be back on track within six to eight weeks.

A separate section of the report read as follows:

Confidential
(Notes from meeting with Dom Updyke and Rich Grillo)

Solution to Partco heads problem
All Partco heads can be reworked (.8 hrs. ea.—cost insignificant) to solve Partco's read problems by grinding an extra three thousandths of an inch off the top of the head. This will reduce the overall pole depth to a point where no read errors occur. The heads will fully

---

*Authors' Note: Error signifies erroneous reading, not an error message. For example, instead of "$200" the head reads "$3005.42."

meet specifications in all respects except one, namely life. Dom estimates that due to the reduced chrome layer (used for wear) the heads' useful life will be 2,500 hours instead of 6,000 hours of actual usage.

Our experience is that no customer keeps accurate records to tell actual usage and life. Moreover the cost is removed since Partco sells drives to MegaComputer who sells systems to end-users. The user at the site hardly knows or rarely complains about extra costs such as the replacement of a head 12 to 18 months down the line instead of the normal 2 years. Besides the service technicians always innovatively believe in and offer plausible explanations—such as the temperature must be higher than average—or they really must be using the computer a lot.

I have directed that the heads be reworked and shipped to Partco. I also instructed John to tell Partco that due to inclement weather this week's shipment will be combined with next week's shipment.

Dinah was flabbergasted. The company planned to sell products deliberately that it knew would not meet life requirements, she said, "risking our reputation as a quality supplier. Partco and others buy our heads thinking they are the best. Didn't we commit fraud through outright misrepresentation?"

Dinah insisted I had to do something. I told her I would look into the matter and get back to her by the end of next week.

Over the weekend I kept thinking about the Partco issue. We had no customer complaints. Partco had always been extremely pleased with our products and technical support. In fact, we were their sole suppliers. MegaComputer had us placed on the preferred, approved ship to stock, vendors list. It was a fact that other vendors were judged against our standards. MegaComputer's Quality Control never saw our product or checked it.

Monday morning I showed the report to Fred. He immediately recollected it and began to explain the situation to me.

MagRec had been under tremendous pressure and was growing rapidly at the time. "That year we had moved into a new 50,000 sq. ft. building and went from 50 or 60 employees to over 300. Our sales were increasing dramatically." Fred was heading Purchasing at the time and every week the requirements for raw materials would change. "We'd started using B.O.A.s (Broad Order Agreements, used as annual purchasing contracts) guaranteeing us the right to increase our numbers by 100% each quarter. The goal was to maintain the numbers. If we had lost Partco then, it could have had a domino effect and we could have ended up having no customers left to worry about."

Fred went on to explain that it had only been a short-term problem that was corrected within the year and no one ever knew it existed. He told me to forget it and to move the file into the back storage room. I conceded. I thought of all the possible hassles. The thing was ancient history anyway. Why should I be concerned about it? I wasn't even here when it happened.

The next Friday Dinah asked me what I had found out. I told her Fred's feelings on the matter and that I felt he had some pretty good arguments regarding the matter. Dinah became angry. She said I had changed since my promotion and that I was just as guilty as the crooks who'd cheated the customers by selling low-life heads as long-life heads. I told her to calm down. The decision was made years ago. No one got hurt and the heads weren't defective. They weren't causing any errors.

I felt bad but figured there wasn't much to do. The matter was

closed as far as I was concerned, so I returned to my afternoon chores. Little was I to know the matter was not really closed.

That night Fred called me at 10:00. He wanted me to come over to the office right away. I quickly changed, wondering what the emergency was. I walked into Fred's office. The coffee was going. Charlie (Personnel Manager) was there. Rich Grillo (V.P. Operations) was sitting on the far side of Fred's conference table. I instinctively headed there for that was the designated smoking corner.

Ken (Director of Marketing) arrived 15 minutes later. We settled in. Fred began the meeting by thanking everyone for coming. He then told them about the discovery of the Partco file and filled them in on the background. The problem now was that Dinah had called Partco and gotten through to their new vice president, Tim Rand. Rand had called Fred at 8 P.M. at home and said he was personally taking the Red Eye to find out what this was all about. He would be here in the morning.

We spent a grueling night followed by an extremely tense few weeks. Partco had a team of people going through our tests, quality control, and manufacturing records. Our production slipped, and overall morale was affected.

Mr. Leed personally spent a week in California assuring Partco that this would never happen again. Though we weathered the storm, we had certain losses. We were never to be Partco's sole source again. We still retained 60 percent of their business, but had to agree to lower prices. The price reduction had a severe impact. Although Partco never disclosed to anyone what the issues were (since both companies had blanket nondisclosure agreements), word got around that Partco was paying a lower price. We were unable to explain to our other customers why Partco was paying this amount. Actually I felt the price word got out through Joe Byrne (an engineer who came to Partco from Systems Tech and told his colleagues back at Systems Tech that Partco really knew how to negotiate prices down). He was unaware, however, of the real issues. Faced with customers who perceived they were being treated unequitably, we experienced problems. Lowering prices meant incurring losses; not lowering them meant losing customers. The next two financial quarters saw sales dollars decline by 40 percent. As the sales manager, I felt pretty rotten presenting my figures to Fred.

With regard to Dinah, I now faced a monumental problem. The internal feeling was she should be avoided at all costs. Because of price erosions, we faced cutbacks. Employees blamed her for production layoffs. The internal friction kept mounting. Dinah's ability to interface effectively with her colleagues and other departments plummeted to a point where normal functioning was impossible.

Fred called me into his office two months after the Partco episode and suggested that I fire Dinah. He told me that he was worried about results. Although he had nothing personally against her, he felt that she must go because she was seriously affecting my department's overall performance. I defended Dinah by stating that the Partco matter would blow over and given time I could smooth things out. I pointed out Dinah's accomplishments and stated I really wanted her to stay. Fred dropped the issue, but my problem persisted.

Things went from bad to worse. Finally, I decided to try to solve the problem myself. I had known Dinah well for many years and had a good

relationship with her before the incident. I took her to lunch to address the issue. Over lunch, I acknowledged the stress the Partco situation had put on her and suggested that she move away for a while to the West Coast where she could handle that area independently.

Dinah was hurt and asked why I didn't just fire her already. I recounted by accusing her of causing the problem in the first place by going to Partco.

Dinah came back at me, calling me a lackey for having taken her story to Fred and brought his management message back. She said I hadn't even attempted a solution and that I didn't have the guts to stand up for what was right. I was only interested in protecting my backside and keeping Fred happy. As her manager, I should have protected her and taken some of the heat off her back. Dinah refused to transfer or to quit. She told me to go ahead and fire her, and she walked out.

I sat in a daze as I watched Dinah leave the restaurant. What the

hell went wrong? Had Dinah done the morally right thing? Was I right in defending *MagRec's* position? Should I have taken a stand with Fred? Should I have gone over Fred's head to Mr. Leed? Am I doing the right thing? Should I listen to Fred and fire Dinah? If not, how do I get my department back on track? What am I saying? If Dinah is right, shouldn't I be defending her rather than *MagRec*?

Review Questions

1. Place yourself in the role of the manager. What should you do now? After considering what happened, would you change any of your behaviors?
2. Do you think Dinah was right? Why or why not? If you were she and you had to do it all over again, would you do anything differently? If so, what and why?
3. Using cognitive dissonance theory, explain the actions of Pat, Dinah, and Fred. ■

CASE 6
It Isn't Fair
....

Developed by Barry R. Armandi, SUNY-Old Westbury

Mary Jones was in her senior year at Central University and interviewing for jobs. Mary was in the top 1 percent of her class, active in numerous extracurricular activities, and was highly respected by her professors. After the interviews, Mary was offered a number of positions with every company with which she interviewed. After much thought, she decided to take the offer from Universal Products, a multinational company. She felt that the salary was superb ($40,000), there were excellent benefits, and good potential for promotion.

Mary started work a few weeks after graduation and learned her job assignments and responsibilities thoroughly and quickly. Mary was asked on many occasions to work

late because report deadlines were moved forward often. Without hesitation she said "Of course!" even though as an exempt employee she would receive no overtime.

Frequently, she would take work home with her and use her personal computer to do further analyses. At other times, she would come into the office on weekends to monitor the progress of her projects or just to catch up on the ever-growing mountain of correspondence.

On one occasion her manager asked her to take on a difficult assignment. It seemed that the company's Costa Rican manufacturing facility was having production problems. The quality of one of the products was highly questionable, and the reports on the matter were confusing. Mary was asked to be part of a team to investigate the quality and reporting problems. The team stayed in poor accommodations for the entire three weeks they were there. This was because of the plant's location near its resources, which happened to be in the heart of the jungle. Within the three-week period the team had located the source of the quality problem, corrected it, and altered the reporting documents and processes. The head of the team, a quality engineer, wrote a note to Mary's manager stating the following: "Just wanted to inform you of the superb job Mary Jones did down in Costa Rica. Her suggestions and insights into the reporting system were invaluable. Without her help we would have been down there for another three-weeks, and I was getting tired of the mosquitos. Thanks for sending her."

Universal Products, like most companies, has a yearly performance review system. Since Mary had been with the company for a little over one year, it was time for her review. Mary entered her manager's office nervous, since this was her first review ever and she didn't know what to expect. After closing the door and exchanging the usual pleasantries, her manager, Tom, got right to the point.

Tom: Well, Mary, as I told you last week this meeting would be for your annual review. As you are aware, your performance and compensation are tied together. Since the philosophy of the company is to reward those who perform, we take these reviews very sincerely. I have spent a great deal of time thinking about your performance over the past year, but before I begin I would like to know your impressions of the company, your assignments, and me as a manager.

Mary: Honestly, Tom, I have no complaints. The company and my job is everything I was led to believe. I enjoy working here. The staff are all very helpful. I like the team atmosphere, and my job is very challenging. I really feel appreciated and that I'm making a contribution. You have been very helpful and patient with me. You got me involved right from the start and listened to my opinions. You taught me a lot and I'm very grateful. All in all I'm happy being here.

Tom: Great, Mary, I was hoping that's the way you felt because from my vantage point, most of the people you worked with feel the same. But before I give you the qualitative side of the review, allow me to go through the quantitative appraisal first. As you know, the rankings go from 1 (lowest) to 5 (highest). Let's go down each category and I'll explain my reasoning for each.

Tom starts with category one (Quantity of Work) and ends with category ten (Teamwork). In each of the categories, Tom has either given Mary a five or a four. Indeed, only two categories have a four and Tom explains these are normal areas for improvement for most employees.

Tom: As you can see, Mary, I was very happy with your performance. You have received the highest rating I have ever given any of my subordinates. Your attitude, desire, and help are truly appreciated. The other people on the Costa Rican team gave you glowing reports and speaking with the plant manager, she felt that you helped her understand the reporting system better than anyone else. Since your performance has been stellar, I'm delighted to give you a 10 percent increase effective immediately!

Mary: (mouth agape, and eyes wide) Tom, frankly I'm flabbergasted! I don't know what to say, but thank you very much. I hope I can continue to do as fine a job as I have this last year. Thanks once again.

After exchanging some departing remarks and some more thank yous, Mary left Tom's office with a smile from ear to ear. She was floating on air! Not only did she feel the performance review process was uplifting, but her review was outstanding and so was her raise. She knew from other employees that the company was only giving out a 5 percent average increase. She figured that if she got that, or perhaps 6 or 7, she would be happy. But to get 10 percent . . . wow!! Imagine . . .

Sue: Hi, Mary! Lost in thought? My, you look great. Looks like you got some great news. What's up?

Susan Stevens was a recent hire, working for Tom. She had graduated from Central University also, but a year after Mary. Sue had excelled while at Central, graduating in the top 1 percent of her class. She had laudatory letters of recommendations from her professors and was into many after school clubs and activities.

Mary: Oh, hi Sue! Sorry, but I was just thinking about Universal and the opportunities here.

Sue: Yes, it truly is . . .

Mary: Sue, I just came from my performance review and let me tell you, the process isn't that bad. As a matter of fact I found it quite rewarding, if you get my drift. I got a wonderful review, and can't wait till next year's. What a great company!

Sue: You can say that again! I couldn't believe them hiring me right out of college at such a good salary. Between you and me Mary they started me at $45,000. Imagine that? Wow, was I impressed. I just couldn't believe

that they would . . . Where are you going, Mary? Mary? What's that you say "It isn't fair"? What do you mean? Mary? Mary . . .

Review Questions

1. Indicate Mary's attitudes before and after meeting Sue. If there was a change, why?
2. What do you think Mary will do now? Later?
3. What motivation theory applies best to this scenario? Explain.

∎

CASE 7
Amoco's Global Human Resource Systems

Developed by Ellen Ernst Kossek, Michigan State University

Headquartered in Chicago, Amoco, formerly Standard Oil of Indiana, began as a sleepy Midwestern U.S. refining company. Historically, Amoco has had a largely domestic focus in its human resources approach. "International human resources" primarily meant the personnel policies of U.S. expatriates—American citizens who work for Amoco abroad. Until several decades ago, most of Amoco's oil reserves were located in the United States; consequently, management had grown up with the view that most of the company's growth would come from within U.S. borders. Today, however, nearly 80 percent of new investment dollars are being targeted toward foreign operations.

Amoco mangement believes that developing a global approach necessitates transformation in attitudes, organizational processes, and human-resource systems. Drivers of global mandates for change in HR practices are as follows:

Global competition: Competitors are increasingly outside the United

Source: This is an abridged version of a case appearing in the Field Guide of E. E. Kossek and S. Lobel, *Managing Diversity: Human Resource Strategies for Transforming the Workplace* (Oxford, England, Blackwell, 1996).

States (British Petroleum, Royal Dutch Shell, ELF Acquitaine, BHP).

Major cash going overseas: Since most oil reserves and markets with most growth potential are now located overseas, operations will increasingly be done outside the United States.

Economic shift: The United States is no longer as dominant an economic base as it has been historically.

Global labor markets: A growing pool of talent will be hired beyond the U.S. labor market. There is also a need to manage cultural and politi-

cal constraints on travel, work permits, type of assignments, and labor market conditions.

Excessive cost of expatriations: Because of the rising cost of expatriates, Amoco must use the talent of local nationals to a greater extent. Yet, in some countries after the costs of social programs are entered into the analysis, staffing local nationals is not always necessarily cheaper.

Culture and value differences of global workforce: State-of-the-art U.S. practices may not favor applicants from non-U.S. cultures (e.g., targeted selection, individual reward and appraisal systems) or may have implementation problems. Expatriation of female employees is limited in some locations.

Increased pressures from foreign governments: Expectations have changed; foreign governments now demand that local nationals be employed.

Increasing need to have a global presence: In many cultures, a long relationship must be developed, and evidence of *staying power* must be shown in order to get business; lack of presence may affect future bids in a country.

Ethics: Amoco's values will not permit it to engage in bribing or violating U.S. laws when abroad, even if it is the custom.

The number one competitive pressure shaping human resource activities is the changing competition of the oil industry. Increasingly, Amoco's competitors are foreign companies, such as British Petroleum and Royal Dutch Shell. Since most investment for new business will be spent overseas, it is essential that Amoco's human resource systems adapt accordingly. Management must also no longer view the United States as the premier economic base.

Because of the need for a global workforce, there will be significantly greater demand to integrate local nationals at all levels of an overseas subsidiary. Contributing to this view is the excessive cost of expatriations; that is, the high cost of moving U.S. employees abroad to run companies. Because of these financial pressures, Amoco must make greater use of the talent of local nationals. Yet, just hiring a great number of local nationals for managerial positions will not necessarily help a company globalize successfully; the ability to balance the parent company's view with local needs is a critical consideration. There is still a nagging (and some might say well-founded) fear in the minds of some Amoco executives that they must cautiously pick people who have allegiance to Amoco and not their local country's government. There is the tendency to be lean and mean in terms of placement of local nationals in key positions in developing countries. As a protective staffing strategy, even in developed countries, the vast majority of critical jobs are held by U.S. expatriates. In Norway, for example, some managers complain of a glass ceiling effect, a barrier that keeps nationals from moving into key positions. And the trend seems to be spiraling downhill, despite the fact that the country's operations are extremely successful, are stable, and mix relatively well with the United States. Even in Northern European countries, cultural differences remain that are barriers to developing a global workforce. Work and family values are different in European countries compared to the U.S. workaholic corporate norm. It is not uncommon to see Norwegian male employees leave at 3:30 in the afternoon to go pick up their children from school, a

practice that is still rare for male employees in the United States. Some U.S. managers have felt that if a lot of high-quality work needs to be done quickly in a short amount of time, U.S. managers are needed to get it done.

Developing worldwide human resource systems means analyzing cultural biases in "leading edge" practices developed with an American view. For example, targeted selection, whereby an interviewer asks questions that target the presence of key abilities found in successful U.S. managers, may not work well for individuals from countries that shun bragging excessively about one's strengths in an interview. Similarly, total quality management, which relies on self-empowerment, may require some modification before being applied abroad in cultures that value individualism less.

Over time, the amount of U.S. expatriation must decrease because of *de facto* cost pressures. Increasingly, a more cost-effective strategy might be to rely on the U.S. workforce more in the consultation role. Greater utilization of local nationals in running international operations might also better blend local laws and customs with Amoco's practices. Yet, typically, when planning new ventures, the human resource plan is usually the last one put in place.

There is also an increasing need to have a presence in a country, in order to get a concession or a government approval to begin energy exploration. In many cultures, a long relationship must be developed and evidence of staying power must be shown to in order to get business. The lack of presence may affect future bids in a country. As one employee commented, "We're very good at managing the technical aspects of the exploration busi-

ness—for instance we have led the industry in seismic techniques related to secondary tertiary recovery, but we're not very good at managing new cultures effectively to obtain entry." In Amoco's defense, some manager's argue that, realistically, Amoco may not know whether it will be in a new country 6 more months or 6 or more years. This uncertainty is dependent on whether a discovery is made, an endeavor that can fail 90 percent of the time. Some managers contend that it makes more sense to use talent from the United States until a discovery is found. Yet a key to developing marketing strength in new markets is to open an office in a country even before a discovery is made. Typically, however, Amoco will not open an office in a new country until after a discovery is made and concessions are given. Because of this policy, Royal Dutch Shell has a 10-month jump on Amoco in Romania, since it was there long before a concession was made. Given the fact that the entitlement and social programs in many countries are very much more costly than in the United States, a counter-argument can be made that it *does* make sense for a U.S. oil company to move slowly when hiring foreign employees. It would be extremely expensive to close a firm and pay off the former workers if no oil were found. Because of these conditions, contract employees are often used heavily in the early stages of development.

Still, many believe that it is not possible for a company the size of Amoco to open as many offices worldwide as larger competitors, such as Royal Dutch Shell or Exxon. Rather, Amoco should focus its efforts on opening offices early in selected countries. Instead of using its technical strengths *after* a discovery is made to gain business, Amoco should do a better job of making the world aware of its strength in applying technology well and leverage this capability to get new contracts.

Increasing pressures to hire locals are also being felt from foreign governments. Expectations today have changed. Foreign governments now demand greater employment of local nationals. This can be a problem in countries such as Trinidad, where lifetime employment is the norm. It is very difficult to be a low-cost operator when the biggest part of the costs come early; then, once the oil platforms are built and the growth is underway, the firm is left with a headcount that is not flexible.

An additional pressure stems from worldwide differences in ethics. Amoco values will not permit it to engage in bribing or violating U.S. laws when abroad, even if it is the custom and competitors are doing so. Ethics also affect the extent to which a multinational chooses to use techniques that minimize damage to the environment, even if there are no foreign environmental laws. Firms that are environmentally cautious may face much higher costs than their competitors. Yet some managers believe that Amoco's ethics could be turned into a competitive advantage to get new business, because many of Amoco's

environmental approaches are leading edge. In Pakistan, for example, the government would not allow the import of beride, a chemical used in the drilling of wells. Amoco spent an extra quarter million dollars on its wells in lining pits and putting up a dustproof room for the lead, which can be hazardous to the environment, if mixed. Similarly, in Burma, where operations were in a jungle, Amoco cut a very narrow path around the area for the oil well and then reforested. In the United States, where environmental regulations are considered to be the most strict in the world, Amoco strives not only to meet but to exceed environmental regulations. As one manager states, "If you spend more now, you'll save a lot later, because you'll be ahead of regulatory changes." Some believe that doing a better job marketing this record will increase global opportunities.

Review Questions

1. What is a global organization?
2. What are the key business pressures driving the globalization of human resource systems?
3. What are some HR practices that would help Amoco Production manage these tensions? ■

For one manager of software projects (based in Los Angeles) who oversees 11 people in a 50-person office based in Dallas, the answer is that telecommuting is very effective, although not without drawbacks. Our manager, a veteran of nine years of telecommuting, is in constant contact with her employees, software technical writers, and quality analysts–testers, through E-mail, with voice mailbox, phone, fax, and, at least once a month, face-to-face visits on site with each employee. One room in her home is fully outfitted as an office, one she can walk away from as a means of separating her personal and professional life. However, she is always connected to those whom she supervises. For example, on a weekend, if an employee has gone in to work, she can answer a question from home by merely walking into her home-based office.

To keep connected with her employees on a physical level, our manager meets individually with each employee on a monthly basis in Dallas. She spends an hour going over the priorities they have listed as activities for the month. Throughout the month, the manager and the employees are in constant contact. Through both physical and electronic communication our manager is able to get to know her employees well. As she has noted, meeting with them in person allows her to "see" them over the phone, judging their psychological "space" by voice intonation when there is no physical face to communicate with. Our manager also interacts with other managers and line personnel through telecommuting. For example, she negotiates over the phone what goes into a product, the time line, the product budget, and all other factors necessary to managing a product effectively.

While our manager likes telecommuting and is able to man-

CASE 8
I'm Not in Kansas Anymore
....

Developed by Anne C. Cowden, California State University, Sacramento

Telecommuting is defined as work done at home or in a remote location using technology as the link. Approximately 7.6 million people currently telecommute. The decision whether to allow employees to telecommute is controversial, owing to the number of managerial control questions raised by people working and/or managing off site.

age effectively, there are both good points and drawbacks. The advantages include the freedom from commuting every day in full office dress, the complexity and challenge to stay well connected with employees, and the time gained by staying at home. The drawbacks can be the isolation that some initially feel when not having daily physical contact with others. Another drawback may be "workaholism" if one is unable to separate life from one's job. Burnout can be a factor if one works all the time.

If you are thinking of telecommuting, our manager would advise the following: get a good headset for talking on the phone; be prepared for the initial feelings of isolation; and keep in daily, close contact with your employees.

Review Questions

1. Is telecommuting the wave of the future, or does top management lose too much control when people are off site?
2. How would you like being a telecommuter, as either a manager or one being managed?
3. Do you think telecommuting is effective for both the employee and the organization? Why or why not? ■

CASE 9
The Forgotten Group Member
....

Developed by Franklin Ramsoomair, Wilfred Laurier University

The Organizational Behavior course for the semester appeared to promise the opportunity to learn, enjoy, and practice some of the theories and principles in the textbook and class discussions. Christine Spencer was a devoted, hard-working student, who had been maintaining an A- average to date. Although the skills and knowledge she had acquired through her courses were important, she was also very concerned about her grades. She felt that grades were paramount in giving her a competitive edge when looking for a job and, as a third-year student, she realized that she'd soon be doing just that.

Sunday afternoon. Two o'clock. Christine was working on an accounting assignment but didn't seem to be able to concentrate. Her courses were working out very well this semester, all but the OB. Much of the mark in that course was to be applied to the quality of groupwork, and so she felt somewhat out of control. She recollected the events of the past five weeks. Professor Sandra Thiel had divided the class into groups of five people and had given them a major group assignment worth 30 percent of the final grade. The task was to analyze a seven-page case and to come up with a written analysis. In addition, Sandra had asked the groups to present the case in class, with the idea in mind that the rest of the class members would be "members of the Board of Directors of the company" who would be listening to how the manager and her team dealt with the problem at hand.

Christine was elected "Team Coordinator" at the first group meeting. The other members of the group were Diane, Janet, Steve, and Mike. Diane was quiet and never volunteered suggestions, but when directly asked, she would come up with high-quality ideas. Mike was the clown. Christine remembered that she had suggested that the group should get together before every class to discuss the day's case. Mike had balked, saying "No way!! This is an 8:30 class, and I barely make it on time anyway! Besides, I'll miss my 'Happy Harry' show on television!" The group couldn't help but laugh at his indignation. Steve was the businesslike individual, always wanting to ensure that group meetings were guided by an agenda and noting the tangible results achieved or not achieved at the end of every meeting. Janet was the reliable one who would always have more for the group than was expected of her. Christine saw herself as meticulous and organized and as a person who tried to give her best in whatever she did.

It was now week five into the semester, and Christine was deep in thought about the OB assignment. She had called everyone to arrange a meeting for a time that would suit them all but seemed to be running into a roadblock. Mike couldn't make it, saying that he was working that night as a member of the campus security force. In fact, he seemed to miss most meetings and would send in brief notes to Christine, which she was supposed to discuss for him at the group meetings. She wondered how to deal with this. She also remembered the incident last week. Just before class started, Diane, Janet, Steve, and herself were joking with one another before class. They were laughing and enjoying themselves before Sandra came in. No one noticed that Mike had slipped in very quietly and had unobtrusively taken his seat.

She recalled the cafeteria incident. Two weeks ago, she had gone to the cafeteria to grab something to eat. She had rushed to her accounting class and had skipped breakfast. When she got her club sandwich and headed to the tables, she saw her OB group and joined them. The discussion was light and enjoyable as it always was when they met informally. Mike had come in. He'd approached their table. "You guys didn't say you were having a group meeting," he blurted. Christine was taken aback.

"We just happened to run into each other. Why not join us?"

"Mike looked at them, with a noncommittal glance. Yah . . . right," he muttered, and walked away.

Sandra Thiel had frequently told them that if there were problems in the group, the members should make an effort to deal with them first. If the problems could not be resolved, she had said that they should come to her. Mike seemed so distant, despite the apparent camaraderie of the first meeting.

An hour had passed, bringing the time to 3 P.M., and Christine found herself biting the tip of her pencil. The written case analysis was due next week. All the others had done their designated sections, but Mike had just handed in some rough handwritten notes. He had called Christine the week before, telling her that in addition to his course and his job, he was having problems with his girlfriend. Christine empathized with him. Yet, this was a group project! Besides, the final mark would be peer evaluated. This meant that whatever mark Sandra gave them could be lowered or raised, depending on the group's opinion about the value of the contribution of each member. She was definitely worried. She knew that Mike had creative ideas that could help to raise the overall mark. She was also concerned for him. As she listened to the music in the background, she wondered what she should do.

Review Questions

1. How could an understanding of the stages of group development assist Christine in leadership situations such as this one?
2. What should Christine understand about individual membership in groups in order to build group processes that are supportive of her work group's performance?
3. Is Christine an effective group leader in this case? Why or why not. ■

Association for Stock Car Auto Racing (NASCAR). The NASCAR Winston Cup Series—its premier league with 34 events at 22 U.S. tracks—kicks off February 7 at Daytona International Speedway and runs through November 21 with the NAPA 500 at Atlanta Motor Speedway in Atlanta.[1]

NASCAR

The Daytona, Florida-based France family owns NASCAR, making it the only family-owned professional league in the United States. In 1998, NASCAR attracted 11 million fans to race tracks and another 252 million to watch races on television.[2] Attendance at NASCAR races has jumped 80 percent since 1990 and the league's television ratings placed second in 1998 behind the NFL in sports programming. Drivers are involved in seven cable network shows and three syndicated radio shows each week. NASCAR's official Web site, at www.nascar.com, is ranked among the five most popular sites on the Internet, receiving 35 million hits each week.[3]

Celebrating its 50th anniversary in 1998, NASCAR has become a marketing powerhouse, with races, merchandise, collectibles, apparel, and co-marketing tie-ins. The Coca-Cola Co. placed images of NASCAR racing teams and drivers on 30 million soda bottles in 1998. It was the biggest promotion the soft drink company had ever done and, the company said that it sold more bottles than its annual favorite starring Santa Claus. NASCAR-licensed products generated more than $900 million in sales in 1998, up from $80 million in 1990, for licensees in 150 categories, including apparel, gifts, accessories, toys and collectibles.[4]

The race cars themselves have been described by some as "200 mile-per-hour billboards." As an

---

CASE 10
NASCAR's Racing Teams

···
Developed by David S. Chappell, Ohio University

When asked to name the fastest growing American team sport, most people respond with basketball, baseball, football, or soccer. However, that distinction, based on total spectator audience, goes to stock car racing. The largest stock car racing group in the world is the National

---

organized sport, NASCAR is unique in that its drivers are treated like independent contractors rather than employees. As such, they must behave in addition to seeking their own sponsors to finance their race teams.[5] Traditional NASCAR sponsors, including RJR Nabisco, Pennzoil-Quaker State, and General Motors have been joined by relative newcomers such as M&M/Mars, Lowe's, and Procter and Gamble. "If you look at where NASCAR was in 1993 and where it is today, you see it's a completely different sport," states Dave Elgena, senior executive vice president in charge of motorsports for MBNA. "Today you see lots of big corporations involved that wouldn't have been here six years ago."[6]

With a history of great drivers, including Richard Petty, Cale Yarborough, and Davey Pearson, a new crop of young drivers is exciting spectators. Compared to the "good-old-boys" who dominated the racing circuit for years, the new crop is younger and more sophisticated. One of the most successful young drivers in the league is Jeff Gordon, racing for Hendrick Motorsport's #24 Dupont Automotive Finishes.

Jeff Gordon—Racing Sensation

Jeff Gordon, on the Winston Cup racing scene since 1993, has been a sensation ever since he started racing go-carts and quarter-midget cars at the age of 5. In 1979 and 1981, he was the quarter-midget national champion, and in 1990 he won the 1990 USAC midget championship.[7] He has captured the imagination of race fans around the world, becoming the youngest driver ever to win three NASCAR Winston Cup overall championships and has over 40 individual race wins in a four-year span.

Gordon, 27, says his strong family upbringing in California and Indiana and his marriage to former Miss Winston beauty queen Brooke Sealy have made it easy. "There's no question Jeff has helped take our sport to the next level as far as image," said Ned Jarrett, a CBS analyst and two-time NASCAR champion during the 1960s. "He's helped raise the level of competition and also helped get the sport places it's never been before."[8] The question becomes, what does Gordon have that others have trouble imitating?

As the driver of a successful race car, Gordon represents the most visible part of an incredibly complex team of individuals—all with a contribution to make on race-day. "To build a winning team, you need three major ingredients—people, equipment and money," states Don Hawk, president of Dale Earnhardt Inc. "You can't do it with only one, not even with two, you need all three. Look at Gordon, his team has crew chief Ray Evernham and the Rainbow Warriors pit crew—their multicolored uniforms match Gordon's multicolored car, the best in the garage area, they have the fastest and most reliable Chevrolet on the track, and they have great finances from DuPont. You couldn't do what they've done with just a great driver, just a great car, or an open pocketbook. You must have all the elements meshing. I liken a winning racing team to a Rubik's Cube. All the pieces must fit, and be in the proper place."[9]

The High Performance TEAM

"Success is a ruthless competitor, for it flatters and nourishes our weakness and lulls us into complacency."

The quote above is found in the shop of Gordon's crew chief, Ray

Evernham, recognized by many in NASCAR as the premier crew chief in the business. While Gordon represents the star attraction, many believe that it's Evernham who pulls the whole act together. He is responsible for a group of over 120 technicians and mechanics and an annual budget estimated between $10 and $12 million. And he has strong opinions as to what it takes to consistently finish first: painstaking preparation, egoless teamwork, and thoroughly original strategizing—principles that apply to any high performance organization.[10]

You win as a team. Evernham believes that teams need to experiment with new methods and processes. When he assembled his Rainbow Warriors pit crew, none of them had Winston Cup experience and none worked on the car in any other capacity. With the use of a pit crew coach, the Rainbow Warriors provide Gordon with approximately one-second advantage with each pit stop, which at a speed of 200 miles-per-hour, equates into 300 feet of race track.

When you coach and support a superstar like Jeff Gordon, you give him the best equipment possible, you give him the information he needs, and then you get out of the way. But racing is a team sport. Everyone who races pretty much has the same car and the same equipment. What sets us apart is our people. I like to talk about our "team IQ"—because none of us is as smart as all of us.

I think a lot about people, management, and psychology: Specifically, how can I motivate my guys and make them gel as a team? I surround them with ideas about teamwork. I read every leadership book I can get my hands on. One thing that I took from my reading is the idea of a "circle of strength." When the Rainbow Warriors meet, we always put our chairs in a circle. That's a way of saying that we're stronger as a team than we are on our own.[11]

Evernham backs up this belief in

team by emphasizing team performance over individual performance. When the car wins a race, everyone shares in the prize money. In addition, when Evernham earns money through personal-service activities such as speaking tours and autograph signings, he shares what he earns with the team. "I wouldn't be in a position to earn that income if it weren't for the team. Everyone should feel as if his signature is on the finished product."[12]

The teamwork during a race can even include adversaries—as in other drivers. In an effort to make races competitive for fans, NASCAR uses several methods to make the cars approximately even in performance, thereby enhancing the competitive environment for the audience. To get ahead, racers depend on their friends in the form of cars that help aerodynamically "slingshot" them ahead of the pack. This may take the form of teammates (Wally Dallenbach and Terry Labonte for Hendrick Motorsports) or opponents.

Push for perfection but accept imperfection. High performance teams are constantly improving, even in small ways. Evernham makes use of every opportunity to learn something new. If the car is running well, Evernham asks Gordon to find something wrong with it. "We always try to make the car perfect. But the car doesn't have to be perfect to win; it just has to be less imperfect than everyone else's car."[13]

Don't strutt your stuff. In the past, most crews concentrated on the car and relied on horsepower and driving talent to win the race. Evernham takes a larger view that keeps the egos in check:

There aren't many secrets in the Winston Cup, so you've got to protect as much information as you can. We want to have the fastest car on the track, but we don't want everybody else to know how fast we are. We don't show our hand until it's time to race or to qualify.

We also try to mix things up on race day. We don't want to fall into patterns or to tip off the competition about our next pit stop. Since everybody can hear us on the scanners, we might use a code word to signal whether we're changing two tires or four. Sometimes, when the car is running well, Jeff might get on the radio and complain to me that the steering's tight, even though he's about to pass another driver. And that driver's crew chief will fall for it: "Yeah, Gordon can't pass you right now, because he's tight." The driver will leave a little opening and—boom—we're past him.[14]

To win the race, drive by different rules. Evernham attacks each race as different from the last. He is constantly looking for even the smallest advantage that can give his race car and driver the edge. The team practices passing cars in unsuspected areas of the track, when their competitors least expect it.[15]

High performance teams do not happen by chance; rather, they are the result of good recruiting and meticulous attention to learning every detail of the job. With 10 wins in 1997 and 13 wins in 1998, the Gordon recipe for success has resulted in three Winston Cup Series Championships. Jeff Gordon wins approximately one of every four races he starts, a pace unmatched in modern times. The question remains, can anyone catch him?

Review Questions

1. Evaluate Jeff Gordon's race team on dimensions discussed under the author's conversation on characteristics of high performance teams.
2. Discuss Jeff Gordon's race team on dimensions discussed under the author's conversation on methods to increase group cohesiveness.
3. Compare Gordon's race team on the methods of team building. Which one most applies to this situation?

References

1. Dodd, Annmarie. "The Fastest Sport on Earth—Fast-Moving and Fast-Growing, NASCAR Uses Its Loud, Folksy Appeal to Find New Racing Fans for the Future," *Daily News Record,* January 25, 1999.
2. Ibid.
3. Ibid.
4. Ibid.
5. Glick, Shav. "Dollar Signs: Sponsorships, Big Money Make NASCAR World Go 'Round," *The Los Angeles Times,* February 14, 1999, p. D1.
6. Yost, Mark. "Companies Use NASCAR Races as Means to Rub Elbows, Boost Their Business," *Wall Street Journal,* February 22, 1999, p. B17B.
7. Dodd, op. cit.
8. "NASCAR Online: Jeff Gordon," http://www.nascar.com/winstoncup/drivers/GordJ01/index.html, February 19, 1999.
9. Cain, Holly. "Gordon Becomes Driving Force," *The Seattle Times,* February 14, 1999, p. D1.
10. Glick, op. cit., p. D1.
11. Slater, Chuck. "Life in the Fast Lane," *Fast Company,* http://www.fastcompany.com/online/18/fastlane.html, October 1998.
12. Ibid.
13. Ibid.
14. Ibid.
15. Ibid.

CASE 11
First Community Financial

Developed by Mark Osborn, Arizona Chamber of Commerce

First Community Financial is a small business lender that specializes in asset-based lending and factoring for a primarily small-business clientele. First Community's business is generated by high-growth companies in diverse industries, whose capital needs will not be met by traditional banking institutions. First Community Financial will lend in amounts up to $1 million, so its focus is on small business. Since many of the loans that it administers are viewed by many banks as high-risk loans, it is important that the sales staff and loan processors have a solid working relationship. Since the loans and factoring deals that First Community finances are risky, the interest that it charges is at prime plus six percent or sometimes higher.

First Community is a credible player in the market because of its history and the human resource policies of the company. The company invests in its employees and works to assure that turnover is low. The goal of this strategy is to develop a consistent, professional team that has more expertise than its competitors.

Whereas Jim Adamany, president and CEO, has a strong history in the industry and is a recognized expert in asset-based lending and factoring, First Community has one of the youngest staff and management teams in the finance industry. In the banking industry, promotions are slow coming, because many banks employ conservative personnel programs. First Community, however, has recruited young, ambitious people who are specifically looking to grow with the company. As the company grows, so will the responsibility and rewards for these young executives. In his early thirties, for example, Matt Vincent is a vice president; at only 28, Brian Zcray, is director of marketing.

Since First Community has a diverse product line, it must compete in distinct markets. Its factoring products compete with small specialized factoring companies. Factoring is a way for businesses to improve their cash flow by selling their invoices at a discount. Factoring clients are traditionally the smallest clients finance companies must serve. Education about the nature of the product is crucial if the company is to be successful since this often is a new approach to financing for many companies. First Community's sales staff is well trained at understanding its product lines and acts as the client's representative as they work through the approval process.

To assure the loans or factoring deals fit within the risk profile of the company, First Community must ask many complex financial questions. Many small businesses are intimidated by credit officers, so First Community handles all of these inquiries through the business development officers. The business development officers, in turn, must understand the needs of their credit officers, who are attempting to minimize risk to the company while maintaining a friendly rapport with the client. By centralizing the client contract through educated sales representatives, First Community is able to ask the hard financial questions and still keep the clients interested in the process. A potential customer can easily be discouraged by

a creditor administrator's strong questioning about financial background. Utilizing the business development officers as an intermediary reduces the fear of many applicants about the credit approval process. Thus, a sales focus is maintained throughout the recruitment and loan application process.

Internally at First Community Financial there is a continual pressure between the business development staff and the credit committee. The business development staff is focused on bringing in new clients. Their compensation in a large part is dependent on how many deals they can execute for the company. Like sales staff in any industry, they are aggressive and always look for new markets for business. The sales staff sells products from both the finance department and the factoring department, so they must interact with credit officers from each division. In each of these groups are credit administrators specifically responsible for ensuring that potential deals meet the lending criteria of the organization. While the business development officer's orientation is to bring in more and more deals, the credit administrator's primary goal is to limit bad loans.

The pressure develops when business development officers bring in potential loans that are rejected by the credit administrators. Since the business development officers have some experience understanding the credit risks of their clients, they often understand the policy reasoning for denying or approving a loan. The business development officers have additional concerns that their loans that have potential to be financed are approved because many of the referral sources of the sales staff will only refer deals to companies who are lending. If First Community fails to help many of a bank's referral clients, that source of business may dry up, as bankers refer deals to other lending institutions.

These structural differences are handled by focused attempts at improving communication. As noted before, the First Community staff experiences an extremely low turnover rate. This allows for the development of a cohesive team. With a cohesive staff, the opportunity to maintain frank and open communication helps bridge the different orientations of the sales staff and the administration divisions. A simple philosophy that the opinions of all staff are to be respected is continually implemented.

Since approving a loan is often a policy decision, the sales staff and the loan administrators can have an open forum to discuss whether a loan will be approved. CEO Jim Adamany approves all loans, but since he values the opinions of all of his staff he provides them all an opportunity to communicate. Issues such as the loan history for an applicant's industry, current bank loan policies, and other factors can be openly discussed from multiple perspectives.

Review Questions

1. What coordinative mechanisms does First Community use to manage the potential conflict between its sales and finance/auditing functions?
2. What qualities should First Community emphasize in hiring new staff to ensure that its functional organizational structure will not yield too many problems?
3. What are the key types of information transfer that First Community needs to emphasize, and how is this transmitted throughout the firm?
4. Why might a small finance company have such a simple structure while a larger firm might find this structure inappropriate? ■

CASE 12
Mission Management and Trust
· · · · · · · · · · · · · · ·

Developed by Mark Osborn, Arizona Chamber of Commerce

With more than 500 business and political leaders in attendance from across the state of Arizona, CEO Carmen Bermudez of Mission Management and Trust accepted the prestigious ATHENA Award. The ATHENA, which is presented by the Arizona Chamber of Commerce, is annually awarded to companies that have a demonstrated track record in promoting women's issues within their company and the community. The 50-pound bronze statute that was presented to Mission Management and Trust was particularly special for the company's leadership because it was a tangible demonstration of their commitment to the community and to women's issues.

Mission Management and Trust is a small newly formed company of just eight employees that has already made great headway in an industry that is dominated by giant corporations. Mission Management and Trust opened its doors just two years ago, and it already manages over $45 million in assets. What makes Mission's development even more impressive is that Mission is the first minority- and women-owned trust company in the nation.

The trust management industry provides services to individuals, organizations, and companies who want their assets managed and protected by specialized outside firms. Mission management provides personal service to its customers at a level of sophistication that is unusual for a firm of its small size. Understanding that the trust management business is highly competitive, Mission developed a unique strategy that highlighted socially conscious policies combined with good business relations.

When the company was formed in 1994, it was created with more than the goal of just making a profit. Founder Carmen Bermudas started Mission with three principal goals in mind. "1. To run a top quality trust company; 2. To promote within the company and, by example, increase opportunities for women and minorities; and 3. To donate a portion of all revenue to charitable projects supported by clients and staff." As these statements demonstrate, Mission Management and Trust was created with a specific purpose in mind that was focused not just on the business of trust management but on the responsibility of being a good corporate citizen.

Even with these lofty goals, Mission faced the problem of finding clients who not only wanted quality services but were not hindered by some of the potential sacrifices a socially conscious investment company might make. Many investors want a high rate of return for their trusts, and social policy is of a much lesser concern. This was not the market Mission wanted to address, so it had to be selective in developing a client base.

Mission needed to find clients

that fit its social philosophy about investing and corporate responsibility. The ideal customers would be individuals and organizations that were committed to socially conscious policies and wanted an investment strategy that reflected this commitment. Mission found a perfect niche in the market with religious institutions. Churches and other civic organizations across the nation have trusts that they use to fund special projects and maintain operating expenses. They need effective service, but in many cases these organizations must be mindful of investing in companies and other projects that do not refelct their ideals. For example, a trust company that invests in companies in the highly profitable liquor and cigarette industries would not be consistent with the philosophy of many religious organizations. Mission services this niche by developing an organization that is structurally designed to make socially conscious decisions.

Mission has already begun to meet one of its principal goals, which is to donate a portion of its profits to charities. By the end of 1994, Mission had already donated $4500 to causes ranging from Catholic Community Services to the Jewish Community Center scholarship program. These donations not only fulfill a goal of the organization but assist in the socially conscious client recruitment. Mission's target client base will find Mission a much more attractive trust company because of its charity programs. A religious organization can be comforted with the reality that some of the dollars it spends on trust management will be recycled into the causes it promotes itself. The mission policy makes good social policy, but it also makes good marketing sense. Understanding your clients is crucial to developing a small business, and Mission has mastered this principle.

Mission makes the most of its commitment to charitable causes by keeping its clients informed about the trust's activities and, more importantly, its community activities. *The Mission Bell,* a regular publication of Mission Management and Trust, details news and issues about the trust industry, company activities, and, most importantly, how Mission's social responsibility philosophy is being implemented. The name *Mission Bell* is more consistent with a religious publication than a corporate investing sheet, but it is consistent with its clients' needs. The name of the publication and its content clarifies Mission's role and purpose. For example, the *Mission Bell Summer Issue* presented articles on new hires, breaking investment news, and an article about how Mission is working with other groups to support socially responsible corporate investing. Thus, the Mission philosophy is clearly defined in its marketing and communication strategies.

To be consistent with the goals of the organizations, Carmen Bremudez collected a small staff of highly experienced individuals whose backgrounds and principles fit Mission's ideals. She frequently comments that the best business decision she ever made was "giving preference to intelligent, talented, compatible people whose main attribute was extensive experience." Mission employees are not just experts in the field of finance but leaders in their communities. These dual qualifications fulfill three important requirements that are crucial for the company's success. With community involvement comes an appreciation of the investment sensitivities that are required by the organizations that Mission services. Second, individuals who are involved in the community have well-developed contacts that can be useful in

business recruitment. Finally, socially active employees are committed to the purpose of the organization and help unify the corporate culture within Mission.

Claire B. Moore, vice president of Mission Management and Trust, is a perfect example of how a corporate philosophy has been translated into practical personnel decisions. Claire was recruited because she had extensive banking experience, as demonstrated by her vice president position in Bank of America (Arizona). Her professional qualifications are augmented by her extensive involvement in the community, which includes the University of Arizona Foundation Planned Giving Council, Tucson Symphony, and the Junior League, to name a few.

The Mission case is a clear example of how matching a philosophy with a market can bear solid results. Mission's commitment to its ideals is evident and reflected in all of their business practices. When human resources, investing, marketing, and strategic planning decisions are made with unified goals in mind, the chances are good that a strong successful corporate culture will develop.

Review Questions

1. How do the mission elements of Mission Management differ from most firms?
2. Does donating to charity before the firm is fully established mean that Mission is not demonstrating financial prudence?
3. Could Mission's unique mission contribute to effective coordination as well as adjustment to the market?
4. Would Mission's unique mission still yield success with more traditional investors? ■

CASE 13
Motorola: Is a High Performance Culture Enough?

Developed by David S. Chappell, Ohio University

Motorola Inc., world famous for its Six Sigma quality control program, was an early success story in the computer/electronics age. Motorola moved from being a decentralized but integrated, narrowly focused electronics firm at $3 billion in 1980 to being a decentralized and disintegrated broad portfolio firm at $27 billion in 1997.[1] Motorola is one of the world's leading providers of wireless communications, semiconductors, electronic systems, components, and services. Its cellular phone and pager products were identified among the very best in the early 1990s. However, increased competition, the Asian economic crisis, and its failure to fully embrace the digital revolution have severely tarnished its operating results and image. Can Motorola return to its high performance ways?

The Evolution of Motorola

Motorola Inc. was founded by Paul V. Galvin in 1928, as the Galvin Manufacturing Corporation. Motorola's long history of technological innovation began in the 1930s with the first car radio. Under the brand name "Motorola," suggesting "sound in motion" the company name was changed to Motorola, Inc. in 1947.[2] Being the sound of innovation, it was Motorola's goal to provide products that would give people the time and freedom to explore new worlds and handle daily tasks in the most efficient way.

Motorola represents a large number of firsts, including the first rectangular television picture tube, first practical car radio, pagers, and more. In 1988, Motorola won the first Malcolm Baldridge National Quality Award in recognition of quality in American business. This is the

Note: The blue underscored words/phrases in this case indicate Internet links provided in the on-line version. See the *Organizational Behavior, Seventh Edition* Web Site at http://www.wiley.com/college/schermerhorn.

same year that George Fisher (now president of Kodak) became president of the firm; he is credited by many with bringing Motorola into the cellular age.

Beginning in 1987, Motorola began the design of IRIDIUM. The system is a satellite-based, wireless communications network. It consists of 66 interconnected, low-orbiting satellites that deliver voice, data, fax and paging through a hand-held phone. The system will simplify communications for business professionals, travelers, residents and other users, permitting them to reach any destination on Earth. Along with Motorola, Sprint and Iridium Canada are contributing to the development of IRIDIUM system to the North American continent. The development of IRIDIUM will provide customers with high-quality service at a reasonable rate.

As Motorola continued to expand its worldwide presence in the global marketplace through products and services, the need for talented personnel to uphold these established standards has increased. In recognition of this essentiality, Motorola has demonstrated a high commitment to seeking and developing a broad base of knowledgeable, highly trained employees, evident through their innovative training programs, through the establishment of Motorola University, and through the offering of expansive benefit plans to all associates.

The Importance of Organizational Culture to Motorola

In the early 1990s, Motorola was recognized as a true high performance organization with its innovations and socially responsible corporate attitude. Indeed, its organizational culture is identified as a source of competitive advantage for the firm. Working in quality teams, members strive to provide the highest level of customer satisfaction, measuring defects in incidents per billion. Motorola earmarks more than $100 million a year for training, with everyone in the organization, however humble, spending at least a week a year back in the classroom at Motorola University, courtesy of the company.[3]

Motorola lists its fundamental objective as total customer satisfaction: "To serve every customer better than our competitors do with products and services of excellent value and quality, and thereby earn continued enthusiastic trust and support."[4] It wishes to accomplish this objective with respect for the individual, a statement it makes clear in its shared beliefs.

People
To treat each employee with dignity, as an individual; to maintain an open atmosphere where direct communication with employees affords the opportunity to contribute to the maximum of their potential and fosters unity of purpose with Motorola; to provide personal opportunities for training and development to ensure the most capable and most effective work force; to respect senior service;

to compensate fairly by salary, benefits and, where possible, incentives; to promote on the basis of capability; and to practice the commonly accepted policies of equal opportunity and affirmative action.

Integrity and Ethics

To maintain the highest standards of honesty, integrity and ethics in all aspects of our business—with customers, suppliers, employees, governments and society at large—and to comply with the laws of each country and community in which we operate.[5]

From a proponent of leadership training to a leader in quality control processes, Motorola has created an internal climate that fosters high standards and a high performance culture. The firm depends on Total Customer Satisfaction Teams (TCS) to ensure the firm's commitment to quality. These teams are now made up of almost 30 percent of Motorola's 150,000 employees, and a goal of 10 times reduction of defects every two years puts pressure on them to constantly devise new ways to develop and deliver their products and services.

Motorola views itself as family and encourages employees to balance their work and family responsibilities. They support onsite child care centers and fund a wellness program for all employees.

Authors John Kotter and James Hesket's study on corporate culture shows that:

1. Corporate culture can have a significant impact on a firm's long-term economic performance.
2. Corporate culture will probably be an even more important factor in determining the success or failure of firms in the next decade.
3. Corporate cultures that inhibit strong long-term financial performance are not rare; they develop easily, even in firms that are full of reasonable and intelligent people.

4. Although tough to change, corporate cultures can be made more performance enhancing.[6]

Organizational culture can be a two-edged sword, however. Strong cultures may contribute to high performance for extended periods of time but may actually result in an inability to adjust when conditions change. It's important to foster a balance between stability and flexibility for change, an objective that is difficult to maintain. For many firms, success in the short term causes problems with inflexibility to changing situations in the long term.

So What Went Wrong?

In early June 1998, Motorola CEO Chris Galvin announced that the company would take a $1.95 billion charge and lay off 15,000 employees. Motorola's semiconductor business, which grew 23 percent in 1995, slowed to a 1 percent growth rate early in 1998. In recent years Motorola's stock has dropped 40 points, to a low of $50 in 1998, and its share of the U.S. cellular phone market has plummeted to 41 percent from 54 percent. "It's kind of depressing," moans one money manager. "It's not as though people weren't barking and screaming to management about what was going wrong."[7]

Maggie Wilderotter, a former top executive with AT&T Wireless Services and its predecessor, McCaw Cellular, lends insight into Motorola's troubles. In the early 1990s, 85 percent of the cell phones McCaw sold to subscribers were made by Motorola, whose flip phones, the most advanced at the time, were in hot demand. Around that time McCaw decided that the future of cellular was digital, and over the next few years Wilderotter met repeatedly with managers at Motorola's Schaumberg, Illinois,

headquarters and in her Seattle office, urging them to develop a digital phone. Motorola said it would work on it. So in the beginning of 1996, not long after AT&T Wireless had rolled out its digital network, Motorola unveiled its StarTAC phone: light, beautiful—and analog. AT&T had no choice but to turn to cellular phone manufacturers Nokia and Ericsson for digital handsets. By the end of 1997, fewer than 40 percent of AT&T Wireless' cell phones were Motorolas.

"It was bizarre," says Wilderotter, now CEO of Wink Communications, an interactive-TV company. "We were very forthright with what we wanted. I don't know if they didn't listen or they thought it wasn't going to happen. It is absolutely amazing to me that they lost their way."[8] In 1998, Nokia replaced Motorola as the leading supplier of mobile handsets, a position Motorola had held since the mobile phone industry began. Nokia sold 37.4 million units (an 81.5 percent increase from the previous year), representing a 22.9 percent market share compared to Motorola's 32.3 million units (only a 27.6 percent increase in volume), representing a 19.8 percent share.[9]

Much of Nokia's success is based on its digital technology, which accounted for 84.6 percent of the 163 million phones sold worldwide in 1998. Motorola remains the world leader in the declining analog handset sector, perhaps because of its presence in the U.S. market where digital has been slower to take off. Even with Motorola's introduction of a digital alternative to its popular StarTAC model, it retails for $500, compared to Nokia's 6100 at $200 and twice the battery life.[10]

Inspection of the company's IRIDIUM satellite system uncovers other weaknesses. The system eliminates "dead cells" by providing complete global coverage for cellular services. However, it comes with a price. The Motorola 9500 phone costs around $3000, and calls are priced anywhere from $1.75 to $7 a minute. The phone is bulky—about the size and weight of cell phones 10 years ago—with a thick, black antenna. In addition, the system needs an unobstructed view of the sky, with tall buildings and even dense foliage blocking transmissions.[11] With AT&T and others offering near unlimited long distance cellular service in the U.S. for under $90 per month, does the Motorola system make sense for anyone but the most remotely located employee?

Some of Motorola's problems are external, including a drop in semiconductor sales due to the Asian economic crisis, increased competition in cellular products, and a decline in pager sales. Motorola is attempting to restructure its operations in combination with cost-cutting measures. However, its situation illuminates the need for a culture that is both strong and responsive to external factors. In the quickly changing high-technology field, companies are forced to make difficult and costly choices among competing technologies.

Another concern for many is the presence of Chris Galvin, 48, as chief executive since January 1997. Unlike his predecessors, Chris has no engineering background; he studied marketing at Northwestern and rose through the sales side of the business. He intends to break down internal rivalries within the company and to create links between Motorola and other technology companies.[12] The question remains: Can Motorola regain its dominant market position without painful adjustments to its organizational culture? And can Chris Galvin lead them into a new era?

Review Questions

1. Discuss Motorola's relative success at the two functions/components of organizational culture discussed by the author.
2. Compare the various levels (observable, shared values, and common assumptions) of corporate culture at Motorola.
3. Discuss the various options managers might use in attempting to change the culture at Motorola.

References

1. Canavan, Patrick. "Motorola: Agility for the Whole Organization," *Human Resource Planning,* September 1998, p. 13(1).
2. "Motorola Homepage— Timeline," http://www.mot.com/General/Timeline/timeln24.html, March 4, 1999.
3. "Managing People: Nicely Does It," *The Economist,* March 19, 1994, p. 84. "Motorola Homepage—Culture," http://www.mot.com/Employment/stand.htm, March 19, 1999.
4. "Organizational Culture Alignment," http://www.msdev.com/culture.htm, March 7, 1999.
5. Ibid.
6. Roth, Daniel. "From Poster Boy to Whipping Boy: Burying Motorola," *Fortune,* July 6, 1998, p. 28(2).
7. Ibid.
8. Cane, Alan. "Nokia Seizes Top Spot in Mobile Phones," *Financial Times* (London), February 8, 1999, p. 22.
9. Ibid.
10. Peltz, Michael. "Hard Cell," *Worth,* March 1999, pp. 45–47.
11. Mossberg, Walter. "Cures for PC Boredom: A Truly Global Phone and a Better Palm Pilot," *Wall Street Journal,* March 11, 1999, p. B1.
12. Peltz, op. cit.

CASE 14
Perot Systems: Can a High Performance Company Have a Human Side?

Although computers have been around for decades, only in the 1990s has their full application potential been realized by companies around the world. Leading the way are internationally recognized Information Technology (IT) service firms, including IBM, Electronic Data Systems (EDS), consulting firms such as Andersen Consulting, Computer Sciences, and Cap Gemini. The U.S. Department of Commerce tabulated 1997 sales in the consulting, systems integration, and project management computer services industry at $90 billion.[1] A relatively recent but important entrant into this field is Perot Systems, which began in 1988 by Ross Perot. As the sixth largest IT firm in the world, can Perot Systems provide solutions for the elusive goal of fully integrated management systems in large, global organizations?

Note: The blue underscored words/phrases in this case indicate Internet links provided in the online version. See the *Organizational Behavior, Seventh Edition* Web Site at http://www.wiley.com/college/schermerhorn.

A Rich History

<u>Ross Perot</u> is one of the true masters of the American economic free enterprise system. Born in Texarkana, Texas on June 27, 1930, he has led a life filled with one significant achievement after another. Having lived his whole childhood in Texarkana, he entered the U.S. Naval Academy in 1949, where he served as class president and battalion commander, an experience that even to this day motivates him to hire many of his top company officers from ex-military personnel.

Upon his discharge from the navy, Ross married and began working for IBM's data processing division as a salesman. In 1962, with $1000, he started a one-man data processing company which he called Electronic Data Systems. Drawing on his experience in the military, in addition to recruiting a large number of ex-military personnel, Perot was able to build his firm into the premier data processing company in the U.S.

In 1984, <u>EDS</u> was sold to <u>General Motors</u> for $2.5 billion. GM wanted to greatly increase its use of technology in its manufacturing process and viewed its EDS purchase as an effective way of meeting this goal. As a result of the purchase, Ross Perot became one of the single largest holders of General Motors and a director in the company. However, Perot had great difficulty adjusting to GM's bureaucratic, autocratic management style, and he was eventually bought out of GM in 1986. After waiting the required two-year noncompete period, he started Perot Systems in 1988.[2] Interestingly, GM spun EDS off in 1996, as it became obvious that the two entities did not make a good fit.

Throughout his career, Ross Perot has always been a model of citizen volunteerism. In 1969, the U.S. government asked him to determine what action could be taken to assist the prisoners-of-war in Southeast Asia. In recognition for his work, he received the Medal for Distinguished Public Service, the highest civilian award presented by the Department of Defense.[3] In 1992 and again in 1996, Ross Perot ran for president of the United States representing a new third party, the <u>Reform Party</u>, which he founded as an alternative to the Republican and Democratic parties.

Perot's campaign efforts forced him to step down from daily involvement in Perot Systems. That year, <u>Mort Meyerson</u>, who had helped him build EDS into a world-recognized leader in data processing, stepped in to assume the chief executive officer duties. Although he had worked closely with Perot at EDS, Meyerson did not share Perot's desire to recreate EDS's "young, male, military model" corporate climate at Perot Systems.[4] He was convinced that times had changed.

In purely financial terms, my seven years running EDS had been unbelievably successful. When I left, I was very proud of the people, the company, and our achievements. From the day I started as president in 1979 to the day I left in 1986, EDS never had a single quarter where we lost money. We never even had a quarter where we were flat—every quarter we grew like gangbusters. That kind of economic performance made a lot of our people very rich. I used to take enormous pride in the fact that I was instrumental in getting a lot of equity into the hands of the people at EDS.

What I realized after I left was that I had also made a lot of people very unhappy. Our people paid a high price for their economic success. Eighty-hour weeks were the norm. We shifted people from project to project and simply expected them to make the move, no questions asked. We called our assignments "death marches"—without a trace of irony. You were expected to do whatever it took to get the job done. In terms of priorities, work was in first place; family, community, other obligations all came after.[5]

Meyerson's concern was the emphasis on profit at the expense of people. He believed that technology, customers, the market, and what people in organizations wanted from their work had all changed from his previous time at EDS.[6] He asked himself two fundamental questions:

1. To get rich, do you have to be miserable?
2. To be successful, do you have to punish your customers?

Meyerson wanted to move Perot Systems toward a corporate model that recognized that the larger issues in life mattered as much as the demands for profit-and-loss. Listening to a senior manager talk about how they handled low performers on teams bothered him.

I heard talk of "drive-by shootings" to "take out" nonperformers; then they'd "drag the body around" to make an example out of them. They may have meant it only as a way of talking, but I saw it as more: abusive language that would influence behavior. Left unchallenged, these expressions would pollute the company's culture.[7]

Meyerson was fully aware that he had not only supported this environment at EDS, but encouraged it. As president for seven years, he had been largely responsible for the high performance atmosphere that demanded so much from EDS employees. He tells a story in which an employee named Max missed a day of work due to a snowstorm and how Meyerson himself called the employee at home to question his loyalty to EDS. The employee took the first opportunity he could and left EDS. He was Max Hopper, who later went on to design the highly successful <u>SABRE</u> reservation system for <u>American Airlines</u>.[8]

None of that happened by accident. I had helped design EDS to operate this way, using the compensation system to motivate people: I tied their pay to profit-and-loss performance. If you ran your project very profitably, you were richly rewarded. If you didn't, you weren't. I routinely spent an extraordinary amount of my time on compensation and rewards—roughly 15 percent. I did it because I knew that compensation mattered most.

The system worked; that is, we got exactly what we wanted. We asked people to put financial performance before everything else, and they did. They drove themselves to do whatever was necessary to create those results—even if it meant too much personal sacrifice or doing things that weren't really in the best interests of customers. Sometimes they did things that produced positive financial results in the short term but weren't in the company's long term interest. That's a charge you'd usually apply to a CEO—but I've never heard it said about individuals down to the lowest ranks of a company. Yet my pay-for-performance approach effectively encouraged that behavior from all of our people.[9]

Upon his arrival at Perot Systems, Meyerson inherited a company of 1500 employees and a revenue of $170 million. His initial effort went into meeting with the top 100 leaders in the company. Through these conversations, Meyerson concluded that he had heard "a laundry list of horrifying bad news."[10] He set about to change the company's culture, including a training seminar that over two-thirds of the firm's employees (including Meyerson) attended. Individuals who could not adjust were asked to leave. Meyerson's objective was clear:

We still tell people we'll give them everything we can in the way of financial rewards. In fact, more than 60 percent of our company is owned by the people who run the company. So if we go public someday, we'll still make a lot of our people very rich.

But we will have done it without having first made them miserable—by offering them another dimension they can't get in most other high performance

companies: a human organization. If any of our people has an interest outside the company, we will encourage and support them; if they have needs outside the company, we will recognize them.[11]

Meyerson's other major concern was how EDS had treated customers. He described negotiations as intense, with EDS's desire to win every penny possible from the customer. Not just to win, but to dominate.[12] At Perot Systems, Meyerson promoted a much closer working relationship with customers and designed the reward system to reflect this newfound cooperation.

Here again, at Perot Systems, I turned to the compensation system to help us live the lesson. We use 360-degree evaluations for our people—asking boss, peers, and subordinates to participate—and always include input from our customers. We also ask our customers to give us report cards—and then we temper bonuses based on customer ratings of how well we support their needs.[13]

Similar to other information technology service firms, Perot Systems concentrates on particular industry groups in order to provide enhanced expertise. These include financial services, energy, travel and transportation, health care, communication, manufacturing, and construction.[14] Several of the contracts that Perot Systems obtained reflect this new corporate vision.

Project: Avis Rent A Car

Avis Rent A Car System, Inc. selected Perot Systems Corporation to provide and maintain a state-of-the-art imaging and workflow solution for customer document processing in its Garden City, N.Y. World Headquarters and Virginia Beach, Va. Processing Center. The decision places Avis on the cutting edge of technological advancements, and the services agreement frees Avis to focus on what they do best, serving their customers.[15]

The change from data processing to systems integration has been motivated by globalization and the need for full supply-chain management. Companies depend on information systems to tie all the functional areas, including marketing, customer support, logistics, service, and operations together into a seamless whole. Rather than develop these competencies on their own, companies are increasingly depending on outside consultants such as Perot Systems to provide the expertise to run these complicated systems.

The New Face of Leadership?

Consistent with Mort Meyerson's new attitude toward business was a new emphasis on the shifting face of leadership. He concludes that the new leadership entails three jobs:

- **Make sure that the organization knows itself.** Meyerson suggests that the leader's primary purpose is to support and embody certain core principles that identify the organization. These values do not have so much to do with business strategy, tactics, or market share; rather, they have to do with human relationships and the obligation of the organization to its individual members and its customers.
- **Pick the right people and create an environment where those people can succeed.** In this sense, the leader is more coach than executive. This requires collaboration and teamwork among people at every level of the company. The leader is not viewed as the final authority in decision making; the team represents the source of knowledge.
- **Be accessible to the people in the organization.** Meyerson

insists that he be in E-mail contact with all employees of the company. He personally answers thousands of E-mail messages every month. No longer is the leader an individual who shows up every six months to deliver a pep rally speech. And the leader must be accessible on issues and concerns that transcend the traditional boundaries of work and the company.[18]

Can a High Performance Company Have a Human Side?

While Mort Meyerson worked to develop his new view of leadership, Perot Systems struggled to earn a consistent profit. As one of the smaller players in the information technology field, Perot Systems' higher costs and lower net earnings troubled Mr. Perot. Operating margins at Perot Systems averaged 5.3 percent versus 7.7 percent at rival EDS.[19] Since 1996, the company has

---

> ### Project: California Electrical Grid
>
> The ISO Alliance, a limited liability company owned jointly by ABB Power T&D Co. and Perot Systems Corp., has been awarded a contract to develop and implement one of the most critical new business systems the state of California will need to operate its electricity markets under deregulation. The new systems will help the state administer the bidding and manage the usage of its power grid to ensure reliable service — much the same way an air traffic control system coordinates take-off and landings at airports to maintain order and manage congestion. California is the largest power market in the United States, with approximately $27 billion in electricity commerce per year.[16]

---

gone through three management changes and in the strongest stock market in history — one led by technology issues — a public offering has been repeatedly delayed. Unhappy with these conditions, Mr. Perot chose to return to day-to-day operations in late 1997.

Initially announced as interim CEO, Perot has evolved into Perot Systems' full-time chief executive officer. "He has centralized reviews of spending and new contracts. He has directed every supervisor to attend a leadership training course that reinforces his precepts. He has cut expenses, stepped up recruiting from the military, reinstated mandatory drug testing, and assigned a reading list including his autobiography. He has promoted executives with military backgrounds who have been with him for decades, since his days as commander in chief of Electronic Data Systems. White shirts are in, and, under his current thinking, same-sex partners' health benefits will be out."[20]

Not everyone is convinced that Mr. Perot can provide the same type of spectacular returns as he did in his EDS heyday. "The wheel he's trying to reinvent is rusty," an executive at a rival company said.[21] When he stepped aside as Perot Systems' chief networked personal computers were just beginning to spread. E-mail addresses (Mr. Perot does not use E-mail; he relies on face-to-face communication) and Internet access were largely the domain of military overlords and university scientists, and Perot Systems was doing mostly standard corporate work on central computers.[22]

"At EDS, he built an organization that was based on command and control," said Allie Young, an analyst at Dataquest, the industry research firm in San Jose, California. "It was 'my way or the highway.' At that time, that type of model worked. Companies wanted that. Today it's very different. Senior executives are involved in the deci-

---

> ### Swiss Air
>
> March 4, 1997 — Perot Systems Corporation today announced it has purchased a controlling stake from SwissAir Corp. in Icarus Consulting AG, a Zurich- and Frankfurt-based management consulting firm that serves the travel and transportation industries in Europe.
>
> Founded in 1988, Icarus had been owned 55 percent by SAir Group, the holding company of SwissAir, and 45 percent by Icarus's management, respectively. After today's agreement, Perot Systems will have a 70 percent stake in Icarus, with a fixed option to purchase the remaining 30 percent from SAir Group over a three-year period.
>
> As an example of its work, Icarus recently conceived and implemented a new air cargo system that combined the services of SwissAir and Sabena Airlines. Under this unique arrangement, Sabena has essentially sold its airline cargo space to SwissCargo, the SAir Group's cargo arm, giving up marketing and operational costs in exchange for a guaranteed revenue stream. SwissCargo gains added capacity and market share and can utilize its existing sales infrastructure much more efficiently.
>
> "This is a good example of the consolidation of core competencies by major air carriers," said Ludwig Bertsch, the Zurich-based managing director of Icarus. "In the coming years we will see some airlines specializing in the design and management of hub systems and routes designs as network managers. Others will excel in flight operations. Still others will create strong niches in catering, cargo services, or maintenance."[17]

---

sion making for contracts, very often the CEO. Information technology is a strategic decision. They don't want anything railroaded by them. They want a business partner."[23] The question is: Will Mr. Perot's command and control approach work in this new environment?

The IPO

On February 2, 1999, Morgan Stanley Dean Witter conducted Perot Systems' IPO at $16 per share, valuing it at $1.35 billion in the New York Stock Exchange flotation. By mid-afternoon, the price had risen $26 1/2 to a value of $42 1/2, thereby increasing Perot Systems' value to $3.6 billion. Analysts credited the movement to the current clamor for information technology shares and the glamour of Ross Perot's name. Perot's personal stake in the firm increased from $553 million to $1.4 billion on the move. (His personal wealth is estimated at $3.7 billion.)[24]

It remains to be seen whether Mr. Perot's leadership style can turn Perot Systems into a major force in the information technology field. With competitors over 12 times larger, competition remains intense. EDS announced a deal with MCI Worldcom in which EDS takes over much of MCI's computer operations while MCI provides telephone and data communications services to EDS. MCI had determined that its computer services unit was just too small to compete for contracts.[25] Can Ross Perot make the difference Perot Systems needs?

Review Questions

1. Compare Mr. Meyerson's leadership style versus Mr. Perot's based on the Michigan and Ohio State behavioral theories of leadership.
2. Utilizing Fiedler's Contingency Theory of Leadership, explain how either Meyerson's or Perot's style might be most appropriate based on specific characteristics of the situation at Perot Systems.
3. Evaluate the situation at Perot Systems from the point of view of the discussion on New Leadership.

References

1. John Mitchell. "Hoovers Industry Snapshot—Computer Software Industry," *Hoovers Online,* http://www.hoovers.com/features/industry/software1.html, February 5, 1999.
2. "Ross Perot Biography," *Perot Official World Wide Web Site,* http://www.perot.org/hrpbio.htm, December 17, 1998.
3. Ibid.
4. Allan Myerson, "Perot's Return to Business: The Vote's Not In," *New York Times,* February 22, 1998, p. 3:1.
5. Mort Meyerson, "Everything I Thought I Knew About Leadership Is Wrong," *Fast Company,* April/May 1996, pp. 5–11.
6. Ibid.
7. Ibid.
8. Ibid.
9. Ibid.
10. Ibid.
11. Ibid.
12. Ibid.
13. Ibid.
14. "Perot Systems Homepage," http://www.perotsystems.com, February 17, 1999.
15. "Avis Selects Perot Systems for Imaging and Workflow Solution," *Business Wire,* April 8, 1996, p. 4081260.
16. "Companies to manage California energy grid," *Electric Light & Power,* September 1997, p. 28.
17. "Perot Systems Takes Major Stake in SwissAir Unit; Consulting Organization, Icarus, Serves European Airlines," *Business Wire,* March 4, 1997, p. 03041322.
18. Meyerson, op.cit., pp. 10–11.
19. Wendy Zellner and Linda Himelstein, "Why Perot May Go with an IPO," *Business Week,* August 10, 1998, p. 65.
20. Meyerson, op. cit.
21. Ibid.
22. Ibid.
23. Ibid.
24. Andrew Cave, "Perot Systems' Shares Leap 165pc During Market Debut," *The Daily Telegraph,* February 3, 1999.
25. Mike Mills, "MCI to Sell Unit to EDS," *Washington Post,* February 12, 1999, p. E01. ∎

CASE 15

Power or Empowerment at GM?

Developed by Aneil Mishra, Pennsylvania State University, Karen Mishra, Pennsylvania State University, and Kim Cameron, Brigham Young University

Introduction

Effective September 25, 1990, the management of the General Motors (GM) Parma, Ohio, stamping plant finalized another three-year local agreement with the United Auto Workers' Union (UAW), Local 1005. It was the second local agreement they had negotiated together *on time* and *without intervention* from Detroit, since Parma's self-described revolutionary agreement seven years previously. It was revolutionary because Parma's management and union had abandoned their old hostilities and incorporated a team-based approach to work, setting Parma in a new direction. The 1990 agreement formally documented their joint priorities of team-based work groups, extensive employee training, and a supportive working environment. The assistant personnel director for hourly employment, Bill Marsh, felt that, although this was another positive step in their ongoing relationship with Local 1005, the negotiating process seemed more "traditional" than the previous negotiation in 1987. Bob Lintz, the plant manager, agreed. Unexpectedly, the new Shop Committee chairman, who is Local 1005's prime negotiator, had introduced over 600 demands at the start of Parma's local contract negotiation. Even though management and the union were still able to finalize an agreement quickly, the tension created by the enormous list of demands still lingered. It could destroy the collaborative relationship that had been built over the past decade between management and the union leadership as well as the openness that Bob Lintz had managed to foster between himself and the hourly employees.

Background

In the early 1980s, Parma's corporate parent, GM, conducted a capacity rationalization study that concluded that almost 75 percent of Parma's operations should either be eliminated or tranferred to other GM facilities within three years. Despite a one-year lapse in formal relations, and with no contract in effect, Parma's management and Local 1005 responded to this threat to plant survival by conducting a joint effort to bring in new business. This joint effort led to a number of competitive assessments of Parma's operations that identified several noncompetitive work practices. To acknowledge

formally this new collaborative relationship, a new labor agreement was drafted and ratified in 1983 by Parma's rank and file that resulted in fewer work classifications and emphasized a team-based approach to managing work groups.[1]

To implement this agreement, Parma's top management and Local 1005 created the Team Concept Implementation Group, or TCIG, to introduce this new Team Concept and spent $40 million on extensive training of the entire workforce in problem solving, group dynamics, and effective communication skills. By 1990, the Team Concept had empowered hourly employees to assume more responsibility in their jobs and to focus on problem-solving and work-related matters and to move beyond status differences exemplified by position titles or neckties.

Roger Montgomery, who had chaired the Shop Committee from 1981 until 1990, felt that he had been able to put aside his past doubts of management's sincerity and work with Bob to create an environment based on teamwork and trust. He credits Bob's sincerity and openness with their ability to respect each other and work together for the good of the plant and its jobs. Roger believed that Bob had to overcome significant obstacles in creating this collaborative relationship at Parma, especially in convincing members of management and supervision. After years of open hostility between management and labor, Roger knew that Bob had supervisors and managers who didn't want to change. After years of fighting for employees by getting doors on bathroom stalls and eliminating hall passes, Roger felt that his union team had achieved greater consensus about the need for change. He felt lucky because even though some of his shop committee might not have agreed with

him about every detail, they did support his efforts out of loyalty to him and to his relationship with Bob. Bob Lintz also felt that his managers and Local 1005's leaders had worked hard to overcome decades-long hostilities and build a positive and collaborative relationship.[2]

Current Situation

Bob and his managers are concerned about the tension that has been created by the new Shop Committee chairman's large number of demands, especially because the union made only about 100 demands during the previous contract negotiations. Roger had publicly endorsed this new chairman of the Shop Committee, yet management was not certain that he would continue Roger's strategy of collaboration within the union and between management and the union. With several new individuals in the union leadership, Parma's management also had to consider the possibility that the entire union leadership was actually becoming more adversarial, especially as the two political factions within the union continued to compete for support among members of Local 1005. Relations between hourly and salaried employees on the production floor could also suffer.

The list of demands from the new chairman of the Shop Committee could have resulted from the uncertainty that existed with the recent announcements of plant closings by GM. Since the mid-1980s, six GM stamping plants had been closed, and Parma's employment level had fallen. These plant closings and pressure from GM were the result of GM losing 10 percentage points of market share in under 10 years and corresponding deterioration in GM's bottom line. By the fall of 1990, GM was losing more than $1100 for every vehicle it produced in North America, in part because of GM's high fixed costs. With over $700 million in sales, Parma is an important plant to GM, but there is no guarantee that it will not be closed if demand for GM's products does not improve. Wall Street is criticizing GM for not being more aggressive in closing plants to remove excess capacity. The corporation is pressuring all of its facilities to reduce expenditures significantly and to eliminate all overtime. Parma has made substantial progress in maintaining revenues amidst declining demand, but it still needs to make significant improvements in productivity. For example, it has still to better utilize the transfer presses that stamp automative doors and hoods. These presses were installed during the $600 million modernization in 1983, and in 1990 their uptime stood at 31 percent.

Parma also needs to improve its quality and customer satisfaction. In 1989, Parma began supplying the metal frame for the minivan produced at GM's Tarrytown, New York, facility. Arthur Norelli, general supervisor of Dimensional Control, remembers that in his first encounters with Parma, "I found them initially, very defensive, almost adversarial. They were always right until we proved them wrong. If we had a part that wouldn't go together properly, they would say 'Well, you're not putting it together right.'" Another customer, a transmission plant within GM's Powertrain Group, has concerns about Parma's ability to produce quality parts in a timely fashion. As recently as 1988, Parma was Powertrain's worst supplier for transmission components. Bill Hurles, a materials manager within the Powertrain Group, remembered Parma back then as "very dependable and very antagonistic."

In addition to pressures to improve costs, quality, and productivity, there are additional pressures on management from the union to bring stamping work in-house that has previously been outsourced. As Parma loses its prop shaft production to another GM facility, the union wants to bring back the production of sheet metal blankings, the first step in the stamping process. Blankings have been outsourced to a supplier, Medina Blanking, Inc., which produces an excellent quality product and has virtually become another department in Parma because of its highly responsive and capable delivery.

As GM closes plants and continues to downsize, Parma's salaried employees, too, are being affected significantly by efforts to reduce salaried employment and eliminate management layers throughout the organization. With fewer salaried employees, workloads are increasing even as promotional opportunities, compensation, and benefits stagnate. As is the case at most GM facilities, Parma's salaried employees are not unionized. As part of its efforts to cut costs, GM has eliminated the salaried year-end bonus, has sharply reduced merit raises, and is considering other benefit reductions. Profit sharing for both hourly and salaried employees has evaporated as losses in GM's North American operations have mounted to several billion dollars annually.

After 10 years of being a top manager at Parma and assuming responsibility for all of Parma's operations, Bob Lintz continues to fashion a top management team based on trust and openness. He also wants his managers to be committed to eliminating hostilities that linger between the stamping and components operations within the plant, as well as between hourly and salaried

employees. He is also looking for people who will support his informal and highly participative management style and who will work to increase the level of involvement among Parma's hourly employees. Although the TCIG has formally disbanded, its efforts are still ongoing. The weekly floor board meetings, where union officials and superintendents discuss plant floor issues, are still active and productive. The biweekly joint meeting of Bob and his staff, along with the Shop Committee chairman, the president of Local 1005, and the Shop Committee, are ongoing as well. These groups are representative of the Team Concept still at work at Parma.

Conclusion

Even though Bob's management team supports his desire to increase the level of involvement among Parma's hourly employees, Dean Baker commented, "Sometimes I get frustrated, though, because I wish he'd have a little bit more confidence in the management organization."

Parma's lead training coordinator, Pat Camarati, is concerned that many of Parma's managers and supervisors see the ongoing Team Concept training as more of a disruption than a necessity. Shop Committee member Ray Kopchak believes that, although they have made great strides, the biggest mistake the union and management can still make is to assume that their relationship can continue to improve without hard work. Seven years after beginning a new collaborative approach, he still feels that the easiest thing to do is "to go back to the old traditional way. But I don't want to do that, it's not necessary. We've proven that management and the union can work together."

Review Questions

1. How would you describe Parma's environment in terms of its level of uncertainty and complexity?

2. How would you characterize Bob Lintz's approach to communication, decision making, and the exercise of power to create change at Parma?

3. What are the most critical issues still facing Parma, and what should be done to address them?

4. How can resistance to change be overcome utilizing the existing workforce? ■

References

1. *Harbour Report,* 1979–1989, p. 235.

2. *Harbour Report,* 1989–1992, p. 69.

3. It costs GM $795 more than Ford to produce a vehicle, [$396 of which is attributed to GM's stamping plants. GM's current contract with the International UAW, to which Parma and all GM's other facilities must adhere, provides union members 95 percent of their take-home pay for up to three years in the event they are laid off. This will cost the Corporation $4 billion over the three-year agreement. In addition, UAW members received wage increases of 17 percent, bringing unions wages and benefits to $36.60/hour.

CASE 16
The Poorly Informed Walrus

Developed by Barbara McCain, Oklahoma City University

"How's it going down there?" barked the big walrus from his perch on the highest rock near the shore. He waited for the good word.

Down below, the smaller walruses conferred hastily among themselves. Things weren't going well at all, but none of them wanted to break the news to the Old Man. He was the biggest and wisest walrus in the herd, and he knew his business, but he had such a terrible temper that every walrus in the herd was terrified of his ferocious bark.

"What will we tell him?" whispered Basil, the second-ranking walrus. He well remembers how the Old Man had raved and ranted at him the last time the herd had caught less than its quota of herring, and he had no desire to go through that experience again. Nevertheless, the walrus noticed for several weeks that the water level in the nearby Arctic bay had been falling constantly, and it had become necessary to travel much farther to catch the dwindling supply of herring.

Someone should tell the Old Man; he would probably know what to do. But who? and how?

Finally Basil spoke up: "Things are going pretty well, Chief," he said. The thought of the receding water line made his heart grow heavy, but he went on: "As a matter of fact, the beach seems to be getting larger."

The Old Man grunted. "Fine, fine," he said. "That will give us a bit more elbow room." He closed his eyes and continued basking in the sun.

The next day brought more trouble. A new herd of walruses moved in down the beach and, with the supply of herring dwindling, this invasion could be dangerous. No one wanted to tell the Old Man, though only he could take the steps necessary to meet this new competition.

Reluctantly, Basil approached the big walrus, who was still sunning himself on the large rock. After some small talk, he said, "Oh by the way Chief, a new herd of walruses seems to have moved into our territory." The Old Man's eyes snapped open, and he filled his great lungs in preparation for a mighty bellow. But Basil added quickly, "Of course, we don't anticipate any trouble. They don't look like herring eaters to me. More likely interested in minnows. And as you know, we don't bother with minnows ourselves."

The Old Man let out the air with a long sigh. "Good, good," he said. "No point in our getting excited over nothing then, is there?"

Things didn't get any better in the weeks that followed. One day, peering down from the large rock, the Old Man noticed that part of the herd seemed to be missing. Summoning Basil, he grunted peevishly. "What's going on, Basil? Where is everyone?" Poor Basil didn't have the courage to tell the Old Man that many of the younger walruses were leaving every day to join the new herd. Clearing his throat nervously, he said, "Well Chief, we've been tightening up things a bit. You know, getting rid of some of the dead wood. After all, a herd is only as good as walruses in it."

"Run a tight ship, I always say," the Old Man grunted. "Glad to hear that all is going so well."

Before long, everyone but Basil had left to join the new herd, and Basil realized that the time had come to tell the Old Man the facts. Terrified but determined, he flopped up to the large rock. "Chief," he said, "I have bad news. The rest of the herd has left you." The old walrus was so astonished that he couldn't even work up a good bellow. "Left me?" he cried. "All of them? But why? How could this happen?"

Basil didn't have the heart to tell him so he merely shrugged helplessly.

"I can't understand it," the old walrus said. "And just when everything was going so well."

Review Questions

1. What barriers to communication are evident in this fable?
2. What communication "lessons" does this fable offer to those who are serious about careers in the new workplace? ∎

CASE 17
Johnson and Johnson: Futuristic Decision Making

Developed by David S. Chappell, Ohio University

With brand names like Tylenol, Band-Aid brands, Neutrogena skin products, and Reach toothbrushes, Johnson and Johnson (J&J) represents the world's largest and most comprehensive manufacturer of health-care products serving the consumer, pharmaceutical, diagnostics, and professional markets.[1] Representative of its conglomerate business model, 15 company group chairpersons, along with their own management boards, oversee over 180 operating companies worldwide.[2] How does such a large company infuse its decision-making process with the energy of a small start-up company?

Johnson and Johnson

J&J was incorporated in 1887 through the combined effort of brothers Robert, James, and Edward Johnson. The brothers pioneered the surgical dressings industry based on work by Sir Joseph Lister, a noted English surgeon who identified airborne germs as a source of infection in the operating room. J&J developed a soft, absorbent cotton and gauze antiseptic dressing that could be mass produced and shipped in quantity to hospitals and every rural physician and druggist in the country.[3]

J&J has had an international focus to its business since its foray into Canada in 1919. It launched a conscious product diversification program in the 1920s with the introduction of its Band-Aid brands and Johnson's baby cream. General Johnson, as the son of one of the original brothers was known, also created the famous J&J Credo around this time. The credo emphasizes the importance of ethical behavior and putting customers first and stockholders last. However, General Johnson was practical enough to infer that such an approach would benefit the owners of the firm in the long run.

J&J is perhaps best known for its advancement of crisis management regarding the cyanide contamination of its flagship Tylenol painkiller. In September 1982, seven Chicago-area individuals died after taking cyanide-laced Extra Strength Tylenol capsules. Representing 7 percent of all of J&J sales and 17 percent of its profits, Tylenol represented a brand that the corporation could not afford to lose.[4]

J&J chose to take a very proactive approach to the crisis. It eventually recalled 31 million bottles worth over $100 million from retail stores, in addition to offering to exchange tablets for capsules for all customers at no charge. It pioneered the tamperproof, triple-sealed packaging that is the industry standard today.

Immediately after the crisis, Tylenol's market share dropped from 35.3 percent of the pain reliever market to 7 percent; however, by May of 1983, its market share returned to 35 percent. The situation was repeated in 1986 when a Westchester, New York woman died of cyanide-laced Extra-Strength Tylenol capsules. Once again, the company recalled all capsules, vowing never again to offer any Tylenol except in the form of tablets or caplets.[5]

J&J does not view itself as just a pharmaceutical firm; it prefers to think of itself as a health-care organization. It represents an autonomous collection of independent entities whose decentralized structure fosters an entrepreneurial culture, insists CEO Ralph Larsen.[6] Not everyone agrees with J&J's conglomerate structure; Paine Webber analyst David Lothson, for example, complains that J&J should be three companies. Of particular concern is the ever-declining roles in sales and profits of the consumer-products line—falling from 44 percent in 1978 to only 28 percent of revenue in 1998. The stock, rather than trading at the attractive high multiples of

---

Note: The blue underscored words/phrases in this case indicate Internet links provided in the on-line version. See the *Organizational Behavior, Seventh Edition* Web Site at http://www.wiley.com/college/schermerhorn.

Johnson and Johnson Conglomerate Structure

DIVISION	1998 SALES (in billions)	MAJOR PRODUCTS
Professional	$8.57	Coronary stents, minimally invasive surgery products, wound-closure products
Pharmaceutical	$8.56	Risperdal for schizophrenia, Levaquin for infections, Procrit for anemia
Consumer	$6.53	Tylenol painkillers, Band-Aids, baby products, Neutrogena skin products[8]

similar pharmaceutical firms, reflects a conservative valuation that is more similar to consumer-good behemoth Procter and Gamble.

Decision making requires the application of information, and perhaps more importantly, knowledge. "Data, information and knowledge are points along a continuum of increasing value and human contribution. Data—the signals about human events and activities that we are exposed to each day—has little value in itself, although to its credit it is easy to store and manipulate on computers.

"Information is what data becomes when we as humans interpret and contextualise it. It is also the vehicle we use to express and communicate knowledge in business and in our lives. Information has more value than data and, at the same time, greater ambiguity—as any manager will attest who has ever argued over how many interpretations the terms 'customer,' 'order' and 'shipment' can have inside the same company.

"Knowledge is information within people's minds; without a knowing, self-aware person there is no knowledge. Knowledge is highly valuable, because humans create new ideas, insights and interpretations and apply these directly to information use and decision making. For managers, knowledge is difficult to 'manage' in other people because (being mental) it is invisible

and its extraction, sharing and use relies on human motivation."[7] Eventually, the companies that prosper with knowledge management will be those that realize that it is as much about managing people as information.

Larsen needs to convince people that his conglomerate business model as a source of knowledge is still practical. Most insiders agree that the strength of J&J is its diversity; the question becomes, how does the company make the most efficient and effective use of this diversity and its associated knowledge base as inputs into its decision making?

FrameworkS at J&J

Conceived in 1993 with the assistance of consulting firm McKinsey & Company, FrameworkS involves a series of focused dialogues between operating company executives, specialists, and most importantly, top management. "FrameworkS is an attempt to democratize how we make strategic choices, how we create our future," says Roger Fine, general counsel of J&J.[9] CEO Ralph Larsen states that never before has "a broad-based group of people been invited to be central, active participants in matters of very substantial corporate significance outside the direct responsibility of their operating companies."[10]

The first FrameworkS looked at the changing nature of the health

care market in the U.S. J&J's nine executive committee members enlisted about 20 senior company executives to explore key topics. After splitting into teams to conduct research, they contacted customers, policy analysis, government officials, and academics regarding the marketplace and their competition. Reconvening after several months, they discussed major changes in how medical care is delivered in the United States, from fee-for-service to HMO institutional decision makers. Dennis Longstreet, head of J&J's Ethicon Endo-Surgery medical devices businesses, argued that the process "caused all levels of management to see things we had not seen before. We listened to our customers, and we looked to the core of our company, down to how we were organized."[11]

One of the critical findings of the investigation was that J&J's largest customers, such as hospital networks, government organizations, and managed care plans wanted a single J&J contract to coordinate purchases from J&J's diverse operating companies. As a result of this finding, in three months J&J created Health Care Systems, Inc. to support a single point-of-contact supplier to its customers. David Cassak, editor of a magazine that tracks the medical industry, states that "it's a truly unique and innovative structure, the perfect vehicle to address customer needs while retaining the culture of autonomous operating companies."[12]

In 1995, in an effort to increase its innovation, J&J launched a FrameworkS project focused on the qualities highly innovative companies exhibited. The team reviewed three J&J companies (Ethicon Endo-Surgery, Janssen Pharmaceutica and Vistakon) and three outside ones (Enron, Hewlett Packard and Nike).[13] They identified three types of innovative activities:

Type of Innovation	Example
Incremental	Glow in the Dark Band-Aid
Substantial (alters market demand with a new generation of product)	Reach Toothbrush
Transformational (alters industry structure)	Vistakon's disposable contact lens

The objective was to identify ways J&J could foster more substantial and transformational innovation in products, services, processes, and management.[14] "What's New" is the program that includes a "toolkit" of actions line managers can take to infuse innovation into their organizations. The intent is to "exercise core competencies and exorcise corporate rigidities."[15]

Does It Work?

While its hard to quantify the impact that FrameworkS has made on J&J's operations, most upper executives support the program. However, things don't always work out as planned. The year 1998 proved to be difficult, with six experimental drugs falling through late in development. J&J's coronary stent, responsible for $500 million of J&J's business, lost 90 percent of its market share to rivals; plans for a cholesterol-lowering margarine suffered a regulatory setback; and the company lost a battle over rights to a future version of a top-selling anemia drug.[16]

Calls to break up the company into separate operating units remain strong. Larsen resists these calls, claiming that "the future belongs to those companies that are broadly based."[17] Do the broad operating companies of J&J offer it a unique opportunity or an unwieldy anachronism? Does FrameworkS offer an institutional mechanism to capture its diversity into a useful and constructive process?

Review Questions

1. How is J&J able to incorporate its organizational diversity into its decision-making process?
2. How does the management of J&J hope that FrameworkS will help with creativity within the organization?
3. How does J&J attempt to infuse ethics into its decision making?

References

1. "Johnson and Johnson Homepage—1998 Fact Book," http://www.jnj.com/who_is_jnj /factbook/98fb_index.html, April 3, 1999.
2. Jones, Gladys Montgomery. "Framing the Future: How Johnson and Johnson Executives Keep in Touch with a Changing Marketplace—and One Another." *Continental Inflight Magazine,* March 1999, pp. 39–41.
3. "Johnson and Johnson Homepage—History," http://www.jnj.com/who_is_jnj /hist_index.html, April 3, 1999.
4. Hartley, Robert F. "Contrast—Johnson & Johnson's Tylenol: Great Crisis Management in Regaining Public Trust." *Management Mistakes and Successes.* New York: John Wiley and Sons, pp. 330–344.
5. Ibid.
6. Langreth, Robert and Winslow, Ron. "Johnson & Johnson Faces Question: Is It Merely an Unwieldy Anachronism?" *The Wall Street Journal,* March 5, 1999, pp. B1, B4.
7. "Is KM just good information management?" *Financial Times* (London), March 8, 1999, p. 2.
8. Langreth and Winslow, op. cit.
9. Jones, op. cit.
10. Ibid.
11. Ibid.
12. Ibid.
13. Ibid.
14. Ibid.
15. Ibid.
16. Langreth and Winslow, op. cit.
17. Ibid.

CASE 18

American Airlines: Trouble in the Air

Developed by David S. Chappell, Ohio University

As one of the major air carriers in the United States, American Airlines conducts thousands of flights daily. After years of operations under Chairman Robert Crandall, Donald Carty took over in May of 1998. One of his first strategic moves was to complete the acquisition of the small, Southwestern, low-fare regional carrier, Reno Air. As a result of this action, in

Note: The blue underscored words/phrases in this case indicate Internet links provided in the on-line version. See the *Organizational Behavior, Seventh Edition* Web Site at http://www.wiley.com/college/schermerhorn.

February 1999, the American Airlines pilots chose to conduct an unauthorized work slowdown, with over 1000 pilots calling in sick. This action served to effectively cripple American's ability to carry out operations at a loss to the carrier of over $150 million. How did the conflict between American and its pilots escalate to this level?

The Airline Industry

The modern era in the U.S. airline industry can be traced to 1978, with the deregulation of the United States' airline industry. Previous to 1978, major airlines had been regulated by the Federal Aviation Administration (FAA) and the Civil Aeronautics Board (CAB) essentially as a government-sponsored oligopoly. Competition was minimized, and entry into the airline industry was difficult, if not impossible. With deregulation, small, low-fare airlines sprang up in many markets, putting severe pressure on the operating profits of the older operators. The flying public benefited with improved service and lower fares, but the established airlines, with their higher operating costs, suffered.

Carrier Classifications

- **Majors**—The majors are airlines whose revenues exceed $1 billion annually. They generally operate international and domestic flights and service only major airports. The majors are characterized as long haul carriers.
- **Nationals**—National airlines are short-haul carriers. Their revenues generally are between $100 million and $1 billion. They fly shorter point-to-point flights that may include a few international flights.
- **Regionals**—Regionals generally make less than $100 million annu-

ally. They concentrate in certain areas of the U.S. and only service that area. They do not usually use large jets, so their capacity is smaller but it allows them to access smaller rural airports that aren't available to the larger carriers.[1]

The following is a listing of the top 10 passenger carriers:

1.	Delta	97,201
2.	United	81,863
3.	American	79,324
4.	US Airways	56,639
5.	Southwest	55,372
6.	Northwest	52,682
7.	Continental	35,743
8.	Trans World	23,281
9.	America West	18,130
10.	Alaska	11,758

Robert Crandall at American Airlines introduced the AAdvantage frequent flier program in 1980, now an industry standard. Intense pressure to slash prices (often to below cost), due to rising energy costs brought on by Gulf War sanctions, an economic recession, and corporate cost-saving measures that forced many business travelers out of first class and into coach led to unprecedented losses for the airlines.

Between 1990 and 1992, airline industry losses of over $5 billion exceeded the combined profits for the previous 67 years.[2] As a result of these losses, airline management pressured various unions representing pilots, flight attendants, and mechanics to agree to labor concessions. With the latter half of the 1990s providing very *attractive profits* for airlines, these unions are now becoming more and more aggressive to win back previous wages and benefits.

Employee salaries (consisting of cabin attendants, ground crews, and flight crews) represent 36 per-

cent of the operating costs for the airline industry. The next largest contributor is ticketing and promotional costs with 17 percent. Finally, fuel costs take 11.7 percent of the expense category. Net income is greatly affected by the fluctuations of these operating costs. Because operating expenses are controlled mainly by volatile forces, the net income of the industry is too dependent on factors outside of its control.[3]

As a result, airlines are looking for innovative ways to control costs, including ticketless travel, Internet sites, lowering or even eliminating travel agents commissions, application of new technology, extensive use of hub-and-spoke traffic systems, code sharing, and alliances. At the same time, labor disputes, including a pilot strike at Northwest in 1998, a narrowly averted flight attendant strike at America West in early 1999, and the American Airlines pilot "sickout" all represent troubling times for airline passengers.

American Airlines

American Airlines, with its rich history of aviation firsts, is a division of AMR Corporation. With major hubs in Chicago, Dallas, and New York City, American Airlines serves about 160 destinations in the Americas and Europe (some through code-sharing alliances with foreign airlines); the airline also leads Oneworld, a global alliance with British Airways and other carriers. AMR operates American Eagle, a group of small regional airlines, owns low-fare carrier Reno Air, and holds 82 percent of the SABRE ("Semi-Automated Business Research Environment") Group, operator of the #1 travel reservation system.

Overall, American Airlines is the second largest domestic carrier behind only United in terms of total

RPMs (Revenue Passenger Miles) and total revenues from flight operations during 1997. Not only must American compete both domestically and abroad with its major brethren, it must also deal with regional and national upstarts, the scrappy entrant carriers to the market. These low-cost carriers usually go head-to-head with the major and regional airlines and try and gain market share by way of offering lower fare prices than the major airlines can. American estimates that as much as 47 percent of its bookings were impacted by competition from lower-cost carriers.

To capitalize on these growth opportunities, American entered into numerous alliances with both domestic and foreign carriers and is looking to expand into certain other markets by means of stock equity acquisitions. For instance, in 1996 British Airways (BA), the largest international passenger airline carrier in the world entered into a strategic alliance with American. Under the conditions of the agreement, both companies would use code sharing and combine some of their passenger and cargo operations, upon regulatory approval by the U.S. Department of Transportation (DOT) and the United Kingdom. Additionally, in 1997 the two companies agreed to implement a common frequent flier program. Finally, in September 1998, American entered into a strategic alliance called Oneworld, which is to rival United and Lufthansa's Star alliance. The members of the Oneworld Alliance include AA, British Airways, Canadian Air, Cathay Pacific, and Qantas.

In the deregulated era, airline competition has become, in part, a contest to build the most ubiquitous network. In that regard, one of American's most critical success factors is the implementation of a strong hub and spoke system. By linking markets on one side of a hub city to markets on another side, airlines are able to exponentially increase the number of origin-destination combinations they serve. The company's success can be linked to its operations at its hub cities which include Dallas/Fort Worth, Miami, Chicago and, to a lesser degree, San Juan, Puerto Rico.[4]

Since 1980, American has evolved from a domestic carrier into one of the world's foremost international carriers. In 1997, international flying generated more than 30 percent of American's passenger revenue. During that year they also did well in Latin America, attracting 7 percent more customers in that year than from the previous year.[5]

American's greatest shortcoming is its weak presence in the Asian market. Compared to many of their rivals, they fly very few routes in and out of Asia. Based on 1996 statistics, American possessed only a 4 percent share of U.S. airline traffic to and from the Asian region. Other weaknesses include their high-cost structure as measured in Cost/ASM (Available Seat-Miles) and Labor Cost/ASM. American's operating costs are among the highest in the industry, especially their labor costs.

The Pilot "Sickout"

Richard Aboulafia, aviation consultant at the Teal Group in Virginia, notes several items that encourage labor strife at the airlines, particularly at American. "Most of the labor-management disputes of the early 1990s were settled at a time of diminished profits for airlines and manufacturing, and now that things are looking up, labor is demanding its fair share."[6] He cites the militant elements of the Allied Pilots Association, especially in New York and Miami, a two-tier wage scale at American, and the difficulty the Railway Labor Act creates in the way of hurdles to strikes. Left with few options, unions resort to various work slowdowns and stoppages. "It got quite adversarial, especially with American Airlines, and now American Airlines is paying the price for that adversarial atmosphere."[7]

American Airlines and its pilots had a close brush with a strike in February of 1997. Minutes after the strike deadline passed, President Clinton declared an emergency, appointed a Presidential Emergency Board, and ordered the parties to continue operating as usual while the board considered recommendations for a solution.[8] Pilots eventually ratified the agreement rather than have Congress impose a contract on them. In the summer of 1998, American pilots stopped volunteering for overtime, forcing American to cancel a small number of flights, when the union found out that American was placing more passengers on Canadian Airlines, one of its foreign partners, than was allowed in an agreement with the union. It was the purchase of small Reno Air that reignited the conflict between American and its pilots. American sought Reno to facilitate expansion into lucrative West Coast markets in addition to travel to the Far East.

The issue came down to how to integrate Reno's 300 pilots, who are paid less than American pilots, into the American system. American discussed the purchase with the Allied Pilots Association's union leaders but closed the deal on December 28, 1998 without first reaching agreement with the pilots union over how it would merge the two airlines.[9] American claims it needs 18 months to combine the two entities, due to crew training and a refit of Reno airplanes. The pilot's union argues that the company is dragging its feet in order to continue to pay Reno's pilots at lower rates, possibly setting a precedent for future acquisitions.[10]

The sickout began in earnest on February 6, 1999, and continued for 10 days, causing American to cancel over 6600 flights with a loss of over $150 million. As a major carrier, American's difficulties stranded huge numbers of passengers, many for days on end. American brought suit in court, and U.S. District Judge Joe Kendall of Dallas issued a temporary restraining order against the union. Kendall also found the union and two of its leaders in contempt of court for not encouraging the pilots to return to work immediately after his order. The judge ordered the union to post $10 million bond—and the leaders to post a total of $15,000—against potential contempt-of-court fines.[11] Eventually, the sickout was called off and pilots returned to their regular work schedule.

Where Do They Go from Here

One of American's primary competitors, UAL, is 60 percent owned by its employees. As a result, in the year 2000 a performance-based pay system for managers will partly be tied to worker satisfaction as measured by an outside survey firm. Coupled with customer satisfaction and on-time performance, the bonus system will account for more than half of what the top 635 UAL managers receive in compensation. Originally rejected by management, it was finally accepted after the union prepared a shareholder resolution, which would have passed given the union's shareholder votes.[12]

In American Airlines' first employee satisfaction survey since 1993, a mere 23 percent said American does an excellent job of inspiring loyalty, while only 31 percent believe what senior management says. And only 30 percent think morale is good. So while 91 percent said they liked their jobs, the overall results were disappointing. Carty says he needs satisfied workers, because only they can provide the superior service that lures high-paying business travelers. Building a happy workforce "remains the last major frontier for us." Carty is already discussing survey details with employees, a first at American, and plans to bring managers and workers together to resolve problems. "Doing a survey like this probably hurts morale in a company unless it leads to some changes," he says. American clearly needs some changes and sooner, rather than later.[13]

Review Questions

1. Discuss the situation at American Airlines in regard to the stages of conflict the author presents.
2. Analyze possible conflict resolution methods using the direct conflict management techniques discussed in the chapter.
3. Suggest possible distributive or integrative negotiation approaches available to the two parties in the American dispute.

References

1. "Air Transport Association," http://www.air-transport.org/data/, March 22, 1999.
2. Johnson, Cynthia, "Hoovers—Airline," http://www.hoovers.com/features/industry/airline.html, March 22, 1999.
3. Ibid.
4. "AMR Corporate," http://www.amrcorp.com/annual/airline_group.htm, March 22, 1999.
5. Ibid.
6. Dine, Philip. "Airlines Face Labor's "Payback" Need: Workers Seek Rewards for Earlier Concessions," *St. Louis Post-Dispatch,* February 16, 1999, p. A1.
7. Ibid.
8. "AMR-Investor Information," http://www.amrcorp.com/annual/year_in_review.htm, March 22, 1999.
9. Zuckerman, Laurence. "Persistent Mistrust and Big Egos Lie at Heart of American Pilots Dispute," the *New York Times,* February 15, 1999, p. A14.
10. Ibid.
11. Pedersen, Daniel. "Stranded and Fuming," *Newsweek,* February 22, 1999, p. 39.
12. Leonhardt, David; Bernstein, Aaron; and Zellner, Wendy. "UAL: Labor Is My Co-Pilot," *Business Week,* March 1, 1999, p. 38.
13. Zellner, Wendy. "Blue Crew at American," *Business Week,* February 22, 1999, p. 8. ■

CASE 19
The New Vice President

[*Note:* Please read only those parts identified by your instructor. Do not read ahead.]

Part A

When the new president at Mid-West U took over, it was only a short time before the incumbent vice president announced his resignation. Unfortunately, there was no one waiting in the wings, and a hiring freeze prevented a national search from commencing.

Many faculty leaders and former administrators suggested that the President appoint Jennifer Treeholm, the Associate Vice President for Academic Affairs, as interim. She was an extremely popular person on campus and had 10 years of experience in the role of associate vice president. She knew everyone and everything about the campus. Jennifer, they assured him, was the natural choice. Besides, Jennifer *deserved* the job. Her devotion to the school was unparalleled, and her energy knew no bounds. The new President, acting on advice from many campus leaders, appointed Jennifer Interim vice president for a term of up to three years. He also agreed that she could be a candidate for the permanent position when the hiring freeze was lifted.

Jennifer and her friends were ecstatic. It was high time more women moved into important positions on campus. They went out for dinner to their every Friday night watering hole to celebrate and reflect on Jennifer's career.

Except for a brief stint outside of academe, Jennifer's entire career had been at Mid-West U. She started out teaching Introductory History, then, realizing she wanted to get on the tenure track, went back to school and earned her Ph.D. at Metropolitan U. while continuing to teach at Mid-West. Upon completion of her degree, she was appointed as an Assistant Professor and, eventually, earned the rank of Associate based on her popularity and excellent teaching.

Not only was Jennifer well liked, but she devoted her entire life, it seemed, to Mid-West, helping to form the first union, getting grants, writing skits for the faculty club's annual follies, and going out of her way to befriend everyone who needed support.

Eventually, Jennifer was elected President of the Faculty Senate. After serving for two years, she was offered the position of Associate vice president. During her 10 years as associate vice president, she handled most of the academic complaints, oversaw several committees, wrote almost all of the letters and reports for the vice president, and was even known to run personal errands for the president. People just knew they could count on Jennifer.

Review Questions

1. At this point, what are your predictions about Jennifer as the Interim Vice President?
2. What do you predict will be her management/leadership style?
3. What are her strengths? Her weaknesses? What is the basis for your assessment?

After you have discussed Part A, please read Part B.

Part B

Jennifer's appointment as interim vice president was met with great enthusiasm. Finally, the school was getting someone who was "one of their own," a person who understood the culture, knew the faculty, and could get things done.

It was not long before the campus realized that things were not moving and that Jennifer, despite her long-standing popularity, had difficulty making tough decisions. Her desire to please people and to try to take care of everyone made it difficult for her to choose opposing alternatives. (To make matters worse, she had trouble planning, organizing, and managing her time.)

What was really a problem was that she did not understand her role as the Number Two person at the top of the organization. The President expected her to support him and his decisions without question. Over time the President also expected her to implement some of his decisions—to do his dirty work. This became particularly problematic when it involved firing people or saying no to old faculty cronies. Jennifer also found herself uncomfortable with the other members of the president's senior staff. Although she was not the only woman (the general counsel, a very bright, analytical woman was part of the group), Jennifer found the behavior and decision-making style to be different from what she was used to.

Most of the men took their lead from the president and discussed very little in the meetings. Instead, they would try to influence decisions

Source: Adapted from Donald D. Bowen, et al., *Experiences in Management and Organizational Behavior,* 4th ed. (New York: John Wiley & Sons, Inc.), 1997.

privately. Often a decision arrived in a meeting as a "fait accompli." Jennifer felt excluded and wondered why, as vice president, she felt so powerless.

In time, she and the President spent less and less time together talking and discussing how to move the campus along. Although her relations with the men on the senior staff were cordial, she talked mostly to her female friends.

Jennifer's friends, especially her close-knit group of long-time female colleagues, all assured her that it was because she was "interim." "Just stay out of trouble," they told her. Of course this just added to her hesitancy when it came to making tough choices.

As the president's own image on campus shifted after his "honeymoon year," Jennifer decided to listen to her friends rather than follow the president's lead. After all, her reputation on campus was at stake.

Review Questions

1. What is the major problem facing Jennifer?
2. What would you do if you were in her position?
3. Would a man have the same experience as Jennifer?
4. Are any of your predictions about her management style holding up?

Part C

When the hiring freeze was lifted and Jennifer's position was able to be filled, the president insisted on a national search. Jennifer and her friends felt this was silly, given that she was going into her third year in the job. Nonetheless, she entered the search process.

After a year-long search, the Search Committee met with the

president. The external candidates were not acceptable to the campus. Jennifer, they recommended, should only be appointed on a permanent basis if she agreed to change her management style.

The president mulled over his dilemma, then decided to give Jennifer the benefit of the doubt and the opportunity. He appointed her permanent Provost, while making the following, private agreement with her.

1. She will organize her office and staff and begin delegating more work to others.
2. She will "play" her Number Two position, backing the president and "echoing" his position on the University's vision statement.
3. She will provide greater direction for the Deans who report to her.

Jennifer agreed to take the position. She was now the University's first female vice president and presided over a council of 11 deans, three of whom were her best female friends. Once again, they sought out their every Friday night watering hole for an evening of dinner and celebration.

Review Questions

1. If you were Jennifer, would you have accepted the job?
2. What would you do as the new, permanent, vice president?
3. Will Jennifer change her management style? If so, in what ways?
4. What are your predictions for the future?

Part D

Although people had predicted that things would be better once Jennifer was permanently in the job, they in fact became more problematic.

People now expected Jennifer to be able to take decisive action. She did not feel she could.

Every time an issue came up, she would spend weeks, sometimes months, trying to get a sense of the campus. Nothing moved once it hit her office. After a while, people began referring to the vice president's office as "the black hole" where things just went in and disappeared.

Her immediate staff were concerned and frustrated. Not only did she not delegate effectively, but her desire to make things better led her to try to do more and more herself.

The vice president's job also carried social obligations and requests. Here again, she tried to please everyone and often ran from one evening obligation to another, trying to show her support and concern for every constituency on campus. She was exhausted, overwhelmed, and knowing the mandate under which she was appointed, anxious about the president's evaluation of her behavior.

The greatest deterioration occurred within her Dean's Council. Several of the male Deans, weary of waiting for direction from Jennifer regarding where she was taking some of the academic proposals of the president, had started making decisions without Jennifer's approval.

"Loose cannons," was how she described a couple of them. "They don't listen. They just march out there on their own."

One of the big problems with two of the deans was that they just didn't take no for an answer when it came from Jennifer. Privately, each conceded that her "no" sounded like a "maybe." She always left room open to renegotiate.

Whatever the problem, and there were several by now, Jennifer's ability to lead was being questioned. Although her popularity was as high as ever, more and more people on campus were expressing their frustrations with what sometimes appeared as mixed signals from her and the president and sometimes was seen as virtually no direction. People wanted priorities. Instead, crisis management reigned.

Questions

1. If you were president, what would you do?
2. If you were Jennifer, what would you do?

Conclusion

Jennifer had a few "retreats" with her senior staff. Each time, she committed herself to delegate more, prioritize, and work on time management issues, but within 10 days or so, everything was back to business as usual.

The president decided to hire a person with extensive corporate experience to fill the vacant position of vice president of Finance and Administration. The new man was an experienced team player who had survived mergers, been fired and bounced back, and had spent years in the number two position in several companies. Within a few months he had earned the respect of the campus as well as the president and was in fact emerging as the person who really ran the place. Meanwhile, the president concentrated on external affairs and fund raising.

Jennifer felt relieved. Her role felt clearer. She could devote herself to academic and faculty issues and she was out from under the pressure to play "hatchet man."

As she neared the magic age for early retirement, she began to talk more and more about what she wanted to do next. ■

EXPERIENTIAL EXERCISES

My Best Manager

Procedure

1. Make a list of the attributes that describe the best manager you ever worked for. If you have trouble identifying an actual manager, make a list of attributes you would like the manager in your next job to have.
2. Form a group of four or five persons and share your lists.
3. Create one list that combines all the unique attributes of the "best" managers represented in your group. Make sure that you have all attributes listed, but list each only once. Place a check mark next to those that were reported by two or more members. Have one of your members prepared to present the list in general class discussion.
4. After all groups have finished Step 3, spokespersons should report to the whole class. The instructor will make a running list of the "best" manager attributes as viewed by the class.
5. Feel free to ask questions and discuss the results.

Graffiti Needs Assessment: Involving Students in the First Class Session

Contributed by Barbara K. Goza, Visiting Associate Professor, University of California Santa Cruz and Associate Professor California State Polytechnic University, Pomona. From *Journal of Management Education*, 1993.

Procedure

1. Complete the following sentences with as many endings as possible.
    1. When I first came to this class, I thought . . .
    2. My greatest concern this term is . . .
    3. In 3 years I will be . . .
    4. The greatest challenge facing the world today is . . .
    5. Organizational behavior specialists do . . .
    6. Human resources are . . .
    7. Organizational research is . . .
    8. The most useful question I've been asked is . . .
    9. The most important phenomenon in organizations is . . .
    10. I learn the most when . . .
2. Your instructor will guide you in a class discussion about your responses. Pay careful attention to similarities and differences among various students' answers.

My Best Job

Procedure

1. Make a list of the top five things you expect from your first (or next) full-time job.
2. Exchange lists with a nearby partner. Assign probabilities (or odds) to each goal on your partner's list to indicate how likely you feel it is that the goal can be accomplished. (*Note:* Your instructor may ask that everyone use the same probabilities format.)
3. Discuss your evaluations with your partner. Try to delete superficial goals or modify them to become more substantial. Try to restate any unrealistic goals to make them more realistic. Help your partner do the same.
4. Form a group of four to six persons. Within the group have everyone share what they now consider to be the most "realistic" goals on their lists. Elect a spokesperson to share a sample of these items with the entire class.
5. Discuss what group members have individually learned from the exercise. Await further class discussion led by your instructor.

What Do You Value in Work?

Procedure

1. The following nine items are from a survey conducted by Nicholas J. Beutell and O. C. Brenner ("Sex Differences in Work Values," *Journal of Vocational Behavior*, Vol.

28, pp. 29–41, 1986). Rank order the nine items in terms of how important (9 = most important) they would be to you in a job.

How important is it to you to have a job that:
____ Is respected by other people?
____ Encourages continued development of knowledge and skills?
____ Provides job security?
____ Provides a feeling of accomplishment?
____ Provides the opportunity to earn a high income?
____ Is intellectually stimulating?
____ Rewards good performance with recognition?
____ Provides comfortable working conditions?
____ Permits advancement to high administrative responsibility?

2. Form into groups as designated by your instructor. Within each group, the *men in the group* will meet to develop a consensus ranking of the items as they think the *women* in the Beutell and Brenner survey ranked them. The reasons for the rankings should be shared and discussed so they are clear to everyone. The *women in the group* should not participate in this ranking task. They should listen to the discussion and be prepared to comment later in class discussion. A spokesperson for the men in the group should share the group's rankings with the class.

3. (*Optional*) Form into groups as designated by your instructor, but with each group consisting entirely of men or women. Each group should meet and decide which of the work values members of the *opposite* sex ranked first in the Beutell and Brenner survey. Do this again for the work value ranked last. The reasons should be discussed, along with reasons that each of the other values probably was not ranked first . . . or last. A spokesperson for each group should share group results with the rest of the class.

Source: Adapted from Roy J. Lewicki, Donald D. Bowen, Douglas T. Hall, and Francine S. Hall, *Experiences in Management and Organizational Behavior,* 3rd ed. (New York: John Wiley & Sons, Inc., 1988), pp. 23–26. Used by permission.

EXERCISE 5

My Asset Base

A business has an asset base or set of resources that it uses to produce a good or service of value to others. For a business, these are the assets or resources it uses to achieve results, including capital, land, patented products or processes, buildings and equipment, raw materials, and the human resources or employees, among others.

Each of us has an asset base that supports our ability to accomplish the things we set out to do. We refer to our personal assets as *talents, strengths,* or *abilities.* We probably inherit our talents from our parents, but we acquire many of our abilities and strengths through learning. One thing is certain: we feel very proud of the talents and abilities we have.

Procedure

1. Printed here is a T chart that you are to fill out. On the right-hand side of the T, list four or five of your accomplishments—*things you have done of which you are most proud.* Your accomplishments should only include those things for which you can take credit, those *things for which you are primarily responsible.* If you are proud of the sorority to which you belong, you may be justifiably proud, but don't list it unless you

can argue that the sorority's excellence is due primarily to your efforts. However, if you feel that having been invited to join the sorority is a major accomplishment for you, then you may include it.

When you have completed the right-hand side of the chart, fill in the left-hand side by listing *talents, strengths,* and *abilities* that you have that have enabled you to accomplish the outcomes listed on the right-hand side.

My Asset Base

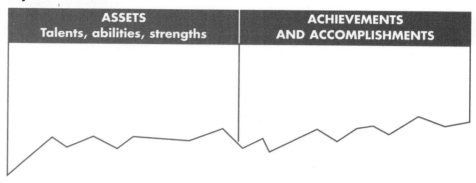

ASSETS Talents, abilities, strengths	ACHIEVEMENTS AND ACCOMPLISHMENTS

2. Share your lists with other team members. As each member takes turn sharing his or her list, pay close attention to your own perceptions and feelings. Notice the effect this has on your attitudes toward the other team members.
3. Discuss these questions in your group:
   (a) How did your attitudes and feelings toward other members of the team change as you pursued the activity? What does this tell you about the process whereby we come to get to know and care about people?
   (b) How did you feel about the instructions the instructor provided? What did you expect to happen? Were your expectations accurate?

Source: Adapted from Donald D. Bowen et al., *Experiences in Management and Organizational Behavior,* 4th ed. (New York: John Wiley & Sons, Inc.), 1997.

EXERCISE 6

Expatriate Assignments

Contributed by Robert E. Ledman, Morehouse College

This exercise focuses on issues related to workers facing international assignments. It illustrates that those workers face a multitude of issues. It further demonstrates that managers who want employees to realize the maximum benefits of international assignments should be aware of, and prepared to deal with, those issues. Some of the topics that are easily addressed with this exercise include the need for culture and language training for the employees and their families and the impact that international assignments may have on an employee's family and how that may affect an employee's willingness to seek such assignments.

Procedure

1. Form into "families" of four or five. Since many students today have only one parent at home, it is helpful if some groups do not have students to fill both

Source: Robert E. Ledman, Gannon University. Presented in the Experiential Exercise Track of the 1996 ABSEL Conference and published in the *Proceedings* of that conference.

parental roles in the exercise. Each student is assigned to play a family member and given a description of that person. Descriptions of family members are given below.

2. Enter into a 20-minute discussion to explore how a proposed overseas assignment will affect the family members. Your goal is to try to reach a decision about whether the assignment should be taken. You must also decide whether the entire family or only the family member being offered the assignment will relocate. The assignment is for a minimum of 2 years, with possible annual extensions resulting in a total of 4 years, and your family, or the member offered the assignment will be provided, at company expense, one trip back to the states each year for a maximum period of 15 days. The member offered the assignment will not receive any additional housing or cost-of-living supplements described in the role assignment if he or she chooses to go overseas alone and can expect his or her living expenses to exceed substantially the living allowance being provided by the company. In your discussion, address the following questions:

  (a) What are the most important concerns your family has about relocating to a foreign country?
  (b) What information should you seek about the proposed host country to be able to make a more informed decision?
  (c) What can the member offered the assignment do to make the transition easier if he or she goes overseas alone? If the whole family relocates?
  (d) What should the member offered the assignment do to ensure that this proposed assignment will not create unnecessary stress for him or her and the rest of the family?
  (e) What lessons for managers of expatriate assignees are presented by the situation in this exercise?

Try to reach some "family" consensus. If a consensus is not possible, however, resolve any differences in the manner you think the family in the role descriptions would ultimately resolve any differences.

3. Share your answers with the rest of the class. Explain the rationale for your answers and answer questions from the remainder of the class.
4. (*Optional*) After each group has reported on a given question, the instructor may query the class about how their answers are consistent, or inconsistent, with common practice of managers as described in the available literature.

Descriptions of Family Members
Person Being Offered Overseas Assignment

This person is a middle- to upper-level executive who is on a fast track to senior management. He or she has been offered the opportunity to manage an overseas operation, with the assurance of a promotion to a vice presidency upon return to the States. The company will pay all relocation expenses, including selling costs for the family home and the costs associated with finding a new home upon return. The employer will also provide language training for the employee and cultural awareness training for the entire family. The employee will receive a living allowance equal to 20 percent of his or her salary. This should be adequate to provide the family a comparable standard of living to that which is possible on the employee's current salary.

Spouse of the Person Offered an Overseas Assignment (Optional)

This person is also a professional with highly transferrable skills and experience for the domestic market. It is unknown how easily he or she may be able to find employment in the foreign country. This person's income, though less than his or her spouse's, is necessary if the couple is to continue paying for their child's college tuition and to prepare for the next child to enter college in two years. This person has spent 15 years developing a career, including completing a degree at night.

Oldest Child

This child is a second semester junior in college and is on track to graduate in 16 months. Transferring at this time would probably mean adding at least one semester to complete the degree. He or she has been dating the same person for over a year; they have talked about getting married immediately after graduation, although they are not yet formally engaged.

Middle Child

This child is a junior in high school. He or she has already begun visiting college campuses in preparation for applying in the fall. This child is involved in a number of school activities; he or she is photographer for the yearbook and plays a varsity sport. This child has a learning disability for which services are being provided by the school system.

Youngest Child

This child is a middle school student, age 13. He or she is actively involved in Scouting and takes piano lessons. This child has a history of medical conditions that have required regular visits to the family physician and specialists. This child has several very close friends who have attended the same school for several years.

Cultural Cues

Contributed by Susan Rawson Zacur and W. Alan Randolph, University of Baltimore

Introduction

In the business context, culture involves shared beliefs and expectations that govern the behavior of people. In this exercise, *foreign culture* refers to a set of beliefs and expectations different from those of the participant's home culture (which has been invented by the participants).

Procedure

1. (10–15 minutes) Divide into two groups, each with color-coded badges. For example, the blue group could receive blue Post-it notes and the yellow group could receive yellow Post-it notes. Print your first name in bold letters on the badge and wear it throughout the exercise.

   Work with your group members to invent your own cultural cues. Think about the kinds of behaviors and words that will signify to all members that they belong together in one culture. For each category provided below, identify and record at least one important attribute for your culture.

Cultural Cues:	Your Culture:
Facial expression:	_____
Eye contact (note: you must have some eye contact in order to observe others):	_____
Handshake:	_____
Body language (note: must be evident while standing):	_____
Key words or phrases:	_____

   Once you have identified desirable cultural aspects for your group, practice them. It is best to stand with your group and to engage one another in conversations involving two or three people at a time. Your aim in talking with one another is to learn as much as possible about each other—hobbies, interests, where you live, what your family is like, what courses you are taking; and so on, all the while practicing the behaviors and words identified above. It is not necessary for participants to answer questions of a personal nature truthfully. Invention is permissible because the conversation is only a means to the end of cultural observation. Your aim at this point is to become comfortable with the indicators of your particular culture. Practice until the indicators are second nature to you.

2. Now assume that you work for a business that has decided to explore the potential for doing business with companies in a different culture. You are to learn as much as possible about another culture. To do so, you will send from one to three representatives from your group on a "business trip" to the other culture. These representatives must, insofar as possible, behave in a manner that is consistent with your culture. At the same time, each representative must endeavor to learn as much as possible about the

Source: Adapted by Susan Rawson Zacur and W. Alan Randolph from *Journal of Management Education,* Vol. 17, No. 4 (November 1993) pp. 510–516.

people in the other culture, while keeping eyes and ears open to cultural attributes that will be useful in future negotiations with foreign businesses. (*Note:* At no time will it be considered ethical behavior for the representative to ask direct questions about the foreign culture's attributes. These must be gleaned from firsthand experience.)

While your representatives are away, you will receive one or more exchange visitors from the other culture, who will engage in conversation as they attempt to learn more about your organizational culture. You must strictly adhere to the cultural aspects of your own culture while you converse with the visitors.

3. (5–10 minutes) All travelers return to your home cultures. As a group, discuss and record what you have learned about the foreign culture based on the exchange of visitors. This information will serve as the basis for orienting the next representatives who will make a business trip.

4. (5–10 minutes) Select one to three different group members to make another trip to the other culture to check out the assumptions your group has made about the other culture. This "checking out" process will consist of actually practicing the other culture's cues to see whether they work.

5. (5–10 minutes) Once the traveler(s) have returned and reported on findings, as a group, prepare to report to the class what you have learned about the other culture.

EXERCISE 8

Prejudice in Our Lives

Contributed by Susan Schor of Pace University and Annie McKee of The Wharton School, University of Pennsylvania with the assistance of Ariel Fishman of The Wharton School

Procedure

1. As a large class group, generate a list of groups that tend to be targets of prejudice and stereotypes in our culture—such groups can include gender, race, ethnicity, sexual orientation, region, religion, and so on. After generating a list, either as a class or in small groups, identify a few common positive and negative stereotypes associated with each group. Consider also relationships or patterns that exist between some of the lists. Discuss the implications for groups that have stereotypes that are valued in organizations versus groups whose stereotypes are viewed negatively in organizations.

2. As an individual, think about the lists you have now generated, and list those groups with which you identify. Write about an experience in which you were stereotyped as a member of a group. Ask yourself the following questions and write down your thoughts:

   (a) What group do I identify with?
   (b) What was the stereotype?
   (c) What happened? When and where did the incident occur? Who said what to whom?
   (d) What were my reactions? How did I feel? What did I think? What did I do?

   (e) What were the consequences? How did the incident affect myself and others?

3. Now, in small groups, discuss your experiences. Briefly describe the incident and focus on how the incident made you feel. Select one incident from the ones shared in your group to role play for the class. Then, as a class, discuss your reactions to each role play. Identify the prejudice or stereotype portrayed, the feelings the situation evoked, and the consequences that might result from such a situation.

4. Think about the prejudices and stereotypes you hold about other people. Ask yourself, "What groups do I feel prejudice toward? What stereotypes do I hold about members of each of these groups? How may such a prejudice have developed—did a family member or close friend or television influence you to stereotype a particular group in a certain way?

5. Now try to identify implications of prejudice in the workplace. How do prejudice and stereotypes affect workers, managers, relationships between people, and the organization as a whole? Consider how you might want to change erroneous beliefs as well as how you would encourage other people to change their own erroneous beliefs.

How We View Differences

Contributed by Barbara Walker

Introduction

Clearly, the workplace of the future will be much more diverse than it is today: more women, more people of color, more international representation, more diverse lifestyles and ability profiles, and the like. Managing a diverse workforce and working across a range of differences is quickly becoming a "core competency" for effective managers.

Furthermore, it is also becoming clear that diversity in a work team can significantly enhance the creativity and quality of the team's output. In today's turbulent business environment, utilizing employee diversity will give the manager and the organization a competitive edge in tapping all of the available human resources more effectively. This exercise is an initial step in the examination of how we work with people whom we see as different from us. It is fairly simple, straightforward, and safe, but its implications are profound.

Procedure

1. Read the following:

Imagine that you are traveling in a rental car in a city you have never visited before. You have a one hour drive on an uncrowded highway before you reach your destination. You decide that you would like to spend the time listening to some of your favorite kind of music on the car radio.

The rental car has four selection buttons available, each with a preset station that plays a different type of music. One plays *country music,* one plays *rock,* one plays *classical,* and one plays *jazz.* Which type of music would you choose to listen to for the next hour as you drive along? (Assume you want to relax and just stick with one station; you don't want to bother switching around between stations.)

Source: Exercise developed by Barbara Walker, a pioneer on work on valuing differences. Adapted for this volume by Douglas T. Hall. Used by permission of Barbara Walker.

2. Form into groups based on the type of music that you have chosen. All who have chosen country will meet in an area designated by the instructor. Those who chose rock will meet in another area, etc. In your groups, answer the following question. Appoint one member to be the spokesperson to report your answers back to the total group.

Question

For each of the other groups, what words would you use to describe people who like to listen to that type of music?

3. Have each spokesperson report the responses of her or his group to the question in step 2. Follow with class discussion of these additional questions:
   (a) What do you think is the purpose or value of this exercise?
   (b) What did you notice about the words used to describe the other groups? Were there any *surprises* in this exercise for you?
   (c) Upon what sorts of data do you think these images were based?
   (d) What term do we normally use to describe these generalized perceptions of another group?
   (e) What could some of the consequences be?
   (f) How do the perceptual processes here relate to other kinds of intergroup differences, such as race, gender, culture, ability, ethnicity, health, age, nationality, etc.?
   (g) What does this exercise suggest about the ease with which intergroup stereotypes form?
   (h) What might be ways an organization might facilitate the valuing and utilizing of differences between people?

Alligator River Story

Source: From Sidney B. Simon, Howard Kirschenbaum, and Leland Howe, *Values Clarification, The Handbook,* revised edition, copyright © 1991, Values Press, P.O. Box 450, Sunderland, MA. 01375. Send for a list of other strategy books from Value Press.

The Alligator River Story

There lived a woman named Abigail who was in love with a man named Gregory. Gregory lived on the shore of a river. Abigail lived on the opposite shore of the same river. The river that separated the two lovers was teeming with dangerous alligators. Abigail wanted to cross the river to be with Gregory. Unfortunately, the bridge had been washed out by a heavy flood the previous week. So she went to ask Sinbad, a riverboat captain, to take her across. He said he would be glad to if she would consent to go to bed with him prior to the voyage. She promptly refused and went to a friend named Ivan to explain her plight. Ivan did not want to get involved at all in the situation. Abigail felt her only alternative was to accept Sinbad's terms. Sinbad fulfilled his promise to Abigail and delivered her into the arms of Gregory.

When Abigail told Gregory about her amorous escapade in order to cross the river, Gregory cast her aside with disdain. Heartsick and rejected, Abigail turned to Slug with her tail of woe. Slug, feeling compassion for Abigail, sought out Gregory and beat him brutally. Abigail was overjoyed at the sight of Gregory getting his due. As the sun set on the horizon, people heard Abigail laughing at Gregory.

Procedure

1. Read "The Alligator River Story."

2. After reading the story, rank the five characters in the story beginning with the one whom you consider the most offensive and end with the one whom you consider the least objectionable. That is, the character who seems to be the most reprehensible to you should be entered first in the list following the story, then the second most reprehensible, and so on, with the least reprehensible or objectionable being entered fifth. Of course, you will have your own reasons as to why you rank them in the order that you do. Very briefly note these too.

3. Form groups as assigned by your instructor (at least four persons per group with gender mixed).

4. Each group should:
   a.   Elect a spokesperson for the group
   b.   Compare how the group members have ranked the characters
   c.   Examine the reasons used by each of the members for their rankings
   d.   Seek consensus on a final group ranking

5. Following your group discussions, you will be asked to share your outcomes and reasons for agreement or non-agreement. A general class discussion will then be held.

• • EXERCISE 11

Teamwork and Motivation

Contributed by Dr. Barbara McCain, Oklahoma City University

Procedure

1. Read this situation.
You are the *owner* of a small manufacturing corporation. Your company manufactures widgets—a commodity. Your widget is a clone of nationally known widgets. Your widget, "WooWoo," is less expensive and more readily available than the nationally known brand. Presently, the sales are high. However, there are many rejects, which increases your cost and delays the delivery. You have 50 employees in the following departments: sales, assembly, technology, and administration.

2. In groups, discuss methods to motivate all of the employees in the organization—rank order them in terms of preference.

3. Design an organization motivation plan that encourages high job satisfaction, low turnover, high productivity, and high-quality work.

4. Is there anything special you can do about the minimum wage service worker? How do you motivate this individual? On what motivation theory do you base your decision?

5. Report to the class your motivation plan. Record your ideas on the board and allow all groups to build on the first plan. Discuss additions and corrections as the discussion proceeds.

Worksheet

Individual Worker	Team Member
Talks	
Me oriented	
Department focused	
Competitive	
Logical	
Written messages	
Image	
Secrecy	
Short-term sighted	
Immediate results	
Critical	
Tenure	

Directions: Fill in the right-hand column with descriptive terms. These terms should suggest a change in behavior from individual work to teamwork.

The Downside of Punishment

Contributed by Dr. Barbara McCain, Oklahoma City University

Procedure

There are numerous problems associated with using punishment or discipline to change behavior. Punishment creates negative effects in the workplace. To better understand this, work in your group to give an example of each of the following situations:

1. Punishment may not be applied to the person whose behavior you want to change.

2. Punishment applied over time may suppress the occurrence of socially desirable behaviors.

3. Punishment creates a dislike of the person who is implementing the punishment.

4. Punishment results in undesirable emotions such as anxiety and agressiveness.

5. Punishment increases the desire to avoid punishment.

6. Punishing one behavior does not guarantee that the desired behavior will occur.

7. Punishment follow-up requires allocation of additional resources.

8. Punishment may create a communication barrier and inhibit the flow of information.

Source: Adapted from class notes: Dr. Larry Michaelson, Oklahoma University.

EXERCISE 13

Annual Pay Raises

Procedure

1. Read the job descriptions below and decide on a percentage pay increase for each of the eight employees.

2. Make salary increase recommendations for each of the eight managers that you supervise. There are no formal company restrictions on the size of raises you give, but the total for everyone should not exceed the $10,900 (a 4-percent increase in the salary pool) which has been budgeted for this purpose. You have a variety of information upon which to base the decisions, including a "productivity index" (PI), which Industrial Engineering computes as a quantitative measure of operating efficiency for each manager's work unit. This index ranges from a high of 10 to a low of 1. Indicate the percentage increase *you* would give each manager in the blank space next to each manager's name. Be prepared to explain why.

_____ *A. Alvarez*   Alvarez is new this year and has a tough work group whose task is dirty and difficult. This is a hard position to fill, but you don't feel Alvarez is particularly good. The word around is that the other managers agree with you. PI = 3. Salary = $33,000.

_____ *B. J. Cook*   Cook is single and a "swinger" who enjoys leisure time. Everyone laughs at the problems B.J. has getting the work out, and you feel it certainly is lacking. Cook has been in the job 2 years. PI = 3. Salary = $34,500.

_____ *Z. Davis*   In the position 3 years, Davis is one of your best people, even though some of the other managers don't agree. With a spouse who is independently wealthy, Davis doesn't need money but likes to work. PI = 7. Salary = $36,600.

_____ *M. Frame*   Frame has personal problems and is hurting financially. Others gossip about Frame's performance, but you are quite satisfied with this second-year employee. PI = 7. Salary = $34,700.

_____ *C.M. Liu*   Liu is just finishing a fine first year in a tough job. Highly respected by the others, Liu has a job offer in another company at a 15-percent increase in salary. You are impressed, and the word is that the money is important. PI = 9. Salary = $34,000.

_____ *B. Ratin*   Ratin is a first-year manager whom you and the others think is doing a good job. This is a bit surprising since Ratin turned out to be a "free spirit" who doesn't seem to care much about money or status. PI = 9. Salary = $33,800.

_____ *H. Smith*   A first-year manager recently divorced and with two children to support as a single parent. The others like Smith a lot, but your evaluation is not very high. Smith could certainly use extra money. PI = 5. Salary = $33,000.

_____ *G. White*   White is a big spender who always has the latest clothes and a new car. In the first year on what you would call an easy job, White doesn't seem to be doing very well. For some reason, though, the others talk about White as the "cream of the new crop." PI = 5. Salary = $33,000.

3. Convene in a group of four to seven persons and share your raise decision.

4. As a group, decide on a new set of raises and be prepared to report them to the rest of the class. Make sure that the group spokesperson can provide the rationale for each person's raise.

5. The instructor will call on each group to report its raise decisions. After discussion, an "expert's" decision will be given.

EXERCISE 14

Tinker Toys

Contributed by Bonnie McNeely, Murray State University

Materials Needed
Tinker toy sets.

Procedure

1. Form groups as assigned by the instructor. The mission of each group or temporary organization is to build the tallest possible tinker toy tower. Each group should determine worker roles: at least four students will be builders, some will be consultants who offer suggestions, and the remaining students will be observers who remain silent and complete the observation sheet provided below.

2. Rules for the exercise:
   a. Fifteen minutes allowed to plan the tower, but *only 60 seconds* to build.
   b. No more than two Tinker Toy pieces can be put together during the planning.
   c. All pieces must be put back in the box before the competition begins.
   d. Completed tower must stand alone.

Observation Sheet

1. What planning activities were observed?

   Did the group members adhere to the rules?

2. What organizing activities were observed?

Source: Adapted from Bonnie McNeely, "Using the Tinker Toy Exercise to Teach the Four Functions of Management, *Journal of Management Education,* Vol. 18, No. 4 (November 1994), 468–472.

Was the task divided into subtasks? Division of labor?

3. Was the group motivated to succeed? Why or why not?

4. Were any control techniques observed?

Was a time keeper assigned?

Were backup plans discussed?

5. Did a clear leader emerge from the group?

What behaviors indicated that this person was the leader?

How did the leader establish credibility with the group?

6. Did any conflicts within the group appear?

Was there a power struggle for the leadership position?

EXERCISE 15

Job Design Preferences

Procedure

1. Use the left column to rank the following job characteristics in the order most important *to you* (1=highest to 10=lowest). Then use the right column to rank them in the order you think they are most important *to others*.

____	Variety of tasks	____
____	Performance feedback	____
____	Autonomy/freedom in work	____
____	Working on a team	____
____	Having responsibility	____
____	Making friends on the job	____
____	Doing all of a job, not part	____
____	Importance of job to others	____
____	Having resources to do well	____
____	Flexible work schedule	____

2. Form work groups as assigned by your instructor. Share your rankings with other group members. Discuss where you have different individual preferences and where your impressions differ from the preferences of others. Are there any major patterns in your group—for either the "personal" or the "other" rankings? Develop group consensus rankings for each column. Designate a spokesperson to share the group rankings and results of any discussion with the rest of the class.

My Fantasy Job

Contributed by Lady Hanson, California State Polytechnic University, Pomona

Instructions

1. Think about a possible job that represents what you consider to be your ideal or "fantasy" job. For discussion purposes, try to envision it as a job you would hold within a year of finishing your current studies. Write down a brief description of that job in the space below. Start the description with the following words—*My fantasy job would be* . . .

2. Review the description of the Hackman/Oldham model of Job Characteristics Theory offered in the textbook. Note in particular the descriptions of the core characteristics. Consider how each of them could be maximized in your fantasy job. Indicate in the spaces that follow how specific parts of your fantasy job will fit into or relate to each of the core characteristics.

    a) Skill variety: _____

    b) Task identity: _____

    c) Task significance: _____

    d) Autonomy: _____

    e) Job feedback: _____

3. Form into groups as assigned by your instructor. In the group have each person share his or her fantasy job and the descriptions of its core characteristics. Select one person from your group to tell the class as a whole about her/his fantasy job. Be prepared to participate in general discussion regarding the core characteristics and how they may or may not relate to job performance and job satisfaction. Consider also the likelihood that the fantasy jobs of class members are really attainable—in other words: Can "fantasy" become fact?

*Eggs*periential Exercise

Contributed by Dr. Barbara McCain, Oklahoma City University

Materials Needed

1 raw egg per group   1 yard of plastic tape

6 plastic straws per group   1 large plastic jar

Procedure

1. Form into equal groups of five to seven people.
2. The task is to drop an egg from the chair onto the plastic without breaking the egg. Groups can evaluate the materials and plan their task for 10 minutes. During this period the materials may not be handled.
3. Groups have 10 minutes for construction.
4. One group member will drop the egg while standing on top of a chair in front of the class. One by one a representative from each group will drop their eggs.
5. Optional: Each group will name the egg.
6. Each group discusses their individual/group behav-iors during this activity. Optional: This analysis may be summarized in written form. The following questions may be utilized in the analysis:

   (a) What kind of group is it? Explain.
   (b) Was the group cohesive? Explain.
   (c) How did the cohesiveness relate to performance? Explain.
   (d) Was there evidence of group think? Explain.
   (e) Were group norms established? Explain.
   (f) Was there evidence of conflict? Explain.
   (g) Was there any evidence of social loafing? Explain.

EXERCISE 18

Scavenger Hunt—Team Building

Contributed by Michael R. Manning and Paula J. Schmidt, New Mexico State University

Introduction

Think about what it means to be a part of a team—a successful team. What makes one team more successful than another? What does each team member need to do in order for their team to be successful? What are the characteristics of an effective team?

Procedure

1. Form teams as assigned by your instructor. Locate the items on the list below while following these important rules:

   a. Your team *must stay together at all times*—that is, you cannot go in separate directions.
   b. Your team must return to the classroom in the time allotted by the instructor.

   The team with the most items on the list will be declared the most successful team.

2. Next, reflect on your team's experience. What did each team member do? What was your team's strategy? What made your team effective? Make a list of the most important things your team did to be succesful. Nominate a spokesperson to summarize your team's discussion for the class. What items were similar between teams? That is, what helped each team to be effective?

Source: Adapted from Michael R. Manning and Paula J. Schmidt, *Journal of Management Education,* Building Effective Work Teams: A Quick Exercise Based on a Scavenger Hunt. (Thousand Oaks, CA: Sage Publications, 1995), pp. 392–398. Used by permission. Reference for list of items for scavenger hunt from C. E. Larson and F. M. Lafas, *Team Work: What Must Go Right/What Can Go Wrong* (Newbury Park, CA: Sage Publications, 1989).

Items for Scavenger Hunt

Each item is to be identified and brought back to the classroom.

1. A book with the word "team" in the title.
2. A joke about teams that you share with the class.
3. A blade of grass from the university football field.
4. A souvenir from the state.
5. A picture of a team or group.
6. A newspaper article about a team.
7. Compose a team song and perform it for the class.
8. A leaf from an oak tree.
9. Stationery from the Dean's office.
10. A cup of sand.
11. A pine cone.
12. A live reptile. (*Note:* Sometimes a team member has one for a pet or the students are ingenious enough to visit a local pet store.)
13. A definition of group "cohesion" that you share with the class.
14. A set of chopsticks.
15. Bring back three cans of vegetables.
16. A branch of an elm tree.
17. Find and share three unusual items with the class.
18. A ball of cotton
19. The ear from a prickly pear cactus.
20. A group name.

(*Note:* Items may be substituted as appropriate for your locale.)

Work Team Dynamics

Introduction

Think about your course work team, a work team you are involved in for another course, or any other team suggested by the instructor. Indicate how often each of the following statements accurately reflects your experience in the team. Use this scale:

1=Always   2=Frequently   3=Sometimes   4=Never

_____ 1. My ideas get a fair hearing.

_____ 2. I am encouraged for innovative ideas and risk taking.

_____ 3. Diverse opinions within the team are encouraged.

_____ 4. I have all the responsibility I want.

_____ 5. There is a lot of favoritism shown in the team.

_____ 6. Members trust one another to do their assigned work.

_____ 7. The team sets high standards of performance excellence.

_____ 8. People share and change jobs a lot in the team.

_____ 9. You can make mistakes and learn from them in this team.

_____ 10. This team has good operating rules.

Procedure

Form groups as assigned by your instructor. Ideally, this will be the team you have just rated. Have all team members share their ratings, and make one master rating for the team as a whole. Circle the items on which there are the biggest differences of opinion. Discuss those items and try to find out why they exist. In general, the better a team scores on this instrument, the higher its creative potential. If everyone has rated the same team, make a list of the five most important things members can do to improve its operations in the future. Nominate a spokesperson to summarize the team discussion for the class as a whole.

Source: Adapted from William Dyer, _Team Building,_ ed. 2 (Reading, MA: Addison-Wesley, 1987), pp. 123–125.

Identifying Group Norms

Procedure

1. Choose an organization you know quite a bit about.

2. Complete the questionnaire below, indicating your responses using one of the following:

> (a) Strongly agree or encourage it.
> (b) Agree with it or encourage it.
> (c) Consider it unimportant.
> (d) Disagree with or discourage it.
> (e) Strongly disagree with or discourage it.

If an employee in this organization were to . . . *Most other employees would:*

1. Show genuine concern for the problems that face the organization and make suggestions about solving them . . . ___
2. Set very high personal standards of performance . . . ___
3. Try to make the work group operate more like a team when dealing with issues or problems . . . ___
4. Think of going to a supervisor with a problem . . .
5. Evaluate expenditures in terms of the benefits they will provide for the organization . . . ___
6. Express concern for the well-being of other members of the organization . . . ___
7. Keep a customer or client waiting while looking after matters of personal convenience . . . ___
8. Criticize a fellow employee who is trying to improve things in the work situation . . . ___
9. Actively look for ways to expand his/her knowledge to be able to do a better job . . . ___
10. Be perfectly honest in answering this questionnaire . . . ___

Scoring

A = +2, B = +1, C = 0, D = −1, E = −2

1. Organizational/Personal Pride
   Score ___
2. Performance/Excellence
   Score ___
3. Teamwork/Communication
   Score ___
4. Leadership/Supervision
   Score ___
5. Profitability/Cost Effectiveness
   Score ___

6. Colleague/Associate Relations
   Score ___
7. Customer/Client Relations
   Score ___
8. Innovativeness/Creativity
   Score ___
9. Training/Development
   Score ___
10. Candor/Openness
    Score ___

•••• **EXERCISE 21** ••

Workgroup Culture

Contributed by Conrad N. Jackson, MPC, Inc.

Source: Adapted from Donald D. Bowen, et al., *Experiences in Management and Organizational Behavior,* 4th ed. (New York: John Wiley & Sons, Inc.), 1997.

Procedure

1. The bipolar scales on this instrument can be used to evaluate a group's process in a number of useful ways.

Use it to measure where you see the group to be at present. To do this, *circle* the number that best represents *how you see the culture of the group*. You can also indicate how you think the group *should* function by using a different symbol, such as a square (□), or a caret (^) to indicate how you saw the group at some time in the past.

2. (a) If you are assessing your own group, have everyone fill in the instrument, summarize the scores, then discuss their bases (what members say and do that has led to these interpretations) and implications. This is often an extremely productive intervention to improve group or team functioning.

(b) If you are assessing another group, use the scores as the basis for your feeback. Be sure to provide specific feedback on behavior *you have*

observed in addition to the subjective interpretations of your ratings on the scales in this instrument.

(c) The instrument can also be used to compare a group's self-assessment with the assessment provided by another group.

1. Trusting	1 : 2 : 3 : 4 : 5	Suspicious
2. Helping	1 : 2 : 3 : 4 : 5	Ignoring, blocking
3. Expressing feelings	1 : 2 : 3 : 4 : 5	Suppressing feelings
4. Risk taking	1 : 2 : 3 : 4 : 5	Cautious
5. Authenticity	1 : 2 : 3 : 4 : 5	Game playing
6. Confronting	1 : 2 : 3 : 4 : 5	Avoiding
7. Open	1 : 2 : 3 : 4 : 5	Hidden, diplomatic

EXERCISE 22

The Hot Seat

Contributed by Barry R. Armandi, SUNY-Old Westbury

Procedure

1. Form into groups as assigned by your instructor.
2. Read the following situation.

A number of years ago, Professor Stevens was asked to attend a departmental meeting at a university. He had been on leave from the department, but a junior faculty member discreetly requested that he attend to protect the rights of the junior faculty. The Chair, or head of the department, was a typical Machiavellian, whose only concerns were self-serving. Professor Stevens had a number of previous disagreements with the Chair. The heart of the disagreements centered around the Chair's abrupt and domineering style and his poor relations with the junior faculty, many of whom felt mistreated and scared.

The department was a conglomeration of different professioral types. Included in the mix were behavioralists, generalists, computer scientists, and quantitative analysts. The department was embedded in the school of business, which had three other departments. There was much confusion and concern among the faculty, since this was a new organizational design. Many of the faculty were at odds with each other over the direction the school was now taking.

At the meeting, a number of proposals were to be presented that would seriously affect the performance and future of certain junior faculty, particularly those who were behavioral scientists. The Chair, a computer scien-

tist, disliked the behaviorists, who he felt were "always analyzing the motives of people." Professor Stevens, who was a tenured full professor and a behaviorist, had an objective to protect the interests of the junior faulty ad to counter the efforts of the Chair.

Including Professor Stevens, there were nine faculty present. The accompanying diagram on the next page shows the seating arrangement and the layout of the room. The ×s signify those faculty who were allies of the Chair. The +s are those opposed to the Chair and supportive of Professor Stevens, and the ?s were undecided and could be swayed either way. The circled numbers represent empty seats. Both ?s were behavioralists, and the + next to them was a quantitative analyst. Near the door, the first × was a generalist, the two +s were behavioralists, and the second × was a quantitative analyst. The diagram shows the seating of everyone but Professor Stevens, who was the last one to enter the room. Standing at the door, Professor Stevens surveyed the room and within 10 seconds knew which seat was the most effective to achieve his objective.

3. Answer the following questions in your group.
   (a) Which seat did Professor Stevens select and why?
   (b) What is the likely pattern of communication and interaction in this group?
   (c) What can be done to get this group to work harmoniously?

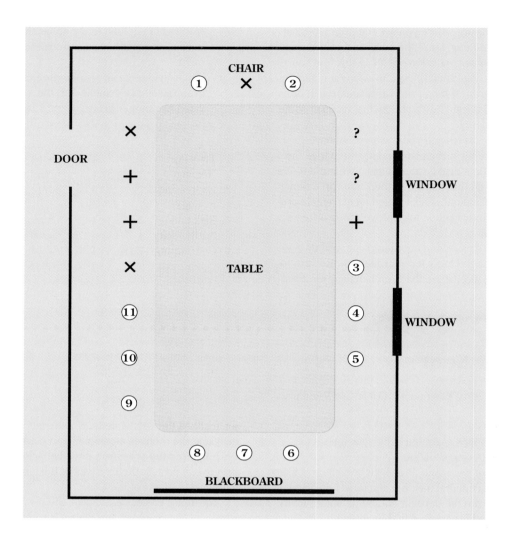

Organizations Alive!

Contributed by Bonnie L. McNeely, Murray State University

Procedure

1. Find a copy of the following items from actual organizations. These items can be obtained from the company where you now work, your parent's workplace, or from the university. Universities have mission statements, codes of conduct for students and faculty, organizational charts, job descriptions, performance appraisal forms, and control devices. Some student organizations also have these documents. All the items do not have to come from the same organization *Bring these items to class.*

Source: Adapted from Bonnie L. McNeely, "Make Your Principles of Management Class come Alive," *Journal of Management Education,* Vol. 18, No. 2, May 1994, 246–249.

(a) Mission Statement   (d) Job Description
(b) Code of Ethics   (e) Performance Appraisal Form
(c) Organizational Chart   (f) Control Device

2. Form groups in class as assigned by your instructor. Share your items with the group, as well as what you learned while collecting these items. For example, did you find that some firms have a mission, but it is not written down? Did you find that job descriptions existed, but they were not really used or had not been updated in years?

EXERCISE 24

Fast Food Technology

Contributed by D. T. Hall, Boston University, and F. S. Hall, University of New Hampshire

Introduction

A critical first step in improving or changing any organization is *diagnosing* or analyzing its present functioning. Many change and organization development efforts fall short of their objectives because this important step was not taken, or was conducted superficially. To illustrate this, imagine how you would feel if you went to your doctor complaining of stomach pains, and he recommended surgery without conducting any tests, without obtaining any further information, and without a careful physical examination. You would probably switch doctors! Yet, managers often attempt major changes with correspondingly little diagnostic work in advance. (It could be said that they undertake vast projects with half-vast ideas.)

In this exercise, you will be asked to conduct a group diagnosis of two different organizations in the fast food business. The exercise will provide an opportunity to integrate much of the knowledge you have gained in other exercises and in studying other topics. Your task will be to describe the organizations as carefully as you can in terms of several key organizational concepts. Although the organizations are probably very familiar to you, try to step back and look at them as though you were seeing them for the first time.

Procedure

1. In groups of four or six people, your assignment is described below.

One experience most people in this country have shared is that of dining in the hamburger establishment known as McDonald's. In fact, someone has claimed that 25th-century archeologists may dig into the ruins of our present civilization and conclude that 20-century religion was devoted to the worship of golden arches.

Your group, Fastalk Consultants, is known as the shrewdest, most insightful, and most overpaid management consulting firm in the country. You have been hired by the president of McDonald's to make recommendations for improving the motivation and performance of personnel in their franchise operations. Let us assume that the key job activities in franchise operations are food preparation, order-taking and dealing with customers, and routine clean-up operations.

Recently the president of McDonald's has come to suspect that his company's competitors such as Burger King, Wendy's, Jack-in-the-Box, Dunkin' Doughnuts, various pizza establishments, and others are making heavy inroads into McDonald's market. He has also hired a market research firm to investigate and compare the relative merits of the sandwiches, french fries, and drinks served in McDonald's and the competitor, and has asked the market research firm to assess the advertising campaigns of the two organizations. Hence, you will not need to be concerned with marketing issues, except as they may have an impact on employee behavior. The president wants *you* to look into the *organization* of the franchises to determine the strengths and weaknesses of each. Select a competitor who gives McDonald's a good "run for its money" in your area.

The president has established an unusual contract with you. *He wants you to make your recommendations based upon your observations as a customer.* He does not want you to do a complete diagnosis with interviews, surveys, or behind-the-scenes observations. He wants your report in two parts. Remember, the president wants concrete, specific, and practical recommendations. Avoid vague generalizations such as "improve communications" or "increase trust." Say very clearly *how* management can improve organizational performance. Substantiate your recommendations by reference to one or more theories of motivation, leadership, small groups, or job design.

Part I

Given his organization's goals of profitability, sales volume, fast and courteous service, and cleanliness, the president of McDonald's wants an analysis that will *compare and contrast McDonald's and the competitor* in terms of the following concepts:

Organizational goals
Organizational structure
Technology
Environment
Employee motivation
Communication
Leadership style
Policies/procedures/rules/standards
Job design
Organizational climate

Part II

Given the corporate goals listed under Part I, what specific actions might McDonald's management and franchise owners take in the following areas to achieve these goals (profitability, sales volume, fast and courteous service, and cleanliness)?

Job design and workflow
Organizational structure (at the individual restaurant level)
Employee incentives
Leadership
Employee selection

How do McDonald's and the competition differ in these aspects? Which company has the best approach?

2. Complete the assignment by going as a group to one McDonald's and one competitor's restaurant. If possible, have a meal in each place. To get a more valid comparison, visit a McDonald's and a competitor located in the same area. After observing each restaurant, meet with your group and prepare your 10-minute report to the executive committee.

3. In class, each group will present its report to the rest of the class, who will act as the executive committee. The group leader will appoint a timekeeper to be sure that each group sticks to its 10-minute time limit. Possible discussion questions include:
   (a) What similarities are there between the two organizations?
   (b) What differences are there between the organizations?
   (c) Do you have any "hunches" about the reasons for the particular organizational characteristics you found? For example, can you try to explain why one organization might have a particular type of structure? Incentive system? Climate?
   (d) Can you try to explain one set of characteristics in terms of some other characteristics you found? For example, do the goals account for structure? Does the environment explain the structure?

EXERCISE 25

Alien Invasion

Procedure

This is an exercise in organizational culture. You will be assigned to a team (if you are not already in one) and instructed to visit an organization by your instructor.

1. Visit the site assigned as a team working under conditions set forth in the "situation" below.
2. Take detailed notes on the cultural forms that you observe.
3. Prepare a presentation for the class that describes these forms and draw any inferences you can about the nature of the culture of the organization—its ideologies, values, and norms of behavior.
4. Be sure to explain the basis of your inferences in terms of the cultural forms observed

You will have 20 minutes to report your findings, so plan your presentation carefully. Use visual aids to help your audience understand what you have found.

Situation

You are Martians who have just arrived on Earth in the first spaceship from your planet. Your superiors have ordered you to learn as much about Earthlings and the way they behave as you can with-

Source: Adapted from Donald D. Bowen et al., *Experiences in Management and Organizational Behavior,* 4th ed. (New York: John Wiley & Sons, Inc.), 1997.

out doing anything to make them aware that you are Martians. It is vital for the future plans of your superiors that you do nothing to disturb the Earthlings. Unfortunately, Martians communicate by emitting electromagnetic waves and are incapable of speech, so you cannot talk to the natives. Even if you did, it is reported by the usually reliable Bureau of Interplanetary Intelligence that Earthlings may become cannibalistic if annoyed. However, the crash course in Earth languages taught by the Bureau has enabled you to read the language.

Remember, these instructions limit your data collection to observation and request that you *not* talk to the "natives." There are two reasons for this instruction. First, your objective is to learn what the organization does when it is simply going about its normal business and not responding to a group of students asking questions. Second, you are likely to be surprised at how much you can learn by simply observing if you put your mind to it. Many skilled managers employ this ability in sensing what is going on as they walk through their plant or office area.

Since you cannot talk to people, some of the cultural forms (legends, sagas, etc.) will be difficult to spot unless you are able to pick up copies of the organization's promotional literature (brochures, company reports, advertisements) during your visit. Do not be discouraged, because the visible forms such as artifacts, setting, symbols, and (sometimes) rituals can convey a great deal about the culture. Just keep your eyes, ears, and antennae open!

EXERCISE 26

Interview a Leader

Contributed by Bonnie McNeely, Murray State University

Procedure

1. Make an appointment to interview a leader. It can be a leader working in a business or nonprofit organization, such as a government agency, school, etc. Base the interview on the form provided here, but feel free to add your own questions.
2. Bring the results of your interview to class. Form into groups as assigned by your instructor. Share the responses from your interview with your group and compare answers. What issues were similar? Different? Were the stress levels of leaders working in nonprofit organizations as high as those working in for profit firms? Were you surprised at the number of hours per week worked by leaders?
3. Be prepared to summarize the interviews done by your group as a formal written report, if asked to do so by the instructor.

Interview Questionnaire

Student's Name _____ Date _____

1. Position in the organization (title):
2. Number of years in current position:
   Number of years of managerial experience:
3. Number of people directly supervised:
4. Average number of hours worked a week
5. How did you get into leadership?
6. What is the most rewarding part of being a leader?
7. What is the most difficult part of your job?
8. What would you say are the *keys to success* for leaders?

Source: Adapted from Bonnie McNeely, "Make Your Principles of Management Class come Alive," *Journal of Management Education,* Vol. 18, No. 2, May 1994, 246–249.

9. What advice do you have for an aspiring leader?
10. What type of ethical issues have you faced as a leader?
11. If you were to enroll in a leadership seminar, what topics or issues would you want to learn more about?
12. (Student's question)

Gender: M____ F____ Years of formal education____

Level of job stress: Very high____ High____ Average____ Low____

Profit organization____ Nonprofit organization____

Additional information/Comments:

Leadership Skills Inventories

Procedure

1. Look over the skills listed below and ask your instructor to clarify those you do not understand.
2. Complete each category by checking either the "Strong" or "Needs Development" category in relation to your own level with each skill.
3. After completing each category, briefly describe a situation in which each of the listed skills has been utilized.
4. Meet in your groups to share and discuss inventories. Prepare a report summarizing major development needs in your group.

Instrument

	Strong	Needs Development	Situation
Communication	_____	_____	_____
Conflict Management	_____	_____	_____
Delegation	_____	_____	_____
Ethical Behavior	_____	_____	_____
Listening	_____	_____	_____
Motivation	_____	_____	_____
Negotiation	_____	_____	_____
Performance Appraisal and Feedback	_____	_____	_____
Planning and Goal Setting	_____	_____	_____
Power and Influence	_____	_____	_____
Presentation and Persuasion	_____	_____	_____
Problem Solving and Decision Making	_____	_____	_____
Stress Management	_____	_____	_____
Team Building	_____	_____	_____
Time Management	_____	_____	_____

Leadership and Participation in Decision Making

Procedure

1. For the ten situations described below, decide which of the three styles you would use for that unique situation. Place the letter A, P, or L on the line before each situation's number.

     A—authority; make the decision alone without additional inputs.

     P—consultative; make the decision based on group inputs.

     L—group; allow the group to which you belong to make the decision.

Decision Situations

_____ 1. You have developed a new work procedure that will increase productivity. Your boss likes the idea and wants you to try it within a few weeks. You view your employees as fairly capable and believe that they will be receptive to the change.

_____ 2. The industry of your product has new competition. Your organization's revenues have been dropping. You have been told to lay off three of your ten employees in 2 weeks. You have been the supervisor for over 1 year. Normally, your employees are very capable.

_____ 3. Your department has been facing a problem for several months. Many solutions have been tried and failed. You finally thought of a solution, but you are not sure of the possible consequences of the change required or the acceptance of the highly capable employees.

_____ 4. Flex time has become popular in your organization. Some departments let each employee start and end work whenever they choose. However, because of the cooperative effort of your employees, they must all work the same 8 hours. You are not sure of the level of interest in changing the hours. Your employees are a very capable group and like to make decisions.

_____ 5. The technology in your industry is changing faster than the members of your organization can keep up. Top management hired a consultant who has given the recommended decision. You have 2 weeks to make your decision. Your employees are capable, and they enjoy participating in the decision-making process.

_____ 6. Your boss called you on the telephone to tell you that someone has requested an order for your department's product with a very short delivery date. She asked that you call her back with the decision about taking the order in 15 minutes. Looking over the work schedule, you realize that it will be very difficult to deliver the order on time. Your employees will have to push hard to make it. They are cooperative, capable, and enjoy being involved in decision making.

_____ 7. A change has been handed down from top management. How you implement it is your decision. The change takes effect in one month. It will personally affect everyone in your department. The acceptance of the department members is critical to the success of the change. Your employees are usually not too interested in being involved in making decisions.

_____ 8. You believe that productivity in your department could be increased. You have thought of some ways that may work, but you're not sure of them. Your employees are very experienced; almost all of them have been in the department longer than you have.

_____ 9. Top management has decided to make a change that will affect all of your employees. You know that they will be upset because it will cause them hardship. One or two may even quit. The change goes into effect in 30 days. Your employees are very capable.

_____ 10. A customer has offered you a contract for your product with a quick delivery date. The offer is open for 2 days. Meeting the contract deadline would require employees to work nights and weekends for 6 weeks. You cannot require them to work overtime. Filling this profitable contract could help get you the raise you want and feel you deserve. However, if you take the contract and don't deliver on time it will hurt your chances of getting a big raise. Your employees are very capable.

2. Form groups as assigned by your instructor. Share and compare your choices for each decision situation. Reconcile any differences and be prepared to defend your decision preferences in general class discussion.

EXERCISE 29

My Best Manager: Revisited

Contributed by J. Marcus Maier, Chapman University

Procedure

1. Refer to the list of qualities—or profiles—the class generated earlier in the course for the "Best Manager."

2. Looking first at your Typical Managers profile, suppose you took this list to 100 average people on the street (or at the local mall) and asked them whether _____ (Trait X, quality Y) was "more typical of men or of women in our culture." What do you think *most* of them would say? That _____ (X, Y etc.) is more typical of *women*? or of *men*? Or of neither/both?[1] Do this for every trait on your list(s). (5 minutes)

3. Now do the same for the qualities we generated in our Best Manager profile. (5 min.)

4. A straw vote is taken, one quality at a time, to determine the class's overall gender identification of each trait, focusing on the Typical Managers profile (10–15 min.). Then this is repeated for the Best Manager profile (10–15 min.).[2]

5. Discussion. What do you see in the data this group has generated? How might you interpret these results? (15–20 min.)

Source: Based on Dr. Maier's 1993 article, "The Gender Prism." *Journal of Management Education,* 17(3), 285–314. 1994 Fritz Roethlisberger Award Recipient for Best Paper (Updated, 1996).

[1] This gets the participants to move outside of their *own* conceptions to their awareness of *societal* definitions of masculinity and femininity.

[2] This is done by a rapid show of hands, looking for a clear majority vote. An "f" (for "feminine") is placed next to those qualities that a clear majority indicate are more typical of women, an "m" (for "masculine") next to those qualities a clear majority indicate would be more typical of men. (This procedure parallels the median-split method used in determining Bem Sex Role Inventory classifications.) If no clear majority emerges (i.e., if the vote is close), the trait or quality is classified as "both" (f/m). The designations "masculine" or "feminine" are used (rather than "men" or "women") to underscore the *socially constructed* nature of each dimension.

Active Listening

Contributed by Robert Ledman, Morehouse College

Procedure

1. Review active listening skills and behaviors as described in the textbook and in class.
2. Form into groups of three. Each group will have a listener, a talker, and an observer (if the number of students is not evenly divisible by three, two observers are used for one or two groups).
3. The "talkers" should talk about any subject they wish, but only *if* they are being actively listened to. Talkers should stop speaking as soon as they sense active listening has stopped.

Source: Adapted from the presentation entitled "An Experiential Exercise to Teach Active Listening," presented at the Organizational Behavior Teaching Conference, Macomb, IL, 1995.

4. The "listeners" should use a list of active listening skills and behaviors as their guide, and practice as many of them as possible to be sure the talker is kept talking. Listeners should contribute nothing more than "active listening" to the communication.
5. The "observer" should note the behaviors and skills used by the listener and the effects they seemed to have on the communication process.
6. These roles are rotated until each student has played every role.
7. The instructor will lead a discussion of what the observers saw and what happened with the talkers and listeners. The discussion focuses on what behaviors from the posted list have been present, which have been absent, and how the communication has been affected by the listener's actions.

Upward Appraisal

Procedure

1. Form work groups as assigned by your instructor.
2. The instructor will leave the room.
3. Convene in your assigned work groups for a period of 10 minutes. Create a list of comments, problems, issues, and concerns you would like to have communicated to the instructor in regard to the course experience to date. *Remember,* your interest in the exercise is twofold: (a) to communicate your feelings to the instructor and (b) to learn more about the process of giving and receiving feedback.
4. Select one person from the group to act as spokesperson in communicating the group's feelings to the instructor.
5. The spokespersons should briefly convene to decide on what physical arrangement of chairs, tables, and so forth is most appropriate to conduct the feedback session. The classroom should then be rearranged to fit the desired specifications.
6. While the spokespersons convene, persons in the remaining groups should discuss how they expect the forthcoming communications event to develop. Will it be a good experience for all parties concerned? Be prepared to observe critically the actual communication process.
7. The instructor should be invited to return, and the feedback session will begin. Observers should make notes so that they may make constructive comments at the conclusion of the exercise.
8. Once the feedback session is complete, the instructor will call on the observers for comments, ask the spokespersons for reactions, and open the session to discussion.

"360" Feedback

Contributed by Timothy J. Serey, Northern Kentucky University

Introduction

The time of performance reviews is often a time of genuine anxiety for many organizational members. On one hand, it is an important organizational ritual and a key part of the Human Resource function. Organizations usually codify the process and provide a mechanism to appraise performance. On the other hand, it is rare for managers to feel comfortable with this process. Often, they feel discomfort over "playing God." One possible reason for this is that managers rarely receive formal training about how to provide feedback. From the manager's point of view, if done properly, giving feedback is at the very heart of his or her job as "coach" and "teacher." It is an investment in the professional development of another person, rather than the punitive element we so often associate with hearing from "the boss." From the subordinate's perspective, most people want to know where they stand, but this is usually tempered by a fear of "getting it in the neck." In many organizations, it is rare to receive straight, non-sugar-coated feedback about where you stand.

Procedure

1. Review the section of the book dealing with feedback before you come to class. It is also helpful if individuals make notes about their perceptions and feelings about the course *before* they come to class.
2. Groups of students should discuss their experiences, both positive and negative, in this class. Each group should determine the dimensions of evaluating the class itself *and* the instructor. For example, students might select criteria that include the practicality of the course, the way the material is structured and presented (e.g., lecture or exercises), and the instructor's style (e.g., enthusiasm, fairness).
3. Groups select a member to represent them in a subgroup that next provides feedback to the instructor before the entire class.
4. The student-audience then provides the subgroup with feedback about their effectiveness in this exercise. That is, the larger class provides feedback to the subgroup about the extent to which students actually put the principles of effective feedback into practice (e.g., descriptive not evaluative; specific not general).

Source: Adapted from Timothy J. Serey, *Journal of Management Education,* Vol. 17, No. 2, May 1993. © 1993 by Sage Publications, Inc. Reprinted by permission of Sage Publications.

Role Analysis Negotiation

Contributed by Paul Lyons, Frostburg State University

Introduction

A role is the set of various behaviors people expect from a person (or group) in a particular position. These role expectations occur in all types of organizations, such as one's

Source: Adapted from Paul Lyons, "Developing Expectations with the Role Analysis Technique," *Journal of Management Education.* Vol. 17, No. 3, August 1993, pp. 386–389. © Sage Publications.

place of work, school, family, clubs, and the like. Role ambiguity takes place when a person is confused about the expectations of the role. And sometimes, a role will have expectations that are contradictory. For example, being loyal to the company when the company is breaking the law.

The Role Analysis Technique, or RAT, is a method for improving the effectiveness of a team or group. RAT helps to clarify role expectations, and all organization members have responsibilities that translate to expectations. Determination of role requirements, by consensus—involving all concerned—will ultimately result in more effective and mutually satisfactory behavior. Participation and collaboration in the definition and analysis of roles by group members should result in clarification regarding who is to do what as well as increase the level of commitment to the decisions made.

Procedure

Working alone, carefully read the course syllabus that your instructor has given you. Make a note of any questions you have about anything for which you need clarification or understanding. Pay particular attention to the performance requirements of the course. Make a list of any questions you have regarding what, specifically, is expected of you in order for you to be successful in the course. You will be sharing his information with others, in small groups.

EXERCISE 34

Lost At Sea

Introduction

Consider this situation. You are adrift on a private yacht in the South Pacific when a fire of unknown origin destroys the yacht and most of its contents. You and a small group of survivors are now in a large raft with oars. Your location is unclear, but you estimate being about 1000 miles south-southwest of the nearest land. One person has just found in her pockets five $1 bills and a packet of matches. Everyone else's pockets are empty. The following items are available to you on the raft.

	A	B	C
Sextant	——	——	
Shaving mirror	——	——	
5 gallons water	——	——	
Mosquito netting	——	——	
1 survival meal	——	——	
Maps of Pacific Ocean	——	——	
Floatable seat cushion	——	——	
2 gallons oil-gas mix	——	——	
Small transistor radio	——	——	
Shark repellent	——	——	
20 square feet black plastic	——	——	
1 quart 20-proof rum	——	——	
15 feet nylon rope	——	——	
24 chocolate bars	——	——	
Fishing kit	——	——	

Source: Adapted from "Lost at Sea: A Consensus-Seeking Task," in *The 1975 Handbook for Group Facilitators.* Used with permission of University Associates, Inc.

Procedure

1. *Working alone,* rank in Column A the 15 items in order of their importance to your survival ("1" is most important and "15" is least important).
2. *Working in an assigned group,* arrive at a "team" ranking of the 15 items and record this ranking in Column B. Appoint one person as group spokesperson to report your group rankings to the class.
3. *Do not write in Column C* until further instructions are provided by your instructor.

•••• **EXERCISE 35** •••

Entering the Unknown

Contributed by Michael R. Manning, New Mexico State University; Conrad N. Jackson, MPC, Inc., Huntsville, Alabama; and Paula S. Weber, New Mexico Highlands University

Procedure

1. Form into groups of four or five members. In each group spend a few minutes reflecting on members' typical entry behaviors in new situations and their behaviors when they are in comfortable settings.
2. According to the instructor's directions, students count off to form new groups of four or five members each.
3. The new groups spend the next 15–20 minutes getting to know each other. There is no right or wrong way to proceed, but all members should become more aware of their entry behaviors. They should act in ways that can help them realize a goal of achieving comfortable behaviors with their group.
4. Students review what has occurred in the new groups, giving specific attention to the following questions:
   (a) What topics did your group discuss (content)? Did these topics involve the "here and now" or were they focused on "there and then"?
   (b) What approach did you and your group members take to the task (process)? Did you try to initiate or follow? How? Did you ask questions? Listen? Respond to others? Did you bring up topics?
   (c) Were you more concerned with how you came across or with how others came across to you? Did you play it safe? Were you open? Did you share things even though it seemed uncomfortable or risky? How was humor used in your group? Did it add or detract?
   (d) How do you feel about the approach you took or the behaviors you exhibited? Was this hard or easy? Did others respond the way you had anticipated? Is there some behavior you would like to do more of, do better, or do less of?
   (e) Were your behaviors the ones you had intended (goals)?
5. Responses to these questions are next discussed by the class as a whole. (*Note:* Responses will tend to be mixed within a group, but between groups there should be more similarity.) This discussion helps individuals become aware of and understand their entry behaviors.
6. Optional individuals have identified their entry behaviors; each group can then spend 5–10 minutes discussing members' perceptions of each other:
   (a) What behaviors did they like or find particularly useful? What did they dislike?

(b) What were your reactions to others? What ways did they intend to come across? Did you see others in the way they had intended to come across?
(Alternatively, if there is concern about the personal nature of this discussion, ask the groups to discuss what they liked/didn't like without referring to specific individuals.)

EXERCISE 36

Vacation Puzzle

Contributed by Barbara G. McCain and Mary Khalili, Oklahoma City University

Procedure

Can you solve this puzzle? Give it a try and then compare your answers with other class-mates. Remember your communicative skills!

Puzzle

Khalili, McCain, Middleton, Porter, and Quintaro teach at Oklahoma City University. Each gets 2 weeks of vacation a year. Last year, each took his or her first week in the first 5 months of the year and his or her second week in the last 5 months. If each professor took each of his or her weeks in a different month from the other professors, in which months did each professor take his or her first and second week?

Here are the facts:

(a) McCain took her first week before Khalili, who took *hers* before Porter; for their second week, the order was reversed.
(b) The professor who vacationed in March also vacationed in September.
(c) Quintaro did not take her first week in March or April.
(d) Neither Quintaro nor the professor who took his or her first week in January took his or her second week in August or December.
(e) Middleton took her second week before McCain but after Quintaro.

Month	Professor
January	
February	
March	
April	
May	
June	
July	
August	
September	
October	
November	
December	

Source: Adapted to classroom activity by Dr. Mary Khalili.

THE OB SKILLS WORKBOOK **515**

The Ugli Orange

Introduction

In most work settings, people need other people to do their job, benefit the organization, and forward their career. Getting things done in organizations requires us to work together in cooperation, even though the ultimate objectives of those other people may be different from our own. Your task in the present exercise is learning how to achieve this cooperation more effectively.

Procedure

1. The class will be divided into pairs. One student in each pair will read and prepare the role of Dr. Roland, and one will play the role of Dr. Jones (role descriptions to be distributed by instructor). Students should read their respective role descriptions and prepare to meet with their counterpart (see steps 2 and 3).
2. At this point the group leader will read a statement. The instructor will indicate that he or she is playing

the role of Mr. Cardoza, who owns the commodity in question. The instructor will tell you
   (a) How long you have to meet with the other
   (b) What information the instructor will require at the end of your meeting
   After the instructor has given you this information, you may meet with the other firm's representative and determine whether you have issues you can agree to.
3. Following the meetings (negotiations), the spokesperson for each pair will report any agreements reached to the entire class. The observer for any pair will report on negotiation dynamics and the process by which agreement was reached.
4. Questions to consider:
   (a) Did you reach a solution? If so, what was critical to reaching that agreement?
   (b) Did you and the other negotiator trust one another? Why or why not?
   (c) Was there full disclosure by both sides in each group? How much information was shared?
   (d) How creative and/or complex were the solutions? If solutions were very complex, why do you think this occurred?
   (e) What was the impact of having an "audience" on your behavior? Did it make the problem harder or easier to solve?

Source: Adapted from Hall et al., *Experiences in Management and Organizational Behavior,* 3rd ed. (New York: John Wiley and Sons, Inc.), 1988. Originally developed by Robert J. Hause. Adapted by D. T. Hall and R. J. Lewicki, with suggested modifications by H. Kolodny and T. Ruble.

Force-Field Analysis

Procedure

1. Choose a situation in which you have high personal stakes (for example: how to get a better grade in course X; how to get a promotion; how to obtain a position).
2. Using a version of the Sample Force-Field Analysis Form below, apply the technique to your situation.
   (a) Describe the situation as it now exists.
   (b) Describe the situation as you would like it to be.
   (c) Identify those "driving forces"—the factors that are presently helping to move things in the desired direction.
   (d) Identify those "restraining forces"—the factors that are presently holding things back from moving in the desired direction.

3. Try to be as specific as possible in terms of the above in relation to your situation. You should attempt to be exhaustive in your listing of these forces. List them all!
4. Now go back and classify the strength of each force as weak, medium, or strong. Do this for both the driving and the restraining forces.
5. At this point you should rank the forces regarding their ability to influence or control the situation.
6. In small groups share your analyses. Discuss the usefulness and drawbacks to using this method for personal situations and its application to organizations.
7. Be prepared to share the results of your group's discussion with the rest of the class.

Sample Force-Field Analysis Form

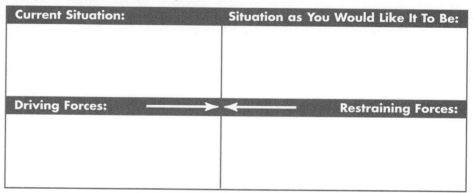

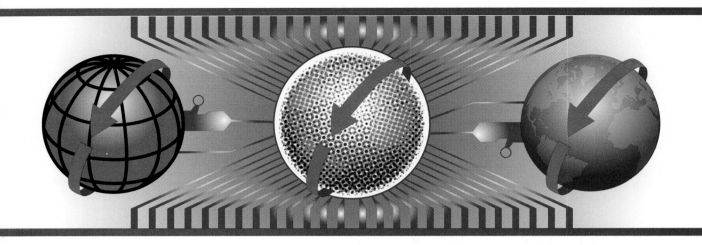

SELF-ASSESSMENT INVENTORIES

ASSESSMENT 1

Managerial Assumptions

Instructions

Read the following statements. Use the space to the left to write "Yes" if you agree with the statement, or "No" if you disagree with it. Force yourself to take a "yes" or "no" position for every statement.

1. Are good pay and a secure job enough to satisfy most workers?

2. Should a manager help and coach subordinates in their work?

3. Do most people like real responsibility in their jobs?

4. Are most people afraid to learn new things in their jobs?

5. Should managers let subordinates control the quality of their work?

6. Do most people dislike work?

7. Are most people creative?

8. Should a manager closely supervise and direct work of subordinates?

Source: Schermerhorn, John R. Jr., *Management*, 5th ed. (New York, John Wiley & Sons, Inc., 1996) p. 51. By permission.

9. Do most people tend to resist change?
10. Do most people work only as hard as they have to?
11. Should workers be allowed to set their own job goals?
12. Are most people happiest off the job?
13. Do most workers really care about the organization they work for?
14. Should a manager help subordinates advance and grow in their jobs?

Scoring

Count the number of "yes" responses to items 1, 4, 6, 8, 9, 10, 12; write that number here as [X = _____]. Count the number of "yes" responses to items 2, 3, 5, 7, 11, 13, 14; write that score here [Y = _____].

Interpretation

This assessment sheds insight into your orientation toward Douglas McGregor's Theory X (your "X" score) and Theory Y (your "Y" score) assumptions. You should review the discussion of McGregor's thinking in Chapter 1 and consider further the ways in which you are likely to behave toward other people at work. Think, in particular, about the types of "self-fulfilling prophecies" you are likely to create.

A 21st-Century Manager

Instructions

Rate yourself on the following personal characteristics. Use this scale.

> S = Strong, I am very confident with this one.
>
> G = Good, but I still have room to grow.
>
> W = Weak, I really need work on this one.
>
> ? = Unsure, I just don't know.

1. *Resistance to stress:* The ability to get work done even under stressful conditions.
2. *Tolerance for uncertainty:* The ability to get work done even under ambiguous and uncertain conditions.
3. *Social objectivity:* The ability to act free of racial, ethnic, gender, and other prejudices or biases.
4. *Inner work standards:* The ability to personally set and work to high-performance standards.
5. *Stamina:* The ability to sustain long work hours.
6. *Adaptability:* The ability to be flexible and adapt to changes.
7. *Self-confidence:* The ability to be consistently decisive and display one's personal presence.
8. *Self-objectivity:* The ability to evaluate personal strengths and weaknesses and to understand one's motives and skills relative to a job.
9. *Introspection:* The ability to learn from experience, awareness, and self-study.

10. *Entrepreneurism:* The ability to address problems and take advantage of opportunities for constructive change.

Scoring

Giving yourself 1 point for each S, and 1/2 point for each G. Do not give yourself points for W and ? responses. Total your points and enter the result here [PMF = _____].

Interpretation

This assessment offers a self-described *profile of your management foundations* (PMF). Are you a perfect 10, or is your PMF score something less than that? There shouldn't be too many 10s around. Ask someone who knows you to assess you on this instrument. You may be surprised at the differences between your PMF score as self-described and your PMF score as described by someone else. Most of us, realistically speaking, must work hard to grow and develop continually in these and related management foundations. This list is a good starting point as you consider where and how to further pursue the development of your managerial skills and competencies. The items on the list are recommended by the American Assembly of Collegiate Schools of Business (AACSB) as skills and personal characteristics that should be nurtured in college and university students of business administration. Their success—and yours—as 21st-century managers may well rest on (1) an initial awareness of the importance of these basic management foundations and (2) a willingness to strive continually to strengthen them throughout your work career.

Source: See *Outcome Management Project,* Phase I and Phase II Reports (St. Louis: American Assembly of Collegiate Schools of Business, 1986 & 1987).

Turbulence Tolerance Test

Instructions

The following statements were made by a 37-year-old manager in a large, successful corporation. How would you like to have a job with these characteristics? Using the following scale, write your response to the left of each statement.

> 4 = I would enjoy this very much; it's completely acceptable.
>
> 3 = This would be enjoyable and acceptable most of the time.
>
> 2 = I'd have no reaction to this feature one way or another, or it would be about equally enjoyable and unpleasant.
>
> 1 = This feature would be somewhat unpleasant for me.
>
> 0 = This feature would be very unpleasant for me.

_____ 1. I regularly spend 30 to 40 percent of my time in meetings.

_____ 2. Eighteen months ago my job did not exist, and I have been essentially inventing it as I go along.

_____ 3. The responsibilities I either assume or am assigned consistently exceed the authority I have for discharging them.

_____ 4. At any given moment in my job, I have on the average about a dozen phone calls to be returned.

_____ 5. There seems to be very little relation in my job between the quality of my performance and my actual pay and fringe benefits.

_____ 6. About 2 weeks a year of formal management training is needed in my job just to stay current.

_____ 7. Because we have very effective equal employment opportunity (EEO) in my company and because it is thoroughly multinational, my job consistently brings me into close working contact at a professional level with people of many races, ethnic groups and nationalities, and of both sexes.

_____ 8. There is no objective way to measure my effectiveness.

_____ 9. I report to three different bosses for different aspects of my job, and each has an equal say in my performance appraisal.

_____ 10. On average about a third of my time is spent dealing with unexpected emergencies that force all scheduled work to be postponed.

_____ 11. When I have to have a meeting of the people who report to me, it takes my secretary most of a day to find a time when we are all available, and even then, I have yet to have a meeting where everyone is present for the entire meeting.

_____ 12. The college degree I earned in preparation for this type of work is now obsolete, and I probably should go back for another degree.

_____ 13. My job requires that I absorb 100–200 pages of technical materials per week.

_____ 14. I am out of town overnight at least one night per week.

_____ 15. My department is so interdependent with several other departments in the company that all distinctions about which departments are responsible for which tasks are quite arbitrary.

Source: Peter B. Vail, _Managing as a Performance Art: New Ideas for a World of Chaotic Change_ (San Francisco: Jossey-Bass, 1989), pp. 8–9. Used by permission.

____ 16. In about a year I will probably get a promotion to a job in another division that has most of these same characteristics.

____ 17. During the period of my employment here, either the entire company or the division I worked in has been reorganized every year or so.

____ 18. While there are several possible promotions I can see ahead of me, I have no real career path in an objective sense.

____ 19. While there are several possible promotions I can see ahead of me, I think I have no realistic chance of getting to the top levels of the company.

____ 20. While I have many ideas about how to make things work better, I have no direct influence on either the business policies or the personnel policies that govern my division.

____ 21. My company has recently put in an "assessment center" where I and all other managers will be required to go through an extensive battery of psychological tests to assess our potential.

____ 22. My company is a defendant in an antitrust suit, and if the case comes to trial, I will probably have to testify about some decisions that were made a few years ago.

____ 23. Advanced computer and other electronic office technology is continually being introduced into my division, necessitating constant learning on my part.

____ 24. The computer terminal and screen I have in my office can be monitored in my bosses' offices without my knowledge.

Scoring

Total your responses and divide the sum by 24; enter the score here [TTT = ____].

Interpretation

This instrument gives an impression of your tolerance for managing in turbulent times—something likely to characterize the world of work well into the next century. In general, the higher your TTT score, the more comfortable you seem to be with turbulence and change—a positive sign. For comparison purposes, the average scores for some 500 MBA students and young managers was 1.5–1.6. The test's author suggests the TTT scores may be interpreted much like a grade point average in which 4.0 is a perfect A. On this basis, a 1.5 is below a C! How did you do?

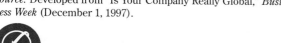

ASSESSMENT 4

Global Readiness Index

Instructions

Rate yourself on each of the following items to establish a baseline measurement of your readiness to participate in the global work environment.

Rating Scale:

1 = Very Poor
2 = Poor
3 = Acceptable

Source: Developed from "Is Your Company Really Global," *Business Week* (December 1, 1997).

4 = Good
5 = Very Good

____ 1. I understand my own culture in terms of its expectations, values, and influence on communication and relationships.

____ 2. When someone presents me with a different point of view, I try to understand it rather than attack it.

____ 3. I am comfortable dealing with situations where the available information is incomplete and the outcomes unpredictable.

____ 4. I am open to new situations and am always

looking for new information and learning opportunities.

_____ 5. I have a good understanding of the attitudes and perceptions toward my culture as they are held by people from other cultures.

_____ 6. I am always gathering information about other countries and cultures and trying to learn from them.

_____ 7. I am well informed regarding the major differences in government, political, and economic systems around the world.

_____ 8. I work hard to increase my understanding of people from other cultures.

_____ 9. I am able to adjust my communication style to work effectively with people from different cultures.

_____ 10. I can recognize when cultural differences are influencing working relationships and adjust my attitudes and behavior accordingly.

Interpretation

To be successful in the 21st-century work environment, you must be comfortable with the global economy and the cultural diversity that it holds. This requires a *global mind-set* that is receptive to and respectful of cultural differences, *global knowledge* that includes the continuing quest to know and learn more about other nations and cultures, and *global work skills* that allow you to work effectively across cultures.

Scoring

The goal is to score as close to a perfect "5" as possible on each of the three dimensions of global readiness. Develop your scores as follows.

Items $(1 + 2 + 3 + 4)/4$
= _____ Global Mind-set Score

Items $(5 + 6 + 7)/3$
= _____ Global Knowledge Score

Items $(8 + 9 + 10)/3$
= _____ Global Work Skills Score

ASSESSMENT 5

Personal Values

Instructions

Below are 16 items. Rate how important each one is to you on a scale of 0 (not important) to 100 (very important). Write the numbers 0–100 on the line to the left of each item.

Not important				Somewhat important				Very important		
0	10	20	30	40	50	60	70	80	90	100

_____ 1. An enjoyable, satisfying job.

_____ 2. A high-paying job.

_____ 3. A good marriage.

_____ 4. Meeting new people; social events.

_____ 5. Involvement in community activities.

_____ 6. My religion.

_____ 7. Exercising, playing sports.

_____ 8. Intellectual development.

_____ 9. A career with challenging opportunities.

_____ 10. Nice cars, clothes, home, etc.

_____ 11. Spending time with family.

_____ 12. Having several close friends.

_____ 13. Volunteer work for not-for-profit organizations, such as the cancer society.

Source: Robert N. Lussier, *Human Relations in Organizations,* 2nd ed. (Homewood, IL: Richard D. Irwin, 1993). By permission.

_____ 14. Meditation, quiet time to think, pray, etc.

_____ 15. A healthy, balanced diet.

_____ 16. Educational reading, TV, self-improvement programs, etc.

Scoring

Transfer the numbers for each of the 16 items to the appropriate column below, then add the two numbers in each column.

	Professional	Financial	Family	Social
	1. _____	2. _____	3. _____	4. _____
	9. _____	10. _____	11. _____	12. _____
Totals	_____	_____	_____	_____
	Community	Spiritual	Physical	Intellectual
	5. _____	6. _____	7. _____	8. _____
	13. _____	14. _____	15. _____	16. _____
Totals	_____	_____	_____	_____

Interpretation

The higher the total in any area, the higher the value you place on that particular area. The closer the numbers are in all eight areas, the more well-rounded you are. Think about the time and effort you put forth in your top three values. Is it sufficient to allow you to achieve the level of success you want in each area? If not, what can you do to change? Is there any area in which you feel you should have a higher value total? If yes, which, and what can you do to change?

ASSESSMENT 6

Intolerance for Ambiguity

Instructions

To determine your level of tolerance (intolerance) for ambiguity, respond to the following items. PLEASE RATE EVERY ITEM; DO NOT LEAVE ANY ITEM BLANK. Rate each item on the following seven-point scale:

1	2	3	4	5	6	7
strongly disagree	moderately disagree	slightly disagree		slightly agree	moderately agree	strongly agree

Rating

_____ 1. An expert who doesn't come up with a definite answer probably doesn't know too much.

_____ 2. There is really no such thing as a problem that can't be solved.

_____ 3. I would like to live in a foreign country for a while.

_____ 4. People who fit their lives to a schedule probably miss the joy of living.

_____ 5. A good job is one where what is to be done and how it is to be done is always clear.

Source: Based on Budner, S. (1962) Intolerance of ambiguity as a personality variable, *Journal of Personality,* Vol. 30, No. 1, 29–50.

_____ 6. In the long run it is possible to get more done by tackling small, simple problems rather than large, complicated ones.

_____ 7. It is more fun to tackle a complicated problem than it is to solve a simple one.

_____ 8. Often the most interesting and stimulating people are those who don't mind being different and original.

_____ 9. What we are used to is always preferable to what is unfamiliar.

_____ 10. A person who leads an even, regular life in which few surprises or unexpected happenings arise really has a lot to be grateful for.

_____ 11. People who insist upon a yes or no answer just don't know how complicated things really are.

_____ 12. Many of our most important decisions are based on insufficient information.

_____ 13. I like parties where I know most of the people more than ones where most of the people are complete strangers.

_____ 14. The sooner we all acquire ideals, the better.

_____ 15. Teachers or supervisors who hand out vague assignments give a chance for one to show initiative and originality.

_____ 16. A good teacher is one who makes you wonder about your way of looking at things.

_____ Total

Scoring

The scale was developed by S. Budner. Budner reports test–retest correlations of .85 with a variety of samples (mostly students and health care workers). Data, however, are more than 30 years old, so mean shifts may have occurred. Maximum ranges are 16–112, and score ranges were from 25 to 79, with a grand mean of approximately 49.

The test was designed to measure several different components of possible reactions to perceived threat in situations which are new, complex, or insoluble. Half of the items have been reversed.

To obtain a score, first _reverse_ the scale score for the eight "reverse" items, 3, 4, 7, 8, 11, 12, 15, and 16 (i.e., a rating of 1 = 7, 2 = 6, 3 = 5, etc.), then add up the rating scores for all 16 items.

Interpretation

Empirically, low tolerance for ambiguity (high intolerance) has been positively correlated with:

- Conventionality of religious beliefs
- High attendance at religious services
- More intense religious beliefs
- More positive views of censorship
- Higher authoritarianism
- Lower Machiavellianism

The application of this concept to management in the 1990s is clear and relatively self-evident. The world of work, and many organizations, are full of ambiguity and change. Individuals with a _higher_ tolerance for ambiguity are far more likely to be able to function effectively in organizations and contexts in which there is a high turbulence, a high rate of change, and less certainty about expectations, performance standards, what needs to be done, etc. In contrast, individuals with a lower tolerance for ambiguity are far more likely to be unable to adapt or adjust quickly in turbulence, uncertainty, and change. These individuals are likely to become rigid, angry, stressed, and frustrated when there is a high level of uncertainty and ambiguity in the environment. High levels of tolerance for ambiguity, therefore, are associated with an ability to "roll with the punches" as organizations, environmental conditions, and demands change rapidly.

Two-Factor Profile

Instructions

On each of the following dimensions, distribute a total of "10" points between the two options. For example:

Summer weather   (7) ....(3) Winter weather

1. Very responsible job   (___) ....(___) Job security

2. Recognition for   (___) ....(___) Good relations
   work accomplishments   with coworkers

3. Advancement   (___) ....(___) A boss who knows
   opportunities at work   his/her job well

4. Opportunities to grow   (___) ....(___) Good working
   and learn on the job   conditions

5. A job that I can   (___) ....(___) Supportive rules,
   do well   policies of employer

6. A prestigious or   (___) ....(___) A high base wage
   high status job   or salary

Scoring

Summarize your total scores for all items in the *left-hand column* and write it here: MF = ____.

Summarize your total scores for all items in the *right-hand column* and write it here: HF = ____.

Interpretation

The "MF" score indicates the relative importance that you place on motivating or satisfier factors in Herzberg's two-factor theory. This shows how important job content is to you. The "HF" score indicates the relative importance that you place on hygiene or dissatisfier factors in Herzberg's two-factor theory. This shows how important job context is to you.

Are You Cosmopolitan?

Instructions

Answer the questions below using a scale of 1 to 5: 1 representing "strongly disagree"; 2, "somewhat disagree"; 3, "neutral"; 4, "somewhat agree"; and 5, "strongly agree."

____ 1. You believe it is the right of the professional to make his or her own decisions about what is to be done on the job.

Source: Developed from Joseph A. Raelin, *The Clash of Cultures, Managers and Professionals* (Harvard Business School Press, 1986).

_____ 2. You believe a professional should stay in an individual staff role regardless of the income sacrifice.

_____ 3. You have no interest in moving up to a top administrative post.

_____ 4. You believe that professionals are better evaluated by professional colleagues than by management.

_____ 5. Your friends tend to be members of your profession.

_____ 6. You would rather be known or get credit for your work outside rather than inside the company.

_____ 7. You would feel better making a contribution to society than to your organization.

_____ 8. Managers have no right to place time and cost schedules on professional contributors.

Scoring and Interpretation

A "cosmopolitan" identifies with the career profession, and a "local" identifies with the employing organization. Total your scores. A score of 30–40 suggests a cosmopolitan work orientation, of 10–20 a "local" orientation, and 20–30 a mixed orientation.

ASSESSMENT 9

Group Effectiveness

Instructions

For this assessment, select a specific group you work with or have worked with; it can be a college or work group. For each of the eight statements below, select how often each statement describes the group's behavior. Place the number 1, 2, 3, or 4 on the line next to each of the 8 numbers.

Usually	Frequently	Occasionally	Seldom
1	2	3	4

_____ 1. The members are loyal to one another and to the group leader.

_____ 2. The members and leader have a high degree of confidence and trust in each other.

_____ 3. Group values and goals express relevant values and needs of members.

_____ 4. Activities of the group occur in a supportive atmosphere.

_____ 5. The group is eager to help members develop to their full potential.

_____ 6. The group knows the value of constructive conformity and knows when to use it and for what purpose.

_____ 7. The members communicate all information relevant to the group's activity fully and frankly.

_____ 8. The members feel secure in making decisions that seem appropriate to them.

Scoring

_____ Total. Add up the eight numbers and place an X on the continuum below that represents the score.

Effective group   8 . . . 16 . . . 24 . . . 32   Ineffective group

Interpretation

The lower the score, the more effective the group. What can you do to help the group become more effective? What can the group do to become more effective?

Organizational Design Preference

Instructions

To the left of each item, write the number from the following scale that shows the extent to which the statement accurately describes your views.

> 5 = strongly agree
> 4 = agree somewhat
> 3 = undecided
> 2 = disagree somewhat
> 1 = strongly disagree

I prefer to work in an organization where:

1. Goals are defined by those in higher levels.
2. Work methods and procedures are specified.
3. Top management makes important decisions.
4. My loyalty counts as much as my ability to do the job.
5. Clear lines of authority and responsibility are established.
6. Top management is decisive and firm.
7. My career is pretty well planned out for me.
8. I can specialize.
9. My length of service is almost as important as my level of performance.

Source: John F. Veiga and John N. Yanouzas, *The Dynamics of Organization Theory: Gaining a Macro Perspective* (St. Paul, MN: West, 1979), pp. 158–160. Used by permission.

10. Management is able to provide the information I need to do my job well.
11. A chain of command is well established.
12. Rules and procedures are adhered to equally by everyone.
13. People accept authority of a leader's position.
14. People are loyal to their boss.
15. People do as they have been instructed.
16. People clear things with their boss before going over his or her head.

Scoring

Total your scores for all questions. Enter the score here [____].

Interpretation

This assessment measures your preference for working in an organization designed along "organic" or "mechanistic" lines. The higher your score (above 64), the more comfortable you are with a mechanistic design; the lower your score (below 48), the more comfortable you are with an organic design. Scores between 48 and 64 can go either way. This organizational design preference represents an important issue in the new workplace. Indications are that today's organizations are taking on more and more organic characteristics. Presumably, those of us who work in them will need to be comfortable with such designs.

Which Culture Fits You?

Instructions

Check one of the following organization "cultures" in which you feel most comfortable working.

1. A culture that values talent, entrepreneurial activity, and performance over commitment; one that offers large financial rewards and individual recognition.

Source: Developed from Carol Hymowitz, "Which Corporate Culture Fits You?" *The Wall Street Journal* (July 17, 1989), p. B1.

2. A culture that stresses loyalty, working for the good of the group, and getting to know the right people; one that believes in "generalists" and step-by-step career progress.
3. A culture that offers little job security; one that operates with a survival mentality, stresses that every individual can make a difference, and focuses attention on "turnaround" opportunities.
4. A culture that values long-term relationships; one that emphasizes systematic career development, regular training, and advancement based on gaining of functional expertise.

Scoring

These labels identify the four different cultures: 1 = "the baseball team," 2 = "the club," 3 = "the fortress," and 4 = "the academy."

Interpretation

To some extent, your future career success may depend on working for an organization in which there is a good fit between you and the prevailing corporate culture. This assessment can help you learn how to recognize various cultures, evaluate how well they can serve your needs, and recognize how they may change with time. A risk taker, for example, may be out of place in a "club" but fit right in with a "baseball team." Someone who wants to seek opportunities wherever they may occur may be out of place in an "academy" but fit right in with a "fortress."

ASSESSMENT 12

Least Preferred Coworker Scale

Instructions

Think of all the different people with whom you have ever worked—in jobs, in social clubs, in student projects, or whatever. Next, think of the *one person* with whom you could work *least* well—that is, the person with whom you had the most difficulty getting a job done. This is the one person—a peer, boss, or subordinate—with whom you would least want to work. Describe this person by circling numbers at the appropriate points on each of the following pairs of bipolar adjectives. Work rapidly. There are no right or wrong answers.

Pleasant	8 7 6 5 4 3 2 1	Unpleasant
Friendly	8 7 6 5 4 3 2 1	Unfriendly
Rejecting	1 2 3 4 5 6 7 8	Accepting
Tense	1 2 3 4 5 6 7 8	Relaxed
Distant	1 2 3 4 5 6 7 8	Close
Cold	1 2 3 4 5 6 7 8	Warm
Supportive	8 7 6 5 4 3 2 1	Hostile
Boring	1 2 3 4 5 6 7 8	Interesting
Quarrelsome	1 2 3 4 5 6 7 8	Harmonious
Gloomy	1 2 3 4 5 6 7 8	Cheerful
Open	8 7 6 5 4 3 2 1	Guarded
Backbiting	1 2 3 4 5 6 7 8	Loyal
Untrustworthy	1 2 3 4 5 6 7 8	Trustworthy
Considerate	8 7 6 5 4 3 2 1	Inconsiderate
Nasty	1 2 3 4 5 6 7 8	Nice
Agreeable	8 7 6 5 4 3 2 1	Disagreeable
Insincere	1 2 3 4 5 6 7 8	Sincere
Kind	8 7 6 5 4 3 2 1	Unkind

Scoring

This is called the "least preferred coworker scale" (LPC). Compute your LPC score by totaling all the numbers you circled; enter that score here [LPC = ____].

Interpretation

The LPC scale is used by Fred Fiedler to identify a person's dominant leadership style. Fiedler believes that this style is a relatively fixed part of one's personality and is there-

Source: Fred E. Fiedler and Martin M. Chemers. *Improving Leadership Effectiveness: The Leader Match Concept,* 2nd ed. (New York: John Wiley & Sons, Inc., 1984). Used by permission.

fore difficult to change. This leads Fiedler to his contingency views, which suggest that the key to leadership success is finding (or creating) good "matches" between style and situation. If your score is 73 or above, Fiedler considers you a "relationship-motivated" leader; if your score is 64 and below, he considers you a "task-motivated" leader. If your score is between 65 and 72, Fiedler leaves it up to you to determine which leadership style is most like yours.

ASSESSMENT 13

Leadership Style

Instructions

The following statements describe leadership acts. Indicate the way you would most likely act if you were leader of a work group, by circling whether you would most likely behave in this way:

> always (A); frequently (F); occasionally (O); seldom (S); or never (N)

A F O S N   1. Act as group spokesperson.
A F O S N   2. Encourage overtime work.
A F O S N   3. Allow members complete freedom in their work.
A F O S N   4. Encourage the use of uniform procedures.
A F O S N   5. Permit members to solve their own problems.
A F O S N   6. Stress being ahead of competing groups.
A F O S N   7. Speak as a representative of the group.
A F O S N   8. Push members for greater effort.
A F O S N   9. Try out ideas in the group.
A F O S N   10. Let the members work the way they think best.
A F O S N   11. Work hard for a personal promotion.
A F O S N   12. Tolerate postponement and uncertainty.
A F O S N   13. Speak for the group when visitors are present.
A F O S N   14. Keep the work moving at a rapid pace.
A F O S N   15. Turn members loose on a job.
A F O S N   16. Settle conflicts in the group.
A F O S N   17. Focus on work details.
A F O S N   18. Represent the group at outside meetings.
A F O S N   19. Avoid giving the members too much freedom.
A F O S N   20. Decide what should be done and how it should be done.
A F O S N   21. Push for increased production
A F O S N   22. Give some members authority to act.
A F O S N   23. Expect things to turn out as predicted.
A F O S N   24. Allow the group to take initiative.
A F O S N   25. Assign group members to particular tasks.
A F O S N   26. Be willing to make changes.
A F O S N   27. Ask members to work harder.
A F O S N   28. Trust members to exercise good judgment.
A F O S N   29. Schedule the work to be done.
A F O S N   30. Refuse to explain my actions.
A F O S N   31. Persuade others that my ideas are best.
A F O S N   32. Permit the group to set its own pace.

A F O S N   33. Urge the group to beat its previous record.
A F O S N   34. Act without consulting the group.
A F O S N   35. Ask members to follow standard rules.

                    T ____   P ____

Scoring

1. Circle items 8, 12, 17, 18, 19, 30, 34 and 35.
2. Write the number 1 in front of a *circled item number* if you responded S (seldom) or N (never) to that item.
3. Write a number 1 in front of *item numbers not circled* if you responded A (always) or F (frequently).
4. Circle the number 1's which you have written in front of items 3, 5, 8, 10, 15, 18, 19, 22, 24, 26, 28, 30, 32, 34, and 35.
5. *Count the circled number 1's*. This is your score for leadership *concern for people*. Record the score in the blank following the letter P at the end of the questionnaire.
6. *Count the uncircled number 1's*. This is your score for leadership *concern for task*. Record this number in the blank following the letter T.

●● ASSESSMENT 14 ●

"TT" Leadership Style

Instructions

For each of the following 10 pairs of statements, divide 5 points between the two according to your beliefs, perceptions of yourself, or according to which of the two statements characterizes you better. The 5 points may be divided between the a and b statements in any one of the following ways: 5 for a, 0 for b; 4 for a, 1 for b; 3 for a, 2 for b; 1 for a, 4 for b; 0 for a, 5 for b, but not equally (2 ½) between the two. Weigh your choices between the two according to the one that characterizes you or your beliefs better.

1. (a) As leader I have a primary mission of maintaining stability.
   (b) As leader I have a primary mission of change.
2. (a) As leader I must cause events.
   (b) As leader I must facilitate events.
3. (a) I am concerned that my followers are rewarded equitably for their work.
   (b) I am concerned about what my followers want in life.
4. (a) My preference is to think long range: what might be.
   (b) My preference is to think short range: what is realistic.

5. (a) As a leader I spend considerable energy in managing separate but related goals.
   (b) As a leader I spend considerable energy in arousing hopes, expectations, and aspirations among my followers.
6. (a) Although not in a formal classroom sense, I believe that a significant part of my leadership is that of teacher.
   (b) I believe that a significant part of my leadership is that of facilitator.
7. (a) As leader I must engage with followers at an equal level of morality.
   (b) As leader I must represent a higher morality.
8. (a) I enjoy stimulating followers to want to do more.
   (b) I enjoy rewarding followers for a job well done.
9. (a) Leadership should be practical.
   (b) Leadership should be inspirational.
10. (a) What power I have to influence others comes primarily from my ability to get people to identify with me and my ideas.
    (b) What power I have to influence others comes primarily from my status and position.

Scoring

Circle your points for items 1b, 2a, 3b, 4a, 5b, 6a, 7b, 8a, 9b, 10a and add up the total points you allocated to these items; enter the score here [**T** = ____]. Next, add up the total points given to the uncircled items 1a, 2b, 3a, 4b, 5a, 6b, 7a, 8b, 9a, 10b; enter the score here [**T** = ____].

Source: Questionnaire by W. Warner Burke, Ph.D. Used by permission.

Interpretation

This instrument gives an impression of your tendencies toward "transformational" leadership (your **T** score) and "transactional" leadership (your T score). You may want to refer to the discussion of these concepts in Chapter 15.

Today, a lot of attention is being given to the transformational aspects of leadership—those personal qualities that inspire a sense of vision and desire for extraordinary accomplishment in followers. The most successful leaders of the future will most likely be strong in both "T"s.

Empowering Others

Instructions

Think of times when you have been in charge of a group—this could be a full-time or part-time work situation, a student work group, or whatever. Complete the following questionnaire by recording how you feel about each statement according to this scale.

> 1 = Strongly disagree
> 2 = Disagree
> 3 = Neutral
> 4 = Agree
> 5 = Strongly agree

When in charge of a group I find:

____ 1. Most of the time other people are too inexperienced to do things, so I prefer to do them myself.

____ 2. It often takes more time to explain things to others than just to do them myself.

____ 3. Mistakes made by others are costly, so I don't assign much work to them.

Source: Questionnaire adapted from L. Steinmetz and R. Todd, *First Line Management,* Fourth Edition (Homewood, IL: BPI/Irwin, 1986), pp. 64–67. Used by permission.

____ 4. Some things simply should not be delegated to others.

____ 5. I often get quicker action by doing a job myself.

____ 6. Many people are good only at very specific tasks, and thus can't be assigned additional responsibilities.

____ 7. Many people are too busy to take on additional work.

____ 8. Most people just aren't ready to handle additional responsibilities.

____ 9. In my position, I should be entitled to make my own decisions.

Scoring

Total your responses; enter the score here [____].

Interpretation

This instrument gives an impression of your *willingness to delegate.* Possible scores range from 9 to 45. The higher your score, the more willing you appear to be to delegate to others. Willingness to delegate is an important managerial characteristic. It is essential if you—as a manager—are to "empower" others and give them opportunities to assume responsibility and exercise self-control in their work. With the growing importance of empowerment in the new workplace, your willingness to delegate is well worth thinking about seriously.

Machiavellianism

Instructions

For each of the following statements, circle the number that most closely resembles your attitude.

Statement	Disagree			Agree	
	A Lot	A Little	Neutral	A Little	A Lot
1. The best way to handle people is to tell them what they want to hear.	1	2	3	4	5
2. When you ask someone to do something for you, it is best to give the real reason for wanting it rather than reasons that might carry more weight.	1	2	3	4	5
3. Anyone who completely trusts someone else is asking for trouble.	1	2	3	4	5
4. It is hard to get ahead without cutting corners here and there.	1	2	3	4	5
5. It is safest to assume that all people have a vicious streak, and it will come out when they are given a chance.	1	2	3	4	5
6. One should take action only when it is morally right.	1	2	3	4	5
7. Most people are basically good and kind.	1	2	3	4	5
8. There is no excuse for lying to someone else.	1	2	3	4	5
9. Most people forget more easily the death of their father than the loss of their property.	1	2	3	4	5
10. Generally speaking, people won't work hard unless forced to do so.	1	2	3	4	5

Scoring and Interpretation

This assessment is designed to compute your Machiavellianism (Mach) score. Mach is a personality characteristic that taps people's power orientation. The high-Mach personality is pragmatic, maintains emotional distance from others, and believes that ends can justify means. To obtain your Mach score, add up the numbers you checked for questions 1, 3, 4, 5, 9, and 10. For the other four questions, reverse the numbers you have checked, so that 5 becomes 1; 4 is 2; and 1 is 5. Then total both sets of numbers to find your score. A random sample of adults found the national average to be 25. Students in business and management typically score higher.

The results of research using the Mach test have found: (1) men are generally more Machiavellian than women; (2) older adults tend to have lower Mach scores than younger adults; (3) there is no significant difference between high Machs and low Machs on measures of intelligence or ability; (4) Machiavellianism is not significantly related to demographic characteristics such as educational level or marital status; and (5) high Machs tend to be in professions that emphasize the control and manipulation of people—for example, managers, lawyers, psychiatrists, and behavioral scientists.

Source: From R. Christie and F. L. Geis, *Studies in Machiavellianism* (New York: Academic Press, 1970). By permission.

Personal Power Profile

Contributed by Marcus, Maier, Chapman University

Instructions

Below is a list of statements that may be used in describing behaviors that supervisors (leaders) in work organizations can direct toward their subordinates (followers). First, carefully read each descriptive statement, thinking in terms of *how you prefer to influence others*. Mark the number that most closely represents how you feel. Use the following numbers for your answers.

> 5 = Strongly agree
> 4 = Agree
> 3 = Neither agree nor disagree
> 2 = Disagree
> 1 = Strongly disagree

To influence others, I would prefer to:	Strongly Disagree	Disagree	Neither Agree nor Disagree	Agree	Strongly Agree
1. Increase their pay level	1	2	3	4	5
2. Make them feel valued	1	2	3	4	5
3. Give undesirable job assignments	1	2	3	4	5
4. Make them feel like I approve of them	1	2	3	4	5
5. Make them feel that they have commitments to meet	1	2	3	4	5
6. Make them feel personally accepted	1	2	3	4	5
7. Make them feel important	1	2	3	4	5
8. Give them good technical suggestions	1	2	3	4	5
9. Make the work difficult for them	1	2	3	4	5
10. Share my experience and/or training	1	2	3	4	5
11. Make things unpleasant here	1	2	3	4	5
12. Make being at work distasteful	1	2	3	4	5
13. Influence their getting a pay increase	1	2	3	4	5
14. Make them feel like they should satisfy their job requirements	1	2	3	4	5
15. Provide them with sound job-related advice	1	2	3	4	5
16. Provide them with special benefits	1	2	3	4	5
17. Influence their getting a promotion	1	2	3	4	5
18. Give them the feeling that they have responsibilities to fulfill	1	2	3	4	5
19. Provide them with needed technical knowledge	1	2	3	4	5
20. Make them recognize that they have tasks to accomplish	1	2	3	4	5

Source: Modified version of T. R. Hinken and C. A. Schriesheim, "Development and Application of New Scales to Measure the French and Raven (1959) Bases of Social Power." *Journal of Applied Psychology,* Vol. 74, 1989, 561–567.

Scoring

Using the grid below, insert your scores from the 20 questions and proceed as follows: *Reward power*—sum your response to items 1, 13, 16, and 17 and divide by 4. *Coercive power*—sum your response to items 3, 9, 11, and 12 and divide by 4. *Legitimate power*—sum your response to questions 5, 14, 18, and 20 and divide by 4. *Referent power*—sum your response to questions 2, 4, 6, and 7 and divide by 4. *Expert power*—sum your response to questions 8, 10, 15, and 19 and divide by 4.

Reward	Coercive	Legitimate	Referent	Expert
1 ____	3 ____	5 ____	2 ____	8 ____
13 ____	9 ____	14 ____	4 ____	10 ____
16 ____	11 ____	18 ____	6 ____	15 ____
17 ____	12 ____	20 ____	7 ____	19 ____
Total ____	____	____	____	____
Divide by 4 ____	____	____	____	____

Interpretation

A high score (4 and greater) on any of the five dimensions of power implies that you prefer to influence others by employing that particular form of power. A low score (2 or less) implies that you prefer not to employ this particular form of power to influence others. This represents your power profile. Your overall power position is not reflected by the simple sum of the power derived from each of the five sources. Instead, some combinations of power are synergistic in nature—they are greater than the simple sum of their parts. For example, referent power tends to magnify the impact of other power sources because these other influence attempts are coming from a "respected" person. Reward power often increases the impact of referent power, because people generally tend to like those who give them things that they desire. Some power combinations tend to produce the opposite of synergistic effects, such that the total is less than the sum of the parts. Power dilution frequently accompanies the use of (or threatened use of) coercive power.

ASSESSMENT 18

Your Intuitive Ability

Instructions

Complete this survey as quickly as you can. Be honest with yourself. For each question, select the response that most appeals to you.

1. When working on a project, do you prefer to:
   (a) Be told what the problem is but be left free to decide how to solve it?
   (b) Get very clear instructions about how to go about solving the problem before you start?
2. When working on a project, do you prefer to work with colleagues who are:
   (a) Realistic?

Source: AIM Survey (El Paso, TX: ENFP Enterprises, 1989). Copyright © 1989 by Weston H. Agor. Used by permission.

   (b) Imaginative?
3. Do you most admire people who are:
   (a) Creative?
   (b) Careful?
4. Do the friends you choose tend to be:
   (a) Serious and hard working?
   (b) Exciting and often emotional?
5. When you ask a colleague for advice on a problem you have, do you:
   (a) Seldom or never get upset if he or she questions your basic assumptions?
   (b) Often get upset if he or she questions your basic assumptions?
6. When you start your day, do you:
   (a) Seldom make or follow a specific plan?
   (b) Usually first make a plan to follow?

7. When working with numbers do you find that you:
  (a) Seldom or never make factual errors?
  (b) Often make factual errors?

8. Do you find that you:
  (a) Seldom daydream during the day and really don't enjoy doing so when you do it?
  (b) Frequently daydream during the day and enjoy doing so?

9. When working on a problem, do you:
  (a) Prefer to follow the instructions or rules when they are given to you?
  (b) Often enjoy circumventing the instructions or rules when they are given to you?

10. When you are trying to put something together, do you prefer to have:
  (a) Step-by-step written instructions on how to assemble the item?
  (b) A picture of how the item is supposed to look once assembled?

11. Do you find that the person who irritates you *the most* is the one who appears to be:
  (a) Disorganized?
  (b) Organized?

12. When an expected crisis comes up that you have to deal with, do you:
  (a) Feel anxious about the situation?
  (b) Feel excited by the challenge of the situation?

Scoring

Total the number of "a" responses circled for questions 1, 3, 5, 6, 11; enter the score here [A = ____]. Total the number of "b" responses for questions 2, 4, 7, 8, 9, 10, 12; enter the score here [B = ____]. Add your "a" and "b" scores and enter the sum here [A + B = ____]. This is your *intuitive score*. The highest possible intuitive score is 12; the lowest is 0.

Interpretation

In his book *Intuition in Organizations* (Newbury Park, CA: Sage, 1989), pp. 10–11, Weston H. Agor states: "Traditional analytical techniques . . . are not as useful as they once were for guiding major decisions. . . . If you hope to be better prepared for tomorrow, then it only seems logical to pay some attention to the use and development of intuitive skills for decision making." Agor developed the prior survey to help people assess their tendencies to use intuition in decision making. Your score offers a general impression of your strength in this area. It may also suggest a need to further develop your skill and comfort with more intuitive decision approaches.

ASSESSMENT 19

Decision-Making Biases

Instructions

How good are you at avoiding potential decision-making biases? Test yourself by answering the following questions:

1. Which is riskier:
  (a) driving a car on a 400-mile trip?
  (b) flying on a 400-mile commercial airline flight?

2. Are there more words in the English language:
  (a) that begin with "r"?
  (b) that have "r" as the third letter?

3. Mark is finishing his MBA at a prestigious university. He is very interested in the arts and at one time considered a career as a musician. Is Mark more likely to take a job:
  (a) in the management of the arts?
  (b) with a management consulting firm?

4. You are about to hire a new central-region sales director for the fifth time this year. You predict that the next director should work out reasonably well since the last four were "lemons" and the odds favor hiring at least one good sales director in five tries. Is this thinking
  (a) correct?
  (b) incorrect?

5. A newly hired engineer for a computer firm in the Boston metropolitan area has 4 years' experience and good all-around qualifications. When asked to estimate the starting salary for this employee, a chemist with very little knowledge about the profession or industry guessed an annual salary of $35,000. What is your estimate?
$____ per year

Source: Incidents from Max H. Bazerman, *Judgment in Managerial Decision Making,* 3rd ed. (New York: John Wiley & Sons, Inc., 1994), pp. 13–14. Used by permission.

Scoring

Your instructor will provide answers and explanations for the assessment questions.

Interpretation

Each of the preceding questions examines your tendency to use a different judgmental heuristic. In his book *Judgment in Managerial Decision Making,* 3rd ed. (New York: John Wiley & Sons, 1994), pp. 6–7, Max Bazerman calls these heuristics "simplifying strategies, or rules of thumb" used in making decisions. He states, "In general, heuristics are helpful, but their use can sometimes lead to severe errors. . . . If we can make managers aware of the potential adverse impacts of using heuristics, they can then decide when and where to use them." This assessment offers an initial insight into your use of such heuristics. An informed decision maker understands the heuristics, is able to recognize when they appear, and eliminates any that may inappropriately bias decision making.

Test yourself further. Before hearing from your instructor, go back and write next to each item the name of the judgmental heuristic (see Chapter 3 text discussion) that you think applies.

Then write down a situation that you have experienced and in which some decision-making bias may have occurred. Be prepared to share and discuss this incident with the class.

Conflict Management Styles

Instructions

Think of how you behave in conflict situations in which your wishes differ from those of one or more persons. In the space to the left of each statement below, write the number from the following scale that indicates how likely you are to respond that way in a conflict situation.

1 = very unlikely	2 = unlikely	3 = likely	4 = very likely

_____ **1.** I am usually firm in pursuing my goals.

_____ **2.** I try to win my position.

_____ **3.** I give up some points in exchange for others.

_____ **4.** I feel that differences are not always worth worrying about.

_____ **5.** I try to find a position that is intermediate between the other person's and mine.

_____ **6.** In approaching negotiations, I try to be considerate of the other person's wishes.

_____ **7.** I try to show the logic and benefits of my positions.

_____ **8.** I always lean toward a direct discussion of the problem.

_____ **9.** I try to find a fair combination of gains and losses for both of us.

_____ **10.** I attempt to work through our differences immediately.

_____ **11.** I try to avoid creating unpleasantness for myself.

_____ **12.** I try to soothe the other person's feelings and preserve our relationships.

_____ **13.** I attempt to get all concerns and issues immediately out in the open.

_____ **14.** I sometimes avoid taking positions that would create controversy.

_____ **15.** I try not to hurt others' feelings.

Scoring

Total your scores for items 1, 2, 7; enter that score here [*Competing* = ____]. Total your scores for items 8, 10, 13; enter that score here [*Collaborating* = ____]. Total your scores

---

Source: Adapted from Thomas-Kilmann, *Conflict Mode Instrument,* Copyright © 1974, Xicom, Inc., Tuxedo, NY 10987. Used by permission.

for items 3, 5, 9; enter that score here [*Compromising* = ____]. Total your scores for items 4, 11, 14; enter that score here. [*Avoiding* = ____]. Total your scores for items 6, 12, 15; enter that score here [*Accommodating* = ____].

Interpretation

Each of the scores above corresponds to one of the conflict management styles discussed in Chapter 15. Research indicates that each style has a role to play in management but that the best overall conflict management approach is collaboration; only it can lead to problem solving and true conflict resolution. You should consider any patterns that may be evident in your scores and think about how to best handle conflict situations in which you become involved.

ASSESSMENT 21

Your Personality Type

Instructions

How true is each statement for you?

	Not True At All				Very True
			Not True or Untrue		
1. I hate giving up before I'm absolutely sure that I'm licked.	1	2	3	4	5
2. Sometimes I feel that I should not be working so hard, but something drives me on.	1	2	3	4	5
3. I thrive on challenging situations. The more challenges I have, the better.	1	2	3	4	5
4. In comparison to most people I know, I'm very involved in my work.	1	2	3	4	5
5. It seems as if I need 30 hours a day to finish all the things I'm faced with.	1	2	3	4	5
6. In general, I approach my work more seriously than most people I know.	1	2	3	4	5
7. I guess there are some people who can be nonchalant about their work, but I'm not one of them.	1	2	3	4	5
8. My achievements are considered to be significantly higher than those of most people I know.	1	2	3	4	5
9. I've often been asked to be an officer of some group or groups.	1	2	3	4	5

Scoring

Add all your scores to create a total score = ____.

Interpretation

Type A personalities (hurried and competitive) tend to score 36 and above. Type B personalities (relaxed) tend to score 22 and below. Scores of 23–35 indicate a balance or mix of Type A and Type B.

Source: From *Job Demands and Worker Health* (HEW Publication No. [NIOSH] 75–160), (Washington, DC: US Department of Health, Education and Welfare, 1975), pp. 253–54.

Time Management Profile

Instructions

Complete the following questionnaire by indicating "Y" (yes) or "N" (no) for each item. Force yourself to respond yes or no. Be frank and allow your responses to create an accurate picture of how you tend to respond to these kinds of situations.

____ 1. When confronted with several items of similar urgency and importance, I tend to do the easiest one first.

____ 2. I do the most important things during that part of the day when I know I perform best.

____ 3. Most of the time I don't do things someone else can do; I delegate this type of work to others.

____ 4. Even though meetings without a clear and useful purpose upset me, I put up with them.

____ 5. I skim documents before reading them and don't complete any that offer a low return on my time investment.

____ 6. I don't worry much if I don't accomplish at least one significant task each day.

____ 7. I save the most trivial tasks for that time of day when my creative energy is lowest.

____ 8. My workspace is neat and organized.

____ 9. My office door is always "open"; I never work in complete privacy.

____ 10. I schedule my time completely from start to finish every workday.

____ 11. I don't like "to do" lists, preferring to respond to daily events as they occur.

____ 12. I "block" a certain amount of time each day or week that is dedicated to high-priority activities.

Scoring

Count the number of "Y" responses to items 2, 3, 5, 7, 8, 12. [Enter that score here ____.] Count the number of "N" responses to items 1, 4, 6, 9, 10, 11. [Enter that score here ____.] Add together the two scores.

Interpretation

The higher the total score, the closer your behavior matches recommended time management guidelines. Reread those items where your response did not match the desired one. Why don't they match? Do you have reasons why your behavior in this instance should be different from the recommended time management guideline? Think about what you can do (and how easily it can be done) to adjust your behavior to be more consistent with these guidelines. For further reading, see Alan Lakein, *How to Control Your Time and Your Life* (New York: David McKay), and William Oncken, *Managing Management Time* (Englewood Cliffs, NJ: Prentice Hall, 1984).

Source: Suggested by a discussion in Robert E. Quinn, Sue R. Faerman, Michael P. Thompson, and Michael R. McGrath, *Becoming a Master Manager: A Contemporary Framework* (New York: John Wiley & Sons, Inc., 1990), pp. 75–76.

Glossary

Ability   A person's existing capacity to perform the various tasks needed for a given job.

Accommodation or **smoothing**   Involves playing down differences and finding areas of agreement.

Achievement-oriented leadership   Emphasizes setting challenging goals, stressing excellence in performance, and showing confidence in people's ability to achieve high standards of performance.

Action research   The process of systematically collecting data on an organization, feeding it back for action planning, and evaluating results by collecting and reflecting on more data.

Active listening   Encouraging people to say what they really mean.

Adhocracy   An organizational structure that emphasizes shared, decentralized decision making; extreme horizontal specialization; few levels of management; the virtual absence of formal controls; and few rules, policies, and procedures.

Affective component   The component of an attitude that reflects the specific feelings regarding the personal impact of the antecedents.

Anchoring and adjustment heuristic   Bases a decision on incremental adjustments to an initial value determined by historical precedent or some reference point.

Aptitude   The capability of learning something.

Arbitration   When a neutral third party acts as judge with the power to issue a decision binding on all parties.

Artificial intelligence (AI)   Studies how computers can be programmed to think like the human brain.

Associative choices   Decisions which can be loosely linked to nagging continual problems but which were not specifically developed to solve the problem.

Attitude   Predisposition to respond in a positive or negative way to someone or something in one's environment.

Attribution theory   The attempt to understand the cause of an event, assess responsibility for outcomes of the event, and assess the personal qualities of the people involved.

Authoritarianism   The tendency to adhere rigidly to conventional values and to obey recognized authority.

Authoritative command   Uses formal authority to end conflict.

Authority decisions   Made by the manager or team leader without involving others using information he or she possesses.

Automation   Allows machines to do work previously accomplished by people.

Availability heuristic   Bases a decision on recent events relating to the situation at hand.

Avoidance   Involves pretending the conflict does not really exist.

Bargaining zone   The zone between one party's

minimum reservation point and the other party's maximum reservation point in a negotiating situation.

Behavioral component An intention to behave in a certain way based on a person's specific feelings or attitudes.

Behavioral decision theory Views decision makers as acting only in terms of what they perceive about a given situation.

Behaviorally anchored rating scales (BARS) A performance appraisal approach that describes observable job behaviors, each of which is evaluated to determine good versus bad performance.

Behavioral perspective Assumes that leadership is central to performance and other outcomes.

Beliefs Ideas about someone or something and the conclusions people draw about them.

Benefit cycle A pattern of successful adjustment followed by further improvements.

Brainstorming Generating ideas through "free-wheeling" discussion and without criticism.

Bureaucracy An ideal form of organization whose characteristics were defined by the German sociologist Max Weber.

Case study An in-depth analysis of one or a small number of settings.

Career planning Creates long-term congruence between individual goals and organizational career opportunities.

Career planning and development Working with managers and/or HR experts on career issues.

Career plateau A position from which someone is unlikely to move to advance to a higher level of responsibility.

Career stages Different points of work responsibility and achievement through which people pass during the course of their work lives.

Causality The assumption that change in the independent variable has caused change in the dependent variable.

Cellular form An organizational structure that emphasizes quasi-independent clusters of self-organizing components.

Central tendency error Occurs when managers lump everyone together around the average, or middle, category.

Centralization The degree to which the authority to make decisions is restricted to higher levels of management.

Centralized communication networks Networks that link group members through a central control point.

Certain environments Provide full information on the expected results for decision-making alternatives.

Change agents People who take action to change the behavior of people and systems.

Changing The stage in which specific actions are taken to create a change.

Channels The pathways through which messages are communicated.

Charismatic leaders Those leaders who, by force of their personal abilities, are capable of having a profound and extraordinary effect on followers.

Classical conditioning A form of learning through association that involves the manipulation of stimuli to influence behavior.

Classical decision theory Views decision makers as acting only in terms of what they perceive about a given situation.

Coercive power The extent to which a manager can use the "right of command" to control other people.

Cognitive components The components of an attitude that are the beliefs, opinions, knowledge, or information a person possesses.

Cognitive dissonance Describes a state of inconsistency between an individual's attitude and behavior.

Collaboration Involves recognition that something is wrong and needs attention through problem solving.

Communication The process of sending and receiving symbols with attached meanings.

Communication channels The pathways through which messages are communicated.

Competition Seeks victory by force, superior skill, or domination.

Compressed work week A work schedule that allows a full-time job to be completed in less than five full workdays.

Compromise Occurs when each party involved in a conflict gives up something of value to the other.

Conceptual skill The ability to analyze and solve complex problems.

Confirmation trap The tendency to seek confirmation for what is already thought to be true, and to not search for disconfirming information.

Conflict Occurs when parties disagree over substantive issues or when emotional antagonisms create friction between them.

Conflict resolution Occurs when the reasons for a conflict are eliminated.

Confrontation meeting An OD intervention designed to help determine how an organization might be improved and to start action toward such improvement.

Conglomerates Firms that own several different unrelated businesses.

Consensus A group decision that has the expressed support of most members.

Consideration A highly considerate leader is sensitive to people's feelings and tries to make things pleasant for the followers.

Constructive stress Stress that has a positive impact on attitudes and performance.

Consultative decisions Decisions made by one individual after seeking input from or consulting with members of a group.

Content theories Profile different needs that may motivate individual behavior.

Contingency approach Seeks ways to meet the needs of different management situations.

Continuous improvement The belief that anything and everything done in the workplace should be continually improved.

Continuous reinforcement A reinforcement schedule that administers a reward each time a desired behavior occurs.

Contrast effects Occur when an individual's characteristics are contrasted with those of others recently encountered who rank higher or lower on the same characteristics.

Control The set of mechanisms used to keep actions and outputs within predetermined limits.

Controlling Monitoring performance and taking any needed corrective action.

Coordination The set of mechanisms used in an organization to link the actions of its subunits into a consistent pattern.

Countercultures Patterns of values and philosophies that outwardly reject those of the larger organization or social system.

Creativity Generates unique and novel responses to problems and opportunities.

Critical incident diary A method of performance appraisal that records incidents of unusual success or failure in a given performance aspect.

Cross-functional teams Brings together persons from different functions to work on a common task.

Cultural relativism The suggestion tht ethical behavior is determined by its cultural context.

Cultural symbol Any object, act, or event that serves to transmit cultural meaning.

Culture The learned and shared ways of thinking and acting among a group of people or society.

Decentralization The degree to which the authority to make decisions is given to lower levels in an organization's hierarchy.

Decentralized communication networks Networks that link all group members directly with one another.

Decision making The process of choosing a course of action to deal with a problem.

Deficit cycle A pattern of deteriorating performance that is followed by even further deterioration.

Delphi technique Involves generating decision-making alternatives through a series of survey questionnaires.

Demographic characteristics Background variables (e.g., age, gender) that help shape what a person becomes over time.

Destructive stress Stress that has a negative impact on both attitudes and performance.

Developmental approaches Systematic models of ways in which personality develops across time.

Directive leadership spells out the what and how of subordinates' tasks

Distributed leadership The sharing of responsibility for meeting group task and maintenance needs.

Distributive justice The degree to which all people are treated the same under a policy.

Distributive negotiation Negotiation in which the focus is on positions staked out or declared by the parties involved who are each trying to claim certain portions of the available pie.

Diversity-consensus dilemma The tendency for diversity in groups to create process difficulties even as it offers improved potential for problem solving.

Divisional departmentation The grouping of individuals and resources by product, territories, services, clients, or legal entities.

Dogmatism Leads a person to see the world as a threatening place and regard authority as absolute.

Dysfunctional conflict Works to the group's or organization's disadvantage.

E-corporation Utilizes the Internet and information technologies to support enterprisewide computer integration of all aspects of operations.

Effective communication When the intended meaning equals the perceived meaning.

Effective groups Groups that achieve high levels of task performance, member satisfaction, and team viability.

Efficient communication Communication that is low cost in its use of resources.

Electronic commerce Where business is transacted through the Internet.

Emotional adjustment traits These traits measure how much an individual experiences emotional distress or displays unacceptable acts.

Emotional conflict Conflict that involves interpersonal difficulties that arise over feelings of anger, mistrust, dislike, fear, resentment, and the like.

Employee involvement The amount of decision making delegated to employees.

Employee involvement teams Members of such teams meet regularly to examine work-related problems and opportunities.

Empowerment The process that allows individuals and groups to make decisions affecting themselves and their work.

Environmental complexity The magnitude of the problems and opportunities in the organization's environment as evidenced by the degree of richness, interdependence, and uncertainty.

Equity theory Adams' theory, which posits that people will act to eliminate any felt inequity in the rewards received for their work in comparison with others.

ERG theory Alderfer's theory, which identifies existence, relatedness, and growth needs.

Escalating commitment The tendency to continue a previously chosen course of action even when feedback suggests that it is failing.

ESOPs Like profit sharing, ESOPs are based on the total organization's performance, but measured in terms of stock price.

Ethical behavior Behavior that is morally accepted as "good" and "right".

Ethical dilemmas Situations that require a person to choose among actions that offer possible benefits while also violating ethical standards.

Existence needs Desires for physiological and material wellbeing.

Expatriate A person who works and lives in a foreign country for an extended time.

Expectancy The probability that work effort will be followed by performance accomplishment.

Expectancy theory Vroom's theory that argues that work motivation is determined by individual beliefs regarding effort/performance relationships and work outcomes.

Expert power The ability to control another's behavior because of the possession of knowledge, experience, or judgment that the other person does not have but needs.

External adaptation Reaching goals and dealing with outsiders. Issues concerned are the tasks to be accomplished, the methods used to achieve the goals, and methods of coping with success and failure.

Extinction The withdrawal of the reinforcing consequences for a given behavior.

Extrinsic rewards Rewards given to the individual by some other person in the work setting.

Feedback The process of communicating how one feels about something another person has done or said.

Field survey A research design that relies on the use of some form of questionnaire for the primary purpose of describing and/or predicting some phenomenon.

FIRO-B theory Examines differences in how people relate to one another based on their needs to express and receive feelings of inclusion, control, and affection.

Flexible benefit plans Pay systems that allow workers to select benefits according to their individual needs.

Flexible manufacturing system Uses adaptive technology and integrated job designs to easily shift production among alternative products.

Flexible working hours Work schedules that give employees some daily choice in scheduling arrival and departure times from work.

Forced distribution A method of performance appraisal that uses a small number of performance categories, such as "very good," "good," "adequate," and "very poor" and forces a certain proportion of people into each.

Formal channels Communication pathways that follow the official chain of command.

Formal groups Officially designated groups for a specific organizational purpose.

Formalization The written documentation of work rules, policies, and procedures.

Functional conflict Results in positive benefits to the group.

Functional departmentation The grouping of individuals by skill, knowledge, and action yields.

Functional silos problem When persons working in different functions fail to communicate and interact with one another.

Fundamental attribution error The tendency to underestimate the influence of situational factors and to overestimate the influence of personal factors in evaluating someone else's behavior.

Gain sharing A pay system that links pay and performance by giving the workers the opportunity to share in productivity gains through increased earnings.

Garbage can model Views the main components of the choice process—problems, solutions, participants, and choice situations—as all mixed up together in the garbage can of the organization.

Generation X (Gold-Collar) workers Workers born between 1965 and 1977 who are knowledge workers in short supply.

Glass ceiling effect A hidden barrier limiting advancement of women and minorities in organizations.

Globalization Involves growing worldwide interdependence of resource suppliers, product markets, and business competition.

Global manager A manager who has the international awareness and cultural sensitivity needed to work well across national borders.

Global organizational learning The ability to gather from the world at large the knowledge required for long-term organizational adaptation.

Goal setting The process of developing and setting motivational performance objectives.

Grafting The process of acquiring individuals, units, and/or firms to bring in useful knowledge to the organization.

Grapevine The network of friendships and acquaintances that transfers information.

Graphic rating scale A scale that lists a variety of dimensions thought to be related to high performance outcomes in a given job and that one is expected to exhibit.

Greenfield sites Those HPO sites started from scratch at a new site.

Group decisions Decisions that are made by all members of the group.

Group dynamics The forces operating in groups that affect the ways members work together.

Groups Involves two or more people working together regularly to achieve common goals.

Groupthink The tendency of cohesive group members to lose their critical evaluative capabilities.

Growth needs Desires for continued personal growth and development.

Halo effect Occurs when one attribute of a person or situation is used to develop an overall impression of the person or situation.

Halo error Results when one person rates another person on several different dimensions and gives a similar rating for each one.

Heuristics Simplifying strategies or "rules of thumb" used to make decisions.

Hierarchy of needs theory Maslow's theory that offers a pyramid of physiological, safety, social, esteem, and self-actualization needs.

High-context cultures Words convey only part of a message, while the rest of the message must be inferred from body language and additional contextual cues.

Higher-order needs Esteem and self-actualization in Maslow's hierarchy.

High performance organization (HPO) An organization that is intentionally designed to bring out the best in people and produce sustainable organizational results.

Hindsight trap A tendency to overestimate the degree to which an event that has already taken place could have been predicted.

Horizontal specialization A division of labor through the formation of work units or groups within an organization.

House's path-goal theory of leadership Assumes that a leader's key function is to adjust his or her behaviors to compliment situational contingencies.

HPO islands Those HPO units engulfed by organizations or units that do not function as HPOs and may even be opposed to them.

Human resource strategic planning Hiring capable, motivated people to carry out the organization's mission and strategy.

Human resources The people who do the work that helps organizations fulfill their missions.

Human skill The ability to work well with other people.

Hygiene factors Factors in a job context, the work setting, that promote job dissatisfaction

Individualism-collectivism The tendency of a culture's members to emphasize individual self-interests or group relationships.

Influence A behavioral response to the exercise of power.

Informal channels Do not follow the chain of command.

Informal groups Unofficial groups that emerge to serve special interests.

Information technology The combination of machines, artifacts, procedures and systems used to gather, store, analyze and disseminate information to translate it into knowledge.

Initiating structure This kind of leader is concerned with spelling out the task requirements and clarifying other aspects of the work agenda.

Innovation The process of creating new ideas and putting them in practice.

Instrumental values Values that reflect a person's beliefs about the means for achieving desired ends.

Instrumentality The probability that performance will lead to various work outcomes.

Integrated production technologies Focus on providing flexibility in manufacturing and services and involve job design and information systems as part of the technology.

Integrative negotiation Negotiation in which the focus is on the merits of the issues, and the parties involved try to enlarge the available pie" rather than stake claims to certain portions of it.

Intellectual capital The sum total of knowledge, expertise and energy available from organizational members.

Interfirm alliances Announced cooperative agreements of joint ventures between two independent firms.

Intergroup conflict Occurs among groups in an organization.

Intergroup team building Helps groups improve their working relationships with one another and experience improved group effectiveness.

Intermittent reinforcement A reinforcement schedule that rewards behavior only periodically.

Interorganizational conflict Occurs between organizations.

Interpersonal conflict Occurs between two or more individuals in opposition to each other.

Intrapersonal conflict Occurs within the individual because of actual or perceived pressures from incompatible goals or expectations.

Intrinsic rewards Rewards received by the individual directly through task performance.

Intuition The ability to know or recognize quickly the possibilities of a situation.

Job analysis The procedure used to collect and classify information about tasks the organization needs to complete.

Job characteristics theory Identifies five core job characteristics of special importance to job designóskill variety, task identity, task significance, autonomy, and feedback.

Job design The process of defining job tasks and the work arrangements to accomplish them.

Job enlargement Increases task variety by adding new tasks of similar difficulty to a job.

Job enrichment Increases job content by giving workers more responsibility for planning and evaluating duties.

Job redesign Creates long-term congruence between individual goals and organizational career opportunities.

Job rotation Increases task variety by shifting workers among jobs involving tasks of similar difficulty.

Job satisfaction The degree to which individuals feel positively or negatively about their jobs.

Job sharing Allows one full-time job to be divided among two or more persons.

Job simplification Standardizes tasks and employs people in very routine jobs.

KISS principle Stands for "keep it short and simple".

Knowledge workers Employees whose major task is to produce new knowledge, typically through computer-oriented means.

Law of contingent reinforcement The view that, for a reward to have maximum reinforcing value, it must be delivered only if the desired behavior is exhibited.

Law of effect   The observation that behavior which results in a pleasing outcome is likely to be repeated; behavior that results in an unpleasant outcome is not likely to be repeated.

Law of immediate reinforcement   The more immediate the delivery of a reward after the occurrence of a desirable behavior, the greater the reinforcing effect on behavior.

Leader match training   Leaders are trained to diagnose the situation to match their high and low LPC scores with situational control.

Leadership   A special case of interpersonal influence that gets an individual or group to do what the leader wants done.

Leadership prototype   An image people have in their minds of what a model leader should look like.

Leading   Creates enthusiasm to work hard to accomplish tasks successfully.

Least preferred coworker (LPC) scale   A measure of a person's leadership style based on a description of the person with whom respondents have been able to work least well.

Legitimate power   The extent to which a manager can use the "right of command" to control other people.

Leniency error   The tendency to give relatively high ratings to virtually everyone.

Line units   Work groups that conduct the major business of the organization.

Long term/short term orientation   The degree to which a culture emphasizes long-term or short-term thinking.

Low-context cultures   Cultures in which messages are expressed mainly by spoken and written words.

Low differentiation errors   What occurs when raters restrict themselves to a small part of the rating scale.

Lower-order needs   Physiological, safety, and social needs in Maslow's hierarchy.

Lump-sum increase   A pay system in which people elect to receive their wage or salary increases in one or more "lump-sum" payments.

Maintenance activities   Activities that support the emotional life of the group as an ongoing social system.

Management by objectives (MBO)   A process of joint goal setting between a supervisor and a subordinate.

Management philosophy   A philosophy that links key goal-related issues with key collaboration issues to come up with general ways by which the firm will manage its affairs.

Managers   People who are formally responsible for supporting the work efforts of other people.

Masculinity-femininity   The degree to which a society values assertiveness or relationships.

Matrix departmentation   A combination of functional and divisional patterns wherein an individual is assigned to more than one type of unit.

MBWA   Involves getting out of the office to directly communicate with others.

Mechanistic type (machine bureaucracy)   Emphasizes vertical specialization and control with impersonal coordination and a heavy reliance on standardization, formalization, rules, policies, and procedures.

Mediation   A neutral third party tries to engage the parties in a negotiated solution through persuasion and rational argument.

Merit pay   A compensation system that bases an individual's salary or wage increase on a measure of the person's performance accomplishments during a specific time period.

Mimicry   The copying of the successful practices of others.

Mission statements   Written statements of organizational purpose.

Mixed messages   Misunderstandings that occur when a person's words say one thing while his or her nonverbal cues say something else.

Monochronic culture   Cultures in which people tend to do one thing at a time.

Motivating potential score   The extent to which the core characteristics of a job create motivating conditions.

Motivation   Forces within an individual that account for the level, direction, and persistence of effort expended at work.

Motivator factors   In job content, the tasks people actually do, are sources of job satisfaction.

Multinational corporation   A business with extensive international operations in more than one country.

Multiskilling   Team members are trained in skills to perform different jobs.

MUM effect Occurs when people are reluctant to communicate bad news.

Need for achievement (nAch) The desire to do better, solve problems, or master complex tasks.

Need for affiliation (nAff) The desire for friendly and warm relations with others.

Need for power (nPower) The desire to control others and influence their behavior.

Negative reinforcement The withdrawal of negative consequences, which tends to increase the likelihood of repeating the behavior in similar settings; also known as avoidance.

Negotiation The process of making joint decisions when the parties involved have different preferences.

New leadership Emphasizes charismatic and transformational approaches and various aspects of vision related to them.

Noise Anything that interferes with the effectiveness of communication.

Nonprogrammed decisions Decisions created to deal uniquely with a problem at hand.

Nonverbal communication Communication that takes place through facial expressions, body movements, eye contact, and other physical gestures.

Norms Rules or standards for the behavior of group members.

Open systems Systems that transform human and material resources into finished goods and services.

Operant conditioning The process of controlling behavior by manipulating, or "operating" on, its consequences.

Operations technology The combination of resources, knowledge, and techniques that creates a product or service output for an organization.

Organic type A professional bureaucracy that emphasizes horizontal specialization, extensive use of personal coordination, and loose rules, policies, and procedures.

Organization charts Diagrams that depict the formal structures of organizations.

Organization development (OD) The application of behavioral science knowledge in a long-range effort to improve an organization's ability to cope with change in its external environment and increase its problem-solving capabilities.

Organization development interventions Activ-

ities initiated to support planned change and improve work effectiveness.

Organizational behavior (OB) The study of individuals and groups in organizations.

Organizational behavior modification (OB Mod) The systematic reinforcement of desirable work behavior and the nonreinforcement or punishment of unwanted work behavior.

Organizational communication The process by which information is exchanged in the organizational setting.

Organizational (or corporate) culture The system of shared actions, values, and beliefs that develops within an organization and guides the behavior of its members.

Organizational design The process of choosing and implementing a structural configuration for an organization.

Organizational governance The pattern of authority, influence, and acceptable managerial behavior established at the top of the organization.

Organizational learning The process of acquiring knowledge and using information to adapt to successfully changing circumstances.

Organizational myth A commonly held cause-effect relationship or assertion that cannot be empirically supported.

Organizational politics The management of influence to obtain ends not sanctioned by the organization or to obtain sanctioned ends through nonsanctioned means and the art of creative compromise among competing interests.

Organizational strategy The process of positioning the organization in the competitive environment and implementing actions to compete successfully.

Organizations Collections of people working together to achieve a common purpose.

Organized anarchy A firm or division in a firm in a transition characterized by very rapid change and a lack of a legitimate hierarchy.

Organizing Dividing up tasks and arranging resources to accomplish them.

Output controls Controls that focus on desired targets and allow managers to use their own methods for reaching defined targets.

Output goals The goals that define the type of business an organization is in.

Paired comparison A comparative method of

performance appraisal whereby each person is directly compared with every other person.

Participative leadership Focuses on consulting with subordinates and seeking and taking their suggestions into account before making decisions.

Perception The process through which people receive, organize, and interpret information from their environment.

Performance appraisal A process of systematically evaluating performance and providing feedback on which performance adjustments can be made.

Permanent part-time work Permanent work of fewer hours than the standard week.

Personal bias error Occurs when a rater allows specific biases, such as racial, age, or gender, to enter into performance appraisal.

Personality Represents the overall profile or combination of characteristics that capture the unique nature of a person as that person reacts and interacts with others.

Personality dynamics The ways in which an individual integrates and organizes social traits, values and motives, personal conceptions, and emotional adjustment.

Planned change Intentional and occurs with a change agent's intentional direction.

Planning Sets objectives and identifies the actions needed to achieve them.

Polychronic culture A culture in which people tend to do more than one thing at a time.

Positive reinforcement The administration of positive consequences that tend to increase the likelihood of repeating the behavior in similar settings.

Power The ability to get someone else to do something you want done or the ability to make things happen or get things done the way you want.

Power distance The willingness of a culture to accept status and power differences among its members.

Problem solving Uses information to resolve disputes.

Procedural justice The degree to which policies and procedures are properly followed.

Process consultation Helps a group improve on such things as norms, cohesiveness, decision-making methods, communication, conflict, and task, and maintenance activities.

Process controls Controls that attempt to specify the manner in which tasks are to be accomplished.

Process innovations Innovations introduced into operations new and better ways of doing things.

Process reengineering The total rethinking and redesign of organizational process to improve performance and innovation; involves analyzing, streamlining, and reconfiguring actions and tasks to achieve work goals.

Process theories Theories that seek to understand the thought processes determining behavior.

Product innovations Innovations that introduce new goods or services to better meet customer needs.

Programmed decisions Decisions that are determined by past experience as appropriate for a problem at hand.

Profit sharing plans Reward employees based on the entire organization's performance.

Projection The assignment of personal attributes to other individuals.

Punishment The administration of negative consequences that tend to reduce the likelihood of repeating the behavior in similar settings.

Quality circle Members of a quality circle meet regularly to find ways for continuous improvement of quality operations.

Quality of work life (QWL) The overall quality of human experiences in the workplace.

Ranking A comparative technique of performance appraisal that involves rank ordering of each individual from best to worst on each performance dimension.

Rational persuasion The ability to control another's behavior because, through the individual's efforts, the person accepts the desirability of an offered goal and a reasonable way of achieving it.

Rational persuasion strategy Uses facts, special knowledge, and rational argument to create change.

Realistic job previews Previews which provide applicants with an objective description of a job and organization.

Recency error A biased rating that develops by allowing the individual's most recent behavior to speak for his or her overall performance on a particular dimension.

Recruitment The process of attracting the best qualified individuals to apply for a job.

Referent power The ability to control another's behavior because of the individual's desire to identify with the power source.

Refreezing The stage in which changes are reinforced and stabilized.

Reinforcement The administration of a consequence as a result of behavior.

Reinforcement theories They emphasize the means through which operant conditioning takes place.

Relatedness needs Desires for satisfying interpersonal relationships.

Reliability The consistency and stability of a score from a measurement scale.

Representativeness heuristic Bases a decision on similarities between the situation at hand and stereotypes of similar occurrences.

Resistance to change An attitude or behavior that shows unwillingness to make or support a change.

Restricted communication networks Link subgroups that disagree with one another's positions.

Reward power The extent to which a manager can use extrinsic and intrinsic rewards to control other people.

Risk environments Business environments that provide probabilities regarding expected results for decision-making alternatives.

Rites Standardized and recurring activities used at special times to influence the behaviors and understanding of organizational members.

Rituals Systems of rites.

Role A set of expectations for a team member or person in a job.

Role ambiguity Occurs when someone is uncertain about what is expected of him or her.

Role conflict Occurs when someone is unable to respond to role expectations that conflict with one another.

Role negotiation A process through which individuals clarify expectations about what each should be giving and receiving as group members.

Role overload Occurs when too much work is expected of the individual.

Role underload Occurs when too little work is expected of the individual.

Romance of leadership People attribute romantic, almost magical qualities to leadership.

Sagas Embellished heroic accounts of the story of the founding of an organization.

Satisficing Decision making that chooses the first alternative that appears to give an acceptable or satisfactory resolution of the problem.

Scanning Looking outside the firm and bringing back useful solutions to problems.

Schemas Cognitive frameworks that represent organized knowledge about a given concept or stimulus developed through experience.

Scientific method A key part of the OB research foundations, which involves four steps: the research question or problem, hypothesis generation or formulation, the research design, and data gathering, analysis, and interpretation.

Selection The series of steps from initial applicant screening to hiring.

Selective perception The tendency to single out for attention those aspects of a situation or person that reinforce or emerge and are consistent with existing beliefs, values, and needs.

Self-concept The view individuals have of themselves as physical, social, and spiritual or moral beings.

Self-directing work teams Teams that are empowered to make decisions about planning, doing, and evaluating their work.

Self-fulfilling prophecy The tendency to create or find in another situation or individual that which one has expected to find.

Self-managing teams Same as self-directing work teams.

Self-monitoring Reflects a person's ability to adjust his or her behavior to external, situational (environmental) factors.

Self-serving bias The tendency to deny personal responsibility for performance problems but to accept personal responsibility for performance success.

Shamrock organizations Firms that operate with a core group of permanent workers supplemented by outside contractors and part-time workers.

Shaping The creation of a new behavior by the positive reinforcement of successive approximations to the desired behavior.

Shared-power strategy Uses participative methods and emphasizes common values to create change.

Simple design An organization configuration involving one or two ways of specializing individuals and units.

Situational control The extent to which leaders can determine what their groups are going to do and what the outcomes of their actions and decisions are going to be.

Skill-based pay A system that rewards people for acquiring and developing job-relevant skills in number and variety relevant to the organization's need.

Social facilitation The tendency for one's behavior to be influenced by the presence of others in a group.

Social information-processing Believes that individual needs and task perceptions result from socially constructed realities.

Social loafing Occurs when people work less hard in groups than they would individually.

Social responsibility The obligation of organizations to behave in ethical and moral ways.

Social traits Surface-level traits that reflect the way a person appears to others when interacting in various social settings.

Socialization Orienting new employees to the firm and its work units.

Societal goals Goals that reflect the intended contributions of an organization to the broader society.

Sociotechnical systems Organizational systems that integrate people and technology into high-performance work settings.

Sources and types of values Parents, friends, teachers, and external reference groups can all influence individual values.

Span of control The number of individuals reporting to a supervisor.

Staff units Groups that assist the line units by performing specialized services to the organization.

Status congruence The consistency between a person's status within and outside of a group.

Stimulus Something that incites action.

Stress Tension from extraordinary demands, constraints, or opportunities.

Stress management An active approach to deal with stress that is influencing behavior.

Stress prevention Involves minimizing the potential for stress to occur.

Stressors Things that cause stress.

Structural redesign Involves realigning the structure of the organization or major subsystem in order to improve performance.

Subcultures Unique patterns of values and philosophies within a group that are not consistent with the dominant culture of the larger organization or social system.

Substantive conflict Fundamental disagreement over ends or goals to be pursued and the means for their accomplishment.

Substitutes for leadership Makes a leader's influence both unnecessary and redundent in that they replace a leader's influence.

Supportive leadership Focuses on subordinate needs, well-being, and promotion of a friendly work climate.

Survey feedback Begins with the collection of data via questionnaires from organization members or a representative sample of them.

Synergy The creation of a whole that is greater than the sum of its parts.

Systems goals Goals concerned with conditions within the organization that are expected to increase its survival potential.

Task activities Actions that directly contribute to the performance of important group tasks.

Team building A collaborative way to gather and analyze data to improve teamwork.

Teams People working actively together to achieve a common purpose for which they are all accountable.

Teamwork Occurs when group members work together in ways that utilize their skills well to accomplish a purpose.

Technical skill An ability to perform specialized tasks.

Telecommuting Working at home or in a remote location that uses computer and telecommunication linkages with the office.

Temporary part-time work Temporary work of fewer hours than the standard week.

Terminal values A person's preferences concerning the "ends" to be achieved.

Theory A set of systematically interrelated concepts, definitions, and hypotheses that are advanced to explain and predict phenomena.

360-degree evaluation A comprehensive approach that uses self-ratings, customer ratings, and others outside the work unit.

Total quality management (TQM) A total commitment to high-quality results, continuous improvement, and meeting customer needs.

Training Provides the opportunity to acquire and improve job-related skills.

Trait perspectives Assumes that traits play a central role in differentiating between leaders and nonleaders.

Transactional leadership Involves leader-follower exchanges necessary for achieving routine performance agreed upon between leaders and followers.

Transformational leadership Occurs when leaders broaden and elevate followers' interests and followers look beyond their own interests for the good of others.

Two-factor theory Herzberg's theory that identifies job context as the source of job dissatisfaction and job content as the source of job satisfaction.

Type A orientation A personality orientation characterized by impatience, desire for achievement, and perfectionism.

Type B orientation A personality orientation characterized by an easygoing and less competitive nature than Type A.

Uncertain environments Business environments that provide no information to predict expected results for decision-making alternatives.

Uncertainty avoidance The cultural tendency to be uncomfortable with uncertainty and risk in everyday life.

Unfreezing The stage of the change process at which a situation is prepared for change.

Unplanned change Change that occurs spontaneously and without a change agent's direction.

Valence The value to the individual of various work outcomes.

Validity The degree of confidence one can have in the results of a research study.

Value congruence Occurs when individuals express positive feelings upon encountering others who exhibit values similar to their own.

Values Broad preferences concerning appropriate courses of action or outcomes.

Vertical specialization A hierarchical division of labor that distributes formal authority.

Virtual team A work team that convenes and operates with its members linked together electronically via networked computers.

Wellness Maintaining physical and mental health to better deal with stress when it occurs.

Workforce diversity Differences based on gender, race and ethnicity, age, and able-bodiedness.

Work-life balance Deals with the demands from one's work and personal affairs.

Zone of indifference The range of authoritative requests to which a subordinate is willing to respond without subjecting the directives to critical evaluation or judgment.

Notes

■ CHAPTER 1

Footnotes

[1] Mirta Ojito, "Making a Good Idea Her Own," *New York Times* (September 23, 1998), p. 4; Gene G. Marcial, "Big Network on Campus?" *Inside Wall Street* (December 21, 1998), p. 73.

[2] John Huey, "Managing in the Midst of Chaos," *Fortune* (April 5, 1993), pp. 38–48. See also Tom Peters, *Thriving on Chaos* (New York: Knopf, 1991); Jay R. Galbraith, Edward E. Lawler III, and Associates, *Organizing for the Future: The New Logic for Managing Organizations* (San Francisco: Jossey-Bass, 1993); William H. Davidow and Michael S. Malone, *The Virtual Corporation: Structuring and Revitalizing the Corporation of the 21st Century* (New York: Harper Business, 1993); Charles Handy, *The Age of Unreason* (Boston: Harvard Business School Press, 1990) and *The Age of Paradox* (Boston: Harvard Business School Press, 1994). Peter Drucker, *Managing in a Time of Great Change* (New York: Truman Talley, 1995); and Tom Peters, "The Brand Called You," *Fast Company* (August/September 1997).

[3] See Gary Hamel and Jeff Sampler, "The e-Corporation," *Fortune* (December 7, 1998), pp. 79–90; and David Kirkpatrick, "The E-Ware War," *Fortune* (December 7, 1998), pp. 115–117.

[4] See Daniel H. Pink, "Free Agent Nation," *Fast Company* (December 1997), pp. 131ff; and Tom Peters, "The Brand Called You," *Fast Company* (August/September 1997).

[5] Thomas Petzinger, Jr., "A New Model for the Nature of Business: It's Alive!" *Wall Street Journal* (February 26, 1999), pp. B1, B4.

[6] Robert B. Reich, "The Company of the Future," *Fast Company* (November 1998), p. 124ff.

[7] Based on Jay A. Conger, *Winning 'em Over: A New Model for Managing in the Age of Persuasion* (New York: Simon & Schuster, 1998), pp. 180–181; Stewart D. Friedman, Perry Christensen, and Jessica DeGroot, "Work and Life: The End of the Zero-Sum Game, *Harvard Business Review* (November–December 1998): 119–129; and C. Argyris, "Empowerment: The Emperor's New Clothes," *Harvard Business Review*, (May–June 1998): 98–105.

[8] The foundation report on diversity in the American workplace is *Workforce 2000: Work and Workers in the 21st Century* (Indianapolis: Hudson Institute, 1987). For comprehensive discussions, see Martin M. Chemers, Stuart Oskamp, and Mark A. Costanzo, *Diversity in Organizations: New Perspectives for a Changing Workplace* (Beverly Hills, CA,: Sage, 1995); and Robert T. Golembiewski, *Managing Diversity in Organizations* (Tuscaloosa, AL: University of Alabama Press, 1995).

[9] David A. Thomas and Suzy Wetlaufer, "A Question of Color: A Debate on Race in the U.S. Workplace," *Harvard Business Review* (September–October 1997): 118–132.

[10] "Change at the Top," *Wall Street Journal* (March 9, 1999), p. B12.

[11] Catalyst Survey 1998 as reported in "Executive Pay Gap Widens," Associated Press, New York, and appearing in *The Columbus Dispatch* (November 10, 1998), p. 2C; and "You've Come a Short Way, Baby," *Business Week* (November 23, 1998), pp. 82–88. For a look at corporate best practices, see Catalyst, *Advancing Women in Business: The Catalyst Guide* (San Francisco: Jossey-Bass, 1998).

[12] James G. March, *The Pursuit of Organizational Intelligence* (Malden, MA: Blackwell, 1999).

[13] See Peter Senge, *The Fifth Discipline* (New York: Harper, 1990); D. A. Garvin, "Building a Learning Organization," *Harvard Business Review* (November/December 1991): 78–91; Chris Argyris, *On Organizational Learning*, 2nd ed. (Malden, MA: Blackwell, 1999).

[14] Information from Reich, op. cit., p. 124ff.

[15] See Jay W. Lorsch ed., *Handbook of Organizational Behavior* (Englewood Cliffs, NJ: Prentice Hall, 1987), for a general overview.

[16] Geert Hofstede, "Cultural Constraints in Management Theories," *Academy of Management Executive*, 7 (1993): 81–94.

[17] For more on mission statements see Patricia Jones and Larry Kahaner, *Say It and Live It: The 50 Corporate Mission Statements That Hit the Mark* (New York: Currency/Doubleday, 1995) and John Graham and Wendy Havlick, *Mission Statements: A Guide to the Corporate and Nonprofit Sectors* (New York: Garland Publishers, 1995).

[18] James C. Collins and Jerry I. Porras, "Building Your Company's Vision," *Harvard Business Review* (September–October 1996): 65–77.

[19] America West Airlines corporate Web site: www.americawest.com.

[20] Reich, op. cit. (1998).

[21] See Michael E. Porter, *Competitive Strategy: Techniques for Analyzing Industries and Competitors* (New York: Free Press, 1980) and *Competitive Advantage: Creating and Sustaining Superior Performance* (New York: Free Press, 1986); Gary Hamel and C. K. Prahalad, "Strategic Intent," *Harvard Business Review* (May–June 1989): 63–76; and Richard A. D'Aveni, *Hyper-*

Competition: Managing the Dynamics of Strategic Maneuvering (New York: Free Press, 1994).

22 Information from Shelley Branch, "The 100 Best Companies to Work for in America," *Fortune* (January 11, 1999), pp. 118–144.

23 Quote from Jeffrey Pfeffer, *The Human Equation: Building Profits by Putting People First* (Boston: Harvard Business School Press, 1998).

24 See Dave Ulrich, "Intellectual Capital = Competence x Commitment," *Harvard Business Review* (Winter 1998): 15–26.

25 "What Makes a Company Great?" *Fortune* (October 26, 1998), p. 218.

26 See Brian Dumaine, "The New Non-Manager Managers," *Fortune* (February 22, 1993), pp. 80–84; and Walter Kiechel III, "How We Will Work in the Year 2000," *Fortune* (May 17, 1993), p. 38.

27 This review is from Henry Mintzberg, *The Nature of Managerial Work* (New York: Harper & Row, 1973). For related and further developments, see Morgan W. McCall, Jr., Ann M. Morrison, and Robert L. Hannan, *Studies of Managerial Work: Results and Methods, Technical Report No. 9* (Greensboro, NC: Center for Creative Leadership, 1978); John P. Kotter, *The General Managers* (New York: Free Press, 1982); Fred Luthans, Stuart Rosenkrantz, and Harry Hennessey, "What Do Successful Managers Really Do?" *Journal of Applied Behavioral Science* 21, No. 2, (1985): 255–270; Robert E. Kaplan, *The Warp and Woof of the General Manager's Job Technical Report No. 27* (Greensboro, NC: Center for Creative Leadership, 1986); and Fred Luthans, Richard M. Hodgetts, and Stuart A. Rosenkrantz, *Real Managers* (New York: HarperCollins, 1988).

28 John R. Schermerhorn, Jr., *Management,* 6th ed. (New York: Wiley, 1999).

29 Mintzberg, op. cit., 1973. See also Henry Mintzberg, *Mintzberg on Management* (New York: Free Press, 1989) and "Rounding Out the Manager's Job," *Sloan Management Review* (Fall 1994): 11–26.

30 Kotter, op. cit. (1982); John P. Kotter, "What Effective General Managers Really Do," *Harvard Business Review*, 60 (November/December 1982): 161. See Kaplan, op. cit., 1984.

31 Herminia Ibarra, "Managerial Networks," Teaching Note #9-495-039, Harvard Business School Publishing, Boston, MA.

32 Robert L. Katz,"Skills of an Effective Administrator, *Harvard Business Review,* 52 (September/October 1974): 94. See also Richard E. Boyatzis, *The Competent Manager: A Model for Effective Performance* (New York: Wiley, 1982).

33 Conger, op. cit., (1998).

34 A good overview is available in Linda K. Trevino and Katherine J. Nelson, *Managing Business Ethics*, 2nd ed. (New York: Wiley, 1999).

35 See Blair Sheppard, Roy J. Lewicki, and John Minton, *Organizational Justice: The Search for Fairness in the Workplace* (New York: Lexington Books, 1992); and Jerald Greenberg, *The Quest for Justice on the Job: Essays and Experiments* (Thousand Oaks, CA: Sage Publications, 1995); Robert Folger and Russell Cropanzano, *Organizational Justice and Human Resource Management* (Thousand Oaks, CA: Sage, 1998).

36 See Steven N. Brenner and Earl A. Mollander, "Is the Ethics of Business Changing?" *Harvard Business Review* 55 (January/February 1977): 50–57; Saul W. Gellerman, "Why 'Good' Managers Make Bad Ethical Choices," *Harvard Business Review* 64 (July/August 1986): 85–90; Barbara Ley Toffler, *Tough Choices: Managers Talk Ethics* (New York: John Wiley, 1986); Justin G. Longnecker, Joseph A. McKinney, and Carlos W. Moore, "The Generation Gap in Business Ethics," *Business Horizons*, 32 (September/October 1989): 9–14; John B. Cullen, Vart Victor, and Carroll Stephens, "An Ethical Weather Report: Assessing the Organization's Ethical Climate," *Organizational Dynamics* (Winter 1990): 50–62; Dawn Blalock, "Study Shows Many Execs Are Quick to Write Off Ethics," *Wall Street Journal* (March 26, 1996), p. C1.

37 Developed in part from Alan L. Otten, "Ethics on the Job: Companies Alert Employees to Potential Dilemmas," W*all Street Journal* (July 14, 1986), p. 17.

38 Based on Gellerman, op. cit. (1986).

39 For research on whistleblowers, see Paula M. Miceli and Janet P. Near, *Blowing the Whistle* (New York: Lexington, 1992).

40 Information from Timothy D. Schellhardt, "An Idyllic Workplace under a Tycoon's Thumb," *Wall Street Journal* (November 23, 1998), p. B1.

41 Douglas McGregor, *The Human Side of Enterprise* (New York: McGraw-Hill, 1960).

42 David A. Nadler and Edward E. Lawler III, "Quality of Work Life: Perspectives and Directions," *Organizational Dynamics* 11 (1983): 22–36; the discussion of QWL, in Thomas G. Cummings and Edgar F. Huse, *Organizational Development and Change* (St. Paul, MN: West, 1990); and Stewart D. Friedman, Perry Christensen, and Jessica DeGroot, "Work and Life: The End of the Zero-Sum Game," *Harvard Business Review* (November–December 1998): 119–129.

43 Pfeffer, *The Human Equation: Building Profits by Putting People First*, op. cit., p. 292.

Source Notes

Information from Jeff Cole, "New Boeing CFO's Assignment: Signal a Turnaround," *Wall Street Journal* (January 26, 1999), pp. B1, B4.

Trilogy information from Robert B. Reich, "The Company of the Future," *Fast Company* (November 1998), p. 124ff; corporate Web site.

Florida A & M University. Diana Kunde, "Black University, Corporations Find Close Ties Benefit Everyone," *The Columbus Dispatch* (October 5, 1998), p. 4).

Great Plains Software information from Robert B. Reich, "The Company of the Future," *Fast Company* (November 1998), p. 124ff.

■ CHAPTER 2

Footnotes

1 This discussion comes from Course Notes for Management 5371, *Managing Organizational Behavior and Organizational Design*, prepared by Barry A. Macy, Texas Tech University, Spring 1999.

2 Personal Communication with Barry A. Macy, March 5, 1999.

3 "What Makes a Company Great?" *Fortune* (October 26, 1998), p. 218.

4 See Thomas A. Stewart, "Planning a Career Without Managers," *Fortune* (March 20, 1995), pp. 72–80.

5 Workplace Visions (September/October 1998), p. 2.

6 Lester Thurow, *Head to Head: The Coming Economic Battle among Japan, Europe, and America* (New York: Morrow, 1992) and Barry A. Macy, *Successful Strategic Change* (San Francisco: Barrett-Koehler, in press).

7 "Unemployment Falls 4.2 Percent to 29-Year Low," *Lubbock Avalanche-Journal* (April 3, 1999), p. E-1.

8 Nina Munk, "The New Organization Man," *Fortune* (March 16, 1998), pp. 63–64.

9 Thurow.

10 See, for example, Jay R. Galbraith, Edward E. Lawler III, and Associates, *Organizing for the Future: The New Logic for Managing Organizations* (San Francisco: Jossey-Bass, 1993); and Peter Drucker, *Managing in a Time of Great Change* (New York: Truman Talley, 1995).

11 Michael Hammer and James Champy, *Reengineering the Corporation* (New York: Harper Collins, 1993).

12 See Gary Hammel and Jeff Sampler, "The e-Corporation," *Fortune* (December 7, 1998), pp. 79–90; and David Kirkpatrick, "The E-Ware War," *Fortune* (December 7, 1998), pp. 115–117.

13 William H. Davidow and Michael S. Malone, *The Virtual Corporation: Structuring and Revitalizing the Corporation of the 21st Century* (New York: Harper Business, 1993). Also, Andrew Kupfer, "Alone Together: Will Being Wired Set Us Free?" *Fortune* (March 20, 1995), pp. 94–104.

14 See Daniel H. Pink, "Free Agent Nation," *Fast Company* (December, 1997), pp. 131ff; and Tom Peters, "The Brand Called You," *Fast Company* (August/September 1997).

15 Charles Handy, *The Age of Unreason* (Boston: Harvard Business School Press, 1990). See also his later book, *The Age of Paradox* (Boston: Harvard Business School Press, 1994).

[16] Jeffrey Pfeffer, *The Human Equation: Building Profits by Putting People First* (Boston: Harvard Business School Press, 1998).

[17] See Dave Ulrich, "Intellectual Capital = Competence x Commitment," *Harvard Business Review* (Winter 1998), pp. 15–26.

[18] Bradley L. Kirksman, Kevin B. Lowe, and Dianne P. Young, "The Challenge in High Performance Work Organizations," *Journal of Leadership Studies*, Vol. 5, No. 2 (Spring 1998): 3–15.

[19] Kirksman, Lowe, and Young, p. 5.

[20] Ibid.

[21] Ibid.; see also Course Notes for Management 5371 (1999).

[22] Kirksman, Lowe, and Young, pp. 5, 6.

[23] Ibid., p. 5.

[24] C. B. Gibson and B. L. Kirksman, "Our Past, Present and Future in Teams: The Role of the Human Resources Professional in Managing Team Performance," in A. L. Kraut and A. K. Korman (eds.), *Changing Concepts and Practices for Human Resources Management: Contributions from Industrial Organizational Psychology* (San Francisco: Jossey-Bass, in press).

[25] P. S. Goodman, R. Devadas, and T. L. Hughson, "Groups and Productivity: Analyzing the Effectiveness of Self Managing Work Teams," in J. P. Campbell and R. J. Campbell (eds.), *Productivity in Organizations: New Perspectives from Industrial and Organizational Psychology* (San Francisco: Jossey-Bass, 1988), pp. 295–237.

[26] Robert E. Markland, Shawnee K. Vickery, and Robert A. Davis, *Operations Management*, 2nd ed. (Cincinnati, OH: Southwestern Publishing, 1998), p. 646.

[27] Lee J. Kraijewski and Larry R. Ritzman, *Operations Management*, 5th ed. (Reading, MA: Addison-Wesley, 1989), pp. 158–159.

[28] Ibid.

[29] See D. A. Garvin, "Building a Learning Organization," *Harvard Business Review* (July–August 1993): 78–91; and Danny Miller, "A Preliminary Typology of Organizational Learning: Synthesizing the Literature," *Journal of Management*, Vol. 22, No. 3 (1996), pp. 485–505.

[30] Kirksman, Lowe, and Young pp. 6–7.

[31] Macy, *Successful Strategic Change.*

[32] Macis, Course Notes, (Spring 1999).

[33] See Jack O'Toole, *Forming the Future: Lessons from the Saturn Corporation* (Cambridge, MA: Basil Blackwell, 1996), p. 15.

[34] Kirksman, Lowe, and Young, pp. 7–12.

[35] Ibid.

[36] Ibid., p. 9.

[37] Macy, Course Notes (Spring 1999).

[38] Ibid.

[39] Kirksman, Lowe, and Young, pp. 10–12.

[40] O'Toole, p. 15.

[41] See B. A. Macy and J. Izumi, "Organizational Change, Design, and Work Innovation: A Meta-Analysis of 131 North American Field Studies— 1961–1991," in W. A. Pasmore and R. W. Woodman (eds.), *Research in Organizational Change and Development*, Vol. 7 (Greenwich, CT: Jai Press, 1993), pp. 235–311.

[42] Macy, Course Notes (Spring 1999).

[43] O'Toole.

[44] Macy, *Successful Strategic Change.*

[45] The discussion in this section is based heavily on Eryn Brown, "VF Corp. Changes Its Underwear," *Fortune* (December 7, 1998), pp. 115–118.

[46] Nina Monk, "How Levi's Trashed a Great American Brand," *Fortune* (April 12, 1999), pp. 82–91.

Source Notes
Information from William B. Brenneman, J. Bernard Keys, and Robert M. Fulmer, "Learning Across a Living Company: The Shell Companies' Experiences," *Organizational Dynamics* (Summer 1998), pp. 67–68.

Information from Katharine Mieszkowski, "Web Commerce As If Customers Mattered," *Fast Company* (November 1998), pp. 98ff.

Information from Eric Sundstrom and Associates, *Supporting Work Team Effectiveness* (San Francisco: Jossey-Bass, 1999), pp. 218–223.

Information from Rhonda Thompson, "An Employee's View of Empowerment," *HR Focus* (July 1993), p. 14.

Information from Eric Sundstrom and Associates, *Supporting Work Team Effectiveness* (San Francisco: Jossey-Bass, 1999), p. 233.

Information from a personal visit to the Benevia plant (October 15–17, 1997), by J. G. Hunt.

Information from Leonard D. Goodstein and Howard E. Butz, "Customer Value: The Linchpin of Organizational Change," *Organizational Dynamics* (Summer 1998), pp. 26–27.

Information from Jack O'Toole, *Forming the Future: Lessons from the Saturn Corporation* (Cambridge, MA: Blackledge, 1996), Ch. 5, 1–5.

Information from Barry A. Macy, *Successful Strategic Change* (San Francisco: Barrett-Koehler, in press).

Developed from E. E. Lawler III, "Total Quality Management and Employee Involvement: Are They Compatible?" *Academy of Management Executive*, Vol. 8, No. 1 (1994), pp. 68–76.

Information from B. A. Macy, *Successful Strategic Change* (San Francisco: Barrett-Koehler, in press).

Adapted from Bradley L. Kirkman, Kevin B. Lowe, and Dianne P. Young, "The Challenge of Leadership in High Performance Work Organizations," *Journal of Leadership Studies*, Vol. 5, No. 2, (1998), p. 8.

Based on Eryn Brown, "VF Corp. Changes Its Underware," *Fortune* (December 7, 1998), p. 117.

■ CHAPTER 3

Footnotes
[1] Information from John Lorinc, "Road Warriors," *Canadian Business* (October 1995), pp. 26–43; and Arthur Johnson, "Editor's Note," *Canadian Business* (October 1995), p. 11; Steven Pearlstein, "Canadian Stores Take on U.S. Rivals," *The Plain Dealer* (January 24, 1999), p. 1H.

[2] "A Way to Measure Global Success," *Fortune* (March 15, 1999), pp. 196–197.

[3] Kenichi Ohmae, *The Borderless World* (New York: Harper Business, 1989); Peter F. Drucker, "The Global Economy and the Nation-State," *Foreign Affairs* (September/October 1997).

[4] See Michael Porter's three-volume series *The Competitive Advantage of Nations, Competitive Advantage*, and *Competitive Strategy* (New York: The Free Press, 1998).

[5] Kenichi Ohmae, *The Evolving Global Economy* (Cambridge, MA: Harvard Business School Press, 1995); Kenichi Ohmae, "Putting Global Logic First," *Harvard Business Review* (January–February 1995), pp. 119–125; and, Jeffrey E. Garten, "Can the World Survive the Triumph of Capitalism?" *Harvard Business Review* (January–February, 1997), pp. 67–79.

[6] William B. Johnston, "Global Workforce 2000: The New World Labor Market," *Harvard Business Review* (March–April 1991), pp. 115–127.

[7] See Porter, op. cit.; Kenichi Ohmae *The End of the Nation State: The Rise of Regional Economies* (New York: The Free Press, 1995); and William Greider, *One World, Ready or Not: The Manic Logic of Global Capitalism* (New York: The Free Press, 1998).

[8] For a discussion of FDI in the United States, see Paul R. Krugman, *Foreign Direct Investment in the United States*, 3rd ed. (Washington, DC, 1995). Statistics on FDI in the United States are available through the Bureau of Economic Analysis, International Accounts Data, [Online] *http://www.bea.doc.gov/bea/di1.htm.*

[9] "Just a Wee Bit of Life in Silicon Glen," *World Business* (March–April 1996), p. 13.

[10] Michael E. Porter, "Clusters and the New Economics of Competition," *Harvard Business Review* (November–December 1998).

[11] See "Alphabet Spaghetti," *The Economist* (October 3, 1998), pp. 19–22; 12 "The Atlantic Century," *Business Week* (February 8, 1999), pp. 64–67.

[12] "Europe Rising," *Business Week* (February 8, 1999), pp. 68–70.

[13] Sarita Kendall and Nancy Dunne, "Business Spurs All-America Free Trade Accord," *Financial Times* (March 22, 1996), p. 3.

[14] One view of the Asian economic crisis is reviewed in George Soros, "Toward a Global Open Society," *Atlantic Monthly* (January 1998).

[15] Michael M. Phillips, "Into Africa," *The Wall Street Journal* (September 18, 1997), pp. R6, R20.

[16] James A. Austin and John G. McLean, "Pathways to Business Success in Sub-Saharan Africa," *Journal of African Finance and Economic Development*, Vol. 2 (1996), pp. 57–76.

[17] Information from "International Business: Consider Africa," *Harvard Business Review*, Vol. 76 (January–February 1998), pp. 16–18.

[18] Robert T. Moran and John R. Riesenberger, *Making Globalization Work: Solutions for Implementation* (New York: McGraw-Hill, 1993); "Don't Be an Ugly-American Manager," *Fortune* (October 16, 1995), p. 225; and, "A Way to Measure Global Success," *Fortune* (March 15, 1999), pp. 196–197.

[19] "Working Overseas—Rule No. 1: Don't Miss the Locals," *Business Week* (May 15, 1995), p. 8.

[20] "Don't Be an Ugly-American Manager," op. cit., p. 225.

[21] Vanessa Houlder, "Foreign Culture Shocks," *Financial Times* (March 22, 1996), p. 12.

[22] Information from Brian O'Reilly, "How Execs Learn," *Fortune* (April 5, 1993), pp. 52–58.

[23] Geert Hofstede, *Culture's Consequences: International Differences in Work-Related Values* (Beverly Hills, CA.: Sage Publications, 1980); and, Fons Trompenaars, *Riding the Waves of Culture: Understanding Cultural Diversity in Business* (London: Nicholas Brealey Publishing, 1993). For an excellent discussion of culture, see also Chapter 3, "Culture: The Neglected Concept," in Peter B. Smith and Michael Harris Bond, *Social Psychology Across Cultures*, 2nd ed. (Boston: Allyn & Bacon, 1998).

[24] Geert Hofstede, *Culture and Organizations: Software of the Mind* (London: McGraw-Hill, 1991).

[25] A good overview of the world's cultures is provided in Richard D. Lewis, *When Cultures Collide: Managing Successfully Across Cultures* (London: Nicholas Brealey Publishing, 1996).

[26] Benjamin L. Whorf, *Language, Thought and Reality* (Cambridge, MA: MIT Press, 1956).

[27] Edward T. Hall, *Beyond Culture* (New York: Doubleday, 1976).

[28] A classic work and the source of our examples is Edward T. Hall, *The Silent Language* (New York: Anchor Books, 1959).

[29] Allen C. Bluedorn, Carol Felker Kaufman, and Paul M. Lane, "How Many Things Do You Like to Do at Once?" *Academy of Management Executive*, Vol. 6 (November 1992), pp. 17–26.

[30] Edward T. Hall's book *The Hidden Dimension* (New York: Anchor Books, 1969; Magnolia, MI: Peter Smith, 1990) is a classic reference and the source of our examples. See also Edward T. Hall, *Hidden Differences* (New York: Doubleday, 1990).

[31] The classic work is Max Weber, *The Protestant Ethic and the Spirit of Capitalism* (New York: Scribner, 1930). For a description of religious influences in Asian cultures, see S. Gordon Redding, *The Spirit of Chinese Capitalism* (New York: Walter de Gruyter, 1990).

[32] Hofstede, op. cit. (1980). Geert Hofstede and Michael H. Bond, "The Confucius Connection: From Culture Roots to Economic Growth," *Organizational Dynamics*, Vol. 16 (1988), pp. 4–21.

[33] Hofstede, op. cit. (1980).

[34] Chinese Culture Connection, "Chinese Values and the Search for Culture-Free Dimensions of Culture," *Journal of Cross-Cultural Psychology*, Vol. 18 (1987), pp. 143–164.

[35] Hofstede and Bond, op. cit., 1988; and, Geert Hofstede, "Cultural Constraints in Management Theories," *Academy of Management Executive*, Vol. 7 (February 1993), pp. 81–94. For a further discussion of Asian and Confucian values, see also Jim Rohwer, *Asia Rising: Why America Will Prosper as Asia's Economies Boom* (New York: Simon & Schuster, 1995), and Chapter 3 on "China" in Lewis, op. cit. (1996).

[36] For an example, see John R. Schermerhorn, Jr., and Michael H. Bond, "Cross-Cultural Leadership Dynamics in Collectivism + High Power Distance Settings," *Leadership and Organization Development Journal*, Vol. 18 (1997), pp. 187–193.

[37] Nancy J. Adler, *International Dimensions of Organizational Behavior*, 2nd ed. (Boston: PWS-Kent, 1991).

[38] Trompenaars, op. cit. (1993).

[39] Alvin Toffler, *The Third Wave* (New York: William Morrow, 1980).

[40] Ibid.

[41] Information from "Sweatshop Wars," *The Economist* (February 27, 1999), pp. 62–63.

[42] See Hofstede, op. cit. (1980, 1993); Adler, op. cit. (1991).

[43] Adler, op. cit. (1991).

[44] Information from Jennifer Scott, "Workers Being Sent Abroad Are Finding More Support," *The Columbus Dispatch* (March 8, 1999), pp. 10–11.

[45] Ibid.

[46] See J. Stewart Black and Hal B. Gregersen, "The Right Way to Manage Expats," *Harvard Business Review* (March–April 1999).

[47] See Rosalie Tung, "Expatriate Assignments: Enhancing Success and Minimizing Failure," *Academy of Management Executive* (May 1987), pp. 117–126; and Adler, op. cit. (1991).

[48] Nancy J. Adler, "Reentry: Managing Cross-Cultural Transitions," *Group and Organization Studies*, Vol. 6, No. 3 (1981), pp. 341–356; and Adler, op. cit. (1991).

[49] For a discussion of international business ethics, see Thomas Donaldson and Thomas W. Dunfee, *Ties That Bind* (Boston: Harvard Business School Press, 1999); Thomas Donaldson, "Values in Tension: Ethics Away from Home," *Harvard Business Review* (September–October 1996), pp. 48–62; and, Debora L. Spar, "The Spotlight and the Bottom Line," *Foreign Affairs* (March–April 1998).

[50] "Cracking Down on Overseas Bribes," *Business Week* (March 1, 1999), p. 41.

[51] "Business Ethics: Sweatshops," *The Economist* (February 27, 1999), pp. 62–63.

[52] Information from Council for Economic Priorities Accreditation Agency Web site: www.cepaa.org.

[53] Donaldson, op. cit. (1996).

[54] Ibid.; Thomas Donaldson and Thomas W. Dunfee, "Towards a Unified Conception of Business Ethics: Integrative Social Contracts Theory," *Academy of Management Review*, Vol. 19 (1994), pp. 252–285; and Donaldson and Dunfee, op. cit. (1999). For a related discussion see John R. Schermerhorn, Jr., "Alternative Terms of Business Engagement in Ethically Challenging Environment," *Business Ethics Quarterly* (1999), forthcoming.

[55] Geert Hofstede, "Motivation, Leadership and Organization: Do American Theories Apply Abroad?" *Organizational Dynamics*, Vol. 9 (1980), pp. 43+; Hofstede, op. cit. (1993).

[56] Two classic works are William Ouchi, *Theory Z: How American Businesses Can Meet the Japanese Challenge* (Reading, MA: Addison-Wesley, 1981); Richard Tanner and Anthony Athos, *The Art of Japanese Management* (New York: Simon & Schuster, 1981).

[57] See J. Bernard Keys, Luther Tray Denton, and Thomas R. Miller, "The Japanese Management Theory Jungle—Revisited," *Journal of Management*, Vol. 20 (1994), pp. 373–402; and "Japanese and Korean Management Systems," Ch. 13 in Min Chen, *Asian Management Systems* (New York: Routledge, 1995).

[58] An example is "Fall of a Keiretsu: How Giant Mitsubishi Group Lost Its Way," Special Report, *Business Week* (March 15, 1999), pp. 85–92.

[59] Wellford W. Wilms, Alan J. Hardcastle, and Deone M. Fall, "Cultural Transformation at NUMMI," *Sloan Management Review* (Fall 1994), pp. 99–113.

Source Notes

Information from "A Global Sightseeing Tour," *Business Week* (February 1, 1999), pp. ENT3.

Information from "Yahoo!," *Business Week* (September 7, 1998), pp. 66–76.

"Just a Wee Bit of Life in Silicon Glen," *World Business* (March/April 1996), p. 13.

Council on Economic Priorities Accreditation Agency Web site, www.cepaa.org.

Developed from Geert Hofstede, *Culture's Consequences* (Beverly Hills, CA: Sage Publications, 1980).

Developed from Fons Trompenaars, *Riding the Waves of Culture* (London: Nicholas Brealey Publishing, 1993).

Developed from Nancy J. Adler, *International Dimensions of Organizational Behavior*, 2nd ed. (Boston: Kent, 1991).

John R. Schermerhorn, Jr., *Management*, 6 ed. (New York: Wiley, 1999), p. 118. Used by permission.

■ CHAPTER 4

Footnotes

[1] J. Laabs, "Interest in Diversity Training Continues to Grow," *Personnel Journal* (October 1993), p. 18.

[2] L. R. Gomez-Mejia, D. B. Balkin, and R. L. Cardy, *Managing Human Resources* (Englewood Cliffs, NJ: Prentice-Hall, 1995), p. 154.

[3] John P. Fernandez, *Managing a Diverse Workforce* (Lexington, MA: D. C. Heath, 1991); D. Jamieson and Julia O'Mara, *Managing Workplace 2000* (San Francisco: Jossey-Bass, 1991).

[4] T. G. Exner, "In and Out of Work," *American Demographics* (June 1992), p. 63, and A. N. Fullerton, "Another Look at the Labor Force," *Monthly Labor Review* (November 1993), p. 34; M. K. Foster and B. J. Orser, "A Marketing Perspective on Women in Management," *Canadian Journal of Administrative Sciences*, Vol. 11, No. 4 (1994), pp. 339–345; L. Gardenswartz and A. Rowe, "Diversity Q & A," *Mosaics* (March/April, 1998), p. 3.

[5] Linda A. Krefting and Frank J. Kryzstofiak, "Looking Like America: Potential Conflicts Between Workplace Diversity Initiatives and Equal Opportunity Compliance in the U.S.," Working paper (Lubbock, TX: Texas Tech University, 1998), p. 10.

[6] Krefting and Kryzstofiak, p. 10.

[7] The following discussion is based on L. Gardenswartz and A. Rowe, *Managing Diversity: A Complete Desk Reference and Planning Guide* (Homewood, IL: Business One Irwin, 1993), p. 405.

[8] Gardenswartz and Rowe, *Managing Diversity*, p. 405; Michelle N. Martinez, "Equality Effort Sharpens Bank's Edge," *HR Magazine* (January 1995), pp. 38–43.

[9] See E. Maccoby and C. N. Jacklin, *The Psychology of Sex Differences* (Stanford, CA: Stanford University press, 1974); G. N. Powell, *Women and Men in Management* (Beverly Hills, CA: Sage Publications, 1988); T. W. Mangione, "Turnover—Some Psychological and Demographic Correlates," in R. P. Quinn and T. W. Mangione (eds.), *The 1969–70 Survey of Working Conditions* (Ann Arbor: University of Michigan Survey Research Center, 1973); R. Marsh and H. Mannari, "Organizational Commitment and Turnover: A Predictive Study," *Administrative Science Quarterly* (March 1977), pp. 57–75; R. J. Flanagan, G. Strauss, and L. Ulman, "Worker Discontent and Work Place Behavior," *Industrial Relations* (May 1974), pp. 101–23; K. R. Garrison and P. M. Muchinsky, "Attitudinal and Biographical Predictions of Incidental Absenteeism," *Journal of Vocational Behavior* (April 1977), pp. 221–230; G. Johns, "Attitudinal and Nonattitudinal Predictions of Two Forms of Absence from Work," *Organizational Behavior and Human Performance* (December 1978), pp. 431–44; R. T. Keller,

"Predicting Absenteeism from Prior Absenteeism, Attitudinal Factors, and Nonattitudinal Factors," *Journal of Applied Psychology* (August 1983), pp. 536–540.

[10] Gomez-Mejia, Balkin, and Cardy, p. 171.

[11] "The Growing Influence of Women," *Workplace Visions* (Sept./Oct. 1998), p. 2.

[12] American Association of Retired Persons, *The Aging Work Force* (Washington, DC: AARP, 1995), p. 3.

[13] Nina Monk, "Finished at Forty," *Fortune* (February 1, 1999), pp. 50–58.

[14] *Mosaics*, Vol. 3, No. 2 (March/April 1997), p. 3.

[15] Paul Mayrand, "Older Workers: A Problem or the Solution?" *AARP Textbook Authors' Conference Presentation* (October 1992), p. 29; G. M. McEvoy and W. F. Cascio, "Cumulative Evidence of the Relationship Between Employee Age and Job Performance," *Journal of Applied Psychology* (February 1989), pp. 11–17.

[16] See Fernandez, p. 236; *Mosaics*, Vol. 4, No. 2 (March–April, 1998), p. 4.

[17] Fernandez; *Mosaics* (March–April, 1998).

[18] See Taylor H. Co and Stacy Blake, "Managing Cultural Diversity: Implications for Organizational Competitiveness," *Academy of Management Executive*, Vol. 5, No. 3 (1991), p. 45.

[19] Literature covering this topic is reviewed in Stephen P. Robbins, *Organizational Behavior*, 8th ed. (Englewood Cliffs, NJ: Prentice-Hall, 1998), Ch. 2.

[20] Robbins, Ch. 2.

[21] Krefting and Krzystofiak, p. 14.

[22] Larry L. Cummings and Donald P. Schwab, *Performance in Organizations: Determinants and Appraisal* (Glenview, IL: Scott, Foresman, 1973), p. 8.

[23] See J. Hogan, "Structure of Physical Performance in Occupational Tasks," *Journal of Applied Psychology*, Vol. 76 (1991), pp. 495–507.

[24] R. Jacob, "The Resurrection of Michael Dell," *Fortune* (August 1995), pp. 117–128.

[25] See N. Brody, *Personality: In Search of Individuality* (San Diego, CA: Academic Press, 1988), pp. 68–101; C. Holden, "The Genetics of Personality," *Science* (August 7, 1987), pp. 598–601.

[26] See Geert Hofstede, *Culture's Consequences: International Differences in Work-Related Values*, abridged ed. (Beverly Hills: Sage Publications, 1984).

[27] Chris Argyris, *Personality and Organization* (New York: Harper & Row, 1957); Daniel J. Levinson, *The Seasons of a Man's Life* (New York: Alfred A. Knopf, 1978); Gail Sheehy, *New Passages* (New York: Ballantine Books, 1995).

[28] M. R. Barrick and M. K. Mount, "The Big Five Personality Dimensions and Job Performance: A Meta Analysis," *Personnel Psychology*, Vol. 44 (1991), pp. 1–26, and "Autonomy as a Moderator of the Relationships Between the Big Five Personality Dimensions and Job Performance," *Journal of Applied Psychology* (February 1993), pp. 111–118.

[29] See Jim C. Nunnally, *Psychometric Theory*, 2nd ed. (New York: McGraw Hill, 1978), Ch. 14.

[30] See David A. Whetten and Kim S. Cameron, *Developing Management Skills*, 3rd ed. (New York: Harper Collins, 1995), p. 72.

[31] Raymond G. Hunt, Frank J. Krzystofiak, James R. Meindl, and Abdalla M. Yousry, "Cognitive Style and Decision Making," *Organizational Behavior and Human Decision Processes*, Vol. 44, No. 3 (1989), pp. 436–453. For additional work on problem-solving styles, see Ferdinand A. Gul, "The Joint and Moderating Role of Personality and Cognitive Style on Decison Making," *Accounting Review* (April 1984), pp. 264–277; Brian H. Kleiner, "The Interrelationship of Jungian Modes of Mental Functioning with Organizational Factors: Implications for Management Development," *Human Relations* (November 1983), pp. 997–1012; James L. McKenney and Peter G. W. Keen, "How Managers' Minds Work," *Harvard Business Review* (May/June 1974), pp. 79–90.

[32] Some examples of firms using the Myers-Briggs Indicators are J. M.

Kunimerow and L. W. McAllister, "Team Building with the Myers-Briggs Type Indicator: Case Studies," *Journal of Psychological Type,* Vol. 15 (1988), pp. 26–32; G. H. Rice, Jr. and D. P. Lindecamp, "Personality Types and Business Success of Small Retailers," *Journal of Occupational Psychology,* Vol. 62 (1989), pp. 177–182; and B. Roach, *Strategy Styles and Management Types: A Resource Book for Organizational Management Consultants* (Stanford, CA: Balestrand Press, 1989).

[33] J. B. Rotter, "Generalized Expectancies for Internal versus External Control of Reinforcement," *Psychological Monographs,* Vol. 80 (1966), pp. 1–28.

[34] Don Hellriegel, John W. Slocum, Jr., and Richard W. Woodman, *Organizational Behavior,* 5th ed. (St. Paul, MN: West, 1989), p. 46.

[35] See John A. Wagner III and John R. Hollenbeck, *Management of Organizational Behavior* (Englewood Cliffs, NJ: Prentice-Hall, 1992), Ch. 4.

[36] Niccolo Machiavelli, *The Prince,* trans. George Bull (Middlesex, UK: Penguin, 1961).

[37] Richard Christie and Florence L. Geis, *Studies in Machiavellianism* (New York: Academic Press, 1970).

[38] See M. Synder, *Public Appearances/Private Realities: The Psychology of Self-Monitoring* (New York: W. H. Freeman, 1987).

[39] Snyder.

[40] Adapted from R. W. Bortner, "A Short Scale: A Potential Measure of Pattern A Behavior," *Journal of Chronic Diseases* Vol. 22 (1969). Used by permission.

[41] See Meyer Friedman and Ray Roseman, *Type A Behavior and Your Heart* (New York: Alfred A. Knopf, 1974). For another view, see Walter Kiechel III, "Attack of the Obsessive Managers," *Fortune* (February 16, 1987), pp. 127–128.

[42] Viktor Gecas, "The Self-Concept," in Ralph H. Turner and James F. Short, Jr. (eds.), Vol. 8, *Annual Review of Sociology* (Palo Alto, CA: Annual Review, 1982), p. 3. Also see Arthur P. Brief and Ramon J. Aldag, "The 'Self' in Work Organizations: A Conceptual Review," *Academy of Management Review* (January 1981), pp. 75–88; and Jerry J. Sullivan, "Self Theories and Employee Motivation," *Journal of Management* (June 1989), pp. 345–363.

[43] Compare Philip Cushman, "Why the Self Is Empty," *American Psychologist* (May 1990), pp. 599–611.

[44] Based in part on a definition in Gecas, p. 3.

[45] Suggested by J. Brockner, *Self-Esteem at Work* (Lexington, MA: Lexington Books, 1988) p. 144; and Wagner and Hollenbeck, pp. 100–101.

[46] See P. E. Jacob, J. J. Flink, and H. L. Schuchman, "Values and Their Function in Decisionmaking," *American Behavioral Scientist,* Vol. 5, Suppl. 9 (1962), pp. 6–38.

[47] See M. Rokeach and S. J. Ball Rokeach, "Stability and Change in American Value Priorities, 1968–1981," *American Psychologist* (May 1989), pp. 775–784.

[48] Milton Rokeach, *The Nature of Human Values* (New York: Free Press, 1973).

[49] See W. C. Frederick and J. Weber, "The Values of Corporate Managers and Their Critics: An Empirical Description and Normative Implications," in W. C. Frederick and L. E. Preston (eds.), *Business Ethics: Research Issues and Empirical Studies* (Greenwich, CT: JAI Press, 1990), pp. 123–144.

[50] Gordon Allport, Philip E. Vernon, and Gardner Lindzey, *Study of Values* (Boston: Houghton Mifflin, 1931).

[51] Adapted from R. Tagiuri, "Purchasing Executive: General Manager or Specialist?" *Journal of Purchasing* (August 1967), pp. 16–21.

[52] Bruce M. Maglino, Elizabeth C. Ravlin, and Cheryl L. Adkins, "Value Congruence and Satisfaction with a Leader: An Examination of the Role of Interaction," unpublished manuscript (Columbia, SC: University of South Carolina, 1990), pp. 8–9.

[53] Maglino, Ravlin, and Adkins.

[54] Daniel Yankelovich, *New Rules! Searching for Self-Fulfillment in a World Turned Upside Down* (New York: Random House, 1981); Daniel Yankelovich, Hans Zetterberg, Burkhard Strumpel, and Michael Shanks, *Work and Human Values: An International Report on Jobs in the 1980s and 1990s* (Aspen, CO: Aspen Institute for Humanistic Studies, 1983).

[55] See Jamieson and O'Mara, pp. 28–29.

[56] Compare Martin Fishbein and Icek Ajzen, *Belief, Attitude, Intention and Behavior: An Introduction to Theory and Research* (Reading, MA: Addison-Wesley, 1975).

[57] See A W. Wicker, "Attitude versus Action: The Relationship of Verbal and Overt Behavioral Responses to Attitude Objects," *Journal of Social Issues* (Autumn 1969), pp. 41–78.

[58] Leon Festinger, *A Theory of Cognitive Dissonance* (Palo Alto, CA: Stanford University Press, 1957).

[59] H. W. Lane and J. J. DiStefano (eds.), *International Management Behavior* (Scarborough, Ontario: Nelson Canada, 1988), pp. 4–5; Z. Abdoolcarim, "How Women Are Winning at Work," *Asian Business* (November 1993), pp. 24–29.

[60] Michelle Neely Martinez, "Health Care Firm Seeks to Measure Diversity," *HR News* (October 1997), p. 6.

[61] Martinez, p. 6.

[62] Jonathan Stutz and Randy Massengale, "Measuring Diversity Iniatives," *HR Magazine* (December 1997), pp. 84, 90.

Source Notes

Information from Timothy D. Schellhardt, "In a Factory Schedule, Where Does Religion Fit In?" *Wall Street Journal* (March 4, 1999), pp. B1, B12.

Information from Christine W. Letts, William P. Ryan, and Allen Grossman, *High Performance Nonprofit Organizations* (New York: Wiley, 1999), pp. 69–70.

Information from "Allstate Creating a World-Class Diversity Program," *BNAC Communicator,* Vol. 15 (Fall 1997), pp. 1 and 6.

Information from Sharon Johnson, "Hospitals Prepare for the International Marketplace," *New York Times Advertising Supplement* (November 12, 1995), p. WF7.

Information from Gary N. Powell, "One More Time: Do Female and Male Managers Differ?" *Academy of Management Executive,* Vol. 4, No. 3 (1990), p. 74.

Information from John P. Fernandez, *Managing a Diverse Workforce* (Lexington, MA: D. C. Heath, 1991); D. Jamieson and Julia O'Mara, *Managing Workplace 2000* (San Francisco: Jossey-Bass, 1991).

Information from Janie Shockley and Coy Gayle, "Diversity on the Border," *MOSAICS; SHRM Focuses on Workplace Diversity* (July/August, 1997), p. 5.

Information from Sharon Johnson, "Hospitals Prepare for the International Marketplace," *New York Times Advertising Supplement* (November, 12, 1995), p. WF16-WF17.]

Information from Bernice Kanner, "Successful Entrepreneurs Share Important Personality Attributes," *Lubbock-Avalanche-Journal* (November 22, 1998), p. 13A.

Information from J. M. Kunimerow and L. W. McAllister, "Team Building with the Myers-Briggs Type Indicator: Case Studies," *Journal of Psychological Type,* Vol. 15 (1988), pp. 26–32.

Information from Sang M. Lee, Snagjim Yoo, and Tosca M. Lee, "Korean Chaebol: Corporate Values and Strategies," *Organizational Dynamics* (Spring 1991), p. 40.

Information from John Cloud, "Why Coors Went Soft," *Time* (November 2, 1998), p. 70.

See Michelle Neely Martinez, "Health Care Firm Seeks to Measure Diversity," *HR News* (October 1997), p. 6.

Chris Argyris, *Personality and Organization* (New York: Harper & Row, 1957).

Information from R. P. McIntyre and M. M. Capen, "A Cognitive Style Perspective on Ethical Questions," *Journal of Business Ethics* 12 (1993): 631; and D. Hellriegel, J. Slocum, and Richard Woodman, *Organizational Behavior,* 7th ed. (Minneapolis: West Publishing, 1995), Ch. 4.

Information from M. Rokeach, *The Nature of Human Values* (New York: The Free Press, 1973).

■ CHAPTER 5

Footnotes

[1]"Clark's Catch Engraved in NFL Lore," *Lubbock Avalanche-Journal* (January 11, 1992), p. D5.

[2] H. R. Schiffmann, *Sensation and Perception: An Integrated Approach*, 3rd ed. (New York: Wiley, 1990).

[3] Example from John A. Wagner III and John R. Hollenbeck, *Organizational Behavior* 3rd ed. (Upper Saddle River, NJ: Prentice-Hall, 1998), p. 59.

[4] See M. W. Levine and J. M. Shefner, *Fundamentals of Sensation and Perception*; Georgia T. Chao and Steve W. J. Kozlowski, "Employee Perceptions on the Implementation of Robotic Manufacturing Technology," *Journal of Applied Psychology*, Vol. 71 (1986), pp. 70–76; Steven F. Cronshaw and Robert G. Lord, "Effects of Categorization, Attribution, and Encoding Processes in Leadership Perceptions," *Journal of Applied Psychology*, Vol. 72 (1987), pp. 97–106.

[5] See Robert Lord, "An Information Processing Approach to Social Perception's, Leadership, and Behavioral Measurement in Organizations," in B. M. Staw and L. L. Cummings (eds.), *Research in Organizational Behavior*, Vol. 7 (Greenwich, CT: JAI Press, 1985), pp. 87–128; T. K. Srull and R. S. Wyer, *Advances in Social Cognition* (Hillsdale, NJ: Erlbaum, 1988); U. Neisser, *Cognition and Reality* (San Francisco: W. H. Freeman, 1976), p. 112.

[6] See J. G. Hunt, *Leadership: A New Synthesis* (Newbury Park, CA: Sage Publications, 1991), Ch. 7; R. G. Lord and R. J. Foti, "Schema Theories, Information Processing, and Organizational Behavior," in H. P. Sims, Jr., and D. A. Gioia (eds.), *The Thinking Organization* (San Francisco: Jossey-Bass, 1986), pp. 20–48; S. T. Fiske and S. E. Taylor, *Social Cognition* (Reading, MA: Addison-Wesley, 1984).

[7]See J. S. Phillips, "The Accuracy of Leadership Ratings: A Categorization Perspective," *Organizational Behavior and Human Performance*, Vol. 33 (1984), pp. 125–138; J. G. Hunt, B. R. Baliga, and M. F. Peterson, "Strategic Apex Leader Scripts and an Organizational Life Cycle Approach to Leadership and Excellence," *Journal of Management Development*, Vol. 7 (1988), pp. 61–83.

[8]D. Bilimoria and S. K. Piderit, "Board Committee Membership Effects of Sex-Biased Bias," *Academy of Management Journal*, Vol. 37 (1994), pp. 1453–1477.

[9] Dewitt C. Dearborn and Herbert A. Simon, "Selective Perception: A Note on the Departmental Indentification of Executives," *Sociometry*, Vol. 21 (1958), pp. 140–144.

[10] J. P. Walsh, "Selectivity and Selective Perception: An Investigation of Managers' Belief Structures and Information Processing," *Academy of Management Journal*, Vol. 24 (1988), pp. 453–470.

[11] J. Sterling Livingston, "Pygmalion in Management," *Harvard Business Review* (July/August 1969).

[12] D. Eden and A. B. Shani, "Pygmalian Goes to Boot Camp," *Journal of Applied Psychology*, Vol. 67 (1982), pp. 194–199.

[13] See B. R. Schlenker, *Impression Management: The Self-Concept, Social Identity, and Interpersonal Relations* (Monterey, CA: Brooks/Cole, 1980); W. L. Gardner and M. J. Martinko, "Impression Management in Organizations," *Journal of Management* (June 1988), p. 332; R. B. Cioldini, "Indirect Tactics of Image Management: Beyond Banking," in R. A. Giacolini and P. Rosenfeld (eds.), *Impression Management in the Organization* (Hillsdale, NJ: Erlbaum, 1989), pp. 45–71.

[14] See H. H. Kelley, "Attribution in Social Interaction," in E. Jones, et al. (eds.), *Attribution: Perceiving the Causes of Behavior* (Morristown, NJ: General Learning Press, 1972).

[15] See Terence R. Mitchell, S. G. Green, and R. E. Wood, "An Attribution Model of Leadership and the Poor Performing Subordinate," in Barry Staw and Larry L. Cummings (eds.), *Research in Organizational Behavior* (New York: JAI Press, 1981), pp. 197–234; John H. Harvey and Gifford Weary, "Current Issues in Attribution Theory and Research," *Annual Review of Psychology*, Vol. 35 (1984), pp. 427–459.

[16] Data reported in John R. Schermerhorn, Jr., "Team Development for High Performance Management," *Training & Development Journal*, Vol. 40 (Nov. 1986), pp. 38–41.

[17] R. M. Steers, S. J. Bischoff, and L. H. Higgins, "Cross Cultural Management Research," *Journal of Management Inquiry* (Dec. 1992), pp. 325–326; J. G. Miller, "Culture and the Development of Everyday Causal Explanation," *Journal of Personality and Social Psychology*, Vol. 46 (1984), pp. 961–978.

[18] A. Maass and C. Volpato, "Gender Differences in Self-Serving Attributions About Sexual Experiences," *Journal of Applied Psychology*, Vol. 19 (1989), pp. 517–542.

[19] See J. M. Crant and T. S. Bateman, "Assignment of Credit and Blame for Performance Outcomes," *Academy of Management Journal* (February 1993), pp. 7–27; E. C. Pence, W. E. Pendelton, G. H. Dobbins, and J. A. Sgro, "Effects of Causal Explanations and Sex Variables on Recommendations for Corrective Actions Following Employee Failure," *Organizational Behavior and Human Performance* (April 1982), pp. 227–240.

[20] See F. Forsterling, "Attributional Retraining: A Review," *Psychological Bulletin* (Nov. 1985), pp. 496–512.

Source Notes

Information from "Vormawha Holds Unique Position as Africa's First Female Sea Captain", *Lubbock Avalanche-Journal* (January 3, 1996), p. 4B.

Data reported in Edward E. Lawler III, Allan M. Mohrman, Jr., and Susan M. Resnick, "Performance Appraisal Revisited," *Organizational Dynamics*, Vol. 13 (Summer 1984), pp. 20–35.

Information from Elizabeth Langton, "Simulated Mayhem Training," *Lubbock Avalanche-Journal* (December 8, 1998), p. 8A.

Information from Kevin Rubens, "Changes in Russia Challenge HR," *HR Magazine* (November 1995), p. 72.

Information from "Marketing Excellence Ontario Award Recipient, 1995 Entrepreneur of the Year," *Canadian Business* (November 1995), pp. 11–12, and information concerning the M.A.C. AIDS Fund (May 1999).

J. Sterling Livingston, "Pygmalion in Management," *Harvard Business Review* (July/August 1969); D. Eden and A. B. Shani, "Pygmalion Goes to Boot Camp," *Journal of Applied Psychology*, Vol. 67 (1982), pp. 194–199.

Information from Christine W. Letts, William P. Ryan, and Allen Grossman, *High Performance Non-profit Organizations* (New York: Wiley, 1999), pp. 93–96.

Information from *Lubbock Avalanche-Journal* (November 19, 1988), p. 1E.

Information from *Lubbock Avalanche-Journal* (March 2, 1997), pp. 1–2H.

Information from "Corporate Identity", *Lubbock Avalanche-Journal* (July 12, 1998), pp. 1–2E.

Data reported in John R. Schermerhorn, Jr; "Team Development for High Performance Management," *Training and Development Journal*, Vol. 40 (Nov. 1986), pp. 38–41.

Information from B. R. Schlinker, *Impression Management: The Self-Concept, Social Identity, and Interpersonal Relations* (Monterey, CA: Brooks/Cole, 1980).

■ CHAPTER 6

Footnotes

[1] Information from Greg Southam, "Unusual Approach Builds a Winner; Company Owner Rejects Traditional Management Teachings," *The Edmonton Journal* (November 30, 1994), p. D6.

[2] See John P. Campbell, Marvin D. Dunnette, Edward E. Lawler III, and Karl E. Weick, Jr., *Managerial Behavior Performance and Effectiveness* (New York: McGraw-Hill, 1970), Ch. 15.

[3] For a review article that identifies a still-relevant need for more integration among motivation theories, see Terrence R. Mitchell, "Motivation—New Directions for Theory, Research and Practice," *Academy of Management Review* 7 (January 1982): 80–88.

[4] Geert Hofstede, "Cultural Constraints in Management Theories," *Academy of Management Executive* 7 (February 1993): 81–94.

5 Geert Hofstede, *Culture's Consequences: International Differences in Work-Related Values*, abridged ed. (Beverly Hills, CA: Sage Publications, 1984).

6 For good overviews of reinforcement-based views, see W. E. Scott, Jr., and P. M. Podsakoff, *Behavioral Principles in the Practice of Management* (New York: Wiley, 1985); Fred Luthans and Robert Kreitner, *Organizational Behavior Modification and Beyond* (Glenview, IL: Scott, Foresman, 1985).

7 Some of B. F. Skinner's work; see his *Walden Two* (New York: Macmillan, 1948), *Science and Human Behavior* (New York: Macmillan, 1953), and *Contingencies of Reinforcement* (New York: Appleton-Century-Crofts, 1969).

8 E. L. Thorndike, *Animal Intelligence* (New York: Macmillan, 1911), p. 244.

9 Adapted from Luthans and Kreitner, op. cit. (1985).

10 This discussion is based on ibid.

11 Both laws are stated in Keith L. Miller, *Principles of Everyday Behavior Analysis* (Monterey, CA: Brooks/Cole, 1975), p. 122.

12 While some have used reinforcement as a springboard to discuss individual learning, we prefer to emphasize the cognitive or thinking aspects of learning.

13 This example is based on a study by Barbara Price and Richard Osborn, "Shaping the Training of Skilled Workers," working paper (Detroit: Department of Management, Wayne State University, 1999).

14 See John Putzier and Frank T. Novak, "Attendance Management and Control," *Personnel Administrator* (August 1989): 59–60.

15 Robert Kreitner and Angelo Kiniki, *Organization Behavior*, 2nd ed. (Homewood, IL: Irwin, 1992).

16 These have been used for years; see K. M. Evans, "On-the Job Lotteries: A Low-Cost Incentive That Sparks Higher Productivity," *Compensation and Benefits Review* 20, No. 4 (1988): 63–74; A. Halcrow, "Incentive! How Three Companies Cut Costs," *Personnel Journal* (February 1986), p. 12.

17 A. R. Korukonda and James G. Hunt, "Pat on the Back Versus Kick in the Pants: An Application of Cognitive Inference to the Study of Leader Reward and Punishment Behavior," *Group and Organization Studies* 14 (1989): 299–234.

18 See "Janitorial Firm Success Story Started with Cleaning Couple," *Lubbock Avalanche-Journal* (August 25, 1991), p. E7.

19 Edwin A. Locke, "The Myths of Behavior Mod in Organizations," *Academy of Management Review* 2 (October 1977): 543–553. For a counterpoint, see Jerry L. Gray, "The Myths of the Myths about Behavior Mod in Organizations: A Reply to Locke's Criticisms of Behavior Modification," *Academy of Management Review* 4 (January 1979): 121–129.

20 Robert Kreitner, "Controversy in OBM: History, Misconceptions, and Ethics," in Lee Frederiksen, ed., *Handbook of Organizational Behavior Management* (New York: Wiley, 1982), pp. 71–91.

21 W. E. Scott, Jr., and P. M. Podsakoff, *Behavioral Principles in the Practice of Management* (New York: Wiley, 1985); also see W. Clay Hamner, "Reinforcement Theory and Contingency Management in Organizational Settings," in Richard M. Steers and Lyman W Porters (eds.), *Motivation and Work Behavior*, 4th ed. (New York: McGraw-Hill, 1987), pp. 139–165; Luthans and Kreitner, op. cit. (1985); Charles C. Manz and Henry P. Sims, Jr., *Superleadership* (New York: Berkley, 1990).

22 Abraham Maslow, *Eupsychian Management* (Homewood, IL: Irwin, 1965), and *Motivation and Personality*, 2nd ed. (New York: Harper & Row, 1970).

23 Lyman W. Porter, "Job Attitudes in Management: II. Perceived Importance of Needs as a Function of Job Level," *Journal of Applied Psychology* 47 (April 1963): 141–148.

24 Douglas T. Hall and Khalil E. Nougaim, "An Examination of Maslow's Need Hierarchy in an Organizational Setting," *Organizational Behavior and Human Performance* 3 (1968): 12–35; Porter, op. cit. (1963); John M. Ivancevich, "Perceived Need Satisfactions of Domestic Versus Overseas Managers," 54 (August 1969): 274–278.

25 Mahmoud A. Wahba and Lawrence G. Bridwell, "Maslow Reconsidered: A Review of Research on the Need Hierarchy Theory," *Academy of Management Proceedings* (1974): 514–520; Edward E. Lawler III and J. Lloyd Shuttle, "A Causal Correlation Test of the Need Hierarchy Concept," *Organizational Behavior and Human Performance* 7 (1973): 265–287.

26 Nancy J. Adler, *International Dimensions of Organizational Behavior*, 2nd ed. (Boston: PWS-Kent, 1991), p. 153.

27 Ibid.; Richard M. Hodgetts and Fred Luthans, *International Management* (New York: McGraw-Hill, 1991), Ch. 11.

28 Clayton P. Alderfer, "An Empirical Test of a New Theory of Human Needs," *Organizational Behavior and Human Performance* 4 (1969): 142–175; Clayton P. Alderfer, *Existence, Relatedness, and Growth* (New York: Free Press, 1972); Benjamin Schneider and Clayton P. Alderfer, "Three Studies of Need Satisfaction in Organization," *Administrative Science Quarterly* 18 (1973): 489–505.

29 Lane Tracy, "A Dynamic Living Systems Model of Work Motivation," *Systems Research* 1 (1984): 191–203; John Rauschenberger, Neal Schmidt, and John E. Hunter, "A Test of the Need Hierarchy Concept by a Markov Model of Change in Need Strength," *Administrative Science Quarterly* 25 (1980): 654–670.

30 Sources pertinent to this discussion are David C. McClelland, *The Achieving Society* (New York: Van Nostrand, 1961); David C. McClelland, "Business, Drive and National Achievement," *Harvard Business Review* 40 (July/August 1962): 99–112; David C. McClelland, "That Urge to Achieve," *Think* (November/December 1966): 19–32; G. H. Litwin and R. A. Stringer, *Motivation and Organizational Climate* (Boston: Division of Research, Harvard Business School, 1966), pp. 18–25.

31 George Harris, "To Know Why Men Do What They Do: A Conversation with David C. McClelland," *Psychology Today* 4 (January 1971): 35–39.

32 David C. McClelland and David H. Burnham, "Power Is the Great Motivator," *Harvard Business Review* 54 (March/April 1976): 100–110; David C. McClelland and Richard E. Boyatzis, "Leadership Motive Pattern and Long-Term Success in Management," *Journal of Applied Psychology* 67 (1982): 737–743.

33 P. Miron and D. C. McClelland, "The Impact of Achievement Motivation Training in Small Businesses," *California Management Review* (Summer 1979): 13–28.

34 The complete two-factor theory is well explained by Herzberg and his associates in Frederick Herzberg, Bernard Mausner, and Barbara Bloch Synderman, *The Motivation to Work*, 2nd ed. (New York: Wiley, 1967); and Frederick Herzberg, "One More Time: How Do You Motivate Employees?" *Harvard Business Review* 46 (January/February 1968): 53–62.

35 From Herzberg, op. cit. (1968), pp. 53–62.

36 See Robert J. House and Lawrence A. Wigdor, "Herzberg's Dual-Factor Theory of Job Satisfaction and Motivation: A Review of the Evidence and a Criticism," *Personnel Psychology* 20 (Winter 1967): 369–389; and Steven Kerr, Anne Harlan, and Ralph Stogdill, "Preference for Motivator and Hygiene Factors in a Hypothetical Interview Situation," *Personnel Psychology* 27 (Winter 1974): 109–124; Nathan King, "A Clarification and Evaluation of the Two-Factor Theory of Job Satisfaction," *Psychological Bulletin* (July 1970): 18–31; Marvin Dunnette, John Campbell, and Milton Hakel, "Factors Contributing to Job Satisfaction and Job Dissatisfaction in Six Occupational Groups," *Organizational Behavior and Human Performance* (May 1967): 143–174; R. J. House and L. Wigdor, "Herzberg's Dual Factor Theory of Job Satisfaction and Motivation: A Review of the Evidence and a Criticism," *Personnel Psychology* (Summer 1967): 369–389.

37 Adler, op. cit. (1991), Ch 6; Nancy J. Adler and J. T. Graham, "Cross Cultural Interaction: The International Comparison Fallacy," *Journal of International Business Studies* (Fall 1989): 515–537; Frederick Herzberg, "Workers Needs: The Same around the World," *Industry Week* (September 27, 1987), pp. 29–32.

38 See, for example, J. Stacy Adams, "Toward an Understanding of Inequality," *Journal of Abnormal and Social Psychology* 67 (1963): 422–436; and J. Stacy Adams, "Inequity in Social Exchange," in L. Berkowitz (ed.), *Advances in Experimental Social Psychology*, Vol. 2 (New York: Academic Press, 1965), pp. 267–300.

[39] Adams, op. cit. (1965).

[40] These issues are discussed in C. Kagitcibasi and J. W. Berry, "Cross-Cultural Psychology: Current Research and Trends," *Annual Review of Psychology* 40 (1989): 493–531.

[41] Victor H. Vroom, *Work and Motivation* (New York: Wiley, 1964).

[42] See Richard T. Mowday, "Equity Theory Predictions of Behavior in Organizations," in Richard M. Steers and Lyman W. Porter (eds.), *Motivation and Work Behavior*, 4th ed. (New York: McGraw-Hill, 1987), pp. 89–110.

[43] See Steers and Porter, op. cit. (1987); Gerald R. Salancik and Jeffrey Pfeffer, "A Social Information Processing Approach to Job Attitudes and Task Design," *Administrative Science Quarterly* 23 (June 1978): 224–253.

[44] See Terence R. Mitchell, "Expectancy Models of Job Satisfaction, Occupational Preference and Effort: A Theoretical, Methodological, and Empirical Appraisal," *Psychological Bulletin* 81 (1974): 1053–1077; Mahmoud A. Wahba and Robert J. House, "Expectancy Theory in Work and Motivation: Some Logical and Methodological Issues," *Human Relations* 27 (January 1974): 121–147; Terry Connolly, "Some Conceptual and Methodological Issues in Expectancy Models of Work Performance Motivation," *Academy of Management Review* 1 (October 1976): 37–47; Terrence Mitchell, "Expectancy-Value Models in Organizational Psychology," in N. Feather (ed.), *Expectancy, Incentive and Action* (New York: Erlbaum & Associates, 1980).

[45] See William E. Wymer and Jeanne M. Carsten, "Alternative Ways to Gather Opinions," *HR Magazine* 37, 4 (April 1992): 71–78.

[46] The Job Descriptive Index (JDI) is available from Dr. Patricia C. Smith, Department of Psychology, Bowling Green State University; the Minnesota Satisfaction Questionnaire (MSQ) is available from the Industrial Relations Center and Vocational Psychology Research Center, University of Minnesota.

[47] Barry M. Staw, "The Consequences of Turnover," *Journal of Occupational Behavior* 1 (1980): 253–273; John P. Wanous, *Organizational Entry* (Reading, MA: Addison-Wesley, 1980).

[48] Charles N. Greene, "The Satisfaction-Performance Controversy," *Business Horizons* 15 (1972): 31; Michelle T. Iaffaldano and Paul M. Muchinsky, "Job Satisfaction and Job Performance: A Meta-Analysis," *Psychological Bulletin* 97 (1985): 251–273; Greene, op. cit. (1972), pp. 31–41; Dennis Organ, "A Reappraisal and Reinterpretation of the Satisfaction-Causes-Performance Hypothesis," *Academy of Management Review* 2 (1977): 46–53; Peter Lorenzi, "A Comment on Organ's Reappraisal of the Satisfaction-Causes-Performance Hypothesis," *Academy of Management Review* 3 (1978): 380–382.

[49] Lyman W. Porter and Edward E. Lawler III, *Managerial Attitudes and Performance* (Homewood, IL: Irwin, 1968).

[50] This integrated model is consistent with the comprehensive approach suggested by Martin G. Evans, "Organizational Behavior: The Central Role of Motivation," in J. G. Hunt and J. D. Blair (eds.), *1986 Yearly Review of Management of the Journal of Management* 12 (1986): 203–222.

Source Notes

WorldCom 1997 Annual Report, pp. 36, 56.

www.omniroyal.com/.

www.Oglebaynorton.com; Jeremy Kahn, "A CEO Cuts His Own Pay," *Fortune* (October 26, 1998), pp. 56, 60, 64.

Starbucks.com/ and Starbucks.com/company mission.

www.patagonia.com; Patagonia Annual Report, 1998.

■ **CHAPTER 7**

Footnotes

[1] For a good discussion of human resource management strategy and its linkage to overall management strategy, see A. J. Templer and R. J. Cattaneo, "A Model of Human Resources Management Effectiveness," *Canadian Journal of Administrative Sciences,* Vol. 12, No. 1, (1995) pp. 77–88.

[2] See J. R. Schermerhorn, Jr., *Management*, 5th ed. (New York: Wiley, 1996), Ch. 12; G. M. Bounds, G. H. Dobbins, and O. S. Fowler, *Management: A Total Quality Perspective* (Cincinnati: South-Western, 1995), Ch. 9; L. R. Gomez-Mejia, D. B. Balkin, and R. L. Cardy, *Managing Human Resources* (Englewood Cliffs, NJ: Prentice-Hall, 1995), chs 2, 6.

[3] Bounds, Dobbins, and Fowler, pp. 313–318.

[4] Bounds, Dobbins, and Fowler, p. 315.

[5] Bounds, Dobbins, and Fowler, p. 317; Gomez-Mejia, Balkin, and Cardy, pp. 97–98.

[6] Summarized from Bounds, Dobbins, and Fowler, pp. 319–321; Gómez-Mejía, Balkin, and Cardy, Ch. 6; Schermerhorn, pp. 290–293.

[7] See "Blueprints for Service Quality: The Federal Express Approach," *AMA Management Briefing* (New York: AMA Publications, 1991).

[8] Based on A. Uris, *Eighty-eight Mistakes Interviewers Make and How to Avoid Them* (New York: AMA Publications, 1988).

[9] G. C. Thornton, *Assessment Centers in Human Resource Management* (Reading, MA: Addison-Wesley, 1992).

[10] B. B. Gaugler, D. B. Rosenthal, G. C. Thornton, and C. Bentson, "Meta-Analysis of Assessment Center Validity," *Journal of Applied Psychology,* Vol. 72 (1987), pp. 493–511; G. M. McEvoy and R. W. Beatty, "Assessment Centers and Subordinate Appraisals of Managers: A Seven-Year Study of Predictive Validity," *Personnel Psychology,* Vol. 42 (1989), pp. 37–52.

[11] P. M. Muchinsky, "The Use of Reference Reports in Personnel Selection: A Review and Evaluaton," *Journal of Occupational Psychology,* Vol. 52 (1979), pp. 287–297.

[12] This training discussion based on Bounds, Dobbins, and Fowler, pp. 326–329; Schermerhorn, pp. 294–295; S. R. Robbins, *Organizational Behavior,* 7th ed. (Englewood Cliffs, NJ: Prentice-Hall, 1996), pp. 641–644.

[13] See Rob Muller, "Training for Change," *Canadian Business Review* (Spring 1995), pp. 16–19.

[14] Much of the initial discussion in this section is based on Daniel C. Feldman, "Careers in Organizations: Recent Trends and Future Directions," *Journal of Management,* Vol. 15 (June 1989), pp. 135–156; Irving Janis and Dan Wheeler, "Thinking Clearly about Career Choices," *Psychology Today* (May 1978), p. 67; Walter Kiechel III, "How We Will Work in the Year 2000," *Fortune* (May 17, 1993), pp. 38–52.

[15] Charles Handy, *The Age of Unreason* (Boston: Harvard Business School Press, 1991).

[16] This discussion combines earlier and later career development literature based on Janis and Wheeler, p. 67; Daniel J. Levinson, *The Seasons of a Man's Life* (New York: Knopf, 1978); Douglas T. Hall, *Careers in Organizations* (Santa Monica, CA: Goodyear, 1975); Lloyd Baird and Kathy Krim, "Career Dynamics: Managing the Superior-Subordinate Relationship," *Organizational Dynamics* (Spring 1983), p. 47; Paul H. Thompson, Robin Zenger Baker, and Norman Smallwood, "Improving Professional Development by Applying the Four-Stage Career Model," *Organizational Dynamics* (Autumn 1986), pp. 49–62; Thomas P. Ference, James A. F. Stoner, and E. Kirby Warren, "Managing the Career Plateau," *Academy of Management Review,* Vol. 2 (October 1977), pp. 602–612; Gail Sheehy, *New Passages: Mapping Your Life across Time* (New York: Ballantine Books, 1995).

[17] "Strategic Issues in Performance Appraisal, Theory and Practice," *Personnel,* Vol. 60 (Nov./Dec. 1983), p. 24; Gómez-Mejía, Balkin, and Cardy, Ch. 8; "Performance Appraisal: Current Practices and Techniques," *Personnel* (May/June 1984), p. 57.

[18] See G. P. Latham and K. N. Wexley, *Increasing Productivity Through Performance Appraisal* (Reading, MA: Addison-Wesley, 1981), p. 80.

[19] See R. J. Newman, "Job Reviews Go Full Circle," *U.S. News and World Report* (November 1, 1993), pp. 42–43; J. A. Lopez. "A Better Way?" *Wall Street Journal* (April 13, 1994), p. R6; M. S. Hirsch, "360 Degrees of Evaluation," *Working Woman* (August 1994), pp. 20–21; B. O'Reilly, "360 Degree Feedback Can Change Your Life," *Fortune* (October 17, 1994), pp. 93–100; See *Leadership Quarterly,* Vol. 9, No. 4 (1998), Special issue on "360-Degree Feedback in Leadership Research," pp. 423–474; Stephen P. Robbins,

Organizational Behavior, 8th ed. (Upper Saddle River, NJ: Prentice-Hall, 1998), p. 568.

[20] Robert C. Hill and Sara M. Freedman, "Managing the Quality Process: Lessons from the Baldrige Award Winner," *Academy of Management Executive,* Vol. 6 (February 1992), p. 84.

[21] For more details, see Latham and Wexley, op. cit. (1981); Stephen J. Carroll and Craig E. Schneier, *Performance Appraisal and Review Systems* (Glenview, IL: Scott, Foresman, 1982).

[22] See George T. Milkovich and John W. Boudreau, *Personnel/Human Resource Management: A Diagnostic Approach,* 5th ed. (Plano, TX: Business Publications, 1988).

[23] For a detailed discussion, see S. J. Carroll and H. L. Tosi, Jr., *Management of Objectives: Application and Research* (New York: Macmillan, 1976); A. P. Raia, *Managing by Objectives* (Glenview, IL: Scott, Foresman, 1974).

[24] For discussion of many of these errors, see David L. Devries, Ann M. Morrison, Sandra L. Shullman, and Michael P. Gerlach, *Performance Appraisal on the Line* (Greensboro, NC: Center for Creative Leadership, 1986), Ch. 3.

[25] E. G. Olson, "The Workplace Is High on the High Court's Docket," *Business Week* (October 10, 1988), pp. 88–89.

[26] Based on J. J. Bernardin and C. S. Walter, "The Effects of Rater Training and Diary Keeping on Psychometric Error in Ratings," *Journal of Applied Psychology,* Vol. 61 (1977), pp. 64–69; see also R. G. Burnask and T. D. Hollman, "An Empirical Comparison of the Relative Effects of Sorter Response Bias on Three Rating Scale Formats," *Journal of Applied Psychology,* Vol. 59 (1974), pp. 307–312.

[27] W. F. Cascio and H. J. Bernardin, "Implications of Performance Appraisal Litigation for Personnel Decisions", *Personnel Psychology,* Vol. 34 (1981), pp. 221–222.

[28] See David Shar, "Comp Star Adds Efficiency and Flexibility to Performance Reviews", *HR Magazine* (October 1997), pp. 37–42.

[29] For complete reviews of theory, research, and practice, see Edward E. Lawler III, *Pay and Organizational Effectiveness* (New York: McGraw-Hill, 1971); Edward E. Lawler III, *Pay and Organization Development* (Reading MA: Addison-Wesley, 1981); Edward E. Lawler III, "The Design of Effective Reward Systems," in Jay W. Lorsch (ed.), *Handbook of Organizational Behavior* (Englewood Cliffs, NJ: Prentice-Hall, 1987) pp. 255–271.

[30] As an example, see D. B. Balkin and L. R. Gómez-Mejía (eds.), *New Perspectives on Compensation* (Englewood Cliffs, NJ: Prentice-Hall, 1987).

[31] Jone L. Pearce, "Why Merit Pay Doesn't Work: Implications from Organization Theory," in David B. Balkin and Luis R. Gómez-Mejía, pp. 169–178; Jerry M. Newman, "Selecting Incentive Plans To Complement Organizational Strategy," in Balkin and Gómez-Mejía, pp. 214–224; Edward E. Lawler III, "Pay for Performance: Making It Work," *Compensation and Benefits Review,* Vol. 21 (1989), pp. 55–60.

[32] See Daniel C. Boyle, "Employee Motivation that Works," *HR Magazine* (October 1992), pp. 83–89. Kathleen A. McNally, "Compensation as a Strategic Tool," *HR Magazine* (July 1992), pp. 59–66.

[33] S. Caudron, "Master the Compensation Maze," *Personnel Journal* (June 1993), pp. 640–648.

[34] N. Gupta, G. E. Ledford, G. D. Jenkins, and D. H. Doty, "Survey Based Prescriptions for Skill-Based Pay," *American Compensation Association Journal,* Vol. 1, No. 1 (1992), pp. 48–59; L. W. Ledford, "The Effectiveness of Skill-Based Pay," *Perspectives in Total Compensation,* Vol. 1, No. 1 (1991), pp. 1–4.

[35] See Brian Graham-Moore, "Review of the Literature," in Brian Graham-Moore and Timothy L. Ross (eds.), *Gainsharing* (Washington, DC: The Bureau of National Affairs, 1990), p. 20.

[36] S. E. Markham, K. D. Scott, and B. L. Little, "National Gainsharing Study: The Importance of Industry Differences," *Compensation and Benefits Review* (Jan./Feb. 1992), pp. 34–45.

[37] Gomez-Mejia, Balkin, and Cardy, pp. 410–411.

[38] Gomez-Mejia, Balkin, and Cardy, pp. 409–410.

[39] C. O'Dell and J. McAdams, "The Revolution in Employee Benefits," *Compensation and Benefits Review* (May/June 1987), pp. 68–73.

Source Notes

Information from Eileen P. Gunn, *Fortune* (October 12, 1998), p. 98.

Information from "Mattell Sets 'Code of Conduct' for its Manufacturers," *Lubbock Avalanche-Journal* (November 24, 1997), p. 10C.

Information from A. Uris, *Eighty-eight Mistakes Interviewers Make and How to Avoid Them* (New York: AMA Publications, 1988).

"Lubbock Company Gives Voice to Customers," *Lubbock Avalanche-Journal* (February 1, 1998), p. 1E.

Information from *Lubbock Avalanche-Journal* (December 31, 1998), p. 8C.

Information from "The Revenge of the Fired," *Newsweek* (February 16, 1987), pp. 46–47.

Information from "Rank-and-File Get CEO-Style Perks," *Lubbock Avalanche-Journal* (September 29, 1998), p. 3A.

Bill Holleran, "Training Resources Are Available on Internet via ALX," *HR News* (October 1998), p. 13.

Information from David Shair, "Comp Star Adds Efficiency and Flexibility to Performance Reviews," *HR Magazine* (October 1997), pp. 37–42.

Information from Ivan Maisel and Steve Richardson, "The Price of Glory," *Dallas Morning News* (June 6, 1993), p. 16B.

Information from J. Zignon, "Making Performance Appraisal Work for Teams," *Training* (June 1994), pp. 58–63.

Adapted from Andrew D. Szilagi, Jr., and Marc J. Wallace, Jr., *Organizational Behavior and Performance,* 3rd ed. (Glenview, IL: Scott, Foresman, 1983), pp. 393–394.

Adapted from J. P. Cambell, M. D. Dunnette, R. D. Arvey, and L. V. Hellervik, "The Development evaluation of Behaviorally Based Rating Scales," *Journal of Applied Psychology,* Vol. 57 (1973), p. 18. Copyright 1973 by the American Psychological Association. Reprinted by permission of the publisher and author.

■ CHAPTER 8

Footnotes

[1] Information from Jessica Guynn, "Peet's Brews Successful Blend for Retaining Workers," *The Columbus Dispatch* (October 26, 1998), pp. 10–11.

[2] Frederick W. Taylor, *The Principles of Scientific Management* (New York: W.W. Norton, 1967).

[3] Information from "Building the S80: More Than a Sum of Its Parts," *Volvo S80* (1998).

[4] Frederick Herzberg, "One More Time: How Do You Motivate Employees?" *Harvard Business Review* 46 (January–February 1968), pp. 53–62.

[5] Paul J. Champagne and Curt Tausky, "When Job Enrichment Doesn't Pay," *Personnel,* Vol. 3 (January–February 1978), pp. 30–40.

[6] For a complete description, see J. Richard Hackman and Greg R. Oldham, *Work Redesign* (Reading, MA: Addison-Wesley, 1980).

[7] See J. Richard Hackman and Greg Oldham, "Development of the Job Diagnostic Survey," *Journal of Applied Psychology,* Vol. 60 (1975), pp. 159–170.

[8] Hackman and Oldham, op. cit. For forerunner research, see Charles L. Hulin and Milton R. Blood, "Job Enlargement Individual Differences, and Worker Responses," *Psychological Bulletin,* Vol. 69 (1968), pp. 41–55; Milton R. Blood and Charles L. Hulin, "Alienation, Environmental Characteristics and Worker Responses," *Journal of Applied Psychology,* Vol. 51 (1967), pp. 284–290.

[9] Gerald Salancik and Jeffrey Pfeffer, "An Examination of Need-Satisfaction Models of Job Attitudes," *Administrative Science Quarterly,* Vol. 22 (1977), pp. 427–456; Gerald Salancik and Jeffrey Pfeffer, "A Social Information Processing Approach to Job Attitude and Task Design," *Administrative Science Quarterly,* Vol. 23 (1978), pp. 224–253.

[10] George W. England and Itzhak Harpaz, "How Working Is Defined:

National Contexts and Demographic and Organizational Role Influences," *Journal of Organizational Behavior* (July 1990), pp. 253–266.

[11] William A. Pasmore, "Overcoming the Roadblocks to Work-Restructuring Efforts," *Organizational Dynamics*, Vol. 10 (1982), pp. 54–67; Hackman and Oldham, op. cit. (1975).

[12] See William A. Pasmore, *Designing Effective Organizations: A Sociotechnical Systems Perspective* (New York: Wiley, 1988).

[13] *The Economist* (October 17, 1998), p. 116.

[14] See Malcolm S. Salter and Wayne A. Edesis, "Wolfsburg at the Center," *Harvard Business Review* (July–August 1991).

[15] Peter Senker, *Towards the Automatic Factory: The Need for Training* (New York: Springer-Verlag, 1986).

[16] See Ramchandran Jaikumar, "Postindustrial Manufacturing," *Harvard Business Review*, Vol. 44 (1986), pp. 69–76.

[17] Michael Hammer, "Reengineering Work: Don't Automate, Obliterate," *Harvard Business Review* (July–August 1990), pp. 104–112.

[18] See Thomas M. Kouloupoulos, *The Workflow Imperative: Building Real World Business Solutions* (New York: Van Nostrand Reinhold, 1995).

[19] For a good overview, see Michael Hammer and James Champy, *Reengineering the Corporation* (New York: Harper Business, 1993); and Michael Hammer, *Beyond Reengineering* (New York: Harper Business, 1997).

[20] Information from "The Business Imperative for Workflow & Business Process Reengineering," *Fortune* (November 27, 1995), special advertising supplement.

[21] Edwin A. Locke, Karyll N. Shaw, Lise M. Saari, and Gary P. Latham, "Goal Setting and Task Performance: 1969–1980," *Psychological Bulletin*, Vol. 90 (July–November 1981), pp. 125–152; Edwin A. Locke and Gary P. Latham, "Work Motivation and Satisfaction: Light at the End of the Tunnel," *Psychological Science*, Vol. 1, No. 4 (July 1990), pp. 240–246; and Edwin A. Locke and Gary P. Latham, *A Theory of Goal Setting and Task Performance* (Englewood Cliffs, NJ: Prentice-Hall, 1990).

[22] Gary P. Latham and Edwin A. Locke, "Goal Setting—A Motivational Technique That Works," *Organizational Dynamics*, Vol. 8 (Autumn 1979), pp. 68–80; Gary P. Latham and Timothy P. Steele, "The Motivational Effects of Participation versus Goal-Setting on Performance," *Academy of Management Journal*, Vol. 26 (1983), pp. 406–417; Miriam Erez and Frederick H. Kanfer, "The Role of Goal Acceptance in Goal Setting and Task Performance," *Academy of Management Review*, Vol. 8 (1983), pp. 454–463; and R. E. Wood and E. A. Locke, "Goal Setting and Strategy Effects on Complex Tasks," in B. Staw and L. L. Cummings (eds.), *Research in Organizational Behavior* (Greenwich, CT: JAI Press, 1990).

[23] See E. A. Locke and G. P. Latham, "Work Motivation and Satisfaction," *Psychological Science*, Vol. 1, No. 4 (July 1990), p. 241.

[24] Ibid.

[25] Information from Joel B. Obermayer, "The Mad Hatters," *The News and Observer on the Web* (January 17, 1999), http://www.news-observer.com.

[26] For a good review of MBO, see Anthony P. Raia, *Managing by Objectives* (Glenview, IL: Scott, Foresman, 1974);

[27] Ibid.; also, Steven Kerr summarizes the criticisms well in "Overcoming the Dysfunctions of MBO," *Management by Objectives*, Vol. 5, No. 1 (1976).

[28] For overviews, see Allan R. Cohen and Herman Gadon, *Alternative Work Schedules: Integrating Individual and Organizational Needs* (Reading, MA: Addison-Wesley, 1978); and Jon L. Pearce, John W. Newstrom, Randall B. Dunham, and Alison E. Barber, *Alternative Work Schedules* (Boston: Allyn & Bacon, 1989). See also Sharon Parker and Toby Wall, *Job and Work Design* (Thousand Oaks, CA: Sage, 1998).

[29] B. J. Wixom, Jr., "Recognizing People in a World of Change," *HR Magazine* (June 1995), pp. 7–8; and "The Value of Flexibility," *Inc.* (April 1996), p. 114.

[30] C. Latack and L. W. Foster, "Implementation of Compressed Work Schedules: Participation and Job Redesign as Critical Factors for Employee Acceptance," *Personnel Psychology*, Vol. 38 (1985), pp. 75–92.

[31] *Business Week* (December 7, 1998), p. 8.

[32] "Aetna Life & Casualty Company," *Wall Street Journal* (June 4, 1990), p. R35; (June 18, 1990), p. B1.

[33] Getsy M. Selirio, "Job Sharing Gains Favor as Corporations Embrace Alternative Work Schedule," *Lubbock Avalanche-Journal* (December 13, 1992), p. 2E.

[34] Ibid.

[35] "Making Stay-at-Homes Feel Welcome," *Business Week* (October 12, 1998), pp. 153–155.

[36] T. Davenport and K. Pearlson, "Two Cheers for the Virtual Office," *Sloan Management Review* (Summer 1998), pp. 51–64.

[37] "Making Stay-at-Homes Feel Welcome," op. cit.

[38] Ibid.

[39] Carol Hymowitz, "Remote Managers Find Ways to Narrow the Distance Gap," *Wall Street Journal* (April 6, 1999), p. B1.

[40] Guynn, op. cit. (1998).

[41] Daniel C. Feldman and Helen I. Doerpinghaus, "Missing Persons No Longer: Managing Part-Time Workers in the '90s," *Organizational Dynamics* (Summer 1992), pp. 59–72.

Source Notes

"When Is a Temp Not a Temp?" *Business Week* (December 7, 1998), pp. 90–91.

Adapted from J. Richard Hackman and Greg R. Oldham, "Development of the Job Diagnostic Survey," *Journal of Applied Psychology*, Vol. 60 (1975), p. 161. Used by permission.

Based on Edwin A. Locke and Gary P. Latham: "Work Motivation and Satisfaction: Light at the End of the Tunnel," *Psychological Science*, Vol. 1, No. 4 (July 1990), p. 244.

Xerox (Canada): Information from Kerry Shapansky, "How Fact-Based Management Works for Xerox," *CMA Magazine*, Vol. 68 (December 1994/January 1995), pp. 20–22.

UPS: Information from Robert Frank, "Efficient UPS Tries to Increase Efficiency," *The Wall Street Journal* (May 24, 1995), pp. B1, B4.

Excite, Inc.: Information from Quentin Hardy, "Aloft in a Career Without Fetters," *The Wall Street Journal* (September 29, 1998), p. B1.

Gap, Inc.: Information from David Kirkpatrick, "The E-Ware War," *Fortune* (December 7, 1998), pp. 102–110.

■ CHAPTER 9

Footnotes

[1] Information from David Kirkpatrick, "The Second Coming of Apple," *Fortune* (November 9, 1998), pp. 86–92. See also Brent Schlender, "The Three Faces of Steve," *Fortune* (November 9, 1998), pp. 96–104.

[2] For a good discussion of groups and teams in the workplace, see Jon R. Katzenbach and Douglas K. Smith, "The Discipline of Teams," *Harvard Business Review* (March–April, 1993), pp. 111–120.

[3] Harold J. Leavitt and Jean Lipman-Blumen, "Hot Groups," *Harvard Business Review* (July–August 1995), pp. 109–116.

[4] See, for example, Edward E. Lawler, III, *High-Involvement Management* (San Francisco: Jossey-Bass, 1986).

[5] Information from "Empowerment That Pays Off," *Fortune* (March 20, 1995), pp. 145–146; and Alex Taylor III, "The Germans Take Charge; Creating DaimlerChrysler Was a Coup for Jurgen Schrempp, But Can He Make the New Company Work?" *Fortune* (January 11, 1999), p. 92.

[6] Marvin E. Shaw, *Group Dynamics: The Psychology of Small Group Behavior*, 2nd ed. (New York: McGraw-Hill, 1976).

[7] Bib Latane, Kipling Williams, and Stephen Harkins, "Many Hands Make Light the Work: The Causes and Consequences of Social Loafing," *Journal of Personality and Social Psychology*, Vol. 37 (1978), pp. 822–832; E. Weldon and G. M. Gargano, "Cognitive Effort in Additive Task Groups: The Effects

of Shared Responsibility on the Quality of Multi-attribute Judgments," *Organizational Behavior and Human Decision Processes*, Vol. 36 (1985), pp. 348–361; John M. George, "Extrinsic and Intrinsic Origins of Perceived Social Loafing in Organizations," *Academy of Management Journal* (March 1992), pp. 191–202; and W. Jack Duncan, "Why Some People Loaf in Groups While Others Loaf Alone," *Academy of Management Executive*, Vol. 8 (1994), pp. 79–80.

[8] D. A. Kravitz and B. Martin, "Ringelmann Rediscovered," *Journal of Personality and Social Psychology*, Vol. 50 (1986), pp. 936–941.

[9] A classic article is by Richard B. Zajonc, "Social Facilitation," *Science*, Vol. 149 (1965), pp. 269–274.

[10] Gerald Salancik and Jeffrey Pfeffer, "A Social Information Processing Approach to Job Attitude and Task Design," *Administrative Science Quarterly*, Vol. 23 (1978), pp. 224–253.

[11] David M. Herold, "The Effectiveness of Work Groups," in Steven Kerr, ed., *Organizational Behavior* (New York: Wiley, 1979), p. 95.

[12] Rensis Likert, *New Patterns of Management* (New York: McGraw-Hill, 1961).

[13] For a good discussion of task forces, see James Ware, "Managing a Task Force," Note 478-002, Harvard Business School, 1977.

[14] See "The Corporate Jungle Spawns a New Species: The Project Manager," *Fortune* (July 10, 1995), pp. 179–180.

[15] Information from Myron Maget, "Who's Winning the Information Revolution?" *Fortune* (November 30, 1992), pp. 110–117; and Paul Taylor, "Big Names Drawn by High Skills and Low Cost Levels," *The Financial Times* (December 2, 1998), p. 2.

[16] Greg L. Stewart, Charles C. Manz, and Henry P. Sims, *Teamwork and Group Dynamics* (New York: John Wiley & Sons, 1999), pp. 139–141.

[17] See, for example, Leland P. Bradford, *Group Development*, 2nd ed. (San Francisco: Jossey-Bass, 1997).

[18] J. Steven Heinen and Eugene Jacobson, "A Model of Task Group Development in Complex Organization and a Strategy of Implementation," *Academy of Management Review*, Vol. 1 (October 1976), pp. 98–111; Bruce W. Tuckman, "Developmental Sequence in Small Groups," *Psychological Bulletin*, Vol. 63 (1965), pp. 384–399; and Bruce W. Tuckman and Mary Ann C. Jensen, "Stages of Small Group Development Revisited," *Group & Organization Studies*, Vol. 2 (1977), pp. 419–427.

[19] Dave Ulrich, "Intellectual Capital = Competence × Commitment," *Sloan Management Review* (Winter 1998), pp. 15–26.

[20] See J. Richard Hackman, "The Design of Work Teams," in Jay W. Lorsch (ed.), *Handbook of Organizational Behavior* (Englewood Cliffs, NJ: Prentice Hall, 1987), pp. 343–357.

[21] Herold, op. cit. (1979). See also the discussion of group tasks in Stewart, Manz, and Sims, op. cit. (1999), pp. 142–143.

[22] Ilgen, et al., op. cit. (1997); and Warren Watson, "Cultural Diversity's Impact on Interaction Process and Performance," *Academy of Management Journal*, Vol. 16 (1993).

[23] L. Argote and J. E. McGrath, "Group Processes in Organizations: Continuity and Change" in C. L. Cooper and I. T. Robertson (eds.), *International Review of Industrial and Organizational Psychology* (New York: Wiley, 1993), pp. 333–389.

[24] See Daniel R. Ilgen, Jeffrey A. LePine, and John R. Hollenbeck, "Effective Decision Making in Multinational Teams," in P. Christopher Earley and Miriam Erez (eds.), *New Perspectives on International Industrial/Organizational Psychology* (San Francisco: New Lexington Press, 1997), pp. 377–409.

[25] William C. Schutz, *FIRO: A Three-Dimensional Theory of Interpersonal Behavior* (New York: Rinehart, 1958).

[26] William C. Schutz, "The Interpersonal Underworld," *Harvard Business Review*, Vol. 36 (July–August, 1958), p. 130.

[27] Katzenbach and Smith, op. cit. (1993).

[28] E. J. Thomas and C. F. Fink, "Effects of Group Size," in Larry L. Cummings and William E. Scott (eds.), *Readings in Organizational and Human Performance* (Homewood, IL: Irwin, 1969), pp. 394–408.

[29] Shaw, op. cit. (1976).

[30] George C. Homans, *The Human Group* (New York: Harcourt Brace, 1950).

[31] Information from "What a Zoo Can Teach You," *Fortune* (May 18, 1992); Thomas Stewart, "The Search for the Organization of Tomorrow," *Fortune* (May 18, 1992); and Nancy Austin, "Making Team Work," *Working Woman* (January 1993). See also Barbara Ettorre, "A Day in the Life: The Wild Life of a Manager—San Diego Zoo Animal Care Manager Curby Simerson," *Management Review*, Vol. 84 (August 1995), p. 28.

[32] For a discussion of intergroup dynamics, see Schein, op. cit. (1988), pp. 106–115.

[33] "Producer Power," *The Economist* (March 4, 1995), p. 70.

[34] This discussion is developed from Schein, op. cit. (1988), pp. 69–75.

[35] Ibid., p. 73.

[36] Developed from guidelines presented in the classic article by Jay Hall, "Decisions, Decisions, Decisions," *Psychology Today* (November 1971), pp. 55–56.

[37] Norman R.F. Maier, "Assets and Liabilities in Group Problem Solving," *Psychological Review*, Vol. 74 (1967), pp. 239–249.

[38] Ibid.

[39] Irving L. Janis, "Groupthink," *Psychology Today* (November 1971), pp. 43–46; Irving L. Janis, *Groupthink*, 2nd ed. (Boston: Houghton Mifflin, 1982). See also J. Longley and D. G. Pruitt, "Groupthink: A Critique of Janis' Theory," in L. Wheeler (ed.), *Review of Personality and Social Psychology* (Beverly Hills, CA: Sage Publications, 1980); Carrie R. Leana, "A Partial Test of Janis's Groupthink Model: The Effects of Group Cohesiveness and Leader Behavior on Decision Processes," *Journal of Management*, Vol. 11, No. 1 (1985), pp. 5–18. See also Jerry Harvey, "Managing Agreement in Organizations: The Abilene Paradox," *Organizational Dynamics* (Summer 1974), pp. 63–80.

[40] Janis, op. cit. (1982).

[41] Gayle W. Hill, "Group versus Individual Performance: Are N1 1 Heads Better Than One?" *Psychological Bulletin*, Vol. 91 (1982), pp. 517–539.

[42] These techniques are well described in George P. Huber, *Managerial Decision Making* (Glenview, IL: Scott, Foresman, 1980); and Andre L. Delbecq, Andrew L. Van de Ven, and David H. Gustafson, *Group Techniques for Program Planning: A Guide to Nominal Groups and Delphi Techniques* (Glenview, IL: Scott, Foresman, 1975); and William M. Fox, "Anonymity and Other Keys to Successful Problem-Solving Meetings," *National Productivity Review*, Vol. 8 (Spring 1989), pp. 145–156.

[43] Delbecq et al., op. cit. (1975); Fox, op. cit. (1989).

[44] R. Brent Gallupe and William H. Cooper, "Brainstorming Electronically," *Sloan Management Review* (Fall 1993), pp. 27–36.

Source Notes

Sony: Information from "Videoconferencing by Sony, Naturally," Business Week (November 16, 1998), special advertising section.

EDS: Information from Eric Matson, "The Seven Sins of Deadly Meetings," *Fast Company Handbook of the Business Revolution* (New York: Fast Company, 1997), p. 31.

W. L. Gore & Associates: Information from Shelley Branch, "The 100 Best Companies to Work for in America," *Fortune* (January 11, 1999), p. 126.

Information from Jennifer Scott, "More Workers Have Option of Taking Stock in Company," *The Columbus Dispatch* (January 25, 1999), pp. 10–11.

Developed from Edgar H. Schein, *Process Consultation*, Vol. 1. Copyright © 1988 (Addison-Wesley Publishing Company), Chapter 6.

■ CHAPTER 10

Footnotes

[1] Information from Tom Redburn, "His Dream Is That We'll All Hear Little Voices," *New York Times* (September 23, 1998), p. 9.

[2] *Fortune* (May 7, 1990), pp. 52–60. See also Ronald E. Purser and Steven Cabana, *The Self-Managing Organization* (New York: Free Press, 1998).

[3] Susan Albers Mohrman, Jay R. Galbraith, Edward E. Lawler III, and Associates, *Tomorrow's Organization: Crafting Winning Capabilities in a Dynamic World* (San Francisco: Jossey-Bass, 1998).

[4] Jon R. Katzenbach and Douglas K. Smith, "The Discipline of Teams," *Harvard Business Review* (March–April 1993a), pp. 111–120; and Jon R. Katzenbach and Douglas K. Smith, *The Wisdom of Teams: Creating the High-Performance Organization* (Boston: Harvard Business School Press, 1993b).

[5] Jay A. Conger, *Winning 'em Over: A New Model for Managing in the Age of Persuasion* (New York: Simon & Schuster, 1998).

[6] Ibid., p. 191.

[7] Katzenbach and Smith, op. cit. (1993a and 1993b).

[8] See also Jon R. Katzenbach, "The Myth of the Top Management Team," *Harvard Business Review*, Vol. 75 (November–December 1997), pp. 83–91.

[9] Information from Robert B. Reich, "The Company of the Future," *Fast Company* (November 1998), p. 124+.

[10] Katzenbach and Smith, op. cit. (1993a and 1993b).

[11] For a good overview, see Greg L. Stewart, Charles C. Manz, and Henry P. Sims, *Team Work and Group Dynamics* (New York: Wiley, 1999).

[12] Katzenbach and Smith, op. cit. (1993a), p. 112.

[13] Developed from ibid. (1993a), pp. 118–119.

[14] See Stewart et al., op. cit. (1999), pp. 43–44.

[15] See Daniel R. Ilgen, Jeffrey A. LePine, and John R. Hollenbeck, "Effective Decision Making in Multinational Teams," in P. Christopher Earley and Miriam Erez (eds.), *New Perspectives on International Industrial/Organizational Psychology* (San Francisco: New Lexington Press, 1997), pp. 377–409.

[16] Ilgen, et al., op. cit. (1997); and Warren Watson, "Cultural Diversity's Impact on Interaction Process and Performance," *Academy of Management Journal*, Vol. 16 (1993).

[17] For a good discussion of team building, see William D. Dyer, *Team Building*, 3rd ed. (Reading, MA: Addison-Wesley, 1995).

[18] Developed from a discussion by Edgar H. Schein, *Process Consultation* (Reading, MA: Addison-Wesley, 1969), pp. 32–37; Edgar H. Schein, *Process Consultation: Volume I* (1988), pp. 40–49.

[19] The classic work is Robert F. Bales, "Task Roles and Social Roles in Problem-Solving Groups," in Eleanor E. Maccoby, Theodore M. Newcomb, and E. L. Hartley (eds.), *Readings in Social Psychology* (New York: Holt, Rinehart & Winston, 1958).

[20] Schein, op. cit. (1988).

[21] For a good description of task and maintenance functions, see John J. Gabarro and Anne Harlan, "Note on Process Observation," Note 9-477-029 (Harvard Business School, 1976).

[22] See Daniel C. Feldman, "The Development and Enforcement of Group Norms," *Academy of Management Review*, Vol. 9 (1984), pp. 47–53.

[23] See Robert F. Allen and Saul Pilnick, "Confronting the Shadow Organization: How to Select and Defeat Negative Norms," *Organizational Dynamics* (Spring 1973), pp. 13–17; Alvin Zander, *Making Groups Effective* (San Francisco: Jossey-Bass, 1982), Ch. 4; Daniel C. Feldman, op. cit. (1984).

[24] For a summary of research on group cohesiveness, see Marvin E. Shaw, *Group Dynamics* (New York: McGraw-Hill, 1971), pp. 110–112, 192.

[25] Information from Stratford Sherman, "Secrets of HP's 'Muddled' Team," *Fortune* (March 18, 1996), pp. 116–120.

[26] See Jay R. Galbraith and Edward E. Lawler III, "The Challenges of Change: Organizing for Competitive Advantage," in Susan Albers Mohrman, Jay R. Galbraith, Edward E. Lawler III, and Associates, *Tomorrow's Organization: Crafting Winning Capabilities in a Dynamic World* (San Francisco: Jossey-Bass, 1998).

[27] See Kenichi Ohmae, "Quality Control Circles: They Work and Don't Work," *Wall Street Journal* (March 29, 1982), p. 16; Robert P. Steel, Anthony J. Mento, Benjamin L. Dilla, Nestor K. Ovalle, and Russell F. Lloyd, "Factors Influencing the Success and Failure of Two Quality Circles Programs," *Journal of Management*, Vol. 11, No. 1 (1985), pp. 99–119; Edward E. Lawler III, and Susan A. Mohrman, "Quality Circles: After the Honeymoon," *Organizational Dynamics*, Vol. 15, No. 4 (1987), pp. 42–54.

[28] See Jay R. Galbraith, *Designing Organizations* (San Francisco: Jossey-Bass, 1998).

[29] Jerry Yoram Wind and Jeremy Main, *Driving Change: How the Best Companies Are Preparing for the 21st Century* (New York: The Free Press, 1998), p. 135.

[30] Jessica Lipnack and Jeffrey Stamps, *Virtual Teams: Reaching Across Space, Time, and Organizations with Technology* (New York: Wiley, 1997).

[31] For a review of some alternatives, see Jeff Angus and Sean Gallagher, "Virtual Team Builders—Internet-Based Teamware Makes It Possible to Build Effective Teams from Widely Dispersed Participants," *Information Week* (May 4, 1998).

[32] Christine Perey, "Conferencing and Collaboration: Real-World Solutions for Business Communications," *Business Week*, special advertising section (1999).

[33] R. Brent Gallupe and William H. Cooper, "Brainstorming Electronically," *Sloan Management Review* (Fall 1993), pp. 27–36.

[34] William M. Bulkeley, "Computerizing Dull Meetings Is Touted as an Antidote to the Mouth That Bored," *Wall Street Journal* (January 28, 1992), pp. B1, B2.

[35] See Gallupe and Cooper, op. cit. (1993).

[36] For early research on related team concepts, see Richard E. Walton, "How to Counter Alienation in the Plant," *Harvard Business Review* (November–December 1972), pp. 70–81; Richard E. Walton, "Work Innovations at Topeka: After Six Years," *Journal of Applied Behavior Science*, Vol. 13 (1977), pp. 422–431; Richard E. Walton, "The Topeka Work System: Optimistic Visions, Pessimistic Hypotheses, and Reality," in Zager and Rosow (eds.), *The Innovative Organization*, Ch. 11.

[37] Information from Vanaja Dhanan and Cecille Austria, "Where Workers Manage Themselves," *World Executive's Digest* (October 1992), pp. 14–16; additional discussion of TI in Malaysia is found in Stewart et al. (1999), pp. 18–26.

Source Notes

Excerpted from "Employee Case Study," Corning Glass Works, located on the corporate Web site at http://www.corning.com/company_info/index.html. Used by permission.

MCI WorldCom: Information from "MCI WorldCom Conferencing," *Business Week* (November 16, 1998), special advertising section; and corporate Web site.

Charles Schwab & Co.: Information from Eric Matson, "The Seven Sins of Deadly Meetings," *Fast Company Handbook of the Business Revolution* (New York: Fast Company, 1997), p. 31.

John R. Schermerhorn, Jr., *Management*, 5th ed. (New York: Wiley, 1996), p. 274. Used by permission.

■ CHAPTER 11

Footnotes

[1] Marcus B. Osborn, "Organizational Structure at First Community Financial," working paper, Department of Public Administration, Arizona State University, Tempe, AZ, 1999.

[2] The bulk of this chapter was originally based on Richard N. Osborn, James G. Hunt, and Lawrence R. Jauch, *Organization Theory: Integrated Text and Cases* (Melbourne, FL: Krieger, 1985). For a more recent but consistent view, see Lex Donaldson, "The Normal Science of Structural Contingency Theory," in Stewart R. Clegg, Cynthia Hardy, and Walter R. Nord (eds.), *Handbook of Organizational Studies* (London: Sage Publications, 1996), pp. 57–76.

[3] H. Talcott Parsons, *Structure and Processes in Modern Societies* (New York: Free Press, 1960).

[4] See Jeffery Pfeffer, "Barriers to the Advance of Organization Science," *Academy of Management Review* 18, No. 4 (1993): 599–620; Richard M. Cyert and James G. March, *A Behavioral Theory of the Firm* (Englewood Cliffs, NJ: Prentice-Hall, 1963). A good discussion of organizational goals is also found in Charles Perrow, *Organizational Analysis: A Sociological View* (Belmont, CA: Wadsworth, 1970) and in Richard H. Hall, "Organizational Behavior: A Sociological Perspective," in Jay W. Lorsch (ed.), *Handbook of Organizational Behavior* (Englewood Cliffs, NJ: Prentice-Hall, 1987), pp. 84–95.

[5] See Terri Lammers, "The Effective and Indispensable Mission Statement," *Inc.* (August 1992): 1, 7, 23, for instance, and I. C. MacMillan and A. Meshulack, "Replacement versus Expansion: Dilemma for Mature U.S. Businesses," *Academy of Management Journal* 26 (1983): 708–726.

[6] See Stewart R. Clegg and Cynthia Hardy, "Organizations, Organization and Organizing," in Clegg, Hardy, and Nord (eds.), *Handbook of Organizational Studies* (1996), pp. 1–28 and William H. Starbuck and Paul C. Nystrom, "Designing and Understanding Organizations," in P. C. Nystrom and W. H. Starbuck (eds.), *Handbook of Organizational Design: Adapting Organizations to Their Environments* (New York: Oxford University Press, 1981).

[7] See Osborn, Hunt, and Jauch (1985).

[8] Janice Beyer, Danta P. Ashmos, and R. N. Osborn, "Contrasts in Enacting TQM: Mechanistic vs. Organic Ideology and Implementation," *Journal of Quality Management* 1 (1997): 13–29, and for an early treatment, see Paul R. Lawrence and Jay W. Lorsch, *Organization and Environment* (Homewood, IL: Irwin, 1969).

[9] For reviews, see Osborn, Hunt, and Jauch (1985); Clegg, Hardy, and Nord (1996).

[10] See Prashant C. Palvia, Shailendra C. Palvia, and Edward M. Roche, *Global Information Technology and Systems Management: Key Issues and Trends* (Nashua, NH: Ivy League Publishing, 1996).

[11] For instance, see J.E.M. McGee, M. J. Dowling, and W. L. Megginson, "Cooperative Strategy and New Venture Performance: The Role of Business Strategy and Management Experience," *Strategic Management Journal* 16 (1995): 565–580 and James B. Quinn, *Intelligent Enterprise: A Knowledge and Service Based Paradigm for Industry* (New York: Free Press, 1992).

[12] See P. Candace Deans *Global Information Systems and Technology: Focus on the Organization and Its Functional Areas* (Harrisburg, PA: Ideal Group Publishing, 1994) and Osborn, Hunt, and Jauch (1985).

[13] Haim Levy and Deborah Gunthorpe, *Introduction to Investments*, 2nd ed. (Cincinnati, OH: South-Western, 1999) and William G. Ouchi and M. A. McGuire, "Organization Control: Two Functions," *Administrative Science Quarterly*, 20 (1977): 559–569.

[14] Adapted from W. Edwards Deming, "Improvement of Quality and Productivity Through Action by Management," *Productivity Review* (Winter 1982): 12, 22; and W. Edwards Deming, *Quality, Productivity and Competitive Position* (Cambridge, MA: MIT Center for Advanced Engineering, 1982).

[15] Beyer, Ashmos, and Osborn (1997).

[16] For related reviews, see W. Richard Scott, *Organizations: Rational, Natural, and Open Systems*, 2nd ed. (Englewood Cliffs, NJ: Prentice-Hall, 1987); Osborn, Hunt, and Jauch, (1985); Clegg, Hardy, and Nord (1996).

[17] Osborn, Hunt, and Jauch (1985), pp. 273–303.

[18] Ibid.

[19] Ibid.

[20] For reviews of structural tendencies and their influence on outcomes, also see Scott (1987); Clegg, Hardy, and Nord (1996).

[21] For a good discussion of the early use of matrix structures, see Stanley Davis, Paul Lawrence, Harvey Kolodny, and Michael Beer, *Matrix* (Reading, MA: Addison-Wesley, 1977).

[22] See P. R. Lawrence and J. W. Lorsch, *Organization and Environment: Managing Differentiation and Integration* (Homewood, IL: Richard D. Irwin, 1967).

[23] See Osborn, Hunt, and Jauch (1985).

[24] Max Weber, *The Theory of Social and Economic Organization*, translated by A. M. Henderson and H. T. Parsons (New York: Free Press, 1947).

[25] These relationships were initially outlined by Tom Burns and G. M. Stalker, *The Management of Innovation* (London: Tavistock, 1961).

[26] See Henry Mintzberg, *Structure in Fives: Designing Effective Organizations* (Englewood Cliffs, NJ: Prentice-Hall, 1983).

[27] Ibid.

[28] Ibid.

[29] See Osborn, Hunt, and Jauch (1984) for an extended discussion.

[30] See Peter Clark and Ken Starkey, *Organization Transitions and Innovation—Design* (London: Pinter Publications, 1988).

[31] Osborn (1984).

Source Notes

electroglas.com/puglic/031698.htm.

ford.com/finaninvest/stockholder/3q98rel.html

Laura Dudio, "How Data General Is Turning Itself Around," http://www.dg.com/news/press-releases/clustrfn.html; LAN Times (January 6, 1992), pp. 26–29.

■ CHAPTER 12

Footnotes

[1] References for General Motors.

[2] R. N. Osborn, J. G. Hunt, and L. Jauch, *Organization Theory: Integrated Text and Cases* (Melbourne, FL: Krieger, 1984), pp. 123–215.

[3] See Henry Mintzberg, *Structure in Fives: Designing Effective Organizations* (Englewood Cliffs, NJ: Prentice-Hall, 1983).

[4] For a comprehensive review, see W. Richard Scott, *Organizations: Rational, Natural, and Open Systems*, 2nd ed. (Englewood Cliffs, NJ: Prentice-Hall, 1987).

[5] See Peter M. Blau and Richard A. Schoenner, *The Structure of Organizations* (New York: Basic Books, 1971).

[6] Joan Woodward, *Industrial Organization: Theory and Practice* (London: Oxford University Press, 1965).

[7] Ibid.

[8] Gerardine DeSanctis, "Information Technology," in Nigel Nicholoson (ed.), *Blackwell Encyclopedic Dictionary of Organizational Behavior* (Cambridge, MA: Blackwell Publishers, Ltd., 1995), pp. 232–233.

[9] James D. Thompson, *Organization in Action* (New York: McGraw-Hill, 1967).

[10] Woodward (1965).

[11] For reviews, see Osborn, Hunt, and Jauch (1984); and Louis Fry, "Technology-Structure Research: Three Critical Issues," *Academy of Management Journal* 25 (1982): pp. 532–552.

[12] Mintzberg (1983).

[13] Charles Perrow, *Complex Organizations: A Critical Essay*, 3rd ed. (New York: Random House, 1986).

[14] Mintzberg (1983).

[15] Prashant C. Palvia, Shailendra C. Palvia and Edward M. Roche, *Global Information Technology and Systems Management: Key Issues and Trends* (Nashua, NH: Ivy League Publishing, 1996).

[16] DeSanctis (1995).

[17] P. Candace Deans, *Global Information Systems and Technology: Focus on the Organization and Its Functional Areas* (Harrisburg, PA: Ideal Group Publishing, 1994).

[18] Osborn, Hunt, and Jauch (1984).

[19] David A. Nadler and Michael L. Tushman, *Competing by Design: The Power of Organizational Architecture* (New York: Oxford University Press, 1997).

[20] David Lei, Michael Hitt, and Richard A. Bettis, "Dynamic Capabilities and Strategic Management," *Journal of Management* 22 (1996): pp. 547–567.

[21] Melissa A. Schilling, "Technological Lockout: An Integrative Model of the Economic and Strategic Factors Driving Technological Success and Failure," *Academy of Management Review* 23, No. 2 (1998): 267–284.

[22] Jack Veiga and Kathleen Dechant, "Wired World Woes:www.help," *Academy of Management Executive* 11, No. 3 (1997): 73–79.

[23] Jaana Woiceshyn, "The Role of Management in the Adoption of Technology: A Longitudinal Investigation," *Technology Studies* 4, No. 1 (1997): 62–99.

[24] Janice Beyer, Danta P. Ashmos, and R. N. Osborn, "Contrasts in Enacting TQM: Mechanistic vs Organic Ideology and Implementation," *Journal of Quality Management* 1 (1997): 13–29.

[25] Veiga and Dechant (1997).

[26] Michael A. Hitt, R. Duane Ireland, and Robert E. Hoskisson, *Strategic Management: Competitiveness and Globalization* (Cincinnati, OH: South-Western College Publishing, 1999).

[27] This section is based on R. N. Osborn and J. G. Hunt, "The Environment and Organization Effectiveness," *Administrative Science Quarterly* 19 (1974): 231–246; and Osborn, Hunt, and Jauch (1984).

[28] See R. N. Osborn and C. C. Baughn, "New Patterns in the Formation of U.S./Japanese Cooperative Ventures," *Columbia Journal of World Business* 22 (1988): 57–65.

[29] R. N. Osborn, *The Evolution of Strategic Alliances in High Technology,* working paper (Detroit: Department of Management, Wayne State University, 1997); and Shawn Tully, "The Modular Corporation," *Fortune* (February 8, 1993).

[30] L. R. Jauch and R. N. Osborn, "Toward an Integrated Theory of Strategy," *Academy of Management Review* 6 (1981): 491–498; Alfred D. Chandler, *The Visible Hand: The Managerial Revolution in America* (Cambridge, MA: Belknap, 1977); Karen Bantel and R. N. Osborn, "The Influence of Performance, Environment and Size on the Identifiability of Firm Strategy," *British Journal of Management* 6 (1995): 235–248.

[31] Hitt, Ireland, and Hoskisson (1999).

[32] M. E. Porter, *Competitive Strategy* (New York: Free Press, 1980).

[33] J. C. Spencer and R. M. Grant, "Knowledge and the Firm: Overview," *Strategic Management Journal* 17 (Winter special issue 1996): 5–10: Spencer and Grant (1996).

[34] G. Huber, "Organizational Learning: The Contributing Process and the Literature," *Organization Science* 2, No. 1 (1991): 88–115.

[35] J. W. Myer and B. Rowan, "Institutionalized Organizations: Formal Structure as Myth and Ceremony," *American Journal of Sociology* 83 (1977): 340–363.

[36] Bandura, *Social Learning Theory* (Englewood Cliffs, NJ: Prentice-Hall, 1977).

[37] See, for example, A. M. Morrison, R. P. White, and E. Van Velsor, *Breaking the Glass Ceiling* (Reading, MA: Addison-Wesley, 1987); J. D. Zalesny and J. K. Ford, "Extending the Social Information Processing Perspective: New Links to Attitudes, Behaviors and Perceptions," *Organizational Behavior and Human Decision Processes* 47 (1990): 205–246; M. E. Gist, C. Schwoerer, and B. Rosen, "Effects of Alternative Training Methods of Self-Efficacy and Performance in Computer Software Training," *Journal of Applied Psychology* 74 (1989): 884–91; D. D. Sutton and R. W. Woodman, "Pygmalion Goes to Work: The Effects of Supervisor Expectations in a Retail Setting," *Journal of Applied Psychology* 74 (1989): 943–950; M. E. Gist, "The Influence of Training Method on Self-Efficacy and Idea Generation among Managers," *Personnel Psychology* 42 (1989): 787–805.

[38] See M. E. Gist, "Self Efficacy: Implications in Organizational Behavior and Human Resource Management," *Academy of Management Review* 12 (1987): 472–485; A Bandura, "Self Efficacy Mechanisms in Human Agency," *American Psychologist* 37 (1987): 122–147.

[39] J. March, *Decisions and Organizations* (Oxford: Basil Blackwell, 1988).

[40] R. N. Osborn, and D. H. Jackson, Leaders, "Riverboat Gamblers on Purposeful Unintended Consequences in the Management of Complex Technologies," *Academy of Management Journal* 31 (1988): 924–947.

[41] See A. L. Stinchcombe, *Economic Sociology* (New York: Academic Press, 1983).

[42] Ibid.

[43] Osborn and Jackson (1988).

[44] Ibid.

[45] O. P. Walsch and G. R. Ungson, "Organization Memory," *Academy of Management Review* 16, No. 1 (1991): 57–91.

[46] A. A. Marcus, *Business and Society: Ethics Government and the World of Economy* (Homewood, IL: Richard D. Irwin, 1993).

[47] Ibid.

[48] Raymond E. Miles, Charles C. Snow, John Mathews, Grant Miles, and Henry Coleman, Jr., "Organizing for the Knowledge Age: Anticipating the Cellular Form," *Academy of Management Executive* 11, No. 4 (1997): 7–20.

Source Notes

George Anders, "Discomfort Zone: Some Companies Long to Embrace the Web But Settle for Flirtation," *Wall Street Journal* (November 4, 1998), pp. 1 and 14; and Jermiah Sullivan, "Functions of the Corporate Web," *Journal of World Business,* in press.

From the 1997 annual report of the Chase Manhattan Corporation and www.chasemanhattan.com.

Warner-Lambert Annual Report 1997, p. 24.

http://www.com/cgi-bin/cgi; Caree P&G Pursues Greatest Growth Ever (September 9, 1998); Douglas G. Shaw and Vincent C. Perro, "Beating the Odds: Five Reasons Why Companies Excel," *Management Review* (August 1992); P&G Annual Report, 1992, 1995, 1997.

www.solutions-4u.com/barter/49063a73.htm/.

■ CHAPTER 13

Footnotes

[1] http.www.cisco.com/; Shawn Tully, "How Cisco Mastered the Net," *Fortune* (August 17, 1998), pp. 23–26; Albert Pang, "E-commerce Bonanza: Is It real or Imagined," *Internet Computing* (February 9, 1998), pp. 3 and 9; Thomas l. Friedman, "The Internet Wars," *New York Times* (April 11, 1998), pp. E8–9.

[2] For a recent discussion of the resurgence of interest in individuals within organizations, see Jeffery Pfeffer, *The Human Equation: Building Profits by Putting People First* (Boston: Harvard Business School Press, 1998).

[3] Edgar Schein, "Organizational Culture," *American Psychologist*, Vol. 45 (1990), pp. 109–119; and E. Schein, *Organizational Culture and Leadership* (San Francisco: Jossey-Bass, 1985).

[4] Schein (1990).

[5] From an interview with Daimler-Chrysler employees after the consummation of the merger between Chrysler and Daimler by Richard Osborn.

[6] This example was reported in an interview with Edgar Schein, "Corporate Culture Is the Real Key to Creativity," *Business Month* (May 1989), pp. 73–74.

[7] For early work, see T. Deal and A. Kennedy, *Corporate Culture* (Reading, MA: Addison-Wesley, 1982); and Peters and R. Waterman, *In Search of Excellence* (New York: Harper & Row, 1982), while more recent studies are summarized in Joanne Martin and Peter Frost, "The Organizational Culture War Games: The Struggle for Intellectual Dominance," in Stewart R. Clegg, Cynthia Hardy, and Walter R. Nord (eds.), *Handbook of Organizational Studies* (London: Sage Publications, 1996), pp. 599–621.

[8] Schein (1985).

[9] For an extended discussion, see J. M. Beyer and H. M. Trice, "How an Organization's Rites Reveal Its Culture," *Organizational Dynamics* (Spring 1987), pp. 27–41.

[10] A. Cooke and D. M. Rousseau, "Behavioral Norms and Expectations: A

Quantitative Approach to the Assessment of Organizational Culture," *Group and Organizational Studies* 13 (1988), pp. 245–273.

[11] Martin and C. Siehl, "Organization Culture and Counterculture," *Organizational Dynamics* 12 (1983), pp. 52–64.

[12] Ibid.

[13] "Is Sony Finally Getting the Hang of Hollywood?" *Business Week* (September 7, 1992), p. 76.

[14] See Pfeffer (1998).

[15] Taylor Cox, Jr., "The Multicultural Organization," *Academy of Management Executive,* Vol. 2, No. 2 (May 1991), pp. 34–47.

[16] Carl Quintanilla, "DU-UDE: CEOs, Feeling Out of Touch with Junior Employees, Try to Get 'Withit' *Wall Street Journal* (November 10, 1998), p. 1.

[17] Schein (1985), pp. 52–57.

[18] Peters and Waterman (1982).

[19] Schein (1990).

[20] H. Gertz, *The Interpretation of Culture* (New York: Basic Books, 1973).

[21] Beyer and Trice (1987).

[22] *Business Week* (November 23, 1992), p. 117.

[23] H. M. Trice and J. M. Beyer, "Studying Organizational Cultures Through Rites and Ceremonials," *Academy of Management Review,* Vol. 3 (1984), pp. 633–669.

[24] J. Martin, M. S. Feldman, M. J. Hatch, and S. B. Sitkin, "The Uniqueness Paradox in Organizational Stories," *Administrative Science Quarterly,* Vol. 28 (1983), pp. 438–453.

[25] Deal and Kennedy (1982).

[26] This section is based on R. N. Osborn and C. C. Baughn, *An Assessment of the State of the Field of Organizational Design* (Alexandria, VA: U.S. Army Research Institute, 1994).

[27] Osborn and Baughn (1994).

[28] R. N. Osborn and D. Jackson, "Leaders, River Boat Gamblers or Purposeful Unintended Consequences," *Academy of Management Journal,* Vol. 31 (1988), pp. 924–947.

[29] G. Hofstede and M. H. Bond, "The Confucius Connection: From Cultural Roots to Economic Growth," *Organizational Dynamics,* Vol. 16 (1991): 4–21.

[30] Martin and Frost (1996).

[31] Warner Burke, *Organization Development* (Reading, MA: Addison-Wesley, 1987); Wendell L. French and Cecil H. Bell, Jr., *Organization Development,* 4th ed. (Englewood Cliffs, NJ: Prentice-Hall, 1990); Edgar F. Huse and Thomas G. Cummings, *Organization Development and Change,* 4th ed. (St. Paul, MN: West, 1989).

[32] Warren Bennis, "Using Our Knowledge of Organizational Behavior," in Lorsch, pp. 29–49.

[33] Excellent overviews are found in Cummings and Huse (1989), pp. 32–36, 45; and French and Bell (1990).

[34] Richard Beckhard, "The Confrontation Meeting," *Harvard Business Review,* Vol. 45 (March/April 1967), pp. 149–155.

[35] See Dale Zand, "Collateral Organization: A New Change Strategy," *Journal of Applied Behavioral Science* 10 (1974): 63–89; Barry A. Stein and Rosabeth Moss Kanter, "Building the Parallel Organization," *Journal of Applied Behavioral Science,* Vol. 16 (1980), pp. 371–386.

[36] J. Richard Hackman and Greg R. Oldham, *Work Redesign* (Reading, MA: Addison-Wesley, 1980).

Source Notes

http.www.cisco.com/; Shawn Tully, "How Cisco Mastered the Net," *Fortune* (August 17, 1998); Albert Pang, "E-commerce Bonanza: Is It Real or Imagined?" *Internet Computing* (February 9, 1998); Thomas l. Friedman, "The Internet Wars," *New York Times* (April 11, 1998), pp .

From interviews with Fred Fernandez.

www.hp.com.

Time David Kirpatrick, "The Second Coming of Apple," *Fortune* (November 9, 1998); Brent Schlender, "The Three Faces of Steve," *Fortune* (November 9, 1998), pp. 8, 27.

Based on work by Jeffrey Sonnenfeld, as reported by Carol Hymowitz, "Which Corporate Culture Fits You?" *Wall Street Journal* (July 17, 1989), p. B1.]

Copyright 1969 by the Regents of the University of California. Reprinted from *California Management Review* 12, No. 2 (1996), p. 26, Figure 1, by permission of the Regents.

■ CHAPTER 14

Footnotes

[1] See J. P. Kotter, *A Force for Change: How Leadership Differs from Management* (New York: Free Press, 1990).

[2] See Bernard M. Bass, *Bass and Stogdill's Handbook of Leadership*, 3rd ed. (New York: Free Press, 1990).

[3] See Alan Bryman, *Charisma and Leadership in Organizations* (London: Sage Publications, 1992), Ch. 5.

[4] Ralph M. Stogdill, *Handbook of Leadership* (New York: Free Press, 1974).

[5] Based on information from Robert J. House and Ram Aditya, "The Social Scientific Study of Leadership: Quo Vadis?" *Journal of Management,* Vol. 23 (1997), pp. 409–474; Shelley A. Kirkpatrick and Edwin A. Locke, "Leadership: Do Traits Matters?" *The Executive,* Vol. 5, No. 2 (1991), pp. 48–60; Gary Yukl, *Leadership in Organizations,* 3rd ed. (Upper Saddle River, NJ: Prentice-Hall, 1998), Ch. 10.

[6] Rensis Likert, *New Patterns of Management* (New York: McGraw-Hill, 1961).

[7] Bass, op. cit., Ch. 24.

[8] Yukl, op. cit.; George Graen, "Leader-Member Exchange Theory Development: Discussant's Comments," *Academy of Management 1998 Meeting,* San Diego, August 7–12, 1998.

[9] Yukl, op. cit.; Peter G. Northouse, *Leadership Theory and Practice* (Thousand Oaks, CA: Sage, 1997), Ch 7.

[10] See M. F. Peterson, "PM Theory in Japan and China: What's in It for the United States?" *Organizational Dynamics* (Spring 1988), pp. 22–39; J. Misumi and M. F. Peterson, "The Performance-Maintenance Theory of Leadership: Review of a Japanese Research Program," *Administrative Science Quarterly,* Vol. 30 (1985), pp. 198–223; P. B. Smith, J. Misumi, M. Tayeb, M. F. Peterson, and M. Bond, "On the Generality of Leadership Style Measures Across Cultures," paper presented at the *International Congress of Applied Psychology,* Jerusalem, July 1986.

[11] G. B. Graen and M. Uhl-Bien, "Relationship-Based Approach to Leadership: Development of Leader-Member Exchange (LMX) Theory of Leadership Over 25 Years: Applying a Multi-Level Multi-Domain Perspective," *Leadership Quarterly,* Vol. 6 (Summer 1995), pp. 219–247.

[12] R. J. House and R. Aditya, "The Social Scientific Study of Leadership: Quo Vadis?" *Journal of Management,* Vol. 23 (1997), pp. 409–474.

[13] Kirkpatrick and Locke; Yukl, Ch. 10; J. G. Hunt and G. E. Dodge, "Management in Organizations," *Handbook of Psychology* (Washington, DC: American Psychological Association, in press).

[14] This section is based on Fred E. Fiedler and Martin M. Chemers, *The Leader Match Concept,* 2nd ed. (New York: Wiley, 1984).

[15] This discussion of cognitive resource theory is based on Fred E. Fiedler and Joseph E. Garcia, *New Approaches to Effective Leadership* (New York: Wiley, 1987).

[16] See L. H. Peters, D. D. Harke, and J. T. Pohlmann, "Fiedler's Contingency Theory of Leadership: An Application of the Meta-analysis Procedures of Schmidt and Hunter," *Psychological Bulletin,* Vol. 97 (1985), pp. 274–285.

[17] Yukl, op. cit.

[18] F. E. Fiedler, M. M. Chemers, and L. Mahar, *Improving Leadership Effectiveness: The Leader Match Concept,* 2nd ed. (New York: Wiley, 1984).

[19] For documentation, see Fred E. Fiedler and Linda Mahar, "The Effectiveness of Contingency Model Training: A Review of the Validation of Leader Match," *Personnel Psychology* (Spring 1979), pp. 45–62; Fred E. Garcia, Cecil H. Bell, Martin M. Chemers, and Dennis Patrick, "Increasing Mine Productivity and Safety through Management Training and Organization Development: A Comparative Study," *Basic and Applied Social Psychology* (March 1984), pp. 1–18; Arthur G. Jago and James W.Ragan, "The Trouble with Leader Match Is that It Doesn't Match Fiedler's Contingency Model," *Journal of Applied Psychology* (November 1986), pp. 555–559.

[20] See Yukl, op. cit.; R. Ayman, M. M. Chemers, and F. E. Fiedler, "The Contingency Model of Leadership Effectiveness: Its Levels of Analysis," *Leadership Quarterly*, Vol. 6 (Summer 1995), pp. 147–168.

[21] This section is based on Robert J. House and Terence R. Mitchell, "Path-Goal Theory of Leadership," *Journal of Contemporary Business* (Autumn 1977), pp. 81–97.

[22] House and Mitchell, op. cit.

[23] C. A. Schriesheim and L. L. Neider, "Path-Goal Theory: The Long and Winding Road," *Leadership Quarterly*, Vol. 7 (1996) pp. 317–321; M. G. Evans, "Commentary on R. J. House's Path-Goal Theory of Leader Effectiveness," *Leadership Quarterly*, Vol. 7 (1996), pp. 305–309.

[24] R. J. House, "Path-Goal Theory of Leadership: Lessons, Legacy, and a Reformulated Theory," *Leadership Quarterly*, Vol. 7 (1996) pp. 323–352.

[25] See the discussion of this approach in Paul Hersey and Kenneth H. Blanchard, *Management of Organizational Behavior* (Englewood Cliffs, NJ: Prentice-Hall, 1988).

[26] R. P. Vecchio and C. Fernandez, "Situational Leadership Theory Revisited," in M. Schnake (ed.), *1995 Southern Management Association Proceedings* (Valdosta, GA: Georgia Southern University 1995), pp. 137–139; Claude L. Graeff, "Evolution of Situational Leadership Theory: A Critical Review," *Leadership Quarterly*, Vol. 8 (1977), pp. 153–170.

[27] See T. R. Mitchell, S. G. Green, and R. E. Wood, "An Attributional Model of Leadership and the Poor Performing Subordinate: Development and Validation," in L. L. Cummings and B. M. Staw (eds.), *Research in Organizational Behavior*, Vol. 3 (Greenwich, CT: JAI Press, 1981), pp. 197–234.

[28] James G. Hunt, Kimberly B. Boal, and Ritch L. Sorenson, "Top Management Leadership: Inside the Black Box," *Leadership Quarterly*, Vol. 1 (1990), pp. 41–65.

[29] C. R. Gerstner and D. B. Day, "Cross-cultural Comparison of Leadership Prototypes," *Leadership Quarterly*, Vol. 5 (1994), pp. 121–134.

[30] Hunt, Boal, and Sorenson, op. cit.

[31] See J. Pfeffer, "Management as Symbolic Action: The Creation and Maintenance of Organizational Paradigms," in L. L. Cummings and B. M. Staw (eds.), *Research in Organizational Behavior*, Vol. 3 (Greenwich, CT: JAI Press, 1981), pp. 1–52.

[32] James R. Meindl, "On Leadership: An Alternative to the Conventional Wisdom," in B. M. Staw and L. L. Cummings (eds.), *Research in Organizational Behavior*, Vol. 12 (Greenwich, CT: JAI Press, 1990), pp. 159–203.

[33] Compare with Bryman; also see James G. Hunt and Jay A. (eds.), Special issue, Part 1, *Leadership Quarterly*, Vol. 10, No. 2 (in press), entire issue.

[34] See R. J. House, "A 1976 Theory of Charismatic Leadership," in J. G. Hunt and L. L. Larson (eds.), *Leadership: The Cutting Edge* (Carbondale, IL: Southern Illinois University Press, 1977), pp. 189–207.

[35] R. J. House, W. D. Spangler, and J. Woycke, "Personality and Charisma in the U. S. Presidency," *Administrative Science Quarterly*, Vol. 36 (1991), pp. 364–396.

[36] R. Pillai and E. A. Williams, "Does Leadership Matter in the Political Arena? Voter Perceptions of Candidates Transformational and Charismatic, Leadership and the 1996 U.S. Presidential Vote," *Leadership Quarterly*, Vol. 9 (1998), pp. 397–416.

[37] See Jane M. Howell and Bruce J. Avolio, "The Ethics of Charismatic Leadership: Submission or Liberation," *Academy of Management Executive*, Vol. 6 (May 1992) pp. 43–54.

[38] Jay Conger and Rabindra N. Kanungo, *Charismatic Leadership in Organizations* (San Francisco: Jossey-Bass, 1998).

[39] Conger and Kanungo, op. cit.

[40] B. Shamir, "Social Distance and Charisma: Theoretical Notes and an Exploratory Study," *Leadership Quarterly*, Vol. 6 (Spring 1995), pp. 19–48.

[41] See B. M. Bass, *Leadership and Performance Beyond Expectations* (New York: Free Press, 1985); A. Bryman, *Charisma and Leadership in Organizations* (London: Sage Publications, 1992), pp. 98–99.

[42] B. M. Bass, *A New Paradigm of Leadership* (Alexandria, VA: U.S Army Research Institute for the Behavioral and Social Sciences, 1996).

[43] Bryman, op. cit., Ch. 6; B. M. Bass and B. J. Avolio, "Transformational Leadership: A Response to Critics," in M. M. Chemers and R. Ayman (eds.), *Leadership Theory and Practice: Perspectives and Directions* (San Diego, CA: Academic Press, 1993), pp. 49–80; Kevin B. Lowe, K. Galen Kroeck, and Nagaraj Sivasubramanium, "Effectiveness Correlates of Transformational and Transactional Leadership: A Meta-Analytic Review of the MLQ Literature," *Leadership Quarterly*, Vol 7 (1996), pp. 385–426.

[44] Bass, *New Paradigm*; Bass and Avolio, op. cit.

[45] See Jay A. Conger and Rabindra N. Kanungo, "Training Charismatic Leadership: A Risky and Critical Task," in Jay A. Conger, Rabindra N. Kanungo, and Associates (eds.), *Charismatic Leadership: The Elusive Factor in Organizational Effectiveness* (San Francisco: Jossey-Bass, 1988), Ch. 11.

[46] See J. R. Kouzes and B. F. Posner, *The Leadership Challenge: How to Get Extraordinary Things Done in Organizations* (San Francisco: Jossey-Bass, 1991).

[47] Marshall Sashkin, "The Visionary Leader," in Conger and Kanungo, *Charismatic Leadership: The Elusive Factor in Organizational Effectiveness*, Ch 5.

[48] See Bradley L. Kirman, Kevin B. Lowe and Dianne P. Young, "The Challenge in High Performance Organizations," *The Journal of Leadership Studies*, Vol. 5, No. 2 (1998), pp. 3–15.

[49] Charles C. Manz and Henry P. Sims, Jr., "Leading Teams to Lead Themselves: The External Leadership of Self-Managed Work Teams," *Administrative Science Quarterly*, Vol. 32 (1987), pp. 106–128; Susan G. Cohen, Lei Chang, and Gerald E. Ledford, Jr., "A Hierarchical Construct of Self-Management leadership and Its Relation to Quality of Work Life and Perceived Work Group Effectiveness," *Personnel Psychology*, Vol. 50 (1997), pp. 275–308.

[50] Manz and Sims, op. cit.

[51] Cohen, Chang, and Ledford, op. cit.

Source Notes

Information from Chuck Salter, "Progressive Makes Big Claims," *Fast Company*, (November 1998), 176–194.

Information from Robert Lamme, "Medicine Man," *Sky* (October 1997), pp. 133–136.

Information from Eryn Brown, "America's Most Admired Companies," *Fortune* (March 1, 1999), pp. 68–73.

Information from Burk Uzzle, "John Deere Runs on Chaos," *Fast Company* (November 1998), p. 173.

Delphi Packers Electric Systems, Brookhaven facility, "Summary Manager's Network Information Packet" (Lubbock, TX: Center for Productivity and Quality of Work Life, Texas Tech University, May 1995).

Robert B. Reich, "The Company of the Future," *Fast Company* (November 1988), pp. 124ff.

David Tarrant, "High Profile: Jack Lowe, Jr.", *Dallas Morning News* (February 21, 1999), pp. E 1–3.

Based on information from Robert J. House and Ram Aditya, "The Social Scientific Study of Leadership: Quo Vadis?" *Journal of Management*, Vol. 23 (1997), pp. 409–474; Shelley A. Kirkpatrick and Edwin A. Locke, "Leadership:

Do Traits Matter?" *The Executive*, Vol. 5, No. 2 (1991), pp. 48–60; Gary Yukl, *Leadership in Organizations* (Upper Saddle River, NJ: Prentice Hall, 1998), Ch. 10.

Adapted from Richard N. Osborn, James G. Hunt, and Lawrence R. Jauch, *Organizational Theory: An Integrated Approach* (New York: Wiley, 1980), p. 464.

From Paul Hersey and Kenneth H. Blanchard, *Management of Organizational Behavior* (Prentice-Hall, Englewood Cliffs, NJ, 1988), p. 171. Used by permission.

Based on Steven Kerr and John Jermier, "Substitutes for Leadership: Their Meaning and Measurement," *Organizational Behavior and Human Performance*, Vol. 22 (1978), p. 387; and Fred Luthans, *Organizational Behavior*, 6th ed. (New York: McGraw-Hill, 1992), Ch. 10.

Based on Boas Shamir, "Social Distance and Charisma: Theoretical Notes and an Exploratory Study," *The Leadership Quarterly*, Vol. 6 (1995), pp. 19–48.

Information from Charles C. Manz and Henry P. Sims, "Leading Workers to Lead Themselves: The External Leadership of Self-Managed Work Teams," *Administrative Science Quarterly*, Vol. 32 (1987), pp. 106–128; and Susan G. Cohen, Lei Chang, and Gerald E. Ledford, Jr., "A Hierarchical Construct of Self-Management Leadership and Its Relationship to Quality of Work Life and Perceived Work Group Effectiveness," *Personal Psychology*, Vol. 50 (1997), pp. 275–308.

■ CHAPTER 15

Footnotes

[1] See "Microsoft and the Browser Wars," *Seattle Times* (November 18, 1998), pp. C1-3; "ASAP Interview with Bill Gates," *Forbes ASAP* (1992), p. 84; "Identity Crises," *Forbes Magazine* (May 25, 1992), p. 82; "Microsoft Aims Its Arsenal at Networking," *Business Week* (October 12, 1992), pp. 88–89; "The PTC and Microsoft," *Business Week* (December 28, 1992), p. 30; "The PC Wars Are Sweeping into Software," *Business Week* (July 13, 1992), p. 132.

[2] We would like to thank Janice M. Feldbauer, Michal Cakrt, Judy Nixon, and Romuald Stone for their comments on the organization of this chapter and the emphasis on a managerial view of power.

[3] Rosabeth Moss Kanter, "Power Failure in Management Circuit," *Harvard Business Review* (July/August 1979): 65–75.

[4] John R. P. French and Bertram Raven, "The Bases of Social Power," in Dorwin Cartwright (ed.), *Group Dynamics: Research and Theory* (Evanston, IL: Row, Peterson, 1962), pp. 607–623.

[5] See French and Raven (1962).

[6] John P. Kotter, "Power, Success, and Organizational Effectiveness," *Organizational Dynamics* 6 (Winter 1978): 27; David A. Whetten and Kim S. Cameron, *Developing Managerial Skills* (Glenview, IL: Scott, Foresman, 1984), pp. 250–259.

[7] David Kipinis, Stuart M. Schmidt, Chris Swaffin-Smith, and Ian Wilkinson, "Patterns of Managerial Influence: Shotgun Managers, Tacticians, and Bystanders," *Organizational Dynamics* 12 (Winter 1984): 60, 61.

[8] Ibid., pp. 58–67; David Kipinis, Stuart M. Schmidt, and Ian Wilkinson, "Intraorganizational Influence Tactics: Explorations in Getting One's Way," *Journal of Applied Psychology* 65 (1980): 440–452.

[9] Warren K. Schilit and Edwin A. Locke, "A Study of Upward Influence in Organizations," *Administrative Science Quarterly*, 27 (1982): 304–316.

[10] Ibid.

[11] Stanley Milgram, "Behavioral Study of Obedience," in Dennis W. Organ (ed.), *The Applied Psychology of Work Behavior* (Dallas: Business Publications, 1978), pp. 384–398. Also see Stanley Milgram, "Behavioral Study of Obedience," *Journal of Abnormal and Social Psychology* 67 (1963): 371–378; Stanley Milgram, "Group Pressure and Action Against a Person," *Journal of Abnormal and Social Psychology* 69 (1964): 137–143; "Some Conditions of Obedience and Disobedience to Authority," *Human Relations* 1 (1965): 57–76; Stanley Milgram, *Obedience to Authority* (New York: Harper & Row, 1974).

[12] Chester Barnard, *The Functions of the Executive* (Cambridge, MA: Harvard University Press, 1938).

[13] Ibid.

[14] See Steven N. Brenner and Earl A. Mollander, "Is the Ethics of Business Changing?" *Harvard Business Review* 55 (February 1977): 57–71; Barry Z. Posner and Warren H. Schmidt, "Values and the American Manager: An Update," *California Management Review* 26 (Spring 1984): 202–216.

[15] Although the work on organizational politics is not extensive, useful reviews include a chapter in Robert H. Miles, *Macro Organizational Behavior* (Santa Monica, CA: Goodyear, 1980); Bronston T. Mayes and Robert W. Allen, "Toward a Definition of Organizational Politics," *Academy of Management Review* 2 (1977): 672–677; Gerald F. Cavanagh, Dennis J. Moberg, and Manuel Velasquez, "The Ethics of Organizational Politics," *Academy of Management Review* 6 (July 1981): 363–374; Dan Farrell and James C. Petersen, "Patterns of Political Behavior in Organizations," *Academy of Management Review* 7 (July 1982): 403–412; D. L. Madison, R. W. Allen, L. W. Porter, and B. T. Mayes, "Organizational Politics: An Exploration of Managers' Perceptions," *Human Relations* 33 (1980): 92–107.

[16] Mayes and Allen, "Toward a Definition of Organizational Politics," p. 675.

[17] Jeffrey Pfeffer, *Power in Organizations* (Marshfield, MA: Pitman, 1981), p. 7.

[18] Michael Sconcolfi, Anita Raghavan, and Mitchell Pacelle, "All Bets Are Off: How the Salesmanship and Brainpower Failed at Long Term Capital," *Wall Street Journal* (November 16, 1998), p. 1, 18–19.

[19] B. E. Ashforth and R. T. Lee, "Defensive Behavior in Organizations: A Preliminary Model," *Human Relations* (July 1990): 621–648; personal communication with Blake Ashforth, December 1998.

[20] See Pfeffer (1981); M. M. Harmon and R. T. Mayer, *Organization Theory for Public Administration* (Boston: Little, Brown, 1986); W. Richard Scott, *Organizations: Rational, Natural and Open Systems* (Englewood Cliffs, NJ: Prentice-Hall, 1987).

[21] Developed from James L. Hall and Joel L. Leldecker, "A Review of Vertical and Lateral Relations: A New Perspective for Managers," in Patrick Connor (ed.), *Dimensions in Modern Management*, 3rd ed. (Boston: Houghton Mifflin, 1982), pp. 138–146, which was based in part on Leonard Sayles, *Managerial Behavior* (New York: McGraw-Hill, 1964).

[22] See Jeffrey Pfeffer, *Organizations and Organization Theory* (Boston: Pitman, 1983); Jeffrey Pfeffer and Gerald R. Salancik, *The External Control of Organizations* (Englewood Cliffs, NJ: Prentice-Hall, 1978).

[23] R. N. Osborn, "A Comparison of CEO Pay in Western Europe, Japan and the U.S.," working paper (Detroit: Department of Management, Wayne State University, 1998).

[24] See the early work of James D. Thompson, *Organizations in Action* (New York: McGraw-Hill, 1967) and more recent studies by R. N. Osborn and D. H. Jackson, "Leaders, Riverboat Gamblers, or Purposeful Unintended Consequences in Management of Complex Technologies," *Academy of Management Journal* 31 (1988): 924–947; M. Hector, "When Actors Comply: Monitoring Costs and the Production of Social Order," *Acta Sociologica* 27 (1984): 161–183; T. Mitchell and W. G. Scott, "Leadership Failures, the Distrusting Public and Prospects for the Administrative State," *Public Administration Review* 47 (1987): 445–452.

[25] J. J. Jones, *The Downsizing of American Potential* (New York: Raymond Press, 1996).

[26] This discussion is based on Cavanagh, Moberg, and Velasquez (1981); and Manuel Velasquez, Dennis J. Moberg, and Gerald Cavanagh, "Organizational Statesmanship and Dirty Politics: Ethical Guidelines for the Organizational Politician," *Organizational Dynamics* 11 (1983): 65–79, both of which offer a fine treatment of the ethics of power and politics.

Source Notes

Linda Corman, "As Good as It Gets: The 1998 Compensation Survey," *CFO* (November 1998), pp. 41–54.

www.catalinamktg.com.

Based on information in John Lornic, "Managing When There Is No Middle," *Canadian Business* (June 1996), pp. 86–89, 94.

Littlecaesars.com; "New Ex Takes Reins at Hospice," *Detroit News* (October 25, 1998), p. C-l.

■ CHAPTER 16

Footnotes

[1] Information and quotes from Sue Shellenbarger, "More Managers Find a Happy Staff Leads to Happy Customers," *Wall Street Journal* (December 28, 1998), p. B1; and Robert D. Hoff, "Sun Power: Is the Center of the Computing Universe Changing?" *Business Week* (January 18, 1999).

[2] Bill Gates, "Bill Gates' New Rules," *Time* (March 22, 1999), pp. 72–84. This is an excerpt from Bill Gates, *The Speed of Thought: Using a Digital Nervous System* (New York: Warner Books, 1999). See Henry Mintzberg, *The Nature of Managerial Work* (New York: Harper & Row, 1973); Morgan W. McCall, Jr., Ann M. Morrison, and Robert L. Hannan, *Studies of Managerial Work: Results and Methods, Technical Report No. 9* (Greensboro, NC: Center for Creative Leadership, 1978); and John P. Kotter, *The General Managers* (New York: Free Press, 1982).

[3] Lucent Technologies, *1998 Annual Report*.

[4] Steve Axley, author of *Communication at Work: Management and the Communication-Intensive Organization* (Westport, CT: Quorum Books, 1996), points out that the ultimate meaning in any communication is created by the receiver or perceiver of the message.

[5] Information from "Cool Company," *Fortune* (February 15, 1999), p. 149.

[6] Developed from J. Stephen Morris, "How to Make Criticism Sessions Productive," *Wall Street Journal* (October 12, 1981), p. 24.

[7] See Axelrod (1996).

[8] See Richard L. Birdwhistell, *Kinesics and Context* (Philadelphia: University of Pennsylvania Press, 1970).

[9] Edward T. Hall, *The Hidden Dimension* (Garden City, NY: Doubleday, 1966).

[10] See D. E. Campbell, "Interior Office Design and Visitor Response," *Journal of Applied Psychology* 64 (1979): 648–653; P. C. Morrow and J. C. McElroy, "Interior Office Design and Visitor Response: A Constructive Replication," *Journal of Applied Psychology* 66 (1981): 646–650.

[11] M. P. Rowe and M. Baker, "Are You Hearing Enough Employee Concerns?" *Harvard Business Review* 62 (May/June 1984): 127–135.

[12] This discussion is based on Carl R. Rogers and Richard E. Farson, "Active Listening" (Chicago: Relations Center of the University of Chicago).

[13] Modified from an example in ibid.

[14] Richard V. Farace, Peter R. Monge, and Hamish M. Russell, *Communicating and Organizing* (Reading, MA: Addison-Wesley, 1977), pp. 97–98.

[15] The statements are from *Business Week* (July 6, 1981), p. 107.

[16] See A. Mehrabian, *Silent Messages* (Belmont, CA: Wadsworth, 1981).

[17] Information from "How Not to Do International Business," *Business Week* (April 12, 1999).

[18] See C. Barnum and N. Woliansky, "Taking Cues from Body Language," *Management Review* 78 (1989): 59; S. Bochner (ed.), *Cultures in Contact: Studies in Cross-Cultural Interaction* (London: Pergamon, 1982); A. Furnham and S. Bocher, *Culture Shock: Psychological Reactions to Unfamiliar Environments* (London: Methuen, 1986).

[19] This research is reviewed by John C. Athanassiades, "The Distortion of Upward Communication in Hierarchical Organizations," *Academy of Management Journal* 16 (June 1973): 207–226.

[20] F. Lee, "Being Polite and Keeping MUM: How Bad News is Communicated in Organizational Hierarchies," *Journal of Applied Social Psychology* 23 (1993): 1124–1149.

[21] Thomas J. Peters and Robert H. Waterman, Jr., *In Search of Excellence* (New York: Harper & Row, 1983).

[22] Portions of this section are adapted from John R. Schermerhorn, Jr.,

Management, 5th ed. (New York: Wiley, 1996), pp. 375–378. Used by permission.

[23] Networking is considered an essential managerial activity by Kotter (1982).

[24] Peters and Waterman (1983).

[25] Information from Amy Joyce, "Latest Office Design Tapping into Benefits of Going 'Casual,'" *Columbus Dispatch* (November 30, 1998), p. 7.

[26] *Business Week* (May 16, 1994), p. 8.

[27] The concept of interacting, coacting, and counteracting groups is presented in Fred E. Fiedler, *A Theory of Leadership Productivity* (New York: McGraw-Hill, 1967).

[28] Research on communication networks is found in Alex Bavelas, "Communication Patterns in Task-Oriented Groups," *Journal of the Acoustical Society of America* 22 (1950): 725–730. See also "Research on Communication Networks," as summarized in Marvin E. Shaw, *Group Dynamics: The Psychology of Small Group Behavior* (New York: McGraw-Hill, 1976), pp. 137–153.

[29] See "e.Biz: What Every CEO Should Know about Electronic Business," *Business Week*, Special Report (March 22, 1999).

[30] See C. Brod, *Technostress: The Human Cost of the Computer Revolution* (Reading, MA: Addison-Wesley, 1984); and G. Brockhouse, "I Have Seen the Future…," *Canadian Business* (August 1993): 43–45.

[31] Deborah Tannen, *Talking 9 to 5* (New York: Avon, 1995).

[32] Deborah Tannen, *You Just Don't Understand: Women and Men in Conversation* (New York: Ballantine Books, 1991).

[33] Deborah Tannen, "The Power of Talk: Who Gets Heard and Why," *Harvard Business Review* (September–October, 1995): 138–148.

[34] Reported by *Working Woman* (November 1995), p. 14.

[35] Ibid.

[36] For an editorial opinion, see Jayne Tear, "They Just Don't Understand Gender Dynamics," *Wall Street Journal* (November 20, 1995), p. A14.

[37] Information from Hal Lancaster, "Performance Reviews: Some Bosses Try a Fresh Approach," *Wall Street Journal* (December 1, 1998), p. B1.

[38] See "My Boss, Big Brother," *Business Week* (January 22, 1996), p. 56.

Source Notes

Eryn Brown, "VF Corp. Changes its Underware," *Fortune* (December 7, 1998), pp. 115–118; and "Stitching Together an E-Corporation," *Fortune* (December 7, 1998), p. 117.

Monsanto: Information from Timothy D. Schellhardt, "Monsanto Best on Box Buddies," *Wall Street Journal* (February 23, 1999), p. B1.

UAL: Information from "UAL: Labor Is My Co-Pilot," *Business Week* (March 1, 1999), p. 38.

American Express: New information from "The Rise of a Star," *Business Week* (December 21, 1998), pp. 60–68.

John R. Schermerhorn, Jr., *Management*, 5th ed. (New York: Wiley, 1996), p. 377. Used by permission.

■ CHAPTER 17

Footnotes

[1] Information from Seth Lubove, "Salad in a Bag," *Forbes* (October 23, 1995): 201–203.

[2] For concise overviews, see Susan J. Miller, David J. Hickson, and David C. Wilson, "Decision-Making in Organizations," in Stewart R. Clegg, Cynthia Hardy, and Walter R. Nord (eds.), *Handbook of Organizational Studies* (London: Sage Publications, 1996), pp. 293–312; George P. Huber, *Managerial Decision Making* (Glenview, IL: Scott, Foresman, 1980).

[3] This section is based on Michael D. Choen, James G. March, and Johan P. Olsen, "The Garbage Can Model of Organizational Choice," *Administrative Science Quarterly* 17 (1972): 1–25 and James G. March and Herbert A. Simon, *Organizations* (New York: Wiley, 1958), pp. 137–142.

[4] This traditional distinction is often attributed to Herbert Simon,

Administrative Behavior (New York: Free Press, 1945), but an available source is Herbert Simon, *The New Science of Management Decision* (New York: Harper & Row, 1960).

5 Ibid.

6 Also see Mary Zey (ed.), *Decision Making: Alternatives to Rational Choice Models* (Thousand Oaks, CA: Sage Publications, 1992).

7 Simon, *Administrative Behavior.*

8 For discussions, see Cohen, March, and Olsen (1972); Miller, Hickson, and Wilson (1996); and Michael Masuch and Perry LaPontin, "Beyond Garbage Cans: An AI Model of Organizational Choice," *Administrative Science Quarterly* 34 (1989): 38–67.

9 Weston H. Agor, *Intuition in Organizations* (Newbury Park, CA: Sage Publications, 1989).

10 Henry Mintzberg, "Planning on the Left Side and Managing on the Right," *Harvard Business Review* 54 (July/August 1976): 51–63.

11 See Weston H. Agor, "How Top Executives Use Their Intuition to Make Important Decisions," *Business Horizons* 29 (January/February 1986): 49–53; and Agor (1989).

12 The classic work in this area is found in a series of articles by D. Kahneman and A. Tversky, "Subjective Probability: A Judgement of Representativeness," *Cognitive Psychology* 3 (1972): 430–454; "On the Psychology of Prediction," *Psychological Review* 80 (1973): 237–251; "Prospect Theory: An Analysis of Decision under Risk," *Econometrica* 47 (1979): 263–291; "Psychology of Preferences," *Scientific American* (1982): 161–173; "Choices, Values, Frames" *American Psychologist* 39 (1984): 341–350.

13 Definitions and subsequent discussion based on Max H. Bazerman, *Judgement in Managerial Decision Making*, 3rd ed. (New York: Wiley, 1994).

14 Cameron M. Ford and Dennis A. Gioia, *Creative Action in Organizations* (Thousand Oaks, CA: Sage Publications, 1995).

15 G. Wallas, *The Art of Thought* (New York: Harcourt, 1926). Cited in Bazerman (1994).

16 E. Glassman, "Creative Problem Solving," *Supervisory Management* (January 1989): 21–26; and B. Kabanoff and J. R. Rossiter, "Recent Developments in Applied Creativity," *International Review of Industrial and Organizational Psychology* 9 (1994): 283–324.

17 Information from Kenneth Labich, "Nike vs. Reebok," *Fortune* (September 18, 1995), pp. 90–106.

18 James A. F. Stoner, *Management*, 2nd ed. (Englewood Cliffs, NJ: Prentice-Hall, 1982), pp. 167–168.

19 Victor H. Vroom and Philip W. Yetton, *Leadership and Decision Making* (Pittsburgh: University of Pittsburgh Press, 1973); Victor H. Vroom and Arthur G. Jago, *The New Leadership* (Englewood Cliffs, NJ: Prentice-Hall, 1988).

20 Barry M. Staw, "The Escalation of Commitment to a Course of Action," *Academy of Management Review* 6 (1981): 577–587; Barry M. Staw and Jerry Ross, "Knowing When to Pull the Plug," *Harvard Business Review* 65 (March/April 1987): 68–74. See also Glen Whyte, "Escalating Commitment to a Course of Action: A Reinterpretation," *Academy of Management Review* 11 (1986): 311–321.

21 Joel Brockner, "The Escalation of Commitment to a Failing Course of Action: Toward Theoretical Progress," *Academy of Management Review* 17 (1992): 39–61; J. Ross and B. M. Staw, "Organizational Escalation and Exit: Lessons from the Shoreham Nuclear Power Plant," *Academy of Management Journal* 36 (1993): 701–732.

22 Bazerman (1994), pp. 79–83.

23 See Brockner (1992); Ross and Staw (1993); and J. Z. Rubin, "Negotiation: An Introduction to Some Issues and Themes," *American Behavioral Scientist* 27 (1983): 135–147.

24 See "Computers That Think Are Almost Here," *Business Week* (July 17, 1995): 68–73.

25 A. R. Dinnis and J. S. Valacich, "Computer Brainstorms: Two Heads Are Better Than One," *Journal of Applied Psychology* (February 1994): 77–86.

26 For an expanded discussion of such ethical frameworks for decision making, see Linda A. Travino and Katherine A. Nelson, *Managing Business Ethics* (New York: Wiley, 1995).

27 B. Kabanoff and J. R. Rossiter, "Recent Developments in Applied Creativity," *International Review of Industrial and Organizational Psychology* 9 (1994): 283–324.

28 Fons Trompenaars, *Riding the Waves of Culture: Understanding Cultural Diversity in Business* (London: Nicholas Brealey Publishing, 1993), p. 6.

29 See ibid., pp. 58–59.

30 For a good discussion of decision making in Japanese organizations, see Min Chen, *Asian Management Systems* (New York: Routledge, 1995).

31 Nancy J. Adler, *International Dimensions of Organizational Behavior*, 2nd ed. (Boston: PWS-Kent, 1991).

32 See Miller, Hickson, and Wilson (1996).

33 We would like to thank Kristi M. Lewis for emphasizing the importance of identifying criteria and weighing criteria and urging us to include this section on ethics.

34 Stephen Fineman, "Emotion and Organizing," in Clegg, Hardy, and Nord *Handbook of Organizational Studies*, pp. 542–580.

35 For an expanded discussion of ethical frameworks for decision making, see Linda A. Travino and Katherine A. Nelson, *Managing Business Ethics* (New York: Wiley, 1995); Saul W. Gellerman, "Why 'Good' Managers Make Bad Ethical Choices," *Harvard Business Review* 64 (July/August 1986): 85–90 and Barbara Ley Toffler, *Tough Choices: Managers Talk Ethics* (New York: Wiley, 1986).

Source Notes
PNCBank.com.

PNCBank.com/whoarewe/corpinfo/officers.html.

Nokia Annual Report, 1997, p. 22.

"The Brain Behind the Brain," *Business Week* (July 17, 1995), p. 71.

Analog.com/publications/DSP; Otis Port and Paul C. Judge, "Chips That Mimic the Human Senses," *Business Week* (November 30, 1998), pp. 158–159.

Information from Mary Scott, "Odwalla, Inc.," *Business Ethics* (November/December 1995), p. 35.

Reprinted from Victor H. Vroom and Arthur G. Jago, *The New Leadership* (Englewood Cliffs, NJ: Prentice-Hall, 1988), p. 184. Used by permission of the authors.

■ CHAPTER 18

Footnotes
1 Information from "From 'Blank Looks' to Blank Checks," *Business Week Enterprise* (December 7, 1998), pp. Ent 18–20.

2 See, for example, Henry Mintzberg, *The Nature of Managerial Work* (New York: Harper & Row, 1973); and John R.P. Kotter, *The General Managers* (New York: Free Press, 1982).

3 One of the classic discussions is by Richard E. Walton, *Interpersonal Peacemaking: Confrontations and Third-Party Consultation* (Reading, MA: Addison-Wesley, 1969).

4 Kenneth W. Thomas and Warren H. Schmidt, "A Survey of Managerial Interests with Respect to Conflict," *Academy of Management Journal* 19 (1976): 315–318.

5 For a good overview see Richard E. Walton, *Managing Conflict: Interpersonal Dialogue and Third Party Roles*, 2nd ed. (Reading, MA: Addison-Wesley, 1987) and Dean Tjosvold, *The Conflict-Positive Organization: Stimulate Diversity and Create Unity* (Reading, MA: Addison-Wesley, 1991).

6 Walton (1969).

7 Ibid.

8 Richard E. Walton and John M. Dutton, "The Management of

Interdepartmental Conflict: A Model and Review," *Administrative Science Quarterly* 14 (1969): 73–84.

[9] Information from Richard Gibson, "Starbucks Plans to Test a Paper Cup That Insulates Hands from Hot Coffee," *Wall Street Journal* (February 22, 1999), p. B17.

[10] Douglas Lavin, "Chrysler's Stallkamp Gets Suppliers to Help Cut Costs," *Asian Wall Street Journal* (May 17, 1993), p. 9.

[10] Geert Hofstede, *Culture's Consequences: International Differences in Work-Related Values* (Beverly Hills, CA: Sage Publications, 1980) and Geert Hofstede, "Cultural Constraints in Management Theories," *Academy of Management Executive* 7 (1993): 81–94.

[11] These stages are consistent with the conflict models described by Alan C. Filley, *Interpersonal Conflict Resolution* (Glenview, IL: Scott, Foresman, 1975); and Louis R. Pondy, "Organizational Conflict: Concepts and Models," *Administrative Science Quarterly* 12 (September 1967): 269–320.

[12] Information from "Capitalizing on Diversity: Navigating the Seas of the Multicultural Workforce and Workplace," *Business Week*, Special Advertising Section (December 4, 1998).

[13] Walton and Dutton (1969).

[14] Rensis Likert and Jane B. Likert, *New Ways of Managing Conflict* (New York: McGraw-Hill, 1976).

[15] Information from Robert L. Simison, "Ford Roles Out a New Model of Corporate Culture," *Wall Street Journal* (January 13, 1999), p. B1.

[16] See Jay Galbraith, *Designing Complex Organizations* (Reading, MA: Addison-Wesley, 1973); David Nadler and Michael Tushman, *Strategic Organizational Design* (Glenview, IL: Scott, Foresman, 1988).

[17] E. M. Eisenberg and M. G. Witten, "Reconsidering Openness in Organizational Communication," *Academy of Management Review* 12 (1987): 418–426.

[18] R. G. Lord and M. C. Kernan, "Scripts as Determinants of Purposeful Behavior in Organizations," *Academy of Management Review* 12 (1987): 265–277.

[19] See Filley (1975); and L. David Brown, *Managing Conflict at Organizational Interfaces* (Reading, MA: Addison-Wesley, 1983).

[20] Ibid., pp. 27, 29.

[21] For discussions, see Robert R. Blake and Jane Strygley Mouton, "The Fifth Achievement," *Journal of Applied Behavioral Science* 6 (1970): 413–427; Kenneth Thomas, "Conflict and Conflict Management," in M. D. Dunnett (ed.), *Handbook of Industrial and Organizational Behavior* (Chicago: Rand McNally, 1976), pp. 889–935; and Kenneth W. Thomas, "Toward Multi-Dimensional Values in Teaching: The Examples of Conflict Behaviors," *Academy of Management Review* 2 (1977): 484–490.

[22] For an excellent overview, see Roger Fisher and William Ury, *Getting to Yes: Negotiating Agreement Without Giving In* (New York: Penguin, 1983). See also James A. Wall, Jr., Negotiation: Theory and Practice (Glenview, IL: Scott, Foresman, 1985).

[23] Roy J. Lewicki and Joseph A. Litterer, *Negotiation* (Homewood, IL: Irwin, 1985), pp. 315–319.

[24] Ibid., pp. 328–329.

[25] For a good discussion, see Michael H. Bond, *Behind the Chinese Face* (London: Oxford University Press, 1991); and Richard D. Lewis, *When Cultures Collide*, Chapter 23 (London: Nicholas Brealey Publishing, 1996).

[26] Following discussion based on Fisher and Ury (1983); and Lewicki and Litterer, (1985).

[27] This example is developed from Max H. Bazerman, *Judgment in Managerial Decision Making*, 2nd ed. (New York: Wiley, 1991), pp. 106–108.

[28] For a detailed discussion, see Fisher and Ury (1983), and Lewicki and Litterer (1985).

[29] Developed from Bazerman (1991), pp. 127–141.

[30] Fisher and Ury (1983), p. 33.

[31] Lewicki and Litterer (1985), pp. 177–181.

Source Notes

John R. Schermerhorn, Jr., *Management*, 6th ed. (New York: Wiley, 199), p. 341. Used by permission.

Honda Motors: Information from "Capitalizing on Diversity: Navigating the Seas of the Multicultural Workforce and Workplace," *Business Week*, Special Advertising Section (December 4, 1998).

Sun Microsystems: Information from Sue Shellenbarger, "More Managers Find a Happy Staff Leads to Happy Customers," *The Wall Street Journal* (December 23, 1998), p. B1.

HRM News: Information from Carol Kleiman, "Performance Review Comes 'Full Circle'," *The Columbus Dispatch* (January 31, 1999), p. 29I.

Deloitte Touche: Information from Sue Shellenbarger, "Three Myths that Make Managers Push Staff to the Edge of Burnout," *The Wall Street Journal* (March 17, 1999), pl. B1.

EEOC: Information from "Suspect Age Bias? Try Proving It," *Fortune* (February 1, 1999), p. 58.

■ CHAPTER 19

Footnotes

[1] Information from Robert Reich, "The Company of the Future," *Fast Company* (November 1998), p. 124+.

[2] See Peter F. Drucker, *Managing for the Future: The 1990s and Beyond* (New York: Truman Talley Books/Dutton, 1992); and Peter F. Drucker, *Peter Drucker on the Profession of Management* (Cambridge, MA: Harvard Business School Press, 1997).

[3] Tom Peters, *Thriving on Chaos* (New York: Random House, 1987); Tom Peters, "Managing in a World Gone Bonkers," *World Executive Digest* (February 1993), pp. 26–29; and Tom Peters, *The Circle of Innovation* (New York: Alfred A. Knopf, 1997).

[4] See David Nadler and Michael Tushman, *Strategic Organizational Design* (Glenview, IL: Scott, Foresman, 1988); and Noel M. Tichy, "Revolutionize Your Company," *Fortune* (December 13, 1993), pp. 114–118.

[5] Jay A. Conger, Edward E. Lawler III, and Gretchen M. Spreitzer (eds.), *The Leaders Change Handbook* (San Francisco: Jossey-Bass, 1999).

[6] Information from "Entrepreneurs Speak at HBS," *Harvard Business School Bulletin* (February 1999), p. 6.

[7] Rosabeth Moss Kanter, Barry A. Stein, and Todd D. Jick, "Meeting the Challenges of Change," *World Executive's Digest* (May 1993), pp. 22–27.

[8] The classic description of organizations on these terms is by Harold J. Leavitt, "Applied Organizational Change in Industry: Structural, Technological and Humanistic Approaches," in James G. March (ed.), *Handbook of Organizations* (Chicago: Rand McNally, 1965). This application is developed from Robert A. Cooke, "Managing Change in Organizations," in Gerald Zaltman (ed.), *Management Principles for Nonprofit Organizations* (New York: American Management Association, 1979). See also David A. Nadler, "The Effective Management of Organizational Change," in Jay W. Lorsch (ed.), *Handbook of Organizational Behavior* (Englewood Cliffs, NJ: Prentice-Hall, 1987), pp. 358–369.

[9] See, for example, Ralph H. Kilmann, *Beyond the Quick Fix* (San Francisco: Jossey-Bass, 1984); Noel M. Tichy and Mary Anne Devanna, *The Transformational Leader* (New York: Wiley, 1986); and Peter M. Senge, *The Fifth Discipline: The Art & Practice of the Learning Organization* (New York: Doubleday, 1990).

[10] Kurt Lewin, "Group Decision and Social Change," in G. E. Swanson, T. M. Newcomb, and E. L. Hartley (eds.), *Readings in Social Psychology* (New York: Holt, Rinehart & Winston, 1952), pp. 459–473.

[11] Tichy and Devanna (1986), p. 44.

[12] The change strategies are described in Robert Chin and Kenneth D. Benne, "General Strategies for Effecting Changes in Human Systems," in Warren G. Bennis, Kenneth D. Benne, Robert Chin, and Kenneth E. Corey (eds.), *The Planning of Change*, 3rd ed. (New York: Holt, Rinehart & Winston, 1969), pp. 22–45.

[13] Example developed from an exercise reported in J. William Pfeiffer and John E. Jones, *A Handbook of Structured Experiences for Human Relations Training*, Vol. II (La Jolla, CA: University Associates, 1973).

[14] Ibid.

[15] Ibid.

[16] Donald Klein, "Some Notes on the Dynamics of Resistance to Change: The Defender Role," in Bennis et al. (eds.), *The Planning of Change* (1969), pp. 117–124.

[17] See Everett M. Rogers, *Communication of Innovations*, 3rd ed. (New York: Free Press, 1993).

[18] Ibid.

[19] John P. Kotter and Leonard A. Schlesinger, "Choosing Strategies for Change," *Harvard Business Review*, Vol. 57 (March/April 1979), pp. 109–112.

[20] A classic work in this area is Peter F. Drucker, *Innovation and Entrepreneurship* (New York: Harper, 1985).

[21] Edward B. Roberts, "Managing Invention and Innovation," *Research Technology Management* (January/February 1988), pp. 1–19. For an extensive case study, see John Clark, *Managing Innovation and Change* (Thousand Oaks, CA: Sage Publications, 1995). For a comprehensive update on innovation in industry, see "Innovation in Industry," *The Economist* (February 20, 1999), pp. 5–18.

[22] Quotes from Kenneth Labich, "The Innovators," *Fortune* (June 6, 1988), pp. 49–64.

[23] Information from Scott Kirsner, "Designed for Innovation," *Fast Company* (November 1998), pp. 54+.

[24] Arthur P. Brief, Randall S. Schuler, and Mary Van Sell, *Managing Job Stress* (Boston: Little, Brown, 1981).

[25] A review of research is available in Steve M. Jex, *Stress and Job Performance* (Thousand Oaks, CA: Sage, 1998).

[26] "Couples Dismayed at Long Workdays, New Study Finds," *Columbus Dispatch* (January 23, 1999), p. 5A.

[27] See Orlando Behling and Arthur L. Darrow, *Managing Work-Related Stress* (Chicago: Science Research Associates, 1984).

[28] Meyer Friedman and Ray Roseman, *Type A Behavior and Your Heart* (New York: Alfred A. Knopf, 1974).

[29] See H. Selye, *The Stress of Life*, rev. ed. (New York: McGraw-Hill, 1976).

[30] Jeffrey Pfeffer, *The Human Equation: Building Profits by Putting People First* (Boston: Harvard Business School Press, 1998).

[31] Quotes are from Alan M. Webber, "Danger: Toxic Company," *Fast Company* (November 1998), p. 152.

[32] Information from organizational Web site: http://www.josephsoninstitute.org/about.htm.

[33] See John D. Adams, "Health, Stress, and the Manager's Life Style," *Group and Organization Studies*, Vol. 6 (September 1981), pp. 291–301.

[34] Robert Kreitner, "Personal Wellness: It's Just Good Business," *Business Horizons*, Vol. 25 (May/June 1982), pp. 28–35.

[35] Information from Mike Pramik, "Wellness Programs Give Businesses Healthy Bottom Line," *Columbus Dispatch* (January 18, 1999), pp. 10–11.

[36] Ibid.

[37] Pfeffer (1998).

Source Notes

John R. Schermerhorn, Jr., *management*, 4th ed. (New York: Wiley, 1999), p. 381. Used by permission.

Richard Pascale, "Change How You Define Leadership and You Change How You Run a Company," *Fast Company, The Professor Series* (Boston: Fast Company, 1998).

General Motors: Information from Craig S. Smith, "GM Seeks Ways to Boost Viability of New China Plant," *The Asian Wall Street Journal* (December 16, 1998), p. 1.

Unilever: Information from Darren McDermott and Fara Warner, "Unilever Finds Brisk Business," *The Asian Wall Street Journal* (November 20, 1998), p. 1.

Red Roof Inns: Information from Mike Pramik, "Wellness Programs Give Businesses Healthy Bottom Line," *The Columbus Dispatch* (January 18, 1999), pp. 10–11.

Lonnie Johnson: Information from Patricia J. Mays, "Gun Showers Wealth on Inventor," *The Columbus Dispatch* (January 24, 1999), p. 6B.

John R. Schermerhorn, Jr., *Management for Productivity*, 4th ed. (New York: Wiley, 1996), p. 661. Used by permission.

■ SUPPLEMENTAL MODULE

Footnotes

[1] See Richard L. Daft, "Learning the Craft of Organizational Research," *Academy of Management Review* Vol. 8 (October 1983), pp. 539–546; Eugene Stone, *Research Methods in Organizational Behavior* (Santa Monica, CA: Goodyear, 1978), p. 21.

[2] Stone, op. cit. (1978), p. 26.

[3] Stone, op. cit. (1978).

[4] C. William Emory, *Business Research Methods,* rev. ed. (Homewood, IL: Irwin, 1980).

[5] Duane Davis and Robert M. Casenza, *Business Research for Decision Making* (Belmont, CA: Wadsworth, 1993), p. 134.

[6] Davis and Casenza, op. cit. (1993), Ch. 5.

[7] Davis and Casenza, op. cit. (1993).

[8] Davis and Casenza, op. cit. (1993), p. 174.

[9] Davis and Casenza, op. cit. (1993), p. 125.

[10] This section based on Davis and Casenza, op. cit. (1993), Ch. 5.

[11] This section based on Stone, op. cit. (1978).

[12] See G. Pinchot, *Intrapreneuring* (New York: Harper, 1985).

[13] See A. D. Aczel, *Complete Business Statistics* (Homewood, IL: Irwin, 1989) for further discussion.

[14] Davis and Casenza, op. cit. (1993).

[15] Davis and Casenza, op. cit. (1993), Ch. 14.

[16] Unreferenced.

Photo Credits

Chapter 1
Page 1: ©Telegraph Color Library/FPG International. Page 4: Dennis O'Clair/Tony Stone Images/New York, Inc. Page 6: Bruce Ayres/Tony Stone Images/New York, Inc. Page 8 (top): Courtesy Trilogy Development Group, Inc. Page 8 (bottom): Courtesy Autodesk, Inc. Page 12: Courtesy Florida A&M University. Page 14: Bob Daemmrich/Stock, Boston/PNI. Page 16: Courtesy SAS Institute, Inc.

Chapter 2
Page 21: George B. Diebold/The Stock Market. Page 23: Courtesy Patricia Seybold Group. Page 26: Roy Wiemann/The Image Bank. Page 27: Courtesy Hampton Inn. Page 28: Keith Brofsky/PhotoDisc. Page 29: Mark Wagner/Tony Stone Images/New York, Inc. Page 30: Courtesy Saturn Corporation. Page 33: Larry Dale Gordon/The Image Bank.

Chapter 3
Page 39: Michael Banks/Tony Stone Images/New York, Inc. Page 41: Courtesy Yahoo. Page 43: Courtesy University of Michigan, Global Leadership Program. Page 49: Walter Hodges/Tony Stone Images/New York, Inc. Page 50: Bob Abraham/The Stock Market. Page 52: Courtesy International Orientation Resources. Page 53: Courtesy Council on Economic Priorities.

Chapter 4
Page 59: AP/Wide World Photos. Page 62: Duncan Smith/PhotoDisc. Page 63: Courtesy The Mount Sinai Hospital of Mount Sinai NYU Health Center, New York. Page 65: Courtesy Scholastic, Inc. Page 69: David Joel/Tony Stone Images/New York, Inc. Page 75: Courtesy Korean

Air. Page 77 (top): Mark Segal/Tony Stone Images/New York, Inc. Page 77 (bottom): Courtesy Coors Brewing Company.

Chapter 5
Page 83: Craig Blankenhorn/AP/Wide World Photos. Page 88: Courtesy Kevin Rubens, Aon Consulting. Page 92: Andy Whale/Tony Stone Images/New York, Inc. Page 93: AP/Wide World Photos. Page 94 (top): C/B Productions/The Stock Market. Page 94 (bottom): Courtesy Deere & Company.

Chapter 6
Page 101: Courtesy Spruceland Millwork, Inc. Page 103: Courtesy Publix Super Markets, Inc. Page 108: Bruce Ayres/Tony Stone Images/New York, Inc. Page 113: Mark Ferri/The Stock Market. Page 116: Courtesy Oglebay Norton Company. Page 119: ©Amy Kumler/Patagonia. Reproduced with permission.

Chapter 7
Page 127: Paul Barton/The Stock Market. Page 129: BARBIE is a trademark owned by Mattel, Inc. ©1999 Mattel, Inc. All rights reserved. Photos courtesy of Mattel, Inc. Page 130: Courtesy Digital Base Productions. Page 134: Peter Fisher/The Stock Market. Page 135: Courtesy America's Learning Exchange. Page 137: Courtesy CompStar.

Chapter 8
Page 153: Courtesy Peet's Coffee. Page 156: Courtesy Volvo Cars of North America. Page 159: Courtesy United Parcel Service. Page 160: ©William Waldron. Page 162: Courtesy Novell Corporation. Page 164 (top): Courtesy Xe-

rox Corporation. Page 164 (bottom): The News & Observer/Jim Bounds. Page 166: Gary Buss/FPG International. Page 168: Elyse Lewin/The Image Bank.

Chapter 9
Page 173: AP/Wide World Photos. Page 175: Gabriel Covian/The Image Bank. Page 178: Courtesy Texas Instruments. Page 179: K.C. Tanner/SUPERSTOCK. Page 182: Kaluzny/Thatcher/Tony Stone Images/New York, Inc. Page 184: Courtesy Zoological Society of San Diego. Page 185: Courtesy W.L. Gore & Associates, Inc.

Chapter 10
Page 193: Courtesy Audible, Inc. Page 195: Jean-Luc Wang/SUPERSTOCK. Page 198: Steven Peters/Tony Stone Images/New York, Inc. Page 200: Courtesy Black Enterprise. Page 207: Courtesy MCI Telecommunications Corp. Page 208: Courtesy Texas Instruments.

Chapter 11
Page 213: Stephen Derr/The Image Bank. Page 217: Courtesy Motorola. Page 225: Courtesy Electroglas, Inc. Page 229: Adam Lubroth/Tony Stone Images/New York, Inc.

Chapter 12
Page 239: John Madere/The Stock Market. Page 241: Bill Gallery/Stock, Boston. Page 247: Ralph Mercer/Tony Stone Images/New York, Inc. Page 249: Courtesy Procter & Gamble. Page 250: Firefly Productions/The Stock Market. Page 252: ©Comstock, Inc. Page 255: L. Wallach, Inc./The Image Bank.

Chapter 13
Page 263: Courtesy Cisco Systems, Inc. Page 266: Courtesy Venus Cleaners. Page 270: Christopher Morrow/Stock, Boston/Picture Network International, Ltd. Page 272: Mark Lewis/Tony Stone Images/New York, Inc. Page 274: Richard T. Nowitz/Photo Researchers. Disney characters are ©Disney Enterprises, Inc. Used by permission from Disney Enterprises, Inc. Page 275: AP/Wide World Photos.

Chapter 14
Page 285: Courtesy Progressive Corporation. Page 288: Courtesy HealthSouth. Page 290: Kenneth Gabrielsen Photography/Liaison Agency, Inc. Page 299: Ron Heflin/AP/Wide World Photos. Page 300: Courtesy Delphi Automotive Systems. Page 302: Courtesy Dell Computer Corporation.

Chapter 15
Page 309: Jeff Christensen/Gamma Liaison. Page 314: Courtesy Cybex Computer Products. Page 317: Courtesy Melita International. Page 322: Courtesy America's Job Bank. Reproduced with permission. Page 323: Courtesy Little Caesars Enterprises, Inc. Page 327: Courtesy Catalina Marketing Corp.

Chapter 16
Page 333: © Sun Microsystems. Page 336: ©Timothy Archibald, Fortune, Feb. 15, 99, p. 149. Page 340: Courtesy Mechanical Mann. Page 341: Kevin Radford/SUPERSTOCK. Page 343: Courtesy CarrAmerica Realty Corp. Page 344: Courtesy Springfield Remanufacturing Corp. Page 346: Courtesy American Express Company. Page 348: John Zoiner/The Stock Market.

Chapter 17
Page 353: Courtesy Fresh International. Page 357: Courtesy PNC Mortgage Corporation. Page 360: Courtesy Nokia, Inc. Page 362: Courtesy Odwalla. Page 367: Courtesy Analog Devices. . Page 368: Courtesy ATR Labls, Kyoto, Japan.

Chapter 18
Page 373: Courtesy Capital Across America, Inc. Page 376: AP/Wide World Photos. Page 378: Lester Lefkowitz/The Stock Market. Page 379: Kwame Zikomo/SUPERSTOCK. Page 381: Kwame Zikomo/SUPERSTOCK. Page 385: Florian Franke/The Image Bank. Page 387: Ken Fisher/Tony Stone Images/New York, Inc. Page 388: Peter Poulides/Tony Stone Images/New York, Inc.

Chapter 19
Page 393: Walter Hodges/Tony Stone Images/New York, Inc. Page 395: ©Markel/Gamma Liaison. Page 397: D E Cox/Tony Stone Images/New York, Inc. Page 401: Courtesy Larami Limited. Page 404: Courtesy Pitney Bowes. Page 405: John Feingersh/The Stock Market. Page 406: Courtesy Josephson Institute of Ethics.

Organization Index

Name Index

Subject Index

Student Leadership Practices Inventory

STUDENT WORKBOOK

James M. Kouzes
Barry Z. Posner, Ph.D.

Jossey-Bass Publishers • San Francisco

ISBN: 0-7879-4425-4

Jossey-Bass is a registered trademark of Jossey-Bass Inc., A Wiley Company.

Printed in the United States of America.

Jossey-Bass books and products are available through most bookstores. To contact Jossey-Bass directly, call (888) 378-2537, fax to (800) 605-2665, or visit our website at www.josseybass.com.

Substantial discounts on bulk quantities of Jossey-Bass books are available to corporations, professional associations, and other organizations. For details and discount information, contact the special sales department at Jossey-Bass.

Printing   10   9   8   7   6   5   4   3   2

 This book is printed on acid-free, recycled stock that meets or exceeds the minimum GPO and EPA requirements for recycled paper.

CONTENTS

People WHO BECOME

leaders

DON'T *always* **seek**

THE challenges

THEY **Face.**

CHALLENGES

also SEEK **leaders.**

1 Leadership: What People Do When They're Leading

"Leadership is everyone's business." That's the conclusion we have come to after nearly two decades of research into the behaviors and actions of people who are making a difference in their organizations, clubs, teams, classes, schools, campuses, communities, and even in their families. We found that leadership is an observable, learnable set of practices. Contrary to some myths, it is not a mystical and ethereal process that cannot be understood by ordinary people. Given the opportunity for feedback and practice, those with the desire and persistence to lead—to make a difference—can substantially improve their ability to do so.

The *Leadership Practices Inventory* (LPI) is part of an extensive research project into the everyday actions and behaviors of people, at all levels and across a variety of settings, as they are leading. Through our research we identified five practices that are common to all leadership experiences. In collaboration with others, we extended our findings to student leaders and to school and college environments and created the student version of the LPI.[1] The LPI is a tool, not a test, designed to assess your current leadership skills. It will identify your areas of strength as well as areas of leadership that need to be further developed.

The *Student LPI* helps you discover the extent to which you (in your role as a leader of a student group or organization) engage in the following five leadership practices:

Challenging the Process. Leaders are pioneers—people who seek out new opportunities and are willing to change the status quo. They innovate, experiment, and explore ways to improve the organization. They treat mistakes as

---

1. For more information on our original work, see *The Leadership Challenge: How to Keep Getting Extraordinary Things Done in Organizations* (Jossey-Bass Publishers).

learning experiences. Leaders also stay prepared to meet whatever challenges may confront them. *Challenging the Process* involves

- Searching for opportunities
- Experimenting and taking risks

As an example of Challenging the Process, one student related how innovative thinking helped him win a student class election: "I challenged the process in more than one way. First, I wanted people to understand that elections are not necessarily popularity contests, so I campaigned on the issues and did not promise things that could not possibly be done. Second, I challenged the incumbent positions. They thought they would win easily because they were incumbents, but I showed them that no one has an inherent right to a position."

Challenging the Process for a student serving as treasurer of her sorority meant examining and abandoning some of her leadership beliefs: "I used to believe, 'if you want to do something right, do it yourself.' I found out the hard way that this is impossible to do. . . . One day I was ready to just give up the position because I could no longer handle all of the work. My adviser noticed that I was overwhelmed, and she turned to me and said three magic words: 'Use your committee.' The best piece of advice I would pass along about being an effective leader is that it is okay to experiment with letting others do the work."

Inspiring a Shared Vision. Leaders look toward and beyond the horizon. They envision the future with a positive and hopeful outlook. Leaders are expressive and attract other people to their organization and teams through their genuineness. They communicate and show others how their interests can be met through commitment to a common purpose. *Inspiring a Shared Vision* involves

- Envisioning an uplifting future
- Enlisting others in a common vision

Describing his experience as president of his high school class, one student wrote, "It was our vision to get the class united and to be able to win the spirit trophy. . . . I told my officers that we could do anything we set our minds on. Believe in yourself and believe in your ability to accomplish things."

Enabling Others to Act. Leaders infuse people with energy and confidence, developing relationships based on mutual trust. They stress collaborative goals. They actively involve others in planning, giving them discretion to make their own decisions. Leaders ensure that people feel strong and capable. *Enabling Others to Act* involves

- Fostering collaboration
- Strengthening people

It is not necessary to be in a traditional leadership position to put these principles into practice. Here is an example from a student who led his team as a team member, not from a traditional position of power: "I helped my team members feel strong and capable by encouraging everyone to practice with the same amount of intensity that they played games with. Our practices improved throughout the year and by the end of the year had reached the point I was striving for: complete involvement among all players, helping each other to perform at our very best during practice times."

Modeling the Way. Leaders are clear about their personal values and beliefs. They keep people and projects on course by behaving consistently with these values and modeling how they expect others to act. Leaders also plan projects and break them down into achievable steps, creating opportunities for small wins. By focusing on key priorities, they make it easier for others to achieve goals. *Modeling the Way* involves

- Setting the example
- Achieving small wins

Working in a business environment taught one student the importance of Modeling the Way. She writes, "I proved I was serious because I was the first one on the job and the last one to leave. I came prepared to work and make the tools available to my crew. I worked alongside them and in no way portrayed an attitude of superiority. Instead, we were in this together."

Encouraging the Heart. Leaders encourage people to persist in their efforts by linking recognition with accomplishments and visibly recognizing contributions to the common vision. They express pride in the achievements of the group or organization, letting others know that their efforts are appreciated. Leaders also find ways to celebrate milestones. They nurture a team spirit, which enables people to sustain continued efforts. *Encouraging the Heart* involves

- Recognizing individual contributions
- Celebrating team accomplishments

While organizing and running a day camp, one student recognized volunteers and celebrated accomplishments through her actions. She explains, "We had a pizza party with the children on the last day of the day camp. Later, the volunteers were sent thank you notes and 'valuable volunteer awards' personally signed by the day campers. The pizza party, thank you notes, and awards served to encourage the hearts of the volunteers in the hopes that they might return for next year's day camp."

Somewhere,

s o m e t i m e ,

THE *leader within*

EACH OF us

MAY get

THE CALL

to STEP forward.

2 Questions Frequently Asked About the *Student LPI*

Question 1: What are the right answers?

Answer: There are no universal right answers when it comes to leadership. The research indicates that the more frequently you are perceived as engaging in the behavior and actions identified in the *Student LPI*, the more likely it is that you will be perceived as an effective leader. The higher your scores on the Student LPI-Observer, the more others perceive you as (1) having personal credibility, (2) being effective in running meetings, (3) successfully representing your organization or group to nonmembers, (4) generating a sense of enthusiasm and cooperation, and (5) having a high-performing team. In addition, findings show a strong and positive relationship between the extent to which people report their leaders engaging in this set of five leadership practices and how motivated, committed, and productive they feel.

Question 2: How reliable and valid is the Student LPI?

Answer: The question of reliability can be answered in two ways. First, the *Student LPI* has shown sound psychometric properties. The scale for each leadership practice is internally reliable, meaning that the statements within each practice are highly correlated with one another. Second, results of multivariate analyses indicate that the statements within each leadership practice are more highly correlated (or associated) with one another than they are between the five leadership practices.

In terms of validity (or, "So what difference do the scores make?"), the *Student LPI* has good face validity and predictive validity. This means, first, that the results make sense to people. Second, scores on the *Student LPI* significantly differentiate high-performing leaders from their less successful counterparts. Whether measured by the leader, his or her peers, or student personnel administrators, those student leaders who engage more frequently, rather than less frequently, in the five leadership practices are more effective.

Question 3: Should my perceptions of my leadership practices be consistent with the ratings other people give me?

Answer: Research indicates that trust in the leader is essential if other people (for example, fellow members of a group, team, or organization) are going to follow that person over time. People must experience the leader as believable, credible, and trustworthy. Trust—whether in a leader or any other person—is developed through consistency in behavior. Trust is further established when words and deeds are congruent.

This does not mean, however, that you will always be perceived in exactly the same way by every person in every situation. Some people may not see you as often as others do, and therefore they may rate you differently on the same behavior. Some people simply may not know you as well as others do. Also, you may appropriately behave differently in different situations, such as in a crisis versus during more stable times. Others may have different expectations of you, and still others may perceive the rating descriptions (such as "once in a while" or "fairly often") differently.

Therefore, the key issue is not whether your self-ratings and the ratings from others are exactly the same, but whether people perceive consistency between what you say you do and what you actually do. The only way you can know the answer to this question is to solicit feedback. The Student LPI-Observer has been designed for this purpose.

Research indicates that people tend to see themselves more positively than others do. The Student LPI-Self norms are consistent with this general trend; scores on the Student LPI-Self tend to be somewhat higher than scores on the Student LPI-Observer. *Student LPI* scores also tend to be higher than LPI scores of experienced managers and executives in the private and public sector.

Question 4: Can I change my leadership practices?

Answer: It is certainly possible—even for experienced people—to learn new skills. You will increase your chances of changing your behavior if you receive feedback on what level you have achieved with a particular skill, observe a positive model of that skill, set some improvement goals for yourself, practice the skill, ask for updated feedback on your performance, and then set new goals. The practices that are assessed with the *Student LPI* fall into the category of learnable skills.

But some things can be changed only if there is a strong and genuine inner desire to make a difference. For example, enthusiasm for a cause is unlikely to be developed through education or job assignments; it must come from within.

Use the information from the Student LPI to better understand how you currently behave as a leader, both from your own perspective and from the perspective of others. Note where there are consistencies and inconsistencies. Understand which leadership behaviors and practices you feel comfortable engaging in and those you feel uncomfortable with. Determine which leadership behaviors and practices you can improve on, and take steps to improve your leadership skills and confidence in leading other people and groups. The following sections will help you to become more effective in leadership.

Perhaps NONE OF us knows OUR *true strength* UNTIL **challenged** TO **bring** *it* **forth.**

3 Recording Your Scores

On pages 13 through 15 are grids for recording your *Student LPI* scores. The first grid (Challenging the Process) is for recording scores for items 1, 6, 11, 16, 21, and 26 from the Student LPI-Self and Student LPI-Observer. These are the items that relate to behaviors involved in Challenging the Process, such as searching for opportunities, experimenting, and taking risks. An abbreviated form of each item is printed beside the grid as a handy reference.

In the first column, which is headed "Self-Rating," write the scores that you gave yourself. If others were asked to complete the Student LPI-Observer and if the forms were returned to you, enter their scores in the columns (A, B, C, D, E, and so on) under the heading "Observers' Ratings." Simply transfer the numbers from page 4 of each Student LPI-Observer to your scoring grids, using one column for each observer. For example, enter the first observer's scores in column A, the second observer's scores in column B, and so on. The grids provide space for the scores of as many as ten observers.

After all scores have been entered for Challenging the Process, total each column in the row marked "Totals." Then add all the totals for observers; do not include the "self" total. Write this grand total in the space marked "Total of All Observers' Scores." To obtain the average, divide the grand total by the number of people who completed the Student LPI-Observer. Write this average in the blank provided. The sample grid shows how the grid would look with scores for self and five observers entered.

Sample Grid with Scores from Self and Five Observers

	SELF-RATING	OBSERVERS' RATINGS										
		A	B	C	D	E	F	G	H	I	J	
1. Seeks challenge	5	4	2	4	4	2						
6. Keeps current	4	4	3	4	4	3						
11. Initiates experiments	3	3	2	2	2	1						
16. Looks for ways to improve	4	3	2	3	5	3						
21. Asks "What can we learn?"	2	3	2	3	3	2						TOTAL OF ALL OBSERVERS' SCORES
26. Lets others take risks	5	3	3	2	3	2						
TOTALS	23	20	14	18	21	13						86

TOTAL SELF-RATING: __23__   AVERAGE OF ALL OBSERVERS: __17.2__

The other four grids should be completed in the same manner.

The second grid (Inspiring a Shared Vision) is for recording scores to the items that pertain to envisioning the future and enlisting the support of others. These include items 2, 7, 12, 17, 22, and 27.

The third grid (Enabling Others to Act) pertains to items 3, 8, 13, 18, 23, and 28, which involve fostering collaboration and strengthening others.

The fourth grid (Modeling the Way) pertains to items about setting an example and planning small wins. These include items 4, 9, 14, 19, 24, and 29.

The fifth grid (Encouraging the Heart) pertains to items about recognizing contributions and celebrating accomplishments. These are items 5, 10, 15, 20, 25, and 30.

Grids for Recording *Student LPI* Scores

Scores should be recorded on the following grids in accordance with the instructions on page 11. As you look at individual scores, remember the rating system that was used:

"1" means that you *rarely or seldom* engage in the behavior.
"2" means that you engage in the behavior *once in a while.*
"3" means that you *sometimes* engage in the behavior.
"4" means that you engage in the behavior *fairly often.*
"5" means that you engage in the behavior *very frequently.*

After you have recorded all your scores and calculated the totals and averages, turn to page 17 and read the section on interpreting scores.

Challenging the Process

	SELF-RATING	OBSERVERS' RATINGS									
		A	B	C	D	E	F	G	H	I	J
1. Seeks challenge											
6. Keeps current											
11. Initiates experiment											
16. Looks for ways to improve											
21. Asks "What can we learn?"											
26. Lets others take risks											
TOTALS											

TOTAL OF ALL OBSERVERS' SCORES

TOTAL SELF-RATING: _____

AVERAGE OF ALL OBSERVERS: _____

Inspiring a Shared Vision

	SELF-RATING	OBSERVERS' RATINGS									
		A	B	C	D	E	F	G	H	I	J
2. Describes ideal capabilities											
7. Looks ahead and communicates future											
12. Upbeat and positive communicator											
17. Finds common ground											
22. Communicates purpose and meaning											
27. Enthusiastic about possibilities											
TOTALS											

TOTAL OF ALL OBSERVERS' SCORES

TOTAL SELF-RATING: _____

AVERAGE OF ALL OBSERVERS: _____

Enabling Others to Act

	SELF-RATING	OBSERVERS' RATINGS									
		A	B	C	D	E	F	G	H	I	J
3. Includes others in planning											
8. Treats others with respect											
13. Supports decisions of others											
18. Fosters cooperative relationships											
23. Provides freedom and choice											
28. Lets others lead											
TOTALS												

TOTAL OF ALL OBSERVERS' SCORES

TOTAL SELF-RATING: _____

AVERAGE OF ALL OBSERVERS: _____

Modeling the Way

	SELF-RATING	OBSERVERS' RATINGS									
		A	B	C	D	E	F	G	H	I	J
4. Shares beliefs about leading											
9. Breaks projects into steps											
14. Sets personal example											
19. Talks about guiding values											
24. Follows through on promises											
29. Sets clear goals and plans											
TOTALS												

TOTAL OF ALL OBSERVERS' SCORES

TOTAL SELF-RATING: _____

AVERAGE OF ALL OBSERVERS: _____

Encouraging the Heart

	SELF-RATING	OBSERVERS' RATINGS									
		A	B	C	D	E	F	G	H	I	J
5. Encourages other people											
10. Recognizes people's contributions											
15. Praises people for job well done											
20. Gives support and appreciation											
25. Finds ways to publicly celebrate											
30. Tells others about group's good work											
TOTALS												

TOTAL OF ALL OBSERVERS' SCORES

TOTAL SELF-RATING: _____

AVERAGE OF ALL OBSERVERS: _____

THE unique ROLE
OF leaders
IS TO *take us*
TO places
WE'VE never
been before.

4 Interpreting Your Scores

This section will help you to interpret your scores by looking at them in several ways and making notes to yourself about what you can do to become a more effective leader.

Ranking Your Ratings

Refer to the previous chapter, "Recording Your Scores." On each grid, look at your scores in the blanks marked "Total Self-Rating." Each of these totals represents your responses to six statements about one of the five leadership practices. Each of your totals can range from a low of 6 to a high of 30.

In the blanks that follow, write "1" to the left of the leadership practice with the highest total self-rating, "2" by the next-highest total self-rating, and so on. This ranking represents the leadership practices with which you feel most comfortable, second-most comfortable, and so on. The practice you identify with a "5" is the practice with which you feel least comfortable.

Again refer to the previous chapter, but this time look at your scores in the blanks marked "Average of All Observers." The number in each blank is the average score given to you by the people you asked to complete the Student LPI-Observer. Like each of your total self-ratings, this number can range from 6 to 30.

In the blanks that follow, write "1" to the right of the leadership practice with the highest score, "2" by the next-highest score, and so on. This ranking represents the leadership practices that others feel you use most often, second-most often, and so on.

Self		Observers
————	Challenging the Process	————
————	Inspiring a Shared Vision	————
————	Enabling Others to Act	————
————	Modeling the Way	————
————	Encouraging the Heart	————

Comparing Your Self-Ratings to Observers' Ratings

To compare your Student LPI-Self and Student LPI-Observer assessments, refer to the "Chart for Graphing Your Scores" on the next page. On the chart, designate your scores on the five leadership practices (Challenging, Inspiring, Enabling, Modeling, and Encouraging) by marking each of these points with a capital "S" (for "Self"). Connect the five resulting "S scores" with a *solid line* and label the end of this line "Self" (see sample chart below).

If other people provided input through the Student LPI-Observer, designate the average observer scores (see the blanks labeled "Average of All Observers" on the scoring grids) by marking each of the points with a capital "O" (for "Observer"). Then connect the five resulting "O scores" with a *dashed line* and label the end of this line "Observer" (see sample chart). Completing this process will provide you with a graphic representation (one solid and one dashed line) illustrating the relationship between your self-perception and the observations of other people.

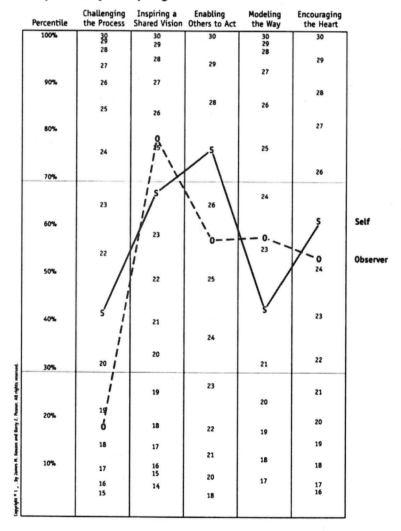

Sample Chart for Graphing Your Scores

Chart for Graphing Your Scores

Percentile	Challenging the Process	Inspiring a Shared Vision	Enabling Others to Act	Modeling the Way	Encouraging the Heart
100%	30 29 28	30 29	30	30 29 28	30
	27	28	29	27	29
90%	26	27			
			28	26	28
	25	26			
80%					27
	24	25	27	25	
70%					26
	23	24	26	24	
60%	22	23		23	25
50%	21	22	25	22	24
40%		21	24		23
	20	20		21	22
30%			23	20	21
	19	19	22	19	20
20%	18	18	21		19
10%	17	17 16 15	20	18	18
	16	14	19	17	17 16
	15		18	16	

Percentile Scores

Look again at the "Chart for Graphing Your Scores." The column to the far left represents the Student LPI-Self percentile rankings for more than 1,200 student leaders. A percentile ranking is determined by the percentage of people who score at or below a given number. For example, if your total self-rating for "Challenging" is at the 60th percentile line on the "Chart for Graphing Your Scores," this means that you assessed yourself higher than 60 percent of all people who have completed the *Student LPI;* you would be in the top 40 percent in this leadership practice. Studies indicate that a "high" score is one at or above the 70th percentile, a "low" score is one at or below the 30th percentile, and a score that falls between those ranges is considered "moderate."

Using these criteria, circle the "H" (for "High"), the "M" (for "Moderate"), or the "L" (for "Low") for each leadership practice on the "Range of Scores" table below. Compared to other student leaders around the country, where do your leadership practices tend to fall? (Given a "normal distribution," it is expected that most people's scores will fall within the moderate range.)

Range of Scores

In my perception				In others' perception			
Practice	**Rating**			**Practice**	**Rating**		
Challenging the Process	H	M	L	Challenging the Process	H	M	L
Inspiring a Shared Vision	H	M	L	Inspiring a Shared Vision	H	M	L
Enabling Others to Act	H	M	L	Enabling Others to Act	H	M	L
Modeling the Way	H	M	L	Modeling the Way	H	M	L
Encouraging the Heart	H	M	L	Encouraging the Heart	H	M	L

Exploring Specific Leadership Behaviors

Looking at your scoring grids, review each of the thirty items on the *Student LPI* by practice. One or two of the six behaviors within each leadership practice may be higher or lower than the rest. If so, on which specific items is there variation? What do these differences suggest? On which specific items are there agreement? Please write your thoughts in the following space.

Challenging the Process

_____

_____

_____

_____

_____

_____

Inspiring a Shared Vision

_____

_____

_____

_____

_____

_____

Enabling Others to Act

_____

_____

_____

_____

_____

Modeling the Way

_____

_____

_____

_____

_____

Encouraging the Heart

_____

_____

_____

_____

_____

Comparing Observers' Responses to One Another

Study the Student LPI-Observer scores for each of the five leadership practices. Do some respondents' scores differ significantly from others? If so, are the differences localized in the scores of one or two people? On which leadership practices do the respondents agree? On which practices do they disagree? If you try to behave basically the same with all the people who assessed you, how do you explain the difference in ratings? Please write your thoughts in the following space.

_____

_____

_____

_____

_____

_____

_____

_____

_____

_____

_____

_____

_____

_____

Wanting TO LEAD AND believing THAT YOU *can lead* ARE THE **departure** POINTS ON THE PATH TO **leadership**. LEADERSHIP IS AN ART— A *performing* art— AND THE **instrument** IS THE **self.**

5 Summary and Action-Planning Worksheets

Take a few moments to summarize your *Student LPI* feedback by completing the following Strengths and Opportunities Summary Worksheet. Refer to the "Chart for Graphing Your Scores," the "Range of Scores" table, and any notes you have made.

After the summary worksheet you will find some suggestions for getting started on meeting the leadership challenge. With these suggestions in mind, review your *Student LPI* feedback and decide on the actions you will take to become an even more effective leader. Then complete the Action-Planning Worksheet to spell out the steps you will take. (One Action-Planning Worksheet is included in this workbook, but you may want to develop action plans for several practices or behaviors. You could make copies of the blank form before you fill it in or just use a separate sheet of paper for each leadership practice in which you plan to improve.)

Strengths and Opportunities Summary Worksheet

Strengths

Which of the leadership practices and behaviors are you most comfortable with? Why? Can you do more?

_____

_____

_____

_____

_____

_____

_____

Areas for Improvement

What can you do to use a practice more frequently? What will it take to feel more comfortable?

_____

_____

_____

_____

_____

_____

_____

Following are ten suggestions for getting started on meeting the leadership challenge.

Prescriptions for Meeting the Leadership Challenge

Challenge the Process

- Fix something
- Adopt the "great ideas" of others

Inspire a Shared Vision

- Let others know how you feel
- Recount your "personal best"

Enable Others to Act

- Always say "we"
- Make heroes of other people

Model the Way

- Lead by example
- Create opportunities for small wins

Encourage the Heart

- Write "thank you" notes
- Celebrate, and link your celebrations to your organization's values

Action-Planning Worksheet

1. What would you like to be better able to do?

_____

_____

_____

_____

_____

_____

_____

2. What specific actions will you take?

_____

_____

_____

_____

_____

_____

_____

3. What is the *first* action you will take? Who will be involved? When will you begin?

Action _____

_____

_____

People Involved _____

_____

_____

_____

Target Date _____

4. Complete this sentence: "I will know I have improved in this leadership skill when . . ."

_____

_____

_____

_____

5. When will you review your progress? _____

About the Authors

James M. Kouzes is chairman of TPG/Learning Systems, which makes leadership work through practical, performance-oriented learning programs. In 1993 *The Wall Street Journal* cited Jim as one of the twelve most requested "nonuniversity executive-education providers" to U.S. companies. His list of past and present clients includes AT&T, Boeing, Boy Scouts of America, Charles Schwab, Ciba-Geigy, Dell Computer, First Bank System, Honeywell, Johnson & Johnson, Levi Strauss & Co., Motorola, Pacific Bell, Stanford University, Xerox Corporation, and the YMCA.

Barry Z. Posner, Ph.D., is dean of the Leavey School of Business, Santa Clara University, and professor of organizational behavior. He has received several outstanding teaching and leadership awards, has published more than eighty research and practitioner-oriented articles, and currently is on the editorial review boards for *The Journal of Management Education, The Journal of Management Inquiry,* and *The Journal of Business Ethics.* Barry also serves on the board of directors for Public Allies and for The Center for Excellence in Non-Profits. His clients have ranged from retailers to firms in health care, high technology, financial services, manufacturing, and community service agencies.

Kouzes and Posner are coauthors of several best-selling and award-winning leadership books. *The Leadership Challenge: How to Keep Getting Extraordinary Things Done in Organizations* (2nd ed., 1995), with over 800,000 copies in print, has been reprinted into fifteen foreign languages, featured in three video programs, and received a Critic's Choice award from the nation's newspaper book review editors. *Credibility: How Leaders Gain and Lose It, Why People Demand It* (1993) was chosen by *Industry Week* as one of the five best management books of the year. Their latest book is *Encouraging the Heart: A Leader's Guide to Rewarding and Recognizing Others* (1998).

Self

Your Name: _____

Instructions

On the next two pages are thirty statements describing various leadership behaviors. Please read each statement carefully. Then rate *yourself* in terms of *how frequently* you engage in the behavior described. *This is not a test* (there are no right or wrong answers).

Consider each statement in the context of the student organization (for example, club, team, chapter, group, unit, hall, program, project) with which you are most involved. The rating scale provides five choices:

(1) If you RARELY or SELDOM do what is described in the statement, circle the number one (1).

(2) If you do what is described ONCE IN A WHILE, circle the number two (2).

(3) If you SOMETIMES do what is described, circle the number three (3).

(4) If you do what is described FAIRLY OFTEN, circle the number four (4).

(5) If you do what is described VERY FREQUENTLY or ALMOST ALWAYS, circle the number five (5).

Please respond to every statement.

In selecting the response, be realistic about the extent to which you *actually* engage in the behavior. Do *not* answer in terms of how you would like to see yourself or in terms of what you should be doing. Answer in terms of how you *typically* behave. The usefulness of the feedback from this inventory will depend on how honest you are with yourself about how frequently you actually engage in each of these behaviors.

For example, the first statement is "I look for opportunities that challenge my skills and abilities." If you believe you do this "once in a while," circle the number 2. If you believe you look for challenging opportunities "fairly often," circle the number 4.

When you have responded to all thirty statements, please turn to the response sheet on the back page and transfer your responses as instructed. Thank you.

STUDENT LEADERSHIP PRACTICES INVENTORY-SELF

How frequently do you typically engage in the following behaviors and actions?
Circle the number that applies to each statement.

1 SELDOM OR RARELY	2 ONCE IN A WHILE	3 SOMETIMES	4 FAIRLY OFTEN	5 VERY FREQUENTLY

1. I look for opportunities that challenge my skills and abilities.   1   2   3   4   5

2. I describe to others in our organization what we should be capable of accomplishing.   1   2   3   4   5

3. I include others in planning the activities and programs of our organization.   1   2   3   4   5

4. I share my beliefs about how things can be run most effectively within our organization.   1   2   3   4   5

5. I encourage others as they work on activities and programs in our organization.   1   2   3   4   5

6. I keep current on events and activities that might affect our organization.   1   2   3   4   5

7. I look ahead and communicate about what I believe will affect us in the future.   1   2   3   4   5

8. I treat others with dignity and respect.   1   2   3   4   5

9. I break our organization's projects down into manageable steps.   1   2   3   4   5

10. I make sure that people in our organization are recognized for their contributions.   1   2   3   4   5

11. I take initiative in experimenting with the way we do things in our organization.   1   2   3   4   5

12. I am upbeat and positive when talking about what our organization is doing.   1   2   3   4   5

13. I support the decisions that other people in our organization make on their own.   1   2   3   4   5

14. I set a personal example of what I expect from other people.   1   2   3   4   5

15. I praise people for a job well done.   1   2   3   4   5

1	2	3	4	5
SELDOM OR RARELY	**ONCE IN A WHILE**	**SOMETIMES**	**FAIRLY OFTEN**	**VERY FREQUENTLY**

16. I look for **ways to improve** whatever project or task I am **involved in.**   1 2 3 4 5

17. I talk with **others about how** their own interests can be met **by working toward** a common goal.   1 2 3 4 5

18. I foster cooperative **rather** than competitive relationships **among people** I work with.   1 2 3 4 5

19. I talk about **the values and** principles that guide my **actions.**   1 2 3 4 5

20. I give people **in our organization** support and express appreciation **for their** contributions.   1 2 3 4 5

21. I ask, "What **can we learn** from this experience?" when things **do not go as** we expected.   1 2 3 4 5

22. I speak with **conviction about** the higher purpose and meaning of **what we are** doing.   1 2 3 4 5

23. I give others **a great deal of** freedom and choice in deciding **how to do their** work.   1 2 3 4 5

24. I follow through on the promises and commitments **I make in this** organization.   1 2 3 4 5

25. I find ways **for us to celebrate** our accomplishments publicly.   1 2 3 4 5

26. I let others **experiment and take** risks even when outcomes **are uncertain.**   1 2 3 4 5

27. I show my **enthusiasm and** excitement about what our **organization is doing.**   1 2 3 4 5

28. I provide opportunities **for** others to take on leadership responsibilities.   1 2 3 4 5

29. I make sure **that we set goals and** make specific plans **for the** projects we undertake.   1 2 3 4 5

30. I make it **a point to tell** others about the good work done **by our** organization.   1 2 3 4 5

Transferring the Scores

After you have responded to the thirty statements on the previous two pages, please transfer your responses to the blanks below. This will make it easier to record and score your responses. Notice that the numbers of the statements are listed *horizontally*. Make sure that the number you assigned to each statement is transferred to the appropriate blank. Fill in a response for every item.

1. _____	2. _____	3. _____	4. _____	5. _____
6. _____	7. _____	8. _____	9. _____	10. _____
11. _____	12. _____	13. _____	14. _____	15. _____
16. _____	17. _____	18. _____	19. _____	20. _____
21. _____	22. _____	23. _____	24. _____	25. _____
26. _____	27. _____	28. _____	29. _____	30. _____

Further Instructions

Please write your name here: _____

Please bring this form with you to the workshop (seminar or class) or return this form to:

_____

_____

_____   _____

_____

If you are interested in feedback from other people, ask them to complete the Student LPI-Observer, which provides you with perspectives on your leadership behaviors as perceived by others.

Jossey-Bass is a registered trademark of Jossey-Bass Inc., A Wiley Company.

No part of this publication may be reproduced, stored in a retrieval system, or transmitted in any form or by any means, electronic, mechanical, photocopying, recording, scanning, or otherwise, except as permitted under Sections 107 or 108 of the 1976 United States Copyright Act, without either the prior written permission of the Publisher or authorization through payment of the appropriate per-copy fee to the Copyright Clearance Center, 222 Rosewood Drive, Danvers, MA 01923, (978) 750-8400, fax (978) 750-4744. Requests to the Publisher for permission should be addressed to the Permissions Department, John Wiley & Sons, Inc., 605 Third Avenue, New York, NY 10158-0012, (212) 850-6011, fax (212) 850-6008, e-mail: permreq@wiley.com.

Printed in the United States of America.

ISBN: 0-7879-4426-2

ISBN 0-7879-4426-2

Jossey-Bass Publishers
350 Sansome Street
San Francisco, California 94104
(888) 378-2537
Fax (800) 605-2665

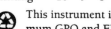
www.josseybass.com

Printing   10   9   8   7   6   5   4   3

This instrument is printed on acid-free, recycled stock that meets or exceeds the minimum GPO and EPA requirements for recycled paper.

STUDENT LEADERSHIP PRACTICES INVENTORY-OBSERVER

Name of Leader: _____

Instructions

On the next two pages are thirty descriptive statements about various leadership behaviors. Please read each statement carefully. Then rate *the person who asked you to complete this form* in terms of *how frequently* he or she typically engages in the described behavior. *This is not a test* (there are no right or wrong answers).

Consider each statement in the context of the student organization (for example, club, team, chapter, group, unit, hall, program, project) with which that person is most involved or with which you have had the greatest opportunity to observe him or her. The rating scale provides five choices:

(1) If this person RARELY or SELDOM does what is described in the statement, circle the number one (1).
(2) If this person does what is described ONCE IN A WHILE, circle the number two (2).
(3) If this person SOMETIMES does what is described, circle the number three (3).
(4) If this person does what is described FAIRLY OFTEN, circle the number four (4).
(5) If this person does what is described VERY FREQUENTLY or ALMOST ALWAYS, circle the number five (5).

Please respond to every statement.

In selecting the response, be realistic about the extent to which this person *actually* engages in the behavior. Do *not* answer in terms of how you would like to see this person behaving or in terms of what this person should be doing. Answer in terms of how he or she *typically behaves*. The usefulness of the feedback from this inventory will depend on how honest you are about how frequently you observe this person actually engaging in each of these behaviors.

For example, the first statement is, "He or she looks for opportunities that challenge his or her skills and abilities." If you believe this person does this "once in a while," circle the number 2. If you believe he or she looks for challenging opportunities "fairly often," circle the number 4.

When you have responded to all thirty statements, please turn to the response sheet on the back page and transfer your responses as instructed. Thank you.

STUDENT LEADERSHIP PRACTICES INVENTORY-OBSERVER

How frequently does this person typically engage in the following behaviors and actions? *Circle* the number that applies to each statement:

1	2	3	4	5
SELDOM OR RARELY	ONCE IN A WHILE	SOMETIMES	FAIRLY OFTEN	VERY FREQUENTLY

He or She:

1. looks for opportunities that challenge his or her skills and abilities.   1   2   3   4   5

2. describes to others in our organization what we should be capable of accomplishing.   1   2   3   4   5

3. includes others in planning the activities and programs of our organization.   1   2   3   4   5

4. shares his or her beliefs about how things can be run most effectively within our organization.   1   2   3   4   5

5. encourages others as they work on activities and programs in our organization.   1   2   3   4   5

6. keeps current on events and activities that might affect our organization.   1   2   3   4   5

7. looks ahead and communicates about what he or she believes will affect us in the future.   1   2   3   4   5

8. treats others with dignity and respect.   1   2   3   4   5

9. breaks our organization's projects down into manageable steps.   1   2   3   4   5

10. makes sure that people in our organization are recognized for their contributions.   1   2   3   4   5

11. takes initiative in experimenting with the way we do things in our organization.   1   2   3   4   5

12. is upbeat and positive when talking about what our organization is doing.   1   2   3   4   5

13. supports the decisions that other people in our organization make on their own.   1   2   3   4   5

14. sets a personal example of what he or she expects from other people.   1   2   3   4   5

15. praises people for a job well done.   1   2   3   4   5

1	2	3	4	5
SELDOM OR RARELY	ONCE IN A WHILE	SOMETIMES	FAIRLY OFTEN	VERY FREQUENTLY

He or She:

16. looks for ways to improve whatever project or task he or she is involved in.   1   2   3   4   5

17. talks with others about how their own interests can be met by working toward a common goal.   1   2   3   4   5

18. fosters cooperative rather than competitive relationships among people he or she works with.   1   2   3   4   5

19. talks about the values and principles that guide his or her actions.   1   2   3   4   5

20. gives people in our organization support and expresses appreciation for their contributions.   1   2   3   4   5

21. asks "What can we learn from this experience?" when things do not go as we expected.   1   2   3   4   5

22. speaks with conviction about the higher purpose and meaning of what we are doing.   1   2   3   4   5

23. gives others a great deal of freedom and choice in deciding how to do their work.   1   2   3   4   5

24. follows through on the promises and commitments he or she makes in this organization.   1   2   3   4   5

25. finds ways for us to celebrate our accomplishments publicly.   1   2   3   4   5

26. lets others experiment and take risks even when outcomes are uncertain.   1   2   3   4   5

27. shows his or her enthusiasm and excitement about what our organization is doing.   1   2   3   4   5

28. provides opportunities for others to take on leadership responsibilities.   1   2   3   4   5

29. makes sure that we set goals and make specific plans for the projects we undertake.   1   2   3   4   5

30. makes it a point to tell others about the good work done by our organization.   1   2   3   4   5

Transferring the Scores

After you have responded to the thirty statements on the previous two pages, please transfer your responses to the blanks below. This will make it easier to record and score your responses. Notice that the numbers of the statements are listed *horizontally*. Make sure that the number you assigned to each statement is transferred to the appropriate blank. Fill in a response for every item.

1. _____   2. _____   3. _____   4. _____   5. _____

6. _____   7. _____   8. _____   9. _____   10. _____

11. _____   12. _____   13. _____   14. _____   15. _____

16. _____   17. _____   18. _____   19. _____   20. _____

21. _____   22. _____   23. _____   24. _____   25. _____

26. _____   27. _____   28. _____   29. _____   30. _____

Further Instructions

The above scores are for (name of person): _____

Please bring this form with you to the workshop (seminar or class) or return this form to:

_____

_____

_____

_____

ISBN: 0-7879-4427-0

Printed in the United States of America.

Jossey-Bass Publishers
350 Sansome Street
San Francisco, California 94104
(888) 378-2537
Fax (800) 605-2665

www.josseybass.com

ISBN 0-7879-4427-0

90000

9 780787 944278

Printing   10   9   8   7   6   5   4   3   2   1

 This instrument is printed on acid-free, recycled stock that meets or exceeds the minimum GPO and EPA requirements for recycled paper.